NAVIES in the 21st CENTURY

NAVIES in the 21st CENTURY

Editor
CONRAD WATERS

Drawings by
JOHN JORDAN

Seaforth
PUBLISHING

Frontispiece: Navies from several European and Pacific countries gathered in the Dardanelles in 2015 to commemorate the anniversary of the 1915 Gallipoli Campaign. More broadly, efforts to increase global naval collaboration between Western nations – so as to make finite resources stretch further – have been a major feature of the post-Cold War era. *(RAN)*

Copyright © Seaforth Publishing 2016
Plans © John Jordan 2016

First published in Great Britain in 2016 by
Seaforth Publishing
An imprint of Pen & Sword Books Ltd
47 Church Street, Barnsley
S Yorkshire S70 2AS

www.seaforthpublishing.com
Email info@seaforthpublishing.com

British Library Cataloguing in Publication Data
A CIP data record for this book is available from the British Library

ISBN 978-1-4738-4991-4

Typeset and designed by Stephen Dent
Printed and bound in China

CONTENTS

Foreword by Geoffrey Till   6

Section 1: Navies in the 21st Century
1.0   **Introduction:** Conrad Waters   8

Section 2: Strategic Overview
2.0   **Post-Cold War Navies:** Ian Speller   16

Section 3: Operational Overview
3.0   **Naval Operations:** Philip Grove   27

Section 4: Fleet Analysis
4.1:   **The Americas:** Conrad Waters   36
4.1.1:   **United States Navy:** Scott Truver   40
4.2:   **Europe & Russia:** Conrad Waters   54
4.2.1:   **The Royal Navy:** Richard Beedall   56
4.2.2:   **Leading Continental European Navies:** Conrad Waters   70
4.2.3:   **The Russian Navy:** James Bosbotinis   83
4.3:   **Asia-Pacific:** Conrad Waters   91
4.3.1:   **People's Liberation Army Navy (PLAN):** Chris Rahman   93
4.3:2   **Royal Australian Navy (RAN):** David Stevens   105
4.3.3:   **Japan Maritime Self-Defence Force (JMSDF):** Alastair Cooper   110
4.3.4:   **Republic of Korea Navy:** Jack McCaffrie   115
4.4:   **Indian Ocean, Middle East & Africa:** Conrad Waters   120
4.4.1:   **Indian Ocean Navies:** Mrityunjoy Mazumdar   122
4.4.2:   **Middle East Navies:** Richard Beedall   130

Section 5: Naval Shipbuilding
5.0   **Global Trends in Warship Design & Construction:** Hartmut Ehlers   135

Section 6: 21st Century Warship Designs
6.1:   **Aircraft Carriers & Amphibious Ships:** Conrad Waters   147
6.2:   **Major Surface Combatants:** Conrad Waters   162
6.3:   **Minor Warships & Auxiliaries:** Conrad Waters   177
6.4:   **Submarines:** Conrad Waters   190

Section 7: Post-Cold War Technical Developments
7.0   **Technology:** Norman Friedman   203

Section 8: Aircraft
8.0   **World Naval Aviation in the 21st Century:** David Hobbs   220

Section 9: Personnel
9.0   **Naval Manning:** Philip Grove   241

Glossary   249
Contributors   252
Index   254

FOREWORD

Geoffrey Till

The challenge of change is a major theme of *Navies in the 21st Century*. It will show that navies all around the world are in a state of constant change as the social, economic, scientific, and technological context in which they operate changes too. Some navies are rising in power and aspiration, others falling. Some are developing new non-traditional roles, others sticking to the old certainties, most oscillating between the two. Nearly all are grappling with the problem of where to strike the balance between high- and low-intensity operations at a time when the international outlook has rarely seemed so unsettled.

On the one hand, the traditional tasks of navies – the defence of the nation that creates them – clearly remains. This mandates developing high-intensity capabilities to control and make strategic use of the sea against other competing navies and air forces. Any idea that this kind of thing is behind us has withered as tensions escalate on either end of the Eurasian land-mass. On the other hand, the sea remains both an invaluable source of resources – oil, gas, fish (and who knows what else in the future) – and the prime means by which goods and people are shifted around the world. On this depends the global sea-based trading system which provides for our peace and prosperity. Helping to defend the maritime security of the international trading system, then, is an increasingly important task for the world's navies, and one in which navies and coast guards co-operate rather than compete. These two strategic imperatives are very different and have very

different requirements – hence the difficult choices navies have to make, often against the background of straitened budgets and falling numbers.

Threats to the system include all forms of maritime crime – piracy, drugs and people smuggling, terrorism and so forth – and often the indirect consequences of natural or man-made disasters. Navies protect the system by what they can do both *at* and *from* the sea. As even the US Navy readily admits, no single navy – however capable it may be – can possibly meet all these challenges, so there is no choice but to co-operate if the job is to be done. To do this, navies have to be aware of what is happening everywhere in the maritime domain. Hence the growing importance of intelligence, surveillance and reconnaissance (ISR), of data fusion and data sharing between co-operating navies and coast guards so that the 'normal' is clearly understood and the abnormal quickly identified. Around the world navies are coming together to share best practice in a common campaign for good order at sea This requires the kind of joined-up strategy at a governmental level that is only slowly being developed around the world. Establishing this is not easy. Even NATO, as the world's foremost collective security organisation, finds it difficult to craft a common and comprehensive position on maritime security; its efforts to expand the Article V operation 'Active Endeavour' counter-terrorism campaign in the Mediterranean into a common and comprehensive maritime security construct that could address a wider range of issues have yet to come to fruition.

The drive for maritime security calls for a fairly low-intensity set of capabilities, weapons, and platforms and a range of procedures, activities, skills sets, and support infrastructure that can be very different from what many navies would regard as their real and potentially much more competitive business – preparation for warfighting. The need to address a maritime security campaign can therefore raise extremely difficult choices, especially in times of tight budgetary constraints.

Moreover, the battle for maritime security is not as cheap an option as is often thought. It calls for maritime domain awareness as delivered by patrol craft and aircraft sufficient in numbers for the areas in question to be covered, supported by means for the timely interception and apprehension of offenders, and all backed by an efficient judicial system able to prosecute offenders. This requirement for awareness explains in no small part the

A Rafale M jet prepares to make a sortie from the French aircraft carrier *Charles de Gaulle*. The ability to conduct high intensity operations remains a core function of many navies but this has to be balanced with the need to perform to lower intensity duties in support of maritime security. *(Dassault Aviation / V Almanza)*

burgeoning market around the world for small, relatively cheap patrol craft, equipped in the main for low-intensity operations in local waters.

As disorder in one geographic area can often seep into, and contaminate, good order elsewhere, there is an 'away game' aspect to this campaign as well. For example, disorder in and off Somalia led to a rise in piracy that threatened international shipping in the Gulf of Aden. The global consequences of this justified a remarkably successful counter-piracy operation there.

'Good order at sea' is not enough, however, as the international system also depends on the confidence that underpins financial investment, and this itself can often be undermined by developments on land, as in the Somali case, which threaten the conditions for trade. Naval action here seeks to instil 'good order *from* the sea', through sea-based interventions. These range from assisting the Philippines in the aftermath of Typhoon Haiyan in 2013 and the relief operation conducted in response to the Ebola outbreak in West Africa that began in 2014 at one end of the scale, to the intervention in Libya in 2011 at the other. The ability to conduct such a range of interventions is an especially important driver of naval policy in Europe and in the Asia-Pacific where the aspiration to be able to contribute to such operations remains a key priority. Hence the push for platforms capable of delivering organic sea-based airpower, for amphibious warfare vessels and large general purpose ships, all able to operate at a distance.

Traditional, more competitive strategic concerns have not, however, gone away. Navies large and small still seek strategic dominance, the capacity for manoeuvre, and the ability to perform tasks in defence of national interest whenever and wherever needed. To deter war they feel they need to be able to show that they can fight it. Hence the continued preoccupation for sea control and/or sea denial and for the platforms, weapons and sensors and for the skill-sets and the experience that make them possible. The proliferation of submarines around the Asia-Pacific illustrates the point exactly. Hence, also, the great emerging debate about the relative balance between strategies of sea denial (Anti-Access/Area Denial) on the one hand and the determination to maintain 'all domain access' on the other. This also relates to the technical debate between those who advocate the concentration of force in relatively fewer, necessarily expensive, platforms as opposed to diffusing it around a much larger number of smaller

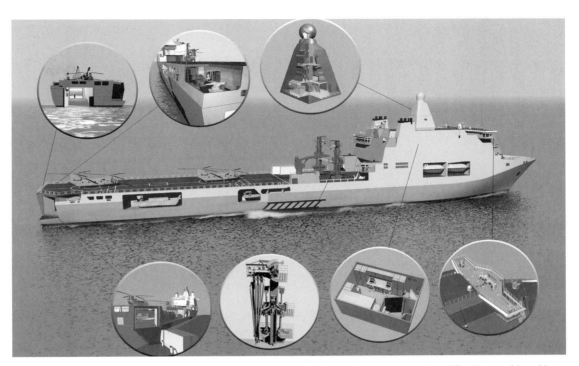

The new Dutch joint support ship *Karel Doorman* is a good example of one of a new generation of flexible warships able to conduct several missions. However, navies still have to make choices as to the roles they are to perform given funding and manpower constraints. *(Royal Netherlands Navy)*

units networked together. As will be shown, much of this is illustrated by the current dynamic between Chinese 'counter-interventionary' concepts of sea denial and the US emphasis on maintaining access through the disciplines of what used to be called Air/Sea Battle but is now labelled as Joint Access and Maneuver for the Global Commons, or JAM-GC. In this crucial, high-intensity dynamic between the means of sea control and of sea denial, the technology involved needs to be cutting edge because so much is expected of it and the stakes are so great.

Investment in amphibious capability is another indicator of the need to focus on the ability to conduct traditional high-intensity warfighting operations. There is plenty of evidence, as the following chapters show, of countries seeking to expand their amphibious and expeditionary forces. It is more difficult to find hard evidence in capability acquisition terms of the continued naval interest in the attack and defence of trade and in the conduct of gunboat diplomacy, since these tasks do not require specialised equipment in quite the same way. Instead, the conduct of these classic naval missions is essentially behavioural – they are exemplified by the

way in which navies use their equipment more than by the characteristics of their equipment. Nonetheless, the requirement to defend national trading interests is a regular feature of naval doctrines around the world.

The increasing flexibility of individual platforms, and groups of platforms is steadily increasing and reduces, to some extent, the need for navies to choose between high- and low-intensity options. Nevertheless, choices have to be made because budgets are tight and manpower levels finite. There are clear limits to the various sleight-of-hand devices sometimes used to conceal the criticality of lower numbers of ships. Because it is future oriented, has to cope with a uniquely uncertain strategic and technological future, takes a very long time and sometimes competes with the government's broader industrial policy, the acquisition of naval platforms, weapons and sensors continues to be an extraordinarily demanding process. The following pages will show just how the world's navies are attempting to cope with this and the other policy challenges they face as they plot their course for the next few decades.

1.0   Conrad Waters

INTRODUCTION

Navies in the twenty-first century exhibit significant changes from their counterparts at the time of the Cold War's end, now a quarter of a century ago. Many of the major fleets that dominated the world's oceans – deprived of longstanding core roles virtually overnight – are now much smaller than they were then. They have, over the same period, been joined by a new cohort of emerging naval powers, many located in Asia. These new fleets have been financed by the shift in world trade towards the broader Asia-Pacific region and justified by rising regional tensions.

However, change extends much further than this.

The evolution of the global political order away from a bipolar stand-off between NATO and the Warsaw Pact (and their respective allies) has been accompanied by a period of instability which has brought new and different missions to replace those lost. These often require different types of warship, as well as changed methods of operation. Technology, increasingly derived from civilian applications in a reversal of the historic direction of travel, has also proceeded apace. This is, perhaps, most evidenced by the accelerating use of unmanned and autonomous vehicles. However, it has also had important implications for such wide-ranging areas as command and control, propulsion, stealth and manning. Meanwhile social change has been reflected in a decisive shift away from conscription towards all-volunteer, professional services and in the growing numbers of women serving at sea.

Since 2010, *Seaforth World Naval Review* has chronicled some of these changes on a yearly basis. However, the short timeframe inherent in this approach is not necessarily the best way to identify and assess trends that might take a decade or more to emerge. *Navies in the 21st Century* therefore attempts to take a longer-term and broader perspective in describing both why and how fleets have evolved in the post-Cold War age. In doing this, the hope is to complement the periodic analysis contained in the *Seaforth World Naval Review* series with a more comprehensive assessment of why things are the way they are now. At the same time, as relations between Russia and the West cool once more as a result of events in Ukraine and the Crimea, the book aims to explain to a broader readership the current importance, objectives, structures and capabilities of the world's major fleets.

Navies in the 21st Century follows the methodology established by the annuals in calling on recognised experts to elaborate on these key themes. This introduction aims to set the financial context to post-Cold War naval developments and outline the major areas addressed in subsequent chapters.

THE FINANCIAL BACKGROUND

One of the biggest factors influencing naval force structures across the world is inevitably the amount of money governments allocate to spending on the military. A good starting point from which to analyse global world naval development is, therefore, to understand this financial backdrop.

Global Trends in Defence Spending: In spite of considerable discussion about the post-Cold War 'peace dividend', it is important to appreciate that the world, at the start of 2015, was actually spending a little more cash on the military than it did at the end of the Cold War. This is graphically illustrated by Diagram 1.1, provided courtesy of SIPRI.[1] Arguably, there are three main reasons for this:

- The world – through the process of economic growth – is now considerably wealthier than it was twenty-five years ago. As such, although the

The US Navy *Los Angeles* class submarine *Pasadena* (SSN-752) prepares to undock from the floating dock *Arco* (ARDM-5) as the *Arleigh Burke* class destroyer *Stockdale* (DDG-106) departs San Diego harbour in January 2016. Although Asian fleets are of growing importance, the US Navy remains the world's largest and best-funded fleet by a considerable margin. *(US Navy)*

The British Royal Navy's technologically advanced Type 45 air-defence destroyer *Diamond* escorting the Danish merchant ship *Ark Futura* in the course of Operation 'Recsyr', part of the UN-sponsored mission to destroy Syria's chemical weapons, in 2014. The post-Cold War era has seen navies acquire new technology and adapt to a broad range of missions. *(Crown Copyright 2014)*

percentage of the world's annual economic output – as measured by gross domestic product (GDP) – allocated to defence has fallen from c.4.5 per cent in 1989 to c.2.3 per cent in 2014, this still means that more cash is available. In 2014, nearly US$1,800bn was spent on the military world-wide.

■ There has, indeed, been a 'peace dividend'. However, this has largely been restricted to Europe and Russia. Elsewhere – particularly in Asia and the Middle East – continued regional tensions have meant that defence spending has remained a priority. Strong economic perform-ance in many economically developing countries has also meant that they have been able to afford to spend more, both in absolute and relative terms. There has therefore been a shift in spending from Europe towards Asia. This is clearly demonstrated by Diagrams 1.2 and 1.3.

■ A big decline in United States' defence spending in the decade after the Cold War was effectively reversed by the terrorist atrocities of 11 September 2001 and the onset of the 'long war' against terrorism. The huge expense of this war explains why the share of world military expendi-ture accounted for by the United States was little different at the end of 2014 than it was in 1989.

Although the impact of the world financial crisis that started in 2008 and a large government deficit have curtailed United States' defence spending since the beginning of the current decade, it remains the world's dominant military power by a considerable margin. The United States spends three times as much on its military as its nearest rival, China, and accounts for around a third of the world's defence spending overall. It also remains by far the largest

1.1: World military expenditure, 1988–2014

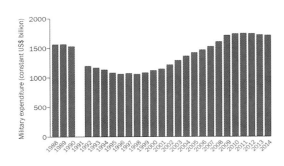

1.2: The share of world military expenditure of the 15 states with the highest expenditure in 1989 *(SIPRI)*

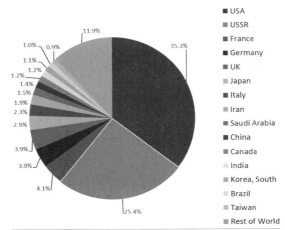

1.3: The share of world military expenditure of the 15 states with the highest expenditure in 2014
(base data courtesy of SIPRI)

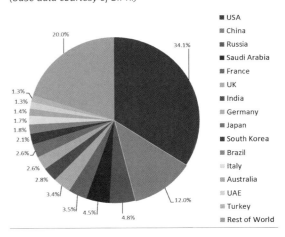

1.4: DoN FY 1999 Budget Estimates
Real Program Trends

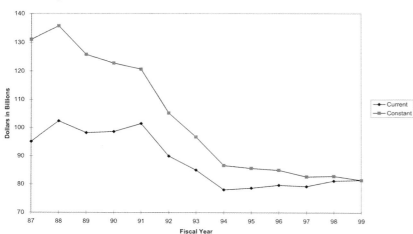

1.5: DON FY 2016 Budget Estimates
Real Program Trends

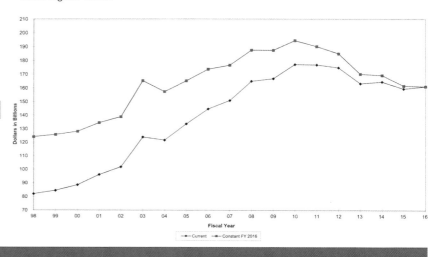

1.6: MAJOR FLEET STRENGTHS – 1990–2015[1]

REGION	THE AMERICAS				EUROPE & RUSSIA										ASIA											IND. OCEAN	
COUNTRY	USA		BRAZIL		UK		FRANCE		ITALY		SPAIN		RUSSIA[2]		CHINA		JAPAN		KOREA(S)		AUSTRALIA		INDIA	
	1990	2015	1990	2015	1990	2015	1990	2015	1990	2015	1990	2015	1990	2015	1990	2015	1990	2015	1990	2015	1990	2015	1990	2015
Carriers & Amphibious																								
CV/CVN	15	10	1	1	–	–	2	1	–	1	–	–	1	1	–	1	–	–	–	–	–	–	1	2
CVS/CVH	–	–	–	–	3	–	1	–	1	1	1	–	6	–	–	–	–	3	–	–	–	–	1	–
LHA/LHD/LPH	13	9	–	–	–	1	–	3	–	–	–	1	–	–	–	–	–	–	–	1	–	2	–	–
LPD/LSD	25	21	2	2	2	5	3	–	2	3	–	2	3	–	–	4	–	3	–	–	–	1	–	1
Submarines																								
SSBN	33	14	–	–	4	4	6	4	–	–	–	–	c.60	13	1	4+	–	–	–	–	–	–	–	–
SSN/SSGN	93	58	–	–	14	7	4	6	–	–	–	–	c.110	c.20	4	6+	–	–	–	–	–	–	1	1
SSK	–	–	5	5	8	–	10	–	9	6	8	3	c.90	c.20	c.100	c.35	15	16	3	14	6	6	18	13
Surface Combatants																								
BB/BC	4	–	–	–	–	–	–	–	–	–	–	–	3	1	–	–	–	–	–	–	–	–	–	–
CGN/CG/DDG	100	82	–	–	13	6	15	11	6	8	–	–	c.60	c.20	–	c.20	34	38	–	12	3	–	5	10
FFG	99	–	6	8	35	13	–	5	12	9	9	10	c.35	c.5	c.15	33	27	6	7	10	9	11	9	14
DD/FGS/FS	–	6	11	4	–	–	21	6	15	6	10	–	c.150	c.45	c.35	c.35	–	–	31	18	–	–	11	10
FAC[3]	6	–	–	–	–	–	–	–	7	–	12	–	c.175	c.35	c.200	c.75	–	6	20+	17	–	–	9	12
Other (Selected)																								
OPV[4]	–	–	9	4	10	4	–	9	4	10	4	15	–	–	–	–	–	–	–	–	–	–	5	10
MCMV	22	13	6	6	33	15	16	14	15	10	12	6	c.225	c.40	c.50	c.30	32	27	11	9	2	6	22	6
AO/AOR	16	18	1	2	13	5	7	3	2	3	–	2	c.35	c.20	2	8	4	5	–	3	2	2	2	4

Notes

1 Numbers are based on official sources, where available, supplemented by news reports, published intelligence data and other 'open' as sources as appropriate. Given significant variations in available data, numbers should be regarded as indicative, particularly with respect to Russia, China and minor warship categories. There is also a degree of subjectivity with respect to warship classifications given varying national classifications and this can also lead to inconsistency.

2 1990 data refers to the Soviet Union, dissolved at the end of 1991. The precise status of the Soviet/Russian fleet at the end of 1990 is rather speculative, as many warships held in official reserve status never returned to operation.

3 FAC numbers relate to ships fitted with or for surface-to-surface missiles.

4 The lack of offshore patrol vessels for some countries reflects the existence of a separate coast guard for the performance of territorial constabulary roles. These can be significant forces.

economy, being over two-thirds larger than China in nominal terms.[2] Moreover, the United States benefits from a network of alliances with many of the other world's major powers, which share a common interest in a global trading economy that relies on a stable international order. In spite of perceived threats to American dominance in Asia and elsewhere, it is difficult to perceive the basic status quo changing materially in the short to medium term. Equally, the US Navy looks firmly anchored to its position as the world's dominant naval force.

Naval Expenditure & Force Structures: Of course, overall trends in and amounts allocated to military expenditure do not necessarily correlate to naval investment. A good case in point is Saudi Arabia, which currently has the fourth largest defence budget in the world but only a comparatively small navy due to the priority attached to land-based forces. Even when money is directed to the naval budget, this does not inevitably result in a more numerous or powerful fleet. The costs of new technology, ill-judged investment decisions and the need to provide adequate conditions of service and compensation to service personnel with growing expectations are just a few examples of factors that can eat away at naval funding.

Given its status as the world's most powerful naval force, it is instructive to look at the development of the US Navy's budget and force structure from the late 1980s with these perspectives in mind. Since then, it has shrunk from the near '600-ship fleet' targeted during the Reagan presidency to somewhat less than 300 ships today. As defence expenditure remains close to 1980s levels, this decline inevitably warrants some explanation. The following factors seem relevant:

- As demonstrated by Diagrams 1.4 to 1.5, US Department of the Navy spending has followed a broadly similar trajectory to overall US Department of Defense expenditure in the post-Cold War era. Real-term budgets initially fell by as much as forty per cent from the Cold War peak, reaching their nadir in the late 1990s. There was subsequently a ramp-up back to Cold War levels as the counter-terrorism war took hold, peaking in FY2010. Expenditure has subsequently declined again – but more moderately – as a result of the winding-down of operations in

The Norwegian *Fridtjof Nansen* class frigate *Thor Heyerdahl* in company with other warships off the Norwegian Coast during exercise Joint Viking 2015, a training drill simulating defence of the northernmost province of Finnmark from Russian attack. Although Europe's fleets have shrunk since the Cold War's end, they remain an important part of a US network of alliances aimed at ensuring a stable world order. *(Petter Brenni Gulbrandsen/ Norwegian Armed Forces)*

the Middle East and increased financial constraints.

- The headline proportion of Department of Defense spending allocated to the US Navy – currently around thirty per cent of the total – has declined a little from the time of the Reagan naval build-up. However, its proportionate share was somewhat less during the peak years of operations in Iraq and Afghanistan given both were predominantly land campaigns. Moreover, the proportion of the naval budget allocated to the US Marine Corps grew from around ten per cent during the Cold War to peak at over twenty per cent between FY2007 and FY2009.

- Efforts to improve conditions of service – including improved housing and medical allowances – have consumed funds that might otherwise have been used on front-line expenditure. This reflects a pattern of pressure from personnel costs experienced elsewhere in the world.

- Much of the post 2001 build-up in defence spending took place under the leadership of Donald Rumsfeld, who served as Secretary for Defense from 2001 to 2006.[3] One of Rumsfeld's key objectives was to transform the military into a more effective post-Cold War force, leading to a greater focus on innovative systems and associated research and development. As a result, the ship-

building account did not expand in line with wider naval budget. In addition, many of the new technologies came at a higher cost than 'legacy' systems and were also associated with delays.

The combined effect of these factors was an initial sharp fall in fleet numbers in the aftermath of the Cold War as old ships were retired and purchases of new vessels significantly reduced. This trend was slowed but not entirely halted by the renewed flow of moneys that followed the '9/11' attacks because warship procurement was not accorded as high a priority as some other areas. In addition, the focus on new technology tended to make new ships more expensive, reducing the numbers that could be ordered. More positively, this problem has been recognised in recent years and efforts – such as a greater focus on established designs and incremental improvements – made to stabilise numbers. In addition, the significant efforts spent on technological R&D should help maintain the US Navy's technical edge into the future. There is always a danger in trying to assess a fleet's strength solely by numbers.

POST-COLD WAR NAVAL DEVELOPMENTS

The ups and downs of the US Navy's development are reflective of the constantly evolving and unpre-

dictable post-Cold War era described more fully by Ian Speller in his opening strategic overview. He explains how the Western navies have steadily sought new roles to supplement or replace those missions that had become less relevant with the Cold War's end. Significant emphasis has been placed on developing maritime expeditionary forces able to project power at distance, especially in the littoral, to tackle causes of instability 'at source'. This is particularly relevant given the emergence of increased maritime terrorist and criminal activity in parts of the world, spurring US-led efforts to emphasise maritime cooperation to support the common good. However, the expansion of Asian navies – particularly that of China's People's Liberation Army Navy (PLAN) – has fostered the re-emergence of more traditional state-on-state rivalries that has produced a renewed focus on warfighting capabilities and driven the United States to refocus its forces towards Asia under the so-called 'Pivot to the Pacific'. The recent return of Russia as a potential military threat certainly reinforces the wisdom of not entirely discounting the need for warships to fight each other at sea.

Philip Grove's review of recent naval operations looks at the same trends from a different perspective. Public perceptions of navies during the Cold War were dominated by the importance of submarines, both in their roles as delivery systems for nuclear weapons and as a potential threat to vital sea lanes in the Atlantic. Whilst these perceptions were never entirely accurate, they tended to force many navies into something of a strategic straitjacket. The return of navies to involvement in a much wider range of operations, heralded by the British Royal Navy's successful expeditionary deployment to the Falkland Islands in 1982 whilst the Cold War was still at its height, has brought greater freedom to demonstrate the flexibility inherent in naval power. It is interesting to note that both writers see the current roles and missions of navies as very much part of an historic continuum in spite of the considerable backdrop of change.

WORLD FLEETS TODAY

Things that have changed, however, are the size and structure of many of the world's largest fleets. This is reflected in Table 1.6, which compares the strengths of the main global navies now with the position twenty-five years ago. The following key conclusions are suggested:

The Australian *Anzac* class frigate *Warramunga* and the PLAN's Type 053H3 counterpart *Luoyang* exercising in the South China Sea in 2010. Whilst China is an important trading partner for nearly all Asian countries, her naval expansion is causing many cause for concern. *(Royal Australian Navy)*

- The major navies highlighted in the table are generally smaller in 2015 than they were in 1990. This reflects both financial considerations and, also, the use of technology to allow a smaller number of more sophisticated ships to do more. This trend towards declining fleets is much less marked in Asia than elsewhere in the world.
- Within this general trend, there has been a marked shift away from lighter surface combatants such as smaller frigates and fast attack craft. This is also the case with respect to mine countermeasures vessels and – to a lesser extent – patrol submarines. In most of the leading Asian navies, this has been counterbalanced by increased numbers of 'high end' units, such as destroyers. This partly demonstrates the progress made by countries such as China and South Korea in refocusing their fleets towards 'blue water' roles. However, unlike some of the traditional Western blue water navies, local considerations still requires both these fleets to retain considerable numbers of smaller ships for offshore defence.
- Nearly all navies have attempted to maintain or increase amphibious forces, whilst support shipping has also faired relatively well. This largely reflects the increased importance attached to long-distance expeditionary warfare described in the opening chapters.
- Although the US Navy has shrunk considerably in size since 1990, the breadth and extent of its capabilities have no significant rival. China's PLAN has certainly grown considerably in potency but nowhere near the extent to rival the potential threat posed by the Soviet Navy at the end of the Cold War. This is even more the case when consideration is given to the US Navy's considerable technological superiority; a factor not evidenced by numbers alone.

There is inevitably significant interest in ranking the leading and, indeed, all navies in accordance with their size and capabilities in spite of the difficulties already referenced with respect to pure numerical comparisons. A number of academic systems exist to provide a more sophisticated basis for such an exercise. Notable examples include the ten-rank Todd/Lindberg classification system (see Table 1.7) and the similar nine rank approach adopted by Eric Grove and Michael Morris.[4] Both ranking systems range from navies capable of global reach power projection – a ranking confined to the US Navy – at

1.7: TODD/LINDBERG CLASSIFICATION SYSTEM

RANK	DESIGNATION	DEFINING CAPABILITIES
BLUE WATER NAVIES		
1	Global-reach power-projection	Multiple, regular and sustained power-projection missions globally in addition to homeland defence
2	Limited global-reach power-projection	At least one major power-projection operation globally in addition to homeland defence
3	Multi-regional power-projection	Power projection missions in regions beyond own EEZ in addition to homeland defence
4	Regional power-projection	Not-at-sea fleet air support other than organic helicopters, therefore limited to area of land-based aircraft range for power-projection missions
NON-BLUE WATER NAVIES		
5	Regional offshore coastal defence	Costal-defence operations at least in own EEZ and slightly beyond
6	Inshore coastal defence	Confined to inner reaches of own EEZ
7	Regional offshore constabulary	Geographic reach as in rank 5, but maritime policing (not maritime defence)
8	Inshore constabulary	Maritime policing confined to inner reaches of own EEZ
9	Inland waterway	Waterborne riverine defence of landlocked states
10	Token navies	Very basic constabulary capabilities if any

Notes
Summarised from *Navies and Shipbuilding Industries: The Strained Symbiosis* (Westport, CT: Prager Publishers, 1996).

the top of the scale to token navies with very limited constabulary forces at the other. Whilst such standardised comparison systems have benefits of consistency – and would certainly accord all the navies in Table 1.6 with some form of power projection (or 'blue water') status – their practical application is fraught with difficulty. To cite just one example, to what extent should Brazil's ranking be adjusted to take account of the fact that its sole aircraft carrier, *São Paulo*, has doubtful operational availability?

As such, no attempt is made to undertake such rankings in our reviews of the larger fleets. Instead, a range of contributors assess the factors influencing how each of the most significant fleets has developed over the past twenty-five years, as well as its current structure and priorities. Inevitably, this analysis is undertaken from a range of perspectives. Scott Truver, for example, looks at the US Navy's progress through the lens of the most significant strategic documents it has promulgated since the end of the Cold War. Richard Beedall highlights how the British Royal Navy's ambitious plans to transform to a more expeditionary posture has been constrained by political neglect. He also explains the current naval environment in the Middle East, where there is widespread reliance on external powers – such as the US Navy and Royal Navy – to provide maritime security. James Bosbotinis, meanwhile, examines

both the benefits and difficulties the Soviet legacy brought to the reconstituted Russian Navy, as well as its current place in Russian military thinking.

Inevitably, there is considerable focus on the Asian navies. A quartet of contributors based in the region – Alastair Cooper, Jack McCaffrie, Chris Rahman and David Stevens – highlight the rise of China's PLAN and its impact on the other major regional fleets. The PLAN's expansion has also had ramifications in the Indian Ocean, as explained in Mrityunjoy Mazumdar's regional review. However, China is only part of the story. For example, North Korean sabre-rattling has had a significant impact on both Republic of Korea Navy and Japanese Maritime Self Defence Force (JMSDF) force structures. Moreover, both Japan and South Korea suffer from a historic legacy that means relations between each other are not necessarily free of tension.

SHIPBUILDING & DESIGN
In addition to changes in fleet sizes and structures, there has also been considerable refinement to the way that warships have been built and designed. Naval architect Hartmut Ehlers, a former employee of the Blohm & Voss yard that originated the modular MEKO concept, takes us through some of the main technical trends. He explains how factors such as stealth, accommodation standards and

modularisation have also contributed to the growth in size that is one of the more readily recognisable features of modern warships across the globe. He also explains how ongoing technological advances will shape the ships of tomorrow. Subsequent chapters look at different warship types, focusing on the more significant classes of the post-Cold War era. It is notable, in spite of the growth of shipbuilding away from its traditional European and North American hubs, how the vast majority of the more sophisticated warship designs currently originate from a relatively small number of established builders. Given the progress achieved in China and South Korea, this may change in the future.

TECHNOLOGY & MANNING

The book's final chapters look at technology and manning. Norman Friedman provides a broad-ranging technological review, focusing on how the rapid rise in computing power typified by Moore's Law has revolutionised naval warfare on, above and under the sea.[5] As well as examining the technical details, he explains how this enhanced capability has been adapted to the new, often littoral-focused operating environment in which navies now find themselves. In many cases, technology derived from the civilian sector has been used to compensate for shrinking financial resources.

Norman Friedman makes the point that naval air power remains particularly relevant at a time when littoral operations are increasingly important, as it provides the only adequate means of engaging the fleeting but numerous targets that might be found in an environment such as Libya or Syria if nearby bases are not available. This is reflected in David Hobbs' comprehensive description of current naval aviation capabilities. One particularly strong theme is the growing popularity of LHD-type 'big deck' amphibious carriers and other aviation-capable shipping as medium-sized navies come to appreciate the capabilities effective naval aviation provides. Another is the development of unmanned aerial vehicles (UAVs) in a broad range of maritime roles.

The concluding chapter looks at the important but often ignored subject of naval manning. History has proved that effectively trained personnel are vital for the maintenance of a capable navy. This remains true in this age of autonomous vehicles and of greater automation generally. Whilst the costs of personnel have resulted in a general reduction in the number of sailors, this has been counterbalanced by

A computer-generated image of the 'Dreadnought 2050' concept produced under the auspices of Startpoint, a new British maritime mission systems initiative in 2015. Although many of the concept's design features are currently hypothetical, elements such as catamaran hulls, mission bays and tethered unmanned vehicles are already in use. *(Startpoint)*

the end of conscription in many navies and much greater levels of overall professionalism. The increased emphasis on naval collaboration referenced in the opening chapters is also relevant here, as it has provided many smaller navies opportunities to broaden their knowledge and experience.

CONCLUSION

It is apparent that the world's navies in the early years of the twenty-first century have faced a fast-evolving situation from a geopolitical, financial and technological perspective. As new uncertainties arise in the West's relations with Russia and tensions in Asia continue, this backdrop is unlikely to change significantly. As such, any definitive conclusions as to the future direction of fleets around the world can only be speculative. However, from the editor's perspective, the following areas are likely to warrant ongoing consideration in the years ahead:

■ **The status of the US Navy as the world's dominant naval power:** The monopolistic position that the US Navy and its allies enjoyed with respect to sea power in the immediate aftermath of the Cold War is now clearly being eroded by the expansion of China and other fleets. Whilst it seems likely

that the US Navy will remain the dominant naval power for the foreseeable future, the strategies it adopts to maintain this position will have a key impact on the extent of its leadership.

■ **Continued tensions in Asia:** There is currently no obvious solution to tensions in Asia, which will likely remain a key focal point from both a military and international relations perspective. Although China's neighbours will inevitably balance the importance of their trading relations with the world's second economy against their concerns over perceived Chinese expansionism, it seems probable that both formal and informal alliances to counter a worst-case scenario of actual conflict will continue to develop. North Korea's likely actions will remain an area of uncertainty. Regional naval and other military expenditure will continue at a relatively high level.

■ **Warfighting capabilities in warship design:** There has been a marked tendency towards emphasising constabulary capabilities in a number of European warship designs, whilst even the US Navy's littoral combat ships have – rather missing the point – been criticised for lack of offensive weaponry. This is in marked contrast to the situation in Asia.[6] Looking forward, however, increased tension in Europe may see a greater emphasis on combat in local warships.

- **Technological Change:** A number of technologies, for example railguns, laser weapons and unmanned carrier aircraft, are currently in their infancy. Many of these weapons are largely the preserve of the US Navy and present only in small numbers. The use of such systems seems likely to grow considerably looking forward.

Doubtless readers will have their own factors to add to this list.

ACKNOWLEDGEMENTS

Just as for the US Navy's hopes of achieving a secure maritime environment based on partnership between co-operating navies, such a wide-ranging book as *Navies in the 21st Century* could only have come about as a result of the collaboration of many people. Foremost amongst these must stand the distinguished group of international contributors, who have provided a diverse range of insights into navies today. I have personally learned much from their various chapters and am grateful for their support. I am indebted to Professor Geoffrey Till FKC for contributing his insightful foreword and guiding me towards contributors for particularly challenging parts of the book. My former fellow student and university flatmate, Professor David H. Dunn, now Head of the Department of Political Science and International Studies at the University of Birmingham, also provided considerable help in this regard. I must especially thank Rob Gardiner of Seaforth Publishing for agreeing to make this one-off supplement to the *World Naval Review* series a reality, as well as Steve Dent for his continuing patience and professionalism in translating the editor's often ill-judged requirements into such an excellent and cohesive design. John Jordan's series of line drawings, many specially produced or adapted for this book, speak for their own excellence but I have also to thank him for his practical advice in the early planning stages. Finally, the support of my wife Susan in continuing the time-consuming and thankless task of undertaking initial proof-reading is acknowledged with affection.

Comments and criticisms from readers are always appreciated; please direct them for my attention to info@seaforthpublishing.com

Conrad Waters
1 January 2016

A US Navy X-47B unmanned combat air vehicle demonstrator pictured alongside a manned FA-18F Super Hornet strike fighter during trials onboard the carrier *Theodore Roosevelt* (CVN-71) in 2014. The development of UAVs in a broad range of maritime roles is an important current naval trend. *(US Navy)*

Notes

1. Information in Diagrams 1.1 to 1.3 is derived from the Stockholm International Peace Research Institute (SIPRI) Database at: http://www.sipri.org/research/armaments/milex/milex_database. The SIPRI Military Expenditure Database contains data on 172 countries over the period 1988-2014. The editor is grateful to Dr Sam Perlo-Freeman, Senior Researcher and Head of the SIPRI Project on Military Expenditure in its Arms and Military Expenditure Programme for his guidance with respect to the usage of comparative expenditure data.

2. These statements are made on the basis of nominal GDP and actual exchange rates. The United States' comparative advantage would reduce – indeed China would be regarded as a larger economy – if purchasing power parity (PPP) adjustments were made to take account of the 'real' cost of living in various economies. PPP adjustments might be regarded as being of limited relevance when considering military expenditure given the fact much of the cost of technology and other expenses (e.g. fuel) are subject to external factors.

3. Rumsfeld had previously also served as Secretary for Defense under President Ford from 1975 to 1977.

4. The Todd/Lindberg system was first set out in their *Navies and Shipbuilding Industries: The Strained*

Symbiosis (Westport, CT: Prager Publishers, 1996). The Grove/Morris system is referenced by Geoffrey Till in *Seapower: A Guide for the Twenty-First Century* (London: Frank Cass Publishers, 2004).

5. Gordon E. Moore (b. 1929) was a co-founder of Fairchild Semiconductor and, later, Intel Corporation. In 1965 he observed the doubling of the number of components in each integrated circuit – essentially an indication of its power – every year and predicted this would last for at least a decade. In 1975, again looking forward, he revised this forecast to a doubling at least every two years. The period is often quoted as eighteen months due to a statement of a fellow Intel executive, David House, that computer performance would double every eighteen months around this time. The prediction has proved remarkably accurate over a sustained period but is now starting to decelerate.

6. The editor is minded of Toshi Yoshihara and James R Holmes' analysis of the relative directions of European and Asian Seapower, 'As one civilization vacates the oceans, another is crowding the seas and skies with ships and warplanes that bristle with offensively orientated weaponry' in *Red Star over the Pacific: China's Rise and the Challenge to US Maritime Strategy,* (Annapolis MD: Naval Institute Press, 2013), p.3.

2.0   Ian Speller

POST-COLD WAR NAVIES

It is now almost thirty years since the Cold War ended with the fall of the Berlin Wall (1989), the reunification of Germany (1990), the dissolution of the Warsaw Pact and the break-up of the Soviet Union (1991). In the space of a few months the old certainties that had dominated strategic thought and practice for decades were swept away. In the years that followed navies had to adjust to a new environment where friends and enemies were less obvious and behaved less predictably than in the past, where established justifications for strategy and policy often did not match new national priorities, and where cherished roles appeared much less relevant than before. For many navies this occurred at a time when the end of the Cold War brought demands for a 'peace dividend' and reductions in expenditure on the armed forces. That the most immediate 'dividend' was not peace but rather a series of minor conflicts, regional wars and humanitarian crises brought additional challenges as navies adjusted to

the shift away from old certainties. These changes had an impact on most navies and none more so than the most powerful and capable during the Cold War, the US Navy.

HISTORICAL BACKGROUND

The United States emerged victorious from the Second World War with the largest and most powerful navy in the world. Its position of dominance was reinforced by the facts that the next largest navy belonged to a close ally (Britain) and the Soviet Union, transformed now from an ally to a potential adversary, had only very limited maritime forces and these focused mainly on coastal defence. For the first decade of the Cold War the United States thus enjoyed a period of what Samuel Huntington described as 'monopolistic sea power'.[1] This gave the United States the chance to enjoy the fruits of global sea control without facing any peer rival, providing them with a major strategic advan-

tage in a series of crises and limited conflicts. This position was never likely to persist unchallenged. After a slow start, the Soviet Union expanded its own navy and, by the 1960s, was beginning to develop blue-water capabilities able to contest United States' dominance beyond Russian waters. Thus, within a decade of their humiliation at the hands of superior United States' maritime power during the 1962 Cuban Missile Crisis, the Soviets were able to challenge their rival at sea. Notably, during the 1973 Yom Kippur War the US Navy's Sixth Fleet in the Mediterranean found itself shadowed by the Soviet 5th *Eskadra*, with the latter gaining diplomatic leverage and political impact in a manner that was discomforting for the West.

By this time the Soviet Navy had surpassed the British as the second largest although it still lagged behind the US Navy in terms of size and capability, particularly in respect of the key United States' offensive platform, their aircraft carriers. Soviet surface ships made regular and high-profile deployments far from home and bases were established in the Mediterranean (Syria) and South East Asia (Vietnam). The most serious challenge to the West was provided by the Soviets' large submarine force and long-range bombers that threatened NATO's vulnerable Atlantic sea lines of communication.

Nevertheless, and despite the very real threat that these posed to transatlantic shipping, by the late 1970s it was recognised that in any conflict the Soviet Navy's major concern would be defensive, and would focus in particular on protecting so-called 'bastions' in the Barents Sea, Arctic Ocean and the Sea of Okhotsk where their strategic nuclear missile submarines (SSBNs) could be protected from attack. This provided an opportunity that, by threatening the bastions, the Soviets could be forced to divert additional assets to their defence, reducing the forces that would be available to attack Allied shipping elsewhere. This approach lay at the heart of the new US Maritime Strategy that evolved during

The US Navy aircraft carriers *Constellation* (CV-64) and *Kitty Hawk* (CV-63) operating together during the 2003 Invasion of Iraq. The build-up of the US Navy during the 1980s produced an offensively-orientated fleet with considerable power projection assets. Many of these proved to be sufficiently flexible to remain of use during the post-Cold War era. *(US Navy)*

NATO warships from Turkey, the United Kingdom, the United States and Denmark exercise together in June 2005. The end of the Cold War brought about a new environment where friends and enemies were less obvious and behaved less predictably than in the past. *(Royal Australian Navy)*

the early 1980s and was published in unclassified form in 1986.[2] That strategy articulated a rather Mahanian focus on seizing the initiative in the war at sea through offensive action in the battle for sea control; carrying the fight to the enemy in order to defeat and destroy their forces at the time and place of America's choosing, rather than fighting a defensive battle on the Soviets' terms. In this way they could secure friendly use of the sea and enable the

reinforcement and support of America's allies in Europe, Japan and elsewhere. They could also use Western maritime superiority to deter the Soviets from taking aggressive military action, using Warsaw Pact vulnerability in the maritime domain to compensate for their numerical superiority on land in central Europe. The strategy reflected the bellicosity of the Reagan administration's approach to the Soviet Union and was accompanied by a

major naval build-up aimed at the creation of a '600-ship Navy'.[3]

Thus, the US Navy approached the end of the Cold War with an offensive mission dominated by a desire to engage and defeat the main enemy in their own backyard. With a fleet that included fifteen aircraft carriers, forty-four battleships and cruisers, sixty-eight destroyers and sixty-five major amphibious vessels, it remained by far the most powerful.[4] The end of the Cold War and the precipitate decline of the Soviet fleet removed at a stroke the existing rationale for this navy and it was clear that the admirals would need to find a new role if they were to justify their share of a reduced budget. That the end of the Cold War would not usher in a period of prolonged peace was soon demonstrated by the Iraqi invasion of Kuwait in 1990 and the subsequent war in the Persian Gulf in 1991. The US Navy was fully involved in the response to the invasion and in the defeat of Iraqi forces, but inevitably it played a supporting role in what was primarily an air and land campaign.

THE US NAVY'S SHIFT TO THE LITTORAL

With the Soviets gone the United States no longer faced a peer rival able to challenge global sea control, but it was clear that there would still be conflicts and crises that would likely involve the United States in some form or another. The US Navy responded to this new era in a series of 'capstone' policy documents that articulated a shift in emphasis away from 'blue water' operations towards a focus on responding to the challenge of what the US Marine Corps described as 'chaos in the littorals'. The first of these documents, entitled *The Way Ahead*, was published in April 1991, shortly after the conclusion of the Gulf conflict. This was followed in 1992 by … *From the Sea*, in 1994 by *Forward From the Sea*, and in 1997 by *Anytime, Anywhere: A Navy for the 21st Century*.[5]

Despite some notable differences in emphasis between these documents they all shared a common focus on a littoral approach and on the kind of capabilities that would enable the navy to influence events on land from the sea in a context where regional crises could occur in unexpected places. Blue-water concerns were never entirely forgotten, and received enhanced prominence in *Forward From the Sea*, but the US Navy had clearly repositioned itself from being one designed primarily to fight for control of the sea against a major peer rival to a force able to exploit its near-monopolistic control in order to influence events ashore in a broad range of contingencies. US Navy interest was matched by that of the US Marine Corps whose concept for *Operational Maneuver from the Sea*, published in 1996, articulated a way for amphibious forces to be employed to decisive effect in the post-Cold War era.[6]

The need to project power ashore was evident in a series of crises including Operations 'Deny Flight' (1994) and 'Deliberate Force' (1995) in Bosnia, where US Navy and US Marine Corps aircraft and sea-launched cruise missiles made an important impact. This was also the case with respect to Operation 'Allied Force' in Kosovo (1999), where sea-launched missiles and carrier aviation made another significant contribution to success ashore. Sea-based missiles and aircraft also contributed to the constant sorties and occasional strikes in the Persian Gulf that marked the interval between the 1991 Gulf War and the 2003 invasion of Iraq. In all three cases the US Navy also undertook embargo operations in support of international sanctions. The growing range of sea-based strikes was illustrated in 1998 when seventy-five sea-launched Tomahawk cruise missiles were fired at targets in Sudan and land-locked Afghanistan in retaliation for the terrorist attacks on United States' embassies in East Africa in August that year. That the US Navy could also fulfil more traditional forward presence and deterrence missions was illustrated during the Taiwan Straits crisis in 1996 when two US Navy carriers were deployed to the straits in response to provocative Chinese missile tests; a rather traditional employment of naval forces to demonstrate United States' capacity and resolve to protect its friends from potential aggression.

By 1999, ten years after the fall of the Berlin Wall, the US Navy had contracted significantly, from almost 600 (actually 566) ships and submarines in commission to 'just' 317. The four old battleships were retired and the navy cut the number of carriers in commission from fifteen to twelve. Particularly heavy cuts were experienced by those forces whose primary rationale related to Cold War missions. Thus, the number of strategic missile submarines was halved from thirty-six to eighteen boats over the course of the decade, nuclear-powered attack submarine numbers were similarly cut from ninety-six to fifty-seven and conventional attack

US Marines embarked on the amphibious assault ship *Tarawa* (LHA-1) undertaking landing exercises in the Persian Gulf in February 2003, shortly before the invasion of Iraq. The aftermath of the Cold War saw the US Navy increasingly preoccupied with being able to exploit its monopolistic control of the sea to influence events ashore. *(US Navy)*

submarines were phased out entirely. The number of frigates, intended primarily for anti-submarine work, was cut by nearly two-thirds, from 100 to just thirty-seven. It should be noted that over the same time period the number of amphibious ships was reduced from sixty-five to forty-one hulls, although the replacement of older ships with newer, more capable vessels mitigated the loss in expeditionary capability. As Amund Lundesgaard has noted, the increase in the number of mine countermeasure vessels, from five to sixteen, reflected the new emphasis on littoral warfare.[7]

MEETING NEW CHALLENGES

One of the features of thinking about security at this time was the growing recognition that concepts based solely on traditional military concerns were no longer sufficient. This impacted on perceptions of security at sea as much as it did the land. It had always been the case that the smuggling by sea of arms, narcotics or people could present a security challenge and that the sea could be used as a medium for attack by terrorists and other sub-state groups. However, these problems appeared particularly acute in the 1990s and 2000s as concerns about a 'new' brand of religiously-motivated terrorism and fears of the proliferation of weapons of mass destruction (WMDs) combined to reinforce established concerns. At the same time there was growing recognition that the security of an increasingly globalised world economy depended on the safe and timely arrival of cargoes that travelled by sea and that could be disrupted at sea or ashore by criminal activity, politically-motivated violence or simply by poor maritime practice. This served to elevate to a new importance maritime security operations (those operations designed to counter terrorism and other forms of illegal activity at sea).

Cynics might argue that Western navies began to emphasise such things because their previous key roles, related to deterrence and warfighting, appeared much less relevant now that they had no conventional adversary to measure themselves against. Whatever the case, that security could be challenged in a variety of unconventional ways was readily apparent even before events such as the attack by al Qaeda on the US Navy destroyer *Cole* in 2000 and the terrorist attacks on targets in Washington and New York on 11 September 2001. These had an important impact on United States' foreign policy, contributing to large-scale military

The Littoral Combat Ships *Fort Worth* (LCS-3) – foreground – and *Freedom* (LCS-1) pass each other off the coast of San Diego. The US Navy's increased interest in littoral operations following the end of the Cold War eventually spawned the Littoral Combat Ship concept. *(Lockheed Martin)*

intervention in Afghanistan (2001) and Iraq (2003) which led, ultimately, to enduring and costly campaigns that achieved rather equivocal results. The US Navy and Marines were heavily involved in both, with strikes conducted by sea-based cruise missiles and carrier aviation and also the landing of troops and supplies from the sea.

While the use of the sea to land United States (and Coalition) forces in Iraq appears unremarkable, the fact that maritime forces could play such a major role in military operations in Afghanistan is noteworthy given the landlocked nature of that state. Despite this, the US Navy supported operations there with the creation of an Expeditionary Strike

The Pentagon burns after the terrorist attacks on the United States on 11 September 2001. Thirty-three sailors and nine other US Navy employees or contractors were amongst the 125 killed at this location. The '9/11' attacks had a significant impact on United States' foreign policy and hence US Navy operations. *(US Navy)*

Force (ESF) consisting of four carrier battle groups and two amphibious ready groups. The ESF contributed strikes deep into Afghanistan and also undertook maritime interdiction operations to intercept cargo intended for the Taliban regime (via Pakistan or Iran). Perhaps most surprising, in November 2001 Marines from the 15th and 26th Marine Expeditionary Units were projected into Afghanistan from amphibious ships in the Arabian Gulf 450 miles away. Joining US Army Special Forces already in theatre, these were the first conventional US ground forces in that country.[8] The success of this operation provided some vindication for the recent preoccupation of the US Navy and Marine Corps with power projection from the sea.

Experience in Afghanistan, and from 2003 also in Iraq, provided a salutary reminder of the costs (human and material) associated with any attempt

A GBU-12 Paveway II laser-guided bomb is loaded onboard a F/A-18 Hornet strike fighter prior to operations over Afghanistan in early 2002. US Navy and Marine forces played a major role in the initial intervention in Afghanistan, somewhat vindicating their emphasis on power projection from the sea. *(US Navy)*

to maintain large ground forces on foreign soil against the wishes of at least a portion of the local people. Within this context the US Navy and Marines were able to emphasise the value of expeditionary forces which could be kept sea based, available to intervene if need be but capable of being forward deployed without a footprint ashore and without infringing the sovereignty of any third parties. By sea basing forces in this manner the US might also be able to maintain a presence in regions where even friendly states might be reluctant to provide permanent bases that could become the focus for political dissent or terrorist activity. The basic idea was far from new, but sea basing in the twenty-first century could be enabled by a range of techniques and technologies that were not available in the Cold War.[9]

The growing appreciation that American and wider global security could be challenged by terrorist activity, criminality and by disorder at sea resulted in an emphasis on wider maritime security designed to deal with transnational threats such as piracy, criminality, terrorism and proliferation activities at sea. It was indicative of this approach that humanitarian assistance/disaster relief and maritime security operations were added by the US Navy to its list of 'Core Capabilities', joining the four traditional tenets of forward presence, deterrence, sea control and power projection. This emphasis on wider maritime security was reflected in the 2002 document, *Seapower 21* and, with even more force, in the 2007 *A Cooperative Strategy for 21st Century Seapower* (CS21).[10] The latter, a joint document produced with the USMC and US Coast Guard, was the first official maritime strategy produced by the United States since the end of the Cold War.

CS21 laid a clear priority on maritime security operations and on the need to secure improved Maritime Domain Awareness (defined as the effective understanding of anything to do with the maritime domain that can have an impact on safety and security). It articulated an understanding that the US Navy alone could not police the global commons but that it could promote partnerships with other navies and agencies in order to create what Admiral Mullen called the '1,000-ship navy'.[11] The notion was not that America would bankrupt itself trying to create a fleet of this size, but rather that friends, allies and partners could work together for the common good. Thus, CS21 identified that US interests would be best served by '… fostering a

peaceful global system comprised of interdependent networks of trade, finance, information and law, people and governance'.[12] It promoted the idea of Global Maritime Partnerships as a means of engaging other nations in defence of this system. It should be noted that CS21 did not neglect more traditional security concerns and it continued to emphasise the importance of forward-deployed, credible combat power as a means of limiting conflict, deterring war and defeating adversaries.

EUROPEAN MARITIME CONCERNS

Many European navies went through a similar change in approach to that adopted by the US Navy. During the Cold War the major concern had been the apparent threat to the east (or west) and naval policy was formulated accordingly. The major emphasis for NATO navies had been on coastal defence, local sea control/denial and anti-submarine operations to keep open the vulnerable Atlantic sea lanes. With the end of superpower confrontation these navies faced both a need and an opportunity to change.

Smaller European navies, such as those of Norway, Denmark and Sweden, underwent a noticeable move away from local concerns towards a new interest in supporting multinational maritime security and humanitarian relief operations further afield. Many invested in enhanced sealift capabilities to enable them to deploy and support forces on overseas missions. Some of the larger navies, including those of Britain, France, Italy, the Netherlands and Spain, focused investment on those assets designed to support the projection of power overseas, and particularly on vessels such as the Spanish assault ship/aircraft carrier *Juan Carlos I* that offered a multi-role capability useful in a wide range of contingencies. Similarly, the perceived requirement to be able to 'go to the crisis before the crisis comes to us' reinforced the desire of some navies (Britain, France, Italy, Spain) to maintain or to substantially enhance their ability to deploy airpower by sea. As with the US Navy, the need to secure and maintain sea control was not forgotten. However, there was a notable emphasis away from blue-water anti-submarine operations and towards the littoral. The European focus on wider maritime security was reflected in the European Union's (EU) first overseas naval mission, the deployment of EU NAVFOR to counter-piracy operations (Operation 'Atalanta') in the Gulf of Aden.

Piracy has been a problem throughout recorded history, although for much of the twentieth century that problem was localised and small scale. An upsurge of piratical activity in South East Asia in the 1970s and 1980s was eventually curtailed (if never entirely eradicated) by concerted activity by the regional states. In the first years of the twenty-first century a combination of disorder ashore and a lack of governance offshore led to a dramatic burst of piratical activity off Somalia, with incidents rising steadily from 2005 and peaking in 2011 with a total of 237 reported attacks. Given the importance of the Gulf of Aden as a major trade route, and the incapacity of the regional states to solve the problem, it was not surprising that the attacks prompted a major international response. To meet the challenge over forty navies contributed ships and/or personnel to anti-piracy patrols operating independently (as did the Chinese Navy) or as part of multinational operations such as NATO's 'Ocean Shield', US-led Combined Maritime Force's CTF-151 or Operation 'Atalanta'.

Typically involving the deployment to the region of between three and six surface combatants and two or three maritime patrol and reconnaissance aircraft, Operation 'Atalanta' was (and is) commanded from Northwood in the UK (the site of a major UK and NATO headquarters). EU NAVFOR has seen contributions from the larger EU navies, including from Britain, France, Germany, Italy and Spain, and also from a variety of smaller navies such as those from Belgium, the Netherlands, Malta and Sweden. The Maltese contribution, which included a staff officer at the UK headquarters and two vessel protection detachments working with the Dutch Navy in *Johann De Witt* and *Zuiderkruis,* provides an example of what a very small navy can do in collaboration with partners. The employment of these two large Dutch vessels in a role for which they were never designed gives a good indication of the kind of flexibility required of post-Cold War navies. A number of non-EU countries have contributed ships (including Colombia, New Zealand, Norway and Ukraine) or staff officers (Montenegro, Serbia, Ukraine) to EU NAVFOR. Undertaken within the framework of the EU's Common Security and Defence Policy, Operation Atalanta reflects that organisation's focus on a 'Comprehensive Approach' to security, tying in political, military, legal, and diplomatic tools in an attempt to address both the cause and effect of insta-

The new Dutch joint support ship *Karel Doorman* arriving at Freetown in Sierra Leone with humanitarian supplies as part of the fight against the Ebola epidemic in West Africa. The Netherlands is one of a number of European countries investing in flexible assets supporting power projection – and wider stabilisation and humanitarian operations – overseas. *(Crown Copyright 2014)*

bility in Somalia. Thus, in addition to dealing with piracy offshore and, much less frequently, taking direct action against pirate facilities onshore, the EU has undertaken capability and capacity building missions within the region in order to help address the root causes of instability.[13]

The European focus on maritime security operations was reflected in the 2014 EU Maritime Security Strategy which emphasised the need for greater co-operation between navies and other parties in building more comprehensive security and better maritime domain awareness.[14] The potential for non-traditional security threats to impact on the maritime sector has been illustrated recently by the plight of thousands of refugees and migrants travelling to Europe by sea in makeshift craft from North Africa and the Middle East and European navies have been very involved in trying to relieve their suffering and to save lives, with some success. They have had less success in stopping the traffic. It is worth noting that the commitment to international security has seen some European navies undertaking significant power-projection operations either as part of a national effort, as with the case of British intervention in Sierra Leone in 2000, or as part of a multinational coalition. The 2011 NATO interven-

tion in Libya provides a good example of the latter, with the navies of Britain, France and Italy making an important contribution to strike and embargo missions during that operation.[15]

In response to this mix of traditional and non-traditional security concerns Geoffrey Till has argued that twenty-first century naval policy has reflected both 'modern' and 'post-modern' tendencies.[16] 'Modern' approaches are those that focus on traditional national security tasks such as deterrence and the capacity to fight other navies while 'post-modern' approaches emphasise mutual cooperation in support of the common good. As Till noted, it was not just the US and European navies that have showed interest in 'post-modern' issues. Navies as diverse as those from China, India, Brazil and South Africa have all focused, to some degree or another, on maritime security operations and have contributed to the international effort to secure good order at sea. It seems likely that in circumstances where a threat is apparent or where one is anticipated then the policies of individual navies will lean towards 'modern' concerns associated with deterrence and warfighting, and in this respect it will be interesting to watch the response of the (currently rather 'post-modern') Scandinavian navies to the recent resurgence of Russian military self-confidence. Nevertheless, it seems unlikely that 'post-modern' concerns will ever retreat quite as far into the background as was once the case.

EMERGENT NAVIES

In many respects the most significant developments during this period occurred beyond Europe and the United States, particularly in Asia. The rapid economic growth experienced by many Asian states, most notably by China, suggested that power might be shifting away from the old world towards the new. The humiliation inflicted on China during the 1996 Taiwan Straits crisis, allied to China's growing dependence on seaborne imports and exports, appears to have spurred the Communist leadership of that state to invest in their navy, previously rather a neglected branch of the armed forces. While the Soviet Navy disintegrated and its successor, the Russian Navy, has made a rather slow and uneven recovery, in the period since the Cold War the Chinese PLAN has grown in size, reach, capability and ambition into a force larger than any of its neighbours and one that may, ultimately, be able to challenge United States' dominance in Asian waters. The furore associated with the commissioning in 2012 of China's first aircraft carrier, the *Liaoning*, reflected growing concern, particularly among American commentators, that this might herald the rise of a new maritime power and one that could, one day, become a true peer rival to the US Navy. China has moved from a policy focused largely on sea denial within its own territorial seas to one that aims to challenge United States' primacy within the so-called First Island Chain (from the Kuril Islands, through Taiwan and the Philippines to Borneo). In a conflict with the US this would likely take the form of approaches designed to deny the US freedom of action within these waters. Against a lesser rival the PLAN would probably aim to achieve and exploit sea control and it has a range of assets designed to allow it to do so.

The Norwegian frigate *Fridtjof Nansen* pictured off the Seychelles in 2013 whilst participating in the NATO Operation 'Ocean Shield' anti-piracy mission in the Indian Ocean. Some smaller European navies have undergone a noticeable shift towards supporting distant multinational security and humanitarian relief operations; controlling the threat from piracy in the Indian Ocean has been a major success. *(Tørbjørn Kjosvold/ Norwegian Armed Forces)*

In time it seems likely that China will be able to challenge the US and others further out into the Pacific and Indian Oceans.[17]

Perhaps inevitably, increasing Chinese investment in its navy has been matched by the expansion of the forces of many of its neighbours, notably South Korea and Japan. The existence of numerous disputes over maritime jurisdiction and the ownership of islands in the East and South China Seas, combined with a rather robust attitude towards the enforcement of their maritime claims on the part of China, has prompted something of a naval arms race within the region. As Geoffrey Till has noted, this has resulted in Asian regional navies outspending those of the 'old West' for the first time in centuries.[18] In response to this, and the apparent challenge posed by the rise of Chinese power, the US government has undertaken a 'pivot to Asia' indicating that in future the Asia-Pacific will be the main priority for the US armed forces. While this does not yet signal a disengagement from Europe it does indicate a reversal of the previous priority given to the Atlantic region.

Chinese investment in maritime facilities in the Indian Ocean (especially in Pakistan and Myanmar) has prompted Indian fears that the PLAN may try to encroach on waters that India considers to be within its own sphere of interest. Despite years of underfunding the Indian Navy has maintained its status as a major regional navy with a balanced fleet. Its acquisition of a nuclear-powered attack submarine (SSN) leased from Russia and the on-going construction of its first ballistic-missile submarine (SSBN), reflect a major step-up in ambition and capability. The Brazilian Navy, which is not nuclear armed, has also declared its intention to develop its own SSNs with assistance from France. In both cases, the Indian and Brazilian acquisition of SSNs will substantially increase their sea control/denial ability far from shore, and they will join a very small and select group of navies that are able to deploy these most advanced and capable weapon systems. Most other navies that aspire to a submarine arm continue to use conventional boats (SSKs), which remain as widely available as ever – and as capable.

TECHNOLOGIES & STRATEGIES

Development of an Indian SSBN offers a reminder that the number of nuclear-armed states has grown since the end of the Cold War, although thus far only India and probably Israel (which likely deploys

The vast new submarine base at Itaguaí, near Rio de Janeiro, is being developed by the Brazilian Navy with assistance from France. It will facilitate the construction of Brazil's first nuclear-powered attack submarine, a capability that will substantially increase its sea control/denial ability far from shore. *(DCNS)*

China's PLAN has grown substantially in size and capability in recent years and may ultimately be able to challenge the US Navy's dominance of Asian waters. This image shows the Type 052C destroyer *Jinan* on a goodwill visit to the east coast of the United States in late 2015. *(US Navy)*

nuclear-armed cruise missiles in its German-built SSKs) have attempted to join Britain, China, France, Russia and the United States in sending nuclear missiles to sea. Their desire to do so reflects the reality that this remains the safest place to deploy a national nuclear deterrent. The discussion about the role of nuclear weapons at sea has moved on since the Cold War, where their employment in a variety of guises, from intercontinental missiles through to nuclear bombs, torpedoes and depth charges, was hotly debated. However, it is clear that the nuclear issue has not gone away. Notably, United States' interest in using the advanced sensors and missiles deployed on its warships to contribute towards ballistic missile defence (BMD) reflects a desire to be able to protect the homeland, allies or in-theatre forces from ballistic missile attacks which, in the worst case scenarios, might be armed with WMDs.

The ability of the US Navy to contribute to BMD reflects the continued advance in naval 'sensors and shooters' that has taken place over the past thirty years. Technological advances have both

enhanced what naval ships, submarines and aircraft can achieve and have also posed new challenges. Some of the most notable advances have related to the increasing range and accuracy of strike operations and the ability of dispersed forces to undertake network centric operations, to remain linked into a 'system of systems' that enables them to operate as far more than the sum of their parts. The growing sophistication of ships, and the things that operate from them, has had an inevitable impact on cost. To take a typical example, the Royal Navy's latest Type 45 destroyers are far more capable vessels than their Cold War predecessors, the Type 42, but the design and production of just six ships has cost the British exchequer over £6bn (c. US$9bn). Few navies can afford large numbers of ships as capable and as costly as these. In such circumstances many fleets, even the US Navy, have seen a need to achieve a balance between the high-value mission critical assets, such as aircraft carriers, cruisers, destroyers and amphibious ships and smaller, cheaper, less capable assets, such as the US littoral combat ship, which can be procured in greater

numbers. There is nothing new in this, it continues a trend evident during the Cold War (and before).

One of the most discussed developments in recent years, which relates partly to new technology, has been the proliferation of so-called anti-access/area denial (A2/AD) weapons and techniques. These systems and approaches are designed either to slow or prevent opposing forces from entering a region (A2) or to limit their freedom of action once within the operational area (AD). The successful attack launched by Hezbollah (a sub-state group in Lebanon) on the Israeli corvette *Hanit* in 2006 provided a graphic illustration of the way in which high-technology weaponry, such as anti-ship guided missiles, was becoming more widely available. The continued improvement of such weapons, and their widespread proliferation, thus threatens to give a growing number of actors the capacity to deny the use of the sea to adversaries. An enterprising opponent could use these new weapons, in conjunction with established capabilities including mines, submarines, land-based aircraft and small fast attack craft, in innovative ways to pose a serious challenge even to a major navy.

Growing United States' concern about this challenge was reflected in the update to CS21, known as CS21R, published in March 2015. That document noted the rising importance of the Indo-Asia-Pacific region and the ongoing development of A2/AD capabilities whilst also continuing to stress the threat posed by criminal and terrorist activity at sea. The tone of the document is notably different to the original, placing greater stress on traditional security concerns. The revised strategy continues to note the importance of a global network of navies but now emphasises the value of such networks in enhancing warfighting effectiveness between partners and allies in addition to retaining the original focus on working together to meet maritime security challenges and to respond to natural disaster.[19]

The debate about A2/AD has often focused on apparently advanced systems such as the Chinese DF-21D anti-ship ballistic missile. However, this should not disguise the reality that in many cases, probably in most cases, the most serious challenges will come from an innovative combination of more established weapons. Threats may occur on the high seas but in most circumstances they are likely to be most challenging within the littoral region. This raises the value of those assets, such as aircraft carriers, which can deploy decisive force from over

The British Royal Navy Type 45 destroyer *Dragon* pictured operating off Gibraltar in March 2013. The growing sophistication of ships has had an inevitable impact on costs – the six ships of the class cost in excess of £6bn. *(Crown Copyright 2013)*

the horizon, projecting into the key danger zone without necessarily having to be there themselves. The confluence of threats within the littoral may also suggest that major assets should not deploy there until enemy defences have been substantially degraded. Prior to this, presence may rest on covert forces or relatively small vessels whose loss could be tolerated. Far from being a new development, this simply reflects a traditional use for submarines, corvettes, frigates and the like. There have always been places where it was not wise to send big ships. In future the use of unmanned vessels, both surface and sub-surface, may provide further options for presence, surveillance and strike into danger zones without having to risk human life or any mission critical asset.

It is a feature of 21st-century thinking about warfighting that challenges are expected to occur in all warfighting domains (sea, air, land, space, cyber and the electro-magnetic spectrum) and that these will call for the close coordination of joint assets in order to overcome them. Joint forces will need to leverage cross-domain synergies in order to secure access in all domains. Once again, this reflects a trend that had been evident for many years; note the 1986 Goldwater-Nichols Act in the United States.[20] Post-Cold War the expeditionary emphasis in the defence policies of many states further encouraged the need for armed forces to think and act in a joint manner. This impetus was reinforced by the realisation that the synergies associated with increased 'jointery' would be necessary in order to mitigate overall reductions in the size of land, sea and air forces. Today it is widely accepted that to meet the complex threats and challenges that they face navies will need to work closely with joint forces and with other agencies. The enhanced level of joint co-operation that future operations will require has been reflected in the emerging concept of Air-Sea Battle, developed by the US Navy in cooperation with the US Air Force as a response to the A2/AD threat.

While for many navies the period since the end of the Cold War was one characterised by changing roles and capabilities this was not the case for all. The Irish Naval Service provides a good example of a force whose role, primarily focused on constabulary duties within the Irish territorial sea and Exclusive Economic Zone (EEZ), did not change much. Sheltered from the realities of the Cold War by favourable geography and a national policy of military neutrality, the collapse of the Soviet Union

The Irish Naval Service provides a good example of a navy whose role has not changed greatly in the post-Cold War era. This image shows the patrol vessel *Aoife* exercising with a helicopter from the Irish Air Corps, in June 2014. *(Irish Defence Forces)*

had little if any immediate effect on the Naval Service. Indeed, Irish naval policy remained broadly unchanged until 2015 when, for the first time, vessels were deployed overseas in support of the European humanitarian effort in response to the refugee/migrant crisis in the Mediterranean. The broader point is worth re-emphasising; for some navies the end of the Cold War did not have an immediate or decisive impact upon them as their roles had never reflected Cold War concerns. For others the demise of one superpower and the shift in focus of the other did remove a potential sponsor, although the recent US interest in global maritime partnerships has seen them provide material and other assistance to a large number of navies in the developing world.

CONCLUSIONS

It is clear that there have been some significant changes in naval strategy and policy since the end of the Cold War. The collapse of the Soviet Union and the end of superpower confrontation brought a reduction in the size of the major Western navies and a change in priority from being prepared to

fight the Soviets towards engagement in a variety of lesser conflicts and crises far from home. For many this brought an increasing priority to power projection and expeditionary forces. The recognition that security could also be challenged by criminal or terrorist activity at sea saw a large number of navies placing a much greater emphasis on maritime security operations and there was a notable trend towards multinational collaboration in order to secure good order at sea.

The US Navy remained the largest and most powerful fleet and, for a period, enjoyed a dominance that was reminiscent of the 'monopolistic' days of the 1950s. The capabilities of other navies waxed and waned, as one might expect. Today the Russian Navy is a pale shadow of its Soviet predecessor but other navies, including those of India and Brazil, are gaining access to capabilities once the preserve only of major powers. Within Asia there has been a major naval build-up and the growth of the PLAN and other Asian navies is one of the most significant developments of the post-Cold War era. This, plus the recognition that A2/AD technologies and techniques may now give weaker forces an

The Chinese PLAN Type 052C destroyer *Jinan* and Type 054A frigate *Yi Yang* seen exercising with the Royal Australian Navy frigate *Darwin* on the first day of 2016. The growth of the PLAN and other Asian navies is one of the most significant developments of the post-Cold War era and may suggest the Western monopoly at sea is coming to an end. *(Royal Australian Navy)*

enhanced capacity to challenge larger rivals across all domains, may suggest that the Western monopoly at sea is coming to an end, if it has not already ended.

Of course, while this is all suggestive of change it also reflects a great deal of continuity. There is nothing new in the concept of rivalry at sea, even if the identity of the rivals may vary. Tactics and techniques have been adjusted in order to accommodate new technology and new ideas but, as has been discussed, often the resulting changes have been evolutionary rather than truly revolutionary, particularly if one takes a broader historical view. It is as true today as it was during the Cold War (or before) that navies undertake military, diplomatic and constabulary duties and different navies place different levels of priority on these different roles.

Some navies seek to establish and then exploit sea control, others are more concerned with denying them the ability to do so. Still more focus primarily on the task of securing their offshore estate and preventing criminality at sea. The ways in which they all do this will continue to evolve but the requirement for navies to police and protect the maritime domain and, if necessary, to fight to secure or deny the use of the sea, has changed little over the years.

Notes

1. Samuel Huntingdon, 'National Policy and the Transoceanic Navy', *Proceedings* (Annapolis, MD: Naval Institute Press, May 1954).

2. John B Hattendorf & Peter M Swartz (eds), *US Naval Strategy in the 1980s: Selected Documents* (Newport, RI: Naval War College Press, 2008), pp.203–29.

3. George Baer, *One Hundred Years of Seapower. The US Navy 1890 to 1990* (Stanford, CA: Stanford University Press, 1996), esp. Chapter 17.

4. Amund Lundesgaard, *US Navy strategy and force structure after the Cold War– IFS Insights – 4/11* (Oslo: Norwegian Institute for Defence Studies, 2011), p.17.

5. *The Way Ahead* (Washington DC: Department of the Navy, 1991); *From the Sea: Preparing the Naval Service for the 21st Century* (Washington DC: Department of the Navy, 1992); *Forward ... From The Sea* (Washington DC: Department of the Navy, 1994); *Anytime, Anywhere. A Navy for the 21st Century* (Washington DC: Department of the Navy, 1997).

6. *Operational Maneuver From the Sea* (Washington DC: Department of the Navy, 1996).

7. Lundesgaard, *US Navy strategy and force structure after*

the Cold War, op. cit., p.17.

8. *Naval Operations Concept 2010: Implementing the Maritime Strategy* (Washington DC: Department of the Navy, 2010), p.62.

9. For example see Sam Tangredi, 'Sea Basing: Concepts, Issues and Recommendations' in *US Naval War College Review – Autumn 2011 Vol. 63, No.4* (Newport, RI: US Naval War College, 2011).

10. *Sea Power 21* (Washington DC: Department of the Navy, 2002); *A Cooperative Strategy For 21st Century Sea Power* (Washington DC: Department of the Navy, 2007).

11. Ronald E Ratcliffe, 'Building Partner's Capacity. The Thousand Ship Navy', in *US Naval War College Review - Autumn 2007, Vol. 60 No.4* (Newport, RI: US Naval War College, 2007).

12. *A Cooperative Strategy For 21st Century Sea Power*, op.cit.

13. For further information, please refer to the EU NAVFOR website at: http://eunavfor.eu/

14. Please refer to the European Commission for Maritime Affairs' website at: http://ec.europa.eu/maritimeaffairs/

policy/maritime-security/index_en.htm

15. Geoffrey Till and Martin Robson, *Corbett Paper No.12 - UK Air-Sea Integration in Libya 2011: A Successful Blueprint for the Future?* (London: King's College London, 2013).

16. See Geoffrey Till, *Seapower: A Guide for the 21st Century*, 3rd edition (London: Routledge, 2013).

17. See Toshi Yoshihara & James R Holmes, *Red Star Over The Pacific Ocean: China's Rise and the Challenge to US Maritime Strategy* (Annapolis, MD: Naval Institute Press, 2013).

18. Peter Dutton, Robert Ross & Oystein Tunsjo (eds), *Twenty-First Century Seapower. Cooperation and Conflict at Sea* (London: Routledge, 2012), p.182.

19. *A Cooperative Strategy for 21st Century Seapower, March 2015* (Washington DC: Department of the Navy, 2015).

20. The Goldwater-Nichols Act essentially revised the command structure of the United States' military, attempting to reduce the effects of inter-service rivalries by increasing the powers of the Chairman of the Joint Chiefs of Staff at the expense of the individual service heads.

3.0

Philip Grove

NAVAL OPERATIONS

If the end of the Cold War can be summed up in terms of winners and losers, then it was a maritime alliance that won the war. This is not an unusual situation, as most major wars in history have been won through the successful employment of naval power, with victory achieved by the maritime nations involved. The Napoleonic Wars, First and Second World Wars, as well as those in Korea and for the Falklands, illustrate this truism well.

Ironically, however, most of the West's politicians and public would have been unaware of the impact of their navies through the course of the forty-year Cold War struggle, let alone their key achievements by its end. For many the Cold War was waged almost solely by the armies and air forces of the alliances on both sides of the Iron Curtain. However, at its heart NATO was and remains a maritime alliance; and its most significant member, the United States, is a maritime nation. There is, after all, a significant clue in NATO's title. Moreover since the end of the communist threat to Europe and the wider world in the late 1980s, Western and now, increasingly, governments globally have resorted to naval power to execute their foreign policies on both regional and world stages.

The former perception that the major threat posed to Europe was from a land offensive by the Eastern Bloc has been replaced by an understanding that current challenges to European security now arise from far further afield and are sometimes global in nature. Likewise many countries elsewhere in the

The British Royal Navy's Trident-armed SSBN *Vigilant* seen returning from a patrol in March 2014. Submarine operations dominate popular perceptions of Cold War naval operations although the reality was somewhat different. Indeed, there is still a widespread lack of understanding of the naval contribution to the Cold War, even though it was a maritime alliance in the form of NATO that 'won' the war. *(Crown Copyright 2014)*

world have come to the conclusion that, whilst their land and air forces might well be key to maintaining the integrity of their own borders, they can be very limited when supporting national interests beyond their territory and, certainly, their coastline. The attributes of maritime power have given 21st-century politicians worldwide the most versatile, politically and economically cost-effective and re-useable tool with which to execute their policies.[1] This has been demonstrated time and time again since 1989 and – given recent developments – is likely to continue into the future. However, it was not always this way.

COLD WAR NAVAL OPERATIONS: AN OVERVIEW

The roles and actions of naval assets during the Cold War were never properly understood nor portrayed. The limited public opinions held on naval power – the traditional view of Cold War naval operations – were dominated by the undoubtedly important role of submarines but with navies otherwise playing a peripheral role to armies and air forces. Air forces, particularly, were seen as providing a crucial military capability in the early stages of the stand-off due to their apparent near-monopoly on the delivery of nuclear weapons. The popular image was somewhat removed from the reality. Navies were often the first and only responses to Cold War crises which were below the nuclear threshold. However, these crises were far removed from European eyes. Transport, logistics, power projection and maritime manoeuvre in the form of carriers, amphibious operations, fleet auxiliaries and naval gunfire support all executed government policy in a myriad of conflicts, but critically outside of Europe's gaze. This is a situation which persists to this day.

Nevertheless, by the late 1950s and early 1960s, navies were increasingly seen as key players in the delivery of nuclear systems for both superpowers and their allies. By the late 1960s, they were arguably the dominant ones. Aircraft carriers initially filled this role but soon both cruise missile and ballistic missile-armed submarines would be joined by the much more versatile, longer-ranged and covert strategic nuclear-powered submarines (SSBNs), whose ballistic missiles could be fired at targets from thousands of miles away. Equipment priorities – and what could loosely be regarded as doctrine – were heavily influenced by this nuclear role. For example, much British Cold War naval investment was focused on bombing the Soviet Union. The potential use of nuclear-armed Buccaneer strike jets in the 1960s simply evolved to the deployment of nuclear-armed Polaris missiles carried in *Resolution* class strategic submarines a decade later.

This strategic role continued to dominate much of the thinking of the key naval powers during the late 1970s and into the early 1980s. A good demonstration is the debate on the future importance of the size of US Navy aircraft carriers during the presidency of Jimmy Carter, a former nuclear submariner whose views had a significantly detrimental influence on the development of other United States' naval capabilities during this time. Equally, in the United Kingdom, the Nott Defence Review of 1981 placed nuclear delivery at the forefront of British naval strategy at the cost of a balanced, globally-deployable force.[2]

Submarine operations also achieved a high profile because of the influence they had on other maritime forces. A significant proportion of NATO and Warsaw Pact maritime assets became focused on either hunting submarines – for example, to ensure North Atlantic communications – or protecting their own sub-surface capability, such as the Soviet Union's defence of the waters of its strategic submarine 'bastions'. This inevitably resulted in a force structure that was less appropriate for a new world order where the primary threat would not be from a vast, well-known military machine but from the re-emergence of a myriad of the historical, racial and social tensions that had been sublimated into prosecuting the Cold War but, with its conclusion, were released upon the world.

ALL CHANGE

Thus, as of the mid-1980s, the equipment and strategy of the major navies, especially those in NATO and the Warsaw Pact, were mostly centred upon conducting a limited range of operations, largely deploying, hunting or protecting submarines.[3] Yet, in reality, many of these navies continued to perform more traditional, balanced naval roles that have now increasingly become the norm. This has suggested to many commentators that the years of the Cold War were actually years of aberration with respect to the fleet structures developed on both sides of the Iron Curtain.

The Falklands War (1982): There had already been hints, in fact more than hints given a number of

naval operations in the 1980s, that the significant limitations inherent in the narrowly-focused fleets of the Cold War era were increasingly recognised. For the United Kingdom, the Falklands War of 1982 was probably a key turning point. It brought the realisation that the Royal Navy specified by John Nott's defence review was incapable of supporting national policy beyond Britain's coastline unless nuclear weapons were to be unleashed; a totally unrealistic proposition. For the United Kingdom, the result was a reversal of many of the defence review's cuts and a commitment to a balanced navy with significant power-projection capabilities that has broadly endured.

The 74-day war – that saw the recovery of the

A map of the British operation to retake the Falkland Islands in 1982, showing the main theatre of operation's vast distance from the home base. The operation resulted in a commitment to maintaining a navy with significant power-projection capabilities that has broadly endured. *(US Military Academy West Point)*

remote British South Atlantic colony after an initially successful Argentine invasion – demonstrated the wide-range of conventional, balanced naval capabilities required to conduct a successful out of area operation, far from a home base. These included the almost total reliance placed on sea-based transportation and logistics, as well the need to gain both sea and air control – even if the latter was a little limited – prior to conducting an amphibious operation. It witnessed the projection of carrier airpower, the deployment of amphibious forces, the use of naval gunfire support and, ultimately, the prosecution of a naval-backed land campaign to successful fruition. It also produced lessons – for example, the importance of airborne early warning and control; the inadequacy of existing area and point defence anti-air systems; and the need to enhance damage control and survivability – that have had a marked effect on both fleet structures and warship design up to the present day. It also provided an important demonstration of the significance of naval airpower that was quick to be recognised internationally.

Late Cold War Operations: The expeditionary style of war represented by the Falklands Conflict has been repeated on numerous occasions subsequently.[4] Indeed, the later years of the Cold War saw a resurgence in the use of naval power by governments exerting their foreign policy at a distance, as seen in the deployment of Western navies in the Persian Gulf during the Iran-Iraq tanker war, as well as off the coast of the Lebanon. Additional examples include the United States' invasion of Grenada, its various actions against Libya and the toppling of the Noriega regime in Panama. A similar pattern of operations can also be seen in the actions of other navies. Some, it could be argued, would become blueprints for the twenty-first century.

Underpinning many of these operations was the US Maritime Strategy of the 1980s. This essentially committed the US Navy to a more offensive naval strategy to counter Soviet naval power, reinforced by a willingness to invest in a '600-ship fleet'.[5] Whether viewed as a scam to bankrupt the Soviet Navy or a realistic offensive strategy – the views of commentators differ widely – the new policy provided both the thinking and the equipment by which many of the US Navy's operations over the past twenty-five years have been conducted.

Iraqi tanks lie abandoned in Kuwait in the aftermath of Operation 'Desert Sabre', the short ground offensive that liberated the country from Iraqi invasion. Although the offensive was a successful demonstration of the US Army and Air Force's 'Air-Land Battle' doctrine, it was naval forces that provided the logistical support and sea control that set the scene for victory. *(US Department of Defense)*

The Gulf War (1990–1): A major test of the concepts behind the US Maritime Strategy occurred just as the Cold War ended, when Iraq unexpectedly invaded neighbouring Kuwait. The subsequent Operations 'Desert Shield' (the defence of Saudi Arabia), 'Desert Storm' (the six-week air and naval bombardment to dislocate Iraqi defences) and 'Desert Sabre' (the four-day ground offensive) were undertaken by an international, US-led coalition to liberate Kuwait. This coalition saw contributions from over forty countries, many of which provided naval forces. As might be expected, these forces were dominated by the US Navy, with a spearhead of no fewer than six aircraft carriers.[6]

As in the Falklands War, these operations demonstrated the value of expeditionary naval forces. In addition to the deployment of the carrier strike groups, the Gulf War saw the first operational Tomahawk Land Attack Missile (TLAM) launches conducted by the US Navy, a major amphibious feint (rather than the full assault suggested by the Maritime Strategy) and numerous Special Forces insertions. Perhaps most significant of all was the successful completion of an enormous maritime logistical undertaking. Ultimately, it was the successful employment of the US Army and US Air Force's 'Air-Land Battle' strategy, originally developed for NATO's Central European Front, against Saddam Hussein's land forces that concluded the war. Yet it was the mass movement of forces by sea, effective blockade and embargo operations, and the neutralisation of the Iraqi sea-denial forces that set the scene for victory in 1991.

WAR'S A DIRTY WORD
Thus, as the Cold War ended, the use of naval power had once again become a key part in the response to global crises. The end of the 'conflict' inevitably saw the shape and size of the major protagonists' naval forces change considerably, mostly shrinking in terms both of manpower and ship numbers. However, this was often accompanied by a process of modernisation, with a loss of submarines and anti-submarine escorts but a growth

in the quantity and quality of power projection forces. Equally, the recent past has seen growth in the size and capabilities of many other navies around the world, as well as significant expansion in their operational deployment.

Certainly navies in the post-Cold War era have found themselves busy, arguably far busier than in the 1970s and 1980s. There has been a constant stream of operations ranging from humanitarian and peacekeeping missions through anti-terrorist and anti-piracy deployments to actual warfighting as instability has increased following the end of the bi-polar world order. Arguably, navies have been consistently employed throughout this period due to their inherent flexibility compared to their land-based counterparts. Strangely, one major role of naval power in the immediate post-Cold War environment was rarely discussed; that of actual war. In fact many missions were described as 'operations other than war' or even 'peace support' operations; terms that could be seen to be all encompassing without mentioning the fighting that normally constituted part of the operation.

Perhaps the euphoria surrounding the Cold War's end and the swift implementation of cuts under the so-called 'peace dividend' blinded many politicians from considering the concept of war in the future. Certainly, at the start of the brief 'New World Order' that followed the Berlin Wall's collapse, any idea of naval forces existing for war was a concept held quietly by both navies and governments. Yet, as the twenty-first century has progressed, warfighting has once again become a staple role for the world's navies and one increasingly accepted by decision makers. The change can be illustrated by looking at the development of Royal Navy maritime doctrine. When the new *The Fundamentals of British Maritime Doctrine BR1806* was first published in 1995, much of the text concerning the roles the navy was associated with were operations below the threshold of war.[7] The navy's warfighting function was certainly not as explicit as many would have expected. By 2011 however, the fourth edition, now re-branded as *Joint Doctrine Publication 0-10, British Maritime Doctrine,* placed warfighting as the first role of naval power. This is supported by 'maritime security' and 'maritime engagement'. Warfighting is now a visually explicit and politically acceptable term for navies to employ. This is clearly justifiable since so many navies have found themselves in so many conflicts since the end of the Cold War.

Post-Cold War Naval Warfighting: In fact navies have found themselves in a succession of warfighting operations since 1989. Two types of warfare have remained constant over this period, viz. inter-state wars and intra-state conflict. Recent inter-state warfare includes the 1990–1 Gulf War already referenced, which was followed closely by the wars in the Balkans throughout much of the 1990s. These include the conflicts in Bosnia and, later, Kosovo with Serbia the target of Western military action on both occasions. Naval forces were involved in the Bosnia crisis as part of Operation 'Sharpguard' (the arms embargo placed upon the protagonists), Operation 'Deny Flight' (no-fly zone policing) and later Operation 'Deliberate Force'. This was the bombing campaign against the Serbs to force them towards negotiations which led to the Dayton Peace Accords. The 1999 Kosovo mission was Operation 'Allied Force'.

The 1990s also saw further actions against Iraq. This was followed by Operation 'Enduring Freedom-Afghanistan', the 2001 intervention in Afghanistan, and Operation 'Iraqi Freedom', the 2003 invasion of Iraq. The former should be remembered as seeing a unique and successful amphibious operation. Although Afghanistan is a landlocked nation, the forces – troops and aircraft – involved flew from carriers and amphibious ships, backed by air support from a multinational carrier force. Even during the later counter-insurgency campaign naval forces made an enormous contribution, especially those of the United States Marine Corps and the Royal Navy. The latter service provided half of Britain's forces on three occasions.[8]

All these operations witnessed naval power being used as a first responder to the crises. Sometimes, perhaps cynically, this was to demonstrate a degree of action on the part of governments wishing to avoid the complications of land basing and host-nation support that more comprehensive intervention would require. In other words, governments could be seen to be doing something but still avoid actually doing anything. However, the ability to send messages from international waters is a key component of naval power. Ultimately, for example with respect to Bosnia, some of these crises resulted in mission creep and the deployment of ground and air forces, supported from the sea.[9] In Bosnia, the naval forces initially deployed for maintenance of an arms embargo and then for peacekeeping eventually found themselves heavily involved in warfighting. As

The advent of the Tomahawk Land Attack Missile (TLAM) has a marked impact on naval operations from the 1990–1 Gulf War to the present day. This picture shows the cruiser *Anzio* (CG-68) launching a TLAM during Operation 'Iraqi Freedom' in 2003. *(US Navy)*

on other occasions, the eventual success of land-based contingents relied heavily on naval logistical support and the use of naval airpower. In Kosovo, this was supplemented by US Navy and Royal Navy TLAM strikes, the latter using cruise missiles in combat for the first time.

Meanwhile, intra-state wars have resulted in long-term counter-insurgency campaigns in Somalia, Sri Lanka, various South American countries, East Timor, Sierra Leone, Iraq, Afghanistan and Libya, to name but a few. Naval forces – whether national government, terrorist or those belonging to external powers – have been involved in all of them. The international dimension of these conflicts often resulted in 'coalitions of the willing' waging large-scale and, sometimes, lengthy wars for humanitarian and stability reasons. Often naval intervention has commenced for humanitarian

A US Marine Corps CH-46 Sea Knight helicopter operating from Camp Rhino, a forward base in Afghanistan, in December 2001. The initial intervention in Afghanistan saw a unique and successful amphibious deployment into a land-locked country. *(US Marine Corps)*

reasons – maritime forces can be used both to protect aid being delivered to an area of conflict and also provide expertise that other governmental and non-governmental agencies lack. However, such intervention does not necessarily ensure the peaceful conclusion to a mission and, on a number of occasions, direct military force has been employed. This can have mixed results; for example, the United States-led forces in Somalia in the 1990s ultimately failed to achieve their objectives. However, the failures have been outweighed by the successes, as evidenced by the following examples:

- **East Timor (1999):** The UN supported an Australian-led multinational peace enforcement mission to return East Timor to stability – after a referendum supporting independence from Indonesia provoked a violent reaction from pro-Indonesian militia – relied heavily on naval expeditionary and logistic forces. The operation achieved its objective with minimal casualties, whilst demonstrating a need to bolster the Royal Australian Navy's amphibious capabilities.
- **Sierra Leone (2000):** Large-scale British intervention in support of the government during the country's civil war – following earlier deployment of a frigate – relied heavily on the carrier *Illustrious* and an amphibious task force. The deployment of forces and the demonstration of carrier power as part of Operation 'Palliser' quelled opposition and led to stabilisation of the country over the following few years.
- **Libya (2011):** The 2011 intervention in Libya's civil war relied heavily on carrier-based air power and TLAM strikes for its ultimate success in degrading the Gadaffi regime's ability to quell opposition forces. The disproportionate contribu-

A US Marine Corps Osprey tilt-rotor landing on the British aircraft carrier *Ark Royal* during an exercise in 2010; a Harrier STOVL jet is seen in the foreground. Expeditionary operations involving naval amphibious and air power have become common from the later years of the Cold War onwards. *(Crown Copyright 2010)*

tion of carrier-based aircraft compared with more numerous land-based aviation assets was particularly notable.[10]

Most recently, operations in Iraq and Syria have often entailed significant naval commitment, especially the use of carriers to prosecute the air campaign against Islamic State forces. In fact American and allied carriers have provided much of the aerial capacity for these operations.

Other limited military operations have also taken place since the Cold War, particularly the creation and implementation of safe zones and no-fly zones. For example, Operation 'Haven' to protect Kurdish refugees in northern Iraq was initiated after 'Desert Storm'. Although a land-locked operation, Britain's contribution was largely provided by Royal Marines and Fleet Air Arm helicopters, all supported from fleet auxiliaries based in Turkey.

IT'S NOT JUST ABOUT WAR

Other naval humanitarian missions have gathered pace over the last twenty-five years. Naval forces have always been employed in the evacuation of nationals in response to wars and natural disasters but increased global instability is seeing these types of operation grow exponentially. They are also drawing in a much greater range of navies than hitherto. For example, the onset of the Libyan conflict in 2011 saw the traditional Western powers being joined by ships from China, India and South Korea in evacuation activities. More recently, in 2015 in Yemen, China's PLAN undertook the evacuation of foreign nationals for the first time. The importance attached to these operations has even resulted in navies acquiring ships which have been part or even wholly funded by national disaster relief funds, relieving strain on defence procurement budgets.[11] Naval evacuations also continue to take place in response to natural disasters, for example after the Indian Ocean tsunami of December 2004 and even the Icelandic ash cloud of 2010. The latter saw the British Royal Navy's larger ships deployed to assist the recovery of stranded tourists.

Natural disasters also see navies being used to insert humanitarian aid into the appropriate areas. More often than not disaster responders find the internal infrastructure of a nation destroyed or inoperable, with immediate access to a devastated nation only possible by helicopter or over a beach. Amphibious and naval aviation assets are clearly particularly valuable in such scenarios; for example the Italian Navy deployed its new carrier *Cavour* to carry aid and helicopters to Haiti on its first ever operational mission after the earthquake of 2010. The new Japanese helicopter carrier *Hyuga* (DDH-181) and the locally-deployed US Navy carrier *George Washington* (CVN-73) were both heavily involved in disaster relief operations after the 2011 Tohoku earthquake and tsunami.

Organised Crime: One other aspect of naval power that has gained renewed prominence in the twenty-first century has been international policing operations against organised crime, most notably drug cartels, people smugglers and pirates. Piracy, particularly, has emerged as a major influence on naval operations in recent years. Often well-organised and equipped, pirates have become the scourge of seas ranging from West Africa through the Indian Ocean and Arabian Sea to South East Asia. Indeed, pirates can be found almost anywhere there is navigable water, including riverine areas such as the Amazon basin.[12] The costs of piracy run into several billion dollars each year through expenses associated with insurance, security and the additional fuel used to avoid high-risk areas.

However, one positive result of the pirate threat to international shipping has been increased co-operation on the high seas to tackle the menace, sometimes between unlikely naval partners. This has been particularly the case in the Indian Ocean, where actions to combat Somali pirates have included the establishment of European Union (under Operation 'Atalanta'), NATO (under Operation 'Ocean Shield') and international (Combined Task Force 151) standing forces. The last-mentioned has been the most remarkable in so far as ships from the 'usual' Western allies have been joined by vessels from other – particularly Asian – nations, whilst there has also been co-operation with independently-deployed national task groups. The combined mission to deny access to interna-

The 2011 international intervention in Libya's Civil War relied heavily on naval power, including carrier-based and cruise missile strikes. This image shows a US Marine Corps Harrier jet operating from the amphibious assault ship *Kearsarge* (LHD-3) in the early stages of the intervention. *(US Navy)*

tional shipping and contain the pirate threat – including the use of ships, maritime patrol aircraft, other aviation assets and targeted operations against pirate strongholds – has been time-consuming and laborious but ultimately successful. Indeed, no reports of piracy incidents were recorded off Somalia or in the Gulf of Aden in the nine months to September 2015. However, piracy continues to be a major threat elsewhere in the world, with current hotspots including the Gulf of Guinea off West Africa and the waters of Indonesia.

Naval operations against other organised crime groups, particularly the global drug cartels, have also gathered tempo. Besides employing traditional smuggling methods such as the use of container ships and fishing vessels, the cartels have deployed more innovative methods, including experiments with homebuilt submarines. The support of extra-regional naval forces in areas such as the Caribbean has been important in combatting trafficking, as they bring capabilities unmatched by most local forces and immune to the influence the cartels can sometimes exert over national security services. The important role played by the larger and more capable navies in training and mentoring some of the less experienced fleets is also worth mentioning at this point.

Terrorism: Maritime terrorism is far from being a new phenomenon. Viet Cong activities from and at sea were experienced by the Americans in the 1960s, whilst British and Irish security forces had to deal with Irish Republican terrorists employing the sea during 'The Troubles' in Northern Ireland in the 1970s and the 1980s. Mediterranean nations had to deal with Arab terrorists – particularly the Palestine Liberation Organisation (PLO) – acting against Israeli and Western interests at around the same time. More recently, attacks against shipping such as those on the French tanker *Limburg* and the US Navy destroyer *Cole* (DDG-67) have highlighted the vulnerability of potential 'status targets'. However, the most notable development is, perhaps, growing evidence that many terrorist groups have learned the attributes of maritime power – such as mobility, flexibility and access – that have traditionally been the preserve of governments. Consequently, terror groups are increasingly moving vital equipment by sea and, increasingly, using the sea to launch attacks. Examples include the operations of the now defunct Tamil Sea Tigers in the civil war in Sri Lanka

A US Navy Sea Hawk helicopter unloads supplies of food and water in Jalan, Sumatra, in the aftermath of the December 2004 Indian Ocean tsunami. Naval forces often provide the only immediate means of access to stricken areas after natural disasters. *(US Navy)*

(1983–2009) and, more famously, the terror attacks on Mumbai in 2008.

The Sea Tigers are worthy of particular note. Beginning initially as a means of smuggling equipment and personnel into Sri Lanka, they quickly evolved an offensive role, employing a powerful force of attack and suicide boats, as well as Special Forces-type units such as frogmen. They proved capable of conducting a series of successful attacks – including amphibious operations behind government lines – and engaged in large-scale battles with the Sri Lanka Navy. The latter adopted the Sea Tigers' swarm tactics but employed larger, faster and more powerful attack boats. These ultimately outclassed the Tigers, regaining control of the sea for the government. The Sri Lanka Navy was also successful in utilising longer-range patrol vessels to interdict Tamil supply routes beyond the range of Sea Tiger vessels, assisted by improved surveillance techniques.[13]

The Sea Tigers ceased to exist with the loss of

their bases during the Sri Lankan government offensive that ended the civil war. However, the tactics adopted by both sides remain relevant in the face of the continued threat posed by well-organised terrorists. For example, India's heavy investment in a network of coastal surveillance radars – that extends to the shores of friendly states in the Indian Ocean – as well as the *Car Nicobar* high-speed patrol vessels appear to reflect key lessons learned from the conflict.

Other Constabulary Duties: In spite of the high profile inevitably attached to operations against piracy and terrorism, it is important to stress that more routine 'bread and butter' patrol activities to ensure the maritime security of domestic territorial waters remains the most important function of many of the world's navies. Extended Exclusive Economic Zones (EEZs) containing vital resources such as food and energy are increasingly seen as requiring naval protection. This has spurred considerable growth in demand for offshore and coastal patrol vessels to safeguard these resources and contribute to the protection of the broader maritime environment. There can also be maritime boundary rights to protect; a particularly live issue in areas such as the South China Sea.

CONCLUSION

In retrospect, the impact of the Cold War had some-thing of a stifling effect on many navies, particularly in the West. Undue focus on what appeared to be the key naval weapons system – the submarine – narrowed operational focus and associated procure-ment. Although navies remained the first responder of choice for many of the era's crises, their true flex-ibility was appreciated by few.

The collapse of the Berlin Wall brought about a period of retrenchment and reorganisation in the fleets of many of the Cold War's protagonists, although growth continued elsewhere. Even more significantly, there were subsequently few moments of rest for the major navies. A series of wars consis-tently demonstrated the importance and flexibility of naval power-projection and logistics. Likewise, frequent humanitarian interventions – whether peaceful or armed – showed the versatility of naval forces in achieving access, often when other forces

The Royal Netherlands Navy's offshore patrol vessel *Holland* is seen operating with a US Coast Guard HC-144 Ocean Sentry maritime surveillance aircraft in the Caribbean during an at sea interdiction when drugs with an estimated wholesale value of US$24m were recovered. Navies have been at the forefront of combatting threats such as terrorism, piracy and organised crime in the post-Cold War era. *(US Navy)*

The European Union Naval Force Somalia's then flagship, the F-100 class air-defence ship *Méndez Núñez*, undertaking a boarding operation in February 2013. The collapse of a bipolar world order has meant that the stabilisation capabilities navies can provide have been in increased demand. *(European Union Naval Force Somalia)*

could not. Navies have also been at the forefront of combatting the threats to regional and global security posed by terrorists, piracy and organised crime. Meanwhile, the extent of more routine policing activity has also greatly expanded.

The reasons for this veritable explosion in naval activity since the early 1990s need to be explored. Certainly, the instability arising from the demise of a bipolar world order has meant that the capabilities provided by naval forces have been in greater demand. Equally, it appears that governments around the world have been both willing and able to deploy naval power to respond to the crises that have arisen. This recognition of the inherent flexibility, mobility and usability of naval forces is only likely to grow in the decades to come.

Notes

1. A fuller explanation of the Attributes of Maritime Power can be found in *Joint Doctrine Publication 0-10, British Maritime Doctrine* (Shrivenham: The Development, Concepts and Doctrine Centre, Ministry of Defence, 2011).

2. The United Kingdom's controversial 1981 Defence Review was led by Defence Secretary John Nott, a former merchant banker. Given the priorities attached to renewal of the strategic submarine force with Trident missile-armed boats and increased investment in the United Kingdom's air defences, cuts had to be made elsewhere. With the then British Army of the Rhine effectively untouchable, it was the Royal Navy's surface fleet – particularly expeditionary assets such as carriers and amphibious assault ships – that were slated for cuts.

3. Clearly this applied to only a limited extent to the US Navy, which retained a balanced set of naval capabilities that were to be significantly expanded during the Reagan era. France's *Marine Nationale* also maintained significant expeditionary capabilities in spite of the high cost of its strategic nuclear submarines.

4. Interestingly, most subsequent British operations have involved deployments far from a home base, albeit allied facilities have sometimes been available. An exception has been recent actions against the Islamic State where, for once, a British base in the form of the sovereign areas in

Cyprus was in close proximity to the theatre of operations.

5. A detailed description of the US Maritime Strategy is beyond the scope of this chapter. For further details see John B Hattendorf and Peter M Schwartz (eds), *US Naval Strategy in the 1980s: Selected Documents* (Newport, RI: Naval War College Press, 2008).

6. The Royal Navy having the second largest contribution as part of Britain's Operation 'Granby'.

7. See *The Fundamentals of British Maritime Doctrine BR1806* (London: Ministry of Defence, 1995). It replaced the previous *The Naval War Manual*.

8. The 2003 Iraq invasion also saw a successful projection of maritime power from the sea, partly due to the limited host-nation support available for this operation. Saudi Arabia, key in 1991, declined use of its territory very early on. Emphasis then shifted to Turkey, from where an air and land thrust would be launched in conjunction with a small naval holding force in the south of Iraq. However, Turkey's parliament rescinded its co-operation and the plan was reversed, with an expansion of naval forces in the northern Persian Gulf key to the invasion's successful execution alongside land forces deployed in Kuwait.

9. The Bosnian crisis is a good example of this, as most

Western governments initially wished to avoid intervention at all costs.

10. The 3,000-plus sorties by the land-based Royal Air Force resulted in 600 targets being attacked. Meanwhile, 1,500 sorties by the French carrier, *Charles de Gaulle,* resulted in some 785 attacks. Similarly, the Italian Navy's Harriers represented just a seventh of their nation's deployed combat strength, yet they flew a fifth of the Italian missions, dropped half of the total ordnance and did so for a tenth of the cost of Italy's land-based Tornadoes and Typhoons.

11. The third *San Marco* class LPD was funded by the Italian disaster relief fund. Meanwhile, the the Thai aircraft carrier *Chakri Naruebet* was funded by three departments, the Royal Thai Navy, the disaster fund and the royal household, the last because it can also act as the royal yacht, with a suite of rooms set aside for the King.

12. Colombia has even set up a centre of excellence for training other navies in riverine skills.

13. A good overview of the Sri Lanka Navy's role in successful countering the Sea Tigers and helping to bring the Sri Lankan civil war to an end is contained in Tim Fish's 'Sri Lanka learns to counter Sea Tigers' swarm tactics', *Jane's Navy International – March 2009* (Coulsdon: IHS Jane's, 2009), pp.20–5.

4.1.   Conrad Waters

THE AMERICAS

The United States Navy inevitably dominates any analysis of 21st-century navies operating in the Americas. This is not only a result of the breadth and depth of its naval forces, as demonstrated in Table 4.1.1, but the extent of the United States' economic, political and military influence across the broader region. To the north, Canada is a long-standing and reliable ally that works closely with the United States, particularly in the context of the NATO framework. Immediately to the south, strong economic and demographic ties with Mexico provide good links in spite of potential strains relating to illegal immigration and narcotics.

These can be the source both of disagreement and collaboration.

Relations with countries deeper into Latin America can be more complex. Ties with Cuba are only slowly warming after half a century of disrepair, whilst Venezuela remains a particular source of hostility. Several other South American countries are distrustful of potential United States' hegemony. The 1947 Inter-American Treaty of Reciprocal Assistance – the Rio Pact – remains in effect but the lack of any real external threat since the end of the Cold War means that the longstanding doctrine of hemispheric defence first heralded by the Monroe Doctrine has limited current relevance.[1] In any event, the last decades have seen growing emphasis on regional defence cooperation within South America. One example is the establishment of the Union of South American Nations (UNASUR) regional security council in 2008. In these – and other regions – the US Navy's presence is limited and focused largely on constabulary activities in collaboration with regional fleets and other agencies. Nevertheless, the US Navy's ability to intervene decisively in its wider 'back yard' should circumstances change is an ongoing influence that should not be overlooked.

A more detailed analysis of the US Navy is contained in Chapter 4.1.1. A brief review of the current status of the other significant fleets in the Americas is set out below.

CANADA

The Royal Canadian Navy's Cold War fleet was essentially an anti-submarine force designed to work in conjunction with is NATO partners in combating the Soviet submarine threat, particularly in the North Atlantic. The end of the Cold War therefore left what was then the Canadian Forces Maritime Command in a similar position to many European navies in so far as the primary threat it was equipped to face had largely ceased to exist.[2] Although an ambitious Canadian programme to acquire an expensive flotilla of nuclear attack submarines had already (in 1989) been cancelled in the face of United States' opposition and budgetary pressures, the renewal of the anti-submarine escort force with the new *Halifax* class had only just commenced.

Operationally, the navy responded well to the revised environment. It was active in using its new surface warships to contribute to international coalition operations as far distant as the Mediterranean and Indian Ocean, notably in the 1990–1 Gulf War. Indeed, the late Cold War fleet modernisation programme had provided a core of new ships that proved to be well-suited to the demands made in these new roles. The new focus on 'engaged internationalism' was reflected in *Landmark: The Navy's Strategy for 2020*, possibly the most important Canadian strategic naval document of the period.[3] A renewed interest in the Arctic – Canada's third 'ocean' and one of the key rationales behind the abortive nuclear submarine programme – was reflected in the 2006 decision to build surface ships capable of operating in the region.

The Royal Canadian Navy frigate *Halifax* pictured exercising with other warships during NATO's Exercise Trident Juncture in the Western Mediterranean in October 2015. The *Halifax* class frigates were only just entering service as the Cold War ended and have provided invaluable as the navy increasingly focused in international coalition operations. *(Royal Canadian Navy)*

Unfortunately, the navy has not been provided with the resources needed to meet the promise of its strategic intent. A series of botched procurement decisions – notably relating to the decommissioned British *Upholder* class submarines and Sikorsky CH-148 Cyclone sea-control helicopters – provided the fleet with equipment that has entered operational service late, has been more expensive than expected and has failed to provide the performance initially anticipated. Even more seriously, ongoing delays in warship procurement has resulted in an increasingly obsolescent fleet that, in some cases, has proved unsafe to operate. A nadir was reached in 2014 when it was announced that two destroyers and the fleet's only two replenishment vessels would be retired without immediate replacement because further repair would either be impractical or uneconomic.

The great hope is the National Shipbuilding Procurement Strategy (NSPS). First announced in 2010, this has allocated the bulk of future naval procurement to two domestic yards, which will work on a series of programmes to recapitalise the fleet. Irving Shipbuilding's Halifax shipyard is currently building a new class of *Harry DeWolf* class Arctic offshore patrol ships in line with the decision first made in 2006 and will move on to replacing the fleet's surface escorts. The twelve *Halifax* class frigates are already well into a modernisation programme aimed to keep them in service until the new ships arrive. Meanwhile, Vancouver Shipyards

on the west coast has been allocated two new *Queenston* class replenishment ships based on the German Type 702 *Berlin* class. However, it will take time to realise these programmes and the cost of indigenous construction is proving expensive. For example, the two *Queenston*s will reportedly cost CAD$2.3bn (US$1.7bn) compared with c. US$900m for the four British *Tidespring* class tankers ordered from Korea.

LATIN AMERICA

The spending spree on new warship procurement that typified many South American navies in the 1970s and early 1980s came to an abrupt halt with the onset of the Latin American debt crisis sparked by Mexico's default in 1982. The so-called 'lost decade' that followed, which resulted in a significant contraction in military expenditure, had widespread ramifications for the region and its defence forces. Notably, greater economic integration across the continent and a progressive reduction in the influence of the military in political life allowed resolution of the large number of border disputes that had previously been a key driver of defence spending. Consequently, the return to economic stability experienced by many countries from the 1990s onwards did not automatically trigger a return to previous spending levels.

The main result of this backdrop is that the inventory of many of the region's navies retain a signifi-

cant element that reflects the programmes of the 1970s and 1980s. True, many of these ships have been subject to significant modernisation, whilst some navies have taken advantage of the post-Cold War peace dividend that saw many NATO fleets shed relatively modern equipment. However, with one or two notable exceptions, it is only recently that regional navies have benefitted from any large-scale degree of material renewal. It is interesting to note that much of this latest investment has tended to focus on constabulary and logistical assets, reflecting the continued absence of external threats, reduced intra-continental tension and the significant expansion in maritime territorial interests that has occurred over recent years.[4]

Of the South American nations, Brazil maintains the most capable and best-funded armed forces. It accounts for over half the region's total defence expenditure in spite of recent reductions driven by Brazil's deteriorating economic performance. These factors are reflected in a fleet that is, perhaps, the only one in the region to have meaningful wider significance. An institutional desire to broaden the fleet's strategic role is reflected both in an ambitious submarine programme and involvement in international peacekeeping operations, notably the United Nations UNIFIL stabilisation mission off Lebanon.

Brazil: As demonstrated by Table 4.1.2, the current *Marinha do Brasil* is a large and reasonably well-

4.1.1: AMERICAN FLEET STRENGTHS – 2015

COUNTRY	SHIP TYPE													
	Aircraft Carriers & Amphibious				Submarines			Surface Combatants				Other (Selected)		
	CV/N	CVS	LHA/D	LPD/SD	SSBN	SSN	SSK	CG/DDG	FFG	FSG/FS	FAC	OPV	MCMV	AOR
United States	10	–	9	21	14	58	–	82	–	6	–	–	13	18
Canada	–	–	–	–	–	–	4	1	12	–	–	–	12	–
Brazil	1	–	–	2	–	–	5	–	8	4	–	4	6	2
Argentina	–	–	–	–	–	–	3	–	4	9	2	–	–	1
Chile	–	–	–	1	–	–	4	–	8	–	3	3	–	2
Peru	–	–	–	–	–	–	6	1	7	–	6	–	–	1
Colombia	–	–	–	–	–	–	4	–	4	1	–	4	–	–
Ecuador	–	–	–	–	–	–	2	–	2	6	3	–	–	–
Mexico	–	–	–	–	–	–	–	–	4	2	2	21	–	–
Uruguay	–	–	–	–	–	–	–	–	–	2	–	–	3	1
Venezuela	–	–	–	–	–	–	2	–	–	3	6	4	–	1

Notes: Numbers are based on official sources where available, supplemented by news reports, published intelligence data and other 'open' sources as appropriate. Given significant variations in available data, numbers and classifications should be regarded as indicative, particularly with respect to minor warships. SSK numbers do not include midget submarines. FAC category includes missile-armed craft only.

4.1.2: BRAZIL – MARINHA DO BRASIL COMPOSITION END 2015

MAJOR BASES & STRUCTURE

Organisationally, the Brazilian Navy is structured into the main surface and submarine commands under the commander-in-chief of the fleet and nine naval districts, seven of which have direct control of a number of minor warships. The major naval bases are at:

Rio de Janeiro: Naval arsenal and cluster of bases, including the new submarine facility being built at Itaguaí to the south.
Aratu (Bahia): Major naval base and maintenance facility.
Val-de-Cães (Pará): Major seagoing and river base and maintenance facility at the mouth of the River Amazon.

There are also smaller naval bases at **Natal** (Rio Grande do Norte), **Rio Grande** (Rio Grande do Sul), **Ladário** (Mato Grosso do Sul) and **Rio Negro** (Amazonas), the last two being for riverine forces.

PERSONNEL

c. 45,000 plus an additional 15.000 marines.

MAJOR WARSHIPS

Type	Class	In Service	Ordered	ISD	Tonnage	Notes
Aircraft Carriers:		1	(–)			
Aircraft Carrier (CV)	*São Paulo*	1	(–)	1963	33,500 tons	CATOBAR. Reliability doubtful.
Major Amphibious Warships:		2	(–)			
Landing Platform Dock (LPD)	*Bahia* (*Foudre*)	1	(–)	1990	12,000 tons	Acquired in 2015. Yet to enter operational service.
Landing Ship Dock (LSD)	*Ceará* (LSD–28)	1	(–)	1956	12,000 tons	Reliability doubtful; major propulsion loss 2015.
Major Surface Escorts:		8	(–)			
Frigate (FFG)	*Greenhalgh* (Type 22 – B1)	2	(–)	1979	4,700 tons	Survivors of class of 4 acquired from UK in 1995.
Frigate (FFG)	*Niterói*	6	(–)	1976	3,700 tons	One additional ship acts as an unarmed training vessel.
Second-Line Surface Escorts		4	(–)			
Corvette (FSG)	*Barroso*	1	(–)	2008	2,400 tons	Four new *Tamandaré* class corvettes are planned.
Corvette (FSG)	*Inháuma*	3	(–)	1989	2,100 tons	A fourth ship has been decommissioned.
Attack Submarines:		–	(1)			
Submarine (SSN)	*Álvaro Alberto*	–	(1)	(c.2025)	Not known	First of up to 6 planned attack submarines.
Patrol Submarines		5	(4)			
Submarine (SSK)	*Riachuelo* ('Scorpène')	–	(4)	(c.2020)	2,200 tons	Under construction in Brazil with DCNS assistance.
Submarine (SSK)	*Tikuna* (Type 209 – mod)	1	(–)	2005	1,600 tons	
Submarine (SSK)	*Tupi* (Type 209)	4	(–)	1989	1,500 tons	

Other Ships

Type	Offshore Patrol Vessels	Sea-going Patrol Vessels	Minehunters	Replenishment Ships	
Number	4	c.20	6	2	Plus various training vessels, landing craft and auxiliaries

NAVAL AVIATION

Brazilian naval aviation is based at NAS São Pedro da Aldeia near Rio da Janeiro. The main seaborne aircraft are:

- **AF-1 series Skyhawk:** Twelve being modernised to remain operational until 2025.
- **S-2 series Tracker/Trader:** Up to eight (four confirmed) being modernised for refuelling, onboard delivery and possible airborne early warning roles.
- **S-70 series Seahawk helicopters:** Eight in service or on order.
- **AW Super Lynx:** Twelve in service.

There are also around twenty-five Eurocopter Squirrel and around fifteen Bell 206 light utility helicopters in service, whilst sixteen new Eurocopter EC-275 transport helicopters are being delivered. The Brazilian Air Force operates around nine P-3 Orion and twelve EMB-111 aircraft in the MPA role.

balanced force that includes aviation, amphibious and blue water surface capabilities. Future procurement is being driven by the long-term PEAMB (*Plano de Articulação e Equipamento da Marinha do Brasil*) naval organisation plan announced at the turn of the current decade. This envisages a significant expansion in current force levels – including two aircraft carriers, four amphibious assault ships and significant fleets of 'blue water' surface ships and both nuclear and conventional submarines – that would appear unachievable under most realistic scenarios. An added complication is a need for considerable constabulary assets to secure the country's extensive littoral waters and broader EEZ, where important energy resources are located.

The major procurement effort to date is undoubtedly the renewal and expansion of Brazil's fleet under the PROSUB (*Programa de Desenvolvimento de Submarinos*) project. This includes construction of a vast submarine manufacturing facility and base at Itaguaí, to the south of Rio de Janeiro. The ultimate aim under PEAMB is for fifteen conventional and six nuclear-powered submarines. The first phase of the programme has seen orders for four conventional submarines of France's 'Scorpène' type – to be named the *Riachuelo* class; a prototype nuclear submarine will follow. Whilst the new facilities being built are impressive, the initial phase of the programme is already delayed by financial pressures and may take a decade or more to complete.

The resources invested in PROSUB are also having an impact of the surface fleet. Most of this dates from the 1970s, or before, and is starting to shrink as ships wear out before replacement. PROSUB's surface counterpart – PROSUPER (*Programa de Obtenção de Meios de Superfície*) – involving local construction of five surface escorts, five offshore patrol vessels and a replenishment ship is currently stalled for lack of funds. This means short-term construction is likely to be dominated by patrol vessels and, perhaps, light frigates. There are also significant concerns relating to naval aviation, where cost-effective steps to renew naval aircraft may be undermined by the increasing age and unreliability of the sole carrier *São Paulo* (the former French *Foch*). In the past, such acquisitions of surplus second-hand ships has proved an effective means of achieving fleet upgrades and Brazil has recently replicated this approach by purchasing the French LPD *Sirocco* for its amphibious fleet. However, the number of ships available for sale is not as great as it once was.

Other Latin American Fleets: Of the other leading Latin American 'ABC' (Argentina, Brazil and Chile) fleets, those of Argentina and Chile have experienced different trajectories. Although substantially reinforced by the arrival of previously-contracted German frigates, corvettes and submarines after the Falklands War, the **Argentine Navy** has been starved of resources subsequently. There has been insufficient money to maintain the existing fleet adequately, let alone embark on significant renewal. As such the real capabilities of the fleet are a shadow of those indicated by its numerical composition. Conversely, the **Chilean Navy** has benefitted from ongoing investment that has been linked to the success of the country's commodity-based economy.[5] This has seen the acquisition of second-hand but reasonably modern British and Dutch frigates to renew the surface fleet, newly-built 'Scorpène' type submarines to reinforce its older German boats and series indigenous production of German-designed offshore patrol vessels. A meaningful amphibious capability has been created by the purchase of *Foudre*, *Sirocco*'s sister-ship, from France.

Elsewhere in Latin America, **Peru** retains a large but elderly fleet built-around German Type 209 submarines and Italian-designed *Lupo* class frigates. Sufficient money is being found to modernise some of these vessels, whilst South Korean help has been sought to re-establish a domestic construction facility. Neighbouring **Colombia**, whose defence spending is second only to Brazil's, has also modernised its escort force, acquired second-hand submarines from Germany and constructed offshore patrol vessels similar to those built in Chile. One of these has recently ventured as far as the Indian Ocean in support of the European Union's Operation 'Atalanta'. The essentially constabulary

This picture shows the Brazilian submarine *Tapajo* arriving at Mayport in Florida to participate in training with the US Navy in May 2013. Brazil is currently renewing its submarine force under the PROSUB project. *(US Navy)*

nature of much of this investment is also reflected in **Mexico's** priorities, which has focused its resources on building a large fleet of indigenous offshore and coastal patrol vessels. The navy has been in the forefront of the war against organised crime; a much more real and immediate threat than any likelihood of external aggression.

Notes

1. The Monroe Doctrine, first stated by President James Monroe in 1823, sought to forestall any efforts by European countries to establish a new presence in the Americas by asserting any such actions would be regarded as acts of aggression, necessitating a US response.

2. The three branches of the Canadian military were amalgamated into the Canadian Forces in 1968. The title Royal Canadian Navy was renewed for the resulting Maritime Command in 2011.

3. See *Landmark: The Navy's Strategy for 2020* (Ottawa: Directorate of Maritime Strategy, 2001). An update was published in 2005 to take account of the post '9/11' environment.

4. The limited willingness of Latin American navies to project power beyond their littoral, particularly into the Pacific was assessed by Robert Farley in an article entitled, 'On the Sidelines: Latin America's Pacific Security Interests' in *The Diplomat – 27 June 2014* (Tokyo: Trans-Asia Inc., 2014).

5. The so-called Copper Law automatically allocated ten per cent of state copper export proceeds to fund military equipment.

4.1.1

Scott Truver

UNITED STATES NAVY

With the Berlin Wall in ruins, the Soviet Union and Warsaw Pact continuing to implode and the Soviet Navy in homeports tied fast to piers, the United States' search for 'peace dividends' in the 1990s was relentless. The end of the Cold War spawned significant uncertainty about US Armed Services' roles, missions and tasks. No stone was left unturned in a search for draconian cuts in American defence spending. No armed service avoided intense scrutiny from the White House, Congress and the American taxpayer. This was particularly true for the US Navy.

'For the first time in at least four decades,' Naval War College professor John B Hattendorf explained, 'the US Navy had neither a peer nor a superior naval adversary; further, no credible naval adversary could be discerned in the foreseeable future.' 'As a result,' he continued, 'the US Navy immediately faced questions as to what its role and functions were, what they should become in the future, and how they should be justified in terms of budget requests to Congress for the future development of naval forces.'[1]

Indeed, the strategic foundation for the US Navy (and the other services) was being questioned throughout the 1990s, much as it had been during the first decade of the Cold War. Clearly, strategic justification of US Navy roles, missions, tasks, forces, force mixes and operations was needed, then and now. In a 1954 article in the US Naval Institute's *Proceedings*, 'National Policy and the Transoceanic Navy', Harvard political scientist Samuel P Huntington wrote, 'The fundamental element of a military service is its purpose or role in implementing national policy. The statement of this role may be called the *strategic concept* of the service. If a military service does not possess such a concept, it becomes purposeless, it wallows about amid a variety of conflicting and confusing goals, and ultimately it suffers both physical and moral degeneration.'[2]

Huntington added, 'If a service does not possess a well-defined strategic concept, the public and the political leaders will be confused as to the role of the service, uncertain as to the necessity of its existence, and apathetic or hostile to the claims made by the service upon the resources of society.'

US NAVY STRATEGIC CONCEPTS

It would take another three decades before *The Maritime Strategy*, the Navy's first-ever official and formal strategic concept, was released publically in 1986 (classified versions began circulating in 1983). To implement the *Maritime Strategy*, Secretary of the Navy John Lehman's '600-ship Fleet' (the actual 'high-water mark' was somewhat less) targeted:[3]

- 15 carrier battle groups and 16 carrier air wings.
- 4 surface action groups centred around reactivated *Iowa*-class battleships.
- 137 battle group escorts (cruisers and destroyers).
- 101 frigates.
- 100 nuclear-powered attack submarines.
- 39 ballistic missile submarines.
- 75 amphibious assault ships (enough for 1 Marine Amphibious Force & 1 Marine Brigade).
- 31 mine-countermeasures vessels.
- An unspecified number of strategic missile submarines.

With the Cold War justifications no longer compelling, from April 1991 to March 2015 some twenty-four strategic concepts, White Papers, visions, assessments, guidance, capstone documents, operational concepts, concepts of operations and policy frameworks were disseminated in reports, briefings, articles, 'glossy' publications, books and Internet 'blogs' (these do not include Secretary of Defense publications such as the *National Security Strategy*, *National Military Strategy*, *Defense Strategic Guidance*, and *Quadrennial Defense Review* reports, among others, at the national level). The objective was to define and articulate the Navy's strategic concepts for a new era. Truth be told, however, in only a few instances did the publication have 'legs' beyond one or two years after publishing; several had 'service lives' measured in months.

This survey focuses on three of the most significant of these strategic publications, assessing their broad implications for US Navy fleet force structures and mixes, viz.

US NAVY: STRATEGIC 'CHURN' 1991–2015

The Way Ahead (1991).
The Navy Policy Book (1992).
Naval Force Capabilities Planning Effort (1991–2).
... From the Sea: Preparing the Naval Service for the 21st Century (1992–3).
Naval Warfare, Naval Doctrine Publication 1 (1994).
FORWARD ... From the Sea (1994).
Naval Operational Concept (1995).
2020 Vision (1996).
Navy Operational Concept (1997).
Anytime, Anywhere: A Navy for the 21st Century (1997).
A Maritime Strategy for the 21st Century (1999).
Navy Strategic Planning Guidance (2000).
Global Concept of Operations (2002).
Sea Power 21 (2002).
Naval Power 21 ... A Naval Vision (2002).
Naval Operating Concept for Joint Operations (2002).
The 3/1 Strategy (2005).
The National Strategy for Maritime Security (2005).
The Navy Strategic Plan (2006).
The Naval Operations Concept (2006).
The Navy Operations Concept (2006).
A Cooperative Strategy For 21st Century Seapower (2007).
Navy Vision Statement/CNO Sailing Direction (2011).
Forward, Engaged, Ready: A Cooperative Strategy For 21st Century Seapower Refresh/Rewrite (2015).

Note: A further strategic document – *A Design for Maintaining Maritime Superiority* – was published at the start of 2016.

The US Navy aircraft carrier *George H. W. Bush* (CVN-77) operating with the British Royal Navy Type 45 destroyer *Defender* in the Middle East in October 2014. Forward presence and combined operations with allied navies are two fundamental principles underlying current US Navy strategy. *(Crown Copyright 2014)*

- ■ ... *From the Sea* (1992–3): the Navy's first post-Cold War strategy.
- ■ *Sea Power 21* (2000): the first post-9/11 strategy.
- ■ *A Cooperative Strategy for 21st Century Seapower* (2015): the recent 'refresh' of the original 2007 document.

... FROM THE SEA: PREPARING THE NAVAL SERVICE FOR THE 21ST CENTURY (1992–3)

On 2 August 1990, with the 'shock and awe' of Operations 'Desert Shield' and 'Desert Storm' yet to be experienced, President George H W Bush delivered an ominous speech during which he announced that he would reduce defence spending by twenty-five per cent, with more cuts to be determined later.

For the US Navy, the Bush defence department decided that the 'Base Force' would see fleet force levels drop to 450 ships, with twelve aircraft carriers and thirteen air wings, about 150 surface warships, fifty-five to eighty attack submarines and fifty-one amphibious ships. The navy – and US Marine Corps (USMC), too – was being challenged by the other services, particularly the US Air Force (USAF), which in 1990 published its *Global Reach, Global Power* pamphlet. Sebastian Bruns noted that the USAF slogan, 'Virtual Presence' had 'bumper-sticker potential and significant political traction'.[4]

By March 1992, with *The Way Ahead* (1991), *The Navy Policy Book* (1992), and the *Naval Force Capabilities Planning Effort* (1991–2) as preludes, a draft White Paper, tentatively entitled 'Power from the Sea', by mid-April had morphed into ... *From the Sea*.[5] Captain Peter Swartz (USN Retired) recalled it being billed as a 'White Paper' and 'combined vision', and there were at least three versions of the 'final' publication – in addition to a four-page article in the November 1992 edition of the US Naval Institute's *Proceedings*.[6] The Navy printed some 140,000 copies of the 'glossy' pamphlet.

Hattendorf noted that the goal of the White Paper was 'to underscore the determination of the Navy's leadership to change, align itself more effectively with the concept of the Base Force ... , apply the lessons the Navy had learned from the First Gulf War [1990–1], and to take into consideration the context of the technology provided by the

Tomahawk [land-attack cruise] missile and the Aegis [anti-air warfare] combat system'. And, as Amund Lundesgaard pointed out, an important objective was 'to engender a fundamental shift in naval thinking – away from the open-ocean confrontation with the Soviet Navy, and toward a much more subtle and more flexible use of naval forces commensurate with a more uncertain strategic environment'.[7] That said, Captain Peter D Haynes (USN) explained, '… *From the Sea* focused on major combat operations, high-tech power projection, and warfighting. Naval leaders were not about to yield the field of major conflict to the Army and the Air Force.'[8]

… *From the Sea* also revealed a growing institutional rapprochement between the navy and the marines, with leading-edge USMC expeditionary and manoeuvre warfare concepts explicit throughout the text. Given the sharp focus on littoral operations, with 'littoral' defined as the 'near land' areas of the world, however, primary concerns – even if not specifically called out – were submarines, mines, cruise missiles and ballistic missiles. The US Navy and USMC divided 'near land' areas into two segments, seaward and landward. The seaward segment was 'the area from the open ocean to the shore which must be controlled to support operations ashore', and the landward segment was 'the area inland from the shore that can be supported and defended directly from the sea'.

It was, however, a tough read. As Sebastian Bruns pointed out … *From the Sea* contained 'no less than six maritime capabilities: powerful presence, strategic deterrence, sea control, extended crisis response, power projection from the sea, and provision of sealift. It later cited four traditional operational means – forward deployment, crisis response, strategic deterrence, and sealift – to which it affixed another four required key operational capabilities (command, control and surveillance; battle space dominance; power projection; and force sustainment).'

'Overall, … *From the Sea* had wide influence within and outside the Navy,' Hattendorf wrote. 'It was extensively used as a basis for flag officer speeches and in testimony before Congress, and it was favourably noted by civilian defence analysts. At the same time, it clearly reflected how the fleet was currently operating and resonated with contemporary thinking about the Navy and Marine Corps.'

But it did not venture into fleet force structure and mix requirements and assessments. While the paper asserted, 'Navy force structure will be prioritized in favour of a ship mix optimized to project power ashore in regional crises in support of the national strategy', there was little effort to increase the proportion of ships or new shipbuilding programs to enhance littoral capabilities. The Base Force US Navy order of battle of 450 ships remained the objective and served as the framework for …

The US Navy *Ticonderoga* class cruiser *Cape St. George* (CG-71) launches a Tomahawk cruise missile against a target in Iraq during Operation 'Iraqi Freedom' in 2003. The importance of new technologies such as Tomahawk and the Aegis weapons system was reflected in US Navy strategic thinking of the 1990s. *(US Navy)*

The *Sea Power 21* Strategy fused three primary elements – Sea Strike, Sea Shield and Sea Basing together by the network-centric concept ForceNet – with the aim of better adapting the US Navy to the post '9/11' strategic environment, where a greater number of threats might need to be dealt with simultaneously. The Sea Basing concept gave rise to the mobile landing platforms of the *Montford Point* (T-ESD-1) class; the lead ship is shown here on exercises in 2014. *(US Navy)*

From the Sea rather than the White Paper driving requirements, assessments, programmes and operations. Indeed, by 1999 the Navy had reduced force levels far further than previously envisaged; by nearly forty-five per cent from the peak to a little over 300 warships.

SEA POWER 21 (2002)

In early 2002, with the September 2001 '9/11' tragedy seared into United States' consciousness, the US Navy began work on a new operational concept. This was in response to the George W Bush administration's new force planning construct and strategy outlined in the 2001 *Quadrennial Defense Review* report (QDR). The QDR outlined a strategy based on four goals: (1) assure allies and friends of America's steadfastness of purpose and ability to fulfil its security commitments; (2) dissuade future military competition; (3) deter aggression by threats and coercion against United States' interests by deploying forward forces able to act decisively; and (4) defeat any adversary if deterrence fails.

The military's new force planning construct was based on a '1-4-2-1' concept, a shift from the 1990s' concept based on fighting two major regional conflicts nearly simultaneously. The 1-4-2-1 architecture represented the need to defend the homeland (1); maintain regionally tailored forces forward-deployed in four regions – Europe, Northeast Asia, the East Asian littoral, and the Middle East/Southwest Asia (4); swiftly defeat attacks in any two of the four more-or-less simultaneously (2); and be able to "win decisively" in one of the two (1). For the US Navy, the problem was how to provide continuous combat-credible forward presence with a fleet that had only enough ships (just over 300) and forward-based infrastructure to support three, not four, regions.

In June 2002, the Chief of Naval Operations (CNO) Admiral Vernon Clark introduced his new strategic White Paper in a speech entitled 'Sea Power 21: Operational Concepts for a New Era'.[9] He explained how *Sea Power 21*'s three primary elements – Sea Strike, Sea Shield, and Sea Basing – were fused together by the network-centric concept – ForceNet – and supported by three 'implementing initiatives' – Sea Trial, Sea Warrior, and Sea Enterprise. Clark laid out *Sea Power 21* in more detail in the October 2002 issue of *Proceedings*. The article was the first in a series of nine directly related articles that were published in *Proceedings* during the

Sea Power 21 re-affirmed the close relationship between the US Navy and the US Marine Corps. This image shows amphibious assault vehicles leaving the well deck of *Ashland* (LSD-48) in August 2015 during relief efforts in Saipan in the aftermath of Typhoon Soudelor. *(US Navy)*

next two years – each written by a high-ranking admiral, each extolling the virtues of the Navy's contributions to the nation's security.

Lundesgaard has compared *Sea Power 21* to the strategic documents of the 1990s, concluding that one of the most apparent changes was the perception of threats. The lack of specificity that characterised the 1990s was replaced by a relative level of certainty, and the impact of 9/11 was obvious: '… events of 11 September 2001 tragically illustrated that the promise of peace and security in the new century is fraught with profound dangers.'

The primary threats were 'nations poised for conflict in key regions, widely dispersed and well-funded terrorist and criminal organizations, and failed states that deliver only despair to their people'. The focus on conventional, regional conflicts broadened to encompass issues that were not traditionally military in nature, as *Sea Power 21* explained: 'threats will be varied and deadly, including weapons of mass destruction, conventional warfare, and widespread terrorism. Future enemies will attempt to deny us access to critical areas of the world, threaten vital friends and interests overseas, and even try to conduct further attacks against the American homeland.'

'*Sea Power 21* was a complex, sprawling, and multi-faceted beast,' Haynes noted. 'Of the Navy's post-war strategic statements, few sought to solve a greater range of problems, including Clark's goal of a 375-ship fleet.' Clark also identified a 265-ship fleet that embraced advanced technology ('SmartShip'), human-centred design and total ownership ('optimal manning'), and crewing ('SeaSwap') innovations that would allow a much smaller fleet to execute the four-region strategy.

Haynes explained *Sea Power 21* was 'more influential inside the Navy over a longer period time than perhaps any strategic statement in the post-Cold War era other than … *From the Sea*, of which it was, in any case, an echo and elaboration. It came after an eight-year drought since the previous major statement, *Forward … From the Sea*. It had a simple construct, which was repeated relentlessly in articles, congressional testimony and speeches by senior Navy leaders. Also unusual, it had the interest and steady backing of the CNO, and benefited from an organised and sustained rollout campaign involving high-ranking admirals to demonstrate consensus.'

Sea Power 21 also represented an affirmation of the close relationship between the US Navy and the USMC. The sea basing section in particular discussed the navy-marine advantages in projecting power by, among other things, replacing on-shore bases with maritime prepositioned equipment and concepts for mobile offshore base vessels.

Sea Power 21 was not influential outside the Navy, however, and Haynes contended it did not resonate in the fleet either. 'It was laden with buzzwords, whose meanings are less self-evident the further one is from the Washington, DC Beltway. Few saw it as new or innovative. Its four-element construct was simple, but abstract. Sea Strike was understandable, but Sea Shield and Sea Basing were not.'

FORWARD, ENGAGED, READY: A COOPERATIVE STRATEGY FOR 21st CENTURY SEAPOWER 'REFRESH' (2015):

In October 2007, *A Cooperative Strategy for 21st Century Seapower* (CS21) was the first 'Tri-Service' US maritime strategy to be signed by all three sea service chiefs, viz. General James T Conway, Commandant, US Marine Corps; Admiral Gary Roughead, Chief of Naval Operations (CNO); and Admiral Thad W Allen, Commandant of the US Coast Guard (USCG). The 2007 CS21 was based on the conviction that the United States sea service – navy, marines, and coast guard – have a uniquely pre-eminent role in protecting the global system and sustaining American leadership. However, as Haynes wrote, CS21 fell on deaf ears in the US Congress, quoting Representative Gene Taylor, chairman of the House Armed Services Committee's Seapower and Expeditionary Forces subcommittee: 'It's a nice, really slick brochure – [but] at the end of the day, it didn't do so much for our country.' When the navy failed to deliver the expected resource plan, Congress dismissed it. Projections of a 285-ship navy, if not even fewer ships, were commonplace.

Four years after the 2007 strategy 'hit the street', the new CNO, Admiral Jonathan W Greenert put in motion what was rumoured to be a 'CS21 Refresh' that would take into account developments since CS21. At first the initiative was only a minimal refresh of the 2007 publication, perhaps to issue a single-service (navy only) addendum. However, subsequent discussions led to a complete bottom-up/clean-sheet-of-paper strategy signed by all three sea service chiefs.

Ultimately, it took more than three years' effort to deliver the final product, which debuted on 13 March 2015. The timeline was lengthened by the mid-stream retirement of two service chiefs: USMC Commandant Joseph R Dunford, Jr. relieved

General James F Amos in October 2014, and, in May 2014, USCG Commandant Admiral Paul F Zukunft relieved Admiral Robert J Papp, Jr. Such 'regime change' meant staffs needed time to figure out what the predecessors had done and whether change was in order. The publication of the 2014 Quadrennial Defense Review report also contributed to CS21-2015's lengthy gestation. The US Navy particularly did not want the update published just prior to or just after the QDR.

CS21-2015 outlines the global, regional and local threats and challenges that confront U.S. naval forces.[10] 'Today's global security environment is characterised by the rising importance of the Indo-Asia-Pacific region, the ongoing development and fielding of anti-access/area-denial (A2/AD) capabilities that challenge our global maritime access, continued threats from expanding and evolving terrorist and criminal networks, the increasing frequency and intensity of maritime territorial disputes, and threats to maritime commerce, particularly the flow of energy.'

The 2007 strategy did not identify China as a challenge, nor did it focus on Chinese A2/AD strategies aimed at the United States and its regional friends. But the 2015 strategy explicitly called-out China six times. CS21-2015 explained, 'China's naval expansion into the Indian and Pacific Oceans presents both opportunities and challenges. For example, China supports counter-piracy operations in the Gulf of Aden, conducts humanitarian assistance and disaster response missions enabled by its hospital ship, and participates in large-scale, multi-

national naval exercises.' However, the strategy also states, 'China's naval expansion also presents challenges when it employs force or intimidation against other sovereign nations to assert territorial claims. This behaviour, along with a lack of transparency in its military intentions, contributes to tension and instability, potentially leading to miscalculation or even escalation. The U.S. Sea Services, through our continued forward presence and constructive interaction with Chinese maritime forces, reduce the potential for misunderstanding, discourage aggression, and preserve our commitment to peace and stability in the region.'

The sea services adjusted essential functions of the original CS21 to account for changes in the global security environment, the 2010/2012/2014 Defense Strategic Guidance, initiatives such as the Air-Sea Battle concept, and a dramatically 'sequestered' fiscal environment.[11] The document features four sections – Global Security Environment, Forward Presence and Partnership, Seapower in Support of National Security, and Force Design: Building the Future Force – and includes a new function called 'All Domain Access' that underscores the challenges forces confront in accessing and operating in contested environments – with clear relevance to cyber space.

The 2015 strategy embraces two fundamental principles. First, forward naval presence of combat-credible forces is essential to defend the homeland, deter conflict, respond to crises, defeat aggression, protect the maritime commons, strengthen partnerships, and provide humanitarian assistance and

One of four US Navy destroyers recently transferred to Rota in Spain to improve European defences against ballistic missile attack, *Porter* (DDG-78) is seen exercising with the Romanian 'Tetal-II' type corvette *Marcellariu* in April 2015. The US Navy is significantly increasing the proportion of forces 'forward deployed' away from the continental United States. *(US Navy)*

disaster response. To meet these needs, 120 ships will be forward deployed by 2020 (up from ninety-seven in 2015), sixty per cent of which will be assigned to the Indo-Asia-Pacific region. Plans include forward-basing four ballistic-missile-defence destroyers in Spain and stationing a fourth attack submarine in Guam by the end of 2015. The navy is scheduled to increase presence in the Middle East from thirty ships in 2015 to forty by 2020.

Second, the strategy re-emphasises combined operations with allies and partners around the world, but particularly in the Indo-Asia-Pacific region. 'Merging our individual capabilities and capacity produces a combined naval effect that is greater than the sum of its parts,' the document notes. Among other things, that means that American naval forces will continue operating in standing NATO maritime groups – a particular priority given Russian 'adventurism' in the Crimea and Ukraine – and participate in Cooperation Afloat Readiness and Training exercises held annually 'to strengthen relationships and enhance force readiness.'

'There is one top-priority, underlying message throughout the new maritime strategy,' retired Admiral James Stavridis wrote in August 2015.[12] 'The need for seapower is greater than ever. Again, this does not diminish the need for other forms of national power – land, air, special operations, cyber. But make no mistake,' he warned, 'extremely difficult international threats and challenges lie in the years ahead. It is essential that we provide the forces and the people the sea services require, and this new strategic vision does a commendable job articulating the case.'

CURRENT US NAVY FORCE STRUCTURE PLANS

On 17 March 2015, almost contemporaneously with the release of CS-21-2015, the US Navy provided Congress with its updated, annual report on long-range shipbuilding plans and force structure requirements.[13] The current targeted force structure level is 308 front-line warships, based on a major Force Structure Assessment (FSA) conducted in 2012 and updated on an interim basis in 2014. The key elements of the targeted force level are:

- 11 aircraft carriers (with 10 air wings).
- 88 large surface combatants (cruisers and destroyers).
- 52 small surface combatants (Littoral Combat Ships and frigates).
- 12 ballistic missile submarines.
- 48 attack submarines.
- 34 amphibious ships.
- 29 supply ships.
- 34 support ships (10 Joint High Speed Vessels, and 24 other ships).

The targeted force level, at least numerically, is little changed from that reached at the end of the 1990s. It shows reasonable consistency with the ten alternative force structure goals (from the 2001 QDR goal onwards), as set out in Table 4.1.1.1. However, it has to take into account the demands of significant changes to the underlying strategic backdrop. These include the strategic rebalancing to the Asia-Pacific region; renewed uncertainties in Europe and the potentially higher demands created by the emphasis on forward deployment embraced by CS-21-2015. Moreover, it is not at all clear the 308-ship ambition can be achieved on a sustained basis given current financial constraints.

The reality in late 2015 is that the US Navy hovers around 280 ships. Absent significant increases in shipbuilding funds, the service might soon find itself crafting yet another strategy to reflect the new normal. Indeed, influential Congressional

4.1.1.1: US NAVY FORCE STRUCTURE GOALS 2001–2015[1]

Ship Type	2001 QDR	2002–04 Navy 375 Ship Plan	2005 Navy 325 Ship Plan	Navy 260 Ship Plan	2006 Navy 313 Ship Plan	2011 Plan Changes 2006–11	2011 Revised 313 Ship Plan	2012 Navy 310–6 Ship Plan	2013 Navy 306 Ship Plan	2015 Navy 308 Ship Plan
Aircraft Carriers	12	12	11	10	11	11	11	11	11	11
Amphibious Ships	36	37	24	17	31	33	33	32	33	34
MPF(F) Ships[2]	–	–	20	14	12	–	–	–	–	–
High Speed Vessels	–	–	–	–	3	21	10	10	10	10
Cruisers & Destroyers	116	104	92	67	88	94	94	90	88	88
Frigates & LCS	0	56	82	63	55	55	55	55	52	52
MCM Vessels[3]	16	26	–	–	–	–	–	–	–	–
Strategic Submarines	14	14	14	14	14	12	12	12–14	12	12
Missile Submarines	2–4	4	4	4	4	0	4	0–4	0	0
Attack Submarines	55	55	41	37	48	48	48	48	48	48
Supply Ships	34	42	26	24	30	30	30	29	29	29
Other	25	25	11	10	17	24	16	23	23	24
Totals	310–312	375	325	260	313	328	313	310–316	306	308

Notes

1 Table simplified from Ronald O'Rourke, *Navy Force Structure and Shipbuilding Plans: Background and Issues for Congress – RL32665* (Washington DC: Congressional Research Service), p.6. It is interesting to note that total ship goals have changed little in the last ten years, with type changes also relatively stable once re–classifications, e.g. of MPF(F) ships, are taken into account.

2 Maritime Positioning Force (Future). Plans for this separate squadron were abandoned post-2006 but many of the ships intended for it were re-allocated to the 'other' category.

3 MCMV tasks will be undertaken by the LCS.

Research Service (CRS) naval analyst Ronald O'Rourke has warned: 'The planned size of the Navy, the rate of Navy ship procurement, and the prospective affordability of the Navy's shipbuilding plans have been matters of concern for the congressional defense committees for the past several years. The Navy's FY2016 30-year (FY2016–FY2045) shipbuilding plan, like many previous Navy 30-year shipbuilding plans, does not include enough ships to fully support all elements of the Navy's 308-ship goal over the entire 30-year period'. 'In particular,' he noted, 'the Navy projects that the fleet would experience a shortfall in small surface combatants from FY2016 through FY2027, a shortfall in attack submarines from FY2025 through FY2036, and a shortfall in large surface combatants (i.e., cruisers and destroyers) from FY2036 through at least FY2045.'[14]

In late 2015, it looked that warship numbers might take a further tumble downwards as reports emerged that the navy had been told to reduce planned Littoral Combat Ship/frigate numbers from fifty-two to forty ships.

FLEET COMPOSITION

Table 4.1.1.2 provides an overview of current US Navy structure and fleet composition. The following comments relate to the main warship types:

Aircraft Carriers: The Navy's nuclear-powered aircraft carriers, with embarked air wings of over seventy fixed-wing aircraft and helicopters, provide the balance between forward presence and surge capability to conduct warfighting operations. Following the inactivation of *Enterprise* (CVN-65) in December 2012, the Navy has been operating with a reduced force structure of ten *Nimitz* (CVN-68) carriers. One of these is undertaking a lengthy mid-life refuelling and modernisation, such that only nine ships are 'deployable'. The force will increase to the statutory requirement of eleven aircraft carriers (including one in complex overhaul/refuelling) when *Gerald R. Ford* (CVN-78) is delivered to the Navy during FY2016, at a cost of c.US$12.9bn, including non-recurring design and engineering expenses.

The next-generation *Ford* class carriers are designed with increased efficiency throughout the ship, aimed at reducing the total lifetime operating costs by approximately US$4bn per hull compared to the *Nimitz* class. All auxiliary systems have been

The new aircraft carrier *Gerald R. Ford* (CVN-78) seen after being floated out of her building dock at HII's Newport News facility in November 2013. Compared with the previous *Nimitz* class, she incorporates enhancements to reduce running costs and improve her ability to conduct air operations. *(US Navy)*

converted from steam to electric power, and the new-design reactor provides an electrical generating capacity nearly three times that of a *Nimitz* carrier, enabling such new technologies such as the electromagnetic aircraft launch system (EMALS), advanced arresting gear (AAG), and Dual-Band Radar. The redesigned flight deck incorporates a smaller island structure located further aft on the ship, which allows greater flexibility during aircraft turnaround and launch-and-recovery cycles. A second *Ford* class vessel, *John F. Kennedy* (CVN-79), is under construction and a third, *Enterprise* (CVN-80), planned.

Amphibious Warships: The *Wasp* (LHD-1) class, comprising eight of these 41,000-ton multi-mission amphibious assault ships, currently form the core of the US Navy's amphibious force. Along with LPD-type amphibious transport docks and LSD-type dock landing ships, they make up the Amphibious Ready Groups (ARGs) that typically deploy with Marine Expeditionary Units (MEUs) as the first 'on-call' response to political and humanitarian crises around the world. Characteristics include a flight deck and hangar for combinations of some forty helicopters and vertical/short take-off or landing aircraft. The latter currently comprise the AV-8B Harrier and MV-22 Osprey aircraft, although all ships will be modified to support F-35B Joint Strike Fighter operations in due course. Each ship also has a well deck to operate air-cushion and conventional landing craft. They can embark up to

1,900 troops and have significant vehicle and ammunition/stores carrying ability. The final ship, *Makin Island* (LHD-8) was modified from the steam turbine configuration of early class members to a hybrid electric propulsion system that uses auxiliary electric motors for low-speed operation, supplemented by direct drive gas turbine propulsion for higher speeds.

The LHD-1 type ships are being supplemented by the new *America* (LHA-6) class amphibious assault ships. These have a similar propulsion system to *Makin Island* but the first two members of the class omit the well deck in favour of enhanced aviation capability (including twice as much aviation fuel capacity as that found on LHD-8). However, ships built from LHA-8 onwards will return to a well-deck configuration; some of the aviation capability lost by this change is being clawed back from a smaller island and other revisions to increase flight deck space. The current long-term force structure plan envisaged eleven amphibious assault ships in commission.

The eight 16,000-ton *Whidbey Island* (LSD-41) and four *Harpers Ferry* (LSD-49) dock landing ships carry, launch and recover amphibious assault vehicles, landing craft, helicopters and MV-22 aircraft. They can accommodate up to 400 troops. The key difference between the LSD-41 class and the LSD-49s is that the latter are cargo variants that have significantly expanded cargo and ammunition stowage space but a shorter docking well. The *Whidbey Island* class is the primary support and

The US Navy's amphibious assault ships are at the heart of its Amphibious Ready Groups (ARGs) and have the aviation capabilities of a medium-sized aircraft carriers. This image shows *Kearsarge* (LHD-3) in the Mediterranean in October 2015. *(US Navy)*

operating platform for LCACs (Landing Craft Air Cushion) and utility landing craft, and can also provide docking and repair services for other small craft. Both classes have two primary helicopter landing spots and can operate helicopters, as well as MV-22 tilt-rotor aircraft. However, neither class has a helicopter hangar, requiring aircraft maintenance and refuelling on the flight deck. In common with other US Navy amphibious ships, both classes are designed with passive and active self-defence capabilities.

The twelve 25,000-ton *San Antonio* (LPD-17)-class amphibious transport docks fall somewhere between the two other types in size and capability. They can accommodate 700 troops (800 in surge conditions), dock up to two LCACS and have aviation facilities that include a hangar and flight deck to operate and maintain a variety of aircraft, including tilt-rotor and rotary-wing aircraft and UAVs. In effect, they have greater troop and aviation capabilities than the more specialized LSDs but do not match the capacity of the much larger amphibious assault ships.

The US Navy has put in place a programme for an eleven-ship LX(R) follow-on class to the LPD-17 as an affordable means to replace the twelve *Whidbey Island* and *Harpers Ferry* dock landing ships. A rigorous analysis of alternatives determined that a derivative of the LPD-17 is now the preferred design to meet the LX(R) operational requirements.

The navy's amphibious forces are being reinforced by a number of auxiliary ships, largely manned by the civilian mariners of the Military Sealift Command. These include the new *Spearhead* (T-EPF-1) joint high speed vessels - now classified as expeditionary fast transports – and the mobile floating offshore bases of the *Montford Point* (T-ESD-1) type.

Surface Warships: The twenty-two remaining *Ticonderoga* (CG-47) class guided-missile cruisers provide multi-mission offensive and defensive capabilities and can operate either independently or as part of aircraft carrier strike groups and surface action groups. They tend to have better command and control facilities than the smaller destroyers; one

Twenty-two *Ticonderoga* class cruisers remain in service with the US Navy; this image shows *Shiloh* (CG-67) undergoing maintenance at Yokosuka in Japan. The facility shared with Japan's JMSDF is the most important outside of the United States and home to the navy's only forward-deployed carrier. *(US Navy)*

4.1.1.2: UNITED STATES –USN COMPOSITION END 2015

MAJOR BASES & STRUCTURE

The US Navy maintains a massive infrastructure of bases and other facilities to support the fleet. Although there have been some reductions since the end of the Cold War, arguably these have not kept pace with shrinkage in the overall fleet size. The following is a summary of the major facilities:

East Coast

Norfolk, VA:	Centre of the main East Coast base cluster, also including the amphibious base at Little Creek. Home to four carriers & three amphibious assault ships plus supporting ships & submarines.
Mayport, FL:	The second most important East Coast naval base. Home to one amphibious assault ship plus supporting ships.
Groton, CT:	Naval submarine base New London is a major attack submarine facility.
Kings Bay, GA:	East Coast base for strategic missile & guided missile submarines. Includes a major submarine refitting facility.

West Coast/Pacific

San Diego, CA:	Centre of the main cluster of bases on West Coast, including the facilities at Coronado. Home to two carriers & four amphibious assault ships plus supporting vessels & submarines.
Puget Sound, WA:	Location of a cluster of bases, including those on the Kitsap peninsula & at Everett. Home to two carriers & strategic submarines. Only naval location for docking carriers on W Coast.
Pearl Harbor, HI:	Pacific Fleet headquarters and large base for surface ships and submarines. Now merged with the US Air Force base as Joint Base Pearl Harbor-Hickam.

Overseas:

Yokosuka, Japan:	Most important overseas base, home to one carrier and supporting ships. In addition an ARG and mine-countermeasures vessels are based at **Sasebo.**
Guam, Pacific:	Submarine and Coast Guard base.
Rota, Spain:	Home to four BMD-equipped destroyers. Facility shared with Spanish Navy.

Other significant overseas facilities include those located in Bahrain, the British Indian Ocean Territory, Cuba (Guantanamo Bay), Greece, Italy and South Korea.

PERSONNEL

c. 324,000 US Navy plus c. 184,000 US Marine Corps. Additional reserve, civilian & US Coast Guard personnel.

NAVAL AVIATION

US Naval Air Stations (NAS) tend to be located near the main naval base clusters, although these are supplemented by additional bases elsewhere, including those used for testing and training (e.g. Naval Air Weapons Station China Lake, CA, NAS Patuxent River, MD and NAS Pensacola, FL). Please refer to Chapter 8 for further detail on US Navy aviation capabilities.

is typically assigned to each carrier strike group under the command of the group's air warfare commander. Like other major US Navy surface combatants, they have a combat system centred on the Aegis Weapon System and the SPY-1 series multi-function phased-array radar. Armament includes the Mk 41 vertical launching system (VLS) equipped with Standard Missile surface-to-air missiles and Tomahawk land-attack cruise missiles; advanced undersea and surface warfare systems; and embarked helicopters. These capabilities are supplemented by extensive command, control and communications systems. The class have been extensively modernised over the past ten years and the navy would like to withdraw half the class from operational service for further upgrades that would extend their lives into the mid-2030s and beyond. However, this plan sparked Congressional opposition, largely over concerns that the no-operational ships would never be returned to service; a modified scheme is now being implemented.

Sixty-two *Arleigh Burke* class destroyers have already been delivered to the US Navy in various configurations and a new Flight III design, incorporating Raytheon's more advanced AN/SPY-6 scalable radar arrays, will enter production soon. This is an early CGI graphic of the revised design. *(Raytheon)*

The *Arleigh Burke* (DDG-51) class guided-missile destroyers' combat system likewise is centred on the Aegis Weapon System and the SPY-1 radar. Like the cruisers, they provide multi-mission offensive and defensive capability, operating independently or as part of an aircraft carrier strike group or surface action group. Twenty-eight Flight I/II and thirty-four Flight IIA variants are currently in service; the

MAJOR WARSHIPS

Type	Class	In-Service	Ordered	ISD	Tonnage	Notes
Aircraft Carriers:		10	(2)			
Aircraft Carrier (CVN)	*Gerald R. Ford* (CVN-78)	–	(2)	(2016)	100,000 tons+	Work on a third ship scheduled to start in 2018.
Aircraft Carrier (CVN)	*Nimitz* (CVN-68)	10	(–)	1975	101,000 tons	One ship generally in long-refit/nuclear refuelling.
Major Amphibious Warships:		30	(4)			
Amphibious Assault Ship (LHA)	*America* (LHA-6)	1	(1)	1989	45,000 tons	Work on a third ship scheduled to start c. 2017.
Amphibious Assault Ship (LHD)	*Wasp* (LHD-1)	8	(–)	2014	41,000 tons	*Makin Island* (LHD-8) has many differences to other ships.
Landing Ship Dock (LPD)	*San Antonio* (LPD-17)	9	(3)	2006	25,000 tons	The last ship will be built to a slightly modified design.
Landing Ship Dock (LSD)	*Whidbey Island* (LSD-41)	12	(–)	1985	16,000 tons	Includes four *Harpers Ferry* (LSD-49) cargo variants.
Major Surface Escorts:		82	(17)			
Cruiser (CG)	*Ticonderoga* (CG-47)	22	(–)	1983	9,900 tons	Survivors of an original class of 27 ships.
Destroyer (DDG)	*Zumwalt* (DDG-1000)	–	(3)	(2016)	15,500 tons	
Destroyer (DDG)	*Arleigh Burke* Flight III (DG-51)	–	(3)	(c.2022)	c. 9,700 tons	First ship to be ordered in FY2016 under multi-year contract.
Destroyer (DDG)	*Arleigh Burke* Flight IIA (DG-51)	34	(11)	2000	9,400 tons	Includes ships authorised under multi-year contract.
Destroyer (DDG)	*Arleigh Burke* Flight I/II (DG-51)	26	(–)	1991	8,900 tons	
Second Line Surface Escorts:		6	(18)			
Corvette (FF/LCS)	*Freedom* (LCS-1)	3	(9)	2008	3,500 tons	Further ships planned to a combined total of 40 of both types.
Corvette (FF/LCS)	*Independence* (LCS-2)	3	(9)	2010	3,000 tons	Further ships planned to a combined total of 40 of both types.
Strategic Submarines:		14	(–)			
Submarine (SSBN)	*Ohio* (SSBN-726)	14	(–)	1981	18,800 tons	To be replaced by *Ohio* replacement class from late 2020s.
Attack Submarines:		58	(16)			
Submarine (SSGN)	*Ohio* (SSGN-726)	4	(–)	1981	18,800 tons	Modification/rebuild of original strategic submarine design.
Submarine (SSN)	*Virginia* (SSN-774)	12	(16)	2004	8,000 tons	Includes ships authorised under multi-year contract.
Submarine (SSN)	*Seawolf* (SSN-21)	3	(–)	1997	9,000 tons	Third boat, *Jimmy Carter* (SN-23), is longer and heavier.
Submarine (SSN)	*Los Angeles* (SSN-688)	39	(–)	1976	7,000 tons	Survivors of an original class of 62.

Other Ships:

Type	Minehunters	Patrol Vessels	Oilers/Combat Support	Dry Stores	
Number	11	13	18	14	Plus many other support ships & auxiliaries

latter support two embarked helicopters, significantly enhancing their sea-control capability. The DDG-51 upgrade plan includes an improved multi-mission signal processor, which integrates air and ballistic missile defence capabilities, and enhancements to radar performance in the littorals. The VLS will be able to support the latest SM-3 and SM-6 variants of the Standard Missile currently entering service. A Flight III variant is also in development and will incorporate the advanced air and missile defence radar (AMDR) and other technology insertions. It would seem that eighty or more DDG-51 series destroyers will ultimately be built.

The *Zumwalt* (DDG-1000)-class guided-missile destroyer is a 15,000-ton optimally-manned (142 crew), multi-mission surface warship tailored for land attack and littoral dominance. The original acquisition strategy identified thirty-two DDG-1000s. This was reduced to three in favour of restarted production of the cheaper DDG-51 design. The lead ship began sea trials in December 2015. With twenty Mk 57 peripheral VLS modules (each with four cells suitable for several missiles) and two 155mm Advanced Gun Systems, the navy's first 'all-electric' warship will provide long-range precision fire in support of forces ashore, operating independently or as part of naval, joint or combined strike forces. To ensure effective operations in the contested littoral, it incorporates signature reduction, active and passive self-defence systems, and enhanced survivability features. It fields an undersea warfare suite capable of mine avoidance, as well as self-defence systems to defeat threats ranging from submarines and cruise missiles to small boats.

Turning to smaller surface combatants, the Littoral Combat Ship (LCS) is a modular, reconfigurable ship that addresses warfighting capability gaps against asymmetric anti-access threats and will eventually comprise a significant portion of the US Navy's future surface combatant fleet. Through its modular design, LCS can be reconfigured for mine-countermeasures, surface warfare, and anti-submarine warfare missions. This versatility enables the Navy to provide warfighters with a capable, cost-effective solution to expeditionary operations in the littoral. There are two variants of LCS, the *Freedom* ((LCS-1) design (odd-numbered ships) and *Independence* (LCS-2) design (even-numbered ships). The *Freedom* variant is a steel semi-planing mono-hull with an aluminium superstructure, whilst the *Independence* variant is an all-aluminium trimaran. As of late 2015, six Littoral Combat Ships had been commissioned and another eighteen were under construction of contract. There has been much debate over the level of capability the LCS offers compared with its cost; this has resulted in a

US NAVY SURFACE COMBATANTS

Missile Destroyer (USA):
Zumwalt (DDG-1000)

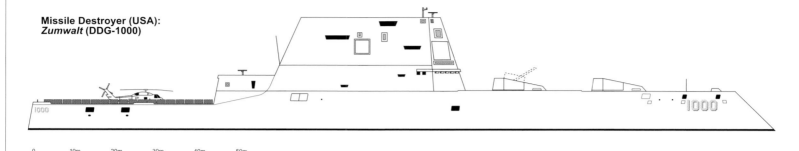

0   10m   20m   30m   40m   50m

Arleigh Burke Class Flight IIA (USA):
Chung-Hoon (DDG-93)

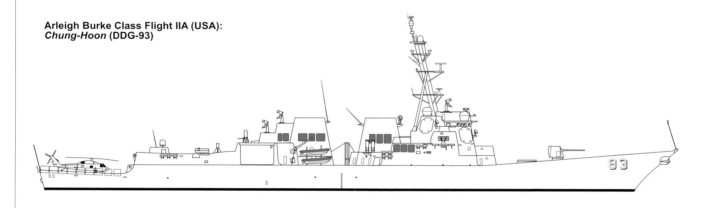

Littoral Combat Ship (USA):
Independence (LCS-2)

Littoral Combat Ship (USA):
Freedom (LCS-1)

The new *Zumwalt* (DDG-1000) class destroyers feature full electric propulsion and a radical stealth design. A product of the US Navy's post-Cold War focus on littoral operations, their cost priced them out of the future construction programme and previous plans for an extensive series have been reduced to just three ships. Instead, production has resumed of the *Arleigh Burke* (DDG-51) class, the current Flight IIA version being represented here by *Chung Hoon* (DDG-93). Construction of a further improved Flight III version will start shortly. Meanwhile, second line surface warships are now concentrated on the *Freedom* (LCS-1) and *Independence* (LCS-2) Littoral Combat Ship designs; a controversial programme that looks set to be truncated to forty ships.
(All drawings © John Jordan 2015)

The US Navy strategic submarine *Henry M. Jackson* (SSBN-730) pictured returning to the submarine base at Bangor – home of the West Coast-based strategic boats – on the Kitsap peninsula in February 2015 after a deterrent patrol. The replacement of the existing *Ohio* class submarines by a new class will be a major undertaking for the US Navy over the next decade and beyond. *(US Navy)*

The *Virginia* class submarines are steadily becoming the core of the US Navy attack submarine forces, with twelve delivered to date. They are being built in flights or series – each showing incremental improvements on the last – by General Dynamics Electric Boat and Huntington Ingalls Industries. This picture shows the launch of *John Warner* (SSN-785) at HII's Newport News yard in September 2014. *(Huntington Ingalls Industries)*

decision to progress to an upgraded light frigate variant from LCS-33 onwards. Whether the recent reduction in the targeted number of small surface combatants to just forty will result in further changes remains to be seen.

Submarines: The US Navy operates fourteen *Ohio* (SSBN-726) class nuclear-powered ballistic missile submarines, the sea-based 'leg' of the United States' strategic deterrence. Each is armed with twenty-four Trident D-5 submarine-launched ballistic missiles and four 21in torpedo tubes for Mk 48 torpedoes. Starting in 2027, the oldest *Ohio* class boat will reach the end of its service life, with the remaining strategic submarines retiring at a rate of approximately one per year thereafter. The highest defence priority is to ensure a seamless and successful transition to the twelve boat *Ohio* Replacement (OR) SSBN, which will maintain strategic deterrence well into the 2080s. The class will be designed to ensure survivability against expected threats into the late twenty-first century. Concurrent with the *Ohio* Replacement, the United Kingdom will recapitalise its own sea-based strategic deterrent platforms, the *Vanguard* class SSBNs, which also host the D5 missile. The OR SSBN programme includes a common missile

compartment under joint development with the British to reduce design and construction costs. Other cost-reduction initiatives include a life-of-ship reactor core, modular construction techniques and selective re-use of in-service submarine systems.

The first four *Ohio*-class boats were converted to Special Forces/guided missile submarines from 2002 to 2007. The SSGN conversion installed systems in three broad groups. The first group includes equipment for a Special Forces campaign: dual lockout chambers, systems to host dry deck shelters and SEAL delivery vehicles, internal and external stowage of special operations equipment and ordnance, and dedicated berthing and fitness facilities. The second comprised the attack weapons system, including space and fire-control systems for as many as 154 Tomahawk cruise missiles. The third group provided major upgrades in mission planning and communications connectivity. Each submarine has a total of 220 bunks and, under normal conditions, can routinely support a Special Operations contingent of up to sixty-six personnel for an extended period of time; as many as 102 troops could be accommodated for shorter periods.

Three classes of nuclear attack submarine (SSN) are in service. The most-recent *Virginia* (SSN-774)

class is specifically designed for multi-mission operations in the littoral while retaining traditional open-ocean anti-submarine and anti-surface capabilities. These submarines have advanced acoustic stealth technology that are intended to allow unimpeded operation within an adversary's defensive perimeter, thereby defeating A2/AD strategies. They are steadily replacing the remaining Cold War-era *Los Angeles* (SSN-688) class boats and are being built in various blocks, each incorporating progressive design enhancements. For example, current development is focusing on a Block V variant that will incorporate a payload module to increase Tomahawk cruise missile capacity, thereby partly compensating for the eventual retirement of the four *Ohio* class SSGNs. Twelve *Virginia* class submarines are currently in service and production may eventually extend to forty-eight boats. The balance of the force comprises three large *Seawolf* (SSN-21) submarines, a class designed towards the end of the Cold War but truncated on cost grounds in the new strategic environment.

WHICH WAY AHEAD?

Retired US Navy Admiral James A Winnefeld, former Vice Chairman of the Joint Chiefs of Staff,

The US Navy destroyer *Paul Hamilton* (DDG-60) operating with other US Navy and Royal Australian Navy warships in 2007. Recent US thinking is tending to see a shift back to 'high end' assets such as destroyers at the expense of overall numbers. One consequence is the likely curtailment of overall Littoral Combat Ship numbers. *(RAN)*

called for the Navy to 'ditch the simplistic benchmark of overall numbers of ships, under which an aircraft carrier counts the same as a frigate. This metric places unhelpful pressure on the Navy to build increased numbers of low-end ships that, while certainly very useful in certain scenarios, will not perform well in a highly contested environment. We need the right combination of vessels, and this requires a far more sophisticated discussion than merely counting ships.'[15]

It requires, as well, the strategic concept to help explain and justify to sometimes-incredulous decision-makers inside as well as outside the Navy the right type, numbers and combination of ships.[16]

Notes

1. John B Hattendorf (ed.), *U.S. Naval Strategy in the 1990s: Selected Documents* (Newport, RI: Naval War College Press, 2006).

2. Samuel P Huntington, 'National Policy and the Transoceanic Navy', *Proceedings - May 1954* (Annapolis, MD: Naval Institute Press, 1954), pp.483–93.

3. The actual composition of the targeted '600-ship fleet' changed over time. These figures are from *Building a 600-Ship Navy: Costs, Timing & Alternative Approaches* (Washington DC: Congressional Budget Office, 1982). There can be inconsistency in the way US Navy force numbers are reported; the most common approach is to focus on 'battle force' ships, as defined by the US Navy's own counting rules.

4. Sebastian Bruns – Dissertation, *U.S. Navy Strategy & American Sea Power from 'The Maritime Strategy' (1982-1986) to "A Cooperative Strategy for 21st Century Seapower' (2007): Politics, Capstone Documents, and Major Naval Operations 1981-2011* (Kiel: Christian-Albrechts University, 2014).

5. *... From the Sea: Preparing the Naval Service for the 21st Century* (Washington DC: Department of the Navy, 1992). The Chief of Naval Information had lobbied for a lower-case 'f' in 'from', to invite the reader's imagination to fill in the ellipses, as in: 'Influence from the Sea', or 'Logistics from the Sea', or 'Disaster Relief from the Sea', as well as

'Power from the Sea'.

6. Captain Peter M Swartz, USN (retired) with Karin Duggan, *Navy Capstone Strategies, Concept, & Context (1970-2010): Insights for the U.S. Navy of 2011 & Beyond* (Arlington, VA: Center for Naval Analyses, 2011).

7. Amund Lundesgaard, *US Navy strategy and force structure after the Cold War – IFS Insights – 4/11*, (Oslo: Norwegian Institute for Defence Studies, 2011).

8. Captain Peter D Haynes, USN – Dissertation. *American Naval Thinking in the Post-Cold War Era: The U.S. Navy and the Emergence of a Maritime Strategy, 1989-2007* (Monterey, CA: Naval Postgraduate School, 2013). This was later published as, *Toward a New Maritime Strategy: American Naval Thinking in the Post-War Era* (Annapolis, MD: Naval Institute Press, 2015).

9. *Sea Power 21* (Washington DC: Department of the Navy, 2002).

10. *A Cooperative Strategy for 21st Century Seapower, March 2015* (Washington DC: Department of the Navy, 2015).

11. The Air-Sea Battle is a US military doctrine that envisages closer cooperation between elements of the US Air Force and US Navy to improve the likelihood of success against A2/AD threats posed by countries such as China and Iran. It has echoes of the Air-Land Battle of the Cold

War. Sequestration refers to the legislation passed to control the American budget deficit, which has had a marked impact on overall defence spending.

12. Admiral James Stavridis USN (retired), 'Incoming: A Maritime Nation Needs 21st-Century Seapower', *Signal – 1 August 2015* (Fairfax, VA: AFCEA International, 2015).

13. *Report to Congress on the Annual Long-Range Plan for Construction of Naval Vessels – March 2015* (Washington DC: US Navy, 2015).

14. See Ronald O'Rourke, *Navy Force Structure and Shipbuilding Plans: Background and Issues for Congress – RL32665* (Washington DC: Congressional Research Service). The publication is regularly updated.

15. Admiral James A Winnefeld USN (retired), 'Charting a New Course for the Navy', *The Boston Globe – 8 November* (Boston: Boston Globe Media Partners, 2015).

16. In January 2016 – just after the formal cut-off date for this book – yet another strategic document, *A Design for Maintaining Maritime Superiority,* was signed off by the new CNO, Admiral John M. Richardson. It was published only ten months after CS21-2015, the supposed legacy of the previous CNO Admiral Jonathan W. Greenert. Out with the old, in with the new! And, it will be important continue to track developments closely, particularly as Admiral Richardson's 2016 *Design for Maritime Superiority* is labelled 'Version 1.0'.

US NAVY ARG COMPONENTS

Amphibious Assault Ship (USA):
Makin Island (LHD-8)

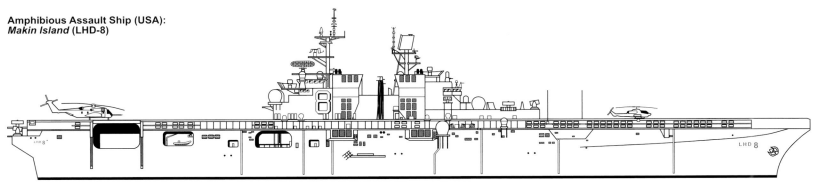

0   10m   20m   30m   40m   50m

© John Jordan 2011

Amphibious Transport Dock (USA):
Anchorage (LPD-23)

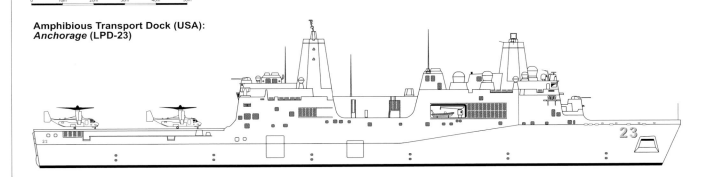

© John Jordan 2015

Dock Landing Ship (USA):
Ashland (LSD-48)

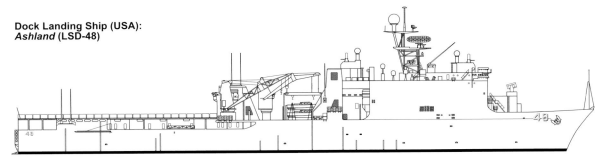

© John Jordan 2015

The Amphibious Ready Groups (ARGs) are at the heart of the forward deployed expeditionary forces that form a key part of current US Navy strategic thinking. The US Navy's ARG structure is typically built around an *America* (LHA-6) or *Wasp* (LHD-1) type amphibious assault ship; a *San Antonio* (LPD-17) class amphibious transport dock; and a dock landing ship of the *Whidbey Island* (LSD-41) or *Harpers Ferry* (LSD-49) classes. The *Makin Island* (LHD-8), represented here, is a transitional type between the *Wasp* and newer *America* classes, featuring the hybrid gas turbine/electric propulsion system found in the *America*s but retaining a traditional well deck. The amphibious assault ships provide the ARG's main aviation capability and can also embark considerable numbers of troops. The smaller amphibious transport docks have a little less than half the troop-carrying capacity of the larger 'flat tops' and much reduced aviation facilities. The LSDs are largely designed to support landing craft operations and, particularly in the *Harpers Ferry* (LSD-49) variant, tend to emphasise cargo carrying capacity.

4.2

Conrad Waters

EUROPE & RUSSIA

The development of Europe's navies since the end of the Cold War has been driven by two primary, related factors. One has been a need for wholesale reconfiguration of force structures after the *raison d'être* for many fleets all but disappeared with the end of the stand-off between NATO and the Warsaw Pact. The other has been a significant reduction in funding as governments seized upon the opportunity for a 'peace dividend' to redirect money into populist social programmes. The latter aspect was subsequently exacerbated by the financial crisis in the latter part of the 2000s and the following Eurozone crisis. The extent to which these factors have impacted European navies has differed on a case-by-case basis. For example, the French fleet was less

focused on NATO sea-control requirements than those of many of its neighbours and, consequently, needed to adapt less. However, restructuring and budgetary constraints are still fairly universal themes that apply throughout the period under consideration. It is also, perhaps, worth noting that the lack of money also had an effect on the extent to which restructuring has been successful.

Turning first to the need for restructuring, the end of the Cold War left many navies with fleets dominated by warships for which there was little immediate use. The most frequently-cited example is, perhaps, the British Royal Navy's large fleet of frigates that had been designed for anti-submarine operations in the North Atlantic. However, there

were many other examples. The Belgian Navy, for instance, had been configured largely around a mine-countermeasures role to protect the major European entry-ports for NATO reinforcements that were no longer likely to be needed. Similarly, the large forces of coastal submarines and fast attack craft maintained by many Baltic and Scandinavian fleets for home defence of their littorals had much less relevance in a post-Cold War environment.

Although the threat of regional conflict in Europe was greatly reduced, new needs for naval forces were quick to emerge. Notably, the end of the bi-polar world order quickly gave rise to new instability and conflict, as evidenced by Iraq's invasion of Kuwait and the break-up of Yugoslavia. The twin plagues of terrorism and piracy also grew in significance. Although none of these challenges was exclusively – even mainly – maritime in nature, a desire to 'reach the crisis before the crisis reaches us' created support for expeditionary forces that often had a significant naval component.

The new environment gave rise to a particular demand for specialised amphibious and logistics assets that could be used as support bases for combined operations in the littoral. The Royal

4.2.0: EUROPEAN FLEET STRENGTHS – 2015

COUNTRY	SHIP TYPE													
	Aircraft Carriers & Amphibious				Submarines			Surface Combatants				Other (Selected)		
	CV/N	CVS	LHA/D	LPD/SD	SSBN	SSN	SSK	DDG	FFG	FSG/FS	FAC	OPV	MCMV	AOR
France	1	–	3	–	4	6	–	11	5	6	–	9	14	3
United Kingdom	–	–	1	5	4	7	–	6	13	–	–	4	15	5
Italy	1	1	–	3	–	–	6	8	9	6	–	10	10	3
Spain	–	–	1	2	–	–	3	5	6	–	–	15	6	2
Germany	–	–	–	–	–	–	6	3	7	5	4	–	15	5
Greece	–	–	–	–	–	–	10	–	13	–	17	8	4	1
Netherlands	–	–	–	2	–	–	4	4	2	–	–	4	6	1
Turkey	–	–	–	–	–	–	13	–	16	8	20	–	15	2
Belgium	–	–	–	–	–	–	–	–	2	–	–	–	6	–
Bulgaria	–	–	–	–	–	–	–	–	–	6	1	–	18	–
Denmark	–	–	–	–	–	–	–	3	2	4	–	2	–	–
Norway	–	–	–	–	–	–	6	–	5	–	6	–	6	–
Poland	–	–	–	–	–	–	5	–	2	1	3	–	20	–
Portugal	–	–	–	–	–	–	2	–	5	4	–	2	–	1
Romania	–	–	–	–	–	–	(1)	–	3	4	3	–	4	–
Sweden	–	–	–	–	–	–	5	–	–	9	–	–	9	–

Notes: Numbers are based on official sources where available, supplemented by news reports, published intelligence data and other 'open' sources as appropriate. Given significant variations in available data, numbers and classifications should be regarded as indicative, particularly with respect to minor warships. Numbers in brackets relate to vessels of doubtful operational status. SSK numbers do not include midget submarines. FAC category includes missile-armed craft only.

A picture of the submarine *Artful* – the third of seven planned *Astute* class attack submarines – departing Barrow-in-Furness on preliminary sea trials in August 2015. European submarine forces have generally shrunk since the Cold War but there has been a continued need for nuclear-powered attack submarines, as well as those equipped with new AIP-technologies, for expeditionary missions. *(BAE Systems)*

Netherlands Navy's JSS joint support ship *Karel Doorman* is, perhaps, the best illustration of this trend. The growing need to support stabilisation operations at extended distances from Europe's shore also saw investment in relatively lightly-armed but technologically-sophisticated offshore or 'oceanic' patrol vessels. The Dutch *Holland* class are a good example of this development, albeit the German Navy's F-125 *Baden-Württemberg* 7,200-ton stabilisation frigates possibly represent the most extreme instance of the trend. The largely constabulary nature of these ships doubtless suited a political mood in which the danger of all-out state-on-state conflict had been banished to the shadows of the past.

Some investment in warfighting vessels has been maintained, particularly where they fill a capability gap that has assumed greater importance in the new operating environment now envisaged. There has been substantial investment in sophisticated air-defence escorts across the majority of Europe's main and second-tier fleets. This presumably reflects the vulnerability of forces operating closer to the shore-line to anti-ship missile attack. Air-independent propulsion (AIP) equipped submarines – better-capable of loitering undetected in a hostile littoral – have also proved popular. In Europe, Germany,

Greece, Italy, Portugal and Sweden are all now currently operating the type. The cynic might also detect the importance of industrial strategy in these choices For example, Germany and Sweden are world-leaders in AIP technology. Similarly a number of European manufacturers have developed the advanced multifunction phased-array radar systems that form the heart of a modern air-defence destroyer.

These changes have taken a very long time to implement. The reason for this has been a lack of willingness – and sometimes means – to devote the money required to wholesale reconfiguration when the overall perception of threat has reduced. The latter has been particularly the case since the Eurozone crisis, given government finances across the region have been severely overstretched. It is also worth noting that European naval restructuring is merely part of a wider military upheaval that has also produced other expensive changes. One example is the end of conscription in many countries. Often, naval programmes have survived as much by dint of social considerations, such as the need to prevent unemployment in depressed industrial areas, than strategic need. It has been reported that the British Royal Navy's flagship *Queen Elizabeth* class carriers only survived the 2010 Strategic Defence and

Security Review because it would have cost more to cancel the programme than continue with it. There is, however, more than a touch of irony in the fact that many of the programmes designed to deliver new constabulary and expeditionary vessels look set to be completed just as the ever-changing strategic environment is starting to swing back to a potentially greater need for warfighting capabilities in local waters.

One group of European fleets have had an additional challenge to deal with. These are the former Warsaw Pact navies of the newly-democratised Eastern European states that have now acceded to the NATO alliance. This has resulted in a pressing need to standardise equipment with their new allies. Although modernisation has sometimes been effectively implemented, for example in the smaller navies formed by the former Soviet Baltic Republics, most of these fleets have struggled to implement the scale of change required. Largely, standardisation has been limited to a handful of major units acquired second-hand from other NATO fleets. It is notable that – some twenty-five years after the pact was dissolved – the vast majority of ships listed for Bulgaria, Poland and Romania in Table 4.2.0 trace their design to Warsaw Pact origins.

4.2.1   Richard Beedall

THE ROYAL NAVY

This chapter considers how the Royal Navy (RN) of the United Kingdom (UK) has evolved since the Cold War ended, and how it is likely to change in the future.[1] In 1991, the RN was the world's third most powerful navy, after the US Navy and the newly-formed Russian Navy. The service was also still benefiting from the prestige of its success in the 1982 Falklands War. Whilst it was expected that the 'peace dividend' being demanded by the public and politicians would mean a reduction in the RN's size, no one anticipated that cuts would occur on a near-annual basis for the next twenty-five years. UK defence expenditure decreased from 4.1 per cent of GDP in 1990/91 to c. 2.0 per cent in 2015/16. The RN suffered disproportionately; excluding nuclear deterrent submarines it lost around two-thirds of its front-line strength during the period. The navies of China, France and India have all arguably now overtaken the RN in size and capabilities.

The current RN is undoubtedly at a low point in numbers, relative strength, and – perhaps – even in its institutional morale and prestige. The US Navy has become openly concerned about the declining capabilities of a navy that has been long been its key partner in arms.

STRATEGY, POLITICS & MONEY
The 'downsizing' of the RN between 1990 to 2015 is landmarked by the publication of a series of government 'White Papers', Ministry of Defence (MOD) policy documents, and various strategies; all intended to guide the changing mission, goals and objectives of the RN.[2] Theoretically the required maritime capabilities and force levels could then be identified and provided. However, this never occurred as the necessary funding was not available. Many described in detail all of the maritime security challenges facing the UK, but then announced cuts to the RN. The most influential of these documents, in chronological order, were:

1990: Options for Change: During most of the Cold War the strategic context was clear – there was only one significant potential threat, the Soviet Union and its Warsaw Pact allies. As a result, the UK's defence priorities were almost self-selecting in the 1970s and 1980s. For the RN, its focus was on providing Britain's nuclear deterrent, contributing to NATO's maritime forces in the Eastern Atlantic and the Channel and protecting home waters and ports. Anything that did not support these missions was always questioned, a notable example being the planned decommissioning of the ice patrol ship *Endurance* in 1982, which encouraged Argentina to invade the Falkland Islands. The only major out-of-area presence was the Armilla Patrol in the Arabian Gulf; this consisted of several frigates and destroyers to help protect UK and Allied merchant ships during the 1980's Iraq-Iran War.

In 1989 the Berlin Wall came down and the Cold War was ending. The need to respond to the changing strategic environment and exploit cost-saving opportunities prompted the *Options for Change* review, published in July 1990. An unambitious document, its stated aim was for 'smaller but better' Armed Forces. For the RN this meant:

- A reduction in personnel (trained and untrained) from 63,000 to 60,000.
- Cutting the number of frigates and destroyers in service from 'about fifty' (actually forty-eight) to forty.
- Reducing   the   number   of   nuclear   attack

The light carrier *Invincible* is welcomed home to Portsmouth amid massive celebrations at the end of the 1982 Falklands War. The Royal Navy was still benefitting from its highly successful role in the campaign at the end of the Cold War. *(Crown Copyright 1982)*

submarines (SSN) to twelve, with five old boats decommissioning early.

■ Limiting the number of conventional submarines (SSK) to the four *Upholder* class already being built; the remaining *Oberon* class boats would decommission without replacement.

The aircraft carrier (three *Invincible* class light carriers with Sea Harrier fighter/attack aircraft) and amphibious forces (primarily two *Fearless* class assault ships) were untouched.

The RN performed well in the First Gulf War of 1990–1 but had a noticeable lack of influence in the command and conduct of operations, perhaps a sign of things to come. In 1991 a further reduction of 5,000 naval personnel was announced. Two years later, further cuts saw:

■ The number of frigates and destroyers reduced to thirty-five.

■ The disposal of twelve 'River' class minesweepers operated by the Royal Naval Reserve.

■ The withdrawal from service of the four new *Upholder* class SSKs, ultimately sold to Canada. This meant that the RN would now only operate nuclear submarines.

1994: Frontline First: The Defence Costs Study: The *Defence Costs Study* was a further assessment of spending, and was intended to maintain the fighting strength of the armed forces whilst achieving significant savings in support costs. In practice the cost savings achieved in the 'tail' were less than hoped, whilst the reduction in logistical support seriously impacted the effectiveness of the RN. The decline in personnel numbers continued, with the expectation that the naval services would be down to 44,000 by 1999.

Neither *Options for Change* or *Frontline First* redefined the role of the RN; they were essentially focused on reducing the defence budget. The main strategic theme of UK defence policy was still Euro-centric, and the MOD attempted to maintain balanced forces by just cutting everything a bit.

Lacking direction from government, senior officers in the RN had, by default, substantial freedom to develop new strategic concepts. Documents such as the *Fundamentals of British Maritime Doctrine* (published in 1995) and the *Maritime Contribution to Joint Operations* (1998) made a considerable impact beyond the service. The concept of expedi-

tionary warfare outside the NATO area began to gain traction. Essential enablers for this would be new amphibious ships (already accepted by the government) and new aircraft carriers (not yet accepted, and potentially controversial given their cost). The RN seized every opportunity to demonstrate the operational flexibility and effectiveness of even small aircraft carriers. In the years 1993–5 the RN maintained a carrier in the Adriatic, helping to enforce the no-fly zone over Bosnia. The RN also regularly deployed a carrier task group to the Arabian Gulf, in support of sanctions against Iraq.

1998: The Strategic Defence Review (SDR): A new Labour government committed to a review of defence policy was elected in May 1997. This was to be a foreign-policy rather than cost-cutting exercise, with the declared goal that British forces would act as a 'force for good' in the world.

When the SDR was published in July 1998, it was clear that the RN's new ideas had often prevailed. The review accepted that in a world of uncertain multi-centric threats, there was a need to create deployable expeditionary forces capable of operations at considerable distances from the UK. One of the SDR's main decisions was to acquire two new large aircraft carriers to function as mobile airbases operating strike aircraft; another was greatly to enhance strategic sea and airlift capabilities. It also established a Joint Rapid Reaction Force (JRRF) which would provide a pool of readily available, rapidly deployable, high capability forces from all three Services. In other initiatives, the SDR created a Joint Helicopter Command, which incorporated British Army, Royal Air Force (RAF) and RN helicopter squadrons; and a combined RAF/RN Harrier and Sea Harrier force (Joint Force 2000, later renamed Joint Force Harrier).

In line with the emphasis on rapid deployment, the SDR required the RN to change its focus from open-ocean warfare in the North Atlantic to force projection and near-coast (littoral) operations worldwide. Shallow water operations in UK waters were also given less importance. There was, however, little immediate change to the composition of the RN, which retained responsibility for maintaining the UK's independent nuclear deterrent. Small cuts in force levels included:

■ A reduction in destroyers and frigates from thirty-five to thirty-two.

The defence reviews that took place in the immediate aftermath of the Cold War were essentially based on securing cost reductions, although forces such as frigates and conventional submarines that were focused on countering Soviet submarine activity suffered disproportionately. Older nuclear-powered attack submarines were also cut back but the more modern boats found new roles, particularly once it was decided to acquire submarine-launched Tomahawk cruise missiles. The image shows the *Trafalgar* class boat *Tireless* in 2007. *(Crown Copyright 2007)*

■ A decline in SSN numbers from twelve to ten (but all equipped with Tomahawk cruise missiles).

■ A modest fall in naval personnel.

As well as the new aircraft carriers, SDR committed the government to building new submarines, destroyers, frigates, amphibious and auxiliary ships, as well as buying a 'Future Carrier Borne Aircraft' (later renamed the Joint Combat Aircraft, or JCA).

The validity of SDR's thinking was vindicated when, in 2000, the UK decisively intervened in the civil war in Sierra Leone to support its government. The RN impressed by quickly assembling a substantial task group off-shore. This included the light carrier *Illustrious* and the ships of the

Amphibious Ready Group, centred on the helicopter carrier *Ocean*.

2002: New Chapter to the Strategic Defence Review: On 11 September 2001, the al-Qaeda terrorist group launched a devastating series of terrorist attacks on the United States of America. Although not immediately clear, this would also have a devastating effect on the RN.

In late 2001, the UK conducted a major exercise in Oman, 'Saif Sareea II', to demonstrate the JRRF concept. The RN committed no less than twenty-one naval vessels, again including *Illustrious* and *Ocean*. Whilst a success, the exercise was overshadowed by the start of American and, soon, British military operations against al-Qaeda and the Taliban in Afghanistan.

In February 2002, the MOD unexpectedly announced that its Sea Harriers would be retired from service by April 2006. Joint Force Harrier (JFH) would operate only RAF-owned Harrier aircraft thereafter. The reason given was that the Sea Harrier required expensive upgrades to remain effective that could not be justified given the aircraft would be replaced from 2012 by the JCA (a date that has since slipped to the end of 2018). It was also decided to evaluate whether the SDR was still adequate 'to cope with the threats faced'.

The resulting *Strategic Defence Review: A New Chapter*, published in July 2002, concluded that the SDR's decisions had been broadly correct, but that changes were needed in the allocation of investment, 'for example to intelligence gathering, network-centric capability … improved mobility and fire power for more rapidly deployable lighter forces, temporary deployed accommodation for troops, and night operations'.[3] Worryingly for the RN, it was not mentioned once in the document. At the end of 2002, the frigate *Sheffield* was paid off without replacement.

2003: Delivering Security in a Changing World: In May 2003, the Royal Navy and Royal Marines contributed significantly to the second Gulf War, the invasion of Iraq. A large force of ships was led by the light carrier *Ark Royal* (operating as a helicopter carrier) and *Ocean*. A particular success was the seizure of the Al Faw Peninsula by 3 Commando Brigade.

At the end of the year, the MOD published a White Paper which again revisited aspects of the SDR. It stated, 'The UK will remain actively engaged in potential areas of instability in and around Europe, the Near East, North Africa and the Gulf. But we must extend our ability to project force further afield than the SDR envisaged. In particular, the potential

for instability and crises occurring across sub-Saharan Africa and South Asia, and the wider threat from international terrorism, will require us both to engage proactively in conflict prevention and be ready to contribute to short-notice peace support and counter-terrorist operations.'[4]

Unfortunately this policy could not be aligned with the immediate reality of costly military operations in Afghanistan and Iraq, and the need for new equipment to support these. As no additional funding was available, cuts had to be made elsewhere. Accordingly, the paper also said: 'Some of our older [naval] vessels contribute less well to the pattern of operations that we envisage, and reductions in their numbers will be necessary.' In practice, this meant:

- The withdrawal of three Type 42 destroyers and three nearly-new Type 23 frigates; the latter sold to Chile.
- The decommissioning of six mine-countermeasures vessels.
- The loss of further SSNs, ultimately taking the force down to seven boats.
- Reductions in planned naval construction, particularly the cancellation of four of twelve planned Type 45 destroyers (another two were cancelled in 2008).

The Royal Navy's emphasis on expeditionary warfare was supported in the 1998 Strategic Defence Review, the last major defence review to be undertaken for twelve years. A central decisions was a commitment to two new large aircraft carriers to improve force-projection capabilities. Preparatory work for these ships continued through the next decade in spite of progressive defence cutbacks. Various alternative design configurations were proposed by consortia led by BAE Systems and Thales. These images show a Thales CATOBAR design (left) and a BAE Systems STOVL variant (right). An 'adaptable' Thales design – initially to be built in STOVL configuration – was finally selected in 2003. *(Thales / BAE Systems)*

A 1,500 reduction in the number of trained personnel to 36,000.

The only compensation was that the paper confirmed, 'The introduction of the two new aircraft carriers [the *Queen Elizabeth* class, or QEC] … early in the next decade'. The White Paper also set out the future roles of each of the services; in the maritime sphere it placed an emphasis on land-attack missiles and amphibious ships to project power ashore.

By mid-2005, the RN was down to twenty-five frigates and destroyers, against a backdrop of increased rather than decreased operational demands. The carrier *Invincible* was withdrawn from operational service in May 2005, five years earlier than previously planned.

2006: The Future Navy Vision: By 2006, the RN faced the reality that its expeditionary strategy was in tatters, its internal plans unrealisable, and that it was in danger of it becoming seen as militarily irrelevant. One of the two remaining carriers was still kept operational in the strike role, but its flight deck was usually empty of fixed-wing aircraft as JFH was stretched maintaining a squadron in Afghanistan. The newly-built amphibious ships were being used for other tasks as the Royal Marines had been committed to Afghanistan. Whilst up to 5,000 naval personnel were sometimes in Afghanistan and Iraq with 3 Commando Brigade, JFH, Joint Helicopter Command and other formations, this was not publicly recognised.

In 2006 the RN tried to make a stand by publishing its own vision for the future. It was drafted under the direction of Admiral Sir Jonathon Band, the First Sea Lord, who wrote, 'Britain is pre-eminently a maritime nation whose people will continue to rely on the unhindered use of the sea for their security, prosperity and well-being. The world faces an uncertain, rapidly changing and competitive global environment in the early decades of the 21st century. My vision envisages a Royal Navy that … will contribute vitally and decisively to the security of the UK, to the preservation of international order at sea and to the promotion of our national values and interests in the wider world.' The vision required a navy capable of Maritime Force Projection (the employment of military power at sea and against the land) and Maritime Security (the defence of the UK home-

Although SDR 1998 gave a high priority to carrier capabilities, financial pressures resulted in an announcement in 2002 that the RN Sea Harrier would be withdrawn in 2006, leaving only RAF Harriers in service. This 2005 image shows aircraft of both types embarked on *Illustrious*. *(Crown Copyright 2005)*

land and sovereign territories), enabled by Maritime Manoeuvre (seaborne access).

The document further stated, 'A broadly balanced Fleet represents the most effective means of delivering this capability, both at home and abroad, as well as providing a reasonable assurance against the unexpected. This means that we will project and sustain Amphibious and Carrier Strike Task Groups simultaneously … [Also] our Fleet should have sufficient flexibility and size to deploy single ships and submarines on sustained, independent tasks on a routine basis, with the potential and capacity to switch quickly to combat and group operations.'

The *Future Navy Vision* document has stood the passage of time well but, unfortunately, has also been largely ignored given subsequent developments.

2010: Strategic Defence and Security Review – SDSR 2010: SDSR 2010, released on 19 October 2015, was a rushed review by a new Conservative/Liberal Democrat coalition govern-

ment, conducted in the context of economic depression and a projected £38bn 'black hole' in the equipment budget. In contrast to the new National Security Strategy (NSS) published a day previously, SDSR 2010's focus was on immediate financial savings; a parliamentary committee could later find no evidence of strategic thinking in the document.[5]

For the RN, the outcome was little short of a disaster. Decisions affecting it included:

Bringing only one of the two new *Queen Elizabeth* class carriers into service; the other would be placed in reserve or sold (the review seriously considered cancelling the ships; however, this would have cost more than completing them).

Joint Force Harrier would disband and the RN's flagship and only operational fixed-wing carrier, *Ark Royal*, decommissioned.

Four Type 22 frigates would decommission,

Sea King transport helicopters operating from the deck of the helicopter carrier *Ocean* during an exercise off Sierra Leone in 2006. In spite of imposing severe overall cuts on Royal Navy capabilities, the Royal Marines and the availability of a high readiness amphibious response group were both protected in SDSR 2010. *(Crown Copyright 2006)*

leaving an escort force of just six destroyers and thirteen frigates.

■ Three RFA ships would be withdrawn from service.
■ The RAF's Nimrod MR4A replacement maritime patrol aircraft (MPA) project was axed.
■ Trained naval personnel would reduce from 35,000 to 30,000 by 2015.

SDSR stated that by 2020, the Royal Navy would be structured to provide:

■ Maritime defence of the UK and Overseas Territories, including the South Atlantic.
■ Nuclear Continuous at Sea Deterrence.
■ A credible and capable presence within priority regions of the world.
■ A very high readiness response force and a contribution to enduring land operations [by the Royal Marines].

The review was implemented as hastily as it had been conducted. *Ark Royal* arrived in Portsmouth on 3 December flying a decommissioning pennant, before being sold for scrap. Joint Force Harrier

The nuclear-powered attack submarine *Triumph* and the Type 45 destroyer *Daring* pictured on exercises in the Middle East in 2012. The maintenance of a credible presence in priority regions such as the Persian Gulf and Middle East was another capability protected from the SDSR 2010 cuts. *(Crown Copyright 2012)*

ROYAL NAVY SURFACE COMBATANTS

Type 45 Destroyer (UK):
HMS *Duncan* (D 37)

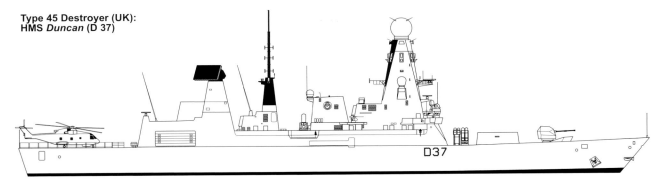

D37

0   10m   20m   30m   40m   50m

Type 23 Frigate (UK):
HMS *Iron Duke* (F 234)

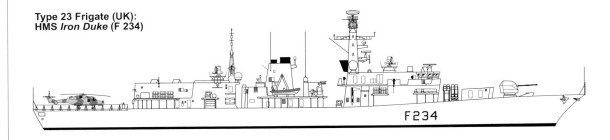

F234

Offshore Patrol Vessel (UK):
HMS *Forth*

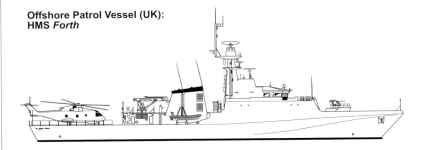

SDSR 2010 consolidated the Royal Navy's surface fleet on two major classes of surface warship. The six modern Type 45 destroyers – half the number initially envisaged – serve in the air defence role but have been steadily upgraded with additional equipment (e.g. Harpoon surface-to-surface missiles, Phalanx CIWS) and may be further modified for BMD. The thirteen remaining Type 23 frigates – three were sold to Chile – are older but are receiving extensive midlife upgrades on an incremental basis that include a new Artisan radar, new surface-to-air missiles (Sea Ceptor), replacement generators and other enhancements. The drawing of *Iron Duke* depicts her with Artisan on her mainmast but before the installation of Sea Ceptor. The class will start to be replaced by the new Type 26 Global Combat Ship from the early 2020s.In addition to these two classes, the 'River' Batch II offshore patrol vessels will enter service from 2017 and be used for constabulary roles. Although the Royal Navy has traditionally been hostile to second-line surface vessels, five 'Rivers' will be in service by 2020 and may serve to take some pressure off an overstretched escort fleet. In the longer term, a new class of light frigate is also planned. *(All drawings © John Jordan 2015)*

ceased to be operational on 15 December 2010; its Harriers were sold to the US Marine Corps for spare parts. Redundancy notices were soon being issued to naval personnel.

Critics of the review could take little satisfaction from the government's discomfort when, in March 2011, it intervened in Libya's civil war as part of an international coalition, and found that many of the required military assets had already been lost, or were about to be lost. For example, French and Italian aircraft carriers conducted intensive air attacks from positions just off the Libyan coast. Lacking an aircraft carrier, the main British air contribution was a small number of sorties by RAF strike aircraft, flying at considerable cost from bases in the UK and Italy. The decommissioning of the Type 22 frigate *Cumberland* had to be delayed by two months, as the ship was busy rescuing British and other foreign nationals from Libyan ports.

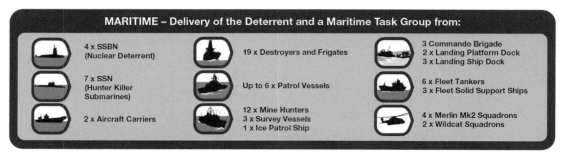

MARITIME – Delivery of the Deterrent and a Maritime Task Group from:

- 4 x SSBN (Nuclear Deterrent)
- 7 x SSN (Hunter Killer Submarines)
- 2 x Aircraft Carriers
- 19 x Destroyers and Frigates
- Up to 6 x Patrol Vessels
- 12 x Mine Hunters
- 3 x Survey Vessels
- 1 x Ice Patrol Ship
- 3 Commando Brigade
- 2 x Landing Platform Dock
- 3 x Landing Ship Dock
- 6 x Fleet Tankers
- 3 x Fleet Solid Support Ships
- 4 x Merlin Mk2 Squadrons
- 2 x Wildcat Squadrons

With the significant exception of the entry into service of the new *Queen Elizabeth* class aircraft carriers, the Royal Navy 'Future Force 2025' structure described by SDSR 2015 is little changed from the current position. *(Crown Copyright 2015)*

2014: National Strategy for Maritime Security: Presented by the Secretary of State for Defence in May 2014, this document defined 'maritime security' to be 'the advancement and protection of the UK's national interests, at home and abroad, through the active management of risks and opportunities in and from the maritime domain, in order to strengthen and extend the UK's prosperity, security and resilience and to help shape a stable world.' Building on the NSS, it established five maritime security objectives:

- Promoting a secure international maritime domain and upholding international maritime norms.
- Developing the maritime governance capacity and capabilities of states in areas of strategic maritime importance.
- Protecting the UK, our citizens and our economy by supporting the safety and security of ports and o?shore installations and Red Ensign Group-flagged passenger and cargo ships.
- Assuring the security of vital maritime trade and energy transportation routes within the UK Marine Area, regionally and internationally.
- Protecting the resources and population of the UK and the Overseas Territories from illegal and dangerous activity, including serious organised crime and terrorism.

The strategy only discussed at a very general level how the Royal Navy and other agencies might meet these objectives, and did not consider required funding and force levels. However, it did commit the RN to deploying ships in order to maintain vital trade routes and ensure freedom of navigation, and also to contributing to three military alliances which help deliver maritime security, namely NATO, the EU and Combined Maritime Forces (CMF).

The veteran replenishment tanker *Gold Rover*, first commissioned in 1974, pictured with the Type 23 frigate *Lancaster* whilst both ships were engaged in Atlantic Patrol Task (South) duties in the South Atlantic in June 2015. Protection of British Overseas territories such as the Falkland Islands formed part of the maritime security objectives set out in the 2014 National Strategy for Maritime Security. *(Crown Copyright 2015)*

2015: National Security Strategy and Strategic Defence and Security Review – SDSR 2015: On 23 November 2015, the recently-elected Conservative government published the results of another defence review. This was undertaken in a very different context to 2010. British combat operations had ended in Iraq (2009) and Afghanistan (2014) but new threats had emerged. Russia was re-asserting herself militarily; China had become a substantial naval power and was claiming sovereignty of large parts of the South China Sea; whilst the Islamic State of Iraq and the Levant (ISIL) was considered a serious threat to UK security. Also, after considerable American pressure, it had been announced on 10 July 2015 that Britain would commit to continuing to spend 2 per cent of its GDP on defence every year until 2020.

SDSR 2015 described how the UK's armed forces might look in 2025 – see schematic on p. 62 for the proposed Royal Navy structure – and sought to plug the worst of the capability gaps created by SDSR 2010. For the RN, there was mixed news. Positively, the review confirmed a decision announced in 2014 that both QEC carriers would, after all, enter service to ensure that one would be continuously available as the core of a maritime task group. More negatively, the previous plan to replace all thirteen remaining Type 23 frigates with the same number of new Type 26 Global Combat Ships was reduced to eight; the cost of the new ships was simply too high. Instead, design studies would begin for a less sophisticated but cheaper general-purpose light frigate, a concept the RN has long resisted. The carrot was that more than five may eventually be built, increasing the size of the escort force.

Other major announcements impacting the RN included:

- Confirmation that four 'Successor' strategic missile submarines would be delivered, although later than previously planned, as part of renewal of the Trident nuclear deterrent.
- Planned orders for two additional 'River' class patrol vessels, as well as three new logistic support ships for the RFA.
- Investigation of the potential for the Type 45 class to operate in a ballistic missile defence role.
- Acceleration of purchases of the F-35B Lightning II (selected for the JCA requirement) to ensure twenty-four will be available for carrier operations by 2023.[6]
- Planned acquisition of nine P-8 Poseidon MPAs to replace the Nimrods cancelled in 2010.
- A slight increase in authorised (trained) personnel numbers to around 30,500 regulars.

A Landing Craft Air Cushioned (hovercraft), of 539 Assault Squadron, Royal Marines, patrolling the Az Zubayr river near Umm Qasr in Iraq. The Royal Marines' light infantry capability remains an important part of the Royal Navy's overall force structure under SDSR 2015. (Crown Copyright 2003)

A P-8 Poseidon MPA in US Navy colours. Re-establishment of a maritime patrol aircraft capability was, perhaps, the major outcome of the British SDSR 2015 defence review. (US Navy)

4.2.1.1: UNITED KINGDOM –ROYAL NAVY COMPOSITION END 2015

MAJOR BASES & STRUCTURE

Portsmouth:	Destroyers, frigates, patrol vessels, mine-countermeasures vessels. Aircraft carriers from 2017.
Devonport (Plymouth):	Amphibious ships; frigates. Remaining attack submarines being transferred to Faslane.
Faslane (Clyde):	Strategic and Attack submarines, mine-countermeasures vessels

Numerous support and training establishments are clustered around the three main bases. There are also minor forward operating bases at **Gibraltar** and the **Falkland Islands,** with a new base being established in **Bahrain**.

PERSONNEL

c. 32,500 regulars, including c.7,000 Royal Marines. There are also c. 5,500 reserves, of which around 1,800 are in the RFA.

MAJOR WARSHIPS

Type	Class	In-Service	Ordered	ISD	Tonnage	Notes
Aircraft Carriers:		–	(2)			
Aircraft Carrier (CV)	*Queen Elizabeth*	–	(2)	(2017)	65,000 tons	STOVL configured strike carriers with secondary amphibious role.
Major Amphibious Warships:		6	(–)			
Helicopter Carrier (LPH)	*Ocean*	1	(–)	1998	22,500 tons	Will be withdrawn as the *Queen Elizabeth* class come into service.
Landing Platform Dock (LPD)	*Albion*	2	(–)	2003	18,500 tons	One normally in reserve.
Landing Ship Dock (LSD)	*Largs Bay*	3	(–)	2006	16,200 tons	Operated by RFA. One ship sold to Australia,
Major Surface Escorts:		19	(3)			
Destroyer (DDG)	*Daring* (Type 45)	6	(–)	2008	7,500 tons	
Frigate (FFG)	Global Combat Ship (Type 26)	–	(3)	(2022)	6,900 tons	Long lead items for 3 ordered. 8 planned.
Frigate (FFG)	*Norfolk* (Type 23)	13	–	1990	4,900 tons	3 additional units transferred to Chile. Midlife upgrades underway.
Strategic Submarines:		4	(4)			
Submarine (SSBN)	'Successor'	–	(4)	(c.2030)	Not known	Long-lead items on order
Submarine (SSBN)	*Vanguard*	4	(–)	1993	16,000 tons	
Attack Submarines:		7	(4)			
Submarine (SSN)	*Astute*	3	(4)	2010	7,800 tons	
Submarine (SSN)	*Trafalgar*	4	(–)	1983	5,200 tons	Survivors of an original class of 7.

Other Ships:

Type	Large Patrol Vessels	Minehunters	Replenishment Ships	
Number	4	15	7	Plus various training vessels, landing craft and auxiliaries, some civilian operated.

NAVAL AVIATION

Main naval air stations (NAS) bases are at Yeovilton & Culdrose. Following the retirement of the Sea Harrier STOVL jets in 2006, front-line fixed wing aircraft operations are carried out jointly with the RAF, with the new F-35B squadrons to be based at RAF Marham. Up to 138 F-35s will ultimately be purchased, with 24 expected to be available for front-line use by 2023. Current main helicopter types are:

- AW-101 'Merlin' HM2 sea control helicopters: 30 in service
- AW-101 'Merlin': HC4 transport helicopters: 25 being converted to new shipborne standard from RAF HC3 configuration, replacing legacy Sea King types.
- AW-159 'Wildcat' HMA2 sea control helicopters: 28 in service or on order. Replacing legacy Lynx HMA8. Additional Wildcat AH1 reconnaissance helicopters drawn from a shared pool.

Additional British Army and RAF Apache attack and Chinook transport helicopters can be embarked as necessary. 3 Insitu Scan Eagle UAVs are also used.

The RAF is to order 9 P-8 maritime patrol aircraft for entry into service from c. 2020 onwards.

The next defence review is expected in 2020.

THE ROYAL NAVY IN 2015

Force Structure: The current Royal Navy force structure is set out in Table 4.2.1.1. The submarine flotilla is focused on four *Vanguard* class SSBN strategic submarines and seven SSN nuclear attack boats, whilst the force of major surface combatants comprises six modern destroyers and thirteen older frigates. Other key components include an amphibious force built around a helicopter carrier, two LPD amphibious transport docks and three auxiliary LSD dock landing ships (operated by the RFA) and an amphibious infantry brigade that includes three Commandos (battalions) of Royal Marines. The Future Force 2025 described by SDSR 2015 will be very similar with the notable exception of entry into service of the two new carriers *Queen Elizabeth* and *Prince of Wales* from 2017 onwards. This will result in the decommissioning (probably in 2018) of the current helicopter carrier *Ocean*, whose crew is needed to help man them. The last *Invincible* class carrier, *Illustrious*, has already been withdrawn from service, in 2014.

After the closure of numerous establishments in the 1990s and early part of the current millennium, most forces are based at or near the three remaining naval bases at the Clyde, Devonport and Portsmouth. In addition to its presence at its main air stations at Culdrose (HMS *Seahawk*) and Yeovilton (HMS *Heron*), the Fleet Air Arm has a growing presence at RAF Marham, from where it will jointly operate the F-35B from 2018.

Organisation: The command and the administrative structures of the Royal Navy had been greatly simplified since the early 1990s. For example, superfluous formations such as frigate and destroyer squadrons have gone, and many senior positions abolished or downgraded. Nevertheless, the RN still receives considerable negative publicity for having more admirals than major warships.

The First Sea Lord & Chief of Naval Staff (1SL) is the professional head of the Royal Navy. Until 1995 he was a 5* Admiral of the Fleet, thereafter a 4* Admiral. 1SL effectively reports to the Chief of the Defence Staff (CDS) – the professional head of the British Armed Forces and the most senior

uniformed military adviser to the Secretary of State for Defence and the Prime Minister.

The 1SL is Chairman of the Naval Board, the body having practical responsibility for running the RN.[7] His key lieutenants are the Second Sea Lord (2SL), a 3* Vice Admiral who is responsible for personnel and infrastructure, and the Fleet Commander & Deputy Chief of Naval Staff, a 3* Vice Admiral based at Navy Command Headquarters at Portsmouth.

Accountable to the Fleet Commander is the most senior sea-going post: Commander United Kingdom Maritime Forces (COMUKMARFOR). A 2* Rear Admiral; he will only go to sea for major exercises or combat operations. The two key RN operational formations in the first decade of the millennium were the UK Carrier Strike Group (UKCSG) and the UK Amphibious Task Group (UKATG), each commanded by a 1* Commodore. The UKCSG was disbanded following the elimination of the RN's strike carrier capability in 2010, with UKATG being renamed the Response Force Task Group (RFTG). However, with the pending entry into service of *Queen Elizabeth*, the UKCSG

Queen Elizabeth being floated out of her building dock in July 2014. The Royal Navy's two new aircraft carriers will enter service from 2017 onwards. *(BAE Systems)*

organisation was re-established in 2015 and the commander of RFTG reverted to being titled Commander Amphibious Task Group.

Operations: By the start of the twenty-first century, the RN seemed to have successfully reorganised itself from its Cold War tasks. The previous focus on anti-submarine warfare in the North Atlantic had been swept away in favour of expeditionary forces capable of global deployment. Indeed, the RN's frigates and destroyers were scattered around the world in a manner not seen since the 1960s.

In the immediate aftermath of SDSR 2010, the RN continued to operate at a high tempo. However, this was not sustainable, placing excessive demands on equipment and personnel. The RN has thus retrenched considerably, cutting some commitments altogether (e.g. participation in many standing NATO maritime groups), and making others part-time (e.g. its presence in the West Indies).

Since 1980, the RN has maintained a near continuous presence in the Arabian Gulf and Indian

4.2.1.2: NAVAL CONSTRUCTION ORDERS (1990–2015)

TYPE	1990s										2000s										2010s					
	0	1	2	3	4	5	6	7	8	9	0	1	2	3	4	5	6	7	8	9	0	1	2	3	4	5
Attack Submarine – SSN								3										1				1		1		1
Aircraft Carrier – CV																		2								
Destroyer – DDG													3	3												
Frigate – FFG			3			3																				
Helicopter Carrier – LPH			1																							
Assault Ship – LPD					2																					
Minehunter – MCMV			7																							
Offshore Patrol Vessel – OPV													3			1								3		
Survey Ships –AGSH						1							2													
Fleet Tanker – AOR							2																	4		
Transport Ship – AKR													6													
Landing Ships Dock – LSD(A)													2	2												

Note: Since 2005 the MOD has begun to order submarines and major warships in stages, so there is an element of subjectivity as to the year allocated.

Ocean, under titles such as Armilla Patrol, Southern Watch and Operation 'Kipion'. These operations were always considered temporary, so only ad-hoc

An image showing the last flight of a Harrier GR9 jet from the aircraft carrier *Ark Royal* in 2010. Re-establishing a fast jet naval aviation capability through introduction of the new *Queen Elizabeth* class aircraft carriers and then developing the concept of CEPP (see p.67) is a key challenge facing the Royal Navy. *(Crown Copyright 2010)*

support arrangements were made. The need for a permanent base in the region was finally recognised in December 2014 when the decision was announced to build the Mina Salman Support Facility in Bahrain, to be named HMS *Juffair* when completed in 2016. A 1* Commodore is already headquartered in Bahrain to command maritime forces in the region.

The new base will be the home port for four mine-countermeasures vessels, plus a 'Bay' class support ship and a repair ship. The base will also be frequently used by other RN assets in the region, typically including a Type 45 destroyer, a Type 23 frigate, a nuclear attack submarine and an RFA replenishment ship. The two escorts regularly participate in maritime security operations such as the multi-national Combined Task Force 150, the NATO-led Operation 'Ocean Shield', and the EU-led Operation 'Atalanta' – all essentially maritime security and counter-piracy operations in the Gulf of Aden and off the Horn of Africa.

Other standing RN commitments include:

- One *Vanguard* class SSBN continuously on patrol, providing the UK's nuclear deterrent.
- One frigate or destroyer at high availability in UK waters (the fleet ready escort).
- A frigate or destroyer, with an accompanying RFA support ship, in the South Atlantic.
- A patrol vessel (normally *Clyde*) based in the Falkland Islands.

- The ice patrol vessel *Protector*, on station in the Antarctic region for most of the year.
- One ship in the West Indies during the winter hurricane season: in 2015 this was the patrol vessel *Severn*.
- Fishery, economic and maritime security protection duties around the UK.

In addition, the RFTG is exercised annually, usually by a four-month deployment to the Mediterranean.

ISSUES & CHALLENGES

The RN currently faces many challenges, the most significant of which include:

Maintaining Britain's Nuclear Deterrent: The current four *Vanguard* class SSBNs are beginning to shows signs of their age and need replacing. They were due to start decommissioning in 2023 but this has had to be delayed, as the first of four new 'Successor' class submarines is not now expected to enter service until the early 2030s. Even this timetable assumes that detailed design and construction work proceeds to schedule.

If the 'Successor' project suffers from the lengthy delays that affected the *Astute* class submarines, there is a serious risk that the RN may eventually be unable to maintain a continuous at-sea nuclear deterrent.

Lack of Personnel: In October 2015, the Royal Navy had 22,480 trained regular personnel, and the Royal Marines 6,970, for a trained total of 29,450 regulars. There were another 3,030 regular personnel under training. This compares with a total of 35,240 trained personnel in October 2010.

Current manpower levels are insufficient to keep the fleet fully manned; in particular a shortage of 500 engineers badly affected operations during 2015. In smaller branches and specialisations (some with less than a hundred personnel), it is also difficult to maintain training capabilities, a coherent career path, and a reasonable work-life balance. The submarine service is a particular concern; it has become so small that the loss of just a few highly skilled and experienced senior rates and officers could cripple the service. Also new joiners (from commanding officers downwards) no longer have the opportunity to learn the ropes in conventional submarines; they now go straight to billion-pound nuclear submarines.

During the SDSR 2015 deliberations, the RN

The 'Successor' class submarine is arguably the most important current British defence project. The existing *Vanguard* class submarines are ageing quickly and there is a risk that the continuous at-sea nuclear deterrent may not be maintained if the new class suffers significant build problems. *(BAE Systems)*

reportedly requested an extra 2,000 regular personnel, but got around 400, which will be slowly added to the 2015 authorised trained strength of 30,270. In spite of the increasing use of reservists, this may not be enough to stop a difficult situation getting worse.

Creating Carrier Enabled Power Projection: A big challenge facing the RN is regenerating its carrier force by bringing the two *Queen Elizabeth* class aircraft carriers in to service and then using these to deliver the concept of Carrier Enabled Power Projection (CEPP).

CEPP was an idea developed as the RN fought to save the carrier programme from cancellation in SDSR 2010. It shifted the rational for the new carriers beyond their original carrier strike role (operating up to thirty-six JCAs). Instead, it emphasised the flexibility of the *Queen Elizabeth* class – particularly with regard to operating helicopters and supporting amphibious operations. This has required changes to the design to allow them to embark a substantial military force and operate a

mixed air-group comprising both fixed-wing aircraft and multiple rotary-wing types effectively. *Prince of Wales* will be completed to the revised design, with – presumably – *Queen Elizabeth* eventually being retrofitted. The operating concept is much closer to that of the US Navy's LHDs than traditional carrier operations, and represents a huge learning curve for the RN. Although *Queen Elizabeth* will enter service in 2017/18, she is not expected to be fully operational and able to deliver all aspects of CEPP before 2022.

CEPP presents a number of risks which will have to be managed. Firstly, it is dependent on the continuous availability of a QEC carrier, and the RN will struggle to keep one always fully manned and operational. Secondly, the QEC will be a hugely expensive, high value unit; accordingly escorting and supporting the carriers will dominate future RN operations. Thirdly, CEPP is 'joint', its application requires the availability and integration of British Army and RAF assets into embarked operations. Finally, the concept has killed a tentative plan for a low-cost replacement for *Ocean*, though there will be

The Type 23 frigate *Kent* pictured in 2010. The thirteen members of the class remaining in Royal Navy service are currently in the middle of a major life-extension programme but replacement by the delayed Type 26 replacement project is becoming increasingly urgent. *(Crown Copyright 2010)*

An image of the new Type 26 global combat ship, which has steadily grown in size and cost in spite of strenuous efforts to design a cost-effective ship. As a result, the British MOD has baulked at the price being quoted by builder BAE Systems – a reduction in class numbers is one consequence, whilst a full build contract has yet to be signed. *(BAE Systems)*

occasions where a helicopter carrier would offer a more appropriate and cost effective presence than a *Queen Elizabeth*-based group. The *Queen Elizabeth*s are now going to have to work closely with amphibious ships such as the *Albion* class; for reasons as basic as differences in maximum speed this will not be easy. New tactics and operational procedures will have to be developed.

Too few Submarines and Escorts: The RN has too few attack submarines and escorts to meet all the demands placed on the force. Operational studies have repeatedly shown that the RN needs at least eight attack submarines but funding permits only seven. Indeed, there are often only six when a *Trafalgar* class boat decommissions before its replacement *Astute* class enters service. The RN currently struggles to deploy even two submarines simultaneously.

The availability of the six Type 45 destroyers is lower than hoped, whilst the availability of the Type 23 frigates is being affected by their life extension programme, involving lengthy refits.[8] No more than five or six escorts can be deployed at the same time – barely enough to meet current commitments. Moreover, a high-value aircraft carrier will need escorting from 2018.

The RN is reluctantly being forced to use patrol vessels for tasks previously fulfilled by escorts. In the long term it is hoped that the new light frigate can be built in sufficient numbers to increase the size of the escort force.

Maintaining the Industrial Base: A *Defence Industrial Strategy* (DIS) published by the MOD in December 2005 said 'For submarines we have endorsed, but not yet committed funding for a 24-month SSN build drumbeat … The longer-term surface ship production drumbeat is of the order of one new platform every one to two years.' This was to prove optimistic.[9]

Table 4.2.1.2 shows ships ordered in the years 1990 to 2015. It can be seen that these peaked in 2000–1 as the MOD began to implement SDR. Indeed, the proposed construction programme was so large that UK shipyard capacity was expected to be inadequate, and the RAND Corporation was asked to develop a plan to optimise its use.[10] Unfortunately by the time RAND completed their report in 2005, much of the construction programme was already in doubt. Progress continued on the £6.5bn *Queen Elizabeth* class aircraft carrier project only by the RN sacrificing almost everything else.

In 2015, despite work on the *Queen Elizabeth* class winding down, SDSR 2015 delayed the first Type 26 order until 2017. As a stop-gap, the MOD is buying five 'River' Batch 2 patrol vessels – three were ordered in 2014, with two more planned for 2016. Capable of world-wide deployment and equipped with a helicopter deck, they are a big step-up from the three Batch 1 ships, which will presumably be sold.

As a result of the lack of RN orders, and a failure to win exports orders, many UK shipyards have closed, most recently the Vosper Thorneycroft (later BAE Systems) facility in Portsmouth in 2014. BAE Systems Maritime – Naval Ships is now the only UK company able to build major warships, with a facility for submarines at Barrow-in-Furness, and two yards in Glasgow (at Govan and Scotstoun) for surface ships. BAE Systems has effectively become a monopolistic supplier, and the MOD is struggling to maintain a UK naval construction capability without paying excessive prices. For example, the MOD has baulked at the price being quoted to it for the Type 26s, and even hinted that it was prepared to order them overseas – a serious threat given the MOD's landmark order in 2012 for four *Tidespring* class Fleet Tankers from DSME of South Korea.

UK naval construction has become shaped not by the needs of the RN, but by budgets and what the Treasury considers to be the lowest rate of naval construction rate that will allow BAE Systems Maritime and key suppliers such as Rolls-Royce to survive and thus preserve critical industrial capabilities.

Poor Public Relations: The Royal Navy has suffered from a relatively poor public image in the early part of the twenty-first century. The glory days of appearances in James Bond films, and the 1970s TV series *Warship* and *Sailor* are long gone. When the RN does feature in the media, it is often in a negative context: cost overruns, ship groundings, excessive drinking and the like. A particular PR disaster was the seizure by Iran in 2007 of two small boats from the frigate *Cornwall* carrying fifteen RN/RM personnel; their subsequent parading in the glare of the world's media was described by Admiral Sir Jonathon Band, then 1SL, as 'one bad day in our proud 400-year history'. An attempt in 2010 to repeat the success of *Sailor* with the TV series *Ark Royal* backfired due to the carrier's obvious lack of aircraft, and the untimely announcement that she was to be decommissioned as a defence cut.

Perhaps even worse is the lack of naval experience and advocacy in political circles; Minister of State for the Armed Forces Penelope Mordaunt (a Sub-

Lieutenant in the RNR) being an important exception. It is also notable that no admiral has held the top post of Chief of the Defence Staff since 2003. One former First Sea Lord, Admiral Sir Jonathon Band, concluded in a speech he made in October 2011, ' …the nation as a whole has forgotten its maritime tradition and nature of existence'. The RN badly needs a high-profile success story. It is also to be hoped that the *Queen Elizabeth* class will become an impressive symbol of British military power in the same way the carrier *Charles de Gaulle* has become for France.

A FINAL COMMENT

The early years of the twenty-first century have been difficult time for the Royal Navy. The UK's military focus on land conflicts during the period has had a negative impact in terms of funding and, consequently, force levels for the naval service.

However, the security of the UK and its national interests are inextricably linked to the sea. The UK is physically an island nation dependent on seaborne trade; it is the fifth largest economy in the world; it has world-wide interests and commitments; and it wants to remain a permanent member of the UN Security Council. Given these factors, the RN may well have reached its nadir; indeed, the advent of the *Queen Elizabeth* class carriers may mark the start of a recovery.

Notes

1. This article often uses the term 'Royal Navy' or RN as being synonymous with the UK naval services. They include the Royal Navy, Royal Marines, Fleet Air Arm, Royal Naval Reserve (RNR) and Royal Fleet Auxiliary Service.

2. Most of the documents referenced in this chapter are available online, for example from the UK National Archives at: www.webarchive.nationalarchives.gov.uk

3. *The Strategic Defence Review: A New Chapter – Cm 5566 Vol 1* (London: Ministry of Defence, 2002), p.29.

4. *Delivering Security in a Changing World – Defence White Paper – Cm 6041-I* (London: Ministry of Defence, 2003), p.7.

5. See further *Securing Britain in an Age of Uncertainty: The Strategic Defence and Security Review – Cm 7948* and *A Strong Britain in an Age of Uncertainty: The National Security Strategy – Cm 7593* (both London: The Prime Minister, 2010).

6. The Lightning II decision should mean that 809 Naval Air Squadron, due to commission in 2018 as an operational conversion unit, will eventually become a full front-line squadron alongside the RAF's 617 Squadron.

7. The Admiralty Board, chaired by the Secretary of Defence, has overall command of RN personnel and responsibility for its administration. In practice, these responsibilities are delegated to the Navy Board.

8. A machinery improvement package for the Type 45 has been approved as part of SDSR 2015.

9. Defence Industrial Strategy – *Defence White Paper- Cm 6697* (London: Ministry of Defence, 2003), p.75.

10. See *The United Kingdom's Naval Shipbuilding Industrial Base: The Next Fifteen Years*, Mark V. Arena et al. (Santa Monica, CA: RAND Publishing, 2005). Available on the RAND Corporation's website at www.rand.org

11. Sources of official information about the current RN are its website: www.royalnavy.mod.uk and newspaper, *Navy News*: www.navynews.co.uk. The National Audit Office's annual Ministry of Defence: Major Projects Report – to be found at www.nao.org.uk – has also become essential reading for naval analysts. Other sources of potential interest include:

D K Brown, *The Future British Surface Fleet: Options for Medium-Sized Navies* (Annapolis, MD: Naval Institute Press, 1991).

Nick Childs, *Britain's Future Navy* (revised edition) (Barnsley: Pen & Sword Maritime. 2012)

Eric J Grove, *Vanguard to Trident: British Naval Policy Since World War II* (Annapolis, MD: Naval Institute Press, 1987).

Lewis Page, *Lions, Donkeys and Dinosaurs: Waste and Blundering in the Military* (London: Heinemann, 2006).

Duncan Redford and Philip D Grove, *The Royal Navy: A History Since 1900* (London: I B Tauris, 2014).

Conrad Waters

LEADING CONTINENTAL EUROPEAN NAVIES

Mainland Europe's leading navies have all had to face common challenges relating to force restructuring and budgetary limitations in the years following the Cold War. However, the extent to which they have been impacted by these challenges – and the way they have addressed them – has varied significantly from fleet to fleet. This chapter aims to examine the strategic decisions Europe's major navies have made over the period and assess the force structures that have resulted.

FRANCE: *THE MARINE NATIONALE*

France's *Marine Nationale* is arguably Europe's leading navy. It maintains a full spectrum of naval capabilities that encompass nuclear-powered strategic and attack submarines; an aircraft carrier and amphibious shipping; and both first-line and second-line surface combatants. The fleet is supported by a well-equipped naval air arm – the *Aéronautique navale* – and a strong domestic defence industry that includes the shipbuilder DCNS and the electronics giant Thales.

Post-Cold War Development: To some extent, the French navy has managed to escape the worst of the force reconfigurations of the post-Cold War years experienced by many of its European neighbours. France spent much of the Cold War as a 'semi-detached' member of NATO – operating outside its main command structures and less influenced by the alliance's military priorities.[1] This, coupled with the realties of geography and a desire to maintain a strong independent interventionist capability, meant that its navy was never as focused towards the Atlantic anti-submarine mission that increasingly

The French aircraft carrier *Charles de Gaulle* operating off the coast of Djibouti in 2015. The French Navy's long focus on expeditionary capabilities meant that it was better placed than many European fleets to face changed requirements following the Cold War's end. *(Crown Copyright 2015)*

dominated the Royal Navy's conventional fleet.[2] As such, the *Marine Nationale* entered the 1990s with a balance of forces – including aircraft carriers, amphibious shipping and constabulary patrol vessels – that were quite well-suited to the changed strategic environment. Subsequent policy decisions in the 1990s – heralded by the *Defence White Paper of 1994* and later implemented by the Chirac administration – tended to support investment in naval expeditionary capabilities. The new nuclear-powered aircraft carrier *Charles de Gaulle* was finally commissioned in 2001, whilst design work commenced in the late 1990s on what were to become the *Mistral* class amphibious assault ships.

The evolution of the French navy throughout this time has, however, not been without its difficulties.

The Cold War focus on the nuclear deterrent and the subsequent expense associated with the move to all-professional armed forces always meant there was insufficient investment in conventional naval forces, particularly the escort force. The inevitable 'peace dividend' also impacted some naval programmes; for example, the final two *Rubis* class attack submarines were cancelled in the early 1990s after work had already commenced and a sixth *La Fayette* class stealth frigate was also axed. Many older classes of surface combatant were retired or reduced. More recently, the ambitious plan to renew the escort fleet with as many as seventeen *Aquitaine* FREMM-type frigates has been steadily scaled back to just eight ships. The reduction in warship numbers was accompanied by a pruning of bases and other infrastructure; the OPTIMAR 95 programme was particularly significant in concentrating the expeditionary fleet at Toulon. Brest became the only other significant operational base in Metropolitan France, specialising in anti-submarine and mine-countermeasures warships in support of the strategic submarines based at the neighbouring Ile Longue.

Having had a fourteen-year gap since a major defence review, France published a new *White Paper on Defence & National Security* in 2008.[3] Amongst a number of decisions, the most significant was to return to full participation in NATO. Although announcing further cuts in personnel and starting the process of scaling back of FREMM construction, the document was largely supportive of naval forces. Notably it confirmed the 'Barracuda' class attack submarine programme, promised a doubling of the *Mistral* class to four ships and held open the possibility of a long-delayed order for a second aircraft carrier. More widely, the White Paper was notable in prioritising intelligence – knowledge and anticipation – as a key strategic priority.

The arrival of the financial crisis almost as soon as the 2008 document had been completed gave rise to a further *White Paper on Defence & National Security* in 2013. Perhaps reflecting the handover of power from President Sarkozy to President Hollande, this was less radical and more cautious than its predecessor, trimming previous plans to take account of financial realities.[4] For the navy, a further reduction in the FREMM programme (partly compensated for by commitment to a new light frigate), the loss of the fourth planned *Mistral* and, most significantly, a definitive abandonment of the second carrier were the main blows. The end result remains a well-rounded fleet with one or two significant limitations, discussed in more detail later.

Strategic Priorities: In line with the strategic objectives set out in the recent White Papers, the *Marine Nationale* has five main missions:

- **Deterrence:** This is achieved principally through the strategic oceanic force – *Force Océanique Stratégique* or FOST – reinforced by Rafale aircraft embarked on the carrier *Charles de Gaulle* that can be armed with the ASMP-A missile.
- **Intervention:** The navy is equipped with a range of assets that can be used in an expeditionary role. The most obvious of these are the *Charles de Gaulle* and the amphibious assault ships of the

Nuclear deterrence – principally achieved through the strategic oceanic force of four ballistic missile-armed nuclear submarines – is one of France's *Marine Nationale*'s main roles. The existing boats are being modernised to embark the new M51 ballistic missile – *Le Triomphant* is shown here towards the completion of her refit in 2015. *(Marine Nationale)*

Mistral class. Also of increasing importance in this role as a result of the acquisition of the MdCN variant of the SCALP cruise missile are the nuclear-powered attack submarine and FREMM frigate forces.

- **Knowledge & Anticipation:** This is also achieved through use of a wide range of ships, from specialised hydrographic and intelligence gathering vessels through ongoing presence in the world's ports, coastal waters and oceans.
- **Prevention:** The crisis avoidance/mitigation task is a major focus of the navy's forward-deployed forces in the French overseas departments. Cooperation with regional allies, particularly in Africa and the Middle East, is also an important part of this role. A new overseas base was opened at Mina Fayed, Abu Dhabi, in the United Arab Emirates in 2009.
- **Protection:** This objective involves both the protection of France's maritime trade and ensuring the security of its territorial waters from threats ranging from pollution through to trafficking and terrorism. The role is frequently carried out in conjunction with other agencies, for example the *Gendarmerie Maritime*.

Of these objectives, the strategic nuclear deterrent continues to be given a high degree of priority. This is not only evidenced by the modernisation of the existing strategic submarine fleet to handle the new M51 ballistic missile but also by the relative importance attached to force protection. This includes construction of the 'Barracuda' attack submarines and the upgrade of maritime patrol aircraft. By contrast, general-purpose surface escorts and the 'presence' assets maintained in the overseas territories have generally been subject to under-investment; for example, orders for a new generation of offshore patrol vessel are now long overdue.

Current Force Structure: The *Marine Nationale*'s current structure and composition is set out in Table 4.2.2.1. The following comments are appropriate on major warship types:[5]

Aircraft Carriers & Amphibious Ships: The sole aircraft carrier *Charles de Gaulle* has taken a leading role in French interventionist operations since first commissioning. Notable missions include strikes against government forces in Libya in 2011 and current actions against the so-called 'Islamic State' in Syria and Iraq. Although providing a unique maritime strike capability within Europe, she has suffered from technical problems in the past and requires a high degree of maintenance. The three modern *Mistral* class amphibious assault ships, commissioned between 2006 and 2012, therefore provide a valuable supplementary aviation capability. The second ship, *Tonnerre*, successfully deployed Eurocopter Tiger attack helicopters during the operations against Libya. The *Mistral*s are being supplemented by four 2,200-ton B2M *bâtiments multimissions* of the *D'Entrecasteaux* class that will conduct logistic support and transport missions on overseas stations.

Submarines: The French submarine fleet of four strategic and six attack submarines is broadly comparable to that maintained by the British Royal Navy. The upgrade of the strategic submarines with M51 missiles will be completed around 2018. By then, *Suffren*, first of the six new 'Barracuda' class attack submarines will have been delivered. The others will follow at roughly two-and-a-half/three-year intervals until the *Rubis* class has been replaced on a like-for-like basis by c. 2030.

Surface Escorts & Patrol Ships: The 2013 White Paper mandated a front-line force of just fifteen surface escorts, a drop of three from those envisaged in 2008 – itself a reduction from previous ambitions. The two *Forbin* class air-defence frigates – destroyers in all but name – produced under the Franco-Italian 'Horizon' programme will be joined by eight *Aquitaine* class FREMM multi-mission frigates. Like the 'Horizons', these ships are of destroyer size and produced in collaboration with Italy. Attention will then turn to constructing a lighter, cheaper frigate to replace the existing five *La Fayette* class, which will receive modernisation in the interim to keep them operational for a further ten or more years.

The navy has traditionally built a series of second-line escorts to make up surface fleet numbers. The six *Floréal* class surveillance frigates – completed to commercial standards some twenty years ago and

The French FREMM-type escort *Aquitaine* undertakes sea trials under gloomy North Atlantic skies in November 2011. The navy hoped to acquire seventeen ships of this type but orders have steadily been cut back to just eight units. *(DCNS)*

The *Marine Nationale* has made reasonable strides modernising its front-line fleet of surface escorts but there are considerable numbers of second-line warships that need replacement. Shipbuilder DCNS hopes that its 'Gowind' series patrol vessel *L'Adroit* will be selected for the role and has lent the prototype – seen here in 2013 – to the navy so they can assess its value. *(EU Naval Force Somalia)*

largely used for 'presence' missions in the overseas departments – will be kept in service for some time. However, there is a need to replace the nine remaining A69 type light frigates of the *D'Estienne d'Orves* class, which all date back to the early 1980s and have now been reclassified as patrol vessels. It seems that a total of around fifteen vessels is envisaged to replace them and other legacy patrol vessel classes but it is not clear how they will be funded. DCNS' experimental patrol vessel, *L'Adroit*, could form the basis for a new design and has been operating on loan to the navy for several years. Two light coastal patrol vessels were ordered in 2015 to operate in the shallow waters off French Guyana and this may herald a more piecemeal approach to fleet renewal.

4.2.2.1: FRANCE – *MARINE NATIONALE* COMPOSITION END 2015

MAJOR BASES & STRUCTURE

Toulon: Main fleet operating base. Aircraft carrier, amphibious ships, surface escorts, attack submarines. Secondary base for mine-countermeasures vessels.
Brest: Surface escorts and mine-countermeasures vessels. Strategic submarine base on neighbouring **Ile Longue**.
There is a minor base at **Cherbourg**, minor overseas bases at **Abu Dhabi, Djibouti, French Guiana, La Réunion, Martinique, New Caledonia** & **Tahiti** plus additional prepositioning facilities.

PERSONNEL
c. 31,000 regulars, plus 3,000 civilian staff in direct support.

MAJOR WARSHIPS

Type	Class	In Service	Ordered	ISD	Tonnage	Notes
Aircraft Carriers:		1	(–)			
Aircraft Carrier (CVN)	Charles de Gaulle	1	(–)	2001	42,000 tons	Conventional CATOBAR configuration.
Major Amphibious Warships:		3	(–)			
Amphibious Assault Ship (LHD)	Mistral	3	(–)	2006	21,500 tons	
Major Surface Escorts:		16	(6)			
Destroyer (DDG)	Forbin ('Horizon')	2	(–)	2008	7,100 tons	Air defence role. Franco-Italian project.
Destroyer (DDG)	Aquitaine (FREMM)	2	(6)	2012	6,000 tons	GP/ASW roles. Franco-Italian project but with major variations.
Destroyer (DDG)	Cassard (FAA-70)	2	(–)	1988	5,000 tons	AA variant of Georges Leygues class.
Destroyer (DDG)	Georges Leygues (FASM-70)	5	(–)	1979	4,800 tons	Survivors of a class of 7. ASW/GP roles.
Frigate (FFG)	La Fayette	5	(–)	1996	3,600 tons	The first 'stealth frigate'. GP role – ASW upgrade planned
Second Line Surface Escorts:		6	(–)			
Frigate (FF)	Floréal	6	(–)	1992	3,000 tons	Built to commercial standards.

The remaining 9 light frigates of the *D'Estienne D'Orves* (A-69) class are now classified as offshore patrol vessels.

Type	Class	In Service	Ordered	ISD	Tonnage	Notes
Strategic Submarines:		4	(–)			
Submarine (SSBN)	Le Triomphant	4	(–)	1997	14,400 tons	Being progressively upgraded with the new M51 ballistic missile.
Attack Submarines:		6	(4)			
Submarine (SSN)	Suffren ('Barracuda')	–	(4)	(2017)	5,500 tons	Proposed class of 6 to replace Rubis class. Four formally ordered.
Submarine (SSN)	Rubis	6	(–)	1983	2,700 tons	All rebuilt to Améthyste standard.

Other Ships:				
Type	Offshore Patrol Vessels	Minehunters	Replenishment Ships	
Number	9	14	3	Plus various training vessels, landing craft and auxiliaries.

NAVAL AVIATION
Main naval air station bases are at Hyères (near Toulon), Landivisiau, Lanveoc (both near Brest) and Lann-Bihoué (near Lorient). Following the retirement of the Super Etendard-Mod aircraft, main types are:

- Rafale M strike fighter: Around forty F3 variant planned to be operational by 2020.
- NH90 Caiman NFH helicopter: Around fifteen in service of twenty-seven on order. Replacing around twenty remaining Westland Lynx.
- AS565 Panther helicopter: Around thirty in service, including around ten Dauphin variants used for search and rescue roles.
- Alouette III helicopter: Around twenty used for utility tasks.

There are also three Hawkeye EC-3 early warning aircraft, whilst fifteen of around twenty remaining Breguet Atlantique 2 MPA aircraft are being modernised for long-term service. Air Force and Army transport and attack helicopters can be embarked on the amphibious assault ships as necessary.

Minor Vessels & Auxiliaries: The core of the navy's mine-countermeasures force comprises eleven remaining 'Tripartite' class vessels completed under a joint programme with Belgium and the Netherlands in the 1980s. They are likely to be eventually replaced by the Maritime Mine Counter Measures (MMCM) 'system of systems' being developed jointly with the United Kingdom under a contract awarded in 2015.

There is a more urgent requirement to replace the three remaining fleet replenishment ships of the *Durance* class, which no longer meet current maritime pollution control standards. A new BRAVE (*bâtiment ravitailleur d'escadre*) design has been proposed by DCNS to meet the requirement but orders are unlikely to be forthcoming until the end of the decade.

Future Prospects: The *Marine Nationale* has adapted to the post-Cold War environment well. However, a combination of increasing commitments and proportionately declining resources currently leave it over-stretched. In the words of one commen-

tator, it is effectively 'The Bare Minimum for the Job'.[6] A particular weakness is the failure to make good the longstanding ambition to return to a two-aircraft carrier structure. This significantly reduces fleet capabilities when *Charles de Gaulle* is undergoing refit or maintenance. There has also been a continued lack of investment in surface ships of all types. This has resulted in quite an elderly age-profile amongst many warship classes, with a consequent impact on operating costs and availability. The ongoing commissioning of the *Aquitaine* class will go some way to alleviating this issue. However, there are still large numbers of second-line warships that require replacing.

Although many of the latest reductions in French defence expenditure are being reversed in the light of the increased terrorist threat, these revisions have inevitably tended to focus on strengthening internal security. As such, the naval force structure envisaged in the 2013 White Paper is essentially unchanged. Even the maintenance of this fleet will entail challenges, particularly as costly renewal of the strategic submarine flotilla will start to draw near as the next

decade progresses. International collaboration may well be one tool used to reduce these growing pressures. Renewed collaboration with the United Kingdom on naval systems – supplementing the more-established relationship with Italy – could well bolster growing operational links between the two fleets.

ITALY: THE *MARINA MILITARE*

The current *Marina Militare* ranks second only to France's amongst continental European navies. Whilst lacking the *Marine Nationale*'s nuclear-powered submarines, its STOVL aircraft carrier, sophisticated surface escorts and growing fleet of AIP-equipped submarines give it powerful warfighting capabilities. These are backed by an extensive fleet of constabulary assets. From an industrial perspective, shipbuilder Fincantieri is one of the world's largest shipbuilding groups with a global footprint. Defence electronics giant Finmeccanica is a leading company in its own sector.

Post-Cold War Development: The end of the Cold War saw the *Marina Militare* positioned as an important partner to the US Navy's Sixth Fleet in the Mediterranean, having steadily filled the gap left by the British Royal Navy's withdrawal from the region during the 1970s. It had particular strengths in areas such as anti-submarine warfare and mine-countermeasures but was also developing broader capabilities. A significant recent development had been legal approval for the navy to operate fixed-wing aircraft at sea.[7] This paved the way for the acquisition of Harrier aircraft to operate from the recently-commissioned carrier *Giuseppe Garibaldi* from the mid-1990s onwards.

The Cold War's aftermath did little, if anything, to reduce the demands placed on the navy in spite of the disappearance of the Soviet Navy from the Mediterranean. The end of the bi-polar Cold War structure acted as a strong destabilising influence on the neighbouring Balkans. This brought a near-decade of conflict in the former Yugoslavia. The navy was heavily involved in ensuring the security of Italy's Adriatic borders during this period and *Garibaldi*'s Harriers were used operationally in 1999 during the Kosovo War. More recently, the 2011 military intervention in Libya and the increasingly severe migration and humanitarian crisis in the waters of the Mediterranean have brought new challenges. The navy has also displayed a steady increase

The Italian Navy gained a major boost from the repeal of laws enacted in the Mussolini era that gave the Italian Air Force a monopoly on operating fixed-wing aircraft. This allowed Harrier jets to be purchased for the light carrier *Giuseppe Garibaldi*, seen here on exercises in the Atlantic in July 2004. *(US Navy)*

4.2.2.2: ITALY – *MARINA MILITARE* COMPOSITION END 2015

MAJOR BASES & STRUCTURE

Taranto: Main southern base including submarines, the carrier *Cavour* and front-line surface escorts. The amphibious ships (including *Garibaldi*) & marines are based at nearby **Brindisi.**

La Spezia: Main northern base including front-line surface escorts and mine-countermeasures vessels. Also supports new ships building at Fincantieri's Riva Trigoso yard.

Augusta: Main base for second-line escorts and patrol craft.

PERSONNEL

c. 34,000 including 2,100 naval infantry.

MAJOR WARSHIPS

Type	Class	In Service	Ordered	ISD	Tonnage	Notes
Aircraft Carriers:		2	(–)			
Aircraft Carrier (CV)	*Cavour*	1	(–)	2008	27,100 tons	STOVL configuration.
Aircraft Carrier (CVS)	*Giuseppe Garibaldi*	1	(–)	1985	13,900 tons	STOVL configuration. Now operating as a helicopter carrier (LPH).
Major Amphibious Warships:		3	(1)			
Amphibious Assault Ship (LHD)	New LHD	(–)	(1)	2022	22,000 tons	New unnamed LHD ordered 2015. Possible secondary carrier role.
Landing Platform Dock (LPD)	*San Giorgio*	3	(–)	1987	8,000 tons	To be replaced by new LHD.
Major Surface Escorts:		17	(6)			
Destroyer (DDG)	*Andrea Doria* ('Horizon')	2	(–)	2007	7,100 tons	Air defence role. Franco-Italian project.
Destroyer (DDG)	*Carlo Bergamini* (FREMM)	4	(6)	2013	6,700 tons	GP/ASW variants. Franco-Italian project but with major variations.
Destroyer (DDG)	*De la Penne*	2	(–)	1993	5,400 tons	
Frigate (FFG)	*Maestrale*	7	(–)	1982	3,100 tons	Being replaced by new FREMM class. 1 already decommissioned.
Frigate (FFG)	*Artigliere*	2	(–)	1994	2,500 tons	Initially built for Iraq. Survivors of 4; being replaced by FREMMs.
Second Line Surface Escorts:		6	(7)			
Frigate (FF)	PPA	–	(7)	(2021)	4,500 tons	Officially classified as patrol vessels. Options for 3 more.
Frigate (FF)	*Minerva*	6	(–)	1992	1,300 tons	Original class of 8. Being decommissioned.
Patrol Submarines:		6	(2)			
Submarine (SSK) – AIP	*Todaro* (Type 212A)	2	(2)	2006	1,800 tons	German design, local assembly.
Submarine (SSK)	*Pelosi*	4	(–)	1988	1,700 tons	Being replaced by additional Type 212A boats on order.

Other Ships:

Type	Offshore Patrol Vessels	Minehunters	Replenishment Ships	
Number	10	10	3	Plus various training vessels, landing craft and auxiliaries.

NAVAL AVIATION

Main naval air station bases are located at Grottaglie (near Taranto), Luni (near La Spezia) and Catania (Sicily). Principal aircraft operated include:

- AV-8B+ Harrier II strike fighters: fourteen aircraft. To be replaced by fifteen F-35B Joint Strike Fighters (with a further fifteen being operated by the Italian Air Force).
- AW-101 helicopter: twenty-two helicopters operating in ASW, early warning & transport roles.
- NH90 helicopter: forty-six ASW and ten transport variants ordered to replace Agusta Bell 212s. Around twenty currently in service.

Scan Eagle and Camcopter 100 UAVs have been trialled. Small numbers of Atlantic, soon to be replaced by ATR-72, maritime patrol aircraft are operated by the Italian Air Force.

---

in its appetite for stabilisation and broader 'flag waving' activities away from the Mediterranean, a trend that had first become evident in Cold War years.

Although there was a general recognition that the axis of threat to Italy had shifted southwards following the end of the Warsaw Pact, it is notable that the period was largely devoid of fundamental strategic reflection on Italy's broader defence policy. Indeed, it has been argued that Italy's recent 2015 *White Paper: Our Defence* was the first document of its kind since 1985.[8] Against an often dysfunctional political backdrop – particularly in the years immediately after the Cold War – it is difficult to escape the conclusion that much naval policy has been driven by the ambitions of the admirals and the interests of Italy's powerful shipbuilding sector. As early as 1989, the then editor of *Jane's Fighting Ships*, Richard Sharpe, was to comment, 'New construction submarine, destroyer, corvette and minehunter programmes are all moving forward,

Italy's navy has been increasingly active outside the Mediterranean – this December 2015 view shows the new FREMM-type escort *Carabiniere* operating in the Indian Ocean with the German corvette *Erfurt* as part of the EU's Operation 'Atalanta' anti-piracy mission. The 2015 Defence White Paper may result in a reorientation of efforts closer to home. *(EU Naval Force Somalia)*

The *Marina Militare*'s escort fleet has benefited from a steady programme of renewal in recent years. This picture shows the sophisticated air-defence destroyer *Andrea Doria* in 2014. *(EU Naval Force Somalia)*

but sometimes the impression is given, perhaps erroneously, that the high-powered shipbuilding industry is the main driving force.'[9] Quite often, incremental funding from economic ministries has been used to supplement the anaemic Ministry of Defence budget to allow shipbuilding programmes to move forward. The latest €5.4bn fleet renewal plan, involving an amphibious assault ship, at least seven frigate-like 'patrol ships' and a new replenishment tanker, has been approved on the basis of this type of special funding.

Force Structure: The *Marina Militare*'s structure is set out in Table 4.2.2.2. The new STOVL carrier *Cavour* forms the core of the carrier fleet and has been designed to operate the F-35B variant of the Joint Strike Fighter. Current Italian plans envisage ordering thirty of these planes. The much smaller *Garibaldi* is now largely used as an amphibious helicopter carrier, supplementing the three *San Giorgio* amphibious transport docks. They will be replaced by the new €1.1bn 22,000-ton amphibious assault ship ordered under the fleet renewal plan in 2015. It seems quite likely the new ship will be able to perform a secondary carrier role in similar fashion to Spain's *Juan Carlos I*.

The front-line surface fleet has benefitted from a steady renewal programme, with ten *Carlo Bergamini* (GP) and *Virginio Fasan* (ASW) FREMM-type 'frigates' steadily entering service to supplement the two *Andrea Doria* class air-defence destroyers commissioned in 2007–8. Attention will then turn to replacing the second-line corvettes and offshore patrol vessels, with contracts for seven new PPA (*Pattugliatore Polivalente D'Altura*) multi-role (plus three options) already signed. These 4,500-ton ships will be configured in light and full versions; the latter incorporating the advanced phased array and missile armament of a modern frigate. Underneath the waves, the submarine flotilla is being reduced to a core of four German-designed but Italian-assembled Type 212A AIP-equipped submarines.

The downside of the investment in modernisation is the withdrawal of significant numbers of older ships, with over fifty vessels expected to be withdrawn from service in the next decade. The number of sailors will also fall. This is in line with wider Defence Ministry plans announced in 2012 to reduce personnel and other support costs to increase expenditure on new equipment.

4.2.2.3: SPAIN – *ARMADA ESPAÑOLA* COMPOSITION END 2015

MAJOR BASES & STRUCTURE

Rota (Cadiz):	The Cadiz area contains a cluster of bases, with some facilities at Rota shared with the United States. Includes amphibious ships and frigates.
Ferrol:	Destroyers and replenishment ships, some patrol vessels.
Cartagena:	Submarines, mine-countermeasures vessels, some patrol vessels.
Las Palmas (Canaries):	Patrol vessels.

PERSONNEL

c. 23,000 plus 6,000 marines.

MAJOR WARSHIPS

Type	Class	In Service	Ordered	ISD	Tonnage	Notes
Major Amphibious Warships:		3	(–)			
Amphibious Assault Ship (LPD)	*Juan Carlos I*	1	(–)	2010	27,100 tons	Two sister-ships sold to Australia, 1 to Turkey.
Landing Platform Dock (LPD)	*Galicia*	2	(–)	1998	13,000 tons	Half-sisters to Dutch *Rotterdam*.
Major Surface Escorts:		11	(–)			
Destroyer (DDG)	*Álvaro de Bazán* (F-100)	5	(–)	2002	6,300 tons	Aegis-equipped. Air-defence destroyers with good GP capabilities.
Frigate (FFG)	*Santa Maria* (FFG-7)	6	(–)	1986	4,100 tons	US design built in Spain.
Patrol Submarines:		3	(4)			
Submarine (SSK) – AIP	*Isaac Peral* (S-80)	–	(4)	(2018)	2,400 tons	Delayed due to design problems.
Submarine (SSK)	*Galerna* (*Agosta*)	3	–	1983	1,800 tons	Survivors of a class of 4. To be replaced by S-80 design.

Other Ships:

Type	Offshore Patrol Vessels	Minehunters	Replenishment Ships	
Number	15	6	2	Plus various minor vessels & auxiliaries.

NAVAL AVIATION

There is a naval air station at Rota near Cadiz. Principal aircraft operated include:

- AV-8B+ Harrier II strike fighters: twelve aircraft.
- SH-60 Seahawk sea control helicopters: c. twelve aircraft.
- SH-3 Sea King helicopters: c. ten aircraft in transport and airborne early warning roles.

The Spanish Air Force operates c .five P-3 Orion and c. ten CN-235 maritime patrol aircraft.

Strategic Priorities & Future Prospects: Whilst the publication of the new defence White Paper has yet to translate into revised plans at individual service level, it does provide a good indication of the likely direction of travel. The new document sets a firm objective of giving Italy's military a central role in the Mediterranean (the 'Euro Mediterranean' region), with the ultimate aim of replicating the stability already achieved to the north (the 'Euro Atlantic' region). Operations beyond these areas will typically be carried out in partnership with other allies. This suggests some potential for a scaling back of the navy's enthusiasm for extra-regional expeditionary operations.

From the perspective of equipment and planned procurement, the navy looks well-placed to meet the maritime requirements of this strategy, albeit its recent focus on procuring 'higher-end' capabilities may need to be tempered by greater focus on its constabulary assets going forward. Attention is also needed to low key but vital areas such as infrastructure and logistics, which have suffered both from under-investment and an unduly parochial approach from the separate services.

SPAIN: THE *ARMADA ESPAÑOLA*

Spain's *Armada Española* has suffered badly as a result of the Eurozone crisis. This saw the early retirement of its sole aircraft carrier and the cancellation or postponement of key construction plans.

Technical problems impacting its submarine renewal programme have dealt it another significant blow. However, the navy maintains a good balance of aviation-capable amphibious assets, modern air-defence escorts and sophisticated long-range patrol vessels from the realisation of previous projects. Plans for new construction are supported by relevant indigenous capabilities, notably Navantia's strong presence in naval shipbuilding and the defence electronics activities of Indra Sistemas.

Post-Cold War Development: The Spanish Navy ended the Cold War on something of a high. The end of the Franco era in 1975 and the subsequent decision in 1982 to join NATO had allowed the navy to benefit from much closer links with its European counterparts. In addition, the realisation of initial fleet renewal plans had seen the delivery of the STOVL carrier *Principe de Asturias*, FFG-7 type frigates and *Agosta* class submarines to form the core of a modern fleet. The ambitious fifteen-year *Plan de Alta Mar* (PAM) announced in 1990 aimed to build on this success through modernisation of the amphibious fleet and expansion of frigate, mine-countermeasures and submarine forces.

As it happened, a dramatic deterioration in Spain's economic climate over the following years significantly impacted procurement plans. It was not until the mid-1990s that construction activity picked up and – like so many naval plans – PAM was never realised in its entirety. However, the next decade saw a virtual transformation of the navy's capabilities, as marked by deliveries of 'state of the art' vessels such as the *Galicia* class amphibious transport docks and F-100 *Álvaro de Bazán* class air-defence ships. The process of modernisation also saw the navy's capabilities grow beyond those needed to defend the territorial integrity of the mainland and the island dependencies in the Atlantic and Mediterranean to a more expeditionary focus. This shift became more marked in the *Armada XXI* fleet recapitalisation plan early in the new millennium,

which was supported by a period of strong economic growth and rising defence spending. Key elements included a LHD-type strategic projection ship and long-range cruise missiles.[10] The latter ambition has subsequently been abandoned, but the strategic projection ship was commissioned in 2010 as *Juan Carlos I*.

The progress achieved from the mid-1990s onwards rapidly ground to a halt with the advent of the serial economic crises that impacted Spain from 2008. To an extent, the navy was fortunate that much new construction had either been delivered or was already committed, ensuring the maintenance of a relatively modern fleet. However, there has been a clear-out of older ships, notably the former flagship *Principe de Asturias*. Fortunately, *Juan Carlos I* was designed to serve in a secondary support carrier role similar to the US Navy's larger amphibious assault ships. This has allowed the navy to maintain a modest fixed-wing aviation capability. With Spain's economic position now stabilising, it seems further reductions in fleet size and capability are unlikely.

Force Structure: Current fleet structure is set out in Table 4.2.2.3. The LHD-type strategic projection ship *Juan Carlos I* provides a powerful amphibious capability and the design has been successfully

exported to Australia and Turkey. She is supplemented by the two *Galicia* class amphibious transport docks, which were designed in conjunction with the Netherlands. The three ships work closely with the Spanish Marine Corps and have a combined lift capacity of over 2,000 troops (roughly the size of the Spanish Marine brigade and supporting elements). There are two replenishment vessels to support deployments at extended distance.

The core of the surface fleet is comprised of the five F-100 destroyers.[11] Equipped with the US Navy's Aegis combat system, they have a primary air-defence role but are equipped to counter a range of threats. The six older FFF-7 type *Santa Maria* class frigates, which started to commission in 1986, are now showing their age. They will be replaced by the long-awaited F-110 design from the early 2020s onwards.

The extended nature of Spain's territorial waters has typically required a large force of constabulary patrol vessels. The downgraded *Descubierta* class corvettes and *Serviola* class offshore patrol vessels that were the most significant units used in this role are now being joined by the new 2,800-ton *Meteoro* BAM (*Buque de Acción Marítíma*) type. This was to be an extended class used in hydrographical and diving support, in addition to their primary patrol configurations. However, the financial crisis has significantly impacted construction plans and only six have been ordered to date.

The small submarine flotilla is currently overstretched, having been reduced to just three of the *Agosta* class boats delivered in the 1980s. The new S-80 *Isaac Peral* class have been badly delayed by a design flaw that has left them seriously overweight and problems have also been reported with the design of their new AIP-propulsion plant. It will not now be until 2018 that the first of four will be delivered.

Strategic Priorities & Future Prospects: The overall strategic direction of the *Armada Española* during the post-Cold War era has been characterised by a desire to supplement its historical territorial defence role with greater capacity in the area of power projection. This ambition has inevitably been tempered by the financial realities of Spain's economic difficulties. However, the successful delivery of much of the ambitious acquisition programmes of the 1990s and 2000s have left the fleet relatively well-equipped to perform both func-

The Spanish Navy's five F-100 air-defence escorts seen operating together during a photographic exercise off the Spanish Atlantic coast in July 2014. The navy benefited from an increasingly ambitious procurement programme before the economic crises of the late 2000s struck. (*Spanish Navy*)

tions. One potential change may be a greater emphasis on maritime security and stabilisation operations considering the deteriorating environment in Africa and the Middle East.[12] The maintained Spanish presence on the North African coast through its possession of the enclaves of Ceuta and Melilla is relevant in this regard.

From a procurement perspective, the immediate priorities would appear to be to resolve the problems with the S-80 programme – so as to maintain a submarine capability – and obtain approval for the delayed orders of the next-generation F-110 surface combatant. The constabulary role probably requires more than the six BAM class vessels authorised to date. The two surface programmes were both key priorities in *Armada 2025*, the latest vision for the future fleet first publicised towards the end of 2011. In the longer term, the renewal of the Harrier fleet will come increasingly to the fore, whist there are also ongoing ambitions to develop land-attack and ballistic missile defence capabilities.

OTHER CONTINENTAL EUROPEAN FLEETS

Some commentary is also warranted on the development and current status of the many other European fleets that remain significant in a regional context.

Scandinavia & the Baltic: The end of the Cold War essentially negated the value of the majority of warships maintained by the Scandinavian fleets. Focused on territorial defence against Warsaw Pact incursions, these navies' warfighting capabilities were built around significant forces of coastal submarines and fast attack craft that had minimal alternative utility once the Soviet threat dissipated. For example, compared with thirty or more submarines in service operated by Denmark, Norway and Sweden in 1990, only eleven are in service today. There are only a handful of fast attack craft in the region as of 2015 compared to around eighty when the Cold War ended.

The post-Cold War period therefore saw the Scandinavian navies refocus from previous structures towards much smaller numbers of ships that remained useful in a territorial defence context but which could be used in a wider range of missions.

The *Armada Española*'s strategic direction since the end of the Cold War has seen a greater emphasis on power projection in addition to its traditional territorial defence role. This trajectory has had to be tempered because of the Eurozone crisis but it has brought economic benefits; for example the sale of 'high-end' warships to Australia. This picture shows the replenishment ship *Cantabria* during a period spent working with the RAN in 2013. *(RAN)*

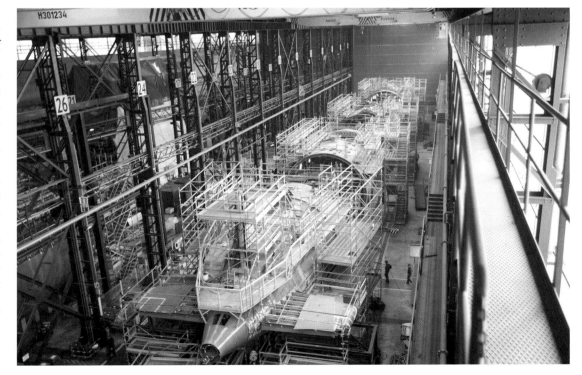

Resolving design problems with the new S80 class AIP-equipped submarines is a major priority for the Spanish Navy. This picture shows work underway on the class at Navantia's facility at Cartagena in 2012. *(Navantia)*

The German Navy's F124 *Sachsen* class air-defence frigates *Hamburg* and *Hessen* replenishing from the combat support ship *Berlin* during a Mediterranean deployment. Today's German Navy is focused heavily on international stabilisation missions. *(German Navy)*

Norway's healthy natural resources-driven economy and robust attitude to defence has provided it with what is probably the region's strongest fleet. A surface flotilla built around the five Aegis-equipped *Fridtjof Nansen* class frigates and six *Skjold* class air-cushion catamaran fast attack craft can be deployed defensively or in support of coalition expeditionary/stabilisation operations. Six coastal submarines have also been retained, providing the most numerous underwater force in the region. Neighbouring **Sweden** has suffered more from the impact of the 'peace' dividend but has slowly brought into service the five *Visby* class stealth corvettes, which have a degree of mission modularity that also makes them useful in defensive and expeditionary roles. Its five operational submarines are all equipped with the indigenous Stirling AIP system and two new boats have been ordered. Meanwhile, **Denmark** has probably moved furthest away from Cold War structures, disbanding its submarine force and decommissioning its Stanflex corvettes. Instead, investment has been focused on three *Iver Huitfeldt* class air-defence ships and the

two *Absalon* hybrid frigate/logistics ships that have already deployed internationally in support of NATO stabilisation activities. The extent to which Denmark remains happy with its choices given the re-emergence of a more assertive Russia is an interesting question.

Elsewhere in the Baltic, structural change has been less pronounced. **Finland's** naval development has largely been marked by recapitalisation of existing capabilities, whilst the **Baltic Republics** have developed modest mine-countermeasures forces in line with the region's maritime topography. **Poland** has replaced most of its important major Warsaw Pact era equipment with second-hand NATO vessels but has only recently embarked on full scale fleet renewal.

Germany: West Germany's Cold War *Deutsche Marine* was split between forward coastal defence in the Baltic and more blue water-orientated operations in protection of trade and convoy routes in the North Sea and Atlantic. The former role demanded large numbers of coastal submarines and fast attack

craft; the latter was more reliant on surface escorts and maritime patrol assets. To an extent, both roles became outdated with the Soviet Union's demise, although reductions in Baltic forces were far more severe. An added complication faced in the immediate aftermath of the Cold War was the need to assimilate the former East German *Volksmarine,* which was officially disbanded on 3 October 1990. In practice, very few of its vessels survived long in *Deutsche Marine* service. However, large numbers were sold to Indonesia in a major fleet modernisation exercise.

In common with many other European fleets, today's German Navy is now much more closely focused on international peacekeeping operations. It has gained considerable experience through its involvement in the maritime component of the UN's UNIFIL mission off Lebanon and has also been heavily involved in EU anti-piracy activities in the Indian Ocean. Upon completion of the new four F-125 'stabilisation frigates' at the end of the decade, the core of the surface fleet will comprise eleven front-line surface escorts and five smaller K-130 corvettes. All these ships are suitable for international deployment and can be sustained by the three large and modern replenishment ships of the *Berlin* class. Six AIP-equipped Type 212A submarines and a substantial mine-countermeasures force will also remain a long-term part of the fleet but the few remaining fast attack craft will soon be withdrawn. There are already signs that Germany is starting to doubt the wisdom of such a significant shift in its structure to stabilisation activities; the new MKS-180 escorts are likely to revert to a much greater warfighting orientation.

The Netherlands: The Royal Netherlands Navy was strongly orientated to oceanic anti-submarine and coastal mine-countermeasures activities during the Cold War. Both these roles had limited value subsequently. The peace dividend extracted from the Netherlands Armed Forces was also heavier than for many of its neighbours. The combined result has been a significant reduction in overall size of a force that included fifteen frigates and over twenty minehunters in 1990.

The restructured fleet of 2015 includes just four 'LCF' type air-defence ships and two 'M' class frigates, supplemented by four of the new *Holland* class oceanic patrol vessels. The latter provide a good indication of the navy's direction of travel, being specifically designed for the conduct of low-intensity stabilisation missions at distance from their home base. The new expeditionary focus is also evidenced by the arrival of two amphibious transport docks and a brand new joint support ship, the latter capable of both amphibious operations and logistical sustainment. Four submarines and a much reduced force of six minehunters comprise the balance of the force.

Portugal: Portugal ended the Cold War with a navy that was largely comprised of ships designed for patrolling the colonial empire it abandoned in the mid-1970s. Subsequent efforts at modernising the fleet have seen the renewal of the front-line surface fleet around a flotilla of three MEKO 200P *Vasco da Gama* class frigates and two former Dutch 'M' class frigates. Two modern Type 214 AIP-equipped submarines built in Germany have replaced the three old *Daphne* class boats. Otherwise, the Eurozone crisis has slowed replacement of constabulary assets. Consequently, a number of colonial-era designs, including four corvettes, remain in service. The resumption of an indigenous offshore patrol vessel programme and the acquisition of former Stanflex vessels from Denmark should allow further progress in the years ahead.

The Aegean & Black Seas: The naval – and wider political – situation in the Eastern Mediterranean has typically been more complicated than elsewhere in Europe. Longstanding troubled relationships between Turkey and European neighbours such as Greece and Bulgaria continued to have as much influence as the stand-off with the Soviet Union throughout much of the Cold War. Events in the Middle East were also close enough to exert an influence at times. A complex network of historical connections goes someway to explaining some unusual developments, possibly including the Hellenic Navy's purchase of Soviet-designed Project 1232.2 'Zubr' class hovercraft. Given this backdrop, it is not surprising that the naval programmes of NATO allies Greece and Turkey have often been as much about maintaining the balance between each other than any potential external threat.

For much of the post-Cold War period, experts considered **Greece**'s navy to have, at least, a qualitative edge over that of its eastern neighbour. The situation today is much less clear-cut after the Greek economic implosion. The arrival of German-designed Type 214 AIP-equipped submarines is

The Royal Netherlands Navy has shrunk considerably since the end of the Cold War but its amphibious forces have benefitted from considerable investment, including two dock landing ships and a hybrid joint support ship. Here, the LPD *Rotterdam* is pictured departing Portsmouth UK in November 2015. *(Conrad Waters)*

Greece's Hellenic Navy is in the unusual position of being a NATO fleet operating Russian-built 'Zubr' hovercraft of Soviet design; *Kerkyra* is pictured here. This is undoubtedly a reflection of the complex network of historical alliances and animosities that exist in the Eastern Mediterranean. *(NATO)*

providing a real boost to an aged underwater fleet. However, significant problems exist elsewhere. For example, whilst the Hellenic Navy's surface fleet is quite large, much of it is ageing badly and only part has been modernised. Financial pressures also resulted in the suspension of fast attack craft production. Efforts to restart the programme have faced technical difficulties.

Meanwhile, **Turkey's** fleet is going from strength to strength. Already numerically superior to that of Greece, it is benefitting from a focus on indigenisation. This has seen the navy progress from the local assembly of foreign designs to local design-and-build, most notably of the new 'Milgem' *Heybeliada* class corvettes. Four of these have already been ordered and an improved version is planned. Turkey is also increasingly setting its sights on expeditionary operations beyond the immediate region. The planned construction of a *Juan Carlos I* type amphibious assault ship is evidence of its ambition in this regard. Further analysis of the Turkish Navy is contained in the Middle East section.

Turkey, of course, needs to keep one eye to the Black Sea, where Russia's local fleet is due for significant reinforcement. The precepts of the 1936 Montreux Convention on the Bosphorus and Dardanelles Straits significantly limit the presence of warships from non-Black Sea nations in this sea.

Turkey has made substantial strides in building its navy, supported by a longstanding policy of improving indigenous capabilities. This image shows *Heybeliada*, the lead ship in the 'Milgem' national corvette programme, in April 2015. *(Devrim Yaylali)*

This leaves Bulgaria, Romania and the Ukraine as the only other countries with a meaningful naval presence in the region. Of these, **Bulgaria** and **Romania** have achieved limited modernisation of their fleets with second hand NATO warships. **Ukraine's** Navy, however, was all but eliminated by Russia's 2014 annexation of the Crimea, where most of the fleet was previously based.

Notes

1. France's somewhat patchy relationship with NATO originated with President Charles de Gaulle's dissatisfaction with Anglo-American domination of the organisation, culminating in the withdrawal of France from NATO's integrated military command in 1966 and a requirement that all foreign NATO forces leave French soil.

2. The French Navy's development during the Cold War era is reviewed by John Jordan in Robert Gardiner (ed.), *Conway's All the World's Fighting Ships 1947-1982 Part I: The Western Powers* (London: Conway Maritime Press, 1983), pp.20–2. There was investment in anti-submarine assets but this was heavily influenced by their role in ensuring the security of the strategic submarines.

3. A good overview of the changes mandated by the 2008 White Paper is contained in Claudia Major's 'The French White Paper on Defense and National Security', *CSS Analyses on Security Policy – Vol 3, No.46* (Zurich: CSS, 2008) at: http://www.css.ethz.ch/publications/pdfs/CSS-Analyses-46.pdf. See also: https://web.archive.org/web/20130914080932/http://www.ambafrance-ca.org/IMG/

pdf/Livre_blanc_Press_kit_english_version.pdf for an English language press kit of the White Paper.

4. For full details see *White Paper on Defence & National Security 2013* (Paris: French Republic, 2013) at: http://www.livreblancdefenseetsecurite.gouv.fr/pdf/the_white_paper_defence_2013.pdf

5. Please refer to Chapter 8 for more details on naval aviation capabilities.

6. See Jean Moulin, 'The *Marine Nationale*: The Bare Minimum for the Job', *Seaforth World Naval Review 2015* (Barnsley: Seaforth Publishing, 2014), pp.76–87.

7. The Italian Air Force had previously been given control over all fixed-wing aviation under laws dating from the Mussolini era.

8. This assertion is made by Alessandro Marrone in Vincenzo Camporini et al's *The White Paper: A Strategy for Italy's Defence Policy* (Rome: IAI, 2015). The White Paper

issued in 2002, as well as a *Staff Strategic Concept* issued in 2005, can be regarded as more in the way of interim updates. An English language translation of the 2015 White Paper can currently be found at: http://www.difesa.it/Primo_Piano/Documents/2015/07_Luglio/White%20book.pdf

9. See Richard Sharpe (ed.), *Jane's Fighting Ships 1989-90* (London: Jane's Defence Group, 1989), p.89.

10. This would almost certainly have been the United States' Tomahawk.

11. The ships are classified as frigates by the Spanish Navy but are of destroyer size and capability; the design was selected by Australia for its air-warfare destroyer programme.

12. The Spanish Navy's future direction post the economic crises was discussed in more detail by Mariano Rajoy in, 'Keeping the Ship Afloat: *Armada Española* sets out its Strategy for Stability', *Jane's Navy International – May 2012* (Coulsdon: IHS Jane's, 2012).

4.2.3   **James Bosbotinis**

THE RUSSIAN NAVY

The Russian Navy, despite a most turbulent recent past, remains one of the world's pre-eminent navies. However, although Russia has the ambition of achieving 'Great Maritime Power' status, its naval future is uncertain. The Russian Navy faces multiple challenges, including its inherited Soviet legacy, contrasting perspectives on the role of the navy within wider Russian military strategy, economic constraints and the trajectory of Russian national policy. Of these, economic constraints pose perhaps the greatest threat to Russia's naval ambitions, in particular to plans for recapitalising the navy's major surface combatant force and replacing its sole aircraft carrier, the *Admiral Kuznetsov*. In this respect, the Soviet legacy of a core of modern ships has been positive.[1]

Much of the Soviet legacy has been, and in several cases, continues to be, a major source of difficulty for the Russian Navy. This includes deficiencies in infrastructure, key elements in the naval (and wider military) industrial base lying outside of Russia (a point particularly relevant to the ongoing crisis with Ukraine), and arguably, the scale of naval ambition. In this regard, the role of the navy in wider Russian military strategy remains an area of continual debate. This is illustrated with reference to, for example, the discussion concerning the abortive acquisition of *Mistral* class amphibious assault ships from France and the continual deferral of a formal programme to build new aircraft carriers. It is also highlighted in the long-term vision for the Russian Navy promulgated by the naval leadership, and ostensibly supported by the Kremlin: that is, a powerful, world-class navy commensurate with the status of a great maritime power.

THE SOVIET LEGACY

The legacy of the Soviet Union, and its subsequent collapse, has had a profound impact on the Russian Navy. The navy's order of battle, in particular in terms of its major units, is dominated by vessels

developed and built (or which commenced building) during the Soviet period; whilst its operational and strategic thinking remains primarily concerned with countering the United States and Western powers in large-scale warfare (as illustrated in numerous exercises). Moreover, the navy had to endure the collapse of and transition from one state to another, and with it, the loss to newly-independent states of critical infrastructure, including bases, training facilities, shipyards and repair facilities, and production centres. In the mid-1990s, for example, the Russian Navy claimed to possess only thirty-four per cent of the ship repair capacity it required.[2] This compounded an already limited naval support base caused by underinvestment in the Soviet period, and combined with the economic situation confronting Russia in the 1990s, resulted

in the Russian Navy being unable to maintain and support major surface combatants, including the *Kiev* class aircraft carriers, *Kirov* class cruisers and *Sovremenny* class destroyers.[3] It had been Soviet practice to send aircraft carriers and cruisers from the Northern and Pacific Fleets back to the shipyard of construction (such as Nikolayev) for refits rather than establish the necessary capability in the fleet areas; this meant Russia could not support the ships properly, nor could it afford to send them to Ukraine for refit.[4]

The loss particularly of the Mykolaiv (formerly Nikolayev) shipyard in Ukraine, then the only shipyard in the former Soviet Union capable of building aircraft carriers, also contributed to the curtailing of the Soviet carrier programme. At the time of the Soviet collapse, the *Varyag* (sister-ship of the *Admiral Kuznetsov*) was eighty per cent complete and construction of the *Ulyanovsk*, an 85,000-ton nuclear-powered catapult-assisted take-off but arrested recovery-configured carrier, was underway. The 1990s were thus a bleak period for Russia's aircraft carrier ambitions: by 1996 all four of the *Kiev* class ships had been decommissioned, the ex-*Varyag* lay incomplete pending disposal or sale at Mykolaiv, and the *Ulyanovsk* had been scrapped. Only the *Admiral Kuznetsov* remained in service,

The Russian Project 1155 *Udaloy* class destroyer *Admiral Panteleyev* sailing with US Navy ships during the 2012 RIMPAC exercises, a photographic opportunity unlikely to be repeated whilst the crisis in Ukraine persists. Although the Russian Navy faces many challenges, the Soviet legacy of a core of modern ships has been positive. *(US Navy)*

The *Mistral* class amphibious assault ships *Vladivostok* and *Sevastopol* seen laid up at Saint-Nazaire in France in March 2015. Part of a plan to renew Russia's amphibious fleet, their acquisition was one of a number of naval programmes impacted by western sanctions following events in the Crimea and Ukraine. The ships have now been sold to Egypt. *(Bruno Huriet)*

The impact of Western sanctions on Russian industry has badly slowed acquisition of new surface ships. As a result, Soviet-era classes such as the Project 1164 *Slava* class – originally laid down in the 1970s – will have to soldier on for a while yet. *(US Navy)*

albeit in a rather less-than-optimal condition.[5]

Arguably, the most significant and enduring legacy of the Soviet Union relates to the relationship between Russia and Ukraine. In naval terms, the Russian Black Sea Fleet's principal bases – current and historical – are situated in Ukraine, namely the Crimea. Additionally, Ukrainian companies, prior to the crisis with Russia in 2014, were key suppliers to the Russian defence industry. For example, Zorya-Mashproyekt, located in Mykolaiv, manufactured the Russian Navy's gas turbines used for ship propulsion. The termination of Ukrainian defence co-operation with Russia following the latter's annexation of Crimea and destabilisation activities focused on eastern Ukraine, has therefore had a significant impact on Russian defence programmes. This includes delays to the construction of the new Project 2235.0 *Admiral Gorshkov* class frigates and the entry into Russian service of only three, rather than the originally planned six, Project 1135.6M *Admiral Grigorovich* class frigates.[6] Further construction of Project 2038.5 *Gremyashchy* class corvettes, an upgraded derivative of the Project 2038.0 *Steregushchy* class, has also had to be abandoned due to the impact of European Union sanctions on the supply of German-manufactured diesel engines.

With regard to the *Admiral Gorshkov* class, Russia has been able to source a domestic substitute (NPO Saturn, a major Russian aircraft engine producer,

collaborated extensively with Zorya-Mashproyekt before the imposition of sanctions). Construction of the third and fourth ships may, however, be delayed. As will be discussed, the *Admiral Gorshkov* class is central to the Russian Navy's long-term modernisation plans. The success – or not – of this import substitution drive will be crucial both to Russian naval rearmament plans and Moscow's long-term defence policy objectives.

A further aspect of the Soviet legacy pertinent to Russia's long-term naval ambitions, and its desire for 'Great Maritime Power' status, is the continuing influence of Admiral Sergei Gorshkov (1910–88), Commander-in-Chief of the Soviet Navy from 1956 to 1985, within the Russian naval establishment. This was particularly highlighted in a 2010 conference marking the centenary of Admiral Gorshkov's birth, at which Admiral Vladimir Vysotsky, then Commander-in-Chief of the Russian Navy, stated: 'Russia's status as successor to the great Soviet Union means that it must have a powerful and balanced ocean navy to defend its interests in any part of the world ocean where such interests exist, and they exist everywhere.' Moreover, Admiral Vysotsky also stated that 'we largely owe it to Admiral Gorshkov that we are now making very considerable efforts to maintain strategic nuclear parity in Russia's interests, at the same time as changing the approaches that were dominant in the 1990s'.[7] The 'approaches that were dominant in the 1990s' are highlighted by comments made by Admiral Valentin Selivanov, then First Deputy Commander-in-Chief and Chief of the Main Staff of the Russian Navy, in 1994: 'Russia needs a relatively small navy, but one which is capable – in co-operation with the other armed services – of supporting her foreign policy, protecting her economic interests and guaranteeing national security.'[8]

The view expressed by Admiral Selivanov did not, however, gain widespread acceptance. The political instability of the 1990s and with it the lack of direction given to the armed forces, resulted in the navy developing its own interpretation of Imperial, Soviet and contemporary naval developments to justify a blue-water fleet. International developments, in particular the accession of former Warsaw Pact states in Eastern Europe to membership of NATO and the latter's intervention in the former Yugoslavia, served to fuel anti-Western sentiment and a Cold War mentality within the Russian military establishment. For the navy, this included a self-defined role of defending Russia from sea-launched cruise missile attacks by the US Navy, thus requiring a fleet sufficiently strong to fulfil that task. The domestic political environment within Russia also underwent a major shift in 1999 with the appointment of Vladimir Putin as prime minister and, subsequently, acting president; he was formally elected as president on 26 March 2000. Significantly, Putin's ascendancy to the presidency meant that the Russian Navy had support in the Kremlin: at a meeting of the Russian Security Council in November 1999 which Putin chaired, he reportedly stated that Russia only became a great power when it became a great maritime power. Despite the *Kursk* disaster in August 2000, the prospects for the Russian Navy improved markedly through the 2000s as Putin sought to restore Russia's position as a great power and reform the armed forces. Notably, this would include an expanded role for the navy in Russian military strategy.[9]

THE RUSSIAN NAVY TODAY

The Russian Navy is currently one of only a handful of navies that can be classed as possessing a full-spectrum capability (alongside those of the United States, France, China and the United Kingdom). Although the Russian Navy's ability to project power globally is limited, especially in comparison to the US Navy, it nonetheless does possess the means to deploy a potent force to areas of interest, especially with respect to anti-surface warfare and air-defence capabilities. Moreover, the Russian Navy has, over the past decade, conducted regular major exercises, including some with Russian Air Force participation (particularly long-range aviation), simulating operations based on high-intensity warfighting scenarios. A number of exercises have also included either the simulated use of nuclear weapons or operations in an environment after an adversary's use of nuclear weapons.

The Russian Navy is also significantly increasing its operational tempo: Admiral Viktor Chirkov, the Navy's Commander-in-Chief, stated at the 'Army 2015' Forum held in Moscow in June 2015, that: 'During the period from January 2014 to March 2015, the time spent underway by submarines and surface ships increased by thirty per cent, the number of manoeuvres by twenty per cent, and the number of combat duty missions by strategic submarines increased by almost fifty per cent, compared to 2013.'[10] Most dramatically, on 7

The Ukrainian Project 641 'Foxtrot' class submarine *Zaporizhzhya* seen berthed alongside the Russian Project 877V 'Kilo' class boat *Alrosa* at a naval base in the Crimea on 22 March 2014, the day the Ukrainian submarine was seized as part of Russia's Crimea annexation. Although Russia achieved its territorial objectives, the termination of supplies of equipment from Ukrainian manufacturers has badly impacted Russian naval programmes. *(Anton Blinov)*

October 2015, the Russian Navy demonstrated for the first time its ability to conduct long-range cruise missile strikes with the launch of twenty-six 'Kalibr' (SS-N-30) land-attack cruise missiles from a light frigate and three corvettes in the Caspian Sea against 'terrorist' targets in Syria.

The Russian Navy's burgeoning operational tempo and the introduction of a nascent long-range strike capability is testament to the efforts made over the preceding decade to reverse the decline of Russian maritime power. It is also reflective of Russia's grand strategic ambitions: the restoration of Russia as a great power and a distinct pole in a multi-polar international system. This ambition has translated into grandiose plans for reequipping the armed forces; in naval terms, this includes new nuclear-powered aircraft carriers and 'destroyers', amphibious assault ships, and a conventional strategic deterrent capability. That is, the acquisition of a navy equipped to project power to a much greater extent than previously possible. It warrants mention that the extent of Russia's naval ambitions

have been tempered somewhat since a peak in 2008–10. Then the naval leadership spoke of plans for constructing up to six nuclear-powered 75,000-ton aircraft carriers, acquiring amphibious assault ships (the abortive *Mistral* purchase) and other amphibious vessels, modernising the four ex-*Kirov* class cruisers and even mooted the construction of new nuclear-powered guided-missile cruisers.[11] However, the scaling back and/or delay to naval rearmament (for example, a new aircraft carrier is not now due to be built until the latter half of the 2020s rather than be in service by 2020) should not be interpreted as a decline in Russia's ambitions: rather it is, perhaps, reflective of an enduring debate on the proper role of the navy in Russian military strategy and national policy.

As a continental power, Russia has traditionally pursued a land power-centric approach to military strategy. However, during the first decade of the twenty-first century, there was a marked shift in Russian thinking. This was promulgated in a report entitled *The Priority Tasks of the Development of the*

Armed Forces of the Russian Federation, and distributed at a conference held in Moscow in October 2003 under the auspices of President Putin and the Russian Defence Ministry. This brought together key figures from the military-security establishment. In this regard, it is notable that Sergei Ivanov, then Defence Minister, and currently Chief of Staff of the Presidential Executive Office, is a close confidant of President Putin, and member of the Kremlin's inner circle. *The Priority Tasks* placed much greater emphasis on aerospace and maritime forces conducting long-range precision strike operations, targeting an adversary's critical infrastructure and, particularly significantly, information warfare (the report did recognise the key role of the ground forces in ultimately securing victory). This has been carried through into Russia's ongoing military reform and rearmament effort, and for the navy (and air force), has resulted in major investment in the development and acquisition of advanced long-range cruise missiles as a core component of an enhanced power projection capability. The development of a conventional long-range strike capability is a central element of the Russian Navy's long-term modernisation plans and is, in part, intended to address its current limited ability to conduct conventional land-attack operations.

The principal role of the Russian Navy, after providing the naval component of Russia's strategic nuclear deterrent, has and continues to be countering opposing naval forces. These are, primarily, the navies of the United States and its NATO allies. In this context, the current edition of Russia's *Maritime Doctrine*, promulgated in 2015, refers to countering NATO expansion. The ships and submarines forming the Russian Navy's current order of battle are, thus, primarily equipped for sea control (anti-submarine, anti-air and anti-surface warfare) operations, or to use Russian terminology, securing a 'favourable operational regime'. The focus on anti-ship (in particular, against US Navy aircraft carriers) operations is reflected in the potent anti-ship cruise missile armaments of three of the four main classes of principal surface combatant in Russian service. More specifically:

4.2.3.1: RUSSIAN NAVY COMPOSITION END 2015

MAJOR BASES & STRUCTURE

Structurally, the Russian Navy is organised into four fleets and the Caspian Sea Flotilla:

Baltic Fleet: HQ at Kaliningrad. Includes major escorts of the *Sovremenny* and *Neustrashimy* types plus *Steregushchy* class corvettes. At least three 'Kilo' & 'Lada' class submarines.

Black Sea Fleet: HQ at Sevastopol. Includes a small flotilla of surface combatants headed by a *Slava* CG. A single Project 877 'Kilo' class submarine is being joined by new Project 636 boats.

Northern Fleet: HQ at Severomorsk. Includes 'Delta IV' SSBNs (being joined by 'Boreis'); 'Akula' & 'Kilo' submarines, the carrier *Kuznetsov* & a surface flotilla with all current CG & DDG types.

Pacific Fleet: HQ at Vladivostok. Includes 'Delta III' SSBNs (being joined by 2 'Boreis'); 'Oscar II', 'Akula' & 'Kilo' submarines; & a surface flotilla focused on a *Slava* CG & *Udaloy* DDGs.

Caspian Flotilla: HQ at Astrakhan. Principal equipment includes 'Gepard' class frigates and 'Buyan/Buyan-M' class corvettes.

Only the Northern and Pacific Fleets operate nuclear submarines, whilst the former is the home of the navy's sole carrier. The Northern Fleet has its main bases clustered around Severomorsk, Murmansk and the adjacent Barents Sea, with shipbuilding facilities further east at Severodvinsk on the White Sea. In addition to its headquarters at Vladivostok, the Pacific Fleet has a cluster of bases on the Kamchatka peninsula. The Baltic Fleet has bases at Baltiysk, Kronshtadt & St. Petersburg. The Black Sea Fleet has a base at Novorossiysk in addition to its facilities in the Crimea.

MAJOR WARSHIPS

Type	Class	In Service	Ordered	ISD	Tonnage	Notes
Aircraft Carriers:		1	(–)			New design to enter service from 2030.
Aircraft Carrier (CV)	Project 1143.5/6 *Kuznetsov*	1	(–)	1991	60,000 tons	
Major Surface Escorts:		c.23 (4)	(10)			
Battlecruiser (BCGN)	Project 1144.2 *Kirov*	1(1)	(–)	1980	25,000 tons	Second ship under modernisation after long-term layup.
Cruiser (CG)	Project 1164 *Slava*	3	(–)	1982	12,500 tons	Fourth ship laid-up incomplete in the Ukraine.
Destroyer (DDG)	Project 1155 *Udaloy*	9	(–)	1980	8,500 tons	Survivors of a class of 12 plus 1 similar Project 1155.1 'Udaloy II'.
Destroyer (DDG)	Project 956/A *Sovremenny*	5(3)	(–)	1980	8.000 tons	Three are reportedly in reserve. Survivors of a class of 17.
Destroyer (DDG)	Project 61 'Kashin'	1	(–)	1962	4,700 tons	Last Russian survivor of 25 ships. Five modified variants for India.
Frigate (FFG)	Project 2235.0 *Gorshkov*	–	(4)	(2016)	4,500 tons	Four ships of a planned 15 being built. First to be delivered soon.
Frigate (FFG)	Project 1135.6M *Grigorovich*	–	(6)	(2016)	4,100 tons	Three ships to be delivered soon; 3 delayed due to lack of turbines.
Frigate (FFG)	Project 1154 *Neustrashimy*	2	(–)	1993	4.400 tons	
Frigate (FFG)	Project 1135 'Krivak I/II'	c.2	(–)	1970	3,700 tons	Remaining ships likely to be replaced with new construction soon.
Second Line Surface Escorts:		c.45	(10)			
Frigate/Corvette (FFG)	Project 2038.0 *Steregushchy*	4	(6)	2008	2,200 tons	Ordered total includes 2 similar Project 2038.5. More planned.
Frigate/Corvette (FFG)	Project 1166.1 'Gepard'	2	(–)	2002	2,000 tons	Caspian Flotilla. Modified variants built/being built for Vietnam.
Corvette (FSG)	Project 2163.0/.1 'Buyan/Buyan M'	8	(4)	2006	950 tons	Largely used in Caspian Flotilla.

Other second line surface escorts include c. 20 Project 1124ME 'Grisha V' and c.8 Project 133.1 'Parchim II' class anti-submarine corvettes.

- The *Kirov* class cruiser *Pyotr Velikiy* is armed with the SS-N-19 'Shipwreck' missile (also found in a twelve-silo installation on the forward section of the flight deck of *Admiral Kuznetsov*).
- The *Slava* class cruisers are armed with the SS-N-12 'Sandbox' or the P-1000 'Vulkan'.
- The *Sovremenny* class destroyers are armed with the SS-N-22 'Sunburn'.

Further, the navy operates dedicated anti-ship missile-armed submarines, notably the 'Oscar II' class armed with SS-N-19 missiles, again primarily intended for the counter-carrier role.

Before discussing Russia's future naval plans, an outline of the current order of battle is appropriate.

At present, the Russian Navy operates across the Northern, Baltic, Black Sea and Pacific Fleets, as well as the Caspian Flotilla. The surface force comprises a single aircraft carrier, *Admiral Kuznetsov*, and almost thirty blue water surface escorts drawn principally from the *Slava*, *Udaloy*, *Sovremenny*, *Neustrashimy* and 'Krivak' classes. These are supplemented by large numbers of smaller surface combatants – including the *Steregushchy* and *Buyan/Buyan-M* class corvettes – and an amphibious force approaching twenty landing ships. *Ivan Gren*, a new 5,000-ton landing ship, the first of two Project 1171.1 ships, is due to enter service at the end of 2015. The submarine force includes three 'Delta III' (armed with 'Vysota' SS-N-18 'Stingray' SLBMs)

and six 'Delta IV' (armed with 'Sineva' SS-N-23 'Skiff' SLBMs) strategic missile submarines, which are being joined by the new 'Bulava' SS-N-32 - armed 'Borei' class. There are also around twenty-five nuclear-powered guided-missile (SSGN) and attack (SSN) submarines, as well as some twenty 'Kilo' class diesel-electric boats. The Russian Navy also has a naval aviation component including land and-sea-based fixed-wing aircraft and helicopters. Further details on force structure are provided in Table 4.2.3.

From the above order of battle, the variety of ships in Russian service becomes apparent. For example, the navy operates two classes of cruiser, three destroyer classes and four frigate classes. A key

PERSONNEL
c.150,000.

NAVAL AVIATION
There are typically three or four naval air bases supporting each of the four fleets. Following the 2008 Russian military reforms, the bulk of the navy's land-based strike aircraft were transferred to the Russian Air Force, although it still operates these aircraft in the Crimea because of treaty requirements. Around twenty-five TU-142M 'Bear' and thirty IL-38 'May' maritime patrol aircraft are also operated by the Northern and Pacific Fleets. Main shipborne aircraft types include:

- Su-33 'Flanker D' strike fighter: Around twelve in service for operation from the *Admiral Kuznetsov*. Being supplemented/replaced by twenty-four MiG-29K/KUB 'Fulcrum D' jets.
- Ka-27/Ka-28/Ka-31 'Helix' helicopter: Around eighty of various variants of the series are in service.
- Ka-52 'Alligator' attack helicopter: Up to thirty-two ordered or planned; requirement may be revised following the collapse of the *Mistral* LHD purchase.

Type	Class	In Service	Ordered	ISD	Tonnage	Notes
Strategic Submarines:		12	(4)			Also 1 Project 941 'Typhoon' trials boat
Strategic Submarine (SSBN)	Project 955/A 'Borei/Borei II'	3	(4)	2013	18,000 tons+	FOC completed 2010 but commissioned 2013. At least 8 planned.
Strategic Submarine (SSBN)	Project 677BDRM 'Delta IV'	6	(–)	1985	18,000 tons	One other modified to non-SSBN role.
Strategic Submarine (SSBN)	Project 677DBR 'Delta III'	3	(–)	1976	18,000 tons	Survivors of a class of 14. To be replaced by 'Borei' class.
Attack Submarines:		c.20–25	(4)			
Attack Submarine (SSGN)	Project 885/M 'Yasen'	1	(4)	2013	13,500 tons+	Possible class of 7 or more.
Attack Submarine (SSGN)	Project 949A 'Oscar II'	c.5	(–)	1986	17,500 tons	A number are in modernisation or reserve.
Attack Submarine (SSN)	Project 971/U 'Akula I/II'	c.10	(–)	1986	9,500 tons	A number are in modernisation or reserve.

There are also around 5 Project 945A 'Sierra II' and Project 671RTM 'Victor III' class submarines operational.

Type	Class	In Service	Ordered	ISD	Tonnage	Notes
Patrol Submarines:		c.20	(4)			
Patrol Submarine (SSK)	Project 677 'Lada'	1	(2)	2010	2,700 tons	
Patrol Submarine (SSK)	Project 877/636 'Kilo'	c.20	(2)	1981	3,000 tons+	Some probably in reserve.

Other Ships:

Type	Missile Attack Craft	Tank Landing Ships	Minehunters	Replenishment Ships	
Number	c.35	c.20	c.40	c.20	Plus support ships & other auxiliaries.
					Many patrol vessels in Border Guard.

element of Russia's long-term naval re-equipment programme is to rationalise its force structure and where possible, operate single classes of ship – such as the forthcoming *Admiral Gorshkov* class frigate, and the 'Lider' class 'destroyer'.

THE FUTURE OF THE RUSSIAN NAVY

The Russian Navy is in the midst of a comprehensive modernisation drive, encompassing the replacement or modernisation of its Soviet-era ships and submarines. Of particular importance are efforts concerning the modernisation of the submarine force; replacing its current fleet of major surface combatants; and developing an eventual replacement for the *Admiral Kuznetsov*. Further, in 2014, Admiral Chirkov, announced that the Navy would contribute to a conventional strategic deterrent force, the core of which would be submarine-based and centred on the new 'Yasen' and modernised 'Oscar II' nuclear submarines and the conventional 'Lada' class; surface ships will also contribute to this force. The SS-N-30, a 2,000km-range land-attack variant of the 'Kalibr' family of missiles, and a naval variant of the Kh-101, an extended-range (5,000km) low-observable cruise missile, will be the principal conventional long-range strike weapons deployed.

The Submarine Force: After a protracted gestation, the Russian Navy has finally inducted into service the first two (of a currently planned eight – up to

The Project 677BDRM 'Delta IV' class currently form the mainstay of Russia's underwater strategic nuclear deterrent, with six operational boats in the Northern Fleet. This is *Tula* in March 2011. They will be replaced by the new 'Borei' class over the next decade. *(Russian Ministry of Defence Mil.ru)*

twelve may ultimately be built) 'Borei' class strategic missile submarines, and the first of possibly seven 'Yasen' class cruise-missile armed attack submarines. The 'Borei' class will, over the next decade or so, replace the 'Delta III/IV' boats and form the core of Russia's naval strategic nuclear forces. Developmental work has also commenced on so-called 'fifth generation' submarines. These include a new SSGN and a new SSN, referred to respectively

as an 'aircraft carrier killer' and 'interceptor'. They are likely to enter service in the 2020s and replace some of the older existing boats. There will also be a fifth-generation diesel-electric submarine, the 'Kalina' class, which will incorporate an AIP system. Given the focus on building a non-nuclear naval long-range strike capability, it will be interesting to see whether the design incorporates a VLS – one variant of the 'Amur' version of the existing Project 677 'Lada' class features a ten-cell VLS.

There are also plans to modernise the 'Oscar II' class, replacing the current armament of twenty-four 'Shipwreck' missiles with either the 'Oniks' (SS-N-26 'Strobile') or 'Kalibr' missile systems; three 'Oniks' or four 'Kalibr' missiles can be installed in lieu of one 'Shipwreck'. It is likely, based on Admiral Chirkov's statement, that modernised 'Oscar II' class submarines will be a significant contributor to the navy's conventional strategic deterrent force. As such, the submarines will be principally configured for the land-attack role and thus be equipped with the appropriate variant of the 'Kalibr'.

Surface Combatants: Two projects are of particular importance to the future of the Russian Navy's surface combatant force: the *Admiral Gorshkov* class frigate and the 'Lider' class 'destroyer'. The former are designed by the Severnoe Design Bureau, displace approximately 4,500 tons and incorporate signature-reduction measures. They are equipped

Russian Fleet units at dusk. The nearest ship is a Soviet-era Project 956 *Sovremenny* class destroyer, with a more modern Project 2038.0 *Steregushchy* class corvette immediately behind. Replacing the fleet of major surface combatants with modern warships is an important priority for the Russian Navy. *(Russian Ministry of Defence Mil.ru)*

with a 'Poliment-Redut' air-defence system that includes a four-faced active phased array and thirty-two VLS cells for 9M96 surface-to-air missiles, as well as sixteen further cells for 'Oniks' or 'Kalibr' missiles. The *Admiral Gorshkov* class are intended to serve as multi-purpose frigates and be capable of countering surface, submarine and air threats and conduct land-attack missions. The Russian Navy hopes to acquire at least fifteen of the ships and potentially as many as thirty to replace the current frigate force: the first-of-class, *Admiral Gorshkov* may enter service around the end of 2015. On a symbolic level, the *Admiral Gorshkov* class are the first major warship design conceived and built entirely in the post-Soviet period in Russia.

The second project, still at the formative stage, is the 'Lider' class. Although referred to as a destroyer, and principally intended to replace the current *Sovremenny* and *Udaloy* classes, the 'Lider' class are planned to offer a level of capability akin to that provided by a cruiser. The ships will displace around 15,000 tons, feature nuclear propulsion and be armed with a naval variant of the S-500 surface-to-air/anti-ballistic missile system currently under development plus anti-ship, land-attack and anti-submarine missiles. A total of twelve are planned (to be divided equally between the Northern and Pacific Fleets). The development of the 'Lider' class's nuclear propulsion system is also intended to provide a foundation for the propulsion system that will equip Russia's projected future aircraft carrier design.

The Russian Navy also intends to retain two nuclear-powered *Kirov* class cruisers in service for the foreseeable future. The *Admiral Nakhimov* is currently undergoing a major overhaul – tantamount to a rebuild – incorporating the renewal of all on-board systems. This includes the replacement of the current principal armament of twenty 'Shipwreck' anti-ship missiles with eighty 'Kalibr' series missiles (comprising land-attack and anti-ship variants) and the fitting of the 'Poliment-Redut' air-defence system also found in *Admiral Gorshkov*. The *Admiral Nakhimov* is due to re-enter service in 2018; the *Pyotr Velikiy* will also be similarly overhauled.

Aircraft Carriers & Amphibious Assault Ships: The Russian Navy remains committed to carrier-based aviation and has stated on numerous occasions an intention to replace the *Admiral Kuznetsov*. Russian thinking toward a future carrier suggests interest in a

The new Project 2235.0 frigate Adm*iral Gorshkov* seen departing on preliminary sea trials in 2014. The class is crucial to the renewal of the Russian Navy's surface component, with at least fifteen planned. *(reflex Yu)*

vessel comparable in size to the US Navy's *Nimitz* (CVN-68) and *Gerald R. Ford* (CVN-78) classes, that is, around 330m long, displacing in excess of 85,000 tons, featuring nuclear propulsion and fitted with electromagnetic catapults. The air group would include a naval variant of the Sukhoi T-50 fifth generation fighter, the MiG-29K currently being acquired for *Admiral Kuznetsov*, helicopters, a fixed-wing airborne early aircraft and unmanned air systems. This vision has remained consistent for approaching a decade. However, in contrast to the period 2007–10, the number of carriers the Russian Navy ultimately hopes to acquire is not now publicly stated: rather, a new carrier is sought by 2030. It may be that the Russian naval leadership has to tread somewhat carefully following the abortive deal to acquire French *Mistral* class helicopter carriers. In this regard, in June 2015, two helicopter carrier concepts were unveiled at the Army-2015 Forum. One, the 'Priboy', is a 14,000-ton vessel designed to embark eight helicopters and 600 troops; the second, the 'Lavina', would be generally comparable to the *Mistral*, displacing 24,000 tons and embarking sixteen helicopters. It is likely that a heli-

copter carrier based on or similar to these concepts will be built for the Russian Navy in the near to mid-term, especially as Russia pursues an active and in cases, interventionist, national policy.

CONCLUSION
The two decades or so since the collapse of the Soviet Union have seen a significant change in the fortunes of the Russian Navy: from the tumultuous 1990s, and doubts over the long-term future of the navy, starkly illustrated by the *Kursk* disaster, through to the growing confidence and grandiose vision of resurgence (naval and national) of the Putin era. However, as highlighted by the Ukraine Crisis and the imposition of sanctions (Ukrainian and Western), Russia's naval future remains vulnerable, in part due to the legacy of the Soviet Union. It therefore remains to be seen whether Russia's ambition for Great Maritime Power status can be achieved. The ability of Russian industry to deliver, and of the economy to afford, the ships and submarines sought by the navy is uncertain. This is especially the case given restricted access to Western technology and the absence of deep economic and

The Russian Navy maintains a significant force of landing ships in its amphibious forces and a number have seen considerable use in providing logistical support to government forces in Syria's civil war. This image shows the Project 775 vessel *Alexander Otravosky* transiting the Bosporus in March 2015. The navy forms a key part of Russia's efforts to achieve 'Great Power' status. *(Devrim Yaylali)*

corvettes and the strategic reach it provides those vessels, may be cited by those in Russia who argue that a blue-water navy is superfluous to requirements. It could be asked, for example, what requirement could justify spending billions on the 'Lider' class when corvettes, at a fraction of the cost, can strike targets 2,000km away from the Baltic, Black and Caspian Seas?

Despite the cost and difficulties associated with building the naval future it seeks, whilst Russia remains committed to striving for the 'Great Power' status it desires, any diminution of military ambition is unlikely. It may not, however, achieve the full extent of its rearmament plans. The slow pace of and difficulties encountered in (highlighted by the dependence on Ukrainian gas turbines) developing the *Admiral Gorshkov* class plus problems with other high-profile programmes (including the 'Bulava' strategic missile and the refit of the carrier *Vikramaditya* for India), illustrate the challenges that must be overcome for the navy's plans to be realised. It should be stressed that progress is being made: the navy is slowly receiving new ships and submarines; its operational tempo and scope of activities are increasing; and it has political support. There are likely to be choppy waters ahead, but the Russian Navy's future appears positive. Even if not a 'Great Maritime Power', the Russian Navy will remain an important naval force in the twenty-first century.

industrial reforms. Moreover, Russia's geographical circumstances, crises and instability along its land borders – or an escalation of tensions in Eastern Europe – may result in a renewed emphasis on land power. Ironically, the integration of the 'Kalibr' long-range cruise missile with light frigates and

Notes

1. These encompass:

– The Project 1143.5/6 aircraft carrier *Admiral Kuznetsov*.
– The Project 1144 *Kirov* class nuclear-powered cruisers.
– The Project 1164 *Slava* class cruisers.
– The Project 1155 *Udaloy* class destroyers.
– The Project 956/956A *Sovremenny* class destroyers.
– The Project 667BDR/BDRM Delta III & IV strategic submarines.
– The Project 949A 'Oscar II' guided-missile armed nuclear-powered submarines.
– The Project 971/971U 'Akula' class nuclear-powered attack submarines.
– The Project 877/636 series 'Kilo' class submarines.

2. Commander Simon E. Airey RN, 'Does Russian Seapower Have a Future?', *RUSI Journal* Vol. 140, No. 6 (London: Royal United Services Institute, 1995), pp.15–22.

3. Mikhail Barabanov, 'The Mistral Problem', *Moscow*

Defense Brief, Issue 3, 2009 (Moscow: Centre for Analysis of Strategies & Technologies, 2009).

4. 'Does Russian Seapower Have a Future?', *op. cit.*, p.20, footnote 12.

5. *Varyag* was eventually completed in China as *Liaoning*. The Mykolaiv shipyard was also responsible for the construction of the *Slava* class cruisers. The first three are in Russian service but the fourth – the former *Admiral Lobov*, launched in 1990 – has languished at the shipyard ever since due to neither Russia nor Ukraine either having the funds or will to complete the ship.

6. The final three ships remain under construction, albeit minus their Ukrainian-made gas turbines.

7. 'Commander argues case for Russia's global naval presence, carrier capability', cited in James Bosbotinis, *The Russian Federation Navy: An Assessment of its Strategic Setting, Doctrine and Prospects* Special Series 10/10

(Shrivenham: Defence Academy of the United Kingdom, 2010), p.18.

8. Admiral Valentin Selivanov, 'A Navy's Job: The Role of the Russian Navy in the System of International Security and Cooperation in the Field of Naval Armaments'; cited in 'Does Russian Seapower Have a Future?', *op. cit.*

9. For further discussion of the period covered in this paragraph see Mikhail Tsypkin, *Rudderless in a Storm: The Russian Navy 1992-2002*, (Sandhurst: Conflict Studies Research Centre, 2002).

10. 'Number Of Russian Navy Drills In 2014-2015 Increases By 20% – Commander', *TASS*, 17 June 2015, reported at: http://tass.ru/en/russia/801350

11. For discussion of this period, see *The Russian Federation Navy: An Assessment of its Strategic Setting, Doctrine and Prospects Special Series 10/10*, *op. cit.*

4.3

Conrad Waters

ASIA-PACIFIC

The major influence on naval force structures in the Asia-Pacific region today is undoubtedly the steady rise in prominence and capacity of China's People's Liberation Army Navy (PLAN). Having spent much of the past twenty years upgrading A2/AD denial capabilities over its near seas, the PLAN has now started to supplement these with the naval forces needed to generate a meaningful 'blue water' presence at greater distance from its shores. Although this development is justified by China's reliance on an extended network of maritime trade routes – SLOC in modern parlance – the country's assertive stance to contentious maritime claims in areas such as the South China Seas and the Senkaku (Diaoyu) islands has made its neighbours from as far apart as India and Japan sit up and take note.

The reaction to China's maritime rise has taken a number of forms. Diplomatically, it has seen a slow coming-together of countries such as Australia, Japan and the Philippines that either feel directly threatened by the PLAN's expansion or are concerned about a potential shift in the current balance of power. The most important of these countries is, inevitably, the United States. Its own 'Pivot to the Pacific' is based both on strengthening its own network of regional alliances and bolstering its regional military presence. Of the local maritime powers, Australia and Japan are taking steps to upgrade their own naval capabilities, with helicopter carriers, air-defence destroyers and long-range patrol submarines high on both countries' shopping lists. The two nations remain firmly wedded to their long-standing bilateral alliances with the United States. Historically, this has tended to see them

invest in naval capabilities intended to complement those deployed by the US Navy. However, their recent investments suggest a desire to generate balanced naval task groups of their own should circumstances require.

The trend of fleet development in the other regional maritime power, South Korea, has been broadly similar to that seen in the Royal Australian Navy (RAN) and the Japan Maritime Self Defence Force (JMSDF). However, an important consideration – also applicable to Japan – is the uncertainty caused by a militaristic, unpredictable North Korea. The danger of incursions and other provocations from its northern neighbour – most notably evidenced by the destruction of the corvette *Cheonan* in March 2010 – has meant that much of the Republic of Korea Navy's budget has been focused on littoral warfare capabilities. North Korea's nuclear weapons programme is an additional complication. It has already resulted in the JMSDF modifying its Aegis-equipped destroyers for an ABM defence role and is the most likely explanation for South Korea's heavy investment in warships that could be similarly modified.

A number of other regional navies – notably those of Taiwan and Vietnam – are also primarily structured as a deterrent against possible Chinese naval

4.3.0: ASIAN FLEET STRENGTHS – 2015

COUNTRY	SHIP TYPE													
	Aircraft Carriers & Amphibious				Submarines			Surface Combatants				Other (Selected)		
	CV/N	CVS	LHA/D	LPD/SD	SSBN	SSN	SSK	DDG	FFG	FSG/FS	FAC	O/CPV	MCMV	AOR
China	1	–	–	4	c.4	c.6	c.35 (10)	c.20	33	c.35	c.75	100+	c.30	8
Australia	–	–	2	1	–	–	6	–	11	–	–	15	6	2
Japan	–	3	–	3	–	–	16 (2)	38 (3)	6	–	6	–	27	5
Korea (South)	–	–	1	–	–	–	14	12	10	18	17	c.70	9	3
Brunei	–	–	–	–	–	–	–	–	–	4	–	4	–	–
Indonesia	–	–	–	5	–	–	2	–	6	26	c.20	50+	11	3
Malaysia	–	–	–	–	–	–	2	–	2	12 (1)	8	8	4	–
New Zealand	–	–	–	–	–	–	–	–	2	–	–	6	–	1
North Korea	–	–	–	–	–	–	50+	–	–	c.10	c.30	c.300	c.30	–
Philippines	–	–	–	–	–	–	–	–	–	14	–	c.50	–	–
Singapore	–	–	–	4	–	–	4	–	6	6	–	11	4	–
Thailand	–	1	–	1	–	–	–	–	7	11	6	50+	6	1
Taiwan	–	–	–	1	–	–	2 (2)	4	20	1	31	c.20	c.10	2
Vietnam	–	–	–	–	–	–	4	–	–	8	18	15+	8	–

Notes: Numbers are based on official sources where available, supplemented by news reports, published intelligence data and other 'open' sources as appropriate. Given significant variations in available data, numbers should be regarded as indicative, particularly with respect to minor warships. Numbers in brackets relate to training vessels; in some cases these could be returned to a front-line role. SSK numbers do not include midget submarines. FAC category includes missile-armed craft only.

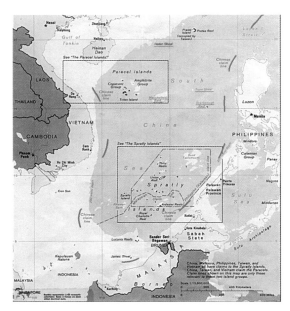

China's assertive stance to various maritime territorial claims have had a significant – and detrimental – influence on relations with its neighbours, A particularly problematic issue has been its 'nine-dashed line' claim to waters that encompass most of the South China Sea. *(CIA)*

The Republic of Singapore Navy is one of the most important and effective of the smaller Asian navies, fielding a balanced force of technologically sophisticated ships. This image shows the *Formidable* class frigates *Supreme* and *Intrepid* exercising with the US destroyer *Lassen* (DDG-82) in July 2015. *(US Navy)*

expansion. Whilst Taiwan's fleet – hampered by ambivalence with respect to relations with the mainland and denied technology by countries fearing damage to their Chinese trade – is in relative decline, Vietnam is investing heavily in Russian submarines, light frigates and fast attack craft. However, neither has a meaningful capacity for extended operations beyond their own littoral without external support. Indeed, as evidenced by the table, most Asian fleets continue to be equipped around constabulary and local defence roles, typically maintaining only a handful of warships capable of high intensity warfare.

A good example is Indonesia's *Tentara National Indonesia Angkatan Laut* (TNIAL), nominally the largest in South East Asia with around 65,000 personnel and some 160 commissioned warships. The vast majority of these are devoted to policing an archipelago that extends to around 17,500 islands and is populated by some 270 million people. Although investments are being made in expanding the small submarine flotilla and acquiring new light frigates under the so-called Minimum Essential Forces (MEF) programme to supplement or replace obsolescent ships, constabulary requirements are

likely to consume the bulk of resources for the foreseeable future. The situation is even worse in the Philippines. It has yet to count one missile-armed ship within fleet numbers, with nine of its fourteen light frigates and corvettes dating from the later years of the Second World War.

Fleets in Asia are, however, benefitting from the region's improving economic prosperity, which is allowing the creation of some modern and capable naval forces. For example, Malaysia, in similar fashion to Vietnam, has a newly-established submarine capability, taking delivery of two French 'Scorpène' type submarines built by DCNS in 2009. A programme is also underway for second-generation patrol vessels – in effect light frigates – that also utilise a DCNS design but which will be assembled locally. This is an increasingly important consideration, with warships of greater or lesser sophistication also being completed in a wide range of other Asian countries. However, it is Singapore that stands out amongst these second-tier fleets as having the most sophisticated local warship-building industry,

having exported indigenous designs to both Thailand and Oman. Indeed, Singapore is undoubtedly the most effective of all the smaller regional navies, with a balanced fleet of up-to date surface combatants, amphibious shipping and submarines that are as capable as any of their type in Asian waters.

One feature of a number of Asian maritime forces – not included in the data in the table – is the growing significance of paramilitary coast guard ships. Some of the larger coast guard and equivalent maritime enforcement agencies, including those of China, Japan and South Korea, comprise several hundred patrol ships and craft. The largest of these are of destroyer size and, whilst lightly armed, are equipped with sophisticated surveillance and communication systems that would be the envy of many smaller navies. Indeed, it is the white-hulled offshore patrol vessels of China's State Oceanic Administration *Weiquan* or 'Rights Protection Fleet' that are increasingly in the forefront of China's territorial dispute across its near seas.

4.3.1

Chris Rahman

PEOPLE'S LIBERATION ARMY NAVY (PLAN)

The steady improvement of China's PLAN in the quarter-century since the end of the Cold War arguably may not have been the most institutionally transformative single naval development of the period. However, it is undoubtedly the naval transformation of by far the greatest strategic consequence. For, while the impressively speedy expansion and modernisation of both the Singaporean and South Korean navies represent perhaps more rapid, even revolutionary, naval change, the continuous and purposeful development of the PLAN signals a moment of great geopolitical significance for the wider Indo-Pacific area. Even if China's navy never becomes a force of truly global presence and capability, its geostrategic expansion in the western Pacific alone – as well perhaps as into the Indian Ocean – will have global as well as regional reverberations.

The PLAN's transformation over the last twenty years can be summarised as being impressive, disruptive and challenging to its neighbours, yet relatively narrowly focused on being able to deter, defend, and dominate throughout the seas adjacent to China's coast.[1] Only in the second decade of the twenty-first century has the Chinese navy begun to seriously add to its force structure capabilities for combat operations beyond the waters of the Yellow, East China and South China Seas. Nonetheless, such capabilities are still limited as of 2015. The A2/AD mission, to use the dominant American terminology, remains the main PLAN priority. Naval missions are driven first and foremost by China's desire to defend its extensive maritime territorial and related jurisdictional and resource claims, most notably over Taiwan itself, but also over the Senkaku (Diaoyu) Islands in the East China Sea, claimed also by Japan

and Taiwan, and the numerous sparsely-situated groups of territorial features claimed by different sets of states in the South China Sea. China has active maritime disputes of these kinds with nine regional states, from contiguous North Korea to relatively distant Indonesia. In addition, Beijing is in dispute with the United States, its allies and other like-minded states over the PLAN's repeated infringe-

ments throughout adjacent seas of the global rights of freedom of navigation and overflight, which are essential for maintenance of the extant world order by US-led alliance and coalition systems.

A second, related factor is Beijing's intent to regain what it perceives as its rightful role as the leading power in Asia. Yet China cannot fully assert its dominance over the region as long as other independent major sea powers such as the United States, India and Japan maintain their political commitments to regional security as part of the broader liberal world order, underpinned by their long-standing naval preponderance in the Pacific and Indian Oceans.

Thirdly, since Deng Xiaoping's opening of the Chinese economy in the late 1970s China has become a highly sea-dependent trading state. Most notably, China has been a net importer of oil since 1993. Most of this must be transported by sea from the Middle East or Africa via potentially vulnerable chokepoints such as the Straits of Hormuz or the Straits of Malacca and Singapore. Thus, security of shipping throughout its most important SLOC has become another task influencing naval development.

The Chinese PLAN Type 052C destroyer *Jinan* leading a formation of Chinese and US Navy ships off the US Atlantic coast in November 2015. Even if China's navy is still some way from becoming a force with a truly global capability, its rapid development has considerable consequences for the Asia-Pacific region. *(US Navy)*

STRATEGIC DEVELOPMENT

Offshore Defence: At the Cold War's close the PLAN remained a technologically backward coastal defence force possessing extremely limited capacity for operations beyond coastal waters. It literally had been focused on supporting the army in defending the Chinese coastal regions from ancillary attacks in the event of war with the Soviet Union. However, changes had been afoot since the early to mid-1980s, when the broader People's Liberation Army (PLA) transformed its overarching strategic guidance (roughly equivalent to the United States' concept of national military strategy) from one fashioned towards fighting a large-scale continental, and nuclear, war against the Soviets, to one focused on fighting local, limited wars along China's periphery, especially the maritime periphery. As a result the PLAN adopted a new strategic concept of offshore defence, which can be viewed as the naval component of the PLA's overarching active defence operational concept.[2]

Of defining interest to China during the 1980s was the South China Sea problem, particularly the contested Spratly Islands. At this time, China was the only claimant other than Brunei not to have occupied territorial features. Spurred by the occupations of other claimants and the economic potential of the marine resources at stake, as well as a growing nationalist ethic and expanding geopolitical ambition, the PLAN was one of several institutional groups with interests in the South China Sea to leverage the issue to their own advantage. In the case of the navy, this meant a redefinition of naval strategy and development of force modernisation plans focused on a need to be able to operate effectively in defence of China's strategic interests throughout its maritime periphery. Taiwan was at this stage less of a priority. This may have been due to a perception that the Taiwan issue was of less urgency, or that military operations against the de facto independent island state were beyond the current capacity of the PLA. It may also have been the case, however, that advocacy for South China Sea contingency-related capabilities meant that the PLAN could pursue development of platforms with greater range and operational flexibility – more attuned to the revised national strategic guidance – that would add more substantively to overall naval modernisation. Taiwan-focused development, on the other hand, could have led to perpetuation of a continued short-legged force with perhaps greater emphasis upon land-based coastal capabilities, rather than naval capabilities able to pursue China's interests farther offshore.

The 'offshore' maritime-strategic concept is sometimes expressed in terms of 'near-sea', as opposed to 'coastal', defence. It evidently was formally endorsed by the navy in 1987, once the dissipation of the Soviet threat had become more conclusive.[3] The new naval thinking is associated with PLAN commander Admiral Liu Huaqing, who led the service from 1982 to 1988, although the central role also of paramount leader, Deng Xiaoping, is often underappreciated.[4] Deng had been involved in maritime-strategic issues at least since his role as co-commander of the offensive operation in 1974 to oust South Vietnam from the Crescent group of islands in the Paracel Islands, thus winning control of the entire archipelago for China. Deng's role as, in effect, political sponsor of Admiral Liu's ascent to navy commander and later senior vice-chairman of the Communist Party's highest military body, the Central Military Commission (CMC), should be recognised. Viewed in this context, Liu's development of naval strategy, operational concepts and force structure can therefore be seen as having had the imprimatur of the highest possible political level.

The PLAN's strategy of offshore, or near-seas, defence is not strictly geographically bounded. However, it has often been described both by Chinese strategists and their foreign interpreters in geostrategic terms. The construct often employed is that of the first and second 'island chains'. The first island chain is generally described as the line of islands stretching from the Kuriles through the Japanese home islands, the Ryukyus, Taiwan and the Philippines, to Borneo. This encompasses the regional seas of most political, economic and strategic importance to Beijing: the Yellow Sea, the East China Sea, and the South China Sea. The second island chain runs from the Kuriles through Japan, the Bonins, the Marianas, Guam and Palau to the Indonesian archipelago.

Liu Huaqing's offshore defence concept has often been characterised in Western writings as being delimited by the first island chain, with an alleged intent for the navy to be able to exert sea control within those waters, with a medium-term aspiration to extend operations, including potentially sea control, out to the second island chain. However, it is unclear that the island chains construct was

The PLAN was a technologically-backward coastal defence force at the Cold War's end. A considerable part of the defensive effort comprised diesel-electric patrol submarines, of which the Type 035 'Ming' class – a redesign of the Soviet 1950s era 'Romeo' design – was the most modern example. These remained in production until the turn of the millennium and gained some export success. This picture shows a boat that was sold to Egypt in the early 1980s. *(Ian Shiffman)*

viewed in such determinative terms by Liu, even though some Chinese strategists did adopt different geographically-bounded views of the offshore defence concept. Such geographically-defined ideas reflect a poor understanding of the nature of the ocean as a medium for mobility, instead taking a land-based conception of the sea, with hypothetical defensive lines drawn across sea areas. Liu's own vision of offshore defence is believed to have encompassed a region beyond the first island chain into the western Pacific east of Taiwan and the northern Pacific Ocean.[5] Whilst not strictly geographically deterministic, this conception nevertheless still represents a typically 'continentalist' perspective on maritime strategy and the employment of naval power. It did signify, though, at the time, a revolutionary change from the intellectual and operational constraints of the coastal defence era.

The PLAN's key tasks under the offshore defence concept have been summarised as, first, preventing invasion from the sea and keeping enemies from encroaching within certain limits; second, protecting China's territorial sovereignty; and third, safeguarding national unity and maritime rights.[6] These latter two tasks are difficult and controversial ones given the disputed nature of most of the island territories and consequent maritime jurisdiction claimed by Beijing. By no means the least is the infamous 'nine-dashed line' claim, encompassing most of the South China Sea, which is seemingly unsupportable on the basis either of historical precedent or international law. It was thus in the Spratlys that much of the PLAN's 1980s activities were focused, including a slowly building naval presence coupled with survey work. China occupied its first Spratly features in 1987, and continued its territorial accumulation into the following year. This led to a clash with Vietnamese forces in March 1988 in which two Vietnamese naval vessels were destroyed and another damaged, with significant casualties.

The 1996 Taiwan Strait Crisis & Its Aftermath: China's strategic guidance was updated in the 1990s as a result of the PLA's increased concern with the extent of the United States' military-technical dominance demonstrated in Operation 'Desert Storm' and other conflicts. Deng Xiaoping's successor, Jiang Zemin, adopted the updated guidance of 'local wars under high-tech conditions' in 1993. The events which had an even greater and more immediate effect upon PLAN development, however, were the

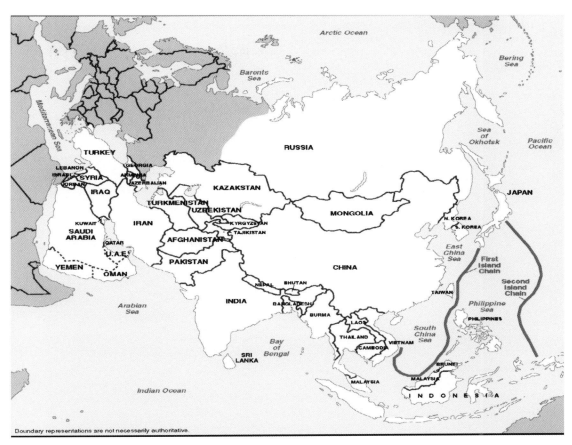

The PLAN's strategy of offshore defence has often been characterised, perhaps somewhat simplistically, as attempting to ensure sea control out to the first and second island chains, depicted on this US Department of Defense map. *(US Department of Defense)*

Taiwan Strait missile crises in mid-1995 and, especially, March 1996. From the late 1980s democratisation on Taiwan had gathered pace, with the first presidential election held in March 1996, with the favoured candidate (and ultimate victor) openly pro-independence. In an attempt to halt this process and undermine pro-independence forces, China launched a series of military exercises and ballistic missile 'demonstrations' in the Strait and close to Taiwan's main ports, partially blockading the island for a brief period. In March 1996, the US Navy intervened by dispatching two carrier groups to the general vicinity of Taiwan. This seemed to come as a major shock to Beijing, and directly informed the immediate development priorities of the PLA.

Aside from the nuclear deterrent, which had been a longstanding priority, most PLA development became A2/AD-focused. In particular, the ability to

deter or deny future American interventions on behalf of Taiwan had become the overwhelming military priority. China's 2000 Defence White Paper complained: 'Hegemonism and power politics still exist … Certain big powers are pursuing "neo-interventionism" [and] "neo-gunboat diplomacy."'[7] It is also worth noting that some Chinese strategists also view the physical occupation and control of Taiwan as an important interim strategic objective, via which China could exert geostrategic control not only within the first island chain and throughout South East Asia, but beyond the island throughout the western Pacific.

The CMC again revised China's national strategic guidance in 2004 under the leadership of Hu Jintao, to that of 'winning local wars under the conditions of informationisation'. This was revised again in 2015 to further emphasise the importance of information operations as 'winning informationised local wars', and 'highlighting maritime military struggle and maritime PMS [preparation for military struggle]'.[8] As the US Office of Naval Intelligence explains, 'informationisation' relates to the incorporation of modern information technology into all relevant military operations A related concept also employed by the PLA is that of 'non-contact warfare', which refers to the ability to detect, target and attack an enemy using long-range precision strikes from beyond the enemy's 'defended zone'.[9] These concepts establish a framework for PLA, and particularly naval, modernisation, and the types of A2/AD capabilities that would be necessary to defeat the world's most capable navy in the waters of the western Pacific.

At a time of double-digit annual defence expenditure increases, the 2004 Defence White Paper stated that the navy increasingly was incorporating such capabilities and had 'expanded the space and extended the depth for offshore defensive opera-

tions'.[10] This reflected the desire to push China's effective defensive perimeter farther out to sea, expanding the extent of the area which it feasibly could deny to United States or allied forces in any Taiwan or other regional contingency.

Blue-Water Operations: China also began to take a much greater strategic interest in waters beyond just the adjacent 'near seas' covered by the strategy of 'offshore defence'. As early as 1997 Jiang Zemin instructed the navy that, in addition to improving combat capabilities within the first island chain and its overall deterrent capability, it 'should gradually develop combat capabilities for distant ocean defence'.[11] Hu Jintao repeated this clarion call in 2002 for the PLAN to 'make the gradual transition to far-seas defence …'.[12] 'Far-seas' areas logically are those that lie beyond 'near seas', presumably the maritime space both within the second island chain and beyond. This concept led to the formation of battle groups of different classes of combatants able

to operate farther out to sea independent of land-based support. The 2012 Defence White Paper refers to the PLAN as developing its blue-water capabilities, including 'improving the training mode of task force formation in blue water … highlighting … remote early warning, comprehensive control, open sea interception, long-range raid, anti-submarine warfare and vessel protection [in] distant sea[s]'.[13] Indicative of this change is the steady growth in PLAN 'combat readiness patrols' and exercises in blue-water environments. The 'Manoeuvre-5' exercise in October 2013 was its largest ever blue-water combat exercise, involving for the first time sea and air assets from all three PLAN fleets, held for fifteen days mostly in the Philippine Sea, while a three-ship surface force undertook the navy's first combat readiness patrol in the Indian Ocean in early 2014.

These naval missions reflect an expanding list of tasking priorities. On the one hand, and still the primary task, is deterrence and denial involving

4.3.1: CHINA – PEOPLE'S LIBERATION ARMY NAVY COMPOSITION END 2015

MAJOR BASES & STRUCTURE

The PLAN is divided into three fleets:

North Sea Fleet: HQ at Qingdao, Shandong Province: Covers the Bohai Gulf, Yellow & East China Sea. Other bases at Guzhen Bay, Huludao, Jianggezhuang, Lushun & Xiaoping Dao.

East See Fleet: HQ at Ningbo, Zhejiang Province: Covers the East China Sea & the Taiwan Strait. Other major bases at Fujian, Shanghai, Xiangshan & Zhoushan.

South Sea Fleet: HQ at Zhanjiang, Guangdong Province: Covers the South China Sea. Other major bases at Guangzhou; Huangfu, Hong Kong & Yulin (Hainan Island).

Many of the major bases – and some of the additional minor bases – are clustered around the naval headquarters or other major locations. For example, Zoushan naval base and the Xiangshan naval base are located close to the East Sea Fleet headquarters at Ningbo, whilst there is a major group of bases on Hainan Island.

PERSONNEL

c. 235,000 plus 10,000 marines of which c. 40,000 conscripts.

MAJOR WARSHIPS

Type	Class	In Service	Ordered	ISD	Tonnage	Notes
Aircraft Carriers:		1	(2–4)			2-4 of an unspecified indigenous class believed ordered.
Aircraft Carrier (CV)	*Liaoning* (*Kuznetsov*)	1	(–)	2012	60,000 tons	Former Soviet design launched in 1988.
Major Amphibious Warships:		4	(2)			
Landing Platform Dock (LPD)	Type 071 *Kunlun Shan* ('Yuzhao')	4	(2)	2007	18,000 tons	Further construction may be planned.
Major Surface Escorts:		c.55	(14)			
Destroyer (DDG)	Type 052D *Kunming* ('Luyang III')	3	(9)	2014	7,500 tons	Total likely numbers approximate. Type 055 cruiser planned.
Destroyer (DDG)	Type 052C *Lanzhou* ('Luyang II')	6	(–)	2004	7,000 tons	Built in one batch of 2 and one much later batch of 4.
Destroyer (DDG)	Type 052B *Guangzhou* '(Luyang I')	2	(–)	2004	6,500 tons	First of Luyang series, all built on common hull.
Destroyer (DDG)	Type 051C *Shenyang* ('Luzhou')	2	(–)	2006	7,100 tons	
Destroyer (DDG)	Project 956E/EM *Sovremenny*	4	(–)	1999	8,000 tons	Currently subject to major mid-life modernisation.
There are also two Type 052 ('Luhu'), a sole Type 051B ('Luhai') and a few remaining Type 051 ('Luda') destroyers in various stages of obsolescence that remain in service.						
Frigate (FFG)	Type 054A *Xuzhou* ('Jiangkai II')	22	(4)	2008	4,100 tons	Includes 2 similar Type 054 *Ma'anshan* ('Jiangkai I') ships.
Frigate (FFG)	Type 053 H2G/H3 *Anqing* ('Jiangwei')	11	(–)	1992	2,500 tons	Three further vessels transferred to Coast Guard.

increasingly sophisticated A2/AD warfighting capabilities. On the other, though, is the growth in China's interests in SLOC security. This had been of interest even in Liu's time, but never a priority for strategy or force development. However, Beijing's rapidly rising dependence upon imported oil, most of which is carried by sea across the Indian Ocean via the Malacca and Singapore Straits, as well as other energy and mineral resource imports, meant that this issue had become increasingly important for China's national security. This concern had been reflected in late 2004 when Hu Jintao introduced his 'new historic missions' for the PLA, which included safeguarding the external environment which had been so permissive to China's rapid economic development, and contributing to international security.

The 2008 Defence White Paper outlined the threats to this environment, including 'struggles for strategic resources', and noting explicitly the piracy threat.[14] Hu's new, more expansive horizons for the PLA in part reflected the stabilisation of cross-Strait

An Italian AW101 helicopter exercising with the PLAN Type 054A frigate *Linyi* in the Indian Ocean in January 2015. Growing Chinese dependence on imported energy is seeing considerable emphasis being placed on SLOC security. *(European Union Naval Force Somalia)*

NAVAL AVIATION

The c. 25,000-strong PLAN Air Force has c. twenty-five airbases split between the three fleets. The majority of aviation assets are land-based. Estimates of the strength of these land-based forces vary significantly dependent on the source consulted but include twenty-four Russian-built Su-30MK2, similar numbers of indigenous J-10 and J-11 and around 120 JH-7 modern strike fighters, plus additional numbers of J-7 and J-8 'legacy' types. Around thirty H-6G (licence-built TU-16 'Badger') bombers can also be used for maritime reconnaissance and are being slowly supplemented by small numbers of modified Y-8 (licence-built AN-12 'Cub') transports for anti-submarine, airborne early warning & electronic gathering. Main shipborne aircraft types include:
- J-15 Flying Shark strike fighter (Su-33 derivative): over ten delivered to date; deliveries ongoing.
- Z-8 Super Frelon helicopter (licence-built SA 321 Super Frelon): over thirty delivered to date; deliveries ongoing. Used in various roles, including utility, anti-submarine and early warning.
- Z-9C/D Haitun helicopter (licence-built AS 365 Panther): over twenty naval variants delivered to date; deliveries ongoing.
- Ka-28/Ka-31 Helix helicopter: Around twenty-five purchased to date, including nine of the Ka-31 airborne early warning variant.

Type	Class	In Service	Ordered	ISD	Tonnage	Notes
Second Line Surface Escorts:		c.35	(c.35)			
Corvette (FSG) -GP	Type 056 *Bengbu* ('Jiangdao')	c. 25	(c.35)	2015	1,500 tons	Series production of Type 056 & 056A ASW variant underway.
There are also a few obsolete frigates of the Type 053 H1/H1G/H2 'Jianghu' series still in service. Total planned numbers of Type 056 corvettes an estimate.						
Strategic Submarines (SSBN):		4+	(c.4)			**Type 094 ('Jin') class in production for total of 5/6. 1 Type 092 'Xia'.**
Attack Submarines (SSN)		6+	(c.4)			**Type 093/093G ('Shang') class replacing Type 091 ('Han') class.**
Patrol Submarines (SSK)		c.35	(c.8)			
Submarine – SSK	Type 039A/39B (Type 041 'Yuan')	12+	(c.8)	2006	c.3,000 tons	Numbers uncertain. May be AIP-equipped.
Submarine – SSK	Type 039/39G ('Song')	13	(–)	1999	2,300 tons	
Submarine – SSK	Project 877 EKM/ Project 636 ('Kilo')	12	(–)	1994	3,000 tons	Acquired from Russia in 3 batches
Additional Type 035 'Ming' class submarines – perhaps 10–15 in total – operate in the training role. There is a single Type 032 'Qing' trials submarine.						

Other Ships:

Type	Missile Attack Craft	Patrol Vessels	Minehunters	Replenishment Ships	
Number	c.75	100+	c.30	8	Plus c. 60 landing ships/transports and numerous support ships and auxiliaries.

relations in the context of the PLA's improved deterrent capability. The White Paper thus elaborated that the navy would develop the ability to conduct 'co-operation in distant waters' and counter 'non-traditional security threats'. Late in 2008 the PLAN embarked upon its first such mission, dispatching a small flotilla to protect shipping from Somali pirates in the Gulf of Aden, a deployment that has been sustained until the present day. This represented a major departure for both China itself, politically, and the PLAN, operationally, making for the first time a welcome contribution to broader maritime and international security. The operation has been an important learning opportunity in conducting and sustaining operations far from home, including replenishment at sea, escort and other counter-piracy tactics, co-operation with international partners, and other operational skills. China further demonstrated its slowly growing ability to operate far from home by assisting with the evacuation of Chinese nationals from Libya in 2011, supporting the operation to

remove chemical weapons from Syria in 2014, searching for Malaysian Airlines flight MH370 in the Indian Ocean and evacuating civilians from Yemen.

The Current Situation: The 2015 Defence White Paper outlines the current transition, stating that the navy 'will gradually shift its focus from "offshore waters defence" to the combination of "offshore waters defence" with "open seas protection" …'. It further notes explicitly China's growing vulnerability to 'international and regional turmoil' with the expansion of its own national interests, and that threats to 'the security of overseas interests concerning energy and resources [and] strategic sea lines of communication' have become 'imminent' issues. Such issues are likely to be compounded by the 'Maritime Silk Road of the 21st Century' concept outlined by current leader, Xi Jinping, to develop closer economic integration with South East Asia, South Asia, the Middle East and Europe, particularly related to the energy trade.[15] For the

navy, this will see greater emphasis being placed upon SLOC security, greater 'far-seas' presence in the Indian Ocean, and improved PLAN access or even basing rights in Indian Ocean ports.

However, for China, SLOC security is not just about protecting shipping or even the broader maritime supply chain from criminal or other non-military threats in an age of terrorism and piracy. With its newfound vulnerability to disruptions to seaborne raw materials, especially oil, the prospect of a more traditional threat by a rival power to blockade such supplies in time of crisis or war is a major concern for Beijing, and the real threat perception underpinning the idea of China's 'Malacca dilemma' coined by Chinese strategists. Notwithstanding the development of alternative transportation routes, including over land, the vast scale of China's seaborne resource imports and geographic locations of their main source regions, cannot be over-emphasised. Given the strength of the United States, Japanese and Indian navies, this potential vulnerability is not practically surmountable in the absence of a blue-water surface fleet, with integrated intelligence, surveillance and reconnaissance (ISR), and support facilities, which would need to be orders of magnitude greater in capability than that of the current PLAN.

A final element of strategy development would seem to be a continuation of China's long-term, gradual expansion throughout the 'near-sea' areas. Its combination of massive island reclamation in the Spratlys, militarisation of disputed features and increasing naval and air presence throughout disputed waters, and challenges to the navigation rights of the US Navy, all point towards an intent to be able to exert some form of sovereign control over those waters even in peacetime, however unrealistic that may seem. This could even lead to military actions to forcibly eject other claimants from their existing occupied features. As a result, power-projection capabilities are back in favour for the first time since at least the early 1990s.

IMPLICATIONS FOR FORCE STRUCTURE DEVELOPMENT

The implications of changes to strategy at both the national and naval levels for navy force structure development have been significant. Prior to the revision to national strategic guidance in 1985, the PLAN had expanded greatly in numbers since the early 1970s. But the coastal-defence focus ensured

Power-projection capabilities are becoming increasingly fashionable in the PLAN as its navy develops additional missions beyond A2/AD defence. Although most media attention has concentrated on the aircraft carrier *Liaoning*, the acquisition of expanded amphibious capabilities – most evidenced by increased use of the Type 071 amphibious transport dock – is at least as significant. This is *Changbai Shan* on a visit to Portsmouth UK in January 2015. *(Conrad Waters)*

that both ships and aircraft mostly had only a relatively short range and limited endurance, with very limited combat capabilities, and were obsolete, in a relative sense, before they even entered service. In part this was due to a lack of access to modern technologies since the Sino-Soviet split of the early 1960s, but also reflected the general backwardness of the Chinese economy. Furthermore, Deng Xiaoping deprioritised military spending during the 1980s, instead emphasising economic development. It thus was not until the 1990s that defence budgets started to surge, expanding quickly on the back of a rapidly growing economy, and due to a perception of increased strategic necessity following the mid-decade Taiwan crises.

Nuclear Submarines: There was, however, one naval programme that had received consistent political support and budgetary prioritisation both before and throughout this period of transition; that of the PLAN's nuclear submarine force.[16] The origins of China's nuclear submarine programme can be traced as far back as the 1950s, and represented a major technological hurdle for a backward autarkic nation starved of foreign technical knowhow. The programme ultimately resulted in the commissioning of five 'Han' class nuclear-powered attack submarines (SSN) between 1974 and 1990, and a single 'Xia' class nuclear-powered ballistic missile submarine (SSBN) in 1987. Despite problems and limitations with these boats, the programme nevertheless represented a significant achievement for Chinese science, technology and industry. It is not clear whether the 'Xia' class boat has ever been fully operational as an SSBN. However, the fact that it is a single boat, with a submarine-launched ballistic missile (SLBM) – the JL-1 – with an estimated range of only 2,150km, ensured that it never represented a survivable, secure second-strike nuclear deterrent capability. Both classes have suffered from problems with their nuclear reactors and are considered relatively noisy, and have been progressively supplanted by the Type 093 'Shang' class SSN and 094 'Jin' class SSBN, from 2006 and 2007, respectively.

Conventional Force Structure Development to the mid-1990s – Gradual Modernisation: The change in strategic guidance to focus on China's maritime periphery only had a gradual impact on force structure, with several classes of vessel remaining in production across eras. In the case of the 'Ming' class

The PLAN destroyer *Qingdao*, one of two experimental Type 052 'Luhu' class destroyers delivered between 1994 and 1996. The early 1990s saw the PLAN in a transitional phase, with small numbers of warships delivered to allow the introduction of new technologies. *(US Navy)*

diesel-electric submarines, production stretched from the early 1970s to 2002; the 'Luda' class guided missile destroyers (DDG) commissioned from the early 1970s to 1991; numerous sub-classes of 'Jianghu' small frigates which entered service between 1975 and 1996; and the 'Yukan' class tank landing ships (LSTs) completed between 1980 and 1995.[17]

New generations of more capable indigenous ships started to emerge in the 1990s, as the PLA began in earnest its attempt to bridge the capability gaps between its own forces and those of potential regional rivals. Such programmes saw greater incorporation of Western technologies and systems into indigenous Chinese platforms. Furthermore, the end of Cold War animosities and ultimate collapse of the Soviet Union meant that Russia once again became a leading supplier of weapons, systems and technologies to China. The importance of Russia as a vendor became greater still following the Western arms embargo imposed upon China as a result of the

1989 Tiananmen Square massacre, although some European Union members have consistently evaded the sanctions, continuing to supply systems and technologies while avoiding the export of complete platforms.

It is worth noting that during the 1980s and into at least the early 1990s, during the Liu Huaqing period, China had a nascent aircraft carrier programme, driven in large part by its desire to protect its maritime claims, exert influence and to project power deep into the South China Sea. China had purchased former Australian and Soviet carriers for scrap or for use as public amusement parks, and possibly to garner technical design insights, and was reported to be training naval aviators for carrier operations in the late 1980s. However, it seems that the programme lacked sufficient high-level political support and it is unclear to what extent carriers ever were a priority. There are likely to have been shipbuilding, technical and budgetary constraints that checked progress too. There also seem to have been divergent opinions within the navy itself over the programme's efficacy, with one school evidently strongly advocating an emphasis instead on submarine development. Ultimately, the submarine emphasis won out.

The first half of the 1990s, however, was mostly a transition period for China's navy, with only small numbers of new, interim designs commissioned. These ships included:

- **Type 053 H2G 'Jiangwei I' class guided-missile frigates:** Four ships of less than 2,500 tons displacement but equipped with six relatively modern YJ-8 (C-801) series surface-to-surface missiles, a short-range SAM capability and helicopter facilities.[18]
- **Type 052 'Luhu' class guided-missile destroyers:** Two ships commissioned in 1994 and 1996, featuring imported turbines, a French combat data system and Crotale-based HQ-7 short-range SAM capability, YJ-8 series anti-surface missiles and helicopter facilities. To an extent, they were demonstrators of the types of technology the PLAN would need to adopt in future.
- **Type 072 III 'Yuting I' class tank landing ships:** Displacing around 4.900 tons and helicopter-capable, these ships started to commission in 1992. Ten ships of the class were built, with ten more of the follow-on 'Yuting II' class commissioned up to 2005.

This period also saw the first new Russian-built platforms enter PLAN service, most notably two Project 877 'Kilo' class submarines in 1994/5. These were followed by a pair of more advanced Project 636 boats in 1998/9.

Force Structure Development from the mid-1990s – A2/AD Capabilities: The mid-1990s crises over Taiwan ensured that power-projection capabilities would be deprioritised in favour of broad-based A2/AD capability development across the PLA. China's 2004 Defence White Paper spelled this out explicitly, stating that 'The PLA will promote co-ordinated development of firepower, mobility and information capability, enhance the development of its operational strength with priority given to the Navy, Air Force and Second Artillery [Strategic Rocket] Force, and strengthen its comprehensive deterrence and warfighting capabilities'. The impact upon the navy was to direct its force development

The then US Navy Chief of Naval Operations Admiral Jonathan Greenert and his Chinese counterpart Admiral Wu Shengli seen after a confidence-building visit to a Type 039B 'Yuan' class submarine and Type 022 'Houbei' class fast attack craft in July 2014. Both types are essential constituents of the PLAN's A2/AD capabilities, which were significantly expanded after the 1996 Taiwan Strait missile crisis. *(US Navy)*

efforts, including its major surface, sub-surface and aviation platforms, towards a comprehensive, combined arms anti-surface warfare capability.

An initial response was to order two *Sovremenny* class guided-missile destroyers from Russia. These ships were significant in that they were designed in the 1970s in combination with the supersonic 160km-range SS-N-22 'Sunburn' (Moskit) surface-to-surface missile as an integrated system with which to attack US Navy carrier battlegroups. Another two were ordered in 2002, with upgraded 240km-range Moskits. China also purchased another eight 'Kilo' class submarines, all armed with SS-N-27 'Sizzler' (Alfa Klub) 180km-range anti-surface missiles. Twenty-four land-based Russian Su-30 Mk 2 fighter aircraft delivered to the navy in 2004 also can carry AS-17 air-to-surface missiles.

The focus on anti-surface warfare also drove indigenous procurement, with most vessels carrying a significant complement of anti-surface missiles. Notably:

- The Type 039/Type 039G 'Song' and Type 039A//Type 039B (Type 041) 'Yuan' class diesel-

electric submarines, as well as the Type 094 'Shang' class SSNs, all carry the submarine-launched YJ-82 (C-801A) variant of the C-801 anti-ship missile. This supplements the submarines' torpedoes and has a c. 40km range. It may well be replaced by the new, longer-range YJ-18 missile in due course.
- Most surface combatants – from destroyers through to the Type 056 'Jiangdao' class corvettes and 'Houbei' class fast attack craft are equipped with variants of the YJ-83 (C-802) series of anti-surface missiles. In addition, the Type 052C 'Luyang II' class destroyers carry the more advanced YJ-62 (C-602) long-range missile and the new Type 052D 'Luyang III' class DDG may be equipped with a next generation missile.
- In addition, the JH-7 maritime strike fighter and H-6G bomber carry a range of air-launched anti-ship missiles including the 200km-range YJ-83K. The H-6 may also carry the new long-range, supersonic YJ-12.[19]

A large inventory of over 50,000 sea mines has also been amassed, while other PLA services also

KEY PLAN SURFACE COMBATANTS

Type 052C Destroyer (China): *Lanzhou*

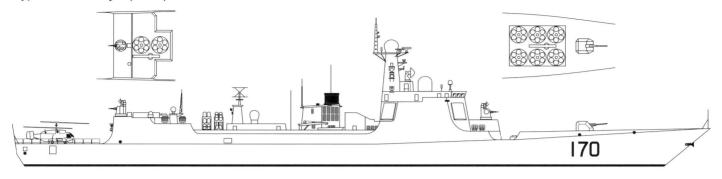

170

0   10m   20m   30m   40m   50m

Type 054A Frigate (China): *Xuzhou*

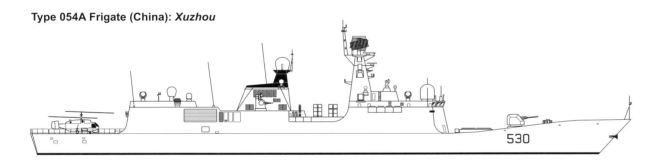

530

Type 056 Corvette (China): *Jian*

586

Type 022 Missile Boat (China)

2208

The drawings represent four of the PLAN's most important surface combatant classes. The Type 022 missile-armed fast attack craft and larger Type 056 corvettes have both been built in large numbers and play an important part of China's A2/AD strategy in littoral waters, where they would likely be used to swarm opposing surface forces with their powerful batteries of surface-to-surface missiles. The Type 056 also offers a more balanced range of general-purpose capabilities, with the Type 056A variant (not depicted) fitted with a towed array for a more potent anti-submarine capability. The significantly larger Type 054A frigates and Type 052C destroyers benefit from possessing area air-defence capabilities and can support the PLAN's 'near seas' defence concept at greater distance. They are also increasingly being used in support of the PLAN's growing interest in blue-water operations. *(All drawings © John Jordan 2015)*

China's increased interest in strategic naval operations beyond her 'near seas' has seen increased deployments far from home. This image shows the Type 052C destroyer *Haikou* participating in the search for the lost Malaysian Airlines flight MH370 in the Indian Ocean in April 2014. *(RAN)*

contribute, with some Air Force fighters able to carry out maritime strike. The Second Artillery's DF-21D anti-ship ballistic missiles (ASBMs) are reportedly capable of striking ships to a range of approximately 1,600km, well beyond the first island chain.

Recent Developments – Power Projection: With the thickening of its A2/AD network of capabilities, the PLAN has pushed its putative defensive perimeter farther out to sea, increasingly beyond the range of land-based air defences. It has also, as we have seen, begun to entertain a possible blue-water future. Anti-air warfare has therefore become a more urgent need, with individual ships and task groups requiring the cover of an organic sea-based area air defence capability. This has developed only over the past decade and has been achieved through a mix of Russian imports and indigenous systems. The former have included the SA-N-12 'Grizzly' fitted to the two Type 052B 'Luyang I' destroyers and modified as the vertically-launched HHQ-16 system found on the numerous 'Jiangkai II' frigates. The 150km-range Russian SA-N-20 'Gargoyle' has also been acquired to equip the two Type 051C 'Luzhou' class destroyers but the domestic 100km-range

HHQ-9 system has been used for the more numerous Type 052C 'Luyang II' and Type 052D 'Luyang III' classes.

The renewed interest in power projection is, however, best illustrated by the commissioning in 2012 of the Soviet-designed *Kuznetsov* class carrier *Liaoning*, which was completed in China after lying unfinished in the Ukraine for years. *Liaoning* does not yet represent a fully operational power projec-

tion asset. The PLAN Air Force is still continuing to build its expertise in carrier-based fixed-wing capabilities through at-sea training with its J-15 fighters, believed to be reverse-engineered variants of the Russian Su-33. However, the navy is advancing quickly in that direction, with between two and four larger Chinese-designed aircraft carriers thought to be under development. Amphibious forces are also receiving considerable attention, as evidenced by the commissioning of four 18,500-ton Type 071 'Yuzhao' class amphibious transport docks, with further ships expected to be built. Each ship can carry up to four 'Yuyi' class air-cushion landing craft and four large helicopters. A follow-on class of flat-deck amphibious assault ship is anticipated, whilst the 'Yuting II' class LSTs have returned to low-rate production.

The new carriers and large amphibious ships will show the flag as a symbol of China's prestige and power, and eventually contribute significantly to blue-water SLOC security missions. Another capability viewed as important to China's naval diplomacy is the 'Anwei' class hospital ship, *Daishandao*, commissioned in 2008. China had been made to look weak and ineffective by its inability to bring serious amphibious and other assets to bear in response to the Indian Ocean tsunami in 2004, unlike not only Western navies but those of its Asian rivals, India and Japan. Perhaps more significantly, fleet replenishment capability is being looked at seriously, not least because continuous deployments to the Gulf of Aden since 2008 and other activities in distant waters have put undue pressure on the small existing replenishment fleet. Five Type 903/903A

Although China has made significant progress in fielding new conventional submarines – one of thirteen Type 039 'Song' class boats is seen nearest the camera – production of nuclear-powered submarines has been more tentative. It has been reported experience with the small numbers of nuclear-powered boats that have been built has not been entirely satisfactory. *(RAN)*

PLAN replenishment capabilities have become stretched as China has increased the number of its blue-water deployments. Series production of the Type 903/903A 'Fuchi' class replenishment ships has been embarked on to remedy the problem; this image shows first of class *Qiandao Hu* on a visit to the United States. *(US Navy)*

'Fuchi' class replenishment ships have now been commissioned and three more will be delivered soon.

CURRENT STATUS & FUTURE EVOLUTION

The PLAN has been in constant transition over the past thirty years. It has developed firstly from a coastal to an offshore defence force, and then from an A2/AD-focused fleet during the mid-1990s onwards to one with multiple missions – including increasing blue-water tasking – today.

The relative success of the force structure improvements implemented to support this transition can be indicated by production numbers. Diesel-electric submarines have been series-built in considerable numbers, a record echoed above the waves in the extended production of recent frigate and corvette classes. Such numbers are indicative of relatively successful designs. However, this track record has not been universal; for example destroyer classes have – until recently – only appeared as single units or in pairs. This may indicate some difficulty, through trial and error, in achieving a successful design. However, the recent appearance of greater numbers of the 'Luyang II' class – and series production of the follow-on 'Luyang III' type – may now indicate that China has mastered the design and production of sophisticated surface warships. It is believed that China is now working on an even more powerful surface vessel, the c. 10,000-ton Type 055.

A similar problem may have occurred with nuclear submarines, with a seven-year break occurring between delivery of the initial two Type 093 SSNs and subsequent improved Type 093A vessels, which only started commissioning in 2014. It has been reported that these vessels have not been entirely successful, including dissatisfaction with their nuclear reactors.[20] It seems that the 093 and

The Chinese Type 920 'Anwei' class hospital ship *Daishandao* (*Peace Ark*) pictured with her US Navy counterpart USNS *Mercy* during the RIMPAC 2014 exercises. The ship forms an important part of China's naval diplomacy. *(US Navy)*

This picture of the Chinese Type 054A frigate *Xuzhou*, seen here in the East China Sea on 20 November 2015, reveals the Russian-design origins of her main search ('Top Plate') and fire control ('Front Dome') radar. The hotchpotch of different indigenous, indigenised and imported systems found in the PLAN is likely to make for logistic and operational difficulties. *(US Navy)*

094 boats may be interim designs, with an improved Type 095 SSN and Type 096 SSBN under development.

Among many weaknesses remaining in the PLAN, three particularly stand out. The first is anti-submarine warfare (ASW), a real shortcoming given the submarine strength of its potential adversaries. Only now is the navy developing a Y-9 ASW variant of its land-based maritime patrol aircraft. However, this will still leave vessels involved in distant water operations relatively unprotected. Power projection is a second shortcoming: with effective operational carriers still years away, the navy lacks a flexible sea-based land-attack capability. This may be rectified in the future by the integration of a new land-attack cruise missile with the latest destroyers and the next-generation SSN. A third issue is the hotchpotch of different indigenous, indigenised and imported systems of various origins currently in service. This must make for logistical, maintenance, training and operational nightmares for navy commanders and may well hamper overall effectiveness.

There remain many further unanswered questions. For example, we know that China still struggles to produce modern, quiet nuclear propulsion systems and, for that matter, gas turbines. But just how effective are its long-range intelligence and targeting capabilities? Its combat data systems? Its submarine quieting technologies? And how successful has the PLAN been in integrating different capabilities into an effective joint force at sea? In the absence of the experience of actual combat, many of these issues are likely to remain clouded.

What does seem certain, though, is that the PLAN will continue to develop its blue-water capabilities. It remains unclear, however, whether it will be able to successfully develop a comprehensive warfighting force able to conduct major combat operations far from home. It is important not to expect equivalence with either the US Navy or even other major blue-water forces, particularly when its most pressing strategic problems lie much closer to home. In this context, no matter how much it may aspire to greater things, strategic necessity and likely contingency mean that the A2/AD focus throughout its 'near seas' and into the western Pacific, will continue to be the PLAN's main priority in the coming decades.

Notes

1. The literature on the PLAN is now vast. Useful sources include the US Office of Naval Intelligence's three reports published in 2007, 2009 and 2015, which are largely factual and judgement free. Ronald O'Rourke's regularly updated CRS Report is a similarly useful factual information source: *China Naval Modernization: Implications for U.S. Navy Capabilities – Background and Issues for Congress* (Washington DC: Congressional Research Service). The annual *Jane's Fighting Ships* (Coulsdon: IHS Jane's) and *The Naval Institute Guide to Combat Fleets of the World* (Annapolis, MD: US Naval Institute Press) publications provide up-to-date data on force structure; various editions of these publications are the primary sources for weapons data in this chapter. Other useful sources are the US Department of Defense's annual reports to Congress on the Chinese military, and the bipartisan congressional US-China Economic and Security Review Commission's annual reports. As a general rule the professional-scholarly literature mostly generated by researchers in the US War College and think tank systems are superior in both quality and quantity to purely academic publications, and more accessible. Most notable is work generated by the Naval War College's China Maritime Studies Institute, as well as articles published in the Naval War College Review; CNA; RAND Corporation; the US Army's Strategic Studies Institute; the US National Defense University; Project 2049 Institute; the Jamestown Foundation China Brief; and related work by the Center for Strategic and Budgetary Assessments. In addition, each year the April edition of the US Naval Institute's *Proceedings* has a China focus.

2. See *China's Navy 2007* (Washington DC: Office of Naval Intelligence [ONI], 2007), pp.24–6.

3. Nan Li, 'The Evolution of China's Naval Strategy and Capabilities: From "Near Coast" and "Near Seas" to "Far Seas"', *Asian Security*, Vol. 5, No. 2 (Philadelphia, PA: Taylor & Francis, 2009), p.156.

4. For a brief summary of Liu's maritime strategic thought, see James R Holmes and Toshi Yoshihara, *Chinese Naval Strategy in the 21st Century: The Turn to Mahan* (London: Routledge, 2008), pp.27–36.

5. *The PLA Navy: New Capabilities and Missions for the 21st Century* (Washington DC: ONI, 2015), p.7.

6. *China's Navy 2007*, *op.cit.*, p.25.

7. *China's National Defense in 2000* (Beijing: Information Office of the State Council of the People's Republic of China, 2000), section I.

8. *China's Military Strategy* (Beijing: The State Council Information Office of the People's Republic of China, 2015), section III.

9. *The PLA Navy, op.cit.*, pp.7–8

10. *China's National Defense in 2004* (Beijing: Information Office of the State Council of the People's Republic of China, 2004), section III.

11. Quoted in *China's Navy 2007*, *op.cit.*, p.26.

12. Quoted in 'The Evolution of China's Naval Strategy and Capabilities', *op.cit.*, p.160.

13. *The Diversified Employment of China's Armed Forces*, (Beijing: Information Office of the State Council of the People's Republic of China, 2013), section III.

14. *China's National Defense in 2008* (Beijing: Information Office of the State Council of the People's Republic of China, 2009), section I.

15. See Xi Jinping, *The Governance of China* (Beijing: Foreign Languages Press, 2014).

16. For further detail refer to John Wilson Lewis and Xue Litai, *China's Strategic Seapower: The Politics of Force Modernization in the Nuclear Age* (Stanford, CA: Stanford University Press, 1994).

17. The 'Jianghu' types lacked even a basic surface-to-air missile (SAM) capability or – with the exception of a single ship – the ability to operate helicopters.

18. Published information on PLAN missile systems is confused, incomplete and often contradictory. The major anti-surface missile of the early 1990s was the YJ-8 series, often referred to under its export designation C-801, which has similarities to the French MM38 Exocet. The NATO reporting name was the CSS-N4 'Sardine'. The longer ranged YJ-83 series, also exported as the C-802 series and designated the CSS-N-8 'Saccade', entered service towards the end of the decade. It is now the most common weapon of its type in service with the PLAN.

19. Office of the Secretary of Defense, *Military and Security Developments Involving the People's Republic of China 2015* (Washington DC: April 2015), p.46.

20. See Lyle Goldstein, 'Emerging from the Shadows', *Proceedings* – April 2015 (Annapolis, MD: US Naval Institute Press, 2015), pp.30–4.

4.3.2   David Stevens

ROYAL AUSTRALIAN NAVY (RAN)

With the release of his *Plan Pelorus* in April 2015, Australia's Chief of Navy, Vice Admiral Tim Barrett, sought to focus his people on what needed achieving over the remaining three years of his appointment.[1] Keenly aware of the more uncertain regional and global security environment, Barrett made clear that, having been the beneficiary of the greatest re-capitalisation in a generation, the Royal Australian Navy (RAN) must evolve into a more innovative, potent and agile force. Rather than continuing the operational habits of the recent past, generally deploying single ships at a distance, the navy intends to regularly generate self-contained task groups, capable of both self-defence and ongoing sustainment, and individually tailored to meet government-directed operational outcomes. As necessary, these task groups will include submarine, afloat support, aviation, mine countermeasures and rapid environmental assessment capabilities

STRATEGIC BACKGROUND
Plans for the current and future navy demonstrate considerable progress in terms of Australia's declared policy to pursue a more robust maritime security strategy. More particularly, they reflect recognition that global power relationships, notably between China and the United States, have become more complex as strategic weight continues to shift between the western and eastern hemispheres. Economic, trade and energy independence is growing across the Indo-Pacific, and by 2050 the region is expected to generate almost half the world's economic output. Already thirty per cent of global trade and sixty per cent of Australia's trade flows through the South China Sea. When combined with persistent tensions over maritime sovereignty, increased risks surrounding extreme weather events, rising sea levels, threats to food and water security, and the continuing potential for mass movement of populations, it is unsurprising that Australia supports good order at sea and encourages all

states to focus on maintaining regional stability.

One hopes that these plans are not too little, too late. Unfortunately, an understanding that Australia is a maritime nation, responsible for one of the world's largest maritime domains, and with a fundamental imperative to maintain its commercial and military sea communications, has not always been widely accepted in political and academic circles. The evolution of security policy during the 1980s, towards self-reliance in the context of a 'Defence of

Australia' strategy, might have been domestically acceptable in the post-Vietnam War era. However, it essentially supported a reactive approach to emerging threats. As a result, strategic thinking tended to favour sea denial over sea control and made thoughts of expeditionary operations anathema. As the then Defence Minister boldly stated in 1990, the 'essentially offensive nature' of an amphibious capability made it inappropriate for Australia's force structure.[2]

The new RAN amphibious assault ship *Canberra* refuelling from the replenishment tanker *Sirius* during first-of-class trials in November 2015. The RAN intends to focus more attention on deploying self-contained task groups capable of self-defence and ongoing sustainment going forward. *(RAN)*

4.3.2.1: AUSTRALIA – ROYAL AUSTRALIAN NAVY COMPOSITION END 2015

MAJOR BASES & STRUCTURE

Fleet Base East (**Sydney**): Amphibious ships; air-defence frigates; general-purpose frigates; minehunters.

Fleet Base West (**Rockingham**): Submarines; general-purpose frigates.

In addition, patrol vessels and minor warships are located at **Cairns** and **Darwin**.

PERSONNEL

c. 14,000 permanent; 8,000 reserve (of which 5,000 active).

MAJOR WARSHIPS

Type	Class	In-Service	Ordered	ISD	Tonnage	Notes
Major Amphibious Warships:		3	(–)			
Amphibious Assault Ship (LHD)	Canberra (Juan Carlos I)	2	(–)	2014	27,100	Project JP2048 Phase 4A/B.
Dock Landing Ship (LSD)	Choules (Largs Bay)	1	(–)	2006	16,200	Acquired second-hand from UK in 2011.
Major Surface Escorts:		11	(3)			
Destroyer (DDG)	Hobart (F-100)	–	(3)	(2017)	6,300	Project SEA 4000. Replace remaining Adelaide class 2017–20
Frigate (FFG)	Adelaide (FFG-7)	3	(–)	1980	4,200	Remainder of original Australian class of 6.
Frigate (FFG)	Anzac (MEKO 200)	8	(–)	1996	3,600	To be replaced on a broadly equivalent basis – Project SEA 5000.
Submarines:		6	(–)			
Patrol Submarine (SSK)	Collins	6	(–)	1996	3,400	To be replaced by 8–12 boats under Project SEA 1000.

Other Ships:

Type	Coastal Patrol Vessels	Minehunters	Survey Vessels	Replenishment Ships
Number	13 (+2 on loan)	6	6	2

NAVAL AVIATION

Naval aviation is focused on NAS **Nowra**, around 80 miles from Sydney. There is no fixed wing capability. Main aircraft types are:

■ MH-60R Seahawk anti-submarine helicopters: twenty-four in service or on order. Replacing existing S-70B Seahawk helicopters.

■ MRH-90 Taipan transport helicopter (NH Industries NH90 TTH): six allocated to the navy from an army/navy pool of forty-seven.

Additional Australian Army MRH-90 and Chinook CH-47F transport helicopters and Tiger ARH reconnaissance aircraft can be embarked as necessary.

The Royal Australian Air Force's AP-3C Orion maritime patrol aircraft will be replaced by eight–twelve P-8A Poseidon and six–eight MQ-4C Triton aircraft by the 2020s.

The constraints of such an outlook were already clear as the Cold War staggered to an untidy close. By the early 1990s, strategic guidance forecast that superpower military competition would be replaced by a more complex, fluid and less certain construct; a world where regional powers, their rivalries and differing levels of economic progress, would assume far greater importance to Australia.[3] Significant new capital equipment such as the *Collins* class submarines and *Anzac* class frigates were then being acquired, but in the latter case were shackled by their original conception as 'tier two' units within the surface fleet, generally tasked for operations in waters proximate to Australia and equipped accordingly. Plans had simultaneously been announced to procure more capable 'tier one' destroyers, and build the major surface combatant fleet up to sixteen–seventeen hulls.[4] However, resource limita-tions soon dropped numbers to a more usual eleven–twelve. In the event, the project to acquire what became the *Hobart* class guided-missile destroyers (DDGs) did not commence until 2007, six years after the last of the three previous DDGs of the *Perth* (*Charles F. Adams*) class decommissioned. The resulting gap in area air warfare capability is only now being filled.

Just as disconcerting, outsourcing became rife and acquisitions were not matched with real growth in the defence vote, meaning that new platforms gener-ally came at an ongoing cost in other areas, notably personnel, maintenance and the provision of fuel and ammunition. Consequently, although from the late 1980s the Australian Defence Force (ADF) could and did engage overseas in low-level activities of limited scope, it never really possessed the sustain-ability or mobility necessary for independent combat operations across the vast empty distances of Australia's continental north, or the sea and air approaches beyond.

Instead, the succession of short-notice ADF deployments in the wake of political instability and natural and manmade disasters pointed to the reality of the emerging strategic situation. Taking place in the near South Pacific and as far away as Somalia, these operations were often only possible because the RAN had managed to retain a minimal sea-lift and amphibious capability in the form of the heavy landing ship, *Tobruk*, six heavy landing craft and a former roll-on roll-off ferry converted to a training ship. Nevertheless, these assets and their relatively small embarked capabilities could only achieve so much, and throughout the 1990s concerns regarding the hollowness of the ADF's force struc-ture were openly discussed.

THE EAST TIMOR INTERVENTION & ITS CONSEQUENCES

Capability limitations eventually came to a head in 1999, when the United Nations called on Australia to lead an international peace enforcement intervention during the humanitarian crisis in East Timor. The ADF's largest overseas commitment since the Vietnam War, this was also a genuinely joint operation, with a requirement for the navy and air force to protect, deploy and sustain combat-ready land forces quickly and in strength. The operation was an undoubted success. However, providing a small-division sized expeditionary force only some 400 miles from the Australian mainland stretched the ADF to breaking point and would have likely proven impossible without the short-term lease of a high-speed catamaran ferry, and the additional maritime and air support provided by Australia's coalition partners.

This support, which variously included additional sea-lift, escort, surveillance, amphibious insertion and logistic services, became an important indicator of international resolve, with the overt presence of surface combatants used to deliberately signal coalition intent up to the final days in theatre. In truth, the ready availability of a comprehensive range of offshore floating capabilities came as a revelation to many in the Australian land forces. In accordance with extant policy, most had generally been expecting to operate in a continental context, with the army maintaining little capability for, or doctrinal interest in, the projection of military power at a distance.

The need for improved amphibious capabilities was immediately reflected in the 2000 Defence White Paper, which introduced both Australia's intention to act proactively, engaging hostile forces as far from its shores as possible, and the associated need for a maritime strategy.[5] In the short term, two ex-US Navy *Newport* class amphibious transports purchased in the mid-1990s finally entered service after substantial and costly modification. Over the next decade these proved of great utility in deployments as far removed as Fiji and the Middle East. Unfortunately, maintenance and personnel issues, that also continued to constrain availability in many other areas of the fleet, forced the early withdrawal of both these vessels in 2011. The elderly and increasingly unreliable *Tobruk* was retained until 2015. Most embarrassingly, the RAN was unable to provide an amphibious platform when Cyclone Yasi

A Sea King helicopter operating with the heavy landing ship *Tobruk* in 1999 during Operation 'Stabilise', the Australian-led peace enforcement mission carried out under UN auspices in East Timor. The successful operation significantly stretched Australian defence capabilities and had a major influence on future procurement. *(RAN)*

devastated North Queensland early in 2011. The 16,000-ton landing ship dock *Choules* (ex-RFA *Largs Bay*), was acquired from the United Kingdom the same year. The following year, the Australian Government procured the Australian Defence Vessel *Ocean Shield*, a civilian-crewed humanitarian and disaster-relief vessel, to provide further capacity until the arrival of purpose-built ships.

EQUIPMENT

Today, the strategic decisions taken in the 2000 Defence White Paper are starting to bear fruit and the RAN's amphibious capabilities, particularly, are much stronger. The self-contained task groups envisaged by *Plan Pelorus* will generally be centred around the two new 27,000-ton amphibious assault ships *Canberra* and *Adelaide*, or *Choules*. They should be capable of achieving significant military effects, either alone or within the joint and combined operational environment. All three amphibious vessels have large flight decks and a docking well for landing craft. Together the two

larger units are able to put ashore over 2,000 troops by helicopter and watercraft, along with all their weapons, ammunition, vehicles and stores. Meanwhile *Choules* has the capacity to load and transport up to thirty-two tanks or 150 light trucks, in addition to 356 troops in normal conditions or up to 700 in overload.

By 2018 the joint warfare and advanced networking capabilities of an Australian naval task group will also benefit from the arrival of the first of three *Hobart* class. Built in South Australia to the Spanish F-100 design, their fit-out includes an Aegis combat system, a 48-cell VLS, canister-launched Harpoon missiles, a 5in Mk 45 gun and surface-launched torpedoes. These extremely capable warships will progressively replace the three remaining guided-missile frigates of the *Adelaide* (*Oliver Hazard Perry*) class commissioned between 1984 and 1993. The latter have all been upgraded during the last decade to ensure that they remain effective and supportable until their final removal from service in 2021. The third of the new DDGs,

The *Anzac* class frigates *Stuart* and *Anzac* pictured operating with the JMSDF destroyer *Kirisame* and the *Collins* class submarine *Rankin* during an event in November 2014 commemorating the departure of the first ANZAC convoy to the First World War. The 1990s saw the Royal Australian Navy benefit from considerable investment in the form of the arrival of *Anzac* and *Collins* class vessels but budgetary conditions meant that availability has, at times, been limited. *(RAN)*

Sydney, the fifth ship of that name, is currently planned to complete in 2020.

Providing additional screen protection will be the eight existing *Anzac* class frigates that first joined the fleet in 1996. These warships were originally built to favour hull numbers over quality, but have successively received an anti-ship missile defence upgrade that includes an Australian-developed CEAFAR active phased-array radar atop a new mast, working in conjunction with a CEAMOUNT multi-channel phased-array missile illuminator. These and other combat system enhancements have greatly improved situational awareness and threat alert in littoral environments, allowing the *Anzac*s to identify, track and engage multiple targets simultaneously and ensuring that they will still provide effective service well into the next decade.

Embarking in all the major surface combatants will be the MH-60R Seahawk naval combat helicopter. Twenty-four aircraft are being procured from the United States to replace the previous fleet of S-70B-2 Seahawks. Equipped with a low-frequency dipping sonar, the Mk 54 lightweight torpedo and Hellfire air-to-surface missiles, they will offer surface forces much improved surveillance, anti-submarine and anti-surface capabilities. With the ADF continuing its path towards becoming a truly integrated joint force, the amphibious ships will also be fully capable of operating a combination of MRH-90 Taipan utility helicopters, CH-47F Chinooks or Tiger armed reconnaissance helicopters.

Elsewhere, the RAN continues its contribution to Australia's whole-of-government effort to safeguard its borders and offshore resource interests. Fourteen *Armidale* class patrol boats began entering service in

The lead *Anzac* frigate is seen departing Portsmouth Harbour UK during a Northern Trident deployment in June 2015. The eight-strong class are being modernised with Australian active phased-array radar systems to improve self-defence capabilities and are likely to remain in service well into the next decade. *(Conrad Waters)*

The *Armidale* class patrol vessels – *Maryborough* is seen here – make an important contribution to securing Australia's borders. *(Royal Australian Navy)*

The RAN has ordered twenty-four MH-60R Seahawk helicopters to provide surveillance, anti-submarine and anti-surface capabilities. This picture shows the newly acquired type on *Perth*, which is the first frigate to deploy the MH-60R operationally. *(RAN)*

2005, but one was lost to a fire in 2014 and ongoing availability issues have since resulted in temporary supplementation by two *Cape* class patrol vessels normally operated by the Australian Border Force. In recent years the priority given to border protection has also required the employment of units from the RAN's mine warfare and hydrographic forces. The hydrographic survey capability currently rests with two *Leeuwin* class survey ships and four *Paluma* class survey motor launches; while six *Huon* class coastal minehunters and two permanent clearance diving teams provide a defensive mine-countermeasures capability.

FUTURE PROCUREMENT PLANS
Looking to the future, the Coalition Government has already announced a twenty-year, AU$89bn investment in multiple new naval systems. These will include: eight to twelve conventionally-powered future submarines to replace the six *Collins* class boats that will likely begin to retire in 2026; future frigates optimised for anti-submarine warfare; and new offshore patrol vessels (OPVs) with improved range, seakeeping and sensor capabilities compared

to the *Armidale*s. Other specialist vessels to be acquired include heavy landing craft for intra-theatre lift and two underway replenishment ships to maintain an east and west coast capability.

The two replenishment ships will be built overseas, but the government has also committed to a transformation of the local naval shipbuilding industry through a continuous build of surface warships. The current plan envisages this beginning with the OPVs and future frigates. Although the build and acquisition strategy for the new submarines remains under consideration, both major political parties publicly support the capability and there is almost certain to be some construction in Australia.

CONCLUSION
The RAN's aim has generally been to field and maintain a balanced fleet, capable of effective action across the spectrum of operations. Looking at its force structure and future planning it would seem that this aim is once again nearly within reach; a situation not really seen since the 1970s. The evidence of *Plan Pelorus* is that the RAN's leadership understands the challenges, particularly those

relating to training, workforce generation and asset management, and is working hard to address them. The fundamental problem, as always, will be to make it all work when so many factors remain outside the navy's control.

Notes
1. See *Plan Pelorus: Navy Strategy 2018* (Canberra: Royal Australian Navy, 2015).

2. K C Beazley quoted by G Cheeseman (ed.) in *The New Australian Militarism* (Leichhardt: Pluto Press, 1990), p.212.

3. *Strategic Review 1993* (Canberra: Commonwealth Government, 1993).

4. This plan was stated in *The Defence of Australia, 1987* (Canberra: Australian Government Publishing Service, 1986).

5. See *Defence 2000: Our Future Defence Force* (Canberra: Commonwealth of Australia, 2000). The decision was affirmed in the 2006–16 Defence Capability Plan, which set out a requirement, inter alia, for the procurement of two amphibious assault ships and three air-defence destroyers.

4.3.3

Alastair Cooper

JAPAN MARITIME SELF-DEFENCE FORCE (JMSDF)

Japan has significant marine resources and a close interest in global maritime communications; these are fundamental inputs to its security and prosperity. It has a complex, advanced economy which is highly leveraged to international trade. Although the Japan Maritime Self-Defence Force (JMSDF) is one of the largest naval forces in the world, the number and geographic span of Japan's maritime interests still exceed the JMSDF's capability to protect them. As a result, co-operative strategies are a necessity. In large part this approach has been driven by Japan's defence alliance with the United States of America. However, the growing proximity and complexity of Japan's defence challenges are likely to require both greater efforts at multilateral co-operation and also unilateral joint-force capabilities. This will make for difficult force structure decisions in coming years, challenging not just the nation's view of what is appropriate under its constitution but also the JMSDF's institutional capacity to deal with strategic and technological change.

JMSDF CAPABILITIES & STRATEGIC RELATIONSHIPS

The JMSDF's capabilities have their greatest strength in anti-submarine (ASW) and mine warfare disciplines, with more recent improvements to ballistic missile defence (BMD) and amphibious warfare. The ASW and mine warfare strengths are the result of the close relationship with the United States Navy through the twentieth-century Cold War period, where the JMSDF played a major role in efforts to track and contain the former Soviet Union's Pacific Fleet, particularly its submarines. In so doing, the JMSDF shaped the operational environment in the Pacific, enabling the US Navy to make best use of its own submarine, amphibious and aircraft carrier task groups. The BMD capability is a response to North Korea's development of nuclear weapons, possibly to be carried by ballistic missiles. The amphibious capability is part of not only changes for the JMSDF, but to the entire Japanese Self Defence Forces, with much greater emphasis being placed on the defence of offshore islands as opposed to Japan's main islands. This is a reflection of the unsettled nature of many territorial and maritime claims, with ongoing disputes or disagreements involving Japan, South Korea, Russia, China,

A large part of the JMSDF's defence strategy has been guided by its alliance with the United States. This image shows the 'helicopter-carrying destroyers' *Izumo* (DDH-183) and *Ise* (DDH-182) exercising with the US Navy carrier *Ronald Reagan* (CVN-76) and surface escorts in 2015. *(JMSDF)*

The JMSDF *Takanami* class destroyer *Makinami* pictured in Sydney Harbour in October 2013. Whilst the JMSDF's relationship with the US Navy will remain its most important, collaboration with other fleets – particularly the RAN and the Indian Navy – is growing. *(RAN)*

Taiwan and many other Association of South East Asian (ASEAN) nations.

Since the end of the Cold War, the rationale for the JMSDF's force structure and capability mix has not been as simple. The slow normalisation of Japan's own security outlook and the growing strength and prosperity of East and South East Asia (in particular the rise of China) have led to questions over the extent to which Japanese and United States strategic interests will coexist in coming decades. It is not that the US-Japan alliance is weakening, but more that the number, geographic span and complexity of security situations both nations have to address are greater. It is, therefore, not certain that their national interests will always be completely congruent. The capabilities provided by the current force structure will continue to have great utility: mine warfare is still an underestimated discipline and anti-submarine warfare is a resource-hungry activity, for which the growing number of submarines in the Asian region will pose ever greater challenges. Outside of the alliance relationship with the United States, the capability mix may not provide Japan with all the options its leaders may think they require. Greater emphasis on amphibious

and organic air capabilities, along with greater priority for joint operations with other arms of the Japanese Self Defence Forces are some of the capability development paths. The 2013 *Japanese National Defense Program Guidelines* (NDPG) reflects the thinking of Japan's defence planners on these issues: while the strategic direction is clear, the practical implementation through force development, personnel, training and relationships with neighbours, partners and allies is still a work in progress and likely to remain so for years to come.[1]

The relationship with the US Navy will remain the JMSDF's most important. However, relationships with the Indian Navy and the RAN show some potential to develop on the back of a renewed understanding that – as maritime democracies – these countries share many values and interests. In addition to some joint exercises, maritime security cooperation in the Middle East and disaster relief in South East Asia provide a practical focus to these embryonic relationships; relationships with the potential to grow very rapidly whether or not Japan starts to export military hardware to either country. There is one concrete proposal for this in the case of Australia, as Japan is a strong candidate in the

competitive evaluation process for the design and construction of Australia's next class of submarine, based on its *Soryu* class. While the sale of arms to India does not have the same definition or focus, there is clear potential.[2]

In recent years the JMSDF has been engaged in counter-piracy operations as part of the Combined Task Force 151 in the Middle East; in 2015 a JMSDF officer took command of the task force for the first time. Both the significant commitment of ships and aircraft, and the deployment of a command team for a multi-national task force, are indicative of the JMSDF effort to engage in cooperative maritime security to the limits of what is constitutionally acceptable for Japan in terms of collective defence. The conduct of their command and the way it is received, internationally and in Japan, will be keys to their future engagement, particularly at a time when there are maritime challenges so close to Japan itself. Moreover, the combined military forces commitment by Japan is the furthest commitment of the JMSDF in support of their trade and energy security. While the trade security task is enduring and closely intertwined with the global trading system on which all nations

4.3.3.1: JAPAN – JMSDF COMPOSITION END 2015

MAJOR BASES & STRUCTURE

Yokosuka, Kanagawa Prefecture: Escort Flotilla 1 (Escort Divisions 1 & 5), Submarine Flotilla, Minesweeping Flotilla, District Flotilla.

Sasebo, Nagasaki Prefecture: Escort Flotilla 2 (Escort Divisions 2 & 6), District Flotilla.

Maizuru, Kyoto Prefecture: Escort Flotilla 3 (Escort Divisions 3 & 7), District Flotilla.

Kure, Hiroshima Prefecture: Escort Flotilla 4 (Escort Divisions 4 &8), Submarine Flotilla, Amphibious Flotilla, District Flotilla.

Ominato, Aomori Prefecture: District Flotilla.

The four **Escort Flotillas** are each split into two divisions of four ships; one headed by a DDH with an air-defence DDG and two GP escorts in support and one headed by an air-defence DDG with three GP escorts in support. They correspond to the longstanding 8-8 structure, under which each flotilla is intended to comprise eight escort ships and eight anti-submarine helicopters (although the latter is being impacted by delivery of the new, higher capacity helicopter carriers). Not all the ships in the escort flotillas are necessarily located in the same base as their assigned flotilla. The **District Flotillas** comprise one or more divisions of older or smaller destroyers plus mine-countermeasures and patrol vessels.

PERSONNEL

c. 45,000 excluding civilian staff.

MAJOR WARSHIPS

Type	Class	In-Service	Ordered	ISD	Tonnage	Notes
Aircraft & Helicopter Carriers:		**3**	**(1)**			**A total force of 4 ships is planned.**
Helicopter Carrier (DDH)	*Izumo* (DDH-183)	1	(1)	2015	27,000	Second ship *Kaga* scheduled for commissioning in 2017.
Helicopter Carrier (DDH)	*Hyuga* (DDH-181)	2	(–)	2009	19,000	
Major Amphibious Warships:		**3**	**(–)**			
Landing Platform Dock (LPD)	*Osumi* (LST-4001)	3	(–)	1998	14,000	Plans for a new, larger replacement class under consideration.
Major Surface Escorts:		**44**	**(3)**			**A total force of 50 ships is planned.**
Destroyer (DDG)	*Atago* (DDG-177)	2	(1)	2007	10,000	Aegis-equipped. One additional ship planned. Modified DDG- 173.
Destroyer (DDG)	*Kongou* (DDG-173)	4	(–)	1993	9,500	Aegis-equipped.
Destroyer (DDG)	*Hatakaze* (DDG-171)	2	(–)	1986	6,300	To be replaced by *Atago* class ships ordered/planned.
Destroyer (DDH)	*Shirane* (DDH-143)	1	(–)	1980	7,500	To be replaced by *Kaga*.
Destroyer (DDG)	*Akizuki* (DD-115)	4	(2)	2012	6,800	Ships under construction are modified DD-119 variants.
Destroyer (DDG)	*Murasame* (DD-101)	14	(–)	1996	6,200	Includes five *Takanami* variants of 6,300 tons delivered from 2003.
Destroyer (DDG)	*Asagiri* (DD-151)	8	(–)	1988	4,900	
Destroyer (DDG)	*Hatsuyuki* (DD-122)	3	(–)	1982	3,800	A further 3 ships serve as training vessels.
Frigate (FFG)	*Abukuma* (DE-229)	6	(–)	1989	2,500	For local district flotillas.
Submarines:		**16**	**(5)**			**A total force of 22 boats is planned.**
Submarine (SSK) – AIP equipped	*Soryu* (SS-501)	6	(5)	2009	4,200	Ongoing production is planned. Improved propulsion in SS-511.
Patrol Submarine (SSK)	*Oyashio* (SS-590)	10	(–)	1998	4,000	One further boat, plus 1 previous SS-583 class boat, used for training.

Other Ships:

Type	Missile Attack Craft	Minehunters	Survey Vessels	Replenishment Ships	
Number	6	27	6	5	Plus various landing ships/craft, support ships, & training vessels.

NAVAL AVIATION

Naval aviation is focused on seven Fleet Air Wings based at the Air Stations of **Kanoya** (Wing 1), **Hachinohe** (Wing 2), **Atsugi** (Wing 4), **Naha** (Wing 5), **Tateyama** (Wing 21), **Omura** (Wing 22) and **Iwakuni** (Wing 31). There is also a major training command at **Shimofusa** and a number of other air bases, including one on **Iwo Jima**. Main front-line aircraft types include:

- P3-C Orion maritime patrol aircraft: c. eighty in service, including some in specialist roles. Being slowly replaced by c. seventy of the new Kawasaki P-1 MPA.
- SH-60J/K anti-submarine helicopters: c. ninety-five in service, of which around half serve in shipboard roles and the other half in coastal defence.
- UH-60J utility helicopters: c. twenty in service, largely in search and rescue roles.
- CH/MCH-101 helicopters: c. fifteen in service or on order for minesweeping and utility roles.

depend, the energy security task is more likely to evolve within the service life of the vessels now entering JMSDF service. Japan's energy mix is likely to evolve over the coming decades and the near complete dependence on Middle Eastern energy sources may not continue, and with it the imperatives to engage in maritime security so far afield. Ongoing recognition of the importance of the relationship with India is likely to keep Japan focussed on both Indian and Pacific regions, but the mix of engagement objectives could change.

An understanding of Japan's maritime relationships cannot be confined to the JMSDF. The Japan Coast Guard is a large and capable organisation, which has led engagement with many South East Asian nations on issues such as piracy and maritime security. More recently, it has been at the forefront of the robust engagement with China over maritime security around disputed offshore islands – the 'grey zone' as Japanese defence planning describes what is also often called the 'salami-slicing' tactics pursued by China to assert its view of its maritime rights. While Japan's Self Defence Forces are building the levels of co-operation between themselves, they will need to include the Japan Coast Guard to enable them to operate as seamlessly as possible across the spectrum of potential operational tasks.

JAPAN'S DEFENCE BUDGET
Spending on defence in Japan has been remarkably consistent over time, showing slow, incremental growth over the last few years when measured in US$, allowing for exchange-rate fluctuations and inflation. The major change in defence spending has been to give greater priority to maritime forces, which has provided the JMSDF with a larger share of the capital budget. It is likely that this will continue for several years to come, underpinning plans for increases in the submarine and surface fleet. The significance of this shift should not be underestimated, particularly in a mature and sophisticated defence organisation such as Japan's. It signifies where Japanese defence planners believe their weight of effort will be concentrated in the medium to long term, and where their strategic centres of gravity face the greatest challenges.

JMSDF PROCUREMENT
Much of the discussion of the JMSDF's most recent acquisitions has focussed on the *Izumo* class ASW carriers, classified as helicopter-carrying destroyers

The JMSDF's *Hyuga* (DDH-181) pictured conducting amphibious operations with the US Navy in September 2014 – a V-22 Osprey tilt-rotor can be seen landing towards the Japanese vessel's stern. Although principally intended for anti-submarine warfare, the two *Hyuga* class vessels – and the larger follow-on design, *Izumo* (DDH-183) – have considerable potential for amphibious warfare and could conceivably be adapted for STOVL fixed-wing jets. *(US Navy)*

(DDH) in Japan. While their Japanese classification clearly reflects their place as part of the JMSDF's anti-submarine capabilities, the *Izumo* class are equally clearly an order of magnitude more capable than the *Shirane* class helicopter destroyers they nominally replace. The *Izumo* class are most accurately classified as a helicopter or ASW carrier, which reflects both their intended use and their more immediate design heritage in the pair of *Hyuga* class ships which preceded them (also euphemistically known as helicopter destroyers in Japanese use). The assessment of the ships as a step toward a fixed-wing aircraft carrier has some self-evident truth; however, that is a long and complicated development path from a pure naval operational perspective, let alone the diplomatic and historical perspective. The lines between a light aircraft carrier, a helicopter carrier and an amphibious assault vessel are not always clear if the physical structure of the vessels is the only determinant. The employment, fit out and capability of the aircraft routinely embarked must be considered to assess the vessels; with this in mind, both the *Hyuga* and *Izumo* class are clearly enhancements to the JMSDF's ASW capability, with obvious potential for amphibious warfare capability, and all the potential flexibility that comes with a substantial organic air wing.

While *Izumo*, which commissioned on 25 March 2015, the same day as *Shirane* decommissioned, has been grabbing most of the attention, the JMSDF's plans to expand their submarine force from sixteen to twenty-two boats has received less public attention. At sixteen boats the JMSDF submarine fleet is already of a similar scale, albeit of quite different composition, to the Russian Pacific Fleet's submarine force; at twenty-two boats it will be greater in numbers at least. With one of the largest fleets of some of the world's most capable conventional submarines, the JMSDF's submarines are a powerful military asset and, alongside its alliance with the United States, Japan's most powerful strategic deterrent. The addition of six boats is a roughly one-third increase in raw numbers and is therefore a much more significant increase in capability than the four *Izumo* and *Hyuga* class vessels, which replaced existing ships on a like-for-like basis.

The JMSDF mine warfare capability, in which submarines could well play a part, is another area which has an impact proportionately greater than the investment or the level of attention. In a similar way to submarines, mine warfare significantly increases the difficulty for China in particular to use military force in a dispute with Japan; without the ability to sweep or hunt, China would risk military action being thwarted in a domain where its burgeoning military has not, yet, demonstrated significant progress.

Japan's ability to quite rapidly scale-up its submarine fleet, with little fuss and, for military hardware at least, relatively small marginal costs, is built on its long-term commitment to a continuous design effort and building programme. Should Japan and China ever come to a military conflict over disputed islands, and leaving to one side any US involvement, the JMSDF's submarine force would be the most significant military problem for the Chinese as submarines would have the capacity to stop a seaborne invasion and make an amphibious lodgement unsustainable. In this sense, Japan's commitment to the current expansion and any future changes to their submarine force are an accurate barometer of Japan's level of military strategic comfort with China.

Along similar lines, the Japan–South Korea relationship is another way of looking at the same subject. The two countries are maritime democracies with huge global trading interests and very similar security interests – their maritime forces have many similarities for this reason, including BMD-capable Aegis destroyers and a large and capable South Korean submarine fleet. Their history and current disputes have meant their military to military co-operation is less intimate than might otherwise be expected. The trajectory of this relationship, both in practice and in the way in which the two countries seek to portray it, will give another good indication of their view of Chinese ambitions.

POTENTIAL IMPACT OF TECHNOLOGICAL CHANGE

At the turn of the nineteenth century, naval technology was on the brink of a period of major and rapid evolution, leading to major changes in surface warship design (the *Dreadnought* revolution, oil-powered turbine-propulsion, wireless communications and gyroscopes), a profusion of complementary warship and aircraft types (submarines, aircraft carriers, destroyers and so on), and consequent changes in naval tactics. All of these changes came in a shorter period of time than the careers of many naval personnel, so the navy they joined and which trained them, was radically different to the navy they left.

Early in the twenty-first century, with directed-

The JMSDF's submarine and mine warfare capabilities have more significance than the amount of attention they have attracted in spite of ongoing investment. This picture shows the launch of the eighth *Soryu* class submarine, *Sekiryu*, on 2 November 2015 and the first *Awaji* class minehunter on 27 October. *(JMSDF)*

energy weapons (lasers and railguns), the expanding influence of the cyber domain, and the increasing number and application of unmanned air, surface and sub-surface vehicles, it is entirely possible that we could experience another period of major and rapid evolution. In many ways the JMSDF is as well placed for such an eventuality as any navy in the world: their close relationship with the US Navy, and their strong industrial base and experience in warship and aircraft design and construction gives the potential for them to innovate or to rapidly follow the innovations of others. The challenge for the JMSDF, along with all established navies, will be how to enable their people to grow beyond the training that characterised their first experiences at sea, to understand and be able to exploit in a tactical and operation sense the capabilities of these new technologies. So the JMSDF's future challenge is one of enduring familiarity: how to have both combat winning equipment and combat winning people – the right technology and the right people and culture.

Notes

1. See *National Defense Program Guidelines for FY2014 and beyond* and the associated *National Security Strategy December 17, 2013* (both Tokyo: Government of Japan, 2013). English translations of both can be found on the President of Japan and His Cabinet's website at http://japan.kantei.go.jp/96_abe/documents/2013/index.html

2. Most notably, there have been numerous reports that the Japanese and Indian governments are in discussion about the latter's potential purchase of ShinMaywa US-2 amphibious search and rescue aircraft.

3. Sources of further reading are plentiful, though observers of the JMSDF writing in English are not as numerous as those for China. Wikipedia is a good first step, not just for the content, but for the bibliographic references, which are the website's most important strength. Defence and international relations think tanks and blogs, such as the United States Naval Institute, the Centre for International and Strategic Studies, the Diplomat, Janes, Information Dissemination and the Lowy Institute all publish content on the JMSDF worth reading.

4.3.4 Jack McCaffrie

REPUBLIC OF KOREA NAVY

Formed in 1948, South Korea's Republic of Korea Navy (ROKN) has only recently emerged as a major regional force with significant blue-water ambitions and capabilities.[1] For much of its early history the ROKN relied on ex-US Navy equipment and focused on local defence needs, especially the threat posed by the Democratic People's Republic of Korea (North Korea). Even as it has turned to local industry for its increasingly capable ships and submarines and has begun to contribute to global maritime security, yet, local concerns continue to demand the navy's attention.

OBJECTIVES & STRATEGY

By the end of the Cold War in the early 1990s the ROKN was still a relatively small force, with a primary operational focus on territorial sea and offshore island defence. The expansion and industri-alisation of the South Korean economy was a major catalyst for change. The growth in manufacturing generated a reliance on imports of raw materials and energy and a corresponding reliance on the export of finished products. Thus the Republic of Korea (South Korea) came to rely on the sea and the secu-rity of its SLOC. Notably, 99.7 per cent of South Korea's imports and exports are moved by sea and the country imports all of its oil.[2] Furthermore, South Korea's industrial development generated both the desire and ability to build its warships locally.

Consequently, from about 1995 there has been a steady upgrading of the ROKN, with the aim of producing a true blue-water navy, primarily for SLOC protection beyond local waters. This emerged from the Defence White Paper of 1994–5 which, inter alia, directed a move towards a policy of 'comprehensive security'. The Navy was helped in this quest, at least indirectly, by the accession in 1993 of South Korea's first civilian president, which reduced the influence on national affairs of the army. The country's trading patterns determined that the most important SLOCs were that between South Korea and China, the sea lane bringing oil from the Middle East, the sea lane supporting trade with the United States and the sea lane with Japan.

Evidence of the ROKN's commitment to blue-water operations and of its broader vision of maritime security exists from the commitment of surface combatants to CTF-151 since 2009. CTF-151 is a multi-national naval force that oper-ates in a counter-piracy role in the waters off Somalia. The ROKN has also begun participating in major international exercises, such as the bien-nial USN-led RIMPAC Exercise based on Hawaii. Force structure development over recent decades

ROKN surface fleet units steam in formation during exercises held in October 2015. The fleet is developing capabilities for expeditionary operations whilst remaining cognisant of the need to maintain littoral security from potential incursions by its northern neighbour. The first three ships in line are, respectively, members of the KDX-III, KDX-II and KDX-I destroyer classes, all intended for blue-water deployment. The fourth ship is an *Incheon* class frigate, designed for littoral operations. *(ROKN)*

4.3.4.1: TRENDS IN REPUBLIC OF KOREA NAVY FLEET STRENGTH

Type	Class	In Service 1990 (On Order)	In Service 2015 (On Order)	Notes
Submarine	Type 209	3 (3)	9	Submarine total does not include midget.
Submarine	Type 214	–	5 (4)	
Destroyer	Sumner	2	–	
Destroyer	Gearing	7	–	
Destroyer	KDX-I	–	3	Planned in 1990 but design work not completed.
Destroyer	KDX-II	–	6	
Destroyer	KDX-III	–	3 (3)	
Frigate	Ulsan	7 (2)	7	Total class of nine, two now decommissioned.
Frigate	Incheon	–	3 (4)	Seven further Batch II ships under order or planned in 2015.
Corvette	Po Hang	22 (4)	18	1990 total includes four similar Dong Hae class.
Mine-warfare	Ex-USN coastal	8	–	
Mine-warfare	Swallow	3 (3)	6	
Mine-warfare	Yang Yang	–	3	
Minelayer	Won San	–	1 (1)	
Fast Attack/Patrol	Various	c.80	c.90	Numbers fluctuating as older types are replaced.
Amphibious – LHD	Dokdo	–	1 (1)	
Amphibious – LST	Various	8	5	Status of two further ex-USN LSTs doubtful as of 2015.
Other Amphibious	Various	23	c.40	
Fleet Replenishment	Chun Jee	– (1)	3	

also provides ample evidence of the ROKN's blue-water ambitions.

Nevertheless, the blue-water ambitions have been tempered with local reality from time to time. Historical tensions between South Korea and its neighbours, together with maritime territorial disputes help to maintain a local security focus. Most of all the unpredictability and aggression of North Korea have concentrated ROKN attention in local waters, especially in recent years. The sinking of the South Korean warship *Cheonan* in March 2010 and the bombardment by North Korea of Yeonpyeong Island in November 2010 indicate that – no matter how much the ROKN has developed in recent years – there are still limits to its capacity to conduct simultaneous operations in widely separated areas.[3]

IMPLICATIONS FOR FORCE STRUCTURE

At the beginning of the 1990s, as the Cold War was coming to an end, the ROKN was transitioning to the blue-water capable navy that it is today. The first of its ocean-going submarines were in service and the Super Lynx anti-submarine helicopter had been ordered. The surface combatant force was also evolving with seven *Ulsan* class frigates and eighteen *Po Hang* class corvettes in service and other new classes planned. New mine-warfare vessels were also being acquired, with three of a planned six *Swallow* class vessels operational.[4]

As shown in Table 4.3.4.1, much of the 'old' navy remained in service as well. The core of the surface combatant force was the mix of two *Sumner* class and seven *Gearing* class destroyers. These were Second World War vintage ships originally operated by the US Navy. Despite their extensive Fleet Rehabilitation and Modernisation (FRAM) upgrades, which optimised the ships for anti-submarine warfare, they had little or no capacity to deal with contemporary air threats.

The destruction of the corvette *Cheonan* in March 2010 as a result of what was concluded to be a torpedo attack by a North Korean submarine demonstrated limitations to the navy's ability to conduct simultaneous operations in separated areas. Unpredictable military activity by North Korea remains the biggest challenge faced by the Republic of Korea Navy and there has been some refocusing back towards littoral warfare as a result of the sinking. This image shows the recovery of the aft part of *Cheonan*'s hull. *(ROKN)*

Naval aviation comprised a fleet of twenty Grumman S2A/F Tracker anti-submarine aircraft and some light unarmed helicopters. The Trackers were nearing the end of their operating lives. Other forces included a gaggle of ex-US Navy landing craft, thirty-one in all. Finally, reflecting the early focus on local coastal security and the threat posed by North Korea, there was a force of about eighty patrol craft, some of which had come from the US Navy.

THE REPUBLIC OF KOREA NAVY TODAY

Turning to the present, the ROKN is a force of about 40,000 personnel and 200 ships. There is also a 27,000-strong Marine Corps. Under the Chief of Naval Operations, the ROKN organisation comprises Navy Headquarters, Operations Command and Marine Corps Command. Under the *Defense Reform 2020* programme, it is evolving at the operational level into three fleet commands,

together with a submarine command, a naval aviation command and a manoeuvre combat group. The three fleets have responsibility for the East and Yellow Seas as well as the Korea Strait. By 2015 the ROKN, therefore, reflects the national, ambition to create a blue-water navy that also remains capable of maintaining local coastal security.

One of the most significant developments has been the expansion of the submarine force to

4.3.4.2: SOUTH KOREA – REPUBLIC OF KOREA NAVY COMPOSITION END 2015

MAJOR BASES & STRUCTURE

Busan, Metropolitan City:	Fleet Headquarters, Maritime Task Flotilla (blue-water operations) squadron.
Jinhae, S. Gyeonsang Province:	Korean Naval Academy, Naval Education & Training Command, Naval Logistics Command, Maritime Task Flotilla (blue-water operations) squadron.
Dongae, Gangwon Province:	First Fleet (littoral operations; eastern naval sector).
Pyongtaek, Gyeonggi Province:	Second Fleet (littoral operations, western naval sector).
Mokpo, S. Jeolla Province:	Third Fleet (littoral operations, southern naval sector).

It is anticipated the Maritime Task Flotilla will relocate to a controversial new base at **Jeju Island** when construction is completed around the end of 2015. Smaller bases include those at **Incheon** (protection of the Seoul littoral under the Second Fleet) and **Pohang** (amphibious shipping).

PERSONNEL

c. 40,000 sailors and 27,000 marines of which c. 20,000 conscripts. Additional reserves.

MAJOR WARSHIPS

Type	Class	In-Service	Ordered	ISD	Tonnage	Notes
Major Amphibious Warships:		1	(1)			
Amphibious Assault Ship (LHD)	*Dokdo*	1	(1)	2007	18,900	At least one further ship planned.
Surface Escorts (Blue Water):		12	(3)			
Destroyer (DDG)	*Sejongdaewang-Ham*	3	(3)	2008	10,000	KDX-III. Aegis-equipped. Batch II ships to a modified design.
Destroyer (DDG)	*Chungmugong Yi Sun Shin*	6	(–)	2003	5,500	KDX-II.
Destroyer (DDG)	*Gwanggaeto-Daewang*	3	(–)	1998	3,900	KDX-I.
Surface Escorts (Littoral):		28	(4)			
Frigate (FFG)	FFX-II	–	(1)	(2016)	3,000	Seven more FFX-II ships planned plus an additional FFX-III. batch
Frigate (FFG)	*Incheon*	3	(3)	2013	3,000	FFX-I.
Frigate (FFG)	*Ulsan*	7	(–)	1981	2,300	One decommissioned. To be replaced by *Incheon* class.
Corvette (FSG)	*Po Hang*	18	(–)	1984	1,200	Five decommissioned; one sunk.
Submarines:		14	(5)			
Submarine (SSK) AIP-equipped	KSS-III	–	(2)	(2022)	c.3,000	A total class of nine planned. To replace Type 209 boats.
Submarine (SSK) AIP-equipped	*Son Won-II* (Type 214)	5	(4)	2007	1,300	KSS-II. Licence-built in South Korea.
Patrol Submarine (SSK)	*Chang Bogo* (Type 209)	9	(–)	1993	1,300	KSS-I. Licence-built in South Korea.

Other Ships:

Type	Missile Attack Craft	Patrol Vessels	Minehunters	Replenishment Ships	
Number	17	c.70	9	3	Plus various landing ships/craft, support ships, & training vessels.

NAVAL AVIATION

Naval aviation bases are located at Jinhae, Pohang and Jeju. Main front-line aircraft types include:

■ P3-C Orion maritime patrol aircraft: c. fifteen in service, including some in specialist roles.

■ Westland Lynx anti-submarine helicopters: c. twenty-five in service. Being supplemented/replaced by eight AW159 Wildcat.

■ UH-60 Blackhawk utility helicopters: c. ten in service. To be replaced by indigenous KUH-1 Surion.

include some of the most advanced ocean-going diesel boats in the world – the German-designed Type 214 – together with a number of mini-submarines suited especially to local waters. The Type 214s have AIP, enabling them to remain submerged, without snorting, for up to two weeks. Nevertheless as events in August 2015 highlighted, North Korea's Navy, the Korean People's Navy (KPN) has a much larger force of primarily smaller submarines which would challenge the ROKN's anti-submarine capacity in any crisis or conflict.[5]

The ROKN's aim to become a blue-water navy is also seen clearly in three other elements of the fleet's development; viz. surface combatants, amphibious shipping and replenishment capability. The cornerstone of the surface fleet is the growing force of *Sejongdaewang-Ham* (KDX-III) destroyers. Larger than the US Navy's *Ticonderoga* class cruisers and incorporating their Aegis combat system, these impressive ships are heavily armed for air, surface and anti-submarine warfare. Their 128 vertical-launch cells house a range of surface-to-air, anti-submarine and cruise missiles, while other armament includes a 5in gun, torpedo tubes and two anti-submarine helicopters. Currently, these ships can track but not engage ballistic missiles. They are supported by the older, less capable but still well-armed KDX-II and KDX-I destroyers. The *Incheon* class frigates, replacing the veteran *Ulsan* and *Po Hang* classes, are primarily intended for coastal operations but also incorporate a 5in gun and surface-to-surface missiles.

Today's ROKN also has a significant patrol force, now approaching a hundred craft of several classes, some missile armed and all responsible for coastal security. Mine-warfare does not have a prominent place in the ROKN force structure, comprising nine mine-countermeasures vessels and one (soon to be two) minelayers.[6] This might seem surprising, especially given the shallow waters around Korea's coast, but few of the world's navies have really substantial mine-warfare forces, despite the vulnerability of merchant shipping to mining threats.

ROKN amphibious capability was expanded with the introduction of the first *Dokdo* class amphibious assault ship (LHD) in 2007. At least two more of these ships are planned, of which one is already under construction. Each is capable of carrying 700 troops, ten UH-60B helicopters and two large landing craft. Some forty-seven other landing craft, including five tank landing ships, round out the force, which

supports the 27,000-strong marines. With the *Dokdo* class ship(s) in particular, the ROKN now has the capacity to contribute robustly to humanitarian aid or disaster relief operations as well as to land a significant ground force for a military operation.[7]

Finally, with the acquisition of three replenishment ships, the ROKN has gained the capacity to conduct extended surface ship deployments without undue reliance on logistics support from other navies or in foreign ports. The presence of these three replenishment ships should ensure that the ROKN could support one or two deployed task groups at any one time.

THE ROKN INTO THE FUTURE

In its quest to become a blue-water navy, the ROKN has acknowledged the reality that the most important maritime security challenges it faces are local. Unpredictable military action by North Korea is the most readily visible aspect of this, while occasionally frosty relations with Japan and China are other manifestations. This situation is unlikely to change in the foreseeable future.

The ROKN's primary operational challenge for the future will be maintaining the ability to counter any North Korean maritime activities or operations aimed at the South. The worst-case scenario for the ROKN would involve the political collapse of the North, in which case ROKN amphibious and patrol forces would be stretched. This would be particularly so if the ROKN had to manage without assistance from allied or friendly countries. In having to counter the KPN the ROKN already has achieved a qualitative advantage, but with respect to submarines it lags in numbers. Indeed, the recently-reported deployment of more than fifty KPN submarines, if replicated in a crisis, would challenge all of the ROKN's anti-submarine forces – submarine, surface and air.

South Korea is trying to strengthen relations with China, which are currently focused on economic activity. Moves to establish deeper military links between the two countries have not yet led to anything more tangible than exchange visits. While China continues to support the North, defence co-operation with South Korea will remain limited and there will always be the potential for tension between the two countries. Long-standing tensions

South Korea's third KDX-III type Aegis-equipped destroyer, *Seoae Ryu Seong-ryong*, pictured in waters off the Dokdo Islands in August 2015. Currently the cornerstone of the blue-water surface fleet, they will be joined by a further three modified ships of the class over the next decade. *(ROKN)*

The Republic of Korea Navy's LHD-type amphibious assault ship *Dokdo* pictured at sea in March 2014. A further member of the class is currently under construction and at least one other is planned. An outstanding question is whether they will be modified to operate F-35B Joint Strike Fighters. *(US Navy)*

Capable ASW forces will also be a vital part of the future force structure, with ongoing consideration given to countering the large number of admittedly less sophisticated North Korean submarines. Finally, the existing emphasis on capable and well-armed patrol forces will need to be maintained to deal with the KPN's own numerous coastal forces, as well as the ongoing potential for maritime disputes with Japan or China.

CONCLUSION

Over the last three decades the ROKN has developed into a powerful regional navy, qualitatively the equal of its neighbours although still smaller than the navies of China and Japan. During that time, South Korea's industrial and economic development has both enabled and demanded the ROKN's transition into a blue-water force. Thus, today the ROKN is a well-balanced force able both to protect distant SLOCs and provide security in coastal waters.

Nevertheless, the ROKN's blue-water ambitions have been tempered by the demands of local maritime security, driven especially by the unpredictable nature of North Korea's leadership. The likelihood that North Korea will continue to provide security challenges, together with the probability that other local maritime disputes will remain unresolved, suggests that tension between local and blue-water operations will continue. Consequently, the ROKN will strive to maintain submarine, surface and air forces with the flexibility needed to respond to a broad range of potential challenges and threats.

between South Korea and Japan will also continue to hamper the development of closer defence ties between them. As an example, a recently formulated intelligence-sharing agreement among Japan, South Korea and the United States excludes direct sharing between Japan and the South – any intelligence will pass from one to the other through United States' authorities.[8]

Thus, the tension between blue-water and local security demands will continue to complicate ROKN force development into the future and procurement plans will very likely reflect this.[9] More

to the point, deployment plans will continue to reflect that reality.

Some of the force structure issues that will demand resolution include the fitting of ballistic missile interception capability to the KDX-III class, including in the planned second batch of ships to be delivered in the 2020s. Another important consideration will be whether all of the mooted *Dokdo* class amphibious assault ships are built and whether fixed-wing aircraft such as the F-35 Joint Strike Fighter could operate from them or – as is possibly more likely – from a larger successor.

Notes

1. See Vice Admiral Yoji Koda, JMSDF (Rtd), 'The Emerging Republic of Korea Navy: A Japanese Perspective', *Naval War College Review* – Spring 2010, Vol. 63 No.2 (Newport, RI: US Naval War College, 2010), p.15. The ROKN began as the Maritime Affairs Association in August 1945, subsequently became the Korean Coast Guard and, in August 1948, became the ROKN.

2. Ian Bowers, 'The Republic of Korea and its Navy: Perceptions of Security and the Utility of Seapower', *Journal of Strategic Studies,* Vol. 37, No. 3 (London: Routledge, 2014), p.445.

3. For further analysis of these two incidents see Captain Duk-ki Kim ROKN, 'The Republic of Korea's Counter-Asymmetric Strategy: lessons from ROKS *Cheonan* and Yeonpyeong Island', *Naval War College Review* - Winter 2012, Vol. 65, No. 1 (Newport, RI: US Naval War College,

2010), p.55.

4. Data from Captain Richard Sharpe, RN, editor, *Jane's Fighting Ships 1990–1* (Coulsdon: Jane's Information Group, 1990). The *Swallows* were a local derivative of the Italian *Lerici* class.

5. See Franz-Stefan Gady, 'North Korea is deploying largest Submarine Fleet Since Korean War', *The Diplomat* – 24 August 2015 at: http://thediplomat.com/2015/08/ north-korea-is-deploying-largest-submarine-fleet-since-korean-war/. The article refers to the deployment of over fifty KPN submarines in response to rising tensions with the South.

6. On the other hand, the Korean Coast Guard does have thirty-seven salvage ships.

7. The ROKN has learned from its lack of capacity to

respond to the 1004 South East Asian tsunami. See 'The Emerging Republic of Korea Navy: A Japanese Perspective', *op. cit.*, p. 25.

8. See Clint Wark, 'Korea and the New Regional Paradigm', *The Diplomat* – 24 April 2015 at: http://thediplomat. com/2015/04/korea-and-the-new-regional-paradigm/

9. See Mingi Hyun, 'South Korea's Blue-water Ambitions', *The Diplomat* – 18 November 2010. http://thediplomat. com/2010/11/south-koreas-blue-water-ambitions/

10. Other reading sources consulted for this chapter include Kyle Mizokami's 'Two Koreas, Three Navies', *USNI News* – 8 May 2014 at: http://news.usni.org/2014/04/ 08/two-koreas-three-navies; *The Military Balance 2015* (London: The International Institute of Strategic Studies, 2015) and various editions of *Jane's Fighting Ships*.

4.4

INDIAN OCEAN, MIDDLE EAST & AFRICA

Although it is the Asian navies that have seen most expansion in their overall capabilities since the end of the Cold War, it is arguably the Indian Ocean and Middle East that has seen most operational naval activity during this period. The wars against the former Saddam Hussein regime in Kuwait and Iraq, the problem of broader instability in the Middle East most recently marked by the abortive 'Arab Spring', and the scourge of piracy off the Horn of Africa following the collapse of centralised government in Somalia have all served to make the region something of a magnet for naval forces. Underlying this interest has been the Indian Ocean's geographical position as a focal point of key sea lines of communication between Asia and Europe. The security of vital Middle Eastern energy supplies to the growing Asian economies, as well as of their exports of manufactured goods to European consumers, are equally vulnerable to disruption of these vital maritime arteries.

With the major exception of India – which has increasingly been using its navy as a key means of ensuring both stability and the maintenance of national interests across the Indian Ocean – it is notable that much of this naval activity has been conducted by external naval powers. The most significant of these is inevitably the US Navy, which stepped into the vacuum created by the run-down of British military forces in the region in the 1960s. France – with ongoing territorial responsibilities in the region – has also been an enduring naval presence. However, Britain never totally abandoned its interests in the region and has maintained significant

4.4.0: INDIAN OCEAN, MIDDLE EASTERN & AFRICAN FLEET STRENGTHS – 2015

COUNTRY	SHIP TYPE													
	Aircraft Carriers & Amphibious				Submarines			Surface Combatants				Other (Selected)		
	CV	CVS	LHA/D	LPD/SD	SSBN	SSN	SSK	DDG	FFG	FSG/FS	FAC	OPV	MCMV	AOR
India	2	–	–	1	–	1	13	10	14	10	12	10	6	4
Bangladesh	–	–	–	–	–	–	–	–	1	9	c.10	c.10	5	–
Myanmar	–	–	–	–	–	–	–	–	3	4	c.15	–	–	–
Pakistan	–	–	–	–	–	–	5	–	10	–	8	–	3	2
Egypt	–	–	–	–	–	–	[4]	–	7	4	c.30	–	c.14	–
Iran	–	–	–	–	–	–	3	–	–	8	c.25	–	–	1
Israel	–	–	–	–	–	–	5	–	–	3	8	–	–	–
Oman	–	–	–	–	–	–	–	–	–	5	4	3	–	–
Saudi Arabia	–	–	–	–	–	–	–	–	7	4	9	–	7	2
United Arab Emirates	–	–	–	–	–	–	–	–	–	4	10	–	2	–
Algeria	–	–	–	1	–	–	4	–	1	6	c.12	–	–	–
Morocco	–	–	–	–	–	–	–	–	1	6	4	1	–	–
Nigeria	–	–	–	–	–	–	–	–	[1]	4	3	4	[2]	–
South Africa	–	–	–	–	–	–	3	–	4	–	3	–	4	1

Notes:
Numbers are based on official sources where available, supplemented by news reports, published intelligence data and other 'open' sources as appropriate. Given significant variations in available data, numbers and classifications should be regarded as indicative, particularly with respect to minor warships. SSK numbers do not include midget submarines. FAC category includes missile-armed craft only. Numbers in brackets relate to ships of limited operational capability.

naval forces in the Persian Gulf since the start of the 1980s. These countries have been the major components in a growing coalition of Western navies committed initially to safeguarding navigation in the strategic Straits of Hormuz against a perceived Iranian threat but whose role has steadily expanded into counter-terrorism and piracy activities. The European Union's Operation 'Atalanta' – launched at the end of 2008 – marked a significant expansion of that organisation's activities in the military sphere.

Perhaps unsurprisingly given the region's significance to their trade, the emerging Asian fleets have also been using the Indian Ocean as the backdrop to their entry onto the international maritime stage. The unbroken presence of a series of Chinese PLAN escort task groups in the Indian Ocean on anti-piracy duties since early 2009 has been the most significant development in this regard. However, countries such as Japan, Malaysia, Singapore and South Korea have also been making their presence felt. It is interesting to speculate the extent to which this upsurge in naval activity has had a significant impact on the pirate threat. Whilst piracy in the region has certainly declined to minimal levels, it is arguable that progress made in rebuilding organised government on the ground have been at least as influential as the enhanced naval presence. Equally, many analysts believe that the need to combat piracy has acted as a cloak to disguise the real interests of countries, such as China, for expanding their regional naval presence.

The rather limited ambitions of local naval forces across the region can be attributed to a variety of factors. These include the priority given to land-based warfare in much of the Middle East and the lack of financial resources across much of Africa. Beyond India, a few navies – including those of Iran and Pakistan – have developed meaningful A2/AD capabilities – in the face of the potential threat posed by more powerful maritime adversaries. However, the overall result has been a predominance of forces with only marginal capabilities beyond the protection of major ports and key coastal interests. This is particularly the case throughout Sub-Saharan Africa. Here it is only South Africa that has any meaningful deployable naval capability.

It is, however, worth noting that the connected influences of enlarged maritime economic zones and a greater appreciation of the potential benefits of exploiting the resources that are contained within them are spurring the creation of more-effective

The South African Navy MEKO A-200 frigate *Spioenkop* on exercises with the Royal Australian Navy in 2005. At this time, the South African frigate's main armament had not been fitted. South Africa is the only country in Sub-Saharan Africa that has any meaningful deployable naval capability. *(RAN)*

naval constabulary forces, albeit from quite a low base. This has been particularly the case in West Africa, which has overtaken the Indian Ocean as a focal point for pirate activity. A number of programmes are underway to provide expanded maritime policing capabilities that range from quite simple patrol craft to reasonably sophisticated corvettes. The growing availability of reasonably-priced vessels from Chinese and other Asian yards is assisting this process. Nigeria has been a notable recipient of Chinese technical assistance, redeveloping naval facilities at Port Harcourt with the aim of being able both to maintain and, potentially, assemble ships of corvette size and above.

No analysis of African naval developments would be complete without reference to the apparent arms race across much of the North African coastline that has seen several navies acquire relatively sophisticated capabilities. Leading the charge has been Algeria, which is reinforcing a navy of largely Soviet-origin equipment with new frigates of German and Chinese origin, as well as additional 'Kilo' class submarines. The 'icing on the cake' is the new

amphibious transport dock *Kalaat Béni Abbès*, an Italian-built derivative of the *San Giorgio* class design which incorporates a powerful area air-defence capability based on an EMPAR radar and Aster surface-to-air missiles. There has to be some doubt as to how easy it will be to mould a navy equipped with such disparate equipment into a cohesive force.

Algeria's investment has certainly been noted by other regional fleets, which have also been building up their own capabilities. Egypt has largely turned to France to assist its own expansion plans, which encompass the two *Mistral* class amphibious assault ships released by the collapse of the deal with Russia, a FREMM-type frigate and 'Gowind' corvettes. Germany is also supplying Type 209 submarines. Morocco's acquisitions, whilst less extensive, have included its own FREMM, three Damen 'Sigma' series light frigates and modernised offshore patrol vessels. There has to be some question over the merits of much of this considerable investment in the absence of any immediate requirement for such sophisticated ships.

4.4.1

INDIAN OCEAN NAVIES

Since 1947, successive governments of the Republic of India have consistently and deliberately rejected formal alliances with other powers. This policy of non-alignment has had a significant impact on the Indian Navy's development, as it has not been able to specialise in any particular role (e.g. as the British Royal Navy focused on anti-submarine warfare in the later stages of the Cold War) and rely on allies to pick up other operational needs. According to retired Indian Admiral Pradeep Chauhan, this has resulted in a need to strive for balance in a number of areas, notably between investment in surface, underwater, aviation and – recently – cyber capabilities, as well as between 'blue-water' and 'brown-water' force structures. This need for balance has also extended to combat-capabilities at sea and onshore support.

Another notable aspect of the Indian Navy's (IN's) development has been a need to struggle for resources against the needs of the army and air force. Although the 1962 military debacle against China spurred higher defence expenditure, it was the army that was the main immediate beneficiary. However, the navy almost doubled in size in the second half of the 1960s and played a major and successful role in the 1971 India-Pakistan War. Spurred on by this experience – and also the entry of the US Navy's Task Force 74 into the Bay of Bengal in a show of support for a beleaguered Pakistan – the IN continued its expansion in the latter half of the Cold War. Helped by Soviet largesse in the form of a windfall of increasingly sophisticated hardware at 'friendship' prices, the IN grew to become the locally dominant fleet with significant 'blue water' potential. 1990 force levels peaked at over 150 ships, including two light carriers, nineteen submarines and sixteen frontline surface escorts, all supported by a credible naval aviation component.

Regrettably, New Delhi's lack of transparency in explaining this build-up, coupled with India's official 'non-aligned' stance but close relations with the Soviet Union, saw the navy being perceived through pink-tinted spectacles in the West. This suspicion was exacerbated by the proactive approach adopted by India's young Prime Minister Rajiv Gandhi during the 1980s. This saw military interventions in the Maldives and Sri Lanka that – despite the support of the relevant governments – caused unease about India's possible long-term hegemonic ambitions in the region. These perceptions would only change from the 1990s onwards as the IN emerged from relative isolation within the context of India's re-evaluation of its geopolitical relationships in the fast changing, multi-polar new world order that emerged in the post-Cold War age. Ultimately this re-evaluation would also strengthen the IN's national importance as maritime concerns became increasingly important to India's overall security. Again according to Admiral Chauhan, a key part of this process was the IN's effort to provide an intellectual and doctrinal foundation upon which the IN's future structure could be built.

The Project 61ME modified 'Kashin' class destroyer *Ranvijay* seen operating off the headquarters of India's Eastern Naval Command at Visakhapatnam in September 2015. The Indian Navy expanded rapidly in both quantitative and qualitative terms in the latter half of the Cold War, assisted by transfer of equipment from the Soviet Union. *(RAN)*

DEVELOPMENTS SINCE THE END OF THE COLD WAR

The decade immediately following the end of the Cold War was marked by several important developments for the IN, not all of them positive. More specifically:

- Force levels declined to a low of around eighty per cent of the 1990 peak as a lack of orders attributable to the Asian financial crisis coincided with the block obsolescence of ships acquired during the previous build-up.
- There were major difficulties keeping Soviet-supplied platforms operational. The collapse of the centrally-controlled but regionally dispersed Soviet military supply chain had disastrous operational consequences for all the Indian armed forces, which struggled to obtain supplies of spares until some order was gradually restored. The Soviet largesse during the Cold War came at a price, as noted by former Indian Chief of Naval Staff Admiral Arun Prakash, 'Through this display of fraternal altruism, Soviet admirals were not just acquiring influence and leverage for Moscow, but also binding India to the USSR for the lifetime of every weapons system sold.'[1]
- The early 1990s saw a lack of funding which was slowly resolved as increased liberalisation improved Indian economic growth. During the period of financial difficulties, the IN focused on acquiring capabilities and sought to 'right size' its force structure with fewer but more capable platforms than it had previously possessed.
- There was a slow, if sporadic, trend towards a greater alignment of political views with the IN's perspective of the importance of the sea for India's security and prosperity. There was also growing political appreciation of the IN's potential as an instrument of statecraft.
- The IN shed its inward perspective, helping to correct earlier misperceptions through increased engagement in naval diplomacy from 1991 onwards. Crucially it led to engagement with the United States through tentative low level 'passexs' with the US Navy. These led to the Malabar Exercises, which remain the most complex foreign naval exercises the IN engages in.

From the late 1990s onwards – and particularly into the new millennium – the IN's fortunes steadily improved on the back of higher funding and – more recently – a strengthening of the civil-naval consensus of the importance of the sea. Underlying reasons for this have included the increased reliance of India's liberalised economy on international

The Russian-built Indian Navy Project 1135.6 *Talwar* class frigate *Tabar* operating with the RAN's *Anzac* in March 2005. Although India has consistently rejected formal alliances with other powers, co-operation with like-minded navies in the Indian Ocean region is increasing. *(RAN)*

trade, leading to a greater appreciation of the need to protect its sea lines of communication. The vulnerabilities within India's coastal security architecture made painfully visible by the Mumbai terrorist attacks have also had significant influence. Most recently, China's growing presence and overlapping aspirations in the Indian Ocean have become an increasing source of concern. The pace of development of China's PLAN has been nothing short of astonishing, leaving the IN in danger of falling behind in capacity and capability. The possibility of some kind of confrontation in the future is becoming more real with time. Of course, India's economic growth has served as a catalyst to free up adequate funds to make expansion possible. The IN's budget has expanded substantially in real terms since the mid-1990s and has also taken a moderately higher proportion of the overall defence budget over time.

In practical terms, higher funding levels have served to halt rather than reverse the previous decline in fleet numbers, although this also ignores a significant qualitative improvement. This has coincided with significant enhancements to aviation capabilities and an improved support infrastructure, for example, the launch of a dedicated naval 'communications' and surveillance satellite, GSAT-7, in August 2013. In spite of stabilised force levels around the 140-ship mark, the IN retains ambitions to expand to a 200-ship force within the next decade.

The IN has continued to focus on naval diplomacy; it holds regular navy-to-navy staff talks with over twenty countries and conducts bilateral or multilateral exercises with ten or more. These numbers are increasing as the navy builds 'bridges of friendship' across the seas. An example of the success of this work is the growing relationship with Myanmar, which signalled its emergence from nearly forty-years of isolation by sending a corvette to the Indian-sponsored MILAN exercises in 2006.

The IN's operational footprint also keeps increasing, including deployments to Europe, Russia, the Mediterranean, and the Pacific – the latter for RIMPAC 2014. Within the last decade, the IN has also engaged in non-combatant evacuation operations in Lebanon (2006), Libya (2011), Iraq – from Kuwait (2014) and Yemen (2015), as well as several humanitarian assistance and disaster relief operations, most notably cyclone relief missions. The scope and tempo of operations has also been increased by anti-piracy efforts off the Horn of Africa and in the Indian EEZ since late 2008.

INDIAN NAVAL DOCTRINE & STRATEGY

Possibly reflecting a need to avoid becoming a 'Cinderella' to the very real land-based requirements of the Indian Army and Indian Air Force, the IN is often regarded as the most strategically-minded of the Indian armed services.[2] The development of Indian naval doctrine and strategy has been assisted by the establishment, early in the new millennium, of a Directorate of Strategy Concepts and Transformation, as well as a quasi-official think-tank, the National Maritime Foundation. Around the same time – in 2004 – the navy published its first official doctrinal statement – the *Indian Maritime Doctrine* – using language not dissimilar to that found in similar US Navy and NATO documents. An initially classified strategy document – *Freedom to Use the Seas: India's Maritime Military Strategy* – followed in 2006. It was published the following year.

Both documents, which place the navy's roles, missions, objectives, operational posture and acquisition policies into a geostrategic perspective, have subsequently been revised. The most recent version of the *Indian Maritime Doctrine* was released in

The Indian Navy aircraft carriers *Viraat* and *Vikramaditya* pictured at sea together with surface escorts at the time of the latter's first arrival in Indian waters in January 2014. The two carriers form the core of the Indian Navy's surface fleet but the veteran *Viraat* will be withdrawn from service in 2016. *(Indian Navy)*

2009, whilst the strategic guidance was updated as *Ensuring Secure Seas: India's Maritime Military Strategy* in 2015.[3] The latest guidance serves to complement current Indian Premier Narendra Modi's four part-framework for the Indian Ocean. Articulated earlier in 2015, this encompasses, (i) the defence of India's maritime territory and interests, (ii) strengthening economic and security co-operation with maritime neighbours, (iii) promoting collective peace and security, and (iv) the achievement of an integrated and co-operative framework for future maritime development.

In general terms, the maritime doctrine lays down the principles governing the intended use of maritime military power, detailing the four basic roles – military, diplomatic, constabulary and benign – that the IN is expected to perform. The strategy provides the contextual framework for employment of maritime forces over a medium term timeframe and is, possibly, more reflective of immediate concerns.

The latest strategic document – in common with previous publications – outlines India's main areas of maritime interest. As might be expected given the IN's enhanced, nodal role in ensuring littoral security in the aftermath of the 2008 Mumbai attacks, it also deals extensively with coastal and offshore constabulary tasks. Whilst it appears no adversaries are specifically named, the influence of China and its links with India's old adversary, Pakistan, are a clear underlying theme. Analysts given access to the as-yet restricted document have, inevitably, reached different conclusions as to its significance. However, long-standing commentator on Indian maritime affairs, Rahul Roy-Chaudhury, suggests that five key elements are of particular note:[4]

- The extent of the areas of Indian maritime interest defined in previous doctrinal and strategic documents have been expanded, with primary interests now encompassing areas such as the Red Sea and Mozambique Channel.
- The importance attached to India being a 'net security provider' to island states in the Indian Ocean is re-emphasised. This would appear to reflect a desire to counter potential Chinese influence, thereby shaping a 'favourable and positive maritime environment'.

The long-awaited arrival of new Project 15A destroyers – lead ship *Kolkata* is pictured here – and Project 17 frigates is allowing the Indian Navy to withdraw older ships. *(Indian Navy)*

- There is official confirmation that the navy plans to develop three carrier battle groups and to be able to deploy two carrier task forces of one or more carrier groups.
- The importance of a punitive nuclear retaliatory capability – for which the *Arihant* class strategic submarines are being developed – is stressed.
- Particular emphasis is placed on strengthening the international legal maritime regime, particularly the United Nations Convention on the Law of the Sea (UNCLOS).

The level of political support for the new strategy was indicated by its release – for the first time – by the Indian defence minister, Manohar Parrikar. The document was subsequently discussed at a combined commanders' conference hosted by Prime Minister Modi onboard the newly-acquired carrier *Vikramaditya*. Whether the consistent investment – and other changes – needed over time to realise the strategy's aims will be forthcoming is, of course, an open question.

CURRENT FORCE STRUCTURE & ORGANISATION

The Indian Navy's current structure is outlined in Table 4.4.1.1. In total, there are nearly 140 warships and submarines currently in commission, of which around fifty can be considered principal combatants. The average age of the fleet is approaching nineteen years, with around a fifth of the fleet past the upper end of a warship's typical lifespan of thirty years. The warships are supported by around a hundred tugs and service craft, whilst there are nearly a further hundred fast interceptors in the *Sagar Prahari Bal* (SPB) force protection unit.

At the core of the fleet are the two carriers *Viraat* (the former Royal Navy *Hermes*) and *Vikramaditya* (the former Russian *Admiral Gorshkov*). The former is at the end of her service life and will be withdrawn – along with her few remaining Sea Harriers – in 2016. Conversely, *Vikramaditya* was only handed over in 2013 after a long refurbishment in Russia. Delays in completing the first indigenous carrier, *Vikrant*, mean that it is unlikely to be much before the end of the decade before a two-carrier fleet is regained.

The surface fleet has ten destroyers and fourteen frigates in service, with the delayed arrival of new indigenous Project 15A and Project 17 types allowing some older, steam-powered frigates to be

The Indian Navy's flagship *Vikramaditya* pictured at sea in February 2015 with Mig-29K strike fighters embarked. In spite of well-publicised challenges, the Indian Navy has made considerable progress in building a balanced force able to secure the country's maritime interests in the Indian Ocean region. *(Sitanshu Kar/Indian Ministry of Defence)*

withdrawn.[5] This process has been assisted by the purchase of a second batch of three Russian-built *Talwar* class frigates that arrived in 2012–13. Future construction will be focused on domestic yards, concentrating on the follow-on Project 15B and Project 17A designs. Given the previous performance of local shipyards, it would be surprising if these were to make a meaningful contribution to force levels before the mid-2020s. Delays have also impacted the first batch of Project 28 *Kamorta* class corvettes. Only two of an initial batch of four have been delivered so far.

Current submarine programmes are focused on licenced construction of the French 'Scorpène' design. Six have been ordered to date and a second batch may follow. The nine remaining 'Kilo' class boats – *Sindhurakshak* was destroyed in 2013 – that form the core of the current underwater flotilla have been given life extensions to keep them operational but replacements are badly needed. More positively, the arrival of the 'Akula II' class attack submarine

Chakra from Russia in 2012 is allowing the IN to regain experience operating nuclear submarines and pave the way for the new strategic submarines currently under construction.

Structurally, the IN is divided into two operational commands: the Western Naval Command with its Western Fleet headquartered in Mumbai and the Eastern Naval Command with its Eastern Fleet headquartered in Visakhapatnam (Vizag). Assets are almost equally divided between the two fleets although the Western Fleet is slightly larger. The Kochi-based Southern Command is the training command responsible for all training units and establishments along with some aviation and secondary afloat assets.

The principal west coast bases are at Mumbai and a new facility at Karwar, near Goa. The latter facility – constructed under Project Seabird – can already accommodate around twenty ships and has a major maintenance facility and ship-lift. It is steadily being expanded with the addition of further berths, weapons preparation and storage facilities, as well as a naval air station. A major factor determining this substantial investment programme was to avoid the security and congestion issues faced by Mumbai's status as a busy commercial port by building a dedicated naval facility. Vizag, the main base of the Eastern Fleet, is home to over thirty warships and submarines including both nuclear boats. A new base – reportedly with underground facilities for India's nascent strategic submarine fleet and aircraft carrier berthing – is being built at Rambili, south of Vizag, under Project Varsha, although details are sparse. According to senior naval officials, the base is expected to be ready in the early 2020s.

In addition to Kochi, there are also a number of smaller but important facilities at mainland loca-tions such as Kolkata, Chennai, Goa and Okha. The main island facility is at Port Blair in the Andaman and Nicobar Islands, which is currently home to around fifteen patrol vessels and landing craft but due for significant expansion. Port Blair is also the Headquarters of the Andaman and Nicobar Command – India's only tri-service formation.

The IN's progress over recent years is highlighted by the recent delivery of *Vikramaditya* and her air group, as well as the long-awaited arrival of the indigenous Project 15A, Project 17 and Project 28 surface escorts. There have also been less immedi-ately apparent improvements in areas such as network-centricity, whilst the pending commis-sioning of the ballistic missile-armed submarine *Arihant* is clearly a significant strategic development.

Major current weaknesses that need to be overcome include the run-down of the conventional subma-rine fleet and a similar reduction in mine-counter-measures capabilities. There is also a critical lack of shipborne sea control and utility helicopters, whilst replenishment assets are insufficient to sustain longer range deployments in spite of recent improve-ments. A series of operational mishaps, most notably the loss of *Sindhurakshak* to an internal explosion in 2013, suggests deficiencies in training and proce-dures that will need to be rectified.

FUTURE DEVELOPMENT PLANS
In line with the importance of achieving balanced forces outlined at the start of this chapter, IN devel-opment plans aim to achieve the expansion of both

4.4.1.1: INDIA –INDIAN NAVY COMPOSITION END 2015

MAJOR BASES & STRUCTURE

The fleet is divided as follows:

Western Naval Command: The largest command. Headquartered in **Mumbai** with another major base at Karwar and significant support facilities in Goa, Okha and Porbandar.
Eastern Naval Command: The other main operational command. Headquartered in **Visakhapatnam,** with support facilities at Chennai and Kolkata. A major base is planned near Rambilli.
Southern Naval Command: This is the main training command. Headquartered at **Kochi** with significant support facilities in Lakshadweep and elsewhere.

In general terms, a number of air stations and support facilities tend to be clustered around the major bases, with the other support facilities being used as forward operating bases. There is also a Tri-Service theatre command in the **Andaman and Nicobar Islands** that incorporates a significant naval component.

PERSONNEL

c.60,000 uniformed personnel, including a small marine Special Forces contingent of less than 1,000. c.50,000 civilian employees.

MAJOR WARSHIPS

Type	Class	In-Service	Ordered	ISD	Tonnage	Notes
Aircraft Carriers:		2	(1)			
Aircraft Carrier (CV)	*Vikrant*	–	(1)	(c.2018)	40,000 tons	Indigenous carrier. ISD may be delayed. Further carriers planned.
Aircraft Carrier (CV)	*Vikramaditya* (P 1143.4 *Gorshkov*)	1	(–)	1987	45,000 tons	Former Soviet STOVL carrier. Converted to STOBAR – ISD 2013.
Aircraft Carrier (CV)	*Viraat* (*Hermes*)	1	(–)	1959	29,000 tons	Acquired from British Royal Navy 1986. To be withdrawn 2016.
Major Amphibious Warships:		1	(–)			
Landing Platform Dock (LPD)	*Jalashwa* (LPD-14 *Trenton*)	1	(–)	1971	17,000 tons	Acquired from USN 2007. Four new amphibious ships planned.
Major Surface Escorts:		24	(12)			
Destroyer (DDG)	Project 15B *Visakhapatnam*	–	(4)	(c.2018)	c.7,500 tons	Modified variant of Project 15A.
Destroyer (DDG)	Project 15A *Kolkata*	2	(1)	2014	7,400 tons	Much-delayed follow-on to Project 15 class.
Destroyer (DDG)	Project 15 *Delhi*	3	(–)	1997	6,700 tons	First class of indigenous destroyers.
Destroyer (DDG)	Project 61ME *Rajput*	5	(–)	1980	5,000 tons	Export version of Soviet 'Kashin' class. Last pair modified.
Frigate (FFG)	Project 17A	–	(7)	(c.2023)	c.6,500 tons	Modified follow-on of Project 17. Construction to start in 2017.
Frigate (FFG)	Project 17 *Shivalik*	3	(–)	2010	6,200 tons	Long delayed indigenous general-purpose frigates.
Frigate (FFG)	Project 1135.6 *Talwar*	6	(–)	2003	4,000 tons	Built in 2 batches of 3 in Russia. More may be constructed locally.
Frigate (FFG)	Project 16A *Brahmaputra*	3	(–)	2000	4,000 tons	Improved Project 16A.
Frigate (FFG)	Project 16 *Godavari*	2	(–)	1983	3,850 tons	Third ship decommissioned in 2015. First locally-designed frigates.

blue water and brown water capabilities. The main guidance for actual procurement decisions is the framework provided by the fifteen-year-forward looking perspective plans, which tend to be updated every five years. The classified *Maritime Capability Perspective Plan 2012-2027* sets out the currently targeted force level of a little over 200 ships. Although the details are classified, reports suggest key elements of the desired structure include three aircraft carriers, around forty front-line surface escorts and about thirty second-line corvettes. There could also be as many as six nuclear-powered strategic and six attack submarines, supplemented by an equivalent number of diesel electric boats. Other significant investment plans include four new amphibious vessels, five replenishment tankers, twelve mine-countermeasures vessels and new light warships for anti-submarine duties in the littorals.

Whilst realisation of these plans would make for a powerful force that would go a long way to ensuring the security of India's key maritime interests in the Indian Ocean, there are indications that there could well be a considerable mismatch between intentions and reality. The following factors are of particular relevance:

The age of the current fleet: Around sixty warships and submarines in the existing fleet are likely to have reached the end of their lifespan within the timescale of the current capability perspective plan. Whilst around fifty vessels are currently under construction or on order, this is insufficient even to counterbalance likely retirements.

A slow contracts process: Whilst construction of around another sixty ships and submarines have been 'approved', there tends to be a considerable delay as requests for information and particulars are considered and actual orders placed. Many key projects appear to find themselves stuck in a bureaucratic quagmire for several years.

A poor track record of delivery: Warship building programmes are still experiencing serious delays due to longstanding factors pointing to poor risk mitigation strategies and weak project management skills. Meanwhile initial cost estimates are not anchored in reality, with some programmes requiring a multiple of the original price to complete. A case in point is

NAVAL AVIATION

Indian naval aviation is headquartered at INS Hansa in **Goa**, where the front-line fixed-wing squadrons are currently based. There are also important air bases at **Mumbai** (for helicopters) and **Kochi** (for helicopters, MPA and UAV), at **Vishakapatnam** (for trainer jets, helicopters and MPA), at **Arakkonam, Ramanathapuram** and **Port Blair** in the Andaman Islands (for MPA). Main shipborne aircraft include:

- MiG-29K/KUB 'Fulcrum D' strike fighters: Forty-five being acquired, replacing existing Sea Harriers once *Viraat* is withdrawn.
- Ka-28/Ka-31 'Helix' helicopter: Ten Ka-28 ASW and fourteen Ka-31 early airborne warning variants currently in service.
- Sikorsky/Westland Sea King helicopter: Seventeen anti-submarine and twelve transport variants in service. Likely to be replaced by the US Seahawk in due course.
- HAL Chetak SA316/319 utility helicopter: Around thirty–forty in service. Small numbers of more modern Dhruv helicopters being brought into service.

At least eight Boeing P-8I Poseidon MPA are being delivered, replacing existing Russian 'Bear' and potentially 'May' types. There are also c. twenty-five second-line Dornier Do-228 MPA (with more being acquired).

Type	Class	In-Service	Ordered	ISD	Tonnage	Notes
Second Line Surface Escorts:		10	(2)			
Corvette (FSG)	Project 28 *Kamorta*	2	(2)	2015	3,400 tons	Last 2 have modified structure. ASW focus. More may be ordered.
Corvette (FSG)	Project 25A *Kora*	4	(–)	1998	1,400 tons	Anti-surface focus. Indigenously built.
Corvette (FSG)	Project 25 *Khukri*	4	(–)	1989	1,400 tons	Anti-surface focus. Indigenously built.
Strategic Submarines:		–	(3+)			
Submarine (SSBN)	*Arihant*	–	(3+)	(2016)	c.6,000 tons	Project details sketchy. At least 3 boats being built & more planned.
Attack Submarines:		1	(–)			
Submarine (SSN)	Project 971U 'Akula II'	1	(–)	2012	9,500 tons+	Former Soviet-era boat completed for and leased to India as *Chakra*.
Patrol Submarines:		13	(6)			
Submarine (SSK)	Project 75 *Kalvari* 'Scorpène'	(–)	(6)	(2016)	c.2,000 tons	Last two boats reportedly to be fitted with AIP. More may be built.
Submarine (SSK)	Project 877EKM *Sindhughosh* 'Kilo'	9	(–)	1986	3,000 tons	A 10th boat was destroyed in 2013.
Submarine (SSK)	Type 209 *Shishumar*	4	(–)	1986	1,900 tons	German-built. Last pair assembled in India. To gain Sub-Harpoon.

Other Ships:

Type	Fast Attack Craft	Large OPVS	AS Corvettes	Minehunters	Replenishment Ships	
Number	12	10	4	6	4	Plus numerous patrol vessels, landing craft and support ships.

the first indigenous aircraft carrier, *Vikrant*, which will be delivered eight years late and US$2.5bn over an initial US$0.5bn budget if a revised delivery date of 2018 is met. It has been hoped that greater involvement of private sector yards in warship construction might improve performance but, to date, it would appear that every one of the contracts allocated under a tentative engagement with private shipbuilders has been delayed.

The focus on indigenisation: Despite continued delays with every indigenous programme, the IN has tried to stay the course and acquire new platforms through the domestic route wherever possible. Moreover, with the Modi administration's 'Make in India' focus, there is a renewed drive to build all future projects in India. However, capacity constraints, slow decision-making, lack of certain technological skills and an appalling track record suggest this approach will create considerable challenges. Imports have previously been used to ensure the delivery of certain critical capabilities but this escape route no longer seems open.

In spite of these question marks, the overall trajectory of development suggests the targeted balance of forces is being successfully maintained, according to Admiral Chauhan. He explains that, from a blue water perspective, the 'carrier battle group' – a synergistic and mutually-supporting force of warships centred on an aircraft carrier – clearly remains a central operational concept to the IN. The adjective 'synergistic' is apt because the combat-capability of

the group as a whole – largely an array of destroyers and frigates – is almost always greater than the sum of its parts. It is therefore important to keep in view that it is the effectiveness of the group – and not the carrier alone – that needs to be analysed in assessing its value. As such, the growing number of relatively sophisticated surface escorts joining the IN is almost as significant to the IN's growing sea-control capabilities as the enhancement of carrier capabilities 'per se'. However, not everything that a balanced navy plans for or does lies within blue waters. Indeed, there are a host of combat missions that must, of operational necessity, be executed within a brown water environment. As such, large numbers of brown-water forces with substantial (i.e. ample) and substantive (i.e., meaningful) offensive and defensive firepower are being acquired, including the associated surveillance chains needed to make full use of their capabilities.

OTHER INDIAN OCEAN NAVIES

Whilst the IN is clearly the dominant indigenous maritime power in the Indian Ocean, the region is also home to a number of significant fleets that warrant brief analysis.

Pakistan: Despite concerns about the Chinese PLAN's growing regional influence, it is the Pakistan Navy (PN) which poses the more immediate threat to the IN given the long history of conflict between the two nuclear-armed neighbours. The PN has long exercised cost-effective sea-denial capabilities, an approach it continues to pursue given it cannot hope

to match the IN's growth. Its submarine service, which is currently comprised of five *Agosta* and *Agosta* 90B boats, is set to expand considerably with the planned acquisition of eight new submarines of Chinese origin, which are reportedly equipped with AIP. Some analysts have suggested that the acquisition of nuclear-powered boats, perhaps with a ballistic missile capability, may be a possibility in time.

China has also assisted with the modernisation of Pakistan's largely obsolescent surface forces, which include five former British Royal Navy Type 21 frigates and a sole FFG-7 class vessel of US Navy origin. It supplied four F22P *Zulfiqar* class frigates – one assembled locally – from 2009 onwards and is helping with the ongoing construction of *Azmat* class fast attack craft at Karachi Shipyard & Engineering Works. The China-Pakistan nexus is a source of serious concern to Indian defence planners, particularly the possibility that the PLAN might obtain bases in Pakistani ports.

Bangladesh: Although Bangladesh can look at Indian ambitions as hegemonic – depending on which political group is in power – there are signs of increasing co-operation between the two navies. The Bangladesh Navy is engaged in a qualitative and quantitative expansion of its fleet involving replacement of surface vessels and establishment of naval air and submarine capabilities under the long-term Forces Goal 2030 – established in 2009 – that aims at creating a three dimensional fleet. As for Pakistan, much of this effort is being supported by Chinese assistance, although ongoing engagement by the United States is also evident as it seeks to maintain influence and thwart Islamic extremism.

The current front-line surface fleet comprises six frigates of largely Chinese and American origin, supplemented by growing numbers of mainly Chinese-designed and/or equipped missile-armed corvettes, patrol vessels and fast attack craft. These will shortly be joined by two Type 035G 'Ming' class submarines that will be largely used for training purposes. The investment in building up considerable sea-denial forces despite settling once contentious maritime boundaries with Myanmar and India raises questions as to the rationale for this investment.

Myanmar: Myanmar has benefitted considerably from both Chinese and, increasingly, Indian assis-

The Pakistan Navy's Chinese-built replenishment tanker *Nasr* and F22P type frigate *Saif* operating with the RAN in 2014. In spite of considerable Chinese-assistance, the Pakistan Navy is outclassed by its larger Indian rival and its main potential lies in its asymmetric capabilities, including its submarines. *(RAN)*

tance as it plays-off the rising powers with whom it shares borders. While China provided the bulk of platforms and weapons during Myanmar's long isolation, India has made considerable inroads in recent times, supplying weapons, sensors, maritime patrol aircraft and training whilst nudging the military junta towards democracy. Meanwhile, an expansion programme based on largely indigenous construction has delivered a fleet of five missile-armed frigates and two corvettes supported by growing numbers of missile-armed fast attack craft. The latest frigates appear to be fitted with a mix of Chinese, Indian, North Korean and Western equipment, which must make for some interesting maintenance challenges.

Indian Ocean Islands: The **Sri Lankan** Navy (SLN) fought a successful campaign against the very effective Tamil Sea Tigers and has benefitted from military assistance from a wide range of nations. As elsewhere, India and China are now both vying for influence in this island nation at India's southern tip. The current SLN, largely structured for asymmetric coastal and inshore operations, operates a preponderance of small heavily armed fast craft along with a handful of larger warships, including two former Indian offshore patrol vessels. It is now seeking to expand these capabilities with more large ships and two Indian-built 105m offshore patrol vessels are slated for delivery in the 2017–18 timeframe.

Elsewhere, the IN has considerable influence in the small but significant island nations of **Mauritius, Seychelles** and the **Maldives**, which have large ethnic Indian populations. While China has, in recent years, stepped up aid to these countries, India provides considerable material assistance and has been working actively to build shared security ties. These, for example, include a linked coastal surveillance radar network that will have stations in all three countries, as well as Sri Lanka and India. Analysts suggest that – once completed – the project will allow India, through its allies, to monitor the movements of all ships transiting the Indian Ocean.

Reference should also be made of the importance of France, which retains a material presence in its overseas region of **Réunion** and has participated in the joint Varuna naval exercises with India since 1993. The **British Indian Ocean Territory** also contains important facilities that are largely used by the US Military.

South Africa: The South African Navy (SAN) is the only navy providing anything beyond purely local influence along the African shores of the Indian Ocean. In partnership with Brazil, it interacts regularly with the IN in the IBSAMAR exercises besides maintaining bilateral relations. Even though it possesses a reasonable combat capability built around three modern Type 209 submarines and four MEKO A-200 frigates acquired under the Strategic Defence Package finalised in 1999, its constabulary assets – a handful of converted former fast attack craft – are inadequate to police its long coastline and considerable maritime economic zone. Its main naval base at Simon's Town, near Cape Town, is also too far from the Indian Ocean to support effective deployments.

The SAN is looking to remedy this deficiency by re-establishing a full naval base at Durban on its eastern coast and build a new fleet of three offshore patrol vessels and three inshore patrol vessels under Project Biro. A further programme, Project Hotel, will see the acquisition of a new hydrographic ship. All the ships will be built in-country and orders should be placed within the next couple of years. The new vessels should allow a greater presence in the Mozambique Channel – a key shipping route between the Atlantic and the Middle East – which has previously received the attention of pirates and is also of increasing focus for the IN. Both fleets are increasingly interacting with the small Mozambique naval force, which is set to be reinforced by the arrival of several patrol craft built by France's CMN.

CONCLUSION

In spite of a number of well-publicised challenges, the Indian Navy has made considerable strides in achieving its aim of building a balanced force that is well-able to contribute to securing the country's maritime interests. Whilst continuing to reject formal alliances, India is also making progress in creating the broader co-operative maritime security architecture across the Indian Ocean that will facilitate the objective of it becoming a net provider of security across the region. It will be interesting to observe to what extent this process results in broadening collaboration with other naval powers operating in the Indian Ocean that have aligned interests; for example Australia, South Africa and – even – the United States.

In the meantime, the navy must continue to devote energy to ensuring better alignment between the ambitious objectives for its force structure and what can be delivered in practice. Obtaining further improvements in the performance of local maritime industry, balancing the expansion of indigenous manufacturing capabilities with the immediate needs of the fleet and ensuring a continuation of adequate funding will all be essential requirements to allow ambitions to be achieved. Nevertheless, the efforts made to develop a coherent naval strategy – and the impetus to the convergence of naval and political thinking as to the utility of naval power that has been given added impetus under the Modi regime – are promising signs for the future.

Notes

1. See Arun Prakash, 'The Rationale and Implications of India's Growing Maritime Power' in Michael Kugelman (ed.), *India's Contemporary Security Challenges* (Washington DC: Woodrow Wilson International Center for Scholars, 2011), p.78.

2. An interesting analysis of the development of Indian naval doctrine is contained in Iskander Rehman's 'India's Aspirational Naval Doctrine' in editor Harsh V Pant's *The Rise of the Indian Navy* (Farnham: Ashgate, 2012), pp.55–79. The chapter stresses the navy's need to develop a convincing doctrine given its largely peripheral role in India's past conflicts. It also makes some interesting comments on the almost schizophrenic split between Western (Royal Navy) and Soviet influences that arose from links with the latter from the 1960s onwards.

3. See *Indian Maritime Doctrine* (New Delhi: Integrated

Headquarters – Navy, 2009) and – in due course – the as yet restricted *Ensuring Secure Seas: India's Maritime Military Strategy* (New Delhi: Integrated Headquarters – Navy, 2015).

4. Rahul Roy-Chaudhury's analysis was contained in 'Five Reasons the World Needs to Pay Heed to India's New Maritime Security Strategy' published on the Indian web-based news publication *The Wire*: http://thewire.in/

5. The Project 15 and Project 17 series have been extensively analysed by the author in *Seaforth World Naval Review 2011* and *Seaforth World Naval Review 2013* (both Barnsley: Seaforth Publishing, 2010/2012).

6. The author would like to thank Vice Admiral Pradeep Chauhan, IN (retired) for his generous assistance on commenting on an early draft of this chapter. All comments remain the author's own.

4.4.2   Richard Beedall

MIDDLE EASTERN NAVIES

This chapter provides a high-level review of the status and capabilities of the navies of Middle Eastern countries at the end of 2015.

The high level of spending on defence by Middle Eastern countries – often over ten per cent of GDP – has not led to the development of proportionally strong navies. Despite the turbulent nature of the region, countries with friendly relations with the United States have chosen to rely heavily on that country for their maritime security, rather than develop their own naval capabilities at considerable expense.[1] In practice the primary role of the fleets of almost all the countries in the region is limited to protecting the safety and security of their ports and offshore installations, and preventing illegal and dangerous activities in their waters, including smuggling and terrorism.[2] This requires modestly-sized patrol vessels with reasonably competent crews, not large and expensive warships with highly-trained

sailors. The bulk of local defence spending has consequently tended to gravitate to other branches of the armed forces.

In the future, both Egypt and Turkey have plans to substantially grow the size and capabilities of their navies, but other countries in the region have had similar unrealised ambitions in the past. It also remains to be seen if Russia will seek to maintain a substantial regional naval presence after its intervention in Syria in late 2015. Another interesting question is whether China will attempt to develop a permanent naval/military presence in the Middle East – or close by in Africa – following the discussions with Djibouti to construct support facilities that were revealed at the end of 2015.

EGYPT

Headquartered in Alexandria on the Mediterranean Sea, the Egyptian Navy has about 18,500 officers

and men. However, this total includes 10,000 conscripts undertaking one to three years of national service, and some 2,000 coast guard personnel.

The Egyptian Navy is set to leap up the world rankings after placing a series of large orders with France during 2014–15. These include contracts to buy the two *Mistral* class amphibious assault ships that France originally built for Russia, a FREMM-type frigate and four 'Gowind 2500' corvettes. The Egyptians wanted the FREMM frigate in a hurry, so the newly completed French ship *Normandie* was transferred in July 2015, being renamed *Tahya Misr*. The country has also recently received four heavily-armed, American-built 'Ambassador IV' *Ezzat* class fast attack craft, ostensibly to defend the Suez Canal.

Egypt is also regenerating its moribund submarine force. Its four remaining Chinese-built 'Romeo' class submarines are over thirty years old, and probably not operational. Their replacement – by four German-built Type 209/1400 submarines – is another very expensive project. Despite reports of Israeli attempts to block the deal, the first of the new submarines was officially named *S41* in December 2015.

Even with French assistance, the Egyptian Navy faces a major challenge developing the ability to maintain and effectively operate a sudden influx of modern, sophisticated and expensive warships. It is also unclear what their role will be. This is particularly the case with respect to *Tahya Misr* and the amphibious assault ships, which are designed for world-wide military operations – a pattern of operations not traditionally associated with the Egyptian Navy. It is puzzling why Egypt is prioritising the costly development of high-end naval capabilities rather than, say, improving its anti-terrorist and anti-piracy maritime security capabilities in the Red Sea and the Mediterranean.

The US Navy coastal patrol craft *Firebolt* (PC-10) pictured in company with the British Royal Navy destroyer *Dragon* during a mine-countermeasures exercise in the Gulf in May 2013. In broad terms, countries in the Middle East have tended to rely on the US Navy and its allies to ensure maritime security in the region. *(US Navy)*

ISRAEL

The Israeli Navy is quite small with just 9,500

personnel (including 2,000 conscripts), but is possibly the most effective of any Middle East Navy. In a regional conflict it seems likely that the five (plus one under construction) German-built *Dolphin 1* and *Dolphin 2* class submarines – the latter being AIP-equipped – operating from the main naval base at Haifa would quickly clear the eastern Mediterranean Sea of the ships of any rival. Additionally, these submarines are almost certainly armed with long-range cruise missiles capable of carrying a nuclear warhead.

The Israeli Navy also has a substantial force of very heavily-armed corvettes and missile patrol craft. The largest are the three American built 1,075-ton 'Sa'ar V' class, whose armament includes eight Harpoon surface-to-surface missiles and thirty-two Barak 1 surface-to-air missiles. The latter is likely to be soon replaced by the more advanced Barak 8, whilst the navy is also considering the possible installation of 'Iron Dome' missile-defence batteries on the ships to help protect the country's offshore gas platforms.

In 2014 Germany's ThyssenKrupp Marine Systems received an order from Israel for four 1,800-ton 'Sa'ar VI' class corvettes, reportedly based on their MEKO A-100 design. The first ship is expected to enter service in 2019. Whilst primarily intended to protect the country's EEZ, their size will nevertheless allow them to be deployed further afield than Israeli warships (excluding the submarines) have traditionally ventured.

The need to ensure coastal security has resulted in the construction of relatively large numbers of indigenous fast patrol boats of the 'Dvora'/'Super Dvora' and 'Shaldag' classes, which have also enjoyed considerable export success.

OTHER MIDDLE EASTERN MEDITERRANEAN NAVIES

Elsewhere in the Mediterranean, **Syria** has never had a strong navy and the civil war that began in 2011 has probably destroyed it as an effective military force. It is unlikely that the two 'Petya III' class frigates and other small ships transferred by the Soviet Union to Syria in the 1970s and 1980s are still operational. At best, the navy may still operate a small number of 'Osa' class missile-armed fast attack craft, plus various small patrol craft, from its main base at Tartus – a facility also used by the Russian Navy.

The small **Lebanese** navy is based at Beirut. It is

The Israeli Sea Corps' flotilla of German-built *Dolphin* class submarines gives it a significant advantage over other regional navies. The submarines are reported to be equipped with nuclear-armed cruise missiles, making them a key strategic asset. A total force of six boats is planned – this image shows the fifth of the class, *Rahav*, undergoing maintenance at Kiel in June 2015 before her delivery voyage to Israel. *(Leo van Ginderen)*

essentially a coast guard operating a force of patrol ships and inshore patrol craft, none displacing more than 130 tons.

IRAN

The Iranian Navy has approximately 21,000 naval personnel (including 2,800 marines), with its fleet headquarters and principal dockyard at Bandar Abbas in the Persian Gulf. Slightly confusingly, there is a second major naval service – the Islamic

Iran acquired three Russian-built 'Kilo' class submarines in the early 1990s – this picture shows the second boat, *Noor*, on her delivery voyage. In practice, difficulties in keeping them operational have meant they have been a less potent weapon than first imagined. *(US Navy)*

Revolutionary Guard Corps Navy – with another 20,000 personnel (including 5,000 marines). In general the Iranian Navy is responsible for longer range and extended duration naval operations in the Arabian Sea and Caspian Sea, whilst the Revolutionary Guard has operational responsibility for the Persian Gulf.

In the 1970s, the Iranian Navy aspired to be a regional superpower, but the 1979 Revolution suspended these ambitions. The 1980s war with Iraq plus decades of American and, later, UN-mandated sanctions have since severely hindered attempts to modernise and strengthen the fleet. The back-bone of the surface fleet remains three small Vosper Mk 5 *Alvand* class frigates, built in Britain in the early 1970s.[3] These have recently been supplemented by three *Mowj* class frigates, built locally and essentially a copy of the *Alvand* design.

In the early 1990s the Iranian Navy received three Russian-built 'Kilo' class submarines. For a time, the threat presented by these severely concerned the US Navy. However it soon became clear that Iran was struggling to operate, maintain and refit the submarines. For example, an attempt to manufacture replacement batteries locally was unsuccessful, and new batteries had to be sourced from India. In 2005 Russia was contracted to modernise the boats at Bandar Abbas, with the first re-entering service in 2012.

Nevertheless, the country is acquiring domestically-built midget submarines, with – perhaps – thirteen or more of the *Chadir* class now in service and improved variants under construction.[4] Their design is probably based on the North Korean *Yono* class. It has been speculated that Iranian submarines may be armed with advanced weapons such as the VA-111 Shkval super-cavitating torpedo developed by the Soviet Union, or the Russian 3M-54E Klub anti-ship missile. However, the likelihood of their deployment has to be regarded with caution – if only because of the dangers associated with using long-range weapons against poorly identified targets in the crowded shipping lanes of the Arabian Gulf.

In terms of naval combat capabilities, Iran has placed a big emphasis on fast attack craft armed with surface to surface missiles – most commonly the Chinese designed C-802 and the smaller C-704. The Iranian Navy is thought to operate over fifty such craft, many built locally using a variety of French, Chinese and North Korean designs. In addition, the Revolutionary Guard Corps operates 200–300 small combatants, Special Forces boats and other patrol craft – again mostly locally built. These tend to be armed with just machine guns and rocket launchers. The 'swarm' tactics of these inexpensive craft have proved highly effective, and has had a significant impact on the operations of other navies in the Arabian Gulf, including those of the US Navy and its allies.

Finally, the Iranian Navy maintains a more substantial amphibious warfare capability than most Middle Eastern navies. This is largely to support the country's claims to many of the numerous small islands located in the Straits of Hormuz, at the eastern end of the Arabian Gulf.

SAUDI ARABIA

Oil-rich Saudi Arabia has one of the highest defence budgets in the world. However, this spending has never been translated into a large navy – ambitious naval expansion programmes have regularly been hinted at, but so far never realised.

Saudi Arabia is a large country that dominates the Arabian Peninsula and has fairly lengthy coastlines on both the Red Sea (970 nautical miles) and Arabian Gulf (450 nautical miles). A significant problem faced by the Saudi Navy is, therefore, the need to split its ships between the Red Sea (the

Western Fleet based at Jiddah) and the Arabian Gulf (Eastern Fleet, based at Al Jubail). Also, whilst the navy is numerically one of the strongest in the region with about 15,500 personnel (including 3,000 marines), in practice it relies heavily on expatriates from the Asian sub-continent to maintain its ships. There is a suspicion that maintaining the superficially smart appearance of its warships might sometimes be considered more important than their combat effectiveness.

Western countries have quietly expressed some disappointment at the failure of the Saudi Arabian Navy to contribute substantially to maritime security and the suppression of piracy in the southern Red Sea and Gulf of Aden areas. However, the Saudi Navy has been reported as being reasonably active supporting the Saudi Arabian-led intervention in Yemen's 2015 Civil War. The United States has provided equipment to help improve communications and interoperability with Western warships operating in the region.

The core of the navy currently consists of three modern *Al Riyadh* class frigates derived from the *La Fayette* design and built in France, as well as four older and smaller *Madina* class frigates that were also French-built. These, together with two replenishment ships and smaller vessels, are based on the Red Sea. The forces in the Arabian Gulf comprise various

corvettes, missile boats and other warships of mainly United States origin supplied under the Saudi Naval Expansion Program (SNEP) of the 1970s. All these US-supplied ships are now over twenty years and often over thirty years old, and probably have only limited operational capabilities.

Saudi Arabia's rivalry with Iran has led to suggestions of a major upgrade of the Eastern Fleet, most likely with United States support under a Saudi Naval Expansion Program II (SNEP II). A significant element of this plan appears to be four Littoral Combat Ships build to a heavily-modified version of the Lockheed Martin *Freedom* (LCS-1) type. However, their purchase has been mooted since 2008 and no firm contract had been announced by the end of 2015 due to the fall in oil prices and other priorities for defence spending.

OTHER GULF NAVIES

The **United Arab Emirates** (UAE) is a confederation of seven small states with unified armed forces. In the naval sphere, Abu Dhabi hosts the main naval base. The UAE Naval Force is small – comprising 2,400 naval personnel plus 1,200 in the coast guard – but very well equipped for a force whose primary role is the patrol and surveillance of the UAE's territorial waters and EEZ.

The United Arab Emirates six *Baynunah* class corvettes – currently in the course of delivery – are set to form the core of its fleet. They are compact, heavily-armed vessels, as evidenced by this picture of lead ship *Baynunah* in the course of preliminary sea trials in 2010. *(CMN)*

The core of the fleet is increasingly comprised of the six 850-ton *Baynunah* class missile corvettes, which are currently being delivered. These are very heavily armed for their size: their weapons include Exocet surface-to-surface and Evolved Sea Sparrow surface-to-air missiles. The lead ship was constructed by CMN in France but five follow on ships are being built in the UAE by Abu Dhabi Shipbuilding, with three completed by the end of 2015.

Another recent acquisition is the 1,650-ton anti-submarine corvette *Abu-Dhabi*; she was built in Italy by Fincantieri and delivered in 2012. Fincantieri is allied with the UAE's other major shipyard, Eithad Ship Building (ESB), and has also delivered two missile armed patrol vessels to add to the very capable force of ten fast attack craft delivered by German yards. Looking forward, the UAE is expected to buy more locally-built vessels from these two major yards and improve its amphibious and mine warfare capabilities.

Further north in the Gulf, **Qatar**, **Bahrain** and **Kuwait** all maintain fleets focused on a core of missile-armed fast attack craft of various ages and effectiveness, supplemented by smaller patrol boats; the latter often manned by the coast guard or police. Bahrain also retains as its flagship the FFG-7 class frigate, *Sabha* – the former US Navy *Jack Williams*

(FFG-24) transferred in 1996. For a few years she regularly trained with other navies in the region, but now rarely leaves her berth. Given the age of the ship, her relatively sophisticated equipment, and her need for a 200-strong crew (almost a quarter of all Bahraini naval personnel), she is probably not kept fully operational. Indeed, Bahrain's main naval significance is as the principal regional base of the US Navy, which is co-located with the Bahraini Navy at the port of Mina Sulman.[5]

Iraq is slowly rebuilding its navy after the international military action that resulted in the overthrow of its former president, Saddam Hussein, in 2003. By the end of that conflict the Iraqi Navy had essentially ceased to exist, and its re-establishment was not an immediate priority. The Iraqi Coastal Defence Force was finally formed in 2004, being renamed the Iraq Navy in January 2005. It has currently only rebuilt itself to around 2,000 personnel, plus 1,500 marines, most located at the Umm Qasr Naval Base, south east of Basra. Its operations focus on the defence of the Al Basra and Khawr al Amaya offshore oil facilities, plus policing the southern end of the Shatt al-Arab and Khawr Abd Allah waterways. For this purpose it has about twenty-one patrol craft – the largest being the four 400-ton *Fateh* class built in Italy in 2006–9.

Headquartered at Wudam As Sahil, west of Muscat and near the mouth of the Persian Gulf, the **Royal Navy of Oman** is relatively small – about 4,200 personnel – but undoubtedly one of the most professional and effective in the region. Unlike many neighbouring countries it has eschewed a dependence on foreign personnel, and its ships are manned solely by Omani nationals. The country traditionally has had strong links with the United Kingdom's Royal Navy and many of its warships have also been built in British yards. These include two *Qahir* class corvettes built in the 1990s and three larger 2,750-ton *Al Shamikh* class corvettes delivered under Project Khareef in 2013–14. However, Oman was disappointed with the performance of the later project – the ships suffered from design problems and were delivered late – and selected Singapore's ST Marine for a contract for four new 'Al-Ofouq' offshore patrol vessels ordered in 2012. Two of the four have now been delivered and will start to replace the 1980s-vintage *Dhofar* class fast attack craft. The focus on commissioning larger vessels probably reflects the increased importance attached to policing Oman's EEZ, which extends far out into the Indian Ocean,

OTHER NAVIES OF REGIONAL SIGNIFICANCE

Although clearly not a Middle Eastern country, the United States is, nevertheless, the dominant naval power in the region maintaining significant forces both in the Mediterranean and the Indian Ocean. Taken as a whole, it probably has more combat power than all the other navies located in the region combined. A number of the United States' allies also maintain a constant presence in the region, with both France and the United Kingdom maintaining bases in the Persian Gulf.

Straddling Europe and Asia, **Turkey's** navy is the largest in the wider region with c. 55,000 personnel (of whom c. 30,000 are conscripts undergoing fifteen months' national service), including 3,000 marines. Headquartered in the capital Ankara and with numerous bases and dockyards around the country, operationally it is divided into a main Fleet Command located at the principal naval base of Gölcük and two regional Commands: a Northern Area Command (covering the Back Sea and Sea of Marmara) run from Istanbul and a Southern Area Command (covering the Aegean and wider Mediterranean seas) based in Izmir.

The Royal Navy of Oman is a modern and effective force built around five corvettes and a number of patrol vessels. This picture shows *Al Rasikh*, the third and final member of the *Al Shamikh* class, during trials in 2013. *(Conrad Waters)*

The old Ottoman Empire used to be a major naval power and the modern Turkish Navy is again becoming a force to be reckoned with. It operates a large flotilla of German-designed Type 209 *Preveze* and *Atilay* class submarines, the latter due to be replaced by new AIP-equipped boats of the Type 214 class. There are also sixteen major surface combatants – split evenly between German MEKO 200 and US Navy FFG-7 types – eight smaller corvettes and over twenty missile-armed fast attack craft. These are complemented by a strong mine-countermeasures force, expanding amphibious capabilities and a modest afloat-support capability. A growing policy of indigenisation is evidenced by the 'Milgem' national ship corvette programme, which is likely to be followed by the planned and much larger TF-2000 air-defence frigates.

In addition to developing indigenous capabilities, the Turkish Navy is intent on expanding its blue water presence. In March 2012, then-commander of the Turkish navy Admiral Murat Bilgel outlined Turkey's strategic objective as '… to operate not only in the littorals but also on the high seas'. He also stated key medium term goals for the coming decade as, 'Enhancing sea denial, forward presence, and limited power projection capacity… '.[6] Reports on Turkey's latest *National Security Policy Document*, updated in 2010, indicate that – unexpectedly – Israel was listed as a key threat alongside traditional rivals such as Greece and Russia. This suggests operations in the Eastern Mediterranean are likely to be particularly significant. Moreover, the Turkish Navy has also been a frequent contributor to NATO deployments in the Indian Ocean, a sign of potentially broader ambitions.

A major statement of Turkey's intention to have the capability to deploy combat forces far from its coasts was made in December 2013 when it announced that it had selected a variant of Navantia's *Juan Carlos I* class design – already in service with the Spanish Navy and the RAN – for its planned new major amphibious ship. The ship was subsequently ordered from local shipyard SEDEF on 7 May 2015. The Turkish National Security Council has decided that the amphibious assault ship – or aircraft carrier, according to some sections of the Turkish media – should be capable of operating STOVL aircraft in similar fashion to *Juan Carlos I* and it is notable that Turkey has already selected the F-35A variant of the Lockheed Martin Joint Strike Fighter for its air force.

Turkish Navy surface escorts of the FFG-7 and MEKO 200 types pictured operating together for a photographic exercise in 2010. Straddling Europe and the Middle East, the Turkish Navy is becoming increasingly influential and has ambitions to extend its 'blue water' presence. *(Turkish Navy)*

Notes

1. Largely because of its acrimonious relations with the United States, Iran is one of a handful of countries to develop a largely indigenous naval capability. It is possible, however, that with the relaxation of sanctions on Iran, local priorities will change.

2. In October 2014, it was announced at a conference in Qatar that the Gulf Co-operation Council (GCC) – whose members are Bahrain, Kuwait, Oman, Qatar, Saudi Arabia and the UAE – had decided to set up a joint maritime security force and enhance co-operation in naval operations in response to increasing regional maritime threats. If followed through, the new force will most likely focus on coastal interdiction and counter-terrorism operations.

3. A fourth member of the class, *Sahand*, was sunk by US Navy forces during Operation 'Praying Mantis' in April 1988.

4. Public sources show considerable variation with respect to numbers of submarines and other craft completed under indigenous Iranian construction programmes.

5. The United Kingdom has effectively based warships at Mina Sulman, in Bahrain since the turn of the millennium, using US navy and Bahraini support facilities. In 2014, it finally decided to build its own permanent base at the port, which will be opened in 2016.

6. Admiral Bigel was quoted in the US Naval Institute's *Proceedings – March 2012* (Annapolis MD, Naval Institute Press, 2012).

7. The main source of reference information for navies in the Middle East is the annually-published *Janes Fighting Ships* (Coulsdon: HIS Jane's), and the less frequently updated *Combat Fleets of the World* (Annapolis, MD: Naval Institute Press). It should be noted that the superficially exact information that these books contain can often be inaccurate and/or dated. The magazines *Jane's Navy International* (Coulsdon: IHS Jane's) and *Naval Forces* (Bad Neuenahr – Ahrweiler: Mönch Publishing Group) publish occasional regional reviews of Middle Eastern navies, as well as more frequent news items.

5.0   **Hartmut Ehlers**

GLOBAL TRENDS IN WARSHIP DESIGN & CONSTRUCTION

In the quarter of a century that has elapsed since 1990 – the year in which the decline of the Warsaw Pact and the decomposition of the Soviet Union finally became a fact with the German reunification – the world's political map has changed significantly. The long-standing Cold War had become history and – in its immediate aftermath – the vision of a peace dividend began to permeate most naval planning departments.

It was to be discovered, however, that there was no such thing. Instead, the naval world soon saw itself confronted with new challenges, which would have significant influences on naval shipbuilding. New 'global players' and/or regional maritime powers such as China and India appeared on the geopolitical scene. Other new developments also emerged that had to be noted by naval designers and planners. These included – but were not limited to – new strategies and tactics, changing tasks and maritime requirements, fresh hull and overall design concepts, advancing techniques and technologies, and new requirements in areas such as combat systems, accommodation and ship services.

HISTORICAL CONTEXT

It is of course the case that challenges from geopolitical and technical developments – as well as the prevalence of trends or even fashions – are by no means new to the shipbuilding world. The nineteenth century saw the revolutionary introduction of steam engines in ships which – in combination with modern breech-loading ordnance and armour – entailed new tactics, concepts and shipbuilding trends. Conversely, after the battle of Lissa in 1866 – where the Austrian Navy succeeded in sinking an Italian battleship by ramming – an ancient tactic became fashionable for a considerable period and larger units were designed with ram bows.

Somewhat later, the French *Jeune École* of Admiral Aube developed a strategic naval concept advocating the use of small, powerful units to combat a larger battleship fleet, and of commerce raiders to curtail the enemy's trade and economy. New ship types such as torpedo boats and submarines made their advent, triggering 'counter-type' designs like the (torpedo boat) destroyer and anti-submarine weapons. Just after the turn of the century, the British 'all-big-gun' battleship *Dreadnought* rendered older 'mixed-gun' battleships obsolete. A similar fate, in turn, eventually befell the battleship after the advent of the aircraft carrier.

More in the way of a fashion, for example, has been the use of raked masts and funnels in both merchant ships and warships to improve their appearance. Similarly, the fitting of the maximum number of funnels possible was highly fashionable for a time. Liner passengers often equated this with a higher level of performance and status, whilst it was even considered that native peoples in the colonies reckoned naval power from the number of funnels in warships 'showing the flag'. The highlight of funnel fashion was, perhaps, reached in the Imperial Russian cruiser *Askold*, launched in 1900, whose flush deck and five tall, narrow funnels gave her a unique appearance. Sometimes a degree of deception was involved. For example, in many of the large, four-funnel ocean liners the fourth stack was a fake and only served a subsidiary purpose, for example as a ventilation trunk.

An example of a more fundamental and permanent trend relates to the shift of officers' living accommodation away from the ship's stern – an arrangement originating in the layout of the old wooden sailing warships – towards the forepart of the ship. This can be seen as part of a steady, albeit initially slow, growth in the importance attached to habitability and accommodation standards that is now a key part of warship design.

CURRENT OVERVIEW

Returning to the present, it is estimated that the global naval shipbuilding could see an investment of nearly US$1,000bn in new warship and submarine construction over the two decades between 2016 and 2035. Interestingly, this investment may take place against a period of a significant downturn in civilian construction. 2015 saw both huge lay-offs from the three largest South Korean shipyards and a fall by around seventy per cent in new orders from Chinese yards in the first half of the year, developments that some commentators see as the first effects of what may become a new merchant shipbuilding crisis.

In preparing for this major phase of renewal of naval capabilities, many countries have been undertaking analysis of the strengths and weaknesses of their naval shipbuilding industries. Specialist studies have been undertaken to take a strategic view of the most effective approach to warship construction, including an examination of the lessons that can be learned from previous programmes and an exploration of the options available to remedy identified shortcomings.

Underlying such an analysis are a number of fundamental factors impacting future naval ship-

The new US Navy destroyer *Zumwalt* (DDG-1000) pictured on preliminary sea trials during December 2015. Her large size, stealthy design, use of integrated electric propulsion and potential to ship new weaponry are all indicative of trends in modern warship design. *(US Navy)*

building over the next decades. Amongst the most important of these are:

- Geopolitical/geostrategic trends and their influence on global maritime requirements.
- Technical developments and their impact on ship design and systems.
- Developments in the fields of standards, rules and regulations, both nationally and globally.
- Trends towards multi-purpose capabilities.
- Associated trends towards modularisation of systems and equipment.
- The growing attention being paid to unmanned systems.
- Industrial trends impacting naval shipbuilding, not least the shift in market influence away from the traditional naval powers towards emerging and developing economies.

The remainder of this chapter examines some of these factors in more detail.

GEOPOLITICAL TRENDS

The end of the Cold War drastically changed both long-standing defence doctrines and the associated geographical focus of many armed forces. For example, from a European perspective, territorial defence (protection against threats to the territory of the European Union) was no longer a primary concern from 1990 onwards. Instead, new threats – terrorism, piracy, the dangers posed by failing states – emerged that required new concepts of operation. There has been increased international interest in areas such as border security and humanitarian intervention. These changes have inevitably had an effect on the requirements set for naval mission capabilities and fleet composition and, accordingly, on ship design and construction. At the same time, navies have remained a crucial means of power projection around the world: a fact of which the United States, Russia and some of the emerging Asian regional powers have been well aware.

For most of the other navies in the world, the trend away from Cold War operational requirements – particularly the associated diminution in floating fleet assets – has become increasingly evident, even to the untrained eye. This effect has been the result both of reduced defence budgets and the steadily rising unit costs of modern warships. However, there have been at least two warship types that have benefitted from new operational requirements. These are

(i) offshore patrol vessels (OPVs) and (ii) multi-role platforms designed to conduct military and security missions, particularly in the littoral.

Driven largely by the extension in national maritime rights established by the evolving United Nations Convention on the Law of the Sea (UNCLOS) regime, OPVs form the fastest-growing segment of the naval vessels market.[1] Around twenty-five countries are known to have a total of about 135 OPVs on order and thirty countries have plans for approximately 275 additional units. Furthermore, the total number of OPVs in operation worldwide had risen to more than 770 as of 2014. Perhaps unsurprisingly, Asian navies account for the largest proportion of both the current fleet and vessels on order (around forty-five per cent in each case). Japan and India together operate about half the Asian vessels, whilst India alone has a quarter of the total number of OPVs on order worldwide. The expansion in the numbers of such vessels is not limited to new construction. For example, in order to acquire OPVs as fast as possible, Bangladesh awarded a contract to Fincantieri in early 2015 to upgrade and convert four *Minerva* class corvettes, being decommissioned by the Italian Navy, into patrol-vessel configuration.

OPVs can be broadly classified into two types, namely (i) high-end warfighting vessels with expensive weapon systems and electronic suites, and (ii) more basic patrol vessels, designed for sustained low intensity missions, equipped with basic armament and standard navigation sensors, and built to commercial standards. Which one of these types a country chooses depends on its particular naval requirements, in turn resulting from its geographic location, political aspirations and the intended role of its naval force. However, the majority of OPV programmes are of the low-cost, constabulary variety. They are being used in an increasing number of roles, including fishery protection, pollution control, fire-fighting, salvage/search and rescue (SAR), counter-narcotics and humanitarian operations within the overall ambit of exclusive economic zone (EEZ) patrol.

Meanwhile, the trend to multi-role platform designs is, perhaps, currently best represented by the US Navy's two Littoral Combat Ship (LCS) types, which are primarily intended for use in coastal waters and to combat 'asymmetric' threats. The two selected type designs incorporate numerous signature-reduction features and are laid out so to be capable of self-

The Swedish *Visby* class corvette *Härnösand* blends into the background of a Norwegian fjord as she participates in Exercise Cold Response 2012. Although very different ships to the *Zumwalt* class, the *Visby*s also reflect many current influences impacting naval shipbuilding and design, including technical developments with respect to stealth and survivability, the trend towards multi-purpose capabilities and the growing use of unmanned systems (in this case to carry out mine-countermeasures operations). *(Tørbjørn Kjosvold, Norwegian Armed Forces)*

The US Coast Guard's national security cutter *James* (WMSL-754) is a 'high end' example of an offshore patrol vessel, the fastest-growing segment in the naval vessels market. This expansion reflects both the extension in maritime rights established by UNCLOS and increased interest in countering piracy, terrorism and other dangers in the littoral in the post-Cold War environment. *(Huntington Ingalls Industries)*

defence and of conducting intelligence, surveillance and reconnaissance operations, as well as interdicting hostile or unknown vessels. Amongst the most prominent design features are a large internal recon-figurable mission bay and the ability to launch and recover rigid inflatable boats (RIBs), small boats, and unmanned surface/subsurface craft from the stern or sides. These features support mission-specific anti-surface, anti-submarine and mine-countermeasures modules. High speed and relatively large size facili-tate rapid global deployment in support of US inter-ests in littoral waters.

TECHNICAL DEVELOPMENTS IN SHIP DESIGN

There have been a number of significant develop-ments in ship design in recent years, many commencing from around the mid-1970s onwards. Some of these developments have resulted from operational experience and fleet planning, whilst others have arisen from administration action such as increasing stringent environmental rules and regulations. Technical change resulting from general technological progress, new inventions and enhance-ments of shipyard production processes have also played a part.

Stealth: One of the most obvious changes in ship design has been the emphasis on stealth evidenced by the introduction of sloped longitudinal and trans-

The French frigate *La Fayette* – seen here in 2007 – was one of the earliest modern examples of stealth at sea.

versal walls, along with smooth superstructure elements in warships of up to frigate and destroyer size. These measures were intended to reduce radar signature – a result that the author can attest was achieved through measurements made on the

Argentine MEKO 360 frigates that were delivered in the first half of the 1980s. The reduction of radar signature can be further enhanced by the deletion of rounded structures (even down to railing stanchions), the omission or concealment of openings in the hull and superstructure, and the avoidance of rectangular corners in substructures exposed to radar radiation. These measures include the undersides of the bridge-wings, deck protrusions, weapon and sensor founda-tions, and attachments to the external walls.

Additional significant signature reduction is achieved by the appropriate shaping of gun houses, antenna elements and – ultimately – the complete concealment of sensors in so-called 'integrated mast modules'. The concealment of items such as life-saving appliances and missile racks is also important. One side-effect has been the emergence of a certain uniformity in new warship designs, not unlike the case with modern cars.

One of the earliest examples of wholesale adop-tion of stealthy design was seen in the French *La Fayette* class frigates of the mid-1990s. The approach was subsequently echoed in types such as Singapore's *Formidable* (Project Delta) class and the Franco-Italian FREMM multi-mission frigates that were influenced by the original ships. Other examples of

The newly-completed US Navy Littoral Combat Ship *Freedom* (LCS-1) seen on trials in the summer of 2008. The LCS designs, which act as platforms for a number of mission-specific modules, are typical of a trend towards ships that can be adapted to carry out a wide range of duties. *(Lockheed Martin)*

the evolution of stealth designs include the smaller vessels of the Swedish *Visby* and UAE 'Falaj 2' classes, as well as the US Navy's much larger *Zumwalt* class (DDG-1000) destroyers. However, it is noteworthy that some leading navies have been relatively late in producing truly stealthy combat ship designs, with China, India, Russia and also Japan being behind the curve in this regard.

Modularisation: Modularisation of equipment with the aim of enhancing mission flexibility is another design trend. It is commonly accepted that this feature was triggered by the German Blohm & Voss MEKO modularised warship concept, which gave rise to the most successful surface combatant export line over the last three decades.

The MEKO concept embraces a flexible methodology for the installation of weapon, sensor, other electronic and major ship service system components in the form of standardised modules and common interfaces. The modules, called Weapon Functional Units and Electronic Functional Units, are configured as containers, pallets or grid pallets and even mast modules. They accommodate weapons, electronic systems and their sub-systems, service systems such as air-conditioning units, and even complete function rooms. In the latter case, the rooms are made up of a single container or are formed by joining two or more containers. As well as interfaces to the ship's data bus, the containerised modules also

5.0 MEKO EXPORT SUCCESSES

TYPE	COUNTRY	NUMBER	CLASS NAME	COMMISSIONED	CONSTRUCTED
MEKO 360H1	Nigeria	1	ARADU	1982	Germany
MEKO 360H2	Argentina	4	ALMIRANTE BROWN	1983–4	Germany
MEKO 140 A16	Argentina	6	ESPORA	1985–2001	Argentina
MEKO 200 TN	Turkey	4	YAVUZ	1987–9	Germany (2), Turkey (2)
MEKO 200 PN	Portugal	3	VASCO DA GAMA	1991–2	Germany
MEKO 200 HN	Greece	4	HYDRA	1992–8	Germany (1), Greece (3)
MEKO 200 ANZ	Australia/New Zealand	8/2	ANZAC	1996–2006	Australia
MEKO 200 TN-IIA	Turkey	2	BARBAROS	1997	Germany (1), Turkey (1)
MEKO 200 TN-IIB	Turkey	2	SALIHREIS	1998–2000	Germany (1), Turkey (1)
MEKO 100 RMN	Malaysia	6	KEDAH	2006–10	Germany (2), Malaysia (4)
MEKO A-200 SAN	South Africa	4	AMATOLA	2006–7	Germany
MEKO 100A	Poland	1	ŚLĄZAK	[2016]	Poland
MEKO A-200 AN	Algeria	2	–	[2016–17]	Germany
TOTALS		**49**			**Germany (21), Overseas (28)**

Notes:

1 In addition to naval exports, the main elements of the MEKO concept were also adopted in the Germany Navy's F-123 class (four ships), F-124 class (three ships) and F-125 class (four ships), the last-mentioned being currently under construction.
2 The trend towards transfer technology and local-build is clearly demonstrated by the fact that over half the MEKO class have been constructed overseas. In addition, considerable final outfitting was carried out by local yards on some German-built vessels.

have standardised connections for ship services (such as power and air-conditioning/ventilation).

This modular outfitting technique allows for the construction of the ship proper in parallel with the

The Turkish Navy's MEKO 200 TN type frigate *Turgutreis* – the second member of the class – which was completed by HDW at Kiel in 1988. The German Blohm & Voss MEKO modularised warship concept has had a significant impact on warship design and was a major export success. *(Devrim Yaylali)*

assembly and testing of the modules. This reduces initial building time and cost, as well as costs associated with subsequent maintenance and modernisation. The installation of weapon modules, for instance, is typically achieved by placing the module in a standard-dimension deck foundation which – in principle – is nothing more than the sill of the deck opening for the module. Subsequent steps include provisionally fixing the module, performing a static alignment at a defined load condition, filling the foundation with a quick-hardening sealant, and bolting it to its foundation. A final dynamic alignment is done during weapon trials. There are four sizes of standard deck foundations for Weapon Functional Modules.

The Royal Danish Navy soon followed the new modularisation trend with its Stanflex concept, which was heavily influenced by MEKO design principles. An initial batch of seven 'Standard Flex' 300 or *Flyvefisken* class convertible patrol vessels with GRP hulls was contracted in July 1985 and a total of fourteen of the class ultimately entered service between 1989 and 1996. Equipped with four positions for Stanflex modules, they could be rapidly reconfigured between anti-surface, anti-submarine,

mine-countermeasures, hydrographic and other roles. Whilst the class has now largely been withdrawn from Danish service, most subsequent Danish warship types since have one or more Stanflex module positions.

The impact of modularisation has now extended from equipment to the ship platform proper, an achievement to which the modular SIGMA (Ship Integrated Geometrical Modularity Approach) concept of the Dutch Damen Schelde Naval Shipbuilding group bears testimony. A number of SIGMA platforms have been ordered or proposed, including SIGMA 10513 and 10514, SIGMA 9813 and 9814, SIGMA 9113, SIGMA 8313, and SIGMA 7513 designs. In each case the figures indicate the length and beam of the platform – a SIGMA 10513 ship therefore has a length of 105m and a breadth of 13m. In essence, all the platforms are based on the geometrically similar SIGMA hull form series, which is adjusted to the required length, beam and draught of the ship.

The basic SIGMA hull structures comprise water-

tight 7.2m compartments. The inner, centre core of the hull is formed of identical structures but the outer sections to port and starboard can be adjusted in width by up to an extra 0.5m each. So, for example, the SIGMA 9813 and SIGMA 10513 class units operated by the Royal Moroccan Navy have

commonality in structure, propulsion and auxiliary systems, with the only difference being the insertion of an additional 7.2m parallel hull section in the 10513 variant amidships. This extra compartment provides added functional spaces and some additional accommodation. Similarly, the SIGMA 10514 uses the same modular 7.2m compartments but with broader outer sections. This variant has been acquired by the Indonesian Navy.[2]

Volume Growth: Another common development in recent years is the considerable growth in volume and, hence, displacement of most warship types. This has also inevitably had an impact on building costs. Growth has been triggered by steadily increasing requirements in the way of enhanced mission capabilities on the one hand and by administrative factors such as accommodation standards, building regulations and rules for outfit and equipment on the other.

There are a number of design features and trends that have had a particular influence on this growth effect. Amongst the most prominent is that of

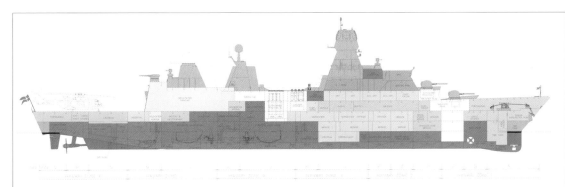

A diagram showing the internal layout of the Danish *Iver Huitfeldt* class frigates, including areas occupied by modular Stanflex weapons containers. A significant amount of internal volume is occupied by crew facilities, representing a major factor in the trend towards larger warships. *(DALO)*

A cabin space on the Venezuelan POVZEE type oceanic patrol vessel *Guaiquerí,* which was delivered by Navantia in 2011. Improvements in accommodation and other crew facilities are driving-up warship size; the relatively lightly armed *Guaiquerí* displaced around 2,500 tons. *(Navantia)*

accommodation facilities. This has not only extended to the amount of living space allocated to crew members but also features such as the dimensions of furniture, the abandonment of three-tier bunks in most navies and reductions in the numbers of crew allocated to each cabin, Other common developments have included a decrease in the slope of stairways – increasing the footprint of staircases – and the ratios of sanitary appliances allocated to each crew member. Even the numbers of life-saving appliances allocated to warships has grown. It is noteworthy that the trend towards growth in accommodation and other crew facilities has expanded even though complement numbers have been reduced.

The effect of certain technical developments, some already mentioned, should not be overlooked. For example, the incorporation of stealth features to reduce radar signature that has already been mentioned and which is manifested in sloping external walls and bulkheads, is a considerable growth stimulator which gains momentum with the angle of slope. Whilst the angle of older designs such as the MEKO 360 was typically around 5.5 degrees, more recent designs such as the new Chilean and Colombian 80m OPVs designed by the German Fassmer shipyard have inward angles of as much as 8 degrees (5 degrees in respect of the outward slopes). It can easily be imagined that a space with vertical walls is better-suited for fitting, for example, standard accommodation modules with vertical boundaries. The same is the case, for example, for vertically arranged two-tier bunks, lockers and other furniture in that there is no unusable triangular void behind. The use of stealth features therefore effectively increases the internal volume required. The same

effect is encountered when installing electronic equipment in a module and mounting the associated container in a ship's room compared with installing similar equipment directly into the room itself. The containerised method will require more space.

Mission Bays/Flexible Decks: The trends towards multi-mission capabilities and modularity previously mentioned are also evident in one promising development that has also been referenced with respect to the US Navy's LCS, viz. the 'mission bay'. In the Danish *Absalon* class combat support ships, designed in accordance with the Stanflex philosophy and commissioned in 2004–05, such a space is provided as a 'multipurpose deck' whilst it features as a 'flex deck' in the new German MKS-180. Although adding further to volume, such decks offer a number of advantages. If properly designed, the

deck will easily and quickly take one of many possible mission packages composed of a varying array of functional units (mission modules), as dictated by mission requirements. It will also ideally encompass the accommodation elements for the required mission crew detachments, and it will house the appropriate boats and unmanned vehicles. It therefore provides inherent modular flexibility whilst simultaneously avoiding interference with the rest of the ship.

The illustrations depict different 'flex deck' variants worked-out for the new MKS-180 type during the design development phase. It should be noted that only the open deck portions are shown and that the mine-countermeasures mission package also comprises a considerable drone component. During

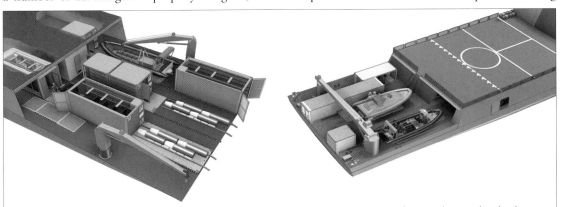

Two conceptual flexible deck layouts developed for the planned German MKS-180 surface combatant showing how different combinations of containerised mission packages, boats and other equipment can be accommodated. Many current surface designs incorporate so-called mission bays or flexible decks. *(MTG Marinetechnik GmbH)*

the MKS design period, which ended in July 2015 with the opening of the procurement procedure, a total of twenty-four steadily-growing design variants were produced by MTG Marinetechnik GmbH. The resulting design – that is being used as the basis for tenders – is a highly capable, versatile platform with considerable inherent mission flexibility. It is also designed to cope with a long period of deployment abroad – up to two years and with 5,000 hours at sea annually. It is anticipated that the German Navy will provide eight crews for a planned minimum of four ships.

New Hull Designs: New bow forms, generally considered a separate design trend, are often incorporated in naval designs. A well-known example is the 'Sea Axe' bow design developed by the Dutch Damen group. It significantly improves the seakeeping performance of a hull and reduces resistance, thus minimising fuel consumption.

Another modern mono-hull design is represented by the French 'C Sword 90' corvette, at present the largest warship ever designed by Construction Mecanique de Normandie (CMN). This concept combines an innovative hull and bow design with a stealthy superstructure. The corvette's design incorporated extensive work on the hull lines so as to reach an optimum in manoeuvrability, performance and resistance. The hydrodynamics of the hull combine excellent seakeeping and speed performance with endurance. The slender stem, with sharp entry lines, also offers performance benefits in terms

of speed. The topside design is described as combining aesthetic and stealth qualities. The CMN group stresses, however, that this resolutely modern corvette does not make concessions to fashion or design trends.

Another truly futuristic platform concept was presented in August 2015 when the British Royal Navy publicised design concepts for a potential warship of the future. Dubbed the *Dreadnought 2050*, the concept was produced under the auspices of Startpoint, a new maritime mission system initiative that was also heavily promoted at the London Defence and Security Equipment International (DSEI) exhibition in September 2015. The concept features an acrylic hull that can be turned translucent to make it nearly invisible to the naked eye – as well as laser and electromagnetic weapons and its own fleet of drone vessels. There will also be a mission bay. An operations room fashioned with a 3D holographic command table to improve the crew's situational awareness is also part of the design. And while most warships of this size are crewed by up to 200 sailors, the *Dreadnought 2050* would require just fifty.

TRENDS IN SHIP PROPULSION

There have been at least two important cornerstones in the history of ship propulsion. These are (i) the advent of the steam engine, ending the era of sail, and (ii) the phasing out of steam propulsion over the past decades with the exception of a 'nuclear niche' for steam turbines.[3] These remain the prime movers

in nuclear aircraft carriers and submarines, as well as in some Russian nuclear icebreakers.

The steady disappearance of steam propulsion from conventional warships can be attributed to a variety of disadvantages. From an operational point of view, steam propulsion requires a long time raising steam prior to sailing. From the designer's point of view, a steam propulsion power plant, be it of the piston or turbine type, is generally characterised by high labour-intensity, high space consumption, and the requirement of bunker spaces for three different working liquids. More specifically, a steam power plant in a warship will require one or more steam generators (boilers) and one or more engines for propulsion, typically divided into two watertight compartments. A crew will be required for each of the boiler room and engine room. In addition, bunker space is required for fuel, feed water and lubricants, whilst provision has to be made for waste liquids.

Current Surface Warship Propulsion Systems: However, the turbine itself has not disappeared from conventionally-powered warships. It was reinvented as the gas turbine in the second half of the twentieth century and has been installed in many types of fast attack craft, surface escorts and larger ships either as the sole type of prime mover or in combination with other types. This has given rise to a range of power plant designations.[4] Gas turbines and diesels, whether separately or in combination, now represent the dominant propulsion types.

Two images of the *Dreadnought 2050* design concept produced under the auspices of Startpoint, a new British maritime mission systems initiative in 2015. The design, incorporating an acrylic trimaran hull, mission bay, fleet of drone vessels and aerial vehicles, provides one view of where warship design is currently heading. An operations room with a 3D holographic command table is also part of the design. *(Copyright Startpoint 2015)*

An important recent trend amongst both main propulsion types is that of increased power output and power density as designs continuously improve. This allows the total number of prime movers required for a ship of a given size or displacement to be reduced. Another recent trend is a move away from mechanical propulsion, for example by means of a diesel engine linked to a shaft line through a gearbox, to diesel-electric and integrated full electric propulsion (IFEP). Under these arrangements, the diesel or gas turbine is used as a generator of electricity that is used to power an electrical motor. Although requiring more components, electric propulsion offers a continuous spectrum of propeller speeds – without gaps and steps – through from idling to maximum speed without the need for elaborate gearboxes. It also means that propulsion and 'hotel needs' can be serviced from a common power source, obviating the need for separate generators to provide for the latter. A final development worthy of mention is the much greater use now seen of sophisticated platform management systems (automation) as a labour saving means, thereby reducing manning figures.

Exhaust Routing & Infra-Red Signature Suppression: Beyond developments in propulsion types, another interesting trend is the increased use of waterline exhaust gas exits. These are found in many smaller and specialised types, where limitations in size, silhouette or other operational considerations make the deletion of exhaust trunks and funnels desirable. For example, the arrangement was often used in tank landing ships of Second World War vintage to simplify construction and avoid interference with the layout of the vehicle deck. In fast attack craft, the volume and deck area that would have been occupied by the trunks and funnels can be used for other equipment or contribute to the minimisation of the platform. Waterline exhausts can pose a significant external and internal exhaust pollution problem in slower, larger ships with moderate exhaust gas velocities.[5] The more common problem of traces of carbon deposits on the hull sides originating from the exhaust gases can be concealed simply by painting the affected hull portion black.

The use of waterline exhaust exits also facilitates efforts towards cooling heat emissions in order to minimise infra-red (IR) signature. It has resulted in their adoption on larger surface combatants that

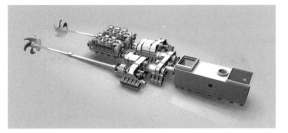 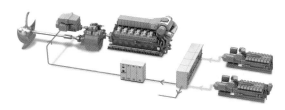

Gas turbines and diesels, whether separately or in combination, now represent the dominant prime movers in warships. A recent trend has been a move away from traditional mechanical propulsion – illustrated by the diagram (left) of a CODAG (combined diesel and gas) propulsion system – by which diesels and/or gas turbines are linked directly to a shaft line by means of a gearbox. Instead, at least part of the propulsion arrangements are provided by electrical motors powered by diesel generators which also produce electrical power for other ship systems. The right-hand image shows a diesel-electrical plant – by which propulsion can be provided either by an electrical motor served by diesel generators or by a direct diesel engine connection with the gearbox. *(Rolls Royce)*

would not otherwise require them for reason of size or silhouette. Cooling arrangements have also been widely installed in more conventional exhaust arrangements.[6] IR signature can also be controlled by other measures, including careful placement of funnels and through the shaping and masking of exhaust openings. For example, the voidance of two funnel exhaust plumes joining into one will contribute significantly to IR signature reduction. Other navies have adopted varying solutions; they tend to be elaborate, voluminous, largely invisible but effective. In combination with careful insulation of respective rooms and compartments and avoidance of hot spots in external structures, a considerable reduction of IR signature can be achieved.

Submarine Propulsion: Today, submarine propulsion is divided between conventional types and those with nuclear propulsion. These two types differ by a factor of about five so far as cost is concerned. This could explain the existence of nuclear submarines in only a handful of navies.

The majority of conventional submarines worldwide have diesel-electric propulsion. A few, such as the former Germany Type 206/206A, have battery-electric propulsion under which the electric propulsion motor is fed exclusively from the batteries. In this variant, the diesels are only used for battery charging and there is no mechanical connection between diesels and propellers. However, all conventional diesel-powered submarines – in contrast to nuclear types – are still dependent on external air. This is a major disadvantage operationally.

Air-independent propulsion (AIP) solutions first appeared a decade before the advent of nuclear propulsion in the last years of the Second World War. German Walter turbine propulsion plant technology utilising hydrogen peroxide was subsequently tested by the United States, Russian and British navies but abandoned once these countries succeeded in developing the small reactors needed for underwater nuclear propulsion. Germany also developed the *kreislaufmotor* or closed-cycle engine as an alternative to the Walter turbine and this was subsequently used in the Russian Project 615 'Quebec' class submarines which were powered by two conventional diesels and one closed-cycle engine. Again, the development of nuclear propulsion meant that this line of development proved to be a dead-end. However, with nuclear boats beyond the budgets of most navies, other AIP technologies emerged. To date, three of these have entered operational service:

- **Stirling AIP System:** The Stirling engine is a piston engine with external combustion. The working medium is helium, which is used in conjunction with liquid oxygen and diesel fuel. The Stirling engine is used to drive 75kW electrical generators, either for propulsion or for charging batteries. In common with other current AIP-equipped submarines, Stirling submarines are hybrid types, since the limited generating capabilities of the AIP plant requires additional propulsion power. The units of the Swedish *Gotland* class were the first Stirling submarines and Japan and Singapore have also used this technology.
- **MESMA AIP System:** The French MESMA (*Module d'Energie Sous-Marine Autonome*) is a closed-cycle steam turbine AIP system under

which a conventional steam turbine power plant is powered by steam generated from the combustion of ethanol (grain alcohol) and stored oxygen at a pressure of 60 atmospheres. Offered for the 'Scorpène' and *Agosta* 90B types, it has only been adopted by Pakistan to date.

■ **Fuel Cell AIP:** A prototype fuel cell was developed by the German Siemens group in the 1980s and trialled in the submarine *U 1* of the Type 205 (mod). To this end, a new 3.8m section containing the fuel cell plant and the required reactive media – hydrogen and oxygen – was inserted in the hull. The 'cold combustion' of these media in the fuel cell results in the production of direct current and of water. A welcome side-effect of the latter is that the boat does not change weight as hydrogen and oxygen are expended. *U 31*, the first of six operational German fuel-cell submarines of the Type 212A class commissioned in October 2005. The technology has proved a success, with fuel-cell equipped submarines of the Type 212A, Type 214, Type 218 and other designs being exported to seven countries to date.

DEVELOPMENTS IN WEAPONS SYSTEMS & EQUIPMENT

Technical developments in ship design are being accompanied by significant changes in weapons systems and other equipment. Amongst the most important potential trends are those relating to new weapons technologies and the growth in unmanned systems.

Weapons Systems: Once deemed utopic, electromagnetic railguns (EMRGs) and lasers are no longer matters of science fiction. Perhaps unsurprisingly, the US Navy is in the forefront of development. It has yet to be seen, however, whether these development efforts will be able to trigger a firm design trend, even if conventional ordnance has reached its final point of development.

The EMRG launcher is a long-range weapon that fires projectiles using electricity instead of chemical propellants. Magnetic fields created by high electrical currents accelerate a sliding metal conductor, or armature, between two rails to launch projectiles at speeds of up to 4,500mph. Given its increased velocity and extended range, the EMRG will provide a considerable multi-mission capability. It should be equally capable undertaking long-range strikes

against land targets, providing precise naval surface gunfire support, conducting engagements against surface warships or providing ship defence. The US Navy plans to test-fire its new EMRG at sea for the first time in the summer of 2016 from on board the *Trenton* (T-EPF-5).

Meanwhile, a prototype solid-state Laser Weapon System (LaWS), deployed aboard the afloat forward staging base *Ponce* (AFSB(I)-15) was successfully tested against air and surface targets during September-November 2014 whilst operating in the Persian Gulf. As well as having a much lower cost per shot compared with onventional projectile weapons, LaWS utilises scalable power levels that can be tuned to provide either a non-lethal or lethal response.

One potential issue relating to these futuristic weapons relates to energy requirements. For example, the US Navy's current EMRG reportedly requires around 25MW of energy to achieve maximum performance. The *Zumwalt* class are the only units in the surface fleet able to meet this need.[7]

Unmanned Systems: Yet another trend to be observed is the growing sector of unmanned surface, subsurface and airborne systems. The first such surface systems were developed as long ago as the late 1950s for mine-countermeasures applications, with drone hulls being in excess of 20m in length. The craft could be operated in manned or in remotely-controlled unmanned modes; the best-known users were the navies of Denmark, Germany, and Russia. An airborne system was introduced at around the same time by the US Navy to serve in the anti-submarine role as the QH-50 DASH (Drone Anti-Submarine Helicopter).

Since then, smaller, multi-faceted unmanned off-board systems have appeared which can be shipped in the form of modular unmanned mission packages. These drones have a varied nomenclature – for example ASV (Autonomous Surface Vehicle) or USV (Unmanned Surface Vehicle); AUV (Autonomous Underwater Vehicle) or UUV (Unmanned Underwater Vehicle); and UAV (Unmanned Airborne Vehicle) – and can operate in a variety of roles. These include mine-countermeasures, hydrography, reconnaissance and threat identification/classification, base defence, force protection and anti-submarine warfare. The systems can be operated both from a host ship or a shore station. It is preferable if host ships are equipped with the 'mission bays' or 'flex decks' already mentioned,

as these are ideal for launch and recovery purposes.

An elaborate new so-called 'system of systems' concept being developed under the Anglo-French Maritime Mine Countermeasures (MMCM) demonstrator programme since March 2015 serves as a good example of how unmanned systems might be used in future. Comprising a portable operations centre, an USV with towed sonar, a remotely-operated delayed disposal system and a number of additional UUVs, it also suggests a trend towards a marked growth in the space needed to support unmanned systems.

Meanwhile, it is interesting to note that one trend relating to unmanned systems in the commercial side of shipbuilding may even lead to the introduction of unmanned merchant ships. For example, 2015 saw the completion of an 'Unmanned Multifunctional Maritime Ships Research and Development Project' set up in 2012 at the Wuhan University of Technology by the Chinese Maritime Safety Administration. In the United Kingdom, the Rolls-Royce group has also undertaken work on the development of drone cargo ships. It is estimated that, by removing the crew, the bridge and other equipment needed to support crew living conditions, ships could be made five per cent lighter and might burn twelve to fifteen per cent less fuel. As a ship's crew typically accounts for just under half the operating expenses of a large container ship, the use of unmanned vessels seems to be an obvious path to savings.

GLOBAL INDUSTRIAL TRENDS IN NAVAL SHIPBUILDING

Shipbuilding is one of the world's oldest and most highly competitive markets. Until the middle of the last century, it was dominated by European countries. In commercial shipbuilding, the rapid growth of the Japanese economy and the establishment of a programme to render shipbuilding a strategic industry, then won market leadership for Japan. In the 1970s, South Korea followed the Japanese strategy and, in combination with low labour costs, began to achieve leadership. Eventually China adopted a similar expansion strategy, ultimately surpassing Japan in 2006 and South Korea in 2009. To make things worse for European shipbuilders, new competitors such as India, Russia, Turkey, and Vietnam also emerged and, together, achieved orders equivalent to European figures.

Technology Transfers: A similar development trend

is obvious in the naval shipbuilding market, where Europe, Russia and the United States had traditionally been the main suppliers of the world's navies. However, when replacement tonnage was sought for ships – many acquired as surplus tonnage from the major powers after the Second World War – from the 1970s onwards, a number of countries with limited existing naval shipbuilding capability commenced a new procurement strategy. This involved a requirement for the transfer of technology and know-how to support local production in new sites or in premises taken over from third parties. The end result was the appearance of new players on the global naval shipbuilding scene and significant structural changes both in the shipbuilding industry and the associated ranks of equipment and weapons suppliers.

A few examples will serve to provide further insight of a developing trend. In the case of Argentina, four MEKO type frigates were built in Germany under a contract authorised in 1979. However, a follow-on contract for six corvettes of the MEKO 140 type could only be concluded under the prerequisite that the corvettes were built in Argentina from material packages supplied by Blohm & Voss and with the provision of complete design documentation. In the case of Turkey, two frigates each of type MEKO 200 TN and MEKO 200 TN-II were built in Germany and two each in

An artist's impression of an electromagnetic railgun onboard a US Navy joint high speed vessel. Tests of the new weapons system are planned to take place on the *Trenton* (T-EPF-5) off the Florida Coast in the summer of 2016. *(US Navy)*

Turkey. Three out of four MEKO 200 HN frigates were constructed in Greece and four of six MEKO 100 RMN corvettes in Malaysia. All ten MEKO 200 ANZ frigates were built in Australia after local design personnel had received design training in Germany. Quite similar arrangements were also agreed with regard to German submarine export business, thus providing the respective countries with a potential submarine export capability.

Global Shipbuilding Groups: Other countries with emerging naval shipbuilding industries have achieved know-how by their own efforts, including transfer of knowledge from the commercial sector. Yet others still have benefited from local production in sites owned by foreign companies. Indeed, several European shipbuilding enterprises have developed production abroad to help their businesses survive. One example is the German Fr. Lürssen group, which founded the Hong Leong Shipyard in Butterworth, Malaysia, as early as the 1970s. Amongst one of the more successful groups to adopt this approach is the well-known Dutch Damen Shipyards Group, which originated in 1927 as a small boat yard. After the Second World War, Damen products slowly gained an excellent reputation in many foreign markets and Damen saw the potential to expand exports. Damen ultimately took over numerous yards specialising in niche markets, leading to the establishment of partnerships and

The Indian Navy's new Project 28 anti-submarine corvette *Kamorta* seen in March 2015. As the chapter's author can attest, the quality of work achieved by local builders GRSE is equivalent to European standards; a far cry from the situation pertaining to Indian warships twenty-five years ago. *(Hartmut Ehlers)*

business co-operation with yards all over the world. Recent developments have included the purchase of a forty-nine percent shareholding in the Vietnamese Ha Long Shipbuilding Co. Ltd. And, most recently, the take-over of the Cyrus Shipyard in Antalya, Turkey, as Damen Shipyards Antalya in late 2014. Italy's Fincantieri is another group adopting this type of strategy, owning the Marinette Marine yard in Wisconsin that builds the LCS-1 variant of the US Navy's Littoral Combat Ship.

A more recent trend is the reverse situation of European shipyards taken over by foreign investors. The most notable example of this is the acquisition of the surface operations of Germany's HDW (part of ThyssenKrupp Marine Systems) at Kiel and Rendsburg by Abu Dhabi-based investors. The company was called Abu Dhabi MAR Kiel (ADMK) until 31 March 2015, when it was renamed German Naval Yards.

China & India: Returning to the global market but especially developments in Asia, it is notable that China is now on the brink of becoming a major – if not even the greatest – emerging competitor to the more established European yards. This makes an interesting contrast with the other largest Asian nation, India, which has gained very limited exposure to warship export markets. This may be attributed to lack of capacity in Indian naval shipyards, which have been more than fully occupied with new construction for their own expanding navy. Indeed, the Indian Navy has placed orders with Russia in recent years to make good a capacity shortfall.

However, India is keen to solve the problem of long delays that many of its major warship construction programmes have experienced whilst furthering the government's 'Made in India' campaign. One recent positive development relates to plans announced during the visit of Indian Prime Minister Modi to South Korea in 2015 for co-operation between Hindustan Shipyard Limited and Hyundai Heavy Industries (HHI) to build warships, including submarines and destroyers. This would also mark an interesting example of a transfer of technology deal involving two Asian countries.

Shipbuilding Quality: A crucial point in the growing competitiveness of designs offered by many Asian and emerging countries in general is an improvement in the quality of their work. A mere twenty-five years ago, this could seldom compare to the standards set by European yards. For example, during a business visit to the Kuwaiti Coast Guard in November 1989, the author had a good opportunity to inspect the Indian Type 16 frigate, *Gomati*, which had called with the replenishment ship *Shakti* in Al Shuwaik port. Built by Mazagon Dock Ltd., Mumbai, *Gomati* had been laid down in 1981 and was commissioned on 16 April 1988. Welding, whether it has been performed automatically or manually, could best be described as sub-standard. In addition, the 'hungry horse' look observed in both hull and superstructure plating was noteworthy. There was a striking difference in quality between *Gomati* and the German-built *Shakti*.

Twenty-six years later, in March 2015 at Porto

Malai, Langkawi, Malaysia, the author was able to examine welding on the new Indian Project 28 corvette *Kamorta*. Built by GRSE, Kolkata, she was laid down in 2006 and commissioned in August 2014. In this ship, welding was found to be up to recent European standards.

CONCLUSION
Warship construction in the last two centuries has seen a breath-taking development far exceeding the imaginative power of contemporary minds. The reader is invited to imagine the reaction of sailors at the battle of Trafalgar in 1805 if the battleship *Dreadnought*, laid down in October 1905, had appeared on the scene. One hundred years later, at the beginning of the twenty-first century, the international naval scene reflects the pace with which warship construction has progressed. Today a battleship from 1905 would make a fine museum exhibit. In addition, the world's political map has changed drastically, and challenges from technical developments have contributed their part.

All told, it remains to be seen what effects continuing geopolitical changes, changes to strategic and operational requirements, progressive technical development and trends in general will entail for the field of warship construction. One thing should be taken for granted. Although the extent is not easy to assess, there will be significant differences by the end of this century. The warship of the year 2105 might – at the extreme – differ from the warship of 2005 as much as the battleship *Dreadnought* differed from the sailing vessels fighting off Trafalgar.

Notes
1. Concluded in 1982 but not taking effect until November 1994, the current UNCLOS III regime formally adopted the concept of a national EEZ. Most significantly, this gave states exclusive rights to marine resources up to 200 nautical miles from their coastline. The convention also provides for more limited rights in respect of a country's continental shelf, which can extend national interests out to 350 nautical miles.

2. It might be worth mentioning that the German Blohm & Voss shipyard also had a comparable patent, covering a 'Ship type series for modular construction with similar fore and aft sections, for all types, and central extension sections for longer ships' (No. DE 4108122 A1). This had been registered in 1991 but lapsed in January 2011 due to non-payment of the annual fee. The author had been a co-inventor of this patent.

3. Steam propulsion itself had quite an interesting history of development. The first steam engines in ships appeared in the early nineteenth century. Mainly of the reciprocating type, they were commonly classified in terms of the cylinder technology used. During the twentieth century, they progressively gave way to steam turbines and diesel engines.

4. Amongst the most common propulsion plant abbreviations are COSAG (combined steam and gas), COGAG (combined gas and gas), CODAG (combined diesel and gas) and CODLAG (combined diesel-electric and gas). Sometimes, the different technologies are used separately rather than together, as for example on CODOG (combined diesel or gas).

5. The author had practical experience of this problem

when – whilst working for MTG Marinetechnik – he was called upon to provide a solution to severe internal exhaust smoke contamination impacting the Royal Navy of Oman's logistic landing ship *Nasr Al Bahr,* first delivered by Brooke Marine of Lowestoft, United Kingdom, in January 1985. Through shipboard inspection and a day at sea, a solution was adopted that included use of a funnel.

6. The first navy to introduce respective measures was the Royal Netherlands Navy which fitted IR signature suppression stack caps to their six *Van Speijk* class frigates in the late 1970s.

7. It has been reported that – should initial EMRG trials prove successful – a railgun will be installed in the third *Zumwalt* class ship, *Lyndon B. Johnson* (DDG-1002), in the place of one of its 155mm guns.

6.1

Conrad Waters

AIRCRAFT CARRIERS & AMPHIBIOUS SHIPS

The changed operating environment faced by navies since the end of the Cold War has tended to favour the use of aviation-capable ships. For the largest navies, such as those of the United States and France, the ability of a fully-fledged aircraft carrier to provide flexible, on-call support against a wide range of objectives almost anywhere in the world is unmatched by any other weapons system. This ability is particular relevant to operations in the littoral, where targets may be numerous, fleeting and warrant a widely varying amount of effort to ensure their destruction. It is no accident that the significant shrinkage in US Navy forces since the end of the 1990s has impacted the carrier fleet much less than other warship types. However, the considerable financial and technical challenges inherent in aircraft carrier operation mean that it remains unaffordable to navies with all but the deepest pockets.

Given this backdrop, many second-tier fleets have attempted to develop options for 'budget' carrier operations. This trend dates back as far as the 1970s, when the availability of the Short Take Off and Vertical Landing (STOVL) capability provided by the Harrier 'jump jet' seemed to offer a new, cheaper entrance ticket to the 'carrier club'. STOVL did allow a number of navies, for example those of Spain, Italy and Russia, to deploy fast jets at sea. Equally significantly, it permitted some fleets, notably the British Royal Navy, an affordable alternative to the increasing cost and complexity of conventional carrier operations. However, in practice, the number of nations developing a new carrier capacity has been broadly balanced by those abandoning fast jet carrier operations.[1] In addition to the still-considerable expense, some nations doubted the cost-effectiveness of the more limited capabilities offered by STOVL aircraft. This may be changing, however. The greater use of commercial standards in warship design, the advent of the more capable F-35B Joint Strike Fighter STOVL variant, and the increasing wealth of many nations – particularly in Asia – may yet combine to see fast jet deployment become more widespread.

Even for those countries without the means or ambition to operate fixed-wing naval aircraft, the growing importance of the littoral has seen increased attention given to the development of amphibious capabilities. These increasingly require the ability to support a considerable number of helicopters to conduct and sustain operations. This has spawned a number of LHD-type amphibious assault ship type programmes utilising a 'through-deck' arrangement to maximise overall flight-deck area.[2] An alternative trend, led by the Royal Netherlands Navy, has seen the combination of amphibious and logistical support characteristics into a vessel resembling a stretched LPD-type amphibious transport dock.

This chapter aims to examine the design characteristics of some of the more significant ships that have resulted from these broad developments.

AIRCRAFT CARRIER DEVELOPMENT

The US Navy continues to dominate conventional Catapult Assisted Take Off But Assisted Recovery (CATOBAR) aircraft carrier development, operating ten of the twelve aircraft carriers in the world that still utilise this technology. All of these ten vessels are members of the c.100,000-ton, nuclear-powered *Nimitz* (CVN-68) class. These typically embark an air group of around seventy aircraft and helicopters.

Preliminary design work began in 1964 and the lead ship was authorised under the FY1967 naval programme. The basic design can be traced back to the conventionally-powered *Forrestal* (CV-59) class of the 1950s; the first post-Second World War 'super carriers' and the earliest designed specifically to operate jet-propelled aircraft.

Nimitz was commissioned in May 1975, whilst *George H. W. Bush* – the tenth and final ship – was accepted in May 2009. The class therefore represents the longest production run of a basic ship design in any modern navy. Incremental improvements have been incorporated as the programme has progressed. *Theodore Roosevelt* (CVN-71) and later ships have better magazine protection, whilst the last two vessels feature a bulbous bow, higher deck levels and a modified island. In spite of these enhancements, it has become increasingly apparent that an essentially fifty-year-old design no longer provides the optimum way to meet current operational requirements. In particular, greater availability of precision weapons means that the ability to conduct an all-out 'Alpha Strike' on a primary target utilising a full deckload of aircraft is of less importance than in Cold War days. The potential to generate a high number of sorties against varying targets over a sustained period is now a more significant consideration. Equally, the *Nimitz* class's high manning levels – the core crew required simply to man each ship is c.3,200 – and legacy systems make it relatively expensive to operate.

Gerald R. Ford (CVN-78) Class: As a result, the US Navy is bringing into service the *Gerald R. Ford* (CVN-78) class, which emerged from the CVX and CVN-21 development programmes. The lead ship was laid down in 2009 but preparatory work started several years previously. It uses the same hull form as the preceding class but has a number of innovations to increase sortie generation rates (SGRs) and lower operating costs.

The most visually obvious change in support of these aims is a major re-design of the flight deck layout to provide flight increased deck space and improve the flow of aircraft movements. These revisions include a reduction in the number of aircraft elevators from four to three and relocation of a smaller, stealthier island further aft. They have been accompanied by a redesign of internal arrangements to produce an improved flow of weapons to refuelling and rearmament 'pit stops'.

Equally significant – if less visually apparent – is

the first-time use of two new technologies to improve CATOBAR operation. These are the Electromagnetic Aircraft Launch System (EMALS) and the Advanced Arresting Gear (AAG). The former replaces the traditional steam catapult, using a linear induction motor to generate a moving magnetic field that propels an aircraft launch carriage down a track until take-off speed is reached. The latter introduces energy-absorbing water turbine technology to replace the less precise hydraulic ram of the current Mk 7 arresting system. Together, the two systems are intended to provide greater reliability and precision than the systems they replace, further speeding aircraft operations. A particular benefit is the fact that they are easier to adjust to handle the new generation of lighter-

weight unmanned aerial vehicles (UAVs) that are likely to enter service over the new class's lifetime. The electrically-powered EMALS also escapes the dependency on steam generation inherent in current carriers. This makes CATOBAR operations a more realistic possibility in non-nuclear-powered ships.[3]

The improvements provided by the *Ford* class's enhanced flight deck design and the superior capabilities of EMALS and AAG are intended to sustain a SGR of at least 160 sorties per day over an extended period, whilst permitting a surge to 270 sorties during a 24-hour fly day surge. Although there is some scepticism these targets will be achieved, they offer a considerable advance over the 120 sustained/240 surge figures permitted by the *Nimitz* class.

The new systems installed in the *Ford* class – which also include a more-effective primary radar – continue a trend towards greater demands for shipboard electrical power.[4] This is being met by a new twin Bechtel A1B nuclear reactor plant that provides around two and a half times the generating capacity of the previous ships. There has also been a redesign of electrical distribution to a zonal system that is lighter and more survivable than the traditional radial arrangement found in older ships. The opportunity has been taken to switch 'hotel' systems such as galleys and laundries to electrical power, often helping to reduce crew size.

Two *Ford* class aircraft carriers – *Gerald R. Ford* herself and *John F. Kennedy* (CVN-69) – are currently under construction and preparatory work is underway on a third. The first ship should be delivered in the course of 2016. She has taken longer and cost more to complete than originally envisaged – total outlays have amounted to US$12.9bn

The first new-generation US Navy nuclear-powered aircraft carrier *Gerald R. Ford* (CVN-78) seen on 9 November 2013, her christening day. She represents a re-working of the previous *Nimitz* class to take account of 21st-century naval aviation requirements. *(Huntington Ingalls Industries)*

(excluding a further US$4.7bn of R&D costs applying to the overall class). This has resulted in the specifications of follow-on ships being paired back to reduce expense. However, a reduction in core crew size of around 500 and other efficiencies should reduce operation costs considerably. Savings of between US$4bn and US$5bn – up to US$100m p.a. – should be achieved over a planned fifty-year service life.

Vikrant: Although both France and Brazil also operate CATOBAR-type aircraft carriers, no other country currently has ships of this configuration under construction. All other carrier programmes since the end of the Cold War have featured naval aircraft with some form of short take-off capability. These aircraft either use the STOVL techniques commonly associated with the Harrier series or the hybrid Short Take Off But Assisted Recovery (STOBAR) method. Under this, aircraft take off under their own power – typically with the help of a ski-jump – but use a traditional barrier arrangement to land.

STOBAR operation originated with the Soviet Union towards the end of the Cold War. It was first employed by the Project 1143.5/6 'heavy aircraft carrying cruiser' *Admiral Kuznetsov*, which was commissioned in January 1991. The technique has been subsequently adopted by China's PLAN following the acquisition, refurbishment and commissioning of *Admiral Kuznetsov*'s incomplete sister-ship *Varyag* as *Liaoning*. The new indigenous Chinese aircraft carrier now under construction at Dalian is also likely to adopt STOBAR configuration. However, the only post-Cold War STOBAR carrier afloat to date is India's first indigenous aircraft carrier *Vikrant*. Launched from Cochin Shipyard Ltd on 12 August 2013, she is scheduled for delivery in 2018 if Indian industry can overturn a terrible track record of late deliveries.

India's adoption of STOBAR – which avoids the complexity of catapult operation but requires the use of aircraft with a sufficiently high thrust/weight ratio

The first indigenously-built Indian aircraft carrier *Vikrant* utilises the Russian STOBAR configuration, under which ski-jump-assisted short take off is combined with arrested recovery. This picture was taken in June 2015, when the ship was undocked for the last time during construction on completion of underwater work. There is a lot to be done if she is to meet a (revised) 2018 commissioning date. *(Indian Navy)*

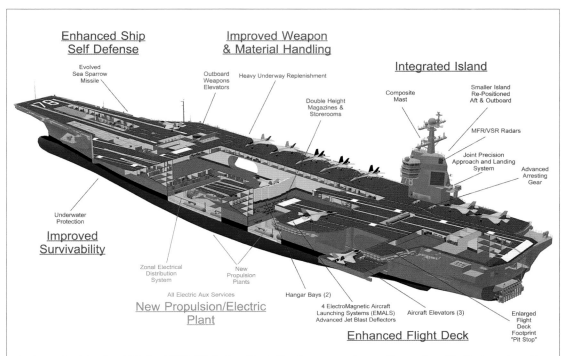

A schematic of the *Gerald R. Ford* (CVN-78) design, illustrating improvements over the previous *Nimitz* class. As well as improving operating performance, the modifications will produce efficiency savings of between US$4bn and US$5bn over the ship's service life. *(US Navy)*

to take-off without catapult assistance – is also the result of Russian influence. The country has recently commissioned the former Russian Project 1143.4 STOVL carrier *Admiral Gorshkov* as *Vikramaditya* following its reconstruction to STOBAR configuration and has acquired MiG-29K strike fighters to operate from both ships. STOBAR-equipped ships have to be reasonably large to allow a sufficient take-off run and - in contrast to STOVL carriers – also need an angled deck to ensure safe operation if the barrier is missed. Consequently, *Vikrant* has a full load displacement of over 40,000 tons and a total flight deck length of around 260m. Even so, one of the two aircraft launch positions – offset from the axial line – is set close to the stern to help fully-loaded aircraft to be launched with safety.

Although *Vikrant*'s STOBAR configuration reflects Russian practice, the ship's design has also been heavily influenced by Western designs and technology in accordance with the 'mix and match'

approach that has typified many recent Indian warships. Notably, Italy's Fincantieri has provided considerable design support and the propulsion system owes much to that installed in the *Marina Militare*'s *Cavour*. Radar and air defence systems feature a mixture of Italian and Israeli technology. A total of up to thirty aircraft – including around twelve MiG-29Ks – will make up the air group.

Vikrant's 2018 delivery date is already eight years later than first planned and she is reportedly likely to

6.1.1: 21st-CENTURY AIRCRAFT CARRIER DESIGNS

Class:	Gerald R. Ford (CVN-78)	Vikrant	Queen Elizabeth	Cavour
Builder:	HII – Newport News Shipbuilding Newport News, Virginia	Cochin Shipyard Limited Kochi, Kerala	Aircraft Carrier Alliance Rosyth, Scotland[1]	Fincantieri Muggiano & Riva Trigoso, Liguria
Country:	United States of America	India	United Kingdom	Italy
Number:[2]	0+2+[1]	0+1+[0]	0+2+[0]	1+0+[0]
Keel Laid:[3]	14 November 2009	28 February 2009	7 July 2009[4]	17 July 2001[4]
Christened:[3]	9 November 2013	12 August 2013	4 July 2014	20 July 2004
Commissioned:[3]	[2016]	[2018 onwards]	[2017]	27 March 2008
Full Load Displacement:	100,000+ tons	40,000+ tons	65,000 tons	27,500 tons
Principal Dimensions:	317m (333m o.a.) x 41m x 12m Flight deck: 333m x 78m	262m o.a. x 62m o.a. x 8m Flight deck: 262m x 62m	263m x (284m o.a.) x 39m x 10m Flight deck: 284m x 73m	244m o.a. x 40m x 8m Flight deck: 234m x 35m
Propulsion:	Nuclear, 30+ knots Unlimited range	COGAG, 28 knots c.8,000nm range	IEP, 25+ knots c.10,000nm range	COGAG, 28 knots c.7,000nm range
Aircraft Capability:	CATOBAR (4 EMALS) 3 elevators c.70 aircraft	STOBAR 2 elevators 6 landing spots c.30 aircraft	STOVL (including ski-jump) 2 elevators 10 landing spots c.40 aircraft	STOVL (including ski-jump) 2 elevators 6 landing spots c.20 aircraft
Armament:	Mk 29 octuple ESSM Mk 49 RAM Mk 15 Phalanx CIWS	Barak 8 SAM 4 x 76mm Oto Melara 2 x Mk 15 Phalanx CIWS	3 x Phalanx CIWS 4 x 30mm 3 x 25mm	4 x 8 cells for Aster-15 SAM 2 x 76mm Oto Melara
Crew:	c.2,800 plus air group	c.1,500 including air group	c.700 plus air group	c.450 plus air group 400+ troops in amphibious role

Notes:

1 The ships are being assembled at Aircraft Carrier Alliance member Babcock's Rosyth shipyard from blocks constructed at yards around the United Kingdom.

2 Refers to ships completed or under construction, with numbers in brackets those firmly planned.

3 Dates relate to the first of the class. Christening dates can vary significantly from actual float-out or launch.

4 Date relates to formal commencement of work on the first major block.

5 Data is largely drawn from official press releases and other official sources. There is a degree of variation with respect to data in the public domain and the table should be regarded as being indicative only.

cost at least six times an initial INR32.6bn (US$0.5bn) budget. As such, the desire to cultivate local industry has come at a heavy price. In addition, it is arguable that historic relations with Russia has resulted in the selection of a STOBAR configuration that does not reflect India's longer-term requirements. Growing co-operation with the United States suggests the second indigenous carrier may result in the EMALS and AAG CATOBAR configuration utilised in the *Ford* class.

***Queen Elizabeth* Class:** Turning to more traditional STOVL operation, the most significant post-Cold War design is undoubtedly represented by the British *Queen Elizabeth* class CVF (future aircraft carrier) programme. Design studies to replace the previous *Invincible* class STOVL support carriers began in the early 1990s and the decision to build two, much larger replacements was taken in the Strategic Defence Review of 1998. However, convoluted discussions as to the merits of CATOBAR, STOBAR and STOVL operation – coupled with significant financial pressures – meant that a full decade was to pass before a formal contact was placed in July 2008.

Whilst the *Queen Elizabeth* class has been built to a STOVL configuration, the ultimate design is nominally adaptable to support other operating methods should the requirement arise. However, when this option was analysed in detail following the 2010 Strategic Defence & Security Review, it was found that the extent of the work involved was such that it was unlikely ever to be cost-effective in practice. Nevertheless, the incorporation of adaptability has resulted in a significant design legacy, not least a 65,000-ton displacement that is second only to the US Navy's nuclear-powered ships.[5]

In addition to the influence of a successful recent track record of STOVL operations, the higher SGR available from STOVL aircraft was a key factor in determining the class's configuration. This outweighed the benefits of lower aircraft acquisition cost, better range and improved inter-operability with allied strike carriers that a CATOBAR carrier would have brought. The baseline air group for the new carriers was established as thirty-six fast jets and four early warning helicopters, reflecting the aim of using them as the core of an expanded expeditionary strike capability. Early plans indicated that up to 150 daily fast jet sorties should be achieved on this basis. However, this had reportedly fallen to a 24-hour

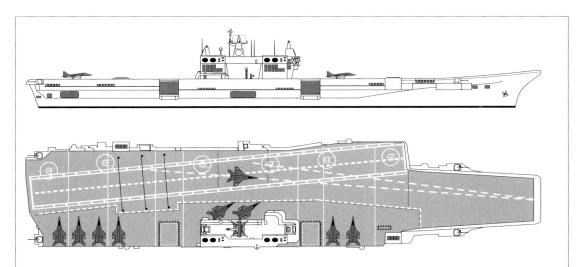

An indicative drawing of the completed *Vikrant*. The drawing provides a good indication of the principal operating features of a STOBAR aircraft carrier. Aircraft take off with the assistance of a ski-jump from one of two launch positions, that aft allowing launch at maximum weight. Recovery is by means of an angled deck fitted with arrester wires. There is room for a deck park and six helicopter landing spots. *(John Jordan)*

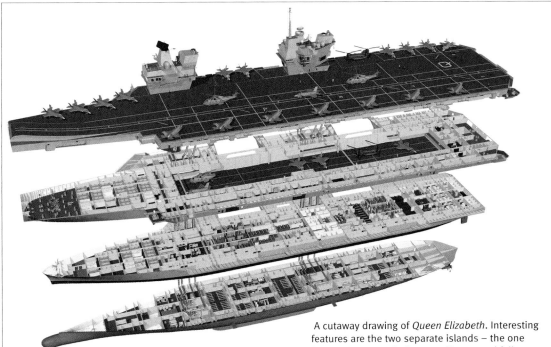

A cutaway drawing of *Queen Elizabeth*. Interesting features are the two separate islands – the one forward for navigation, the one placed aft for aviation control. The use of integrated full electric propulsion allows the ship's gas turbines to be placed immediately below the islands, allowing shorter exhausts and easier maintenance. The large lifts are capable of handling two F-35Bs or a Chinook helicopter with rotor blades extended. The hangar is small compared with the total size of the ship but is high enough to stow a wide range of aircraft. *(Aircraft Carrier Alliance)*

surge rate of 108 fast jet sorties (i.e. three per aircraft), dropping to seventy-two sorties per day (two per aircraft) thereafter, by the time the ships were ordered.

As for the US Navy's *Ford* class, the SGR requirement has had a major impact on the ship's overall design. For example, the innovative twin-island arrangement helps to maximise flight deck area.[6] The 'pit stop' servicing arrangement has also been adopted to speed aircraft turnaround times, whilst an automated cargo handling system facilitates rapid

delivery of munitions from the magazines to the single hangar and flight deck. This also helps achieve a significant reduction in crew size – the core complement of c. 680 is around the same as that required for the legacy *Invincible* class.

As for STOBAR operation, STOVL places greater limitations on aircraft operation compared with a more traditional CATOBAR arrangement. The *Queen Elizabeth* class's c.280m long flight deck and ski-jump allow the F-35B to be launched with a full weapons load. However, recovery with an un-

depleted payload could still be problematic, particularly in hot conditions where jet engines work less effectively. A Shipborne Rolling Vertical Landing (SRVL) technique is being developed to mitigate this limitation, using a new landing reference system, the Bedford Array. However, the lack of an angled deck suggests this may be a more risky method than the STOBAR alternative.

The expense of nuclear propulsion meant this was unaffordable for the cost-limited *Queen Elizabeth* design. Instead, the ships use the 'in vogue' integrated full electric propulsion (IFEP) arrangement. The ship's gas turbines and diesel generators provide electricity to a distribution network. This supplies

The first British *Queen Elizabeth* class carrier being floated out of her construction dock in July 2014. It is interesting to compare her state of completion with the image of *Vikrant*. (BAE Systems)

power to the electric motors that propel the ship as well as meeting the requirements of other electrical equipment from radar through to internal lighting. Nevertheless, the two ships have not been inexpensive, with a series of cost increases resulting in a total budget of £6.2bn (c.US$10bn). Indeed, there have been occasions when the whole project has come close to cancellation. However, with the first ship scheduled to start trials towards the end of 2016, there is now greater appreciation of the class's potential. This has broadened somewhat beyond the initial strike focus, with the Carrier Enabled Power Projection (CEPP) concept now envisaging them being equipped with a wide range of tailored air groups to meet different roles.

Cavour: The only other 'pure' STOVL carrier ordered since the end of the Cold War is the Italian *Cavour*. She is the outcome of another protracted design process. This commenced in the late 1980s, when a second major unit was sought to supplement the new carrier *Giuseppe Garibaldi* and replace the veteran helicopter cruiser *Vittorio Veneto*. Originally based on an improved *Garibaldi*, the resultant design when through numerous iterations as the navy debated the extent to which the new ship should be optimised for amphibious operations. The potential inclusion of a well deck was a significant factor driving up overall size. Ultimately, however, the desirability of configuring the ship to support the next generation F-35B STOVL strike fighter and the possibility of using helicopters for amphibious projection resulted in a ship configured primarily for naval air operations, but with a subsidiary amphibious transport capability. This is the opposite of the more common post-Cold War trend of amphibious assault ships being designed with potential to perform a secondary carrier role.

The resultant ship was ordered from Italy's Fincantieri in 1999, being delivered on 27 March 2008. Displacing around 27,500 tons in full load condition, she is somewhat smaller than the other new carriers considered in this chapter, although considerably larger than the preceding *Garibaldi*. This has had an impact on the baseline air group of around eighteen to twenty aircraft, some twelve of which can be accommodated in the hangar. This reflects the reality that Italy would be unlikely to deploy an air group – particularly of fast jets – of the size envisaged by some of the larger fleets.

The main emphasis in *Cavour*'s design is on flexi-

The Italian STOVL aircraft carrier *Cavour* is the smallest of recent 'pure' aircraft carriers, perhaps stretching the limits of what can be done to minimise size (and cost) whilst retaining a meaningful aviation capability. This image shows her on trials in 2008. *(Italian Navy)*

bility. For example, the hangar can be used as a garage for army vehicles as well as to house aircraft. It can be accessed by side and stern ramps and is capable of supporting a vehicle weight of up to 60 tons. Whilst the core crew is in the order of 450, sufficient accommodation is provided for over 1,200 personnel. This would be sufficient for an air group, headquarters staff and in excess of 400 troops. *Cavour*'s defence systems are also of a higher standard than in many other Western carrier designs, aiding deployment in higher-threat areas. In particular, the SAAM-IT system – combining the EMPAR multifunction radar and Aster 15 surface-to-air missile – provides a powerful air-defence capability.[7] There is also a comprehensive command and control suite. Propulsion is by means of a conventional COGAG arrangement, providing a maximum speed of 28 knots.

All-in-all, *Cavour* provides Italy with a relatively sophisticated aviation capability at an affordable cost – total outlays were reportedly in the region of €1.3bn (c. US$1.5bn) at 2001 prices. The main constraint is the impact that her relatively modest size might have on future operations. Although the requirements of the next-generation F-35B were taken into account in the design, overall flight deck length of some 234m may not be sufficient to take full advantage of the new aircraft type.

AMPHIBIOUS ASSAULT SHIPS & HELICOPTER CARRIERS

It is evident from the above overview that purpose-built aircraft carriers remain the preserve of only a few, relatively well-funded navies. However, the attraction of naval aviation capabilities has been far more widespread. This has spurred a number of ships that provide considerable scope to support a range of naval air activities in addition to their primary role. This has been particularly the case with respect to amphibious warships.

Juan Carlos I: An alternative approach to Italy's *Cavour* is presented by Spain's *Juan Carlos I* amphibious assault ship. Approved in September 2003 to meet a requirement for a strategic projection ship to support Spain's growing post-Cold War appetite for expeditionary operations, *Juan Carlos I* was ordered the following year and delivered in the autumn of 2010. Two virtually identical ships – the *Canberra* class – have been delivered to the RAN under Project JP2048 (phase 4A/B). In addition, a close derivative has been ordered by Turkey to meet its own amphibious requirements.

Conceptually similar to – but smaller and cheaper – than the US Navy's larger *Tarawa* (LHA-1), *Wasp* (LHD-1) and *America* (LHA-6) types, the *Juan*

Carlos I type is an excellent example of a ship optimised to undertake amphibious assaults but with potential to host a broader range of expeditionary activities. The former mission demands a significant amount of internal volume to transport up to 900 troops and associated stores and equipment, as well

as a large flight deck area to allow the operation of sufficient helicopters to support an airborne assault. An internal well deck is also important to support the subsequent deployment of heavier equipment and vehicles in the absence of more specialist shipping. Meanwhile, a secondary requirement to be able

6.1.2: 21st-CENTURY AMPHIBIOUS ASSAULT SHIP & HELICOPTER CARRIER DESIGNS

Class:	*Juan Carlos I*	*Mistral*	*Dokdo*	*Hyuga* (DDH-181)	*America* (LHA-6)
Builder:[1]	Navantia	DCNS	Hanjin Heavy Ind.	IHI Marine United	HII – Ingalls Shipbuilding
	Ferrol, Galicia	Brest, Brittany[2]	Busan	Yokohama, Kanagawa	Pascagoula, Mississippi
Country:	Spain	France	South Korea	Japan	United States of America
Number:[3]	3+1+[0]	5+0+[0]	1+1+[0]	2+0+[0]	1+1+[0]
Keel Laid:[4]	20 May 2005	9 July 2002	2003	11 May 2006	17 July 2009
Christened:[4]	10 March 2008	6 October 2004	12 July 2005	23 August 2007	20 October 2012
Commissioned:[4]	30 September 2010	27 February 2006	3 July 2007	18 March 2009	11 October 2014
Full Load Displacement:	27,100 tons	21,500 tons	18,900 tons	19,000 tons	45,000 tons
Principal Dimensions:	231m x 32m x 7m	199m x 32m x 6m	200m x 31m x 7m	197m x 33m x 7m	237m (257m o.a.) x 32m x 9m
	Flight deck: 202m x 32m	Flight deck: 199m x 32m	Flight deck: 200m x 30m	Flight deck: 195m x 33m	Flight deck: 249m x 36m
Propulsion:	IEP (pods), 21 knots	Diesel-electric (pods), 19 knots	Diesel, 22 knots	COGAG, 30 knots	Hybrid Electric Drive, 24 knots
	c.9,000nm range	c.11,000nm range	c.6,000nm range	c.8,000nm range	
Aircraft Capability:	STOVL (including ski-jump)	Helicopters only	Helicopters only	Helicopters only	STOVL (no ski-jump)
	6 landing spots	6 landing spots	5 landing spots	4 landing spots	9 landing spots
	c.30 aircraft	c.16 helicopters	10+ helicopters	c.10 helicopters	c.35+ aircraft
Armament:	4 x 20mm	2 x Simbad PDMS	1 x Mk 49 RAM	2 x 8 Mk 41 cells (ESSM/ASROC)	2 x Mk 29 octuple ESSM
			2 x Goalkeeper CIWS	2 x Phalanx CIWS	2 x Mk 49 RAM
				2 x triple 324mm TT	2 x Phalanx CIWS
Lift Capacity:	c. 1,200 troops, staff & air crew	c. 900 troops & air crew	c. 700 troops + air crew	Hangar only	c. 1,850 troops
	2,375m² lower vehicle deck	2,650m² vehicle deck	Hangar & well deck		Significant cargo capacity
	2,045m² upper deck/hangar	1,800m² hangar			No well deck
	69m x 17m well deck	58m x 15m well deck			
Core Crew:	260	160	c. 300	c. 350 (including air group)	c. 1,050 (including air group)

Notes:

1 Builders relate to the first of the class.

2 *Mistral* was built in two sections; the forward section at Chantiers de l'Atlantique at Saint Nazaire and the latter at DCNS in Brest. The two halves were joined and fitting-out completed at Brest.

3 Refers to ships completed or under construction, with numbers in brackets those firmly planned. *Juan Carlos I* column includes two ships built for Australia (integrated locally) and one ordered by Turkey (built locally). *Mistral* column includes two ships built for Russia and now acquired by Egypt.

4 Dates relate to the first of the class. Christening dates can vary from actual float out or launch. *Mistral*'s commissioning date refers to delivery; she was formally commissioned on 15 December 2006.

AVIATION SUPPORT SHIPS

Amphibious Assault Ship (Spain):
Juan Carlos I (L 61)

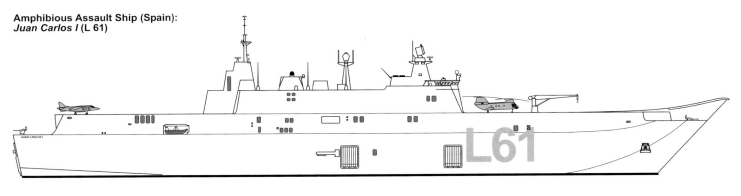

© John Jordan 2011

Amphibious Assault Ship (France):
Tonnerre (L 9014)

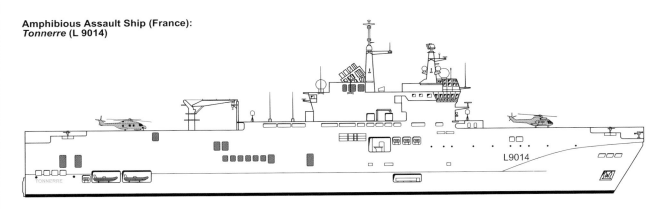

© John Jordan 2011

Helicopter-Carrying Destroyer (Japan):
Hyuga (DDH-181)

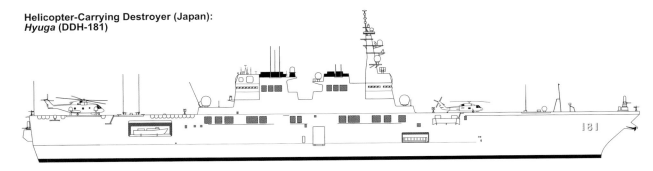

© John Jordan 2012

These drawings represent profiles of the two principal European amphibious assault ship designs: Spain's *Juan Carlos I* and France's *Mistral* class (here represented by second of class *Tonnerre*), as well as the Japanese helicopter-carrying destroyer *Hyuga*. The Spanish design is fitted with a ski-jump for STOVL aircraft operation, a function assisted by her overall length. The French ship is designed purely as a helicopter carrier, with the omission of a ski-jump providing additional landing space on the shorter flight deck. *Hyuga* has a broadly similar length and beam to *Tonnerre*, also reflecting her use as a pure helicopter carrier. However, her principal role is for anti-submarine operations and she does not require the same internal volume as the French warship.

to operate STOVL fast jets is reflected in the incorporation of a ski-jump and relatively long flight deck, as well as the use of hangar/garage spaces that can be used by both vehicles and aircraft. Overall hangar and garage area is around 4,400m² or nearly double the 2800m² provided by *Cavour*'s hangar. A sophisticated command and communications capability supports operation in a range of roles.

The combination of all these requirements has resulted in a relatively large ship – full-load displacement is very similar to that of *Cavour* – that would not be readily affordable by many second-tier fleets without significant design compromises. One of these is the widespread use of commercial building and design standards, with military specifications only being used in a number of key areas (e.g. flight deck facilities and ammunition storage). There is also a very light defensive armament, whilst the otherwise advanced IFEP system is limited to a maximum speed of around 21 knots. These economies resulted in the Spanish lead ship's cost being limited to just €375m (c.US$450m) or significantly less than a modern air-defence frigate. Further lifetime economies will be realised from a core crew numbering a little over 250.

***Mistral* Class:** Of course, not all fleets require the flexibility that is a key part of the *Juan Carlos I* design concept. A case is the French *Mistral* amphibious assault design, three of which have been delivered to the *Marine Nationale* from 2006 onwards. In addition, a pair of slightly modified ships constructed to Russian order have now been acquired by Egypt after events in Crimea and Ukraine scuppered the original deal.

Required to replace existing 1960s-era LPD/LSD ships, the *Mistral* class *bâtiments de projection et de commandement* (BPC) – projection and command ships – were intended to provide French amphibious forces with an expanded organic aviation capacity. However, the French Navy's continued focus on conventional CATOBAR carrier operations and

Australia's *Juan Carlos I* type amphibious assault ships *Canberra* and *Adelaide* pictured together in Sydney after the latter's delivery in 2015. Turkey is also building a vessel of the same type, which provides a pragmatic mix of amphibious and aviation capabilities. *(RAN)*

The French amphibious assault ship *Mistral* seen in company with British Royal Navy frigate *Argyll* in March 2013. In contrast to the Spanish *Juan Carlos I* design, the Mistral type does not have a STOVL capability. *(Crown Copyright 2013)*

consequent lack of STOVL aircraft meant that a fixed-wing aviation capability was not required. This is reflected in the absence of the ski-jump that usually features prominently in STOVL carriers, as well a relatively short, 199m-long flight deck. The lack of a ski-jump does have the significant advantage of releasing deck space for helicopter operations, six of which can use the flight deck simultaneously. The larger *Juan Carlos I* only has the same capacity.[8]

The French ships also offer broadly equivalent capabilities to the Spanish ships with respect to other amphibious functions, being able to transport a similarly-sized assault force but having a slightly less capacious well deck. Equally, investment in command-and-control facilities has taken precedence over defensive armament and there has been acceptance of a low maximum speed. Both designs share the same use of commercial standards to lower overall construction and operating costs.[9] Published sources suggest the purchase cost of the third *Mistral*, *Dixmude*, was c. €300m (US$360m).

Asian Designs: Whilst Europe has taken the lead in

South Korea's *Dokdo* is the only Asian-designed amphibious assault ship to be commissioned to date. Her design reflects the influence of the US Navy's much larger amphibious assault ships but is broadly comparable in size to the *Mistral*s. Although there have been rumours she might be modified to operate F-35B jets, she is probably a little too small to deploy them effectively. *(ROKN)*

developing innovative aviation platforms, reference also needs to be made to South Korea's amphibious assault ship *Dokdo*, which commissioned in July 2007. A second ship is currently under construction. As for the European vessels already discussed, her design owes much to larger US Navy amphibious assault ships. In spite of a different profile, she is quite similar to the *Mistral* type in overall dimensions and displacement. Her flight deck is laid out to allow the simultaneous operation of up to five helicopters, whilst two LCAC hovercraft can be shipped in the well deck. There is currently no provision for STOVL aircraft in spite of ongoing reports that consideration is being given to operating F-35B aircraft from the ships.

Neighbouring Japan has taken a slightly different route to developing maritime aviation capabilities. It has constructed two new classes of through-deck 'helicopter-carrying destroyers' to replace more conventionally-configured ships of this type. The initial pair of *Hyuga* (DDH-181) class ships are heavily orientated towards anti-submarine warfare. Despite a carrier-like appearance, a relatively small hangar and flight deck – laid out with only four helicopter spots – mean that abilities to sustain a wider range of roles are quite limited. However, the following *Izumo* (DDH-183) – with an overall length of 248m and a full load displacement of

c. 27,000 tons – is a different proposition. The first of the class was commissioned in March 2015 and a second ship will be delivered in 2017.

This enlarged design sacrifices onboard weapons and sensor fit to accommodate a larger aviation complement. Notably, there are five main helicopter operating spots on deck, each sufficiently spacious to handle a heavy helicopter. Overall helicopter-carrying capacity is also increased, whilst access arrangements to the hangar are improved to allow heavy vehicles to be embarked. These developments clearly increase utility in an amphibious role. The Japan Ground Self Defence Force is acquiring the V-22 Osprey tilt-rotor to improve its ability to defend the southern island chain and its use onboard the new ships would seem likely. As for Korea, there has also been ongoing speculation about Japan operating the F-35B STOVL Joint Strike Fighter variant. However, this would be a very significant political development.[10]

***America* (LHA-6) Class:** Meanwhile, the US Navy has also adopted the evolutionary process evident in its CATOBAR aircraft carriers to post-Cold War amphibious assault ship construction. Its fleet of large-deck, LHA/LHD-type amphibious assault ships are bigger than many aircraft carriers in other fleets and – like the *Juan Carlos I* design – can provide a

meaningful fixed-wing aviation capability based around embarked STOVL aircraft. The latest iteration of the type is the *America* (LHA-6) class. Although retaining a strong resemblance to preceding ships, this reflects recent trends both in amphibious operations and with respect to propulsion.

The former is evidenced by much greater emphasis on aviation facilities than in previous ships. The majority of amphibious force deployments – at least in their initial stages – are now more likely to be carried out by embarked aircraft rather than by landing craft. As a result, the traditional well deck is dispensed with to provide space for a larger aircraft hangar and increased storage for aviation fuel and spare parts. The intention is to allow more effective use of aircraft such as the MV-22B Osprey tilt-rotors and F-35B strike fighters with which the US Marine Corps is now being re-equipped. However, there has been a considerable backlash against the deletion of landing craft facilities and they seem set to be reinstated from the third ship of the class onwards.[11]

Propulsion is by means of a new hybrid electric drive system, combining gas turbine and electrical propulsion in lieu of the rather dated steam turbines used in the bulk of the *Wasp* class. The system essentially uses auxiliary electric motors powered from the ship's electrical grid for low speed operation up to speeds of c.12 knots, with gas turbine propulsion being clutched in when greater speed is necessary. The arrangement was trialled in the last *Wasp* class ship, *Makin Island* (LHD-8), providing considerable operating economies. A zonal electrical distribution system similar to that found on the *Ford* class has also been introduced. *America* was commissioned in October 2014 and a second ship, *Tripoli* (LHA-7) laid down in June of the same year.

OTHER AMPHIBIOUS SHIPS
The growing focus on expanding aviation capabilities that has driven investment in amphibious assault ships has not – to quite the same extent – been replicated in increased purchases of other major amphibious types. The US Navy – with greater resources to allocate to specialised warships – has continued to acquire LPD-type amphibious transport docks to form part of its amphibious ready groups as older ships retire. No fewer than twelve *San Antonio* (LPD-17) vessels have now been authorised and the once-troubled design is earmarked as the basis for replacing existing dock landing ships. The United Kingdom also replaced its former

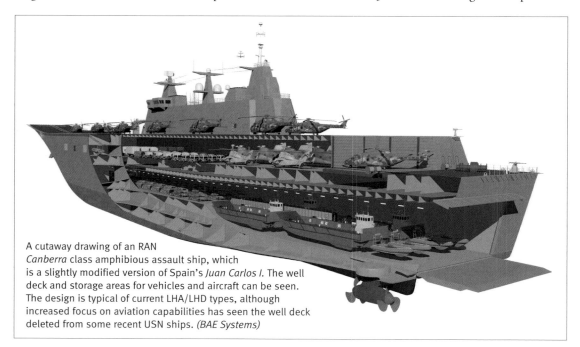

A cutaway drawing of an RAN *Canberra* class amphibious assault ship, which is a slightly modified version of Spain's *Juan Carlos I*. The well deck and storage areas for vehicles and aircraft can be seen. The design is typical of current LHA/LHD types, although increased focus on aviation capabilities has seen the well deck deleted from some recent USN ships. *(BAE Systems)*

Fearless class on a like-for-like basis with the current pair of *Albion* type LPDs as part of a renewal of its amphibious fleet that saw acquisition of the helicopter carrier *Ocean* and – later – the 'Bay' class LSDs. However, new operators – essentially China, Singapore and Thailand in Asia and the Netherlands and Spain in Europe – have been more limited than might be expected when considering the greater expense associated with the larger LHDs. It would seem that those countries that have been able to commit significant resources have opted for the ships offering the greatest aviation potential; the other have either made second-hand acquisitions (for example, Chile) or restricted investment to smaller, tank landing ship types.

One interesting alternative to this general approach has been provided by the Netherlands, whose Joint Support Ship (JSS) concept combines amphibious and logistical support requirements into a single hull. One ship – *Karel Doorman* – has been built to this arrangement. She resembles an enlarged LPD. A conventional forward structure provides accommodation for the ship's crew and a small embarked force, as well as space for a large helicopter hangar. Replenishment rigs for 'at sea' transfers are located aft of the superstructure. The rest of the ship is reserved for a large helicopter deck capable of supporting two heavy-lift helicopters simultaneously, beneath which is a garage for vehicles and stores. Whilst there is no traditional well deck, utility landing craft can moor and transfer stores at an indented berthing point in the stern and personnel landing craft are carried on davits. A defensive package of armament and sensors – that includes a Thales integrated mast – is quite similar to that used in the *Holland* class offshore patrol vessels but also includes Goalkeeper close-in weapons systems.[12]

The overall combination is a logical one given the obvious synergies between maritime sustainment, strategic sea lift and sea basing missions. It could prove attractive for navies not wishing to use the amphibious route to develop broader aviation capacity. The Royal Canadian Navy appears to have considered something similar before opting for the more traditional German *Berlin* class replenishment design for its own JSS project. The concept may also influence the new generation of British logistic support ships.

One potential weakness of the Dutch JSS is the relatively high expense associated with such a

The US Navy's *America* (LHA-6) class represent an incremental improvement on its previous amphibious assault ships. They place particularly heavy emphasis on aviation capabilities. Although omitting a ski-jump to maximise flight deck area for helicopter operations, their size makes them well-suited for F-35B STOVL operations. This image shows her on trials before final delivery. *(Huntington Ingalls Industries)*

The Japanese 'helicopter carrying destroyer' *Izumo*, commissioned in March 2015, is one of a pair of enlarged *Hyuga* class vessels. The two *Hyuga*s were heavily focused on anti-submarine warfare but the new ships have much greater potential to operate in a range of roles. *(JMSDF)*

The US Navy's *Masa Verde* (LPD-19) and British Royal Navy *Albion* (respectively left and below) are both relatively recent examples of LPD-type amphibious transport docks. The increasing importance of aviation facilities in amphibious operations means that new LPD designs have not been as numerous as might have been expected. *(US Navy/Crown Copyright 2008)*

bespoke vessel – *Karel Doorman* has reportedly cost some €360m (c. US$430m) at 2009 prices. This is more than a *Mistral* class amphibious assault ship. A possible solution is the adaptation of commercial designs for service in second-tier roles. As in so many other fields, the US Navy has taken the lead here, using a commercial fast ferry as the basis for the Joint High Speed Vessel (JHSV) intra-theatre transports. The resulting *Spearhead* (T-EPF-1) class – still not particularly cheap at a cost of around US$180m per unit – has seem a helicopter deck and berthing ramp added to an existing catamaran design, providing the ability to deploy up to 400 troops and equipment over a distance of over 1,000 nautical miles at speeds

The *Karel Doorman* replenishing the air-defence ship *Tromp* in 2014. The combination of logistical and amphibious support requirements into a combined vessel is but one example of the Royal Netherlands Navy's innovative thinking in naval design. *(Royal Netherlands Navy)*

of around 35 knots. The class appears to be providing a useful capability in low-intensity operations but is limited by poor seakeeping in higher sea states and an inability to survive unsupported in higher threat areas given an almost total lack of defensive armament. The United States has also adapted commercial designs for other amphibious roles, notably the giant *Montford Point* (T-ESD-1) mobile landing platforms. Adapted from an Alaskan oil tanker, these ships act as floating transhipment points and forward operating bases for amphibious forces.

Notes

1. As of late 2015, Brazil, China, France, India, Italy, the Russian Federation, Spain and the United States all have the capacity to deploy fixed-wing aircraft at sea. In addition, the United Kingdom is building the new *Queen Elizabeth* class with the intention of resuming aircraft carrier operation by c. 2020. Since the end of the Second World War, Argentina, Australia, Canada, the Netherlands and Thailand have all commenced – but subsequently abandoned – fixed-wing carrier aviation.

2. A through deck is, of course, also an essential characteristic for those navies wanting to use their amphibious ships to develop a basic aircraft carrier capability.

3. The United Kingdom considered installing EMALS in the second *Queen Elizabeth* class aircraft carrier, *Prince of Wales*, but abandoned the plan because the cost of conversion was too high. The Indian Navy is also reportedly interested in the system for their next indigenous aircraft carrier.

4. *Gerald R. Ford* is to be equipped with a new Dual Band Radar (DBR). This integrates two radars operating in different frequency bands through a single interface to the combat management system. However, this sophisticated system is regarded as being too expensive and follow-on ships will have a simpler array.

5. More accurately, the larger air group envisaged for the ships drove an increase in size that allowed alternative configurations to be considered. The subsequent decision to produce an adaptable design then had a further impact on ship dimensions.

6. The arrangement also allows ship navigation (located in the forward island) and flight control (based in the aft island) to be located in the best locations and provides a degree of redundancy in the event of action damage.

7. The system is similar to the PAAMS system installed in the Franco-Italian 'Horizon' type air-defence destroyers. However, the destroyers can also deploy longer-range Aster 30 missiles and also benefit from being equipped with the S1850M volume-search radar.

8. The *Juan Carlos I* design does, however, offer greater flexibility in so far as all the operating spots can be used by heavy helicopters.

9. Construction of the first two *Mistral*s was actually split in two. The forward halves were built at the Saint-Nazaire-based Chantiers de l'Atantique yard of what is now STX France SA, whose experience is based on the construction of passenger ships such as cruise liners. The main accommodation spaces are in these sections. Construction of the sterns – containing more military features – were carried out under the leadership of prime contractor DCNS. Overall integration took place at DCNS Brest. The third of class, *Dixmude*, was constructed entirely at Saint-Nazaire. However, there was a reversion to the split arrangement for the two ships built to Russian order, with the sterns fabricated in Russia. These ships were specifically modified to Russian requirements and they were considerably more expensive than the French versions.

10. The Japanese Constitution's prohibition on the maintenance of armed forces – in practice, interpreted to forbid possession of the means to wage an aggressive war – has often been taken to exclude the acquisition of aircraft carriers. Any Japanese deployment of strike aircraft at sea would therefore be hugely controversial.

11. Other aspects of the ship – including the island – will be redesigned to provide compensating space for aviation capabilities.

12. The *Holland* class is described in Chapter 6.3. Another interesting hybrid is Algeria's new amphibious transport dock, *Kalaat Béni Abbès*. Based on the Italian *San Giorgio* class design, she combines the transportation and deployment facilities of a small amphibious ship with the air defence capabilities of a destroyer. The combination appears to meet a unique Algerian requirement and it is unlikely more of the type will be seen.

13. The following principle sources used in the production of this chapter provide more detailed analysis:

David Architzel, 'The US CVN 21 Aircraft Carriers Programme: Capability Requirements, Concepts and Design', *RUSI Defence Systems – Summer 2006* (London: Royal United Services Institute, 2006), pp.44–6.

Michele Cosentino, '*Cavour*: A Multi-Role Aircraft Carrier for the Italian Navy' in John Jordan (ed.), *Warship 2014* (London: Conway, 2014), pp. 93–111.

Christian Herrou, 'Embarqement sur le Mistral', *Marines & Forces Navales – No 108* (Rennes: Marines Éditions, 2007), pp.18–39.

Charles Oldham (Editor in Chief), *HMS Queen Elizabeth* (Tampa, FL: Faircount LLC, 2014).

Ronald O'Rourke, *Navy Ford (CVN-78) Class Aircraft Carrier Program: Background and Issues for Congress RS20643* (Washington DC: Congressional Research Service).

In addition, many of the ships reviewed in this section have featured in past editions of *Seaforth World Naval Review* (Barnsley: Seaforth Publishing) or been discussed by the author in the annual *Warship* (London: Conway).

Conrad Waters

MAJOR SURFACE COMBATANTS

The last twenty-five years have seen a marked reduction in numbers of major surface combatants in service across the world's navies. This trend has been combined with a tendency for these remaining combatants to have grown greatly in size and sophistication. The reasons for the numerical decline – the end of the Cold War and a sharp reduction in the need and willingness of the main protagonists to pay for such ships – are not hard to understand, but the trend towards larger, more complex ships warrants further explanation. So far as size is concerned, design influences such as improvements to accommodation and other crew facilities, the additional space utilised by stealth techniques, and even the impact of greater use of modular equipment have already been explained in some detail in Chapter 5. The increased focus on expeditionary activities, far from home bases, has also tended to emphasise further the benefits of volume for accommodation, fuel and stores.

Meanwhile, greater sophistication has been driven by evolving threats and the availability of technology, increasingly assisted by developments in consumer electronics, to provide an effective counter. Of these threats, that posed by saturation attack from anti-ship missiles had commonly been perceived as the most severe by the latter half of the Cold War. During this time, the expansion of the Soviet naval bomber force armed with stand-off air-to-surface missiles had particularly exercised US Navy planners. The capability of such systems, albeit of Western origin, were vividly demonstrated by the success of Argentine Exocet missile attacks on *Sheffield* and *Atlantic Conveyor* in the 1982 Falklands War. By this stage, however, the US Navy was already on the point of deploying its new *Ticonderoga* (CG-47) class cruisers, which provided a potent answer to the problem.[1]

Existing warships had been vulnerable to air attack because defensive missiles needed a dedicated fire-control radar to guide them onto any target

The deployment of the Aegis weapons system – combining SPY-1 phased arrays with an unprecedented level of command and control automation – revolutionised US Navy air-defence capabilities towards the end of the Cold War. The system was first deployed operationally on the *Ticonderoga* class cruisers; the third ship of the class, *Vincennes* (CG-49) is pictured here with the two aft SPY-1 arrays clearly visible. In July 1988 *Vincennes* shot down a civilian Iranian Airbus jetliner with the loss of 300 lives in an incident that demonstrated how even the most sophisticated system is open to human error. *(US Navy)*

identified by the main search-and-surveillance radar. Essentially, each engagement required a separate fire-control radar throughout its entire course and only a small number of such radars could be carried. The *Ticonderoga* class were the first equipped with the Aegis weapons system, including its associated AN/SPY-1 electronically scanned or 'phased' radar arrays. The greater flexibility and precision of phased arrays – which use electronics to form and direct their radar beams – allowed Aegis to direct modified

Standard series missiles (the Standard SM-2) towards incoming threats via mid-course guidance. This avoided the need for a separate fire-control radar until the final stages of an engagement. At this stage, 'slaved' illuminators were used to guide the semi-active Standard missiles onto the relevant target.[2] This permitted a far greater number of incoming targets to be engaged than previously. The system's precision and automated nature also allowed for fast reaction times. This is useful against

6.2.1: 21st-CENTURY US NAVY MAJOR SURFACE COMBATANTS

Class:	Ticonderoga (CG-47) VLS Variant: CG-52 onwards	Arleigh Burke (DDG-51) Flight I Variant	Arleigh Burke (DDG-51) Flight IIA: DDG-79 onwards	Zumwalt (DDG-1000)
Builder:	HHI – Ingalls, Mississippi GD Bath Iron Works, Maine	GD Bath Iron Works, Maine HHI – Ingalls, Mississippi	GD Bath Iron Works, Maine HHI – Ingalls, Mississippi	GD Bath Iron Works, Maine
Number:	22 (+5 non VLS, now retired)	28	34+11[1]	0+3
Keel Laid:[2]	11 January 1984	6 December 1988[3]	9 October 1997	17 November 2011
Launched:[2]	11 March 1985	16 September 1989	7 November 1998	28 October 2013
Commissioned:[2]	20 September 1986	4 July 1991	19 August 2000	[2016]
Full Load Displacement:	9,900 tons	8,900 tons	9,400 tons	15,500 tons
Principal Dimensions:	173m x 17m x7m	154m x 20m x 7m	155m x 20m x 7m	183m x 25m x 8m
Propulsion:	COGAG 30+ knots 6,000nm range	COGAG 30+ knots 4,400nm range	COGAG 30+ knots 4,400nm range	IFEP 30+ knots 4,500nm range
Armament:	122 x VLS cells (Standard/ESSM/ASROC/TLAM) 2 x quad Harpoon SSM 2 x 127mm guns 2 x triple 324mm TT 2 x Phalanx CIWS 2 x helicopters	90 x VLS cells (Standard/ESSM/ASROC/TLAM) 2 x quad Harpoon SSM 1 x 127mm gun 2 x triple 324mm TT 2 x Phalanx CIWS Helicopter deck	96 x VLS cells (Standard/ESSM/ASROC/TLAM) 1 x 127mm gun 2 x triple 324mm TT 1/2 x Phalanx CIWS[4] 2 x helicopters	80 x VLS cells (Standard/ESSM/ASROC/TLAM) 2 x 155mm guns 2 x 30mm guns 2 x helicopters
Crew:[5]	c.350	c.300	c.330	c.150

Notes:

1 Based on plans at the end of 2015. Production is scheduled to transition to a Flight III variant once the Flight IIA programme is completed.

2 First of class.

3 Some sources suggest fabrication commenced significantly earlier.

4 Some ships are fitted 'for and not with'.

5 Published figures on crew size vary significantly and, for older ships, have fallen since construction as greater automation has been introduced during refits. All data should be regarded as being indicative only.

'pop-up' missiles – such as those fired from a submerged submarine – that may be a more likely threat in post-Cold War naval scenarios.

It was to be some years before other navies deployed weapons systems of equivalent capability to Aegis. Congressional reluctance to release the technology outside the US Navy meant that ten years were to elapse before Aegis was deployed by a foreign navy – onboard Japan's *Kongou* (DDG-173) in 1993 – and only a handful of fleets have acquired the system to date. Moreover, Aegis' sophistication was such that it was to be a further decade still before

equivalent systems were developed by the main European navies, commencing with the Dutch *De Zeven Provinciën* in 2002. Initially largely installed in dedicated air-defence ships, phased arrays and their associated control systems are now increasingly common in all types of new surface combatants as the relevant technology becomes more affordable. Some of the emergent navies are also developing similar systems, rather than relying on imports from the United States or Europe. Notable examples include China's Type 346 series of active phased arrays and the Israeli EL/M-2248 MF-STAR.[3] The

latter is being used in conjunction with the Indo-Israeli Barak 8 surface-to-air missile system onboard the new Indian-built *Kolkata* class destroyers.

Whilst this expansion of warship building and associated maritime technology industries to new countries has been another trend in 21st-century warship construction, it is important to note that its influence on major surface combatant design remains quite limited. With the exception of China – and possibly India – most major warship classes remain heavily influenced by prototypes and, certainly, weapons and systems developed in the traditional naval hubs of the United States and Europe. Even China, it is reported, has first relied on technology extracted from Russia and the West to build its own indigenous capabilities. Although it seems likely that this will change in future as emergent economies continue to broaden their skills, it remains a fact that the majority of the twenty-first century's major surface combatant designs are essentially of Western or Russian origin.

UNITED STATES

Construction of major surface combatants for the US Navy since the end of the Cold War has been dominated by series production of the *Arleigh Burke* (DDG-51) class destroyers. Displacing nearly 9,000 tons in their original guise, the class is a multi-mission combatant with an emphasis on anti-air warfare. Preliminary design studies for the class started in the late 1970s as part of plans to replace older surface escorts. An important aim was to develop an affordable complement to the

Ticonderoga class cruisers, the target cost being three-quarters of that of the larger cruiser. Principal sacrifices to achieve this aim included a reduction in fire-control illuminators (used in the final stages of an engagement) from four to three, omitting a helicopter hangar and air-warfare command and control facilities and a reduction in Mk 41 VLS missile cells to ninety from 122. Otherwise, the ships benefitted from being a purpose-designed platform for the Aegis system – the *Ticonderoga* class was a modification of the existing *Spruance* (DD-963) class hull – with a broader, more stable hull, improved survivability features and a significantly reduced radar cross-section. Propulsion is by means of a traditional COGAG plant. The lead ship was procured under the FY1985 construction programme. She was launched in September 1989 and commissioned on 4 July 1991.

Twenty-eight of the original Flight I and slightly modified Flight II *Arleigh Burke*s were completed between 1991 and 1999 before production switched

to the modified Flight IIA design. These ships are around 500 tons heavier than the early ships and remedied a major perceived weakness of the original design by incorporating a hangar for two helicopters. They also have an additional six VLS cells. Thirty-four of this upgraded variant, benefitting from a series of incremental improvements as production progressed, were delivered from 2000 to 2012 before construction was halted in favour of the radical new *Zumwalt* (DDG-1000) class. However, a subsequent decision to terminate the *Zumwalt* programme – largely on cost grounds – meant that further orders were placed for the Flight IIA type from FY2010 onwards for delivery from 2016. Eleven additional ships will be built to this design before construction switches to a further improved Flight III variant, which will incorporate Raytheon's improved air and missile defence radar (AMDR) in place of the SPY-1 arrays. AMDR – now designated AN/SPY-6 – will be particularly useful in improving capability against the threat from ballistic missiles. Ballistic missile defence (BMD) has become an important additional role for Aegis in the twenty-first century given the proliferation of first-generation tactical systems such as the Russian 'Scud'. The greater potential of more recent ballistic weapons – not least China's DF-21D anti-ship ballistic missile – means that an array conceived with this threat in mind is now desirable.

The longevity of DDG-51 class production is a tribute to the flexibility inherent in the original design, which now has the longest production run of any post-Second World War US Navy surface combatant. This has also brought the benefits of economies of scale from a long production run, with current ships costing around US$1.6bn –US$1.7bn per unit. However, there are signs that scope for further growth in the current design is now limited in terms of both internal volume and electrical generation and distribution capabilities. For example, although generation and cooling capacity is being increased in the Flight III ships, the version of the AMDR to be shipped is smaller and less-capable than that initially envisaged in a purpose-built ship. The *Arleigh Burke*s are also arguably expensive to operate compared with more modern, optimally-manned designs in spite of efforts to reduce crew size. For example, current complement of a little over 300 in the Flight I variant compares with c.190 in a British Type 45 air-defence destroyer.

The US Navy did have the answer to many of

The Flight IIA *Arleigh Burke* class destroyer *Chafee* (DDG-90) seen alongside the carrier *George Washington* (CVN-73) during a refuelling manoeuvre in 2015. The ship's fixed SPY-1 radar panels provide 360-degree coverage, with the use of electronics to direct radar beams meaning they do not need to rotate in the same way as a mechanical radar. The Mk 41 VLS launchers are principally used for Standard and Evolved Sea Sparrow surface-to-air missiles but can house other types. *(US Navy)*

these issues in the *Zumwalt* class, a lean-manned (c.150 crew) cruiser-sized vessel of c.15,500 tons full load displacement incorporating a series of innovations in terms of hull form (use of a tumblehome hull), propulsion (integrated full electric propulsion), signature reduction, weapons systems and sensors. Armament includes two 155mm Advanced Guns Systems (AGS) optimised for shore bombardment and twenty quad Mk 57 peripheral VLS cells that are distributed around the ship's outer shell to enhance survivability. A Dual Band Radar (DBR) similar to that specified for the new carrier *Gerald R. Ford* (CVN-78) was also originally planned but Raytheon's AN/SPY-3 array has now been modified to perform all the functions intended for DBR as one of a number of cost-saving measures.[4] However, an original programme that envisaged twenty-four ships being procured from FY-2005 onwards has ultimately seen production truncated at just three vessels as costs have spiralled upwards. Current estimates suggest total programme expenses of over US$12bn or more than US$4bn per ship. All-in-all, it seems that the US Navy were overly ambitious in attempting to introduce too many innovations simultaneously in one class of ship. At the same time, a renewed effort will have to be made to progress from the basic *Burke* hull sometime soon if the US Navy is not to lose its qualitative edge to foreign designs.

In the meantime, the DDG-51 design has formed the basis of Japan's *Kongou* and *Atago* (DDG-177) classes, as well as the somewhat larger South Korean KDX-III *Sejongdaewang-Ham* type. The Aegis/SPY-1 combination has also been used in Spain's F-100 *Álvaro de Bazán* class 'frigates' and their Australian *Hobart* class near-sisters. Finally, a 'cut down' version of the system, featuring smaller SPY1-F arrays with fewer than half the individual elements found in the standard panels, has been used in Norway's *Fridtjof Nansen* class anti-submarine orientated frigates.

WESTERN EUROPE

As previously mentioned, the development of air-defence ships with comparable capabilities to Aegis took some considerable time to achieve in Europe in spite of the very real threat posed by Soviet anti-ship missiles. To some extent, this reflects the failure of the NATO Frigate Replacement programme or NFR-90. Somewhat ironically, this was originally driven forward by the United States in the mid-1980s as a means of persuading NATO allies to adopt anti-air capabilities similar to Aegis. The costly programme was partly to be achieved through the economies of scale inherent in a programme for almost sixty ships. The project collapsed between 1989 and 1990 due to considerable differences in the requirements and industrial interests of the eight partner members.

NFR-90 was beneficial, however, in that it identi-

The US Navy has brought sixty-two *Arleigh Burke* class destroyers into service to date. The earlier ships – *Arleigh Burke* (DDG-51) herself is shown at the top – lacked a helicopter but the later Flight IIA ships – depicted by *Gravely* (DDG-107) above – were modified to provide this facility and additional VLS cells. These can be used to fire a range of munitions, notably Standard and ESSM surface-to-air missiles, Tomahawk land attack cruise missiles and the ASROC anti-submarine weapon. *(Huntington Ingalls Industries, US Navy)*

fied the broad type of warship and equipment required to combat current anti-ship missiles, which were considered to remain a threat in the post-Cold War environment. This saw the emergence of new, smaller European groupings that were ultimately to produce the next generation of European surface combatants. These essentially comprised the Common New Generation Frigate (CNGF) grouping – also known as Project Horizon – of France, Italy and the United Kingdom and a somewhat looser alliance of Germany, the Netherlands and Spain.

Active Phased-Array Radar (APAR) Equipped Air Defence Ships: Of the two alliances, the more flex-

6.2.2: 21st-CENTURY EUROPEAN AIR-DEFENCE SHIPS

Class:	De Zeven Provinciën (LCF)	Sachsen (F-124)	Iver Huitfeldt	Forbin ('Horizon')[1]	Daring (Type 45)	Álvaro de Bazán (F-100)
Builder:	Royal Schelde, Vlissingen	ARGE-F124[2]	Odense Steel Shipyard	DCNS, Lorient[1]	BAE Systems, Clyde[3]	Navantia, Ferrol
Country:	Netherlands	Germany	Denmark	France/Italy	United Kingdom	Spain/Australia[4]
Number:	4	3	3	4[1]	6	5/(3)[4]
Keel Laid:[5]	1 September 1998	1 February 1999	2 June 2008	4 April 2002	28 March 2003	14 June 1999
Launched:[5]	8 April 2000	20 January 2001	11 March 2010	10 March 2005	1 February 2006	31 October 2000
Commissioned:[5]	26 April 2002	4 November 2004	11 January 2011[6]	14 October 2010[7]	23 July 2009	19 September 2002
Full Load Displacement:	6,100 tons	5,600 tons	6,600 tons	7,100 tons	7,500 tons	6,300 tons
Principal Dimensions:	144m x 19m x 5m	143m x 17m x 5m	139m x 20m x 5m	153m x 20m x 5m	152m x 21m x 5m	147m x 19m x 5m
Propulsion:	CODOG 30 knots 5,000nm range	CODAG 29 knots 4,000nm range	CODAD 28+ knots 9,000nm range	CODOG 29+ knots 7,000nm range	IFEP 30+ knots 7,000nm range	CODOG 28 knots 4,500nm range
Armament:	40 x VLS cells (Standard/ESSM) 2 x quad Harpoon SSM 1 x 127mm gun 2 x twin 324mm TT 1/2 x Goalkeeper CIWS 1 x helicopter	32 x VLS cells (Standard/ESSM) 2 x quad Harpoon SSM 1 x 76mm gun 2 x triple 324mm TT 2 x RAM PDMS 2 x helicopter	32 x VLS cells (Standard/ESSM) 24 x VLS cells[8] (ESSM only) 2 x quad Harpoon SSM 2 x 76mm guns 2 x twin 324mm TT 1 x 35mm CIWS 1 x helicopter	48 x VLS cells (Aster15/Aster 30) 2 x quad Exocet SSM 2 x 76mm guns 2 x 324mm TT 2 x helicopters	48 x VLS cells (Aster15/Aster 30) 2 x quad Harpoon SSM 1 x 115mm gun 2 x Phalanx CIWS 2 x helicopters	48 x VLS cells (Standard/ESSM) 2 x quad Harpoon SSM 1 x 127mm gun 2 x twin 324mm TT 1 x helicopter
Principal Sensors:	APAR/SMART-L	APAR/SMART-L	APAR/SMART-L	EMPAR/S-1850M	SAMPSON/S-1850M	SPY-1/SPG-52
Crew:	c.200	c.250	c.100+	c.195	c.190	c.200+

Notes:

1 Project Horizon encompassed two French and two Italian ships; the Italian ships being built by Fincantieri at Riva Trigoso and Muggiano. They have minimal differences to the French ships, notably a third 76mm gun.

2 Comprised a consortium of Blohm & Voss, HDW and Thyssen Nordseewerke, each of which assembled one ship. Blohm & Voss built the lead ship.

3 The lead ship was assembled at the Yarrow yard on the Clyde from blocks constructed at Yarrow, Govan (also on the Clyde) and Portsmouth. Subsequent ships were assembled at Govan.

4 The fifth Spanish ship and three Hobart class ships being built in Australia for the RAN have slight modifications. The Australian ships will be delivered from 2017 onwards.

5 Dates relate to lead ship.

6 Further work scheduled after delivery meant the ship was not fully operational at this date.

7 The ship was delivered in December 2008.

8 The Danish Stanflex system means there is considerable optionality around weapons load-out. These details relate to a fully-equipped ship.

EUROPEAN AIR-DEFENCE SHIPS

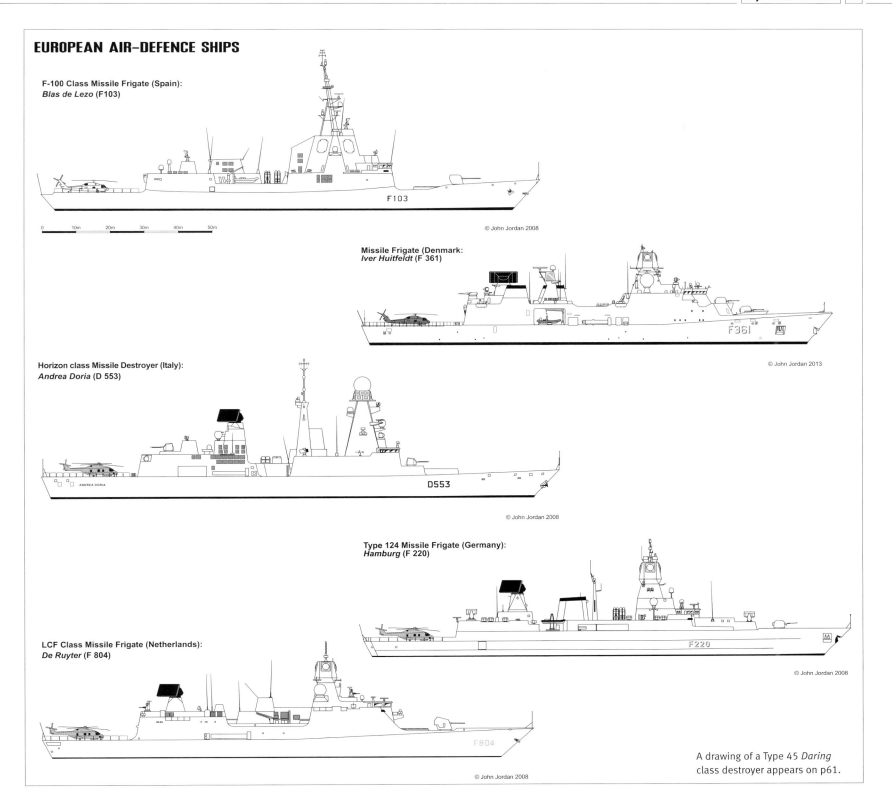

F-100 Class Missile Frigate (Spain):
Blas de Lezo (F103)

F103

0   10m   20m   30m   40m   50m

© John Jordan 2008

Missile Frigate (Denmark:
Iver Huitfeldt (F 361)

F361

© John Jordan 2013

Horizon class Missile Destroyer (Italy):
Andrea Doria (D 553)

ANDREA DORIA

D553

© John Jordan 2008

Type 124 Missile Frigate (Germany):
Hamburg (F 220)

F220

© John Jordan 2008

LCF Class Missile Frigate (Netherlands):
De Ruyter (F 804)

F804

© John Jordan 2008

A drawing of a Type 45 *Daring* class destroyer appears on p61.

The Royal Netherlands Navy's LCF *De Zeven Provinciën* class – *Tromp* is shown here in 2011 – were the first European air-defence ships to use phased-array technology. The first ship commissioned in 2002, nearly twenty years after *Ticonderoga* was delivered. During this time technology had developed and the pyramid like APAR array on the foremast is an active phased array, with separately energised modules. *(Royal Netherlands Navy)*

APAR is also used in the German Navy's three *Sachsen* class warships; second of class *Hamburg* is shown in this image. The system is typically combined with the Thales L long-range search array seen on the mainmast as APAR is optimised for short-range precision tracking and guidance at the expense of long-range search functions. *(German Navy)*

ible partnership of Germany, the Netherlands and Spain brought the quicker results. Spain quickly determined that the Aegis system met its needs; the F-100 class referenced previously was the result. Co-operation between the German and Netherlands navies proved more enduring and they both ultimately built ships designed around the Thales Nederland APAR (Active Phased-Array Radar) and SMART L surveillance radar. The latter system is used to detect and track targets at long ranges (in excess of 300 nautical miles), handing over to the shorter-ranged APAR for later stage tracking and fire control purposes. APAR has four fixed panels similar to Aegis SPY-1 that are typically arranged in a distinctive pyramid-like mast. However, its use of active technology means that it is more flexible than Aegis and it is sufficiently precise to be able to carry out both tracking and fire-control functions. This means that it does not need the separate 'slaved' fire-control illuminators found in the US Navy CG-47 and DDG-51 classes.

The APAR/SMART L combination is used in conjunction with the Standard SM-2 missiles and shorter-ranged Evolved Sea Sparrow Missiles (ESSM) that are also found in Aegis-equipped ships. Three different classes totalling ten warships have been built with the system to date, viz.

***De Zeven Provinciën* class:** Also known as the air defence and command frigates (*luchtverdedigings en commando fregat* or LCF), the four ships in this class were ordered in pairs in June 1995 and February 1997. The first vessel was completed in 2002 and the following units delivered at roughly yearly intervals. Although described as frigates, a full load displacement in excess of 6,000 tons – nearly twice that of the preceding *Karel Doorman* or 'M' class – puts them firmly in the destroyer category. The total cost of the programme has been quoted as around €1.9bn (US$2.2bn) or over US$500m per ship.

The LCF type combines the air-defence capabilities provided by APAR and SMART L with a broad range of general-purpose capabilities that include Harpoon surface-to-surface missiles, a medium-calibre gun and a sea-control helicopter. Sufficient space is available for six eight-cell Mk 41 VLS modules but only five of these are normally carried. This means total missile load-out is less than half that found in the DDG-51 class, partly reflecting the latter's use of a broader range of vertically-launched munitions such as Tomahawk cruise missiles and ASROC anti-submarine weapons. The Netherlands considered the acquisition of Tomahawk for the class but the programme was eventually cancelled on political grounds. However, the SMART-L radar has proved effective in tracking ballistic missiles and it is possible the class could be modified to provide a full BMD capability in due course.

The LCF design reflects its more recent design antecedents than its US Navy counterparts in the incorporation of the latest signature-reduction techniques and the use of automation to reduce manning requirements to c.200 sailors. CODOG machinery provides a maximum speed of 30 knots and a range of around 5,000 nautical miles. Significant attention has also been paid to survivability, a feature that has gained increased priority since the Cold War's end.[5] All in all, the LCF represents a sophisticated, cost-effective and survivable design that has provided the Royal Netherlands Navy with its 'high-end' warfighting capability over the last decade.

Sachsen class: The three *Sachsen* or F-124 class frigates were ordered in June 1997 and commissioned from November 2004 following a lengthy period of sea trials. Full load displacement is 5,600 tons, again placing them in a destroyer-sized category. Programme cost is reported to be around €2.0bn (US$2.4bn) or c.US$800m per ship. The greater expense compared with the Dutch programme may reflect division of construction between three shipyards to support the industrial base.

The F-124 class is conceptually very similar to the LCF type. However, a different appearance betrays variations in national design approaches, equipment choices and operating priorities. Structurally, the *Sachsen* class owes much to the previous F-123 *Brandenburg* class, which was itself heavily influenced by the successful German MEKO modular design system. As described in Chapter 5, this allows major weapons and sensor modules to be installed and changed without structural alteration. Propulsion is by means of a CODAG arrangement, with only one gas turbine being used compared with two in previous German escort classes. The use of stealth technology also evolved compared with previous designs. This includes use of an X-form design, under which the ship's hull and structure are inclined at different angles to reduce radar cross-section. Overall crew size does, however, remain

The three Dutch *Iver Huitfeldt* class air-defence ships pictured at sea in various stages of completion in 2012. A combination of civilian design standards and the use of existing Stanflex modules to outfit much of the class's weaponry meant they were remarkably cost-effective to build. *(DALO)*

comparatively large at some 250 personnel. Given the ship is the smallest of contemporary European air-defence ship designs, this leaves it somewhat more crowded than its contemporaries.

As for the LCF class, the *Sachsen* class is primarily focused on the air-defence role but also incorporates a range of general-purpose weaponry that includes a 76mm gun and provision for up to two helicopters. There are only thirty-two cells (four eight-cell modules) for the principal air-defence system. However, these are supplemented by two twenty-one cell Mk 49 launchers for the RAM (Rolling Airframe Missile) point defence system that Germany developed in conjunction with the United States. When combined with the Standard SM-2 and ESSM missiles controlled by APAR, these provide a capable layered defence system well-suited to the high-threat littoral waters that comprise both the German Navy's traditional operating area and the likely environment for current era expeditionary missions.

Iver Huitfeldt class: The APAR/SMART L combination achieved a major export success in 2006 when the system was selected for Denmark's three *Iver Huitfeldt* class frigates. These were a follow-on to two previous *Absalon* class flexible support ships commissioned in 2005, which effectively combined the capabilities of a general-purpose surface escort with a multi-purpose flex deck that could be used to transport the vehicles and stores of a small military force. Surplus accommodation for around 200 personnel over the ships' crews was also provided for this purpose. The *Iver Huitfeldt* class are derived from the basic *Absalon* class design. However, they omit the flex deck and have a modified hull form to accommodate twice the installed power. This is provided through four MTU diesels in CODAD arrangement. Like all current-generation air-defence ships, the class are relatively large ships displacing over 6,600 tons. This may also partly reflect the use of heavier-grade steels in a design that is largely built to commercial standards. Construction of many blocks was sub-contracted to foreign yards to control costs.

The ships make full use of the Danish Stanflex modular system, incorporating pre-prepared positions for containerised weapon and system modules under an approach that reflects German MEKO principles. As such, whilst the principle components of the air-defence system – for example its sensors and Mk 41 VLS – were acquired specifically for the ship, many of its remaining weapons systems comprise Stanflex modules refurbished from previous use. The cost of the ships and the air-defence system sensors are understood to have amounted to a little over US$1bn or around

The French 'Horizon' class air-defence destroyer *Chevalier Paul* seen operating with the US Navy carrier *John C. Stennis* (CVN-74) in 2013. Like all modern air-defence ships, *Chevalier Paul*'s main role is the defence of high-value units from air and missile attack. However, she carries a wide range of weapons systems suitable for other roles. *(US Navy)*

A picture of the Royal Navy Type 45 destroyer *Daring*'s mainmast, with the Sampson radar system concealed under the dome. It features two rotating back-to-back arrays, reducing cost and weight in comparison with fixed arrays. This allows it to be installed higher in the ship, extending the ship's radar horizon. *(RAN)*

US$350m per ship before weapons systems are taken into account. Core crew is c.100 sailors, although some reservations have been expressed whether this is enough for expeditionary employments. All-in-all, however, the *Iver Huitfeldt* class are an impressive example of what can be achieved on a limited budget.

Project Horizon & the Type 45 Destroyer Programmes: Originally a trilateral alliance, Project Horizon was carried forward as a Franco-Italian programme after the United Kingdom decided to withdraw from the partnership to pursue the national Type 45 design in April 1999. In spite of this parting of the ways, the Type 45 design was heavily influenced by previous collaborative work and uses the same missile system as the Horizon destroyers, albeit controlled by a different radar.

Two pairs of 'Horizon' class destroyers were ordered by France and Italy in October 2000. All four were commissioned between 2007 and 2009. Their air defence capabilities are focused on the PAAMS(E) variant of the Principal Anti-Air Missile

System developed in collaboration with the United Kingdom. This comprises an EMPAR (European Multifunction Phased-Array Radar) passive array and Aster 15 (short-range) and Aster 30 (medium-range) surface-to-air missiles housed in a Sylver VLS. In similar fashion to APAR-equipped ships, a modified S-1850M variant of the SMART L radar performs long-range search functions. EMPAR is a passive array similar to SPY-1 but uses a single rotating array to achieve 360-degree coverage compared with the four fixed panels seen in US ships. This cheaper and lighter approach allows the radar to be positioned higher in the ship but increases risks of mechanical malfunction and reduces overall capabilities. To some extent, this is balanced by the capabilities of the Aster missiles that form a key part of the system. These use the capabilities of the phased array to assist initial guidance towards incoming missiles in similar fashion to SM-2 but also incorporate an active seeker that is able to find and track its target autonomously. As such, there is no need for separate fire-control illumination in an engagement's terminal phase. The missile bodies

of the Aster 15 and Aster 30 are identical but the longer-ranged weapon has a larger booster.

The 'Horizon' class are otherwise similar to previously described air-defence ships in fielding a range of secondary weapons to broaden their primary air-defence role, although lack of a medium-calibre gun would lessen their usefulness in an amphibious support mission. There are a few minor differences between the French and Italian ships – for example, in the selection of nationally-produced surface-to-surface missiles – but they are largely identical in most key respects. At a little over 7,000 tons full load displacement they are amongst the largest European vessels of the type and also owe much to the comprehensive French approach to stealth first displayed in the light frigates of the *La Fayette* class. Propulsion is by means of a conservative CODOG arrangement but automation has kept crew size below 200. The

French programme reportedly cost €2.2bn (US$2.6bn) or c. US$1.3bn per unit.

The British Type 45 programme that followed withdrawal from Project Horizon saw orders for three ships placed in December 2000 and a further batch of three in February 2002.[6] The lead ship, *Daring*, commissioned in July 2009 and *Duncan*, the sixth and final ship, in September 2013. In spite of the longer production run, the British ships were the most expensive of the new generation of European air-defence ships. Total programme costs were around £6bn or c. US$1.5bn per ship. To some extent, this reflected the Type 45s' greater sophistication compared with the other warship programmes, notably the use of the PAAMS(S) air-defence system and integrated full electric propulsion (IFEP) in the design. The Type 45s are also the largest of the European designs, with full load displacement approaching 7,500 tons.

The architecture of PAAMS(S) is similar to that of the PAAMS(E) variant used in the 'Horizon' ships with the key difference that the British designed and built Sampson radar is substituted for the EMPAR system in the French and Italian ships. Sampson is an active phased array similar to APAR, with two rotating radar panels installed back-to-back in the Type 45. It has a substantially greater performance than EMPAR, particularly in providing area defence for a group of ships, to meet British requirements that reflected the bitter lessons of the Falklands War. As such, it is possibly the most advanced air-defence system in service anywhere in the world today. The Type 45s were also the first surface combatants to be equipped with IFEP, which – less positively – has proved to be something of an Achilles heel due to persistent unreliability problems. The expense of the innovative technology used in the design also left insufficient money available for the full range of non-air defence equipment found in other ships. The propulsion problems are to be fixed through a programme of refits authorised in the 2015 Strategic Security and Defence Review, whilst additional equipment is being installed in a series of incremental upgrades. Ongoing research is also being undertaken into their potential as BMD assets.

Multi-Mission Frigates: The completion of the air-defence ship projects initiated in the 1990s has allowed the major European navies to contemplate renewal of their fleets of general-purpose surface combatants, most dating back to the Cold War era.

The French FREMM multi-mission frigate *Normandie* seen on trials in 2014. The main European navies turned to renewing the fleets of general-purpose escorts once the new generation of air-defence ships had been completed and the Franco-Italian FREMM project is by far the largest programme to date. *Normandie* was sold to Egypt in 2015 before ever having commissioned in the *Marine Nationale*. (DCNS)

Many of these programmes remain in the pre-production phase, notably the United Kingdom's Type 26 Global Combat Ship, Spain's F-110 frigate and a proposed joint project between the Netherlands and Belgium to replace their remaining multi-purpose 'M' class frigate fleets. Germany is somewhat further advanced, being in the course of constructing four large c.7,500 ton F-125 stabilisation 'frigates'. These are optimised towards undertaking lengthy peacekeeping duties in low threat areas, a specialisation that appears something of a luxury given renewed tensions on European borders. The following MKS-180 design will have more of a combat orientation.

The most significant programme to deliver ships to date has been that for Franco-Italian FREMM multi-mission frigates, which followed on from Project Horizon. Again, this has produced ships of c.6,000 to 6,500-ton destroyer size. However, in contrast with Project Horizon, the participating countries have been given considerable flexibility in adjusting the design to meet national military and industrial requirements. This has resulted in national variants of significantly different appearance in spite of a basically common design approach. Whilst, therefore there has been considerable pull through of equipment from previous designs – for example, Aster missiles – to reduce costs, equipment outfit differs significantly. For example, the Italian ships use an upgraded active version of the EMPAR phased array whilst the French FREMMS are equipped with the less capable Herakles radar previously used in the *Formidable* class frigates exported to Singapore. The original programme called for no less than ten Italian and seventeen French ships. Whilst Italian numbers have been maintained, the French requirement has been steadily cut back to just eight units. By way of compensation, France has managed to export single ships to both Morocco and Egypt.[7]

Export Designs: The success of the French FREMM variant in export markets reflects the fact that European warship construction has traditionally extended beyond the requirements of its own fleets. In comparison to the Cold War years, export contracts were less than plentiful in its immediate

The UK's shipbuilding industry has achieved some post-Cold War success in exports of major surface combatants, notably the sale of two *Lekiu* type frigates to Malaysia. *(RAN)*

The Republic of Singapore Navy frigate *Formidable* pictured on exercises with the Royal, Royal Australian and Royal Malaysian Navies in 2013. Built by France's DCNS, she has strong similarities with the French FREMM variant, with both classes having been influenced by the 1990s stealth frigate *La Fayette*. *(RAN)*

The UK's shipbuilding industry has achieved some post-Cold War success in exports of major surface combatants, notably the sale of two *Lekiu* type frigates to Malaysia. *(RAN)*

aftermath, largely because of the availability of surplus but still relatively modern tonnage from shrinking NATO fleets. However, markets have improved in recent years and have undoubtedly help secure the future of some facilities in the absence of domestic orders.

In addition to its recent successes with FREMM sales, France had previously achieved considerable exports based on its associated *La Fayette* class stealth frigate design. The first of these was laid down just as the Cold War was ending. Six modified versions were subsequently sold to Taiwan as the *Kang Ding* class in 1992, marking one of the few major contracts of the immediate post-Cold War era. Further success was achieved with the somewhat larger *Al Riyadh* design for Saudi Arabia under a programme confirmed in the mid-1990s but not formally commenced until the first of three ships was laid down in September 1999. An order for six *Formidable* frigates from Singapore – five to be assembled locally – was placed in the following year. These c.3,500-ton ships resemble miniature versions of the French *Aquitaine* class FREMMs but have a simpler diesel propulsion system and a lower missile capacity.

Although the United Kingdom has also achieved exports of major surface combatants through the Royal Malaysian Navy's two *Lekiu* class frigates that were delivered in 1999, it is Germany's modular MEKO series that has been the principal rival to France in the twenty-first century. These have previously been detailed in Chapter 5. Earlier ships closely resemble the first MEKO – Nigeria's *Aradu* commissioned in 1992 – but the more recent A-200 series exhibit considerable stealth characteristics. Four of these were commissioned by South Africa as the Valour class between 2006 and 2007. A pair of similar vessels will soon be delivered to Algeria.

RUSSIA & ASIA

The collapse of the Soviet Union after the end of the Cold War brought an effective end to the construction of new Russian major surface combatant designs for a number of years. In addition to a severe lack of funding, the dispersal of naval shipbuilding infrastructure across the union's various republics caused significant dislocation once these republics became independent. This legacy of the Soviet era

Two images of Indian Navy *Talwar* class frigates – a broadside view of *Trikand* and a detail of *Tarkash*'s forward armament. Both ships – members of a class of six – were built in Russia to the Project 1135.6 design. Both Indian and Russian surface combatant design has been heavily influenced by Russian technology. *(Conrad Waters)*

continues to cast a shadow to the present time, not least in the cessation of supplies of marine gas turbines from Ukraine following Russia's seizure of the Crimea and intervention in the Donbass region. When naval construction did resume, the immediate priority was modernisation of the nuclear deterrent and the assets needed to protect it, the latter including the Project 2038.0 *Steregushchy* class corvettes/light frigates.

Project 2235.0 *Admiral Gorshkov* Class: Russia, did, however retain a significant warship design capability after the Cold War in the form of the various research institutes and design bureaux established in Soviet times. This had two important consequences. First it has allowed Russia to recommence major warship construction as greater stability and economic prosperity has returned. The foremost example of this is the new Project 2235.0 *Admiral Gorshkov* class, the first of which was laid down in February 2006 and is currently running final trials. The new 4,500-ton general-purpose design has a much greater emphasis on stealth than seen in previous Russian ships but retains the Soviet-era propensity for a heavy weapons outfit. This includes the 'Poliment-Redut' air-defence system

that benefits from a four-faced phased array and a thirty-two cell VLS, believed to be for the 9M36 surface-to-air missile that is derived from the S400 (NATO: SA-21 'Growler') land-based weapon. This is supplemented by sixteen additional strike-length cells for long-range surface-to-surface missiles, as well as anti-submarine torpedoes and a flight deck and hangar for a Ka-27 Helix sea-control helicopter. A total of four of the class are currently under production and an extended series is planned. Nevertheless, the ten-years taken to complete the first ship is an indication of the difficulties of restarting warship production once key skills are lost.

India: The availability of warship design expertise in Russia was also significant in that it was drawn upon heavily by both India and China to develop their own indigenous warship building capabilities. This has typically taken the form of limited acquisitions of entire warships, supplemented by larger purchases of equipment and associated technical know-how. In India's case, a total of six Project 1135.6 *Talwar* class frigates, a significant enhancement of the Cold War 'Krivak III' design, were commissioned between 2003 and 2013.[8] The principal rationale behind the acquisition was to make good a shortfall in warship

procurement during the 1990s. However, the experience gained from the possession of modern warships will undoubtedly have helped indigenous programmes. So far, as major surface combatants are concerned, these have been focused on two main series of warships; the Project 15 and successor destroyers and the Project 17 series frigates. Both series display the heavy influence of Russian design principles in their basic design but incorporate a bewildering mix of Russian, Western and indigenously-designed equipment. The reliance on Russia has had an unfortunate side-effect in so far as the disruption of equipment supplies that has impacted the Russian fleet has also been felt by Indian shipbuilders. This has been a significant factor in producing extended construction times, which have averaged around nine-years or more.

The most modern designs currently in service are the 6,200-ton Project 17 *Shivalik* class general-purpose frigates and the larger 7,400-ton Project 15 *Kolkata* class destroyers, the latter having a heavy emphasis on anti-air warfare. Three of each type have been – or are close to being – commissioned and improved variants are planned. The former class were ordered at the end of the 1990s and commissioned between 2010 and 2012. They incorporate some stealth features and a Western propulsion system. However, enhancements to automation are not fully reflected in a crew of c.270 once a helicopter is embarked. The main weapons systems are of Russian origin. Whilst the 'Klub' export variant of the SS-N-27 'Kalibr' cruise missile provides a powerful anti-surface punch, the Shtil-1 (SA-N-12) medium-range surface-to-air system – with just a single launcher – does not have the capability of more modern Western designs to combat saturation attacks. The use of the vertically-launched Israeli Barak 1 surface-to-air missile system for point defence may reflect its

limitations. The Indo-Israeli-developed Barak 8 medium-range missile, which is deployed in conjunction with the EL/M-2248 MF-STAR active phased array on the *Kolkata* class appears to be a far more potent system. The *Kolkata* class also carry the Indo-Russian BrahMos supersonic cruise missile, which will be retrofitted to other types.

China: China's naval construction programmes have followed a slightly different track than India's in so far as the Western ban on imports of military systems following the Tiananmen Square massacre

has resulted in a rather less diverse approach to procurement. This appears to have accelerated a transition from imported, largely Soviet-era technology, to the deployment of designs fielding almost entirely indigenous weapons and sensors. The extent to which the underlying technology has been acquired by entirely legitimate means has divided the opinion of commentators.

Direct imports of Russian surface vessels were limited to two pairs of Project 956E/EM *Sovremenny* class destroyers commissioned between 1999 and 2006. However, these acquisitions appear to have

6.2.3: 21st-CENTURY SPECIMEN GENERAL-PURPOSE SURFACE COMBATANTS

Class:	*Fridtjof Nansen*	*Carol Bergamini* (FREMM)	*Xuzhou* (Type 054A)	*Shivalik*	*Akizuki* (DD-115)
Builder:	Navantia, Ferrol, Galicia	Fincantieri, Liguria[1]	Huangpu Shipyard, Guangzhou	Mazagon Dock, Mumbai	Mitsubishi HI., Nagasaki
Country:	Norway	Italy	China	India	Japan
Number:	5	4+4+[2][2]	20+4	3[3]	4[3]
Keel Laid:[4]	9 April 2003	4 February 2008	2005	11 July 2001	17 July 2009
Launched:[4]	3 June 2004	16 July 2011	30 September 2006	18 April 2003	13 October 2010
Commissioned:[4]	5 April 2006	29 May 2013	29 January 2008	29 April 2010	14 March 2012
Full Load Displacement:	5,200 tons	6,700 tons	4,100 tons	6,200 tons	6,800 tons
Principal Dimensions:	133m x 17m x5m	144m x 20m x 5m	134m x 16m x 5m	143m x 17m x 5m	151m x 18m x 5m
Propulsion:	CODAG	CODLAG	CODAD	CODOG	COGAG
	27 knots	27+ knots	27+ knots	30+ knots	30 knots
	4,500nm range	6,500nm range	5,000+ nm range	5,000nm range	No published range
Armament:	16 x VLS cells	16 x VLS cells	32 x VLS cells	1 x S3-90 launcher	32 x VLS Cells
	(ESSM)	(Aster 15/30)	(HHQ-16 SAM)	(Shtil-1 SAM)	(ESSM)
	2 x quad Kongsberg NSM	4 x twin Teseo Mk 2/A SSM	2 x quad YJ-83 SSM	4 x octuple Barak 1 PDMS	2 x quad Mitsubishi SSM
	1 x 76mm gun	1 x 127mm gun	1 x 76mm gun	8 x VLS cells for Klub-N SSM	1 x 127mm gun
	2 x twin 324mm TT	1 x 76mm gun	2 x triple 324mm TT	1 x 76mm gun	2 x triple 324mm TT
	1 x helicopter	2 x triple 324mm TT	2 x 30mm CIWS	2 x 12-tube A/S rocket launchers	2 x Phalanx CIWS
		2 x helicopters	1 x helicopter	2x twin 533mm TT	2 x helicopters
				2 x helicopters	
Crew:	c.120	c.150+	c.190	c.260	c.200

Notes:

1 Construction split between Riva Trigoso and Muggiano yards.

2 Italian ships are being built in general-purpose and anti-submarine variants; data refers to the GP type. Eight broadly similar vessels have been built or are building for France, which has also sold a ship to each of Morocco and Egypt.

3 Orders have been placed for additional ships of modified variants.

4 First of class.

been supplemented by additional purchases of entire systems, such as the Shtil-1-based air defence system used in the Type 052B 'Luyang I' destroyers, the Rif-M (SA-N-20) missiles of the Type 051C 'Luzhou' class and the Fregat MAE (Top Plate) search radar found on many current surface combatants. Russian influence remains particularly strong in the Type 054A 'Jiangkai II' or *Xuzhou* class frigates, which have been in series production from 2005 onwards. Over twenty of these ships have been commissioned to date and they provide the mainstay of the People's Liberation Army Navy's blue water deployments. However, the larger Type 052C and Type 052D destroyers that form the 'high end' combatant force use largely indigenous equipment, including the Type 346 (Dragon Eye) series phased array and the vertically-launched HHQ-9 surface-to-air missile.[9] Interestingly, however, HHQ-9 reflects Russian practice in being derived from a land-based system and has been reported to rely heavily on technology found in the 'Luzhou' type's Rif-M.

In contrast to India, China appears to be able to produce its warships at considerable speed. Build times for major combatants of around three years are comparable with the most productive Western and Japanese yards. It is also starting to enter the market for exports of major surface combatants. Pakistan's F-22P *Zulifiqar* class possibly represents its most important export success to date.

Japan: Elsewhere in Asia, China's principal naval rival, Japan, has long-established warship design and build capabilities. Whilst Japan's most advanced surface combatants – notably its Aegis-equipped ships – have been heavily influenced by overseas designs, it has otherwise built a series of anti-submarine optimised surface escorts that reflect local operational requirements. These tend to use a mix of Western – largely US Navy but some European – weapons and propulsion systems that are then integrated into Japanese platforms that benefit considerably from local electronics 'know-how'. Orders have been purposely placed to a regular 'drumbeat' of one to two major units each year. This protects the industrial base and facilitates incremental improvement.

The latest surface escorts to be commissioned are the *Akizuki* (DD-151) class. Four of these were brought into service between 2012 and 2014. Displacing some 6,800 tons in full load condition, the class is derived from the previous *Takanami* (DD-110) and *Murasame* (DD-101) classes but exhibits a

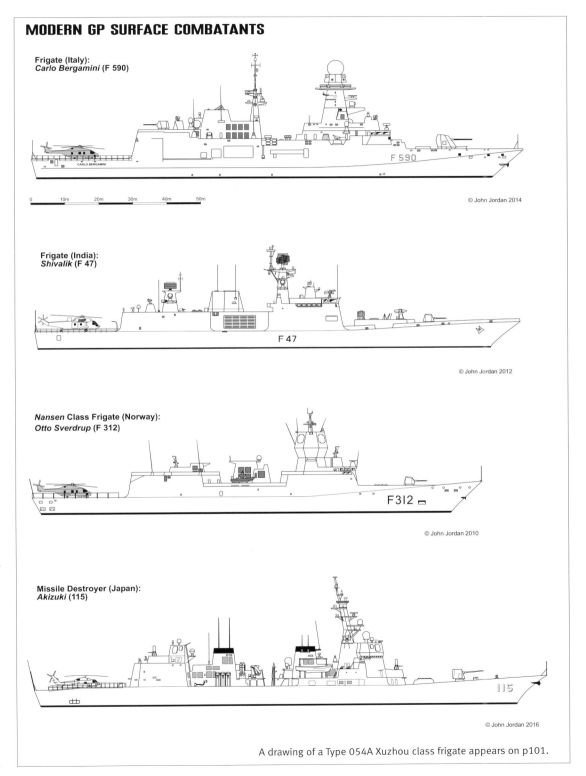

MODERN GP SURFACE COMBATANTS

Frigate (Italy): *Carlo Bergamini* (F 590)
© John Jordan 2014

Frigate (India): *Shivalik* (F 47)
© John Jordan 2012

Nansen Class Frigate (Norway): *Otto Sverdrup* (F 312)
© John Jordan 2010

Missile Destroyer (Japan): *Akizuki* (115)
© John Jordan 2016

A drawing of a Type 054A Xuzhou class frigate appears on p101.

general enhancement in stealth features and has an upgraded propulsion system. Most notably, however, the class has enhanced air-defence capabilities based on the indigenous Melco FC-3 phased array. This was first installed in the 'helicopter-carrying destroyer' *Hyuga* and incorporates some elements of APAR technology. The incorporation of more sophisticated air-defence equipment reflects the class's primary role as general-purpose escorts for the helicopter carriers and Aegis-equipped destroyers, particularly when the latter are carrying out BMD taskings.

South Korea is also a major shipbuilding nation and its KDX-I and KDX-II series destroyers are another important example of Asian designed major surface combatants. The subsequent Aegis-equipped KDX-III series was heavily influenced by the DDG-51 class. However, a planned second batch will probably incorporate more local ideas. Local industry is also heavily involved producing the new FFX *Incheon* class littoral combatants. These approach major surface combatant status in terms of size and capability.

The Japanese *Akizuki* destroyer class is a development of previous escort destroyer classes with a greater emphasis on local air defence requirements; most previous destroyers were heavily anti-submarine focused. This excellent aerial view shows the fixed FCS-3 phased arrays fitted to the forward and aft superstructures. One of each pair of fixed arrays is used for search and tracking functions, the other for fire control. *(JMSDF)*

Notes

1. *Ticonderoga* – the first of twenty-seven CG-47 class cruisers – was commissioned on 22 January 1983.

2. With semi-active guidance, the missile seeks radiation reflected from the target by the fire-control illuminator. The latest generation of Standard SM-2 missiles also incorporate an infra-red seeker for use against targets over the horizon or with a low radar cross-section.

3. The original phased arrays – such as SPY-1 – were passive, using a single source of radio energy to power their individual elements. Digitally-controlled phase shifters are used to create and direct the radar beams. With the latest generation active phased arrays, each individual transmit-receive module is separately energised and can therefore operate within a range of different frequencies. Active arrays are more flexible than their passive predecessors in being able to form multiple beams simultaneously and have greater inherent reliability.

4 The DBR was developed to take advantage of the different properties of radar frequencies. In general terms, higher-frequency radars produce a sharper, more accurate beam for a given size of antenna but have a shorter range and are less suitable for volume search. DBR was intended to achieve the best of both worlds by combining the X band (NATO I/J band) 8-12 GHz frequency AN/SPY-3 antennae with the lower 2-4 GHZ frequency AN/SPY-4 S Band (NATO E/F band) arrays in a common system. The

removal of AN/SPY-4 from the *Zumwalt* class means that AN/SPY-3 will have to undertake volume search functions, for which it is not best suited.

5. The swift, all-out conflict envisaged during the Cold War meant saving battle-damaged ships – that were unlikely to be repaired before the end of combat – was a low priority. However, lessons learned from the Falklands War, as well as the Iraqi Exocet missile attack on the US Navy frigate *Stark* (FFG-31) in 1987, tended to increase the emphasis placed on survivability. The different operating environment of the current age, where damage from asymmetric attack is a particular risk, has accelerated this trend.

6. It was originally planned to build twelve Type 45 destroyers but the number was reduced to eight, then six. Orders for 'Horizon' class vessels were also reduced, as France originally wanted four of the type and Italy as many as six.

7. The Egyptian ship was launched as the French *Normandie* but transferred to Egypt when almost ready to enter the *Marine Nationale* to meet an urgent Egyptian requirement for the ship.

8. The Russian Navy has subsequently ordered six of the type for its own use as the *Admiral Grigorovich* class, reflecting the need for modern vessels as a result of the pause in construction following the Soviet Union's

collapse. The status of the last three is, however, uncertain due to inability to source their Ukrainian-built gas turbines.

9. The Type 052D class incorporates a modified phased array derived from the Type 346 system.

10. The following principle sources used in the production of this chapter provide more detailed analysis:

Norman Friedman, *The Naval Institute Guide to World Naval Weapons Systems – Fifth Edition* (Annapolis, MD: Naval Institute Press, 2006).
Hartmut Manseck, 'Frigate Type 124 Sachsen Class', *Naval Forces – Volume 25, Issue 1* (Bonn: Mönch Publishing Group, 2004).
Jean Moulin, 'Le Chevalier Paul & les fregates Horizon', *Marines & Forces Navales* (Rennes, Marines Éditions, 2009), No. 120, pp.8–27, and No. 121, pp.14–33.
Norman Polmar, *The Naval Institute Guide to the Ships and Aircraft of the U.S. Fleet – Nineteenth Edition* (Annapolis, MD: Naval Institute Press, 2013).
Ronald O'Rourke, *Navy DDG-51 and DDG-1000 Destroyer Programs: Background and Issues for Congress RL32109* (Washington DC: Congressional Research Service).

In addition, many of the ships reviewed in this section have featured in past editions of *Seaforth World Naval Review* (Barnsley: Seaforth Publishing) or been discussed by the author in the annual *Warship* (London: Conway).

6.3

Conrad Waters

MINOR WARSHIPS & AUXILIARIES

Most naval commentary on warship designs inevitably tends to focus on the carriers, amphibious vessels and major combatants that have been discussed in previous chapters. However, for the majority of the world's navies, it is minor surface warships such as corvettes, fast attack craft, mine-countermeasures vessels and patrol ships that comprise the bulk of their fleets. These vessels typically have their home in the littoral waters that have come increasingly to dominate 21st-century naval operations and therefore warrant greater attention.

They can be broadly sub-divided between ships built for a primary warfighting role and those which have been acquired for constabulary-type policing duties. Sometimes, however, the distinction between the two can be quite blurred.

Turning first to warfighting combatants, the latter half of the Cold War saw the increasing popularity of surface-to-surface missile-armed fast attack craft. At the time, it was thought that these offered a quick and relatively cheap means of levelling the playing field with the better equipped and funded blue water

navies. As has often been the case with such 'disruptive technologies' in the military sphere, the promise fell somewhat short of the reality. The experience of the 1990–1 Gulf War, in particular, revealed the hideous vulnerability of many of these vessels to air and helicopter attack from outside the range of their (usually limited) air defences. Nevertheless, fast attack craft remain useful littoral combatants in geographical locations – such as archipelagos – that best suit their employment, particularly when operating as part of a 'system of systems' that takes requirements such as appropriate air defence into account.

Another minor warship type that has somewhat reduced popularity in the early years of the twenty-first century has been the classic mine-countermeasures vessel. Partly a response to the reduced threat from mine warfare in the post-Cold War environment, this trend also reflects the development of remote – and, increasingly, autonomous – underwater vehicles that are described further in Chapter 7. This means that the use of expensive non-magnetic warships in the mine-countermeasures role is less necessary than previously. In turn, this has opened up the possibility of a new generation of offshore combatant that can be configured to undertake several traditional littoral warfare roles, a trend evidenced by vessels such as Sweden's *Visby* class. The most interesting aspect of this trend, however, is the development and deployment of such specialist warships offensively against anti-access forces in the littoral. The US Navy's two Littoral Combat Ship designs are the most obvious examples of this type of ship.

Turning to constabulary vessels, the rise of the specialist offshore patrol vessels (OPVs) in response to growing maritime territorial rights has already been discussed in Chapter 5. These policing duties were often carried out in the past by downgrading life-expired or obsolescent front-line warships into what was perceived as a secondary role. To an extent, the practice still continues. However, in addition to the fact that the numbers of ships available for such tasking are somewhat less than in the past, the use of ships in roles for which they were not designed can be inefficient and uneconomical. Often, the development of patrol vessels can also assist developing economies to start on the path towards developing their own warship construction capabilities. An example is the adoption of the Fassmer OPV-80 design for local construction by Chile and Colombia.

Gepard, the lead German Type 143A fast attack craft, pictured operating with her sister *Nerz* and other NATO units off the Scottish coast in 2005. The vulnerability and other inherent limitations of missile-armed fast attack craft has meant that they have lost popularity in the twenty-first century, albeit they remain useful in certain scenarios. *(RAN)*

As in the case of minor combatants, it is interesting to note that the development of offshore patrol vessels has also extended to ships capable of deployment on expeditionary tasks such as peace-keeping or anti-piracy missions. To some extent, this has merely been a demonstration of the flexibility inherent in most warship designs. For example one of Colombia's OPV-80 type vessels – *7 de Agosto* – was deployed halfway round the world to the Indian Ocean in the second half of 2015 to work with the EU Operation 'Atalanta' and the NATO Operation 'Ocean Shield' anti-piracy missions. However, a number of patrol vessels – notably the Spanish *Meteoro* and the Dutch *Holland* classes – have been purposely designed with such extended deployments in mind. This reflects the wider focus on expeditionary stabilisation missions also evidenced by the German F-125 *Baden-Württemberg* class stabilisation frigates and the Dutch *Karel Doorman* JSS.[1]

The latter ship is indicative of the unglamorous but critical role of fleet and logistical support which is becoming ever-more vital to the growing number of navies seeking to deploy at distance. This seems to have been a key limiting factor on China's PLAN's extension of its blue-water deployments and what appears to be almost a 'crash' programme of replenishment ship construction has been put in place to remedy the deficiency. The development of multi-role logistical shipping, as well as multi-role auxiliary vessels similar to the British Royal Fleet Auxiliary *Diligence*, in much greater numbers than hitherto, certainly seems likely to be a major trend over the next decade and more.

Two images of the Colombian Fassmer OPV-80 type offshore patrol vessel *7 de Agosto* operating with European Union and NATO forces in support of anti-piracy activities in the Indian Ocean in 2015. Her deployment halfway around the world reflects the flexibility inherent in most warship designs; however a number of patrol vessels are now being built with expeditionary and stabilisation missions in mind. *(European Union Naval Force Somalia, NATO)*

LITTORAL COMBATANTS

The large number of littoral combatants in service today, as well as the inevitably varying approaches to littoral operations adopted by different countries, means that it is only possible to make generalisations about 21st-century design trends.

Clearly, most littoral combatants are designed for defensive purposes. The most common approach still appears to be to design specific warships for specific warfighting roles. These are often linked together as part of a broader, integrated defence concept. A frequent modus operandi is to utilise small, missile-armed fast attack craft in conjunction with larger, anti-submarine orientated corvettes. A good example of this is the Chinese PLAN's construction of its Type 056 series corvettes – particularly the Type 056A variant with variable-depth sonar – to supplement the anti-surface warfare focus

of the Type 022 missile boats with additional anti-submarine capabilities. The Republic of Korea Navy appears to have adopted a similar strategy with simultaneous construction of *Incheon* class littoral warfare frigates with PKX series missile-armed fast attack craft. There are also echoes of the approach in India's new Project 28 *Kamorta* class anti-submarine corvettes given its history of operating a combination of anti-surface and anti-submarine orientated light warships for littoral defence.[2]

***Skjold* Class:** In general terms the capabilities of individual vessels in the littoral force mix has grown considerably in recent years. An example of this is provided by Norway, whose Aegis-equipped *Fridtjof Nansen* class frigates and *Skjold* class fast attack craft represent a quantum leap over their predecessors. Both classes originated from studies around the end of the Cold War to replace existing ships, with the proximity of Russia's Northern Fleet remaining a major influence. The *Nansen*s are of a size and capability to deploy at distance in the role of major general purpose surface combatants in addition to their primary defensive anti-submarine mission. The *Skjold* class, meanwhile, utilise an air-cushion catamaran/surface effect ship (ACC/SES) configuration in conjunction with a fibre reinforced plastic construction in their key role as platforms for high speed anti-surface warfare in the Norwegian littoral.[3] They rely heavily on stealth for survivability, including the use of a visual camouflage scheme designed to blend in with Norwegian topography. Their combination of speed, stealth and firepower – they ship an enclosed battery of up to eight Kongsberg NSM Naval Strike Missiles – make them particularly well-suited for this specific role.

Republic of Korea Navy corvettes and fast attack craft depicted on exercises off the South Korean coast in October 2012. The South Korean Navy is one of a number that tend to utilise fast attack craft focused on anti-surface warfare in conjunction with larger corvettes, which tend to have greater anti-submarine warfare capabilities, on littoral operations. *(Republic of Korea Navy)*

6.3.1: 21st-CENTURY SPECIMEN LITTORAL COMBATANTS

Class:	Skjold	Visby	Freedom (LCS-1)	Independence (LCS-2)	Type 056 'Jingdao'	Type 022 'Houbei'
Type	Fast Attack Craft/Corvette	Corvette	Littoral Combat Ship	Littoral Combat Ship	Corvette	Fast Attack Craft
Builder	Umoe Mandal, Vest-Agder	Saab Kockums, Karlskrona	Marinette Marine,[1] Marinette, WS	Austal USA,[2] Mobile, AL	Various	Various
Country:	Norway	Sweden	United States of America	United States of America	China	China
Number:	6	5	3+11[3]	3+11[3]	c.25+c.35	c.80
Keel Laid:[4]	4 August 1997	17 December 1996	2 June 2005	19 January 2006	2011	2003
Launched:[4]	22 September 1998	8 June 2000	23 September 2006	26 April 2008	May 2012	April 2004
Commissioned:[4]	17 April 1999[5]	10 June 2002[6]	8 November 2008	16 January 2010	February 2013	2004
Full Load Displacement:	275 tons	650 tons	3,500 tons	3,000 tons	c.1,500 tons	c.225 tons
Principal Dimensions:	48m x 14m x 2m[7]	73m x 10m x 3m	118m x 18m x 4m	128m x 32m x 4m	89m x 12m x 4m	43m x 12m x 2m
Propulsion:	COGAG + waterjets c.60 knots 800nm range	CODOG + waterjets 35+ knots 2,500nm range	CODAG + waterjets 40+ knots 3,500nm range	CODAG + waterjets 40+ knots 4,300nm range	CODAD c.30 knots	Diesel + waterjets c.40 knots
Armament:	2 x quad Kongsberg SSM 1 x 76mm gun	2 x quad Saab RBS-15 SSM Provision for SAM module 1 x 57mm gun 4 x 400mm torpedo tubes Platform for 1 x helicopter	1 x 57mm gun 1 x RAM PDMS 2 x helicopters Mission-specific module[8]	1 x 57mm gun 1 x Sea RAM PDMS 2 x helicopters Mission-specific module[8]	2 x twin YJ-83 SSM 1 x 76mm gun 2 x triple torpedo tubes 1 x FL-3000N PDMS 2 x 30mm CIWS Platform for 1 x helicopter	2 x quad YJ-83 SSM 1 x 30mm gun
Principal Sensors:	Thales MRR 3D-NG search	Saab Sea Giraffe search Hydra multi-sonar	EADS TRS-3D search Sonar in mission module	Saab Sea Giraffe search Sonar in mission module	Type 360 search Sonar (VDS on T-056A)	Type 362 search
Crew:	c.21	c.43 Accommodation for c. 53	c.40+ mission crew Accommodation for c. 75	c.40+ mission crew Accommodation for c. 75	c.80–90	c.15

Notes:

1 The prime contractor for the programme is Lockheed Martin.

2 The prime contractor for the prototype vessels was General Dynamics.

3 A total of forty Littoral Combat Ships is currently planned, of which eight will be a more heavily-armed frigate variant. It is not currently known how this final number will be split between the two types.

4 Relates to first of class, as far as is known. Some dates relate to start of fabrication.

5 The first of class was delivered in prototype form on this date. It was subsequently rebuilt to full operational configuration, recommissioning as the final 'full specification' ship of the class in April 2013.

6 Relates to initial delivery to the Swedish defence materiel organisation. Formal delivery to the Swedish Navy was delayed until 2012.

7 Draught is less than 1m with the air cushion turned on.

8 Ships are designed for fitting with a mission-specific module, including additional weapons, sensors and crew. There are currently anti-surface, anti-submarine and mine-countermeasures modules.

However, they have a very limited capacity for other operations and are heavily reliant on the support of other units to counter air and underwater threats.

Visby Class: The limitations of such capable but single role-orientated vessels as the *Skjold*s has, along with the other factors identified in the opening remarks to this chapter, led to efforts towards developing minor surface combatants with multi-role capabilities. As already mentioned, a good example of this trend is Sweden's *Visby* class of littoral warfare corvettes. These are broadly contemporaries with the Norwegian ships in terms of conception and entry into operational service. Conceived as a replacement for existing fast attack craft, the class shares the *Skjold* type's emphasis on stealth and has significant anti-surface warfare capabilities. However, possibly reflecting Sweden's previous use of FAC type vessels for anti-submarine operations, *Visby* is also designed

with significant anti-submarine and mine-counter-measures potential. This essentially requires a combat management system that can easily integrate the weapons and sensors that might be required to perform a wide range of roles, as well as enough space to accommodate a variety of mission equipment. A spacious equipment deck underneath the flight deck provides room for anti-submarine torpedoes, mines, depth charges and anti-submarine sonar and is linked to a working area used to deploy unmanned vehicles. Delays to the class's entry into operational service means that it is not yet clear to what extent the design has been a success. However, studies into larger vessels suggest the 650-ton design might be a little cramped to be fully effective as a true multi-mission combatant.

Littoral Combat Ships: The ships which currently best represent the multi-mission littoral warship in

the public's eyes are undoubtedly the US Navy's Littoral Combat Ships (LCS). As previously mentioned, these are somewhat atypical, however, in so far as they are largely designed to support offensive, expeditionary deployments away from the United States rather than act in a purely defensive role. This fundamental factor has had a significant impact on overall design, particularly in terms of the size and speed the ships require to deploy globally. It has been reflected in the need for innovation in the terms of hull design and propulsion arrangements, as well as a relatively high unit cost that approaches that of a major surface combatant.[4]

Developed from conceptual studies such as the 1990s 'Streetfighter', the LCS programme was formally launched in 2001. After assessment of a number of rival proposals, two very different designs were finally selected for series production. The Lockheed Martin *Freedom* (LCS-1) variant incorpo-

The Norwegian *Skjold* class fast attack craft – also designated as littoral corvettes – are an enlarged and modernised version of the traditional type. Their high speed, stealth and powerful battery of surface-to-surface missiles make them ideal for their role as the anti-surface component of a network of defensive systems. They are, however, inevitably less well-suited to independent operation. This is *Steil* in June 2013. *(Peder Torp Mathisen/ Norwegian Armed Forces)*

rates a semi-planing steel mono-hull and an aluminium superstructure. A combined diesel and gas (CODAG) propulsion arrangement based around two Rolls-Royce MT-30 gas turbines and two Colt-Pielstick diesels is connected to four Rolls-Royce Kamewa waterjets. The General Dynamics/Austal *Independence* (LCS-2) variant, on the other hand, is based on an all-aluminium trimaran design. This provides much greater volume and deck area than a conventional mono-hull of similar displacement. The hull arrangement also has lower hull resistance, allowing a lower-powered arrangement of GE gas turbines and MTU diesels to be specified. Again, these are connected to waterjet propulsors. In spite of the differences, both LCS variants displace in the region of 3,000–3,500 tons and can achieve speeds of around 45 knots.

The key element of similarity in the two LCS designs is, however, their use of common modular mission packages. These have similarities with the Danish Stanflex system discussed in previous chapters but also benefit from incorporation of a large mission bay for use with conventional and unmanned vehicles. Sensibly, the US Navy's concept of operations includes embarkation of specialised mission personnel with each package. The LCS programme originally encompassed three specific packages aimed at countering threats particularly prevalent in the littoral. These are anti-submarine warfare, mine warfare and surface warfare. Unfortunately, development of the packages has lagged behind commissioning of the new ships, adding to criticism of a design that has suffered from concerns over construction problems, cost overruns, and manning and support issues. Perhaps as significantly, the overall LCS concept has been condemned as putting insufficiently survivable ships into a high-threat environment. This criticism rather misunderstands the typical US Navy approach of operating its ships as a network of mutually reliant but force enhancing units. As such, LCS operations would likely take place under the protection of major surface combatants. However, concern has been such that later LCS hulls will be recast as light frigates, receiving additional weaponry but losing some of their modularity. Production will also be capped at forty ships rather than the fifty-two originally called for.

The US Navy's LCSs have not been the only small warships designed with expeditionary deployments in mind. Germany's K-130 *Braunschweig* class are –

The Swedish *Visby* class are designed to operate in a similar littoral environment to the *Skjold* class but are larger ships with a much greater capability for multi-mission deployment. For example, they have been designed with a spacious equipment deck and adjacent area for unmanned vehicle deployment that provides them with considerable potential in anti-submarine and mine-countermeasures operations. This image shows *Härnösand* in March 2012. *(Torbjørn Kjosvold / Norwegian Armed Forces)*

This stern view of the US Navy *Independence* (LCS-2) variant *Coronado* (LCS-4) in August 2015 gives an impression of the significant volume and deck area produced by her trimaran structure. The large working area helps to house the various multi-mission modules that are key to the LCS concept. *(US Navy)*

The US Navy Littoral Combat Ship has been built to two distinct designs. This image shows the *Freedom* (LCS-1) class variant *Fort Worth* (LCS-3) on deployment to the Indian Ocean in October 2015. *(US Navy)*

The most sophisticated end of the constabulary patrol vessel spectrum is represented by the US Coast Guard's *Bertholf* or 'Legend' class national security cutters. Eight ships have been ordered; this image shows the fifth vessel *James* (WMSL-754) on acceptance trials in the spring of 2015. The class's CODAG propulsion provides sufficient speed to operate with naval task groups and much of their equipment is common to frontline US Navy warships. *(Huntington Ingalls Industries)*

to some extent, an attempt to recast Cold War missile-armed attack craft concepts to a warship suitable for overseas missions in littoral areas. Equally, the *Heybeliada* class light frigates that are emerging from Turkey's Milgem 'national ship' programme are being used to support international deployments. The latter carry more than a passing resemblance to the LCS-1 *Freedom* variant. However, neither warship has the ability to switch between different minor combatant roles – nor the capability for rapid global deployment – that is inherent in the LCS type.

PATROL VESSELS

Just as for warfighting vessels, the range of patrol vessels put into service around the world varies significantly according to topography, financial resources and the specific requirements of different countries. They range, at one extreme, from small coastal patrol vessels of less than 100 tons to the giant oceanic ships – the latest approaching or even exceeding 10,000 tons – operated by China and Japan at the other. Most, of course, fall somewhere between these two extremes. Of these, offshore patrol vessel types have become increasingly important in the current century, not least because maritime territorial rights are now much more extensive than before. A range of current designs is discussed further below. In spite of national differences, all share the same combination of range, endurance, habitability, communications

systems and capability to conduct boarding operations required for successful long-range constabulary duties.

Bertholf (WMSL-750) Class: The *Bertholf* (WMSL-750) class national security cutters – otherwise known as the 'Legend' class – form the high end of the US Coast Guard's cutter force. Five of the 4,500-ton ships have been commissioned from 2008 onwards and a total of eight is planned. They will replace twelve 1960s-generation *Hamilton* (WHEC-715) class cutters. Their use as part of a 'system of systems' that includes manned and unmanned aerial vehicles accounts for the fall in numbers. The new ships are regarded as the first line in a defence-in-depth of the homeland, undertaking long-distance patrols of United States territorial waters out as far as Alaska and Hawaii. They are also often assigned to participating in capability-building exercises with national allies. Their design is intended to facilitate operations with front-line US Navy warships and many of their weapons and other systems are common to one or other LCS variant. A degree of stealth is also evident in the ships; for example the mast is based on a stealthy design used in DDG-51 class destroyers.

The ships' ability to deploy at distance is reflected in a maximum range of no less than 12,000 nautical miles. In line with other US Navy warships, manning is relatively heavy. A typical crew size is

around 110 personnel and accommodation is provided for nearly 150. An enclosed stern ramp facilitates the deployment of fast interceptor craft for boarding operations and up to two medium helicopters can be embarked and supported. Military grade communications facilities are provided to allow the ships to undertake a command role in the aftermath, for example, of a major terrorist attack on a busy port or waterway.

Holland Class: An interesting comparator to *Bertholf* is the Dutch *Holland* class design. Tracing their origins to a 2005 Naval Study that aimed to achieve the optimum structure for the future Dutch fleet, the four ships in the class were ordered in December 2007.[5] All were in commission by the end of 2013. Of broadly comparable size to the 'Legend' class, they are specifically designed for operations at 'the lower end of the spectrum of

The Dutch *Holland* class offshore patrol vessel *Zeeland* pictured departing Portsmouth Harbour in November 2014. The class's distinctive pyramid-like integrated mast gives them excellent surveillance capabilities but they are not intended for front-line operations. They are designed to police Dutch territorial waters in Europe and the Caribbean, as well as to undertake broader stabilisation missions overseas. *(Conrad Waters)*

violence'. Built largely to civilian standards, a good level of protection is provided against the asymmetric threats (such as attack by lightly-armed terrorists or pirates) that might be encountered whilst operating in the littoral. However, overall weapons fit – a 76mm gun and light weapons – provides a slightly lower level of overall capability than that found on their US Navy counterparts and is certainly not suitable for unsupported deployment in higher-threat areas.[6]

There are, however, three areas where the *Holland* class excels. The first is the provision of a comprehensive range of sensors housed in the class's most visually prominent feature – the pyramid-like Thales integrated mast located immediately aft the bridge. This is a separate, airtight module that incorporates all the ship's major sensors and communications equipment. It is fabricated separately to the rest of the ship and simply bolted on when complete. Important advantages claimed for the structure are the avoidance of interference between sensors, more efficient manufacture and much easier maintenance. The range of Thales Nederland equipment installed includes active phased arrays and electro-optical surveillance devices. The combination provides a more effective surveillance capability than that found in many front-line frigates. In spite of this level of sophistication, extensive use of automation allows the class to be manned by a core crew of fifty, saving considerably on operating costs. Finally, total capital costs of €468m (c.US$565m) for all four ships are relatively affordable, amounting to little more than the acquisition expense associated with a single *Bertholf.*

***Meteoro* Class:** Another example of a recent European offshore patrol vessel design is represented by the Spanish Navy's *Meteoro* type, which are also designated as the *Buque de Acción Maritima* or BAM class. A contract for an initial four ships was placed in 2006; these entered service from 2011 onwards. It was initially intended to order many more of the class to perform a variety of roles, including hydrog-

The Spanish Navy's *Meteoro* of BAM class has a broadly similar function to the Dutch *Holland* but does not have such a sophisticated sensor suite. However, the basic hull has been built with flexibility in mind and can be adapted to a number of roles. *(Navantia)*

The Irish Naval Service's new *Samuel Beckett* class represents a lower level of capability than some of its contemporaries but is ideal for patrolling the harsh waters of the North Atlantic, where Ireland has significant territorial waters. This is second of class *James Joyce* in July 2015. *(Irish Defence Forces)*

raphy and submarine rescue. However, these plans have been significantly curtailed by Spain's economic crisis and it was not until 2014 that a further order, for just two ships, was placed.

Whilst smaller than the *Holland* class at c. 2,600 tons full load, *Meteoro* and her sisters are remarkably similar from a conceptual perspective. Designed to counter asymmetric threats in lower-risk environments and to carry out surveillance and broader constabulary duties, the class replaces a range of vessels ranging from light frigates to coastal patrol ships. As for the Dutch ships, this requirement has been met through combining commercial construction standards and a light armament with the provision of extensive communications and control facilities. The combined diesel or electric (CODOE) power plant also provides a comparable level of capability to the equivalent system on the Dutch ships. It allows diesel-powered transit to an assigned patrol area, where the lower-powered but more energy efficient electric motors can be used for lower-speed loitering. Yet another similarity is the use of automation to drive down crew size. A BAM is usually operated by only forty-five crew, albeit considerably more are needed for more extended deployments.

***Samuel Beckett* Class:** Somewhat less capable than the previous ships is the Irish Naval Service's new *Samuel Beckett* class. An enlarged development of the previous pair of *Róisín* class vessels delivered around the turn of the Millennium, two ships were commissioned in 2014–15. A third is currently under construction. Both designs were produced by STX Canada (now part of Fincantieri's Vard Marine subsidiary) and built by the British Babcock group at Appledore in Devon. The new ships are optimised for constabulary operations in the low threat but climatically harsh conditions of the North Atlantic. Key requirements are therefore an ability for effective deployment in adverse weather – assisted by extending the hull by some 11m over the original 79m design – along with sustained endurance on station. The latter is achieved by use of a similar CODOE propulsion arrangement to that fitted to the *Holland* and BAM types. The main 76mm Oto

The Mexican Navy's *Oaxaca* class offshore patrol vessel *Independencia* exercising with US Coast Guard and British Royal Navy units in the Caribbean in September 2012. The Mexican navy has built a successful series of austerely-equipped but successful 'gunships' for local constabulary missions. *(US Navy)*

Melara gun is also equivalent to the main armament found on these ships but there is no place for their sophisticated military-grade command and communications systems. Equally, there is no provision for helicopter operations. The quid pro quo is a unit cost of only a little over €50m (US$60m) per vessel for the two ships that have already been delivered.

A little smaller than the *Beckett* class, probably reflecting a typically more confined and less climatically challenging area of operations, are Mexico's *Oaxaca* class. These are the latest in a long line of locally-built 'gunships' which date back to the *Holzinger* class of the early 1990s. The *Oaxaca* type vessels are the latest iteration of the basic design, which now extends to four different classes. The main armament is, again, a 76mm Oto Melara gun but the different – potentially more hostile – environment the ships are called to operate in has seen the incorporation of a helicopter deck in addition to a well deck housing a fast interceptor.[7] The design represents, yet again, the significance of specific local operational requirements in shaping warship design.

Warfighting Offshore Patrol Vessels: Another good example of this can be seen in the various adaptations of the basic British-built 'River' class offshore patrol vessel design constructed from the early 2000s onwards. The original three *Tyne* class variants were largely intended for fishery protection and other policing duties in home waters. As such, a cheap, functional 80m design with minimal combat capability was selected. The design was subsequently developed to meet the need for a new Falkland Islands patrol vessel. The resulting *Clyde* was fitted with a long-range search radar, a basic combat management system and a helicopter flight deck. The next variant was an enlarged, 90m design including many core platform systems used on the previous ships but featuring a different hull form and more powerful propulsion package for greater maximum speed. Three of these ships were built for Trinidad and Tobago as the *Port of Spain* class but subsequently sold to Brazil. A locally-built variant of the design for the Royal Thai Navy has been further upgraded with a Thales TACTICOS combat management system, Variant search radar and 76mm gun.[8] In short, the original ships have been continuously adapted so as to span the gap between basic patrol vessel to light corvette, dependent on various owners' needs.

Sometimes, the extent to which patrol vessels have

The British-built 'River' series of offshore patrol vessels has gone through a series of iterations to meet the needs of customers extending from Brazil to Thailand. This image shows the Brazilian *Araguari* – originally ordered by Trinidad and Tobago – on sea trials off Portsmouth in 2013. The Royal Navy's *Forth* (see p.61) is a further development of the design. *(Conrad Waters)*

The Royal Navy of Oman's corvette *Al Shamikh* is a good example of an offshore patrol vessel design that has been upgraded to achieve light frigate characteristics. Basic design similarities with the 'River' class vessel above are obvious. *(Conrad Waters)*

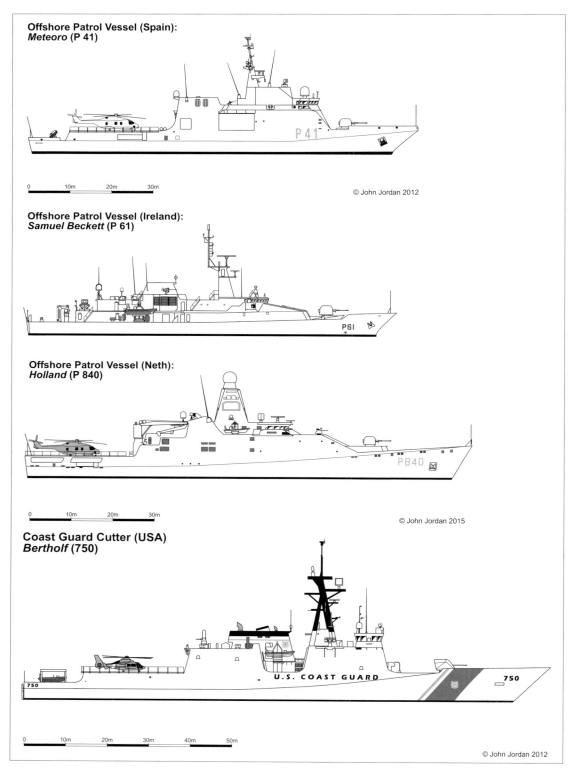

Offshore Patrol Vessel (Spain):
Meteoro (P 41)

0   10m   20m   30m

© John Jordan 2012

Offshore Patrol Vessel (Ireland):
Samuel Beckett (P 61)

P61

Offshore Patrol Vessel (Neth):
Holland (P 840)

0   10m   20m   30m

P840

© John Jordan 2015

Coast Guard Cutter (USA)
Bertholf (750)

750

U.S. COAST GUARD   750

0   10m   20m   30m   40m   50m

© John Jordan 2012

been upgraded make them the equivalent of warfighting combatants. Oman's *Al Shamikh* class are one example. Originally designated as oceanic patrol vessels, the ships have a full outfit of surface-to-surface and surface-to-air missiles, as well as guns and a helicopter, that place them firmly in the light frigate category. Similar ships include the Malaysian MEKO-based *Kedah* class offshore patrol vessels and the Chinese Type 056 patrol vessel export variants sold to Bangladesh and Nigeria. In both these cases, this reflects the potential inherent in a fundamentally combat-orientated design that has ostensibly been acquired for a constabulary role.

Coastal Patrol Vessels: Damen StanPatrol: Turning to the other end of the scale, the range of smaller coastal patrol vessels in service today is possibly even more varied than that for larger ships. However, one post-Cold War trend that does warrant a reference is the remarkable success of the Dutch Damen Group's StanPatrol design series. Originating from the firm's development of a series of standardised, modular workboats and tugs from the 1970s onwards, the firm claims that around 500 standardised patrol vessels have been delivered to date. Currently advertised designs range from the StanPatrol 1204, a small aluminium harbour patrol craft to the StanPatrol 6011, a large seagoing patrol ship. In each case, the four figures relate to the length and beam of the platform. Particular success has been achieved by the mid-sized StanPatrol 4207, of which over sixty have been sold to ten navies and coast guards. The slightly larger 4708 design forms the basis for the US Coast Guard's *Bernard C. Webber* (WPC-1101) or 'Sentinel' class fast response cutter. Around fifteen of these have been delivered to date out of a planned total of almost sixty. The broad StanPatrol modularisation concept has also been applied to larger Damen group ships; for example the successful SIGMA-type corvettes already described in Chapter 5.

AUXILIARIES & SUPPORT VESSELS

In contrast to the significant growth in the market for constabulary patrol assets, recent procurement of logistic support ships has been rather more restrained. To a large extent, this reflects the shrinkage in many of the larger fleets that previously invested heavily in support vessels and a decision to funnel limited resources into front-line warships. One consequence of this is the growing age of many

6.3.2: 21st-CENTURY OFFSHORE PATROL VESSEL DESIGNS

Class:	Berthof (WMSL-751)	Holland	Meteoro (BAM)	Samuel Beckett
Builder:	HII Ingalls Shipbuilding, Pascagoula, MS	Damen Schelde Naval Shipbuilding, Vlissingen[3]	Navantia, San Fernado/Puerto Real, Cadiz	Babcock Marine, Appledore, Devon
Country:	United States of America	The Netherlands	Spain	UK (for Ireland)
Number:[1]	5+3	4+0	4+2	2+1
Keel Laid:[2]	29 March 2005	8 December 2008	13 March 2009	18 May 2012
Launched:[2]	29 September 2006	2 February 2010	16 October 2009	3 November 2013
Commissioned:[2]	4 August 2008	6 July 2012	28 July 2011	17 May 2014
Full Load Displacement:	4,500 tons	3,750 tons	2,600 tons	2,250 tons
Principal Dimensions:	127m x 17m x 7m	108m x 16m x 5m	94m x 14m x 4m	90m x 14m x 4m
Propulsion:	CODAG, 30+ knots 12,000nm range	CODOE, 22 knots 5,000nm range	CODOE, 21 knots 8,000nm range	CODOE, 23 knots 6,000nm range
Principal Armament:	1 x 57mm gun 1 x Phalanx CIWS 2 x helicopters	1 x 76mm gun 1 x 30mm gun 1 x helicopter	1 x 76mm gun 2 x 25mm guns 1 x helicopter	1 x 76mm gun 2 x 20mm guns
Boarding Capabilities:	Stern launch ramp 1 x 11m & 2 x 7m RHIBs	Stern slipway 2 x 12m RHIBs, 1 x rescue boat	2 x RHIBs	3 x 8m RHIBs
Principal Sensors:	EADS TRS-3D search radar SPQ-9B surface search/fire control	Thales IM-400 mast	Indra Aires search	Kelvin Hughes search
Crew:	110 Accommodation for 148	50 Accommodation for 90 Temporary facilities for 100 refugees	45[4] Accommodation for c.70	44 Accommodation for 54

Notes:

1 Refers to completed ships and ships under construction or on order.

2 Dates relate to first ship of class.

3 Two of the class were fabricated at the Damen yard in Galati, Romania, with only final integration work carried out in the Netherlands.

4 It was originally intended to operate the class with as few as thirty-five crew but this has increased in practice.

logistical assets that remain in service. For example, the British Royal Fleet Auxiliary (RFA) is still operating tankers and stores ships dating from the 1970s and the earlier members of the French *Durance* class are not much younger. There has, of course, been some ongoing construction to replace life-expired vessels. The US Navy put fourteen of the *Lewis and Clark* (T-AKE-1) class ammunition cargo ships into service between 2006 and 2012, whilst the RFA's two 'Wave' class tankers were delivered a little earlier.

Other orders have come from navies with developing 'blue water' naval ambitions. China's increasing fleet of Type 903/903A replenishment ships and India's two *Deepak* class replenishment tankers are examples of this.

The majority of these newly-built support ships have been orientated towards a specific function. This is the case with respect to one of the larger ongoing construction programmes; that for four 'Tide' class fleet tankers being built by South Korea's

DSME to a BMT Group Aegir-derived design for the RFA. The new 37,000-ton ships are primarily designed to carry out the replenishment of marine and aviation fuel at sea and have very limited stores capacity. Secondary roles include humanitarian and constabulary operations. The ability to stow and maintain a single helicopter – also used for vertical replenishment – is a key enabler in this regard. A separate class of solid support ships, authorised in the British 2015 defence review, will provide

replenishment of ammunition and other dry cargo.

Looking forward, there are indications both of growth in the overall market and a move towards logistic ships with greater multi-role functionality. The former trend is being influenced by the growing focus on expeditionary operations but also by the fact that many current vessels are obsolescent. There is a particular issue with respect to non-compliance with MARPOL standards mandating double-hulled tanker construction, as significant numbers of single-hulled naval tankers remain in service.[9] Meanwhile, trends to multi-role vessels are evidenced, amongst others, by the German Type 702 *Berlin* class delivered between 2001 and 2013, which are officially designated as 'task force suppliers'. As well as significant fuel capacity, the ships can also carry around 600 tons of mixed cargo in addition to nearly eighty standard 20ft containers. The ships have significant surplus accommodation for use in embarking additional forces or supporting humanitarian operations. The latter is assisted by the potential to embark a containerised 45-bed hospital. The ships are also able to house and support two medium helicopters and are fitted 'for but not with' the RAM point-defence missile system.

Broadly similar in concept to the three *Bonn* class ships is the Norwegian *Maud,* which is scheduled for delivery in 2016. Like the 'Tide' class she is a derivative of the BMT Aegir design and built in South Korea but has a much greater multi-role capability. This includes ability to supply a wide range of liquids and dry stores, as well as permanent hospital facilities for eight patients that can be expended to as many as forty-eight if required. She is sufficiently flexible to undertake a wide range of secondary roles, notably as a forward-based 'mothership' for other Norwegian units such as submarines or Special Forces. Other possible tasking includes supporting salvage and repair activities or even operating as a floating headquarters for a network based defence.

The potential to extend multi-role support concepts still further to encompass amphibious

The use of converted civilian offshore support ships for naval roles has provided a useful forward maintenance capacity. This image shows the British Royal Fleet Auxiliary *Diligence* preparing to provide support to the Type 22 frigate *Cornwall* in the Middle East in 2010. Looking forward, it seems likely that specially-built designs will be able to assist with a broader range of naval operations. *(Crown Copyright 2010)*

A number of more recent replenishment ships have been designed to carry out a wide range of roles, which can include humanitarian support, salvage and repair or even service as a floating headquarters. An example is the new Norwegian logistics support vessel *Maud*, which is being built by DSME in Korea to a BMT Defence Services design. *(BMT Defence Services)*

operations is evidenced by the Dutch JSS *Karel Doorman*, which has already been discussed in Chapter 6.1. Another potential development is the construction of multi-role utility auxiliaries, which would expand on existing offshore commercial designs to create a type better optimised for naval operations. Such a ship would extend the use of existing types for repair and maintenance to a much wider range of roles, including the deployment of unmanned vehicles, submarine rescue and embarked force logistics. The overall aim would be to reduce numbers of both class and ship types to achieve both capital and through-life savings.

Notes:

1. The F-125 class is a rather unique concept that falls a little between the typical characterisation of warships into major and minor surface combatants. Displacing c.7,500 tons, the new ships are equal to the size of a Second World War cruiser and place a heavy emphasis on survivability. This includes the duplication of much equipment, notably through a twin island arrangement that divides important equipment between two distinctive deckhouses. However, armament is entirely focused on low/medium-intensity stabilisation operations and would be insufficient to ensure survival in a higher-threat environment. In this regard, they are somewhat more akin to a large, well-equipped patrol vessel.

2. This, in turn, reflects heavy Russian Cold-War investment in a range of single-mission anti-submarine and anti-surface orientated littoral surface combatants to secure its core maritime 'bastions'. The current Project 2038.0 *Steregushchy* class corvettes have inherited this role but, like the *Kamorta* class, have more general purpose capabilities.

3. A surface effect ship combines the air cushion of a hovercraft with the rigid twin hulls of a catamaran. The ship is supported by the buoyancy of the catamaran hulls when the cushion is turned off, rising so that less of the fixed hull area remains in the water when the air cushion is turned on. The *Skjold* class can operate in less than 1m of water in air-cushion mode.

4. Average costs for LCS-5 to LCS-24, the first to be subject to multi-year procurement, are c. US$450m when

government-furnished equipment is taken into consideration.

5. The study concluded that – in a post-Cold War environment where constabulary and stabilisation missions were growing in importance – the navy was too centred upon warfighting ships. The *Holland* class were regarded as being better-suited for patrolling the Dutch EEZ in the waters of the North Sea and Caribbean. They would also be used to support international peacekeeping missions.

6. This judgement is somewhat subjective. However, as currently outfitted, the Dutch ships have little capacity for anything other than surface engagements against relatively lightly-armed enemies, particularly as the 76mm gun is not currently configured for use against aircraft. By contrast, the US Coast Guard class's 57mm gun and Phalanx CIWS provide a limited anti-air capability.

7. The Mexican Navy has been heavily involved in the fight against drug trafficking and other forms of organised crime that currently plague Mexico. Its offshore patrol vessels need to be well-equipped to counter any resistance from criminal gangs, some of which are heavily armed.

8. Subsequently, a further three of these 'Batch II River' type patrol vessels have been ordered by the Royal Navy as the *Forth* class. There are plans for two additional ships.

9. Single-hulled commercial tankers have now been phased out and – although naval tankers are not covered by the MARPOL regulations – the pressure to follow suit is

increasing. A presentation given by BMT Defence Services' Head of Business – Auxiliaries, Rob Steel and Chief Naval Architect, Andy Kimber at the 2015 DSEI exhibition in London indicated that around seventy new replenishment vessels were needed to replace existing ships. This is a significant driver of a market that research analysts at HIS Jane's estimate to amount to c. US$20bn over the next decade.

10. The following principle sources used in the production of this chapter provide more detailed analysis:

Barry Clarke, Jurgen Fielitz & Malcolm Touchin (Editor Professor G Till), *Coastal Forces* (London: Brassey's UK Ltd, 1994).

Tim Fish, 'Cruising Ahead: Briefing – Offshore Patrol Vessels', *Jane's Defence Weekly – 17 March 2010* (Coulsdon: IHS Jane's, 2010), pp.22–7.

Hartmut Manseck, 'Ship Special: the "Holland" Class', *Naval Forces – Issue III, 2011* (Bonn: Mönch Publishing Group, 2011), pp.75–80.

Ronald O'Rourke, *Navy Littoral Combat Ship (LCS)/Frigate Program: Background & Issues for Congress RL33741*, (Washington DC, Congressional Research Service).

Stuart Slade, 'Fast Attack Craft', in *Conway's History of the Ship, Navies in the Nuclear Age* (London: Conway, 1993). pp 98-109

In addition, many of the ships reviewed in this section have featured in past editions of *Seaforth World Naval Review* (Barnsley: Seaforth Publishing) or been discussed by the author in the annual *Warship* (London: Conway).

6.4

Conrad Waters

SUBMARINES

If the submarine was the weapon that best typified Cold War naval operations, then the stand-off's immediate aftermath saw the rapid demise of its popularity. No US Navy submarines were authorised for construction between FY1992 and FY1998; the longest period since the first introduction of the submarine that no new boats were approved by the United States. The collapse in submarine production in the Soviet Union was even more marked.[1] Some countries, for example Denmark, decided to abandon underwater operations altogether.

In spite of this rather patchy run-up to the begin-

ning of the twenty-first century, submarines remain a key instrument of naval warfare. Their perceived invulnerability in oceanic waters – and the retaliatory capability this provides – means that ballistic missile-carrying submarines remain the weapon of choice for countries wishing to field a strategic nuclear deterrent. Equally, the range, endurance and flexibility of operations – from reconnaissance through to land attack – provided by nuclear-powered attack submarines make them essential for those navies wishing to project blue-water power. Indeed, some countries have maintained these

forces at the expense of other underwater capabilities. Of the main Western naval powers, the US Navy retired its last diesel-electric submarine just as the Cold War was coming to an end.[2] Both the United Kingdom and France have subsequently also decided to consolidate on an all nuclear-powered underwater force.

Of course, many countries cannot afford the unique capabilities, notably prolonged underwater operation, offered by nuclear power. However, this does not mean that alternatives are unavailable. Notably, progress made in the area of air-independent propulsion (AIP) has extended the underwater endurance of conventionally-powered submarines. The system is a popular choice for many second-tier navies. Moreover, even traditional diesel-electric powered submarines – that need to periodically surface for air – offer a combination of stealth and firepower that is attractive, particularly in areas where there is less risk of detection when coming close to the surface to snorkel. In contrast to the period immediately after the Cold War, the number of countries operating submarines is expanding again. Unsurprisingly, this trend is particularly marked in South East Asia, where Malaysia and Vietnam have recently joined the submariners' club.

Even more so than for major surface combatants, the ability to design and construct submarines – even conventionally-powered ones – remains the preserve of a very few nations. Whilst many countries have been involved in the assembly of submarines, key components such as torpedo and other weapons handling systems, propulsion and even parts of the pressure hull have often to be sourced from overseas. One consequence of this is that the number of new submarine designs put into service has been quite limited, as the following overview demonstrates.

STRATEGIC MISSILE SUBMARINES

At the present time five countries are known to have operational nuclear-armed ballistic missile submarines, viz. the United States, Russia, the United Kingdom, France and China. In addition, India will soon bring its first strategic submarine, *Arihant*, into service and Israel is believed to have developed a nuclear-armed cruise missile capability for its *Dolphin* class submarines.

Until recently, there had been very little in the way of new strategic submarine design and construction since the end of the Cold War, at least in the

The US Navy's *Seawolf* class nuclear-powered attack submarine *Connecticut* (SSN-22) pictured in November 2009. A product of the Cold War focus on hunting Soviet submarines, the design proved too large and expensive for the post-Cold War era and only three were completed. However, submarines have remained an important naval asset in the twenty-first century and a number of different production programmes are currently underway. *(US Navy)*

West. The Western nuclear powers – the United States, United Kingdom and France – all had replacement strategic submarine programmes well underway as the Cold War ended. These, sometimes in reduced numbers, were sufficient, once completed, to meet the lesser needs of the new era. Indeed, the requirements of the START II strategic nuclear arms reduction treaty – which was finally signed in 1993 but never took effect – were even to lead to the US Navy reducing its flotilla of modern *Ohio* (SSBN-726) Trident submarines from eighteen to fourteen. This was achieved by rebuilding the first four boats to carry conventionally-armed cruise missiles.[3] It should be noted, however, that some enhancements to existing boats were carried out through this time. For example, some of the earlier US Navy Trident boats – that had initially been equipped with the early Trident C-4 weapons – were retrofitted with the improved D-5 variant of the missile between 2000 and 2005. Similarly, the older members of the French *Triomphant* class are being re-equipped with the new M51 ballistic missile, which first entered service on *Terrible* in 2010. The planned service lives of existing boats are also being stretched; the *Ohio* class were originally designed for a thirty-year service life but this has been extended to over forty years.

Both the US and British Royal Navy's strategic submarines need replacement from the early 2030s. Work to ensure new boats are ready within this timescale is now well underway. The two programmes – involving twelve SSBN(X) *Ohio* Replacement Submarines for the US Navy and four 'Successor' class boats for the Royal Navy – are being managed separately but have a degree of overlap. This is most evident in the development of a common missile compartment for the two classes. The new PWR3 nuclear reactor being built for the new British submarines has also benefitted from US Navy input. Although publicly-available details are scarce, the overall intention of both programmes appears to be to reduce costs by adapting technologies developed for post-Cold War nuclear attack submarine programmes whilst pursuing innovation where this will enhance operational or cost performance.[4] It seems that both new classes will adopt the X-form control planes found in many recent diesel-electric submarine designs and the use of integrated electric propulsion also seems likely. This should improve overall acoustic performance, a key design driver. There is no immediate intention of replacing

The US Navy strategic submarine *Nevada* (SSBN-773) seen in June 2013. Both the US Navy's and British Royal Navy's Trident missile-equipped boats are now quite elderly. The plan is to replace the submarines but retain the missiles, which have already been subject to a life-extension programme.

the Trident missiles that form the main armament of existing strategic boats. These have already benefitted from a life-extension programme that will keep them operational into the 2040s.

Turning to Russia, the navy has long been struggling to deploy its Project 955 'Borei' class strategic submarines, on which development work reportedly started during the 1980s. The submarines have been desperately needed to replace the existing Soviet-designed and built strategic submarine fleet, most of which was commissioned in the 1980s. The first submarine, *Yuri Dolgoruky*, was laid down in 1996. However, its completion was badly delayed by the abandonment of the original ballistic missile intended for the boat. The replacement RSM-56 Bulava (SS-NX-30/SS-N-32) also suffered a protracted and problematic development process that included a number of missile malfunctions during test firings. As such, although *Yuri Dolgoruky* finally commenced sea trials in 2009, it was not until 2014 that she became fully operational. There

is little information available on the extent to which the class is an advance on previous designs, although she is reported to be fitted with pump-jet propulsion and feature hydrodynamic improvements. Published sources suggest that parts from incomplete Soviet-era submarines were used in the first boats. Three of the initial Project 555 type are now in commission, with work underway on four of at least five of an improved Project 555A variant.

There is little meaningful information on the even more secretive Chinese and Indian strategic submarine programmes. However, it would seem likely that both have benefitted from access to the Russian technology and know-how that has assisted a wide range of other domestic military programmes. The Indian Navy has yet to integrate its relatively short-ranged K-15 ballistic missile with the new submarine *Arihant* and the longer-ranged K-4 is still in development. China's equivalent JL-2 – deployed in the latest Type 094 'Jin' class – has a much longer range and is viewed as providing a

The second British *Vanguard* class submarine *Victorious* transiting the River Clyde in April 2013. The class will start to reach the end of its lifespan by the early 2030s and work on the 'Successor' replacement programme is well underway. An image of the 'Successor' design can be seen in Chapter 4.2.1. *(Crown Copyright 2013)*

credible sea-based deterrent. However, all its nuclear-powered submarines remain noisy compared with Western and Russian designs. This constitutes a major operational weakness.

NUCLEAR-POWERED ATTACK SUBMARINES

Although the Cold War's end saw a lengthy hiatus in construction of strategic submarines, nuclear-powered attack submarine programmes have been a little more active. Production of these boats is confined to the same countries currently operating strategic submarines, although India operates the nuclear-powered *Chakra* on lease from Russia and has plans for its own production line. Brazil also has an active submarine construction programme that incorporates a nuclear-powered element.

Virginia Class (SSN-774): The *Virginia* class programme had its origins at the end of the Cold War, when concerns over the cost of the existing *Seawolf* (SSN-21) design gave rise to a decision to pursue a complementary design to maintain overall force numbers. The *Seawolf* design was optimised for anti-submarine warfare against an anticipated

A series of images showing a test launch of a Trident D5 missile from the US Navy's *Ohio* class strategic ballistic missile submarine *West Virginia* (SSBN-736) in June 2014. Although the Trident missile system is intended to remain in service well into the 2040s, the American and British submarines that carry it will require replacing before then. *(US Navy)*

new generation of very stealthy Soviet boats. The new submarine – initially termed 'Centurion' – was intended to provide a more balanced range of capabilities, including support for operations in the littoral. In addition to having a substantially lower cost than Seawolf, the 'Centurion' design was also intended to be better suited to upgrade as new technologies became available.[5]

The first *Virginia* class submarines were ordered in 1998. The lead boat was laid down in September 1999 and commissioned on 23 October 2004. Early production efforts were focused on reducing unit costs to c.US$2bn in FY2005 terms, thereby allowing the purchase of two submarines each year. This was achieved by FY2012 and indeed, a steady production 'drumbeat' of two boats p.a. has been in place since FY2011. Most of the class have been ordered under multi-year contractual arrangements, thereby assisting with economies of scale. To help maintain the US industrial base, assembly is split between Electric Boat at Groton, Connecticut and Newport News Shipbuilding, Virginia. Each yard builds the same sections of each boat, with the reactor module and final assembly being assigned on an alternating basis.

Displacing c.8,000 tons submerged, the *Virginia* class revert to the relatively long, narrow hull lines seen in the *Los Angeles* (SSN-688) class, which first entered service in the 1970s. They use the upgraded HY-100 steel introduced with the *Seawolf* boats – thereby providing a deeper operating depth – as well as a pump-jet propulsor derived from British attack submarine practice. Otherwise, they introduce a number of innovations into US Navy submarine

The *Virginia* class submarine *California* (SSN-781) being floated out at Newport News Shipbuilding, Virginia, in November 2010. Construction of the class has been split between the Huntington Ingalls Industries yard and GD Electric Boat at Groton, Connecticut to maintain the US industrial base. *(Huntington Ingalls Industries)*

construction, largely to improve affordability. These include a new reactor with a core designed to last the life of the boat (saving expensive refuelling costs) and a sonar system using open system architecture (facilitating the periodic upgrade of both software and hardware). The boats are also the first US Navy

submarines fitted with non-hull penetrating photonics masts in place of traditional periscopes. The inherent flexibility of the design has been demonstrated by the incorporation of a series of upgrades as different blocks or series have been ordered. For example, the Block III boats include a

Russia has struggled to replace the Soviet-era submarines that form the sea-based element of its strategic nuclear deterrent. However, persistent effort to correct deficiencies in a new generation of strategic missiles has achieved results. These images show the Project 941 'Typhoon' class strategic submarine *Dimitry Donskoy*, which acted as the testbed for new RSM-56 Bulava ballistic missile. This has subsequently been displayed operationally on the new 'Borei' class submarines; second of class *Aleksandr Nevsky* is shown here. *(Russian Ministry of Defence)*

new sonar – the Large Aperture Bow (LAB) array – in place of the US Navy's traditional sonar sphere and two large-diameter missile tubes instead of the smaller vertical-launch systems found in older members of the class. The planned Block V submarines are scheduled to receive an additional mid-body section – the *Virginia* Payload Module (VPM) – so as to be able to deploy more Tomahawk cruise missiles or other payloads.

Twelve *Virginia* class submarines have been commissioned to date and orders for a further sixteen have been placed, with more planned. Whilst, at a current cost of c. US$2.8bn per unit they are certainly not cheap to procure, the programme has met its objective of producing a comparatively cost-effective design that has proved capable of progressive upgrade.

Astute **Class:** The British Royal Navy equivalents to the *Virginia* class boats are the *Astute* class nuclear-powered attack submarines.[6] Three of these boats have now been delivered and a further four are in various stages of construction. The *Astute* class was conceived immediately after the end of the Cold War as a cheaper alternative to the previously planned 'W' or SSN-20 programme. In comparison to the all-new 'W' class design, the alternative programme was based on an evolution of the previous *Trafalgar* class, including the use of an enlarged hull to accommodate the PWR-2 reactor developed for the much-larger *Vanguard* class strategic submarines. The *Astute* class hull form is therefore very different to their US Navy comparators, with a length to breadth ratio of around 8.5:1 compared with 11.5:1 on a *Virginia* making them much squatter than the American boats. Displacement is, however, similar at c.7,800 tons submerged.

Initial orders for three *Astute* class submarines were placed in March 1997 at a total cost of c.£2bn (US$3bn). At this stage it was anticipated that the first of class would enter service in June 2005. However, largely due to a significant erosion of submarine construction skills since the completion of the previous *Vanguard* class, the programme proved extremely problematic. Significant time-

Table 6.4.1: 21st-CENTURY NUCLEAR POWERED ATTACK SUBMARINES[1]

Class:	*Virginia* (SSN-774)	*Astute*	*Suffren* ('Barracuda')	*Severodvinsk* (Project 885 'Yasen')	Type 093
Builder:	GD Electric Boat, Groton CT HII Newport News Shipbuilding, VA	BAE Systems, Barrow-in-Furness	DCNS, Cherbourg	Severodvinsk Shipyard	Bohai Shipyard, Huludao
Country:	United States of America	United Kingdom	France	Russia	China
Number:[2]	12+16+[10+]	3+4	0+4+[2]	1+4+[2+]	2+[4]
Keel Laid:[3]	2 September 1999	31 January 2001	19 December 2007	21 December 1993	1994
Launched:[3]	16 August 2003	8 June 2007	[2016]	15 June 2010	24 December 2002
Commissioned:[3]	23 October 2004	27 August 2010	[2018]	30 December 2013	December 2006
Submerged Displacement:	8,000 tons	7,800 tons	5,100 tons	13,500+ tons	c.7,000 tons
Principal Dimensions:	115m x 10m x 9m	97m x 11m x 10m	99m x 9m x 7m	120m x 14m x 9m	110m x 11m x 8m
Propulsion:	Nuclear, direct drive 35+ knots	Nuclear, direct drive c.30 knots	Nuclear, hybrid drive 25+ knots	Nuclear, direct drive 35+ knots	Nuclear, poss. turbo-electric c.30 knots
Diving Depth (Test):	c. 400m–450m	'Over 300m'	'Over 350m'	c.600m	Not known
Armament:	4 x 533mm torpedo tubes 12 x VLS cells c.38 weapons	6 x 533mm torpedo tubes 38 weapons	4 x 533mm torpedo tubes 24 weapons	4 x 630mm torpedo tubes 4 x 533mm torpedo tubes 24 VLS cells c.50+ weapons	6 x 533/630mm torpedo tubes
Crew:	c.135	c.100	c.60	c.90	Not known

Notes:

1 Information on submarine operations is subject to significantly less disclosure than for other types of warship and there is also probably a significant amount of disinformation spread. Some of the above details should therefore be regarded as speculative, particularly with respect to diving depth.

2 Refers to ships completed or under construction, with numbers in brackets those firmly planned.

3 Dates relate to the first of the class. Some dates in the 'Keel Laid' line relate to start of fabrication.

consuming and expensive remedial efforts were ultimately required, including assistance from *Virginia* class constructors, Electric Boat. As such, *Astute* did not finally commission until August 2010 and the cost of the first three submarines – at some £3.5bn – was over fifty per cent higher than initially envisaged.[7] However, the programme now seems to be on a more stable footing, with all key design requirements reportedly met and construction of the final three boats back on schedule. These will have an average cost (in current prices) of c. £1.5bn (US$2.3bn) a boat, somewhat less than a *Virginia*.

Technically, the *Astute*s are reported as being broadly equivalent to the *Virginia* class submarines. For example, the most recent 'Core H' incorporated in the PWR-2 reactor provides a similar 'whole boat life' endurance as the US Navy class and they have similar, non-hull penetrating optronic masts. The performance of the Thales Sonar 2076 – arguably the most significant combat system on the boats – is reported to have performed well in trial exercises against the US Navy. However, the *Astute*s lack the US Navy's vertical-launch systems, launching both torpedoes and cruise missiles from traditional 533mm torpedo tubes. A capacity to carry a total of thirty-eight weapons is, however, similar to that of a current member of the *Virginia* class.

Suffren **Class:** France, the third Western power to operate nuclear powered-submarines, has traditionally followed a different course from the US Navy and the Royal Navy in the design of its boats. The existing *Rubis* class – with a submerged displacement of c. 2,700 tons – is much more compact than its contemporaries. It also features nuclear-powered turbo-electric propulsion compared with the direct steam-powered drive employed by the United States

France's 'Barracuda' design is much smaller than other contemporary nuclear-powered attack submarines, perhaps reflecting the need to operate regularly in the confined waters of the Mediterranean. This is an early computer-generated image of the design, which features an X-plane stern for better shallow-water manoeuvrability. (DCNS)

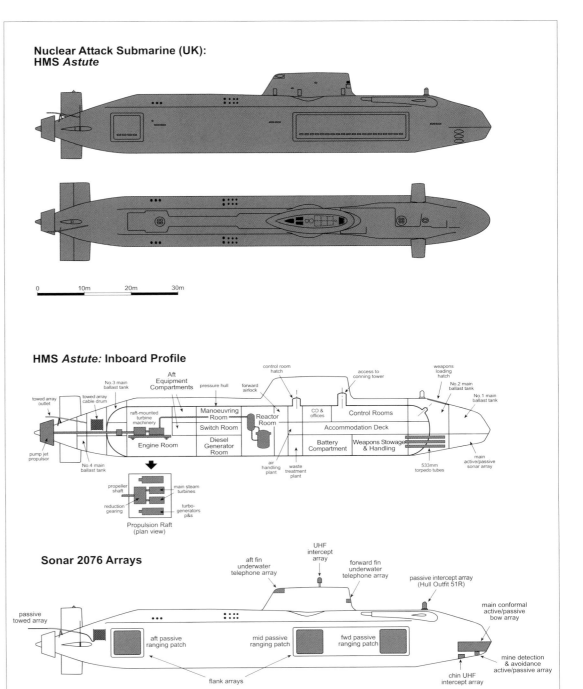

Nuclear Attack Submarine (UK): HMS *Astute*

0   10m   20m   30m

HMS *Astute*: Inboard Profile

Sonar 2076 Arrays

These internal and external drawings of the British Royal Navy nuclear-powered attack submarine *Astute* show the typical layout of a modern SSN. The forward end of the boat is largely taken up with weapons systems, accommodation and storage spaces, with the whole area aft of the fin given over to the propulsion system. This is a major determining factor on the submarine's overall size. The extent of the sophisticated sonar system is also clear. *(Drawings © John Jordan 2010)*

and United Kingdom. This could, theoretically, provide acoustic benefits, although deficiencies in the class's initial hull design generated much more noise than anticipated until this was modified.

Design studies for the replacement 'Barracuda' or *Suffren* class commenced in the late 1990s. However, post-Cold War budgetary constraints meant that it was not until December 2006 that the first order was placed. The intention is to replace the *Rubis* class on a like-for-like basis. The lead submarine should be launched in 2016 and delivered by 2018, a slight delay on previous plans. All six boats are scheduled to be in service by the end of 2029.

Whilst larger than the previous class with a submerged displacement of 5,100 tons, the new French design remains significantly smaller than the other attack submarines already discussed. This has benefits in terms of programme expense, particularly in terms of allowing the continued use of existing support infrastructure, and boat-handling. Unit coast as of 2013 was reported as being c.€1.3bn (US$1.6bn). The penalty is a reduced weapons-carrying capacity, with a total load-out of twenty-four weapons less than two-thirds of that found on Royal and US Navy nuclear-powered attack submarines.

Interestingly, propulsion on the 'Barracuda' class will comprise a new hybrid system. This retains turbo-electric drive for low-speed operation but substitutes direct steam-powered mechanical for higher speeds. The K-15 nuclear reactor is a variant of those used to power the aircraft carrier *Charles de Gaulle* and utilises low-enriched, civilian-grade fuel. This means that refuelling will continue to be required during the lifespan of the boats, albeit a ten-year core life is longer than that for the *Rubis* class. More importantly, the design-choice leverages the capabilities of the substantial French civilian nuclear infrastructure in a move that should reduce overall support costs.

Given that Brazil is relying heavily on France's DCNS for its conventional submarine programme, which is based on indigenous assembly of the company's 'Scorpène' design, it would seem likely that its planned nuclear-powered attack submarine will also reflect French influence. However, the reactor will reportedly be of entirely Brazilian design.

The first of the new 'Barracuda' class submarines seen under construction at DCNS' Cherbourg facility in 2015. Her launch is scheduled for 2016 and delivery for 2018. *(DCNS)*

The French nuclear-powered attack submarine *Améthyste* pictured on a visit to the United States in 2008. She is one of the existing *Rubis* class that will be replaced by the new 'Barracuda' design from towards the end of the current decade onwards. *(US Navy)*

The German PEM fuel cell-based AIP system has been both an operational and commercial success. It was first used in the Type 212A submarines, which were initially designed with operation in the confined waters of the Baltic in mind. AIP is particularly suitable for this environment. The image shows *U-35*, the first of a second batch of two, improved members of the class, on initial sea trials in 2013. *(ThyssenKrupp Marine Systems)*

Russian & Chinese Designs: Just as in other areas of naval construction, work on Russian nuclear-powered attack submarines virtually ceased at the end of the Cold War. At that time, work on a derivative of the Project 971 'Pike' (NATO: 'Akula') class by the Malakhit bureau was one of several submarine design efforts underway. This work resulted in the first Project 885 'Yasen' class boat, *Severodvinsk*, being laid down at the end of 1993. As for many Russian projects of the era, the programme was hit by significant financial difficulties, as well as the priority given to the 'Borei' strategic submarines. As a result, the much-delayed trials of the lead submarine did not commence until 2011. By this time a second unit, built to an improved Project 885M specification was underway. Four further Project 885M submarines have been ordered subsequently and a total of at least seven is expected. The class is reportedly very expensive, possibly more than a US Navy *Virginia* class boat, to construct. Work on new 'fifth generation' submarines suggests a more cost-effective replacement is being sought.

Published details for the class are largely speculative and frequently contradictory. In line with Soviet-era submarine practice, the 'Yasen' class are large submarines, reportedly displacing as much as 13,800 tons. They benefit from the progress the Soviet Union achieved in improving acoustic signature during the later years of the Cold War. However, they are not thought to be as silent as the most recent Western types. The reactor reflects American and British practice in being designed for the life of the boat and – given the capabilities of Soviet-era submarines – a high underwater speed is likely. There is a strong emphasis on anti-surface weaponry, with eight vertical-launch tubes for at least twenty-four submarine-launched cruise missiles being supplemented by eight torpedo tubes for, possibly, thirty further weapons. Some reports suggest a form of surface-to-air missile system is fitted for self-defence.

Meanwhile, Chinese nuclear attack submarine construction is focused on the Type 093 'Shang' class. Very few firm details on these submarines are in the public domain. They appear to displace in the order of 6,000–7,000 tons and are equipped with torpedo tubes and, possibly, vertical launch systems. They are reported as being noisy compared with foreign contemporaries, a charge also levelled at earlier Type 091 'Han' class. Very slow and limited production – an initial run of just two units was followed by a pause of several years before construction of an improved variant commenced – suggests that they are principally being used to gain technological and operational experience pending the arrival of an improved Type 095.

AIP-EQUIPPED SUBMARINES

Given the immense capital outlays associated with the acquisition of nuclear-powered submarines, not to mention the additional costs associated with ongoing operation and ultimate decontamination and disposal of decommissioned boats, it is not surprising that so few countries can afford the costs involved. However, the growing proficiency of anti-submarine countermeasures targeted towards detecting surfaced boats as the Cold War progressed spurred a number of second-tier fleets towards seeking an alternative source of power for prolonged underwater operation.[8] Not unsurprisingly, much of this work was carried out by navies with significant experience of operating in enclosed, hostile waters. It is this environment where the risk of detection is greatest. This work gave rise to a new generation of submarines equipped with auxiliary air-independent propulsion (AIP). AIP typically supplements a boat's main diesel-electric plant with a low-powered source

Drawings of a German Type 212A submarine showing both the main diesel-electric and the auxiliary AIP propulsion systems. Both oxygen tanks and hydrogen cylinders are stowed outside the pressure hull on safety grounds. The overall internal arrangement is conceptually similar but more compact than the larger nuclear attack submarine, *Astute*. This similarity extends to the general arrangement of the sonar suite. *(All drawings © John Jordan 2013)*

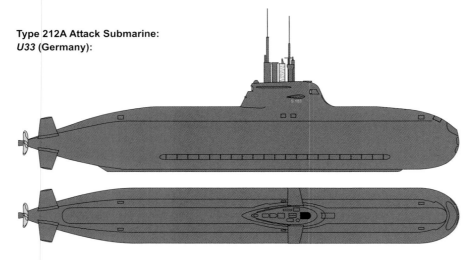

Type 212A Attack Submarine:
U33 (Germany):

Type 212A Batch 1: General Arrangement

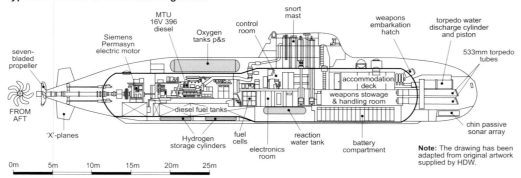

MTU 16V 396 diesel • Siemens Permasyn electric motor • Oxygen tanks p&s • control room • snort mast • weapons embarkation hatch • torpedo water discharge cylinder and piston • 533mm torpedo tubes • accommodation deck • weapons stowage & handling room • chin passive sonar array • seven-bladed propeller • FROM AFT • 'X'-planes • diesel fuel tanks • Hydrogen storage cylinders • fuel cells • electronics room • reaction water tank • battery compartment

Note: The drawing has been adapted from original artwork supplied by HDW.

0m 5m 10m 15m 20m 25m

Type 212A Batch 1: Sensor Outfit

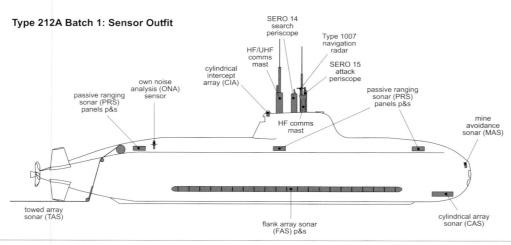

SERO 14 search periscope • Type 1007 navigation radar • HF/UHF comms mast • SERO 15 attack periscope • cylindrical intercept array (CIA) • own noise analysis (ONA) sensor • passive ranging sonar (PRS) panels p&s • passive ranging sonar (PRS) panels p&s • mine avoidance sonar (MAS) • HF comms mast • towed array sonar (TAS) • flank array sonar (FAS) p&s • cylindrical array sonar (CAS)

of propulsion that can be used to extend underwater endurance to several weeks at low speed.

Type 212A and Type 214 Class Submarines: As explained in Chapter 5, three different types of AIP systems have entered service to date. These are based on Stirling, MESMA and fuel cell technologies.[9] Of the three, the German-designed, fuel-cell based system has been by far the most successful. This originated from prototype trials using an alkaline-based fuel cell plant in the 1980s and was subsequently developed into an operational system based on Siemens' polymer electrolyte membrane (PEM) technology. The German Type 212A submarines, which have also been built by Italy, were the first to incorporate the new system. An initial order for four boats, designed by HDW and Thyssen Nordsee-werke in conjunction with IKL, was authorised in July 1994. The first of these – *U 31* – commissioned in October 2005. When combined with contracts for a second batch of two improved German submarines and two pairs of Italian boats, a total of ten have now been ordered.

The Type 212A is a small and stealthy submarine design – underwater displacement is in the region of 1,800 tons – that was heavily influenced by the requirements of Cold War operations in the shallow waters of the Baltic. The design is also notably short and broad, with a length to breadth ratio of around 8:1. This partly reflects an unusual one and a half-deck configuration, under which the pressure hull narrows to just one deck aft the fin where the

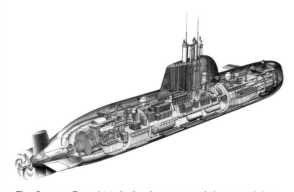

The German Type 214 design incorporated the propulsion system first used in the Type 212A submarines into a modified Type 209 design to create an AIP-equipped submarine suitable for export. The resulting submarine is longer and narrower than the Type 212A with a greater weapons-carrying capacity but less suitability for shallow-water operations. *(ThyssenKrupp Marine Systems)*

propulsion system is located. This comprises a MTU 16V 396 diesel and Piller electric generator; a lead-acid battery; the auxiliary AIP plant encompassing nine Siemens BZM34 fuel cell modules; and a Permasyn electric motor. Maximum underwater speed is around 20 knots, falling to around 8 knots for AIP operation. In line with the emphasis on stealth, extensive use is made of non-magnetic steel, supplemented by lightweight GRP for outer hull coverings and the fin. Overall size limits weapon loadout to twelve torpedoes or equivalent, whilst extensive automation facilitates operation by under thirty crew. The use of an X rudder configuration assists with manoeuvrability in shallow waters, as well as reducing underwater resistance.

Much of the technology used in the Type 212A design has been incorporated in the longer but narrower Type 214 class. It has been described as an evolution of the long-established Type 209 design with the addition of a number of innovations found in the Type 212A. This includes the use of a similar,

Table 6.4.2: 21st-CENTURY SPECIMEN DIESEL-ELECTRIC SUBMARINES

Class:	Type 212A	Type 214	'Scorpène'	Project 636 'Kilo'	A-26	*Soryu*
Principal Builder:[1]	TKMS HDW	TKMS HDW	DCNS	Admiralty, St. Petersburg[2]	Saab Kockums	Mitsubishi Heavy Industries / Kawasaki Heavy Industries
Country:	Germany	Germany	France	Russia	Sweden	Japan
Number:[3]	Germany 5+1 Italy 2+2	Greece 3+1 Portugal 2+0 South Korea 5+4 Turkey – 6 ordered	Brazil 0+4 Chile 2+0 India 0+6 Malaysia 2+0	Algeria 2+2 China 10+0 Russia 4+2 Vietnam 4+2	2 ordered	6+5
Keel Laid:[4]	1 July 1998	7 March 2005	18 November 1999	16 July 1996	[2016/7]	31 March 2005
Launched:[4]	20 March 2002	15 July 2008	1 November 2003	26 April 1997	[2021]	5 December 2007
Commissioned:[4]	19 October 2005	17 June 2010	8 September 2005	26 August 1997	[2022]	30 March 2009
Submerged Displacement:	1,800 tons	1,900 tons	1,700 tons[5]	3,000+ tons	c.1,900 tons	4,200 tons
Principal Dimensions:	56m x 7m x 6m	65m x 6m x 6m	66m x 6m x 6m[5]	73m x 10m x 7m	62m x 7m x 6m	84m x 9m x 9m
Propulsion:	Diesel-electric Auxiliary Fuel Cell AIP 20 knots	Diesel-electric Auxiliary Fuel Cell AIP 20 knots	Diesel-electric 20 knots	Diesel-electric 17+ knots	Diesel-electric Stirling AIP 'Over 12 knots'	Diesel-electric Stirling AIP 20 knots
Diving Depth (Test):	Over 250m	Over 250m	Over 300m	c.300m	Over 200m	Over 300m
Armament:	6 x 533mm torpedo tubes 12 weapons	8 x 533mm torpedo tubes 16 weapons	6 x 533mm torpedo tubes 18 weapons	6 x 533mm torpedo tubes 18 weapons	4 x 533mm torpedo tubes c.15 weapons	6 x 533mm torpedo tubes c.30 weapons
Crew:	c.30	c.30	c.30	c.50	c.25	c.70

Notes:

1 Relates to current main building yard. Some domestic submarine construction has been split between yards and many exported submarines have been subject to local assembly.

2 The Komsomolsk Shipyard was the lead yard for the original Project 877 'Kilo' and other yards have been involved. However, most current construction appears to be focused on St. Petersburg.

3 Numbers relate to those completed to date and those under construction or firmly ordered.

4 Dates relate to first of class to be completed. The Type 214 figures relate to Portugal's Type 209(PN), which appears identical to the Type 214.

5 Data relates to Chilean and Malaysian boats.

6 Information on submarine operations is subject to significantly less disclosure than for other types of warship and there is also probably a significant amount of disinformation spread. Some of the above details should therefore be regarded as speculative, particularly with respect to diving depth.

The Japanese *Soryu* class submarines are an incremental improvement on previous classes, with the incorporation of Sterling AIP being a major improvement. This picture shows third of class *Hakuryu* visiting Pearl Harbor in 2013. *(US Navy)*

The Italian AIP-equipped Type 212A submarine *Salvatore Todaro* seen on a US deployment. The class have quickly proved themselves capable of extended deployment. *(US Navy)*

but more compact, fuel cell system with a smaller number of more powerful modules, as well as a Permasyn electric motor. The design is not, however, optimised for shallow-water operations to the same extent as the Type 212A and non-magnetic steel is therefore not specified. Over twenty units have been exported to Greece, Portugal (Type 209PN), South Korea and Turkey, the majority for local assembly. It is also worth noting that later units of the Israeli *Dolphin* class, as well as Singapore's New Type 218 submarines, also use fuel cell-based AIP.

The potential inherent in this new generation of fuel cell-equipped boats was quickly demonstrated when *U 32* completed a submerged transit from the German Bight to the Bay of Cadiz between 11 and 25 April 2006 on AIP propulsion alone. The class has also proved itself capable of extended deployment, best demonstrated by the despatch of Italy's *Salvatore Todaro* and *Sciré* to North America for exercises with the US Navy during 2008 and 2009. *Todaro*'s deployment was the first time that an Italian submarine had crossed the Atlantic since the Second World War.

Other AIP-Equipped Boats: Other AIP systems have typically been less of a commercial success; for example, the French MESMA has only been installed in Pakistan's *Agosta* 90B class to date. There have been a number of reports that China's Type 039A/B has some form of AIP – although the precise type has not been specified – whilst Russia also intends to deploy the capability in late members of its troubled Project 677 *Sankt Peterburg* type. Meanwhile, Spain's Navantia has encountered significant difficulties in completing the new S-80 *Isaac Peral* class, which includes a new ethanol based fuel plant. A design error has resulted in the four submarines being significantly overweight and a major redesign effort has been required that has badly delayed the project.

For the time being, therefore, Sweden's Stirling system is the only major competitor to Siemens PEM technology. This was developed towards the end of the Cold War and first installed in the Type A14 submarine *Näcken* during 1987–8 through insertion of an 8m-long hull-plug. It was subsequently fitted as new to the three A-19 *Gotland* class submarines ordered in March 1990 and a further iteration of the system has been specified for the new A-26 type boats. The latter appear to be roughly the same displacement as the German Type 212A design but will be longer and narrower and have a higher weapons-carrying capacity. Overseas, Stirling AIP has been retrofitted to the former Swedish submarines sold to Singapore as the *Archer* class, as well as installed from new in Japan's *Soryu* type submarines.[10]

The *Soryu* class continues the practice of incremental design improvements in Japanese warships that is also evident in its surface combatants. Its hull is based on the preceding *Oyashio* class, eleven of which were completed between 1998 and 2008. Six *Soryus* have been commissioned to date and a further five are currently on order. Their submerged displacement of c. 4,200 tons makes them amongst the largest conventionally-powered submarines built to date, reflecting the requirements of extended Pacific Ocean operations. They have considerable weapons-carrying capacity – a loadout of up to thirty torpedoes and Harpoon missiles has been quoted – and a sophisticated sonar system. Japan is reported as being willing to sell the design to regional allies and the RAN has expressed considerable interest as it looks to replace the existing *Collins* class.

CONVENTIONAL SUBMARINES

Whilst AIP has proved to be a popular technological innovation, it is important to stress that it is essentially an auxiliary propulsion system that provides an operating performance far removed from the speed and range of deployment provided by nuclear propulsion. The advantages it confers are largely related to the additional stealth it furnishes when

The French 'Scorpène' design has proved popular with those navies that do not have a requirement for AIP, with fourteen of the type sold to date to countries in South America and Asia. Chile was the first customer; the Chilean Navy's *Carrera* is pictured on sea trials in November 2005. *(Navantia)*

The veteran German Type 209 submarine design, which is now almost fifty years old, has continued to secure new exports after the end of the Cold War. This is one of the South African 'Heroine' class boats delivered between 2005 and 2008. *(ThyssenKrupp Marine Systems)*

A Russian 'Kilo' class submarine. Modernised versions of the design have continued to attract orders throughout the post-Cold War era. *(US Navy)*

boats are operating in a relatively high threat and confined environment where snorkelling would produce undue risk. As such, it is arguably less valuable for submarines operating in oceanic and other open-water conditions. This is reflected in the continued acquisition of submarines equipped solely with conventional diesel-electric propulsion. For example, not one boat with AIP installed has been deployed throughout the Americas to date.

This geographical pattern has been particularly useful for the French submarine-building sector, whose 'Scorpène' design has gained export success in Chile and Brazil in spite of the less than enthusiastic reception for its MESMA system. None of the 'Scorpène' type boats sold to date have been AIP-equipped.[11] The 'Scorpène', which has also been

acquired by India and Malaysia, was originally produced in conjunction with Spain's Navantia but there was a parting of the ways when the Spanish company decided to develop the S-80 design.

The main competitors to the 'Scorpène' have been Germany's veteran Type 209 design and the only moderately more recent Russian 'Kilo'.[12] Both have been progressively updated to provide a cost-effective underwater capability and have continued to attract orders throughout the post-Cold War era. At the current time, Germany is building new Type 209s for Egypt whilst Algeria and Vietnam have joined Russia in buying new 'Kilos'. A new entrant to the market is China, which has been marketing an export variant of its Type 039B submarine – possibly AIP-equipped – to Pakistan, Thailand and others. Whilst Pakistan reportedly committed to a purchase in August 2015, other contracts have proved difficult to finalise, perhaps reflecting a bias towards more tried and tested designs.

Notes

1. See Norman Polmar and Kenneth J. Moore, *Cold War Submarines: The Design & Construction of U.S. and Soviet Submarines* (Washington DC: Potomac Books Inc., 2004), pp.331–2. This situation contrasted to the years of the Cold War, with no fewer than 936 submarines delivered between August 1945 and the end of 1991. 401 of these boats were nuclear powered.

2. The *Barbel* class submarine *Blueback* (SS-581) was the last combat-capable diesel-electric submarine in the US Navy, decommissioning in October 1990. The research submarine *Dolphin* (AGSS-555) was stricken in January 2007.

3. For more detail on the Trident guided-missile submarine conversion programme see Ronald O'Rourke's *Navy Trident Submarine Conversion (SSGN) Program: Background and Issues for Congress RS21007* (Washington DC: Congressional Research Service).

4. According to a briefing paper released by the US *Ohio* Replacement Class Submarine Program Office (PMS 397) in September 2014, the new US Navy submarines will benefit from the ship control system, pump jet propulsor and modular construction used in the *Virginia* class submarines and will retain elements of the existing *Ohio* class's weapons and fire-control system. The use of a life-of-ship reactor core also reflects recent practice in both American and British nuclear attack submarines. In addition to electric drive and an X-stern, other innovations include enhancements to work stations, networks and cyber security.

5. For further background to the *Virginia* class, see Norman Polmar, *The Naval Institute Guide to the Ships and Aircraft of the U.S. Fleet – Nineteenth Edition* (Annapolis, MD: Naval Institute Press, 2013). Ronald O' Rourke's periodically updated *Navy Virginia (SSN-774) Class Procurement: Background and Issues for Congress RL32418*, (Washington DC, Congressional Research Service) is a good source of information on current programme issues.

6. Details of the protracted design and entry into service of the *Astute* class are provided by Richard Beedall in *'Astute Class Submarines: A Quantum Leap in Capability for the "Silent Service"', Seaforth World Naval Review 2011* (Barnsley, Seaforth Publications, 2010).

7. The UK National Audit Office's annual reports are an excellent source of information on the cost, schedule and performance of various weapons systems. The latest report available on the *Astute* class can be found in *Major Projects Report 2015 & the Equipment Plan 2015 to 2025: Appendices and project summary sheets* (London: National Audit Office, 2015), pp.26–53.

8. As further explained in Chapter 5, work on AIP technologies dates back to German efforts to produce an alternative to the established diesel/electric battery combination in the Second World War. The initial emphasis was on increasing underwater speed rather than reducing the inherent vulnerability in the diesel-powered submarine's frequent need for atmospheric oxygen. This work was continued by the Allied powers after the war's end with the assistance of captured technology but was ultimately overtaken by the success of nuclear power.

9. A more elaborate description of the detailed development and fundamentals of current AIP-technologies is contained in the editor's 'Modern Air-Independent Propulsion Equipped Submarines' in *Warship 2012* (London: Conway, 2012) pp.65–80. He also discusses the origins and designs of the Type 212A class in 'Germany's Type 212A Submarines', *Seaforth World Naval Review 2014* (Barnsley: Seaforth Publishing, 2013), pp.136–52.

10. The acquisition of Swedish warship builder Kockums by German rival ThyssenKrupp Marine Systems – manufacturer of the Type 212A and Type 214 classes – appears to have had some impact on the enthusiasm with which the Stirling system was promoted. This is likely to change with the company's return to Swedish ownership through its acquisition by SAAB under a deal actively supported by the Swedish government.

11. 'Scorpènes' can be equipped with MESMA but there have been no sales to date. The later Indian-built submarines will reportedly be fitted with an indigenous AIP system based on phosphoric acid fuel cells.

12. The first Type 209 submarine, the Hellenic Navy's *Glavkos*, was commissioned in 1971. The first 'Kilo' class boat – built to the original Project 877 design – was delivered to the Soviet Navy in 1980. Although the Russian Navy intended to focus construction of new diesel-electric submarines on the new Project 677 type, problems with the prototype boat resulted in resumed production of the improved Project 636 variant of the 'Kilo' in 2010.

7.0

Norman Friedman

TECHNOLOGY

Navies are built to meet stated or implicit strategic needs (requirements) within financial limits, using what is available from the technological menu. Since the end of the Cold War, the main drivers of change have been a dramatic shift in naval requirements, particularly for Western (NATO) navies; the crash in funding due to the end of the Cold War, which has been pronounced in the West but which has not occurred at all in the Asia-Pacific region; and dramatic changes in technology, particularly in computer technology. In contrast to the Cold War, the technology menu is now dominated by the civilian sector rather than by military research and development.

THE NEW ENVIRONMENT

The Importance of the Littoral: For the US Navy and its NATO allies, the Cold War's end profoundly affected the relevance of what had until then been primary naval concerns. The huge Soviet submarine fleet, against which NATO had concentrated vast resources, was no longer a central concern – and it was shrinking dramatically. The US Navy no longer concentrated on a Maritime Strategy which emphasised a decisive battle to destroy the Soviet Union's other main anti-shipping resource, its powerful force of missile-carrying bombers. The primary post-Cold War naval mission became power projection in the littoral – an area the US Navy defines as the strip of sea directly affected by events ashore and the strip of shore affected directly by events offshore. The geography of sea power also changed, as the North Atlantic was no longer likely to be the focus of naval warfare. Land attack thus became far more important than in the past. For example, standard anti-ship missiles such as Harpoon have been given alternative GPS guidance so that they may be fired at targets ashore. Moreover, with the end of the Cold War, defence spending in Western countries fell sharply. No existential threat like the Soviet Union seemed in sight. Cold War force structure was no

longer affordable. The numerical strength of the US Navy, by far the strongest in NATO, was quickly nearly halved.

Navies built mainly around surface combatants have only a limited capacity to strike at land targets. Individual Harpoons or Tomahawks can certainly hit targets ashore, but there is only so much that a few warheads can do. More and more frequently, navies are used to strike ashore in support of troops. Close-support targets pop up suddenly, and often in considerable numbers. The missions envisaged in the past for naval strike weapons were typically precision attacks on what seemed to be extremely important point targets. That was probably never an altogether realistic image of future war, but in recent

wars it has become even less meaningful. What handful of targets would be decisive in a place like Syria or Afghanistan?

The problem, which no one has solved, is that surface ships accommodate limited numbers of missiles and cannot easily be replenished at sea. Any operation requiring the ability to strike at will in support of a fight ashore requires not only substantial numbers of ready-use weapons but also the ability to keep feeding more weapons into the fight. Given the inability to replenish surface warships and the relative simplicity of replenishing aircraft carriers, the new reality favours the latter. Britain learned as much during the Libyan civil war in 2011. It wanted to support the anti-Gaddafi rebels, which required an ability to strike at government troops massing suddenly to attack these rebel forces. That needed nearby weapons which could quickly be deployed. The British were aware that aircraft orbiting near Libya were the best solution, but aircraft flying from the UK lacked the necessary endurance (eventually NATO used Italian bases near Libya). Without a carrier, the national decision to support the rebels could not really be exercised. It was clear that existing British frigates, each armed

The end of the Cold War has meant that the primary mission for the US Navy and – to an extent – many of the other major fleets became power projection in the littoral. This has demonstrated the utility of aircraft carriers compared with precision missiles on surface combatants, which cannot carry enough munitions to make a decisive contribution. Unsurprisingly, many countries are trying to gain some sort of carrier capability. This view shows the Japanese 'helicopter-carrying destroyers' *Izumo* and *Ise* from the flight deck of *Ronald Reagan* (CVN-76) in 2015. *(US Navy)*

The British lack of an operational aircraft carrier made operations during the 2011 Libyan intervention much more difficult, as it meant there was a lack of substantial numbers of ready-use weapons to support the anti-Qadaffi rebels. The use of British Army Apache attack helicopters from the amphibious carrier *Ocean* provided a partial solution. *(Crown Copyright 2011)*

with eight Harpoons, could not contribute effectively to the fight. This experience heavily influenced the British decision to commission both new carriers shortly about to enter service. Even the few aircraft carried by the previous *Invincible* class light carriers would have been effective.

Re-configuration in NATO: Soon after the collapse of the Soviet Union in 1991, every NATO navy discarded large numbers of frigates designed primarily for open-ocean anti-submarine warfare (ASW). That was a particular blow to navies, like that of the Netherlands, which had virtually specialised in ASW. Navies also slashed maritime patrol plane strength.[1] The great fixed submarine detection system in the Atlantic, SOSUS, was no longer likely to be useful. Much of it was discarded (some arrays were turned to scientific purposes such as tracking whales). Similarly, the Cold War orientation of the Scandinavian and German navies, towards stopping possible Soviet invasions through the Baltic, was suddenly no longer nearly as relevant. For a time, these navies argued that their main value was in teaching the oceanic navies how to deal with littoral defenders like themselves. However, ultimately they wanted to join international operations far from home. They needed new fleets of larger combatants.

The US Navy was fortunate in that its Cold War Maritime Strategy emphasised an approach to seizing and holding sea control through projecting power from the sea (or, at the least, through threatening such projection). As a consequence, much American naval investment of the 1980s remained relevant after the Cold War ended. The French Navy, too, had concentrated on power projection

The German Type 143A class fast attack craft *Wiesel* pictured supporting UNIFIL operations off the Lebanese coast in 2013. The Cold War orientation of the Scandinavian and German navies towards stopping positive Soviet invasion through the Baltic meant that they operated many warships that were much less relevant once this threat had dissipated. Although some found alternative uses, these navies really needed larger combatants. *(German Navy)*

and limited investment in open-ocean ASW. It maintained a strike carrier, although the ambition to build a second ship proved unaffordable. The British Royal Navy slowly re-orientated itself towards force projection, ultimately including the construction of two large carriers. However, it was striking that it took about fifteen years for the 1998 decision favouring new carriers to be implemented, and that the British carrier force has been eliminated altogether for several years before the new ships enter service. This was particularly unfortunate in that so much of British naval investment over the period had been concentrated on the needs of a strike or power projection.[2] Italy and Spain also built substantial ships capable of operating STOVL aircraft, but they could accommodate such aircraft only in limited numbers.

The Chinese Dimension: The situation in the Far East has been rather different. There, after the Soviet Union's fall, the principal fact of politics was the rise of Chinese (PRC) sea power. The Chinese government has a stated goal of securing control of the island chains off its coast, which happen to belong to other governments unwilling to accept Chinese suzerainty. Since the United States is the other main guarantor of security in the area, China has been investing in anti-carrier technology and forces reminiscent of those of the Cold War Soviet Union. More and more, the key question for the US Navy has been how to deal with this new threat. Chinese naval expansion has also fuelled the expansion of other Asian navies, particularly those of Japan and Korea. Since the Chinese Navy (PLAN) still resembles that of the old Soviet Union, naval development in the Far East broadly continues along Cold War lines.

The PLAN has stated another rationale: China is increasingly dependent on overseas sources of energy and critical materials. In theory, this rationale should push the PLAN towards the sort of sea-control emphasis NATO navies showed during the Cold War, particularly since so many countries around China are buying submarines as an equaliser against growing Chinese sea power. The United States already has a large, capable nuclear submarine fleet, which – at least in theory – might also be used to interdict Chinese sea lines of communication. However, the PLAN is still oriented mainly towards anti-ship operations. It is certainly buying modern ASW ships, but there does not seem to be any indi-

The Chinese *Sovremenny* class destroyer *Taizhou*, which was built in Russia. China was a major beneficiary of the collapse of the Soviet Union, benefitting from imports of complete systems and technology from Russia and the Ukraine. These helped accelerate development of indigenous systems. *(David Yang under creative commons licence 2.0)*

The heavily-damaged US Navy destroyer *Cole* (DDG-67) being towed away from the port of Aden in Yemen following a terrorist attack on 12 October 2000. Ship survivability has become more important in the post-Cold War environment. *(US Marine Corps)*

cation of the sort of massive maritime patrol aircraft fleet which NATO felt compelled to field. Nor is there any indication, at least in public, of a Chinese equivalent of SOSUS to direct such a force.

China has been, perhaps, the main beneficiary of the collapse of the Soviet Union. This suddenly removed the lavish funding which had supported Soviet military development, leaving numerous organisations desperate for money and, thus, desperate to export their work. Particularly immediately after 1991, the central Russian and Ukrainian governments had little ability to control exports of complete equipment and of technology. The Soviet state had deliberately distributed research institutes around its territory, partly in hopes of promoting national unity. Now these dispersed research and development institutes found themselves competing for that market.

Only two potential customers had enough demand and enough money to rescue the Soviet-era military-industrial base: China and India. China was in a leading position because it had a healthier economy. Russian and Ukrainian technology made up for the break in a nascent NATO export programme.[3] More recently, China has extracted considerable Western technology by cyber-espionage. This combination of purchases, copying, and espionage is a classic path to home-grown military power: first buy and then copy foreign technology, then steal the bits which cannot be produced locally and meld them into initial locally-conceived systems.[4] Indeed, that is what the United States did in the late nineteenth and early twentieth centuries. For the West, which has been unable to protect its intellectual property, the result is anything but benign.

The Impact of Terrorism: The new environment requires a different approach to ship survivability. During the Cold War, survivability seemed less important, the theory being that the big war (if it came) would be short; any ship which could be put out of action for several months was as good as sunk. Now that the West faces a protracted period of low-level conflict, this approach is no longer valid. Moreover, survivability may be linked to the vital role of naval presence. That is a vital way of convincing friends in turbulent places of support, but it also presents enemies with attractive targets. The main case in point was the attack on the *Cole* (DDG-67) in Aden on 12 October 2000. The bomb

exploded alongside was far more powerful than any anti-ship missile in current or contemplated service. However, the ship survived, limiting casualties and damage, and denying the attackers the prestige of actually sinking a major warship. The immediate lesson was that ships visiting ports in potentially hostile areas had to be defended at all times. For example, the US Navy developed a system of night-vision cameras linked to remote-controlled machine guns. Another lesson is that ship survivability is far more valuable than had been imagined during the Cold War.[5]

For the US Navy, the main implication of the 'war against terror' from 2001 onwards has been that it must mount operations in many places at once. The past doctrine of two-war capability (typically major involvement in one and a holding action elsewhere) was swept aside.[6] This caused the navy to seek ways to create more strike groups. For a time that meant Expeditionary Strike Groups (ESGs) and new Surface Action Groups (SAGs). Deep involvement in Iraq and in Afghanistan seems to have stopped plans for this kind of dispersion, but the reality which led to it remains. The navy needed more surface combatants to fill out the new formations. They had to be affordable; for a period the only requirement imposed on the new ships was that they should cost a quarter as much as a missile destroyer. The only project which seemed relevant was designated the Littoral Combat Ship (LCS). From the outset, the only way in which the cost goal could be met involved some form of modularity; this has marked the LCS programme.

In some sense, navies and other armed forces are now acting more as police forces than as traditional military forces, attempting to hold a continuing problem down to manageable proportions. For this purpose, numbers of surface ships with substantial endurance is the key issue, and investment in such ships is an alternative to naval strike forces. The most prominent recent case of this need is the naval effort to control the massive flow of refugees across the Mediterranean.

THE IMPACT OF RISING COSTS

Well before the Cold War's end, all Western navies had to confront the rising cost of operating, not to mention procuring, new ships and weapons. In most countries personnel costs were a large part of overall operating costs, to the point that it was worthwhile to spend heavily to reduce numbers. For example, the

US Navy conceived its *Zumwalt* (DDG-1000) class destroyer as a less expensive replacement for the Cold War *Spruance* (DD-963) class. The emphasis was not so much on reducing the ship's purchase cost as the cost of running it – it had to operate with many fewer crew and more efficient propulsion. Initially, the really radical feature of *Zumwalt* was minimum crewing, not stealth. Electric drive was adopted largely because it allowed operation on fewer gas turbines, at a much lower cost in fuel consumption (it also offered better survivability, though this seems not to have been emphasised in the design). The unusual shape of the ship, and its enormous cost, can be attributed mainly to the addition of stealth requirements to the initial concept. As it was, the *Zumwalt* class priced itself out of production.

Rising ship unit costs made it impossible for navies to replace ships on a one-for-one basis; they had to find some way to do the same things with fewer ships. During the latter part of the Cold War, the Royal Danish Navy found a way out of this problem in the form of modularity, a system it called StanFlex. Initially the key perception was that increasing computer capacity made it possible to store a variety of combat system programmes in the ship's central computer. Modules in the form of standard blocks could be placed onboard as needed; because the software was already on board, and the combat management system designed for all envisaged roles, conversion was relatively simple and very quick. Denmark envisaged a sequence of wartime naval roles; its limited number of StanFlex ships fulfilling them in turn. With the end of the Cold War, these short-range ships were no longer adequate, but the StanFlex concept remained relevant. The Danes built a series of frigate-sized ships with large open inboard spaces into which containers or trailers could be placed, so that the ships could rotate various roles. This arrangement has apparently been quite successful.

The US Navy has taken the idea a step further in its LCS programme. Initially something like StanFlex seems to have been envisaged. However, the choice has been to create modules using unmanned vehicles of various kinds, including unmanned helicopters. The LCS operating such vehicles serves as a processing node for whatever information they generate, and other vehicles on board may be used to deal with whatever is found. The LCS itself is sometimes called a 'seaframe', to analogise it to an airframe which can carry alterna-

The US Navy's *Zumwalt* destroyer class was initially conceived as a way of reducing through-life costs by minimising operating expenses such as crewing and fuel costs. A subsequent focus on stealth raised acquisition cost so much that the class essentially priced itself out of production. This image shows *Zumwalt* departing Bath Iron Works' yard in Maine on initial sea trials on 7 December 2015. (*General Dynamics Bath Iron Works*)

BQM-74E target drones being prepared for launch. Unmanned aircraft are nothing new – drones were used in the Second World War and the MQM/BQM series dates from the mid-1960s – but today's UAVs are far more sophisticated. (*Northrop Grumman*)

tive payloads. As the LCS concept evolved, it was also required to achieve an unusually high speed; to some extent the desire to achieve this performance has overshadowed the development of the modules.[7] Complement has been limited to restrict overall cost, but many modules require substantial deck-handling parties. It can be argued that an LCS is now more like a small carrier (of unmanned systems) than a traditional surface combatant. Carrier experience suggests that aircraft within air wings should be mixed and matched, not limited to just a few of one type – this probably also applies to unmanned vehicle systems.

THE TECHNOLOGY MENU: VARIOUS APPLICATIONS OF MOORE'S LAW

The key fact of modern technology is Moore's Law: computer power doubles at least every eighteen months. As originally stated, the unit cost of computing would halve every eighteen months, which is not quite the same thing. Either way, it is clear that the same performance can be obtained in smaller and smaller packages over time. No one knows when this frantic rate of improvement will flatten out, but all other technologies have shown a pattern of exponential growth followed by a dramatic slowing.

Unmanned Vehicles: Perhaps the most spectacular application of Moore's Law has been to unmanned and partly autonomous vehicles, both in the air and in and under the sea. Unmanned aircraft are nothing new; drones existed during the Second World War and were flown into North Korean targets during the Korean conflict. Drones were also used extensively for reconnaissance during the Vietnam War and later. Modern unmanned aerial vehicles (UAVs), however, are different. In the past, drones flew on autopilot except when they were remotely piloted. Modern UAVs are generally fed with waypoints; they fly themselves between these waypoints and manoeuvre as planned, but with the option of changing their flight plans as ordered – not merely making ordered turns. Another change is shrinking size and increasing sensor payloads. For nearly all navies, this has given frigates – and even small combatants – a means of peering over the horizon. The US Navy has demonstrated something more: the X-47B capable of flying onto a carrier deck, and of being refuelled in the air. The navy is currently developing a new-generation armed (or reconnaissance) UAV termed UCLASS (unmanned carrier-launched airborne surveillance and strike).

Unmanned vehicles are usually described as a way of keeping valuable people out of danger, for

example in mine countermeasures. However, this is just one of their potential advantages. Unmanned aircraft can operate beyond the human limits which ultimately define operational endurance. In the case of a UAV more or less equivalent to a manned attack plane, the UAV also offers enormous potential savings. It is in effect a reusable cruise missile (cruise missiles like Tomahawk can already be redirected in flight). Unlike a manned plane, it need not fly frequently in order to maintain a pilot's proficiency; there is no need for numerous aircraft in the training pipeline either. The cost of planes is so high that any dramatic reduction in required numbers or in maintenance can have enormous impact on a navy's overall budget.

The underwater equivalent of a UAV needs greater onboard intelligence, as it cannot remain in constant communication with its base (not least in order to remain undetected). It must have a considerable degree of autonomous capability, which is why underwater unmanned vehicles are sometimes called autonomous underwater vehicles (AUVs). There is a considerable difference between a submarine offshore conducting reconnaissance using onboard sensors and a submarine lying further offshore launching multiple AUVs to conduct similar reconnaissance over a wider area. As submarines become more expensive and less numerous, AUVs should allow the footprint of a single submarine to be extended. That applies much more to reconnaissance than to traditional attack missions (although armed AUVs are sometimes proposed). However, for the major Western navies reconnaissance is probably the primary mission of long-range submarines. It may well have been their primary Cold War mission, too.

Mine-countermeasures ships commonly operate close-in remote vehicles carrying minehunting sonars and even counter-mine charges, reducing the need to limit their signatures near mines. However, the minehunter still has to examine mine-like objects one by one. A minehunter launching multiple unmanned vehicles to examine a potential minefield from a distance should search much more quickly, even if (as is likely) it takes human analysis to decide whether what the AUV sees is really a mine. AUVs are currently in use by several navies

Autonomous underwater vehicles (UAVs) have the potential to considerably extend the more limited number of submarines that many of the major navies can now afford. This picture shows a Saab AUV62 on the surface. *(Copyright Saab AB)*

for mine countermeasures, but the potential for rapid minehunting has not yet been realised. The rate at which a minefield can be cleared (or a poten-

tial field searched) has enormous tactical significance and will surely lead to the use of multiple AUVs in parallel.

Moore's Law & Aircraft: Aircraft stealth is another consequence of Moore's Law, in the sense that it takes enormous computing power to calculate the radar reflection from a given complex shape in various directions. It seems clear, for example, that the reason the F-117, a first-generation stealth fighter, has a faceted shape is that the computers used in its design could not deal with a continuously curved shape. Modern stealthy aircraft like the B-2 benefitted from more powerfully designed computers. However, it seems that stealth is no longer considered as important as it was in, say, the late 1980s. For example, the US Navy accepted a wide range of sacrifices in order to minimise the radar cross-section of the *Zumwalt* class but then returned to the more efficient *Burke* (DDG-51) design.[8]

US naval fighter development also illustrates the impact of Moore's Law. In the past, radar signals were generated by specialised tubes such as the Second World War magnetron. The physical configuration of the tube determined the sort of signal it would produce. The Swedish Philips company prospered at one time because it produced a magnetron which could be tuned to change its signal over time,

The bat-like Northrop Grumman X-47B unmanned demonstrator aircraft pictured being prepared for launch from the deck of *Theodore Roosevelt* (CVN-71) in November 2013. The US Navy has yet to decide whether a follow-on operational type will be optimised for reconnaissance or strike. *(US Navy)*

confusing countermeasures systems. Similarly, a major post-1945 countermeasures development was a tuneable tube called a Carcinotron that could mimic the signals produced by a variety of radars

Thus the roles of aircraft radars were set largely by what sort of power tubes they contained. A single-seater could be a fighter or it could be an attack bomber – it could have a Doppler air-to-air radar or an air-to-surface radar. In the 1960s, however, a new generation of radar signal tubes appeared. They were broad-band amplifiers, either TWTs (travelling wave tubes) or Klystrons. A computer could produce a very low power signal of whatever type was needed. It could be amplified to useful strength using a Klystron or TWT. Thus the same radar could have multiple, different functions. The first plane to exploit this possibility seems to have been the F-14 Tomcat. It happened that the Tomcat was not initially used as a fighter-bomber because of a peculiarity of its aerodynamics: the tunnel under the engines tended to suck bombs back up after they had been released. The full potential offered by the plane's radar was not realised until much later, when GPS-guided bombs were explosively released clear of the plane.

Moore's Law meant that the same sort of computer power which required a huge F-14 in the early 1970s could be packed into a much smaller plane a few years later. That made it possible to designate the McDonnell Hornet an F/A-18 rather than an F-18 or A-18. The navy had considered buying two aircraft with much the same airframes and engines but different radars and weapon systems, but it found that a TWT-oriented radar could switch from one role to the other. During the 1991 Gulf War two F/A-18s on a bombing mission were jumped by Iraqi aircraft. They switched radar mode, shot down the Iraqis, then switched back and bombed their target. In the past, they would probably have jettisoned their bombs and fled. More than twenty years later, it is possible to pack a much more complicated radar performance into the same package – for example, to provide a radar with a more varied set of waveforms, far more difficult for any countermeasures receiver to recognise.

Distributed Systems: Later in the 1990s, the US Navy found a very different application for Moore's Law. The latest Russian submarines were far quieter than their predecessors. The last US Cold War submarines, the *Seawolf* (SSN-21) class countered

Soviet silencing by adopting massive new sonar arrays, which made for a larger hull and enormous expense. What should the navy do in the face of further Russian silencing and a badly-slashed defence budget? It analysed the sonar as an integrated system, not merely the expensive sonar arrays. The only affordable way to improve net sonar performance was to change the way in which sonar data were processed – there was more affordable potential to be found in signal processing and handling than in seeking ever more massive and sensitive arrays. A programme called ARCI (Acoustic Rapid COTS [Commercial Off The Shelf] Insertion) was instituted. It installed high-capacity data buses leading data from its sonars to servers whose computer chips could be regularly replaced. Every time the chips were replaced, new software could be written to exploit the new capacity provided. The navy sought to keep pace with the 'state of the practice' rather than with the 'state of the art' as a compromise between capability and reliability; for some years it has not had to

repair computer servers for the duration of a submarine patrol.

The ARCI idea was later applied to surface ships and to naval aircraft. It explains why the Aegis anti-air warfare programme was so determined to shift from specialised computers (UYK-7 and then UYK-43) to commercial computers in a distributed system. The latter could include more powerful servers, which could accommodate whatever software the latest 'state of the practice' computers could handle. The transition from the single bespoke computers to commercial types has turned out to be difficult. However, by 2015, it had been accomplished in later versions of Aegis.

Each ARCI generation costs very little to insert into existing ships or aircraft, because the physical installation which accepts the new processors is already there. New software can be reproduced for free (except for licensing charges). This contrasts dramatically with the high cost of changing major hardware such as sonar arrays. Moreover, the improvements can be extremely rapid.

The US Navy submarine *Connecticut* (SSN-22), seen here in 2009, is the second of just three *Seawolf* class boats. The navy was able to avoid installing the massive sonar arrays that were a feature of these submarines in the subsequent *Virginia* class through enhancements to the way shipboard computers handled and processed data. *(US Navy)*

A Tomahawk cruise missile flying over land on a test flight. When it first entered service, Tomahawk achieved precision by correlating the elevation of land under it with its desired course; GPS targeting made mission planning considerably simpler. *(Raytheon)*

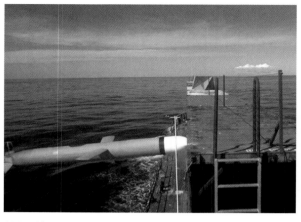

GPS guidance allows the Tomahawk cruise missile to hit a moving target at sea, as demonstrated in these images of a trial undertaken in January 2015. There are also plans to add a terminal seeker to the missile to improve targeting in the last seconds of an engagement. *(Raytheon)*

The submarine programme eradicated one cost of constantly inserting new technology. It is one thing to find a far better way of detecting and tracking underwater targets, but quite another when the same computers can fire weapons. Any US system capable of firing weapons requires certification, meaning insurance against inadvertent firing. The US Navy's solution has been to separate the fire-control function (which has to be certified) from the sonar/command function of detecting, tracking and interpreting the underwater environment. This type of separation is not difficult to embody in a large submarine, but in smaller ones the different functions are often carried out by the same computers at the same consoles.

The Significance of GPS: GPS, the Global Positioning System, is another application of Moore's Law. By the 1970s it was clear that timed satellite signals could be used to provide precision navigation. Navies already exploited satellites for navigation in the form of the US Transit system and its Soviet counterpart. The computation involved was relatively complex and required a substantial computer. By the late 1980s, however, the same computing power could fit into a hand-held device – or into a bomb or a missile. The result was astonishing.

Prior to GPS, it was certainly possible to guide a missile into a designated target using a laser as a pointer or a television seeker concentrating on an edge or an area of contrast in the target. A plane could only hit one target at a time, and debris thrown up by a bomb could ruin the aim of subsequent ones. There was also no way of automatically designating a bomb or missile to hit a target revealed by reconnaissance; the attack had to await the arrival of an attack aircraft trying to identify the target or at least that of a photograph to be used as the basis for a strike. During the 1970s it became clear that, with the advent of inexpensive inertial guidance, a pilot could point a bomb at a target he could see; he did not have to loiter to continue to guide the bomb. This was still a relatively cumbersome proposition. About 1989 however, with GPS deployment imminent, it became possible to envisage the widespread

A British F-35B Lightning II undergoing maintenance at Elgin Air Force Base in Florida. The advanced software packages used in the aircraft have involved such a high cost that they might impact overall demand for the aircraft. *(Crown Copyright 2014)*

use of inexpensive GPS-guided weapons. Suddenly a single strike plane could quickly attack many targets in sequence.

The use of Tomahawk missiles gives an idea of what happened. When Tomahawk entered service, it achieved precision by correlating the elevation of the land under it with its desired course. Arranging a single Tomahawk flight was a massive undertaking. As the first Iraq War loomed, the United States found itself having to map Iraq precisely; the Defense Mapping Agency ran on a 24/7 schedule. Ships firing Tomahawks against Iraq had to send their weapons along paths which made terrain-comparison navigation possible. It was relatively easy to adjust the missile path near the target, but not along the whole path. Iraq learned that Tomahawks approaching Baghdad flew predictable paths for part of the time, and hence could be shot down. Also, Tomahawks could not approach directly from the sea, which offered them no navigational updates; they had to fly ashore and then fly a considerable distance there in order to determine their positions.

GPS solved this problem. Flying a Tomahawk over a trackless sea no longer presented any difficulties. Moreover, a potential target area no longer had to be mapped; all that was needed was a target position and sufficient information to allow the missile to fly a low-altitude path over defended areas. Tomahawk became a flexible weapon suited to post-Cold War uncertainties. This new capability was demonstrated during the 1994 attacks against Serbia. Ultimately GPS guidance makes it possible to order a missile to fly to the predicted position of a moving target, such as a vehicle or a ship – as the US Navy has demonstrated. Prediction is of course tricky, and it is better to give the missile a terminal seeker. However, the terminal seeker need not have anything like the range (or detectability) of past ones, so it is likely to be far more difficult to confuse or defeat.

GPS had wider significance. As previously mentioned, earlier precision weapons homed on some sort of signal, such as the reflection of a laser beam, or the centroid of an identifiable area of light or darkness in the target. Precision attack without such a signal was impossible, as in the example of debris thrown up by an initial bomb ruining the signal for follow-on weapons. To the extent that GPS signals are effective, none of this matters. Once the position of the target has been identified accurately, weapons can be directed into it. Moreover, the

attacking plane need not loiter near the target to keep it in sight, as would be the case with a laser weapon. For carriers this has meant that a single aircraft can attack multiple targets per sortie. The change has been remarkable. During the Vietnam War, it took a concentrated strike (an Alpha Strike) to damage a point target, and even then all the bombs might miss. For radar bombing, accuracy within a thousand feet was considered acceptable. When the first laser-guided bombs (Paveways) were introduced, a single sortie might be expected to hit the target. A carrier might launch, say, thirty attack aircraft to hit thirty targets a day. With GPS, each sortie might hit multiple targets. Thus, the same carrier might hit as many as 160 targets each day.

By 2015, so much of the West's precision fire-power has come to depend on GPS that GPS itself is a possible target. Satellites fly high enough to be difficult to destroy physically, but their signals can certainly be jammed or distorted. In the past, the argument has always been that navigation is so valuable to both sides that neither is likely to attack a navigational system. That may be no more than self-deception. Land-attack missiles, for example, may yet need to fall back on some form of terrain recognition, albeit a more sophisticated one given computer memory is now so much more capacious.

The F-35: The Potential Cost of Moore's Law: Increasing computer power often seems to offer an alternative to increasing investment in platform technology. The F-35 Lightning II is a case in point. It was conceived as a simple, inexpensive attack bomber. To that end, platform capabilities such as performance and stealth were sacrificed. Early in the programme, someone decided that much of what had been given up could be clawed back using computer power generated by Moore's Law. For example, the F-35 has an extremely sophisticated electronic intelligence system, one object of which is to provide the pilot with unprecedented situational awareness. It has underbody sensors whose images are blended together to give the pilot the illusion that he can see through the plane. The main lesson of the programme seems to be that such software solutions can still be horrifically expensive, and that they can also cause long delays. These can be blamed on the reality that no one has been able to predict either the cost or the timetable of software development. Often programme managers interpret this reality as though software is free – however, it is

anything but. On the other hand, once software works, the marginal cost of reproducing it really is virtually nil. In that sense the cost of building twice as many F-35s is far lower than twice the cost of the current programme. It remains to be seen whether the high cost of the plane will dramatically cut production and sales.[9]

COMMAND & CONTROL

Increasing computer power has shown itself most spectacularly in advances in command and control. This encompasses the proliferation of individual ship automated command systems and the appearance of ever more powerful means of co-ordinating forces.

During the Cold War, individual ship automation was a relatively expensive feature initially restricted to high-end ships, such as carriers. By the end of the Cold War, many frigates had computerised command systems, but they were usually fairly simple. In the following decade, computer systems spread to virtually all warships, from fast missile boats upwards. For example, the US Navy adopted the Ship Self Defense System (SSDS), which began as a means of creating a unified tactical picture from disparate sensors aboard carriers and amphibious ships. Very soon that unified tactical picture – extending to the surface situation around the ship – was being displayed on large screens comparable to those on board Aegis ships. Despite its name, SSDS was providing much the same functions as the large-ship computer command system of the past, the Naval Tactical Data System (NTDS). It had, moreover, a major advantage. Instead of inhabiting a single time-shared computer, it employed multiple processors, and was thus amenable to the sort of growth inherent in Moore's Law. Within a few years the US Navy found itself abandoning a large-ship system descended from NTDS in favour of multi-processor versions of SSDS, the name no longer being particularly meaningful.

The command systems of the past employed bespoke consoles and computers, and could be characterised by, for example, the number of tracks they could handle or the update rate applied to those tracks. The effect of Moore's Law has been to open up these systems, which now use current processors (chips) and whatever consoles a customer may choose. In theory they can run whatever software a user selects. It is no longer possible to characterise them concretely. Yet, just like commercial computer operating systems, they are quite different, and some are more flexible than others. One interesting feature is that it is no longer possible to characterise the underlying software in any concrete way. For example, brochures describing modern command systems are largely indistinguishable, yet users know that the systems themselves are quite different.

Then there is the interaction between ships and between ships, aircraft and submarines. During the Cold War that was entirely a matter of formatted data links, the most important being NATO Links 4 and 11, with Link 16 (JTIDS) entering service. These links still exist, whilst the most important new one is Link 22 (Link 16 messages on Link 11 HF media). For HF links, the main new development has been much higher data rates, thanks to computer mediation of transmission. Computer mediation of transmission through a distorting medium has also made high-capacity underwater

data transmission possible, at least over limited ranges. At least in theory, the latter capability should ultimately affect unmanned underwater vehicle operation.

The formatted links connect ship command systems at what is called the vector level; they provide the position, course, and speed of an object. The vector level was chosen because data was provided by search radars and sonars with limited precision. With the advent of the high-precision SPY-1 Aegis radar something more was envisaged. Instead of vectors, created by a ship's own command system based on a stream of data from its own radars, it might be possible to merge the streams of data from the high-precision radars on board several ships to create more precise target tracks. For example, if several ships were operating together off a coast, a target might be obscured from some of

them as it flew behind, say, an island. If data from the others were in the stream, and the stream were shared, all of the ships in the group might see the target all the time. Sharing data might also be effective against stealthy aircraft and missiles. Generally no vehicle is stealthy from all angles. All observers see it occasionally, but typically not long enough to form a viable track. Adding those quick observations can, however, make it possible to create a viable target track, and a defensive missile can be fired at the target's computed position. The US Navy developed this concept into the Co-operative Engagement Capability (CEC). Other radars, particularly that on board the E-2C Hawkeye airborne command and control plane, were brought into the system. CEC tracks could also be transmitted to non-CEC ships. CEC was first announced about 1996, but software problems delayed entry into service until about 2001. After that CEC was supported not only for fleet air defence but also for missile defence.

While the formatted links and CEC were evolving, the civilian world was transformed by the Internet. There was an obvious extension to the sea. Features like chatrooms and e-mail had vital naval applications. Chat rooms made it possible for a commander to link up with his ships in a way not formerly possible except by shipboard conferences. The ability to transmit entire documents, such as charts, proved vitally important during and after the Gulf War of 1991. The kind of high-bandwidth ship-to-ship communication involved also made possible video teleconferences, which made for much better unity of purpose among widely-separated ships. None of this seems at all unusual from a civilian perspective, but the sort of unformatted communication involved makes a stark comparison with a past of formatted and stereotyped naval message traffic.

Digital communication has made an enormous difference in carrier and other strike operations. In the past, strikes were planned on the basis of whatever intelligence data might be on board the carrier, plus whatever the carrier reconnaissance aircraft could collect. It was a major advance in the late 1960s for the new carrier reconnaissance aircraft (the RA-5C) to unload its product into a computerised integrated intelligence system. High-capacity satellite systems now make it possible for a carrier to receive images from files kept ashore, some of them generated by reconnaissance satellites. Missions can

A picture of the operations room on the new British Royal Navy Type 45 destroyer *Daring*. The use of computerised command systems evolved slowly during the Cold War and were initially the preserve of major ships. However, the significant increase in computer power driven by Moore's Law means that nearly all warships now employ sophisticated computer systems. *(Crown Copyright 2009)*

The US Navy destroyer *Fitzgerald* (DDG-62) fires two SM-2 missiles during a test engagement. The advent of co-operative engagement capability means that data gathered by several ships' sensors can be used to engage a hostile threat. *(US Navy)*

be planned much more quickly using computer systems. The combination of far greater information resources and quick planning and precise navigation (using GPS) makes the carrier strike system far more supple than in the past.

A case in point is Saddam Hussein's burial of arms in dumps under Baghdad before the 2003 attack. Satellites observed the city while the tunnels were dug and arms moved into them; the Iraqis could never be sure of what the satellites saw. Previously, the fruits of this intelligence might have been flown out to the fleet, where photos would be processed and attacks planned. To the extent that the right material had been sent, the process would have been quick and relatively smooth. However, as attacks were planned, questions would arise, and more material required. There is a huge difference between a process in which the central intelligence system pushes out what is thought to be needed, and one in which the fleet (or other prospective attackers) pull in what they need. In 2003, the attackers got what they needed in the form of sufficient data to know where arms had been buried – and they were able to destroy the arms caches. A particular advantage of the system is that the fleet need not necessarily fly reconnaissance sorties before striking, so that reconnaissance does not warn a prospective target of the fleet's intentions.

CEC provides a force with a unified air picture, but the US Navy is looking towards a unified force weapon system. The argument is that, given a sufficiently unified picture, a command system should be able to select the best weapon anywhere in the force to engage any chosen target. This idea obviously applies to all forms of warfare, but was first applied to anti-air operations. The idea is also to integrate all available fleet sensors, an obvious new candidate being the sophisticated electronic intelligence system onboard the F-35. Airborne sensors are of particular interest because they can be manoeuvred into favourable positions. The implication is that a single system will wield both shipboard and airborne anti-air weapons. The new system was declared operational in 2015 as part of a larger programme of making fuller use of weapons and platforms in each naval formation.

NAVAL AVIATION

The most significant difference between the US Navy and its allies – and, indeed, all other navies – during and since the Cold War has been in naval

A F/A-18C Hornet strike fighter landing on *Harry S. Truman* (CVN-75) in November 2015. The US Navy decided that they could do without a long-range attack plane in the cash-constrained aftermath of the Cold War but this has proved to be something of a false economy. *(US Navy)*

Royal Navy Sea Harrier FA2 aircraft of 801 Naval Air Squadron pictured in July 2005, a few months before the type was withdrawn from service. Although the original Sea Harrier was improved with the addition of better radar and longer-range missiles in the form of the FA2, plans for a supersonic Harrier were abandoned in the late 1970s, effectively capping the Harrier's performance. Britain will therefore use the US-built F-35B in its new aircraft carriers. *(Crown Copyright 2007)*

aviation. All major navies have naval air components, but only the US Navy has masses of carrier-based aircraft plus a powerful land-based patrol component. It also deploys far more land-attack cruise missiles than any other. The first question post-Cold War US Navy planners had to decide was how to balance the new capacity for land attack from surface combatants against continuing investment in long-range carrier striking power. As previously discussed, planes could deliver much heavier sustained attacks than Tomahawk missiles fired by surface ships and submarines. However, if there were only a few point targets, Tomahawks might be considered a viable alternative.

In 1991, the project for a stealthy long-range attack bomber (the A-12 Avenger II) had just died; the service had to choose either to develop a new long-range attack aircraft or hand the long-range attack role to long-range missiles. The navy leadership decided that deep strikes would generally be attacks against discrete point targets. However, it seemed likely that there would be frequent littoral operations for which naval aircraft would often provide the main supporting fire. These mass attacks by naval aircraft would, therefore, be made mainly at relatively short ranges. No new long-range attack aircraft was needed; the F/A-18 Hornet was enough.[10] For a while, the navy retained some deep-strike capability in the form of modified F-14 'Bombcats'. However, these aircraft were ageing and expensive to maintain and to operate compared to the F/A-18.

In practice, this has been a mistake. In Iraq and Afghanistan, carriers have supplied support to troops far from the sea because of obstacles to basing aircraft on land, closer to the ground battles. A few hundred Tomahawks would not have offered anything like the same impact, and no local power would have welcomed American aircraft enthusiastically. However, carrier-based F/A-18s needed tanking, an expensive complication. The decision favouring short-range air strike has also had significant consequences in the Far East, where are carriers both the main means of power projection and the main targets of forces based in China. In 1996 the presence of US Navy carriers helped defuse Chinese threats to Taiwan. Ever since, China has sought means of threatening the US Navy sufficiently to avoid carriers again being deployed under similar circumstances. The closer the carriers have to come to the Chinese coast to provide effective air cover,

the greater the threat the Chinese can mount at an affordable cost.

In 2015, the US Navy is finally about to receive a new strike fighter, the F-35C Lightning II. Unfortunately it is more expensive than the aircraft it is replacing, probably because of the elaborate software it uses to sense its environment. Its cost has led some to suggest that the F-35C will never be bought in quantity; instead the navy may invest in heavy, high-performance unmanned aircraft. This is a contentious point, as there is considerable debate whether the future UCLASS system should primarily be a deep-strike reconnaissance system or a full strike aircraft. Key unresolved questions include just how reliable the elaborate software involved would be, and how well communications and navigation (both dependent on satellites) would likely perform in a future war.

For the British Royal Navy, the most important naval aviation fact of the Cold War era was that the Falklands War (1982) demonstrated a continuing need for carriers and strike aircraft, in its case STOVL jets of the Harrier/Sea Harrier series. The advent of this aircraft made it possible for several navies to operate aircraft at sea despite limits on carrier size – India, Italy, Spain, and even Thailand. The US Marine Corps also operates Harriers from its large-deck amphibious ships. In the late 1970s a supersonic follow-on was considered but not ordered, Rolls-Royce did not develop an improved engine on the basis of which a much more capable STOVL aircraft might have been built, and the performance of the Harrier was effectively capped.[11] Sea Harriers performed effectively in the land strike role during the NATO war against Serbia, whilst Harriers were sent to Afghanistan to support British troops from extemporised land bases. Performance under 'hot and high' conditions proved limited and they were eventually retired early under defence cuts.

When it contemplated new carriers, the Royal Navy had to decide whether to revert to conventional (CATOBAR) aircraft or to persist with STOVL. It decided that in either case it would adopt a version of the F-35 Lightning II strike fighter. STOVL cost range and payload but the British Government chose it over the conventional version. The decision against 'cats and traps' makes it impossible for the new British carriers to cross-deck conventional aircraft, such as those flown by the US Navy and *Marine Nationale*.

ANTI-AIR WARFARE

Anti-air warfare includes defence against enemy anti-ship missiles. During the later stages of the Cold War, the US Navy and its allies faced a major Soviet missile threat, much of it from naval bombers. These same bombers were probably the most effective threat against North Atlantic shipping; in effect they were the main Soviet fleet. Possibly the most important perception leading to the development of the US Navy's Maritime Strategy was that – unless the Soviet naval bomber force could be destroyed – it would be impossible for NATO supply shipping to survive in the North Atlantic. No surface escort force could deal with this threat. The Maritime Strategy therefore envisaged mounting a carrier-borne threat so severe that the Soviets would feel compelled to use their naval bombers to deal with it. The Soviet naval air force would then be destroyed in the air, much as the Japanese naval air force had been eliminated in the 'Turkey Shoot' of the Battle of the Philippine Sea in June 1944. To do this required massive firepower in the air (mainly onboard F-14s) and backup to deal with any missiles the Soviet bombers launched before being attacked. The latter role justified construction of numerous escorts equipped with the Aegis system, and modernisation of many older ships under the New Threat Upgrade (NTU) programme.[12]

The anti-air situation changed radically after 1991. Now the greatest threat was pop-up missiles fired largely from the shore – weapons whose launchers could not be dealt with before ships were exposed to their weapons. In this context the great virtue of the Aegis system was that, because its fire control was so intimately linked to its tactical picture, it could react extremely quickly. Older modernised ships, which could handle the saturation problem presented by masses of Soviet bombers, could not react nearly as quickly. They were decommissioned.[13]

Aegis gained its quick-reaction capacity from its anti-saturation design. Instead of assigning a tracker and a guidance channel to each target, it employs a search/track radar which creates an overall picture of the air environment so accurate that a missile can be directed on this basis. The missile is periodically updated using an uplink. Ultimately a slaved illuminator is turned on briefly, the missile homing on reflected radar energy. Because homing begins only near the target, the system has a reasonable chance of overcoming stealthy targets. The system's reliance on its tactical picture has made it adaptable to new roles, such as defence against ballistic missiles. Several other navies have adopted it. The step beyond is to provide the missile with a homing head, so that it only has to be commanded into a 'basket' near the target. That is the case with the Anglo-French-Italian PAAMS system.[14]

The effect of Moore's Law has been to extend the search/track concept to smaller and smaller systems. For example, the Enhanced Sea Sparrow Missile System (ESSM) applies an up-link to a longer-range version of the earlier Sea Sparrow. That both extends its effective range (the missile can be fired beyond the horizon) and offers the sort of anti-saturation performance provided by Aegis.[15] Current missiles have active seekers, as in PAAMS. The Royal Navy's new Sea Ceptor, which replaces the Sea Wolf point-defence missile, offers somewhat shorter range with an active radar seeker and an uplink, supported by a search/track radar. The South African Umkhonto (adopted by South Africa and Finland) combines an uplink with an infra-red terminal seeker. The picture/up-link combination also appears in recent Chinese systems (as is evident from the lack of dedicated illuminators) and in the Israeli Barak 8.

Perhaps the chief exception to the picture/up-link combination is the US-German RAM (Rolling Airframe Missile). In its current incarnation, this has an infra-red seeker. The launcher is slewed in the direction of an incoming missile, and the RAM missile detects and engages its target entirely on the basis of its seeker. The anti-saturation feature is that this is a fire-and-forget weapon.[16]

Many navies also have back-up close-in defensive weapons, such as the American Phalanx and the Dutch Goalkeeper. They were developed during the Cold War, and, unlike missiles, have not seen extensive development since. The genuinely new close-in weapon is the laser; in 2014 the US Navy announced that it was deploying such a device to a base ship in the Gulf. The challenge to any such weapon is that salt mist rising off the sea may absorb (or distort) the beam it generates. A deeper question is whether the damage the device inflicts is sufficient to destroy (or redirect) an incoming missile. There is, after all, considerable evidence that badly-damaged aircraft can continue flying.

In recent years, China has publicised the develop-

A test firing of an Aster 30 missile. Aster 15 and Aster 30 missiles are used in the PAAMS system that equips the Franco Italian 'Horizon' and British Type 45 destroyers, as well as the frigates of the FREMM programme and French-designed warships exported to Saudi Arabia and Singapore. The missile uses an active seeker to target incoming missiles in the final stages of an engagement, thereby avoiding the need for a slaved illuminator required by the Standard series missiles associated with the US Navy's Aegis weapons system. (MBDA)

ment of ballistic anti-ship missiles with bomblet (area) warheads. These missiles are so much faster than conventional anti-ship weapons that their advocates argue they cannot be countered. However, they follow a much more predictable path: China claims they reduce predictability by shaping the missile trajectory, but physics limits what they can do. At the least, these missiles require their user to solve substantial problems of reconnaissance and command and control: the target has to be found and tracked, and commands to the missile have to be generated promptly and accurately. Despite the area character of the warhead, it still has to burst quite close to its target. Bomblets, moreover, may not suffice to put a large carrier with an armoured flight deck out of action, although they may sweep away aircraft on deck. As of 2015, the system had yet to be tested against a seagoing target, and its operational status is unclear.

A close-up view of the SPY-1 radar panels on the Arleigh Burke class destroyer Hooper (DDG-70). Closely associated with the Aegis system, the SPY-1 multifunction radar was able both to detect targets and direct anti-air missiles towards them, giving a much-enhanced capability against saturation attack. It also allowed for quick reaction times against 'pop-up' missile attack. (US Navy)

The Chinese threat coincides with the maturation of the anti-ballistic missile version of the Aegis system, which had been under development since the mid-1990s. The relevant version of the Aegis radar is capable of tracking a ballistic missile at considerable range, and the interceptor – carried by an SM-3 missile – locks-on and manoeuvres into the target. The combination of radar, command system and missile have demonstrated the ability to hit incoming ballistic missiles, most spectacularly when Lake Erie (CG-70) destroyed a tumbling satellite in 2007. It can be argued that, because it was moving randomly, the satellite presented greater problems than a guided anti-carrier missile. Several navies have shown interest in this Aegis variant and Japan is actively involved in SM-3 development. In addition, SM-3 arms a shore-based version of Aegis, which is being emplaced in Romania and Poland.

The US Navy has taken the lead in deploying anti-ballistic missile systems at sea, using Raytheon's SM-3 interceptor in conjunction with the Aegis system. This image shows the destroyer *Hooper* (DDG-70) undertaking a successful test engagement against a ballistic missile target in 2009 and a Raytheon graphic showing how the interceptor is being

A MQ-8B Fire Scout UAV undertaking night-time operations from the Littoral Combat Ship *Fort Worth* (LCS-3) in May 2015. The US Navy has examined the use of LCS-deployed unmanned aerial vehicles in conjunction with underwater sonar arrays to attack diesel submarines with ultra-lightweight torpedoes. *(US Navy)*

ANTI-SUBMARINE WARFARE

As with anti-air warfare, the nature of ASW changed sharply after the Cold War. It seemed that future warfare would be conducted mainly in the littoral – meaning shallower, warm water – and that the threat would be presented mainly by diesel-electric submarines. During the Cold War, NATO's major weapon against Soviet nuclear boats was passive detection. Nuclear submarines must run certain machinery continuously; this produces regular sounds which can be detected and enhanced using signal processing. Onboard ships, the shift to passive detection was reflected in the rise of towed-array sonars. In airborne ASW, the passive systems employed narrow-band processing, a technique called Jezebel. Narrow-band passive processing made long-range detection possible. These systems began as ways of detecting diesel submarines when they snorkelled, but they were most effective against nuclear submarines. By contrast, a diesel submarine is sometimes loud (when it snorkels) and sometimes much quieter (running on battery or sitting on the bottom). It can be detected using active sonar, but shallow warm water presents serious propagation problems.

Western navies have tried a number of solutions. Both the US Navy and Royal Navy became interested in using active sources (explosions in the US Navy, pressure pingers in the Royal Navy) to create sounds whose echoes can be received by sonobuoys. Explosive echo-ranging (Julie) was tried during the Cold War but rejected due to confusion between submarine echoes and reverberation off the sea bottom. Computer technology has solved that problem, and the solution now fits manageable dimensions.[17] For ships, the equivalent is a low-frequency pinger, echoes being received using a towed array. The current case in point is the Royal Navy's 2087, which is onboard some Type 23 frigates.

The US Navy became interested in another approach. A diesel submarine under battery power may be quiet, but generates waves if it moves. In shallow water, an array on the bottom will register that a submarine has passed overhead. Multiple arrays will register places where the submarine passes. Because detection is entirely passive, the submarine never knows that it has been detected, so it does not manoeuvre evasively. Its future path can be plotted and a weapon dropped where it should be. This idea was the basis of interest in an ultra-lightweight (6.75in diameter) torpedo. In simple terms, the idea was behind the plan to have the new LCS support lightweight unmanned helicopters that could deliver the torpedo to a precise point computed by the LCS combat system based on inputs from underwater arrays.

The post-Cold War strategic reality of fewer warships also suggests that it is now more important to protect valuable units from torpedo attack. Escorts do not offer such protection directly: they are deterrents. Submarine commanders expect that once they attack, escorts will react. However, they may assume that they can escape anyway. The idea of, in effect, shooting down an incoming torpedo has been very attractive for a long time, as has the idea of deceiving the torpedo seeker.

During the Cold War, Western anti-ship torpedoes homed on the target's noise; for example, propeller noise typically radiated out of a ship's bow. What was not understood until late in the Cold War was that Soviet homing torpedoes exploited a ship's wake, not the noise generated.[18] The difference was profound. It is quite possible to mimic the sound of a ship in a towed or projected noise-maker. Such a device attracts a noise-homing torpedo. There is, apparently, no way of mimicking a wake. The torpedo must be either evaded or directly destroyed. Direct attack is complicated by the short distances involved, and the need to decide instantly that a torpedo is approaching. On the other hand, a direct-kill torpedo countermeasure can deal not only with homing weapons but also with spreads of straight- or pattern-running torpedoes. Given that the Soviets almost exclusively developed only wake-followers for anti-ship use, it follows that any country operating Russian-built 'Kilo' class submarines is likely to use wake-following torpedoes.[19]

Another important development has been the rise of air-independent propulsion (AIP) for submarines. Forms of AIP developed in Sweden (Stirling) and in Germany (fuel cell) are currently in service; other versions are on offer. Current versions of AIP produce enough power to move a diesel submarine at low speed for a period of weeks. Advocates point to the possibility that, within a few years, AIP may generate enough power to replace a submarine's batteries altogether. It is not clear what sort of speed they would offer. In either case, AIP is not a poor man's form of nuclear power; it does not confer nuclear speed on a submarine. It does allow a submarine to operate without snorkelling; if a submarine is in danger of detection only when it is snorkelling, AIP should be quite valuable.

The navies which have made the most effort to develop AIP operate in the Baltic, which was under intense Soviet surveillance, making snorkelling there extremely dangerous. In most of the world, however, submarines are not under wide-area passive acoustic surveillance. The most sophisticated Western navies have adopted low-frequency active sonar for use against diesel submarines, and AIP has no effect whatever on that form of detection. Nor would it beat the envisaged US bottom (looking-up) system. Western nuclear submarines do rely heavily on passive acoustics, but it is not clear that eliminating the noise of snorkelling is enough to protect a diesel-electric submarine against them.

MINE WARFARE

Moore's Law has had an enormous impact on mine warfare. During the Cold War, the principal means of dealing with mines was hunting; examining mine-like objects one by one to decide which ones had to be destroyed. Minehunters were expensive both because they needed sophisticated onboard sensors, and because their various signatures had to be drastically limited so that they could approach mines without triggering them. Typically a minehunter would direct a remote-controlled submersible, such as the widely-used French PAP 104, to examine a mine-like object at close range, using very high-frequency sonar and underwater television. If those on board the minehunter decided that the object was, indeed, a mine, the submersible might be withdrawn and a charge dropped near the mine. Generally no vehicle could actually touch the mine-like object, because it might well detonate. However, in really shallow water, mine-like objects were detected and examined by divers, using hand-held sonars and hand-emplaced charges.

Once it has been submerged for months, a mine can be difficult to distinguish from other objects in the sea. In the past, it was accepted that an experienced operator on board a minehunter was needed to decide whether an object really was a mine. The problem is complicated by the reality that the seafloor near harbours is cluttered with junk which may or may not resemble bottom mines (a moored mine is a far less ambiguous object).

An early computer-generated image of the US Navy's RMS Remote Minehunting System, a programmable autonomous underwater vehicle (AUV) that can remotely scan a potential mined area using the attached AN/AQS-21 minehunting sonar. The system offers the prospect of much quicker identification of minefields but development has not been altogether straightforward. (Lockheed Martin)

A schematic of the different components of the Maritime Mine Counter Measures (MMCM) system being developed by Thales for the Royal Navy in conjunction with France's Marine Nationale. The main objectives in modern mine-hunting are to remove the mine-detection element away from the hunter and accelerate mine clearance. The deployment of autonomous vehicles is an important contributor to the latter aim. (Thales)

Modern mines are designed to survive nearby explosions. A minehunter's attack would therefore more likely ruin the mine's detonator than physically – hence visibly – destroy the mine proper. Minehunting therefore requires precise reporting and navigation, so that once a mine is accounted for no other hunters re-examine and re-attack it later.

Quite aside from the considerable danger all of these practices entailed, they made clearance of a suspected minefield very slow. It was one thing to clear one's own harbours. During the Cold War, for example, some NATO navies periodically examined the bottom over Q-Routes to which merchant ships might be limited in wartime. At least in theory, re-examination once hostilities began would allow mine countermeasures to be limited to objects not detected in earlier runs. If, however, the possibly mined area was not periodically surveyed, the situation was far worse. This had potentially ruinous tactical implications. For example, amphibious operations are effective to the extent that they are surprise attacks; otherwise the enemy can build up enough forces to drive the attackers into the sea. Modern mine-countermeasures ships are so expensive that no navy, and probably no coalition, can afford to clear the waters off more than one prospective beachhead at a time. Mine clearance thus can become the warning which makes amphibious assault impossible. The lengthier the clearance effort, the worse the tactical problem.

In the Gulf in 1990, the US Navy substituted mine reconnaissance for minehunting. This is a simpler effort to identify areas which are probably mined. Mine stocks are generally limited, so an enemy cannot mine every possible landing beach. In this case, it was not realised that Iraq was laying mines from dhows and other small craft; the movements of two Iraqi T-43 minesweepers/minelayers were associated with the mining effort. When two major American warships, including the mine-countermeasures flagship *Tripoli*, were mined, it was not in water that had been swept but rather in water which reconnaissance had decided was safe. The method of reconnaissance used before the war was discredited, but not the idea of reconnaissance.

Modern improvements in minehunting have had two objects. One is to cut the cost of hunting by moving the mine-detection element away from the hunter, which no longer needs the drastically reduced signatures of the past. A second is to make

Notes

1. Several countries, including the United Kingdom, disbanded their land-based maritime patrol aircraft (MPA) arms altogether. In the British case, that proved embarrassing when Russian submarines began snooping around British submarine bases; the MPAs had been used – in part – to 'delouse' submarines going on patrol. In 2015, Britain changed policy and decided to reconstitute its MPA arm with American-built P-8 Poseidon aircraft.

2. The Royal Navy's adoption of submarine-launched Tomahawk missiles can be read as a means of smashing air defences and thus making limited carrier-based strike forces more effective. The Royal Navy built a force of air-warfare destroyers (Type 45s) intended specifically to shield the striking force of carriers from air attack (British SSNs and Type 23 frigates offered protection against submarines). It abandoned diesel submarines because only nuclear attack submarines could work with strike forces far from home. It also built a substantial amphibious force, far more powerful than the one which had been maintained during most of the Cold War.

3. NATO exports were authorised in the 1980s in hopes that rising Chinese power would divert Soviet forces to Asia. At that time the deep Sino-Soviet rift precluded Chinese purchases of Soviet equipment, even though much of it fitted better into Chinese thinking and organisation. NATO exports were banned after the Tiananmen Square massacre in 1989, though much dual-use technology continued to go to China. As Russia stabilised, the authorities came to regret its own sales to China, as China's main aim was to duplicate technology, rather than continue buying it from Russia. However, continued Russian cash problems have produced further sales to China in recent years, despite the loss of design information.

4. Chinese military development was severely affected by Mao's Cultural Revolution of 1965–72, which closed schools, killed many teachers, and sent many educated people to the countryside. Although the Cultural Revolution ended over forty years ago, echoes remain in the absence of the experienced development team leaders found in Western countries. Chinese accounts of weapons development in the 1970s and 1980s show that even copying Soviet weapons took decades, and that some, more ambitious projects had to be cancelled Another problem for Chinese weapon development is that, at least until recently, the military was unable or unwilling to tap civilian industry, for example in software, for purely military applications. In the West, the existence of a vibrant civilian industry has often made military development much faster.

5. During the Cold War, passive survivability, except possibly for the largest ships, was generally denigrated. It was assumed that a missile hit would so damage a ship's electronics as to put her out of action; she could then easily be sunk. In reality, late in the Cold War, much electronic equipment was solid-state, and could have stood up to substantial damage. In the case of *Cole*, sheer size contributed to the ship's survival: an explosion against the side of a ship destroys the outer hull over a finite length. It helped considerably that *Cole* had been designed with survivability in mind, and that she therefore had internal protected bulkheads intended to limit the extent of damage. It was also very important that she was attacked in a harbour, in calm weather. On the other hand, at sea she would have faced much smaller warheads (*Cole* was attacked by about 2,000lbs of explosive).

6. The two-war idea was based partly on the reality that the United States is a two-ocean power, and that a crisis in one ocean might not be linked to one in the other. During the Cold War this was realistic because the main source of crisis, the Soviet Union, was relatively cautious: the Soviets wanted to weaken the West, but they also feared that local aggression by their allies could touch off a ruinous major war. They considered that creating too many crises at the same time could push their enemies too hard. For the US Navy, the point of the 9/11 attacks was that many uncorrelated crises might be possible.

7. The speed may have been associated with Gulf operations and the modular concept. The fleet requires several different roles, but they could arguably be sequenced. Thus an LCS might race from its base (say at one end of the Gulf), carry out a mission, and then race back to switch to another. High speed might be justified on the grounds that time to change missions – including passage back and forth to the base – had to be minimised. Since the first ships have been completed, the idea of changing missions has been more or less abandoned with the realisation that it is better for a crew to become expert at a particular mission.

8. The *Zumwalt*'s tumblehome hull form was adopted to eliminate the corner reflector formed by the side of the ship and the reflecting sea around her. It was effective only if the ship did not roll, and if her freeboard was fixed. To that end the ship has large ballast tanks (so that she is always at a fixed displacement). Even so, the original extreme form of tumblehome performed very poorly in tank tests, and the degree of tumblehome was considerably reduced. The hull is designed to pierce waves (i.e., to take green water over the deck) rather than to ride over them. At the very least, that has limited what can be placed on deck. The unusual superstructure also seems to have been

mine countermeasures much faster and, possibly, less visible.

The simplest form of signature reduction is to place the mine-detection sonar on the submersible, which can run well ahead of the minehunter. This 'dog on a leash' approach was devised before the end of the Cold War. It makes hunting safer and less expensive, but it does not affect the speed of hunting: there is only one dog per minehunter. However, Moore's Law now makes it possible to build Autonomous Underwater Vehicles. At the very least, an AUV can be sent on a programmed trip through a potentially mined area, collecting data which it can then dump into some kind of head-quarters. The Autonomous Underwater Vehicle may be a mine-reconnaissance device. Alternatively, it may duplicate the earlier function of minehunting

sensors (it can get relatively close to a real mine). Some manufacturers have claimed in recent years that advances in artificial intelligence make it possible for an AUV to distinguish the kinds of mine-like objects that minehunters attack. Others argue that human intervention remains indispensable.

In either case, Autonomous Underwater Vehicles offer a very different approach to hunting, because a single vessel can support multiple AUVs, operating in parallel. They have inherently small signatures, and they need not neutralise a mine-like object before moving on. Instead, multiple Autonomous Underwater Vehicles can rapidly explore a potential minefield, leaving neutralisation to the minehunter or to other platforms. For example, many mine-hunters now deploy anti-mine torpedoes. Since the

anti-mine weapon is intended to destroy itself and the mine, there is no reason not to guide it directly into a mine. It is far more likely than the earlier type of anti-mine charge actually to destroy the mine, and thus to preclude any confusion caused when another hunter encounters a ruined but apparently intact mine.

AUVs were first used during the clearance of Iraqi ports in 2003, as an alternative both to divers and the marine mammals that had previously been used in mine detection. At the time, they were advertised as a far safer alternative but, because many of them could be used in parallel, the ports were cleared quite rapidly. This had important consequences: until the port of Basra was made usable, Coalition forces ashore lacked such vital equipment as armour and heavy artillery.

---

chosen for low radar visibility, with all antennas (including those for communication) built into the sides or the top of it. The 155mm guns have low cross-section shields. Despite all of these efforts, it is difficult to imagine that the ship does not leave a very visible wake. Also, stealthy shapes are typically not stealthy from some angles, so that stealthy objects may be revealed if multiple separate radars are used and their outputs integrated.

9. Commercial software illustrates this reality. Software seems inexpensive because standard packages, such as those for offices, deliver considerable capability for what seems a very low price. The hidden reality is that the cost of development is spread over tens of millions of buyers. If there were only a thousand buyers, development cost would loom much more.

10. The longer-ranged F/A-18E/F Super Hornet was first proposed as the low end of a high-low mix, the upper end of which would have been the A-12. This project was not announced as long as the A-12 remained viable, but it was revealed in May 1992 (the A-12 was cancelled in January 1991). The Super Hornet was justified as a relatively simple development of the Hornet. In fact it was a considerably larger aircraft, and development was somewhat protracted.

11. In the wake of the Falklands War the Royal Navy did develop a new FA2 variant of the Sea Harrier, equipped with a more sophisticated radar system and armed with long-range air-to-air missiles. It entered service after the Cold War but it fell victim to the new requirements of the post-Cold War world.

12. Like Aegis, NTU relied on a form of command guidance

(via data link) to bring air defence missiles into homing range of the target. However, the search radars of NTU ships were not anything like as precise as the SPY-1 radar of Aegis ships. In NTU, once a missile was within homing range of the target, it had to be handed over to a tracking/illuminating radar. This radar was tied up for considerably longer than the slaved illuminator of the Aegis system, so an NTU ship could not handle nearly as many targets. Also, most of the NTU missiles could not be fired nearly as quickly as the missiles of the Aegis system. For example, the longer-range missiles (modified versions of the two-stage SM-1 descended from Terrier) had to have booster fins manually inserted before launch. NTU was more a means of extending air-defence range than of dealing with short-range pop-up targets.

13. Disposal was also justified on the grounds that they typically used steam plants requiring large, expensive crews. Cynics argued that by disposing of these ships instead of retaining them in reserve, the navy hoped to increase pressure for replacement. The only pre-Aegis air-defence ships surviving the axe were the gas turbine-powered *Perry* (FFG-7) class frigates, which, however, had their air-defence missile systems discarded.

14. PAAMS is Principal Anti-Air Missile System. The missile is Aster with a numerical suffix indicating nominal range against a missile target. In British Royal Navy service PAAMS utilises the Sampson radar and is known as Sea Viper.

15. In a pure semi-active system, such as the original NATO Sea Sparrow, the missile must detect reflected energy from a target before it can be fired. The target therefore has to be inside the horizon before it can be engaged, whatever the range set by the missile motor. However, data relayed

from other ships may indicate the presence, course and speed of a target invisible from the firing ship. The missile can therefore be commanded to fly out in the expectation that it will meet the target at a point at which shipboard illumination will be possible.

16. The original version of RAM homed initially on the radar emissions of the seeker of the incoming missile; unfortunately not all anti-ship missiles use radar seekers. All do generate heat plumes from their engines, although there are ways of doping such a plume to shift its emissions into bands which are rapidly absorbed in the atmosphere.

17. In the 1990s, sufficient electronics could fit in a shoebox-sized package; data from multiple sonobuoys could be correlated within ten minutes to form a usable picture of the bottom (which might include a bottomed submarine).

18. Wake-following torpedoes approach from the side of the wake, detect its onset and then its other side. They follow a programmed turn, re-crossing the wake again and again until they detect the bottom of the ship. Wake-following is now common in Western anti-ship torpedoes

19. The Soviets also developed very fast straight-running torpedoes (the 200-knot 'Shkval'), which has been bought in small numbers by China and by Iran. They are probably relatively ineffective without the nuclear warheads for which they were originally designed.

20. All views expressed are the author's own, and do not necessarily reflect those of the US Navy or of any other organisation with which he has been associated.

8.0: David Hobbs

NAVAL AVIATION IN THE 21st CENTURY

Aircraft operating from carrier task forces had become a dominant factor in warfare by 1945. They continued to provide an unrivalled means of projecting power in the dangerous era of Cold War and limited conflict which followed. The break-up of the Soviet Union at the end of the Cold War and the perceived lack of short-term threats led

politicians in many countries to seek a significant reduction in defence expenditure but, despite its own reduction in size, the US Navy retained a powerful, balanced naval aviation capability and became the effective guarantor of Western maritime interests. It has managed to convince successive governments that carriers are a vital part of national

strategy and a US Navy without them would be difficult to imagine. On the other hand, cuts were especially severe in the United Kingdom, the West's other most significant carrier operator for much of the Cold War. Here politicians took sea power for granted and forgot that once run down, navies take a long time to recover. The 'bow wave' of increased

The US Navy's nuclear-powered aircraft carrier *Ronald Reagan* (CVN-76) pictured off Iwo Jima in September 2015 en route to her new homeport of Yokosuka in Japan. She is one of ten *Nimitz* class carriers currently in service with the US Navy. The aircraft carrier has continued to play a prominent part in American power projection throughout the post-Cold War period and it is difficult to imagine a US Navy without them. *(US Navy)*

cost when a whole class of ships and their aircraft had to be replaced in a relatively short space of time was a further, associated, problem. The United Kingdom's Strategic Defence Review (SDR) of 1998 proposed a sensible maritime strategy with two new aircraft carriers as its 'cornerstone'. However, politics and the malign influence of lobby groups opposed to carrier-based strike forces dogged their design and the selection of aircraft to operate from them.

Whilst the overall number of traditional aircraft carriers has decreased, there are growing numbers of big-deck amphibious carriers, designated as LHA and LHD, with the ability to act either as amphibious ships, light carriers or even – in the case of the biggest ships – to combine both roles. Among the aircraft that operate from them, the AV-8B Harrier has served the US Marine Corps (USMC) well since the mid-1980s and the last are not due to be replaced until 2025. It has proved to be afford-able, adaptable and very effective; virtues that its replacement, the F-35, has yet to demonstrate. Unmanned combat air vehicles have now come into operational service and have demonstrated impres-sive capabilities to spend long hours on surveillance at peak efficiency with no need for human continu-ation training. The US Navy leads in this field but has yet to find the optimal balance between manned and unmanned options.

AIRCRAFT CARRIERS AND THEIR AIR WINGS

United States: The United States Navy currently has ten ships of the *Nimitz* class in service, with the first of a new class, *Gerald R. Ford* (CVN-78), scheduled to join the fleet in the spring of 2016. All eleven ships are nuclear-powered. The second unit of the *Ford* class, *John F. Kennedy* (CVN-79), was laid down in 2015 at Huntington Ingalls Industries' shipyard at Newport News and a third ship, *Enterprise* (CVN-80) is projected in the FY2018 construction programme. However, the US Navy has accepted that construction cost for the latter two ships must be driven down substantially from *Ford*'s US$12.9bn.[1] Consequently, both will be fitted with more affordable air surveillance radars – the Enterprise Air Surveillance Radar (EASR) – being competitively developed by Northrop Grumman and Raytheon, while the cost of the new Electro-Magnetic Aircraft Launch System (EMALS) and Advanced Arrester Gear (AAG) is expected to lower as more are produced. The newer ships will also

Elements of the US Navy's carrier air wing CVW-5 pictured on the flight deck of *George Washington* (CVN-73) in August 2015. Comprising a mix of F/A-18C Hornet, F/A-18-E/F Super Hornets and EA-18G Growler fast jets plus supporting early warning aircraft and helicopters, the combat power of a c. seventy-strong carrier air wing surpasses that of many national air forces. *(US Navy)*

feature improved construction techniques expected to reduce cost.

However, these efforts may not be sufficient to ensure continued production of the class. Indeed, the US Navy revealed during a Congressional hearing in March 2015 that it is carrying out a study into potential alternative aircraft carrier designs. Sean Stackley, the Assistant Secretary of the Navy for Research, Development & Acquisition, described the study as a search for 'a sweet spot … that would provide the power projection we need … from our aircraft carriers but at the same time put us in a more affordable position to provide that capability'. The work has some influential political supporters but aspirations for cheaper ships are not new.[2] Notably, the CVV aircraft carrier (medium) conventional carrier studies of the 1970s considered ships of about 50,000 tons standard displacement, little more than half that of the *Ford* design. However, these were ultimately rejected as being slow, second-rate ships with considerable limitations on the air groups they could embark.[3] Various hidden costs, such as the increased number of replenishment tankers that

might be required should conventional propulsion be selected, would also need to be considered. In addition, the US Navy will be conscious of the fact that Congress has approved total numbers of aircraft carriers, not their total tonnage or the total number of aircraft they are capable of embarking.[4] In this environment – absent a credible political pledge to buy significantly more CVVs than the larger CVNs they would ultimately replace – requesting a second rate, conventionally-powered carrier that would require an intellectual investment similar to that put into the *Ford* design is unlikely to be attractive.

In truth, although the CVNs might be expensive, they have an unlimited radius of action and can project an air wing of about seventy aircraft from anywhere on the oceans that cover seventy per cent of the earth's surface. They contain the infrastructure – including maintenance, weapons, fuel and accom-modation – to begin operations the moment that they arrive at a crisis point. Carrier-borne aircraft operate as part of a seamless, network-enabled system which also includes cruise missiles that can be launched to considerable distances inland from

TABLE 8.1: US NAVY CARRIER AIR GROUPS

CURRENT/FUTURE AIRCRAFT TYPE	CURRENT CARRIER AIR WING (2015) COMPOSITION	NUMBER	FUTURE CARRIER AIR WING (C. 2025) COMPOSITION	NUMBER
Fighter/Attack	1 or 2 squadrons of F/A-18C Hornet	44	2 squadrons of F-35C Lightning II	44
	2 or 3 squadrons of F/A-18E/F Super Hornet		2 squadrons of F/A-18E/F Super Hornet	
Electronic Attack	1 squadron of EA-18G Growler	5	1 squadron of EA-18G Growler	5
Airborne Early Warning	1 squadron of E-2C Hawkeye	4	1 squadron of E-2D Advanced Hawkeye	4/5
Intelligence & Surveillance	N/A	–	1 squadron of RAQ-25A UAVs[1]	6
Helicopter – Sea Control	1 squadron of MH-60R	11	1 squadron of MH-60R[2]	11
Helicopter – Utility	1 squadron of MH-60S	8	1 squadron of MH-60S[2]	8
Total		72	Total[2]	78/79
	Plus attachment of 1–2 C-2A Greyhound COD		Plus attachment of 1–2 V-22A Osprey COD	

Notes:

1 The precise future role of the US Navy's future UCLASS capability is subject to ongoing debate between the US Navy and Congress.

2 The US Navy plans to base eight of the helicopters currently embarked on its carriers on other ships in the carrier strike group.

submarines and surface ships with anti-aircraft capabilities that can also be used to defeat attack by ballistic missiles. This combined capability continues to provide the United States with enormous international leverage. Whilst, therefore, the outcome of current US Navy deliberations cannot be predicted with certainty, a cost-constrained continuation of the *Ford* design – taking full advantage of the economies of scale inherent with this approach – seems the most likely outcome.[5]

The US Navy requires ten carrier air wings (CVWs) to support its eleven strike carriers, although this has temporarily fallen to nine in the face of budget constraints and pending *Gerald R. Ford*'s delivery. Each CVW comprises around seventy aircraft, with present and likely future composition as set out in Table 8.1.[6] The focus of the air wings are the four strike fighter squadrons (VFAs), currently encompassing a mix of F/A-18E/F Super Hornet and earlier F/A-18C/D Hornet squadrons.[7] These aircraft have carried out all carrier strike and interception roles since the withdrawal of the F-14 Tomcat dedicated naval interceptor in 2006. The Boeing Super Hornet currently dominates the US Navy's tactical fighter force. A total of 563 of the type have been ordered to date and it equips nearly thirty squadrons. The balance of the force comprises around ten US Navy and USMC Hornet squadrons drawn from around 300 of the legacy type that remain operational.

A good example of the rationalisation in aircraft procurement that took place in the immediate aftermath of the Cold War, the Super Hornet is an enlarged development of the older McDonnell Douglas Hornet design. The F/A-18E/F was originally authorised as a contingency against the possible failure of aircraft projects begun late in the Cold War, including the A-12 stealth strike aircraft. When these were cancelled as savings measures the Super Hornet became the most important project in US naval aviation. Initial contracts were placed with McDonnell Douglas in 1992, prior to the firm's acquisition by Boeing in 1997. Development was completed on time and under budget, with the first flight taking place in late 1995. Production aircraft were built in multi-year procurement packages, which further drove down acquisition costs. Many aircraft were delivered early. Delays to the F-35C Lightning II's development have required the procurement of extra Super Hornets to avoid a potential 'fighter gap' in the mid-2020s.

Technical details of the Super Hornet (and other fixed-wing aircraft described in this section) are included in Table 8.2. Sensors have been steadily upgraded over time and, with current versions equipped with the APG-79 active electronically scanned array (AESA) radar; the AN/ASQ-228 advanced targeting forward-looking infrared system (ATFLIR); the SHARP reconnaissance pod and a comprehensive outfit of radar-warning receivers,

jammers, countermeasures dispensers and a towed decoy. Information from the sensors is 'fused' through multi-source integration software and fed to 'glass panel' cockpit displays and the aircrew helmet-mounted cueing system. In the two seat 'F' model the crew can engage separate targets using fused onboard or off-board sensor information which can be networked using Link 16. Both 'E' and 'F' have identical systems but the 'E' has an extra fuel tank in place of the second cockpit giving a slightly greater radius of action. Both can carry the complete US Navy range of air-to-air and air-to-surface weapons and – with up to 30,000lbs of fuel in a five external tank configuration – can be used as in-flight refuelling tankers to accompany a strike force or extend a combat air patrol (CAP) on station. They can act as their own escorts on strike missions or as a CAP over the fleet. Eleven hardpoints provide considerable flexibility in selecting the appropriate loadout for a wide range of operations. Typical weapon loads include four AIM-9 Sidewinders and eight AMRAAM for a pure fighter mission or two Sidewinders, two AMRAAM and seven Joint Direct Attack Munitions for a strike mission.

Early in the Super Hornet's development, it was appreciated that the airframe could be adapted to provide an electronic attack variant as a replacement for the venerable EA-6B Prowler. Designated the EA-18G Growler, this variant first flew in 2006 and had completely replaced the EA-6B in the CVWs by 2015. It retains the same basic systems as the Super Hornet but additionall, carries ALQ-218 RF receivers, ALQ-227 communications countermeasures and ALQ-99 tactical jamming pods, as well as a multi-mission advanced tactical terminal (MATT). This receives and fuses off-board sensor information through a satellite link. A total of 151 Growlers have been ordered to date, with five typically allocated to the electronic attack squadron (VAQ) that forms part of each carrier air wing. Additional squadrons are assigned to expeditionary, land-based roles.

The US Navy has also carried out well-considered modernisations of other elements of its carrier air wings. Most notably, the E-2D Advanced Hawkeye airborne early warning aircraft achieved initial operational capability (IOC) in 2015. The major new feature which differentiates it from the earlier 'C' variant is the AN/APY-9 advanced electronically-scanned radar. This operates in the UHF band and uses high digital computing power to detect targets as diverse as stealth-configured aircraft and even

TABLE 8.2: CARRIER STRIKE FIGHTERS IN SERVICE 2015

Aircraft:[1]	F/A-18C/D Hornet	F/A-18E/F S. Hornet	Su-33 'Flanker D'	MiG-29K 'Fulcrum D'	J-15 'Flying Shark'	Rafale M F3
Manufacturer:	McDonnell Douglas	Boeing	Sukhoi	Mikoyan	Shenyang AC	Dassault
Country:	United States	United States	Russia	Russia	China	France
Length:	17.1m	18.3m	21.9m	17.3m	21.9m	15.3m
Wingspan:	12.3m	13.6m	14.7m	12.0m	14.7m	10.9m
Max Take-off Weight:	23,500kg	29,900kg	33,000kg	24,500kg	33,000kg	24,000kg
Engines:	2 x GE F404-GE-402	2 x GE F414-GE-400	2 x Saturn AL-31F3	2 x Kilmov RD-33MK	2 x Shenyang WS-10A	2 x SNECMA M88-2
	79.2kN each	97.9kN each	125.5kN each	88.3kN each	135kN each	75.6kN each
Maximum Speed:	Mach 1.8	Mach 1.8	Mach 2.2	Mach 2	Mach 2	Mach 1.6
Max Altitude:	50,000ft (15,200m)	50,000ft (15,200m)	56,000ft (17,000m)	57,000ft (17,500m)	66,000ft (20,000m)	50,000ft (15,200m)
Ferry Range:	1,800 NM	1,800NM	1,600NM	1,100NM	1,800NM	1,000NM
Principal Sensor:	AN/APG-73	AN/APG-79	N-019 'Slot Back'	Zhuk-ME	AESA radar	Thales RBE2
Weapons	1 x 20mm cannon	1 x 20mm cannon	1 x 30mm cannon	1 x 30mm cannon	1 x 30mm cannon	1 x 30mm cannon
	9 hardpoints	11 hardpoints	12 hardpoints	9 hardpoints	12 hardpoints	13 hardpoints
	c.6,000kg capacity	c.8,000kg capacity	c.6,500kg capacity	c.5,500kg capacity	Unknown capacity	c.9,000kg capacity
Crew:	1/2	1/2	1 (2: SU-33UB)	1 (2: MiG-29KUB)	1	1
Number:	627 produced[2]	563 produced[2]	c.20 produced	45 produced for India	Production ongoing	40–50 Ms planned
	c. 300 operational		c.12 operational	24 ordered for Russia	c.10 delivered to date	c.40 operational

Notes:

1 Data has been compiled from manufacturers' documentation and other publicly-available information. Due to considerable variations in published information, data should be regarded as indicative only.

2 Does not include production for land-based air forces overseas, EA-18G Growler variants nor five additional aircraft authorised in December 2015 but not yet contracted.

small objects, including people, on land. The E-2D is able to use its sensors to provide networked information to guide fleet weapons such as AMRAAM and SM-6 onto targets beyond the range of their launch platform's sensors. The E-2D will replace the four E-2Cs that equip the airborne early warning (VAW) squadron in each CVW on a like for like basis, with total orders of seventy-five aircraft ultimately planned.

Meanwhile, by 2016, the MH-60R and MH-60S versions of the Sea Hawk helicopter will have completely replaced the legacy SH-60F, both in carrier air wings and on other warships. In 2015 *Theodore Roosevelt* (CVN-71) marked this process of transition by carrying out a round-the-world deployment with VAW-125 (the 'Tigertails') – the first operational E-2D squadron embarked – together with HS-11 (the 'Dragonslayers'), the last SH-60F helicopter anti-submarine squadron. Also

The FA/18-E/F Super Hornet is the current mainstay of the US Navy's carrier air wings with some 563 delivered or on order as of the end of 2015. This shows a F/A-18E single seat variant from Strike Fighter Squadron (VFA) 115 launching from the carrier *George Washington* (CVN-73) in July 2015. *(US Navy)*

The eyes of the US Navy's carrier groups are formed by its E-2 Hawkeye airborne early warning aircraft, the initial variant of which first flew as long ago as 1960. The current E-2C version, pictured here on the deck of *George Washington* (CVN-73) in June 2015, is in the course of replacement by the new E-2D Advanced Hawkeye, which incorporates the AN/APY-9 electronically-scanned radar. *(US Navy)*

The MH-60R Sea Hawk is the latest sea-control iteration of the popular Sea Hawk helicopter series, being deployed both on US Navy aircraft carriers and surface warships. *(Lockheed Martin)*

in 2015, the US Navy announced that the long-serving C-2A Greyhound carrier-on-board delivery (COD) aircraft will be replaced from 2020 onwards by a modified version of the MV-22 Osprey tilt-rotor aircraft, which has demonstrated the ability to carry bulky loads – such as the F-35's PW-135 engine – internally. The COD variant is to have increased range and represents a wise selection as it is also capable of operating from undeveloped airfields around the world, and of landing on big-deck STOVL (short take-off and vertical landing) carriers – such as *America* (LHD-6) and *Queen Elizabeth* – which do not have arrester wires.

The twenty-first century has also seen the significant development of US Navy unmanned combat air vehicles (UCAV). The Northrop Grumman X-47B system demonstrator carried out the first arrested carrier landings in 2013 and the first air-to-air refuelling in 2015; it was not 'flown' by a remote pilot but used its own sensors and artificial intelligence to fly a briefed mission autonomously. The type ceased flying in 2015 when its demonstration programme was complete but the US Navy intends to build on its achievements by procuring an unmanned carrier-launched air surveillance and strike system designated the RAQ-25A. This was originally intended to achieve IOC with a single unit forming part of a carrier air wing in 2020. However, a lack of consensus between Congress and the US Navy on the type's primary mission has delayed the formulation of a staff requirement and prevented a request for proposals being sent out to industry.[8] The projected IOC has now moved out to 2023 and RAQ-25A's capabilities will, therefore, have to be balanced against F/A-XX, the aircraft that the USN wants as an eventual F/A-18E/F replacement beyond 2030. Secretary of the Navy Ray Mabus stated in 2015 that the F-35 'should, and almost certainly will, be the last manned strike fighter the … Navy will ever buy or fly'. However, the Chief of Naval Operations, Admiral Greenert, expressed his own alternative view that F/A-XX should have 'interchangeable manned and unmanned options'. Detailed requirements for both types will evolve over the next few years.

India: The Indian Navy's longstanding ambitions to modernise and expand its carrier force have been largely focused on indigenous construction. Design work on the country's first indigenous carrier, the 40,000-ton STOBAR *Vikrant* II started around the turn of the millennium and she is currently being fitted out in Cochin, India, after formal launch in August 2013.[9] The programme has proved challenging for the Indian Navy to manage and construction is running late and substantially over-budget. Although work is being accelerated in the hope of achieving a planned 2018 delivery, previous experience of Indian Navy construction programmes suggests this may be optimistic.

A second, more advanced, indigenous carrier, provisionally named *Vishnal*, is projected and, in January 2015, US President Barack Obama announced an agreement with the Indian government covering the transfer of aircraft carrier technology that may well be applied to the new ship. A delegation led by Vice Admiral Cheema subsequently visited the USA in August 2015 to establish a working group that will assist this process. The Indian Navy is believed to want a ship of about 65,000 tons fitted with catapults and arrester gear which can be in service by 2033. EMALS and AAG together with other US carrier-related technologies are obviously attractive and the US Department of Defense has stated its willingness to make them available.

Meanwhile, the elderly *Viraat* (the former Royal Navy *Hermes*) – currently the world's oldest operational carrier – will be withdrawn from service in 2016 when she will be fifty-seven years old. Her seven remaining Sea Harriers will likely be withdrawn at the same time. Until the new *Vikrant* enters service this leaves the Indian Navy with only *Vikramaditya*, the former Russian *Admiral Gorshkov*, in operation. Modernised at a reported cost of US$2.4bn to meet Indian requirements after a substantial period in reserve following a serious fire, modifications included the installation of a new forward flight deck and a 14.3-degree 'ski-jump' together with a number of new hull sections necessitating some 2,500 tons of extra steel work. Despite being reboilered, she suffered a number of machinery problems both during trials and after delivery and her mechanical state might therefore be a cause for concern in the years ahead. Like its Russian and Chinese equivalents – and the new *Vikrant* – *Vikramaditya* uses the STOBAR system under which high performance strike fighters take off using the 'ski-jump' but have tail-hooks to make conventional arrested landings. Aircraft require a high thrust-to-weight ratio to utilise the technique and the Indian Navy has procured the Russian twin RD-33-engined MiG-29K for this purpose.

The Indian Navy's newly-delivered carrier *Vikramaditya*, pictured at sea early in 2015. Her air group is focused on MiG-29K strike fighters which – like the ship – are Russian in origin. They are operated in STOBAR configuration. *(Sitanshu Kar)*

Vikramaditya can also embark Sea King, Kamov Ka-28 and Ka-31 helicopters for anti-submarine and airborne early warning tasks as part of a c. thirty-strong air group.

Total Indian Navy orders for the MiG-29K are understood to amount to forty-one aircraft, to which must be added four MiG-29KUB two-seat variants. All of these are expected to be delivered by 2017. The aircraft have a maximum launch weight of 24,500kg (54,000lbs) and a thrust, in full re-heat, approaching 180kN (40,000lbs). Sensors include what is described as an 'electronic intelligence system' and a Phazotron Zhuk-ME radar, which has a 'track-while-scan' capability. The jet is capable of

The Indian Navy intends to procure its future aircraft carriers indigenously, although construction of the first vessel, *Vikrant*, has proved to be far more expensive and time consuming than initially envisaged. *Vikrant* will be operated in STOBAR configuration but future vessels may have US Navy-sourced electro-magnetic catapults and arrester gear. *(Indian Navy)*

engaging four targets simultaneously. It carries a wide range of air-to-air and air-to-surface missiles on eight under-wing hardpoints, with another under the fuselage centreline.

The Indian Navy ultimately plans to augment the MiG-29K in embarked air wings with a naval variant of the indigenous Tejas light combat aircraft (LCA), which is being developed jointly with the Indian Air Force. Tejas has a tailless delta configuration and is supersonic at all heights with a maximum speed of over Mach 1.6. The current Mk 1 version has a maximum launch weight of 13,200kg (29,100lbs) and its single General Electric F404-GE-IN20 delivers up to 90kN (20,000lbs) thrust. Two navalised prototypes based on the Mk1 variant of the aircraft have flown to date out of a reported initial batch of six. Series production of at least forty jets will be focused on an improved Mk 2 version with a more powerful engine. The fully-developed version is to have an internal 23mm cannon and six under-wing hardpoints and a further one under the fuselage capable of carrying up to 5,000kg (11,000lbs) of weapons including air-to-air, air-to-surface, anti-ship missiles, laser-guided and 'dumb' bombs. A further hardpoint under the port intake is intended for a targeting pod and the type's multi-mode radar is to have 'track-while-scan' with the ability to engage ten targets simultaneously.

The veteran Indian aircraft carrier *Viraat*, first commissioned as the Royal Navy *Hermes* in 1959. She is scheduled to be withdrawn – along with her Sea Harrier STOVL aircraft – in the course of 2016 *(US Navy)*

Russia: In contrast with the relatively healthy situation that persists with respect to the United States Navy, carrier aviation in Russia has struggled to survive the end of the Cold War and the subsequent breakup of the Soviet Union in 1991. At that time, four Project 1143 *Kiev* class 'heavy aviation cruisers' were in various states of operational readiness and the newly-commissioned STOBAR carrier *Admiral Kuznetsov* was in the course of completing trials. A particular complication was that all these ships had been completed in the Nikolayev Shipyard that had, by then, become part of the independent Ukraine. The yard was also building a second *Kuznetsov* class vessel, *Varyag*, which had been launched in 1988. She was ultimately sold and towed to China where, after years of restoration and reconstruction, she was commissioned in 2012 as *Liaoning*. Work on a further aircraft carrier, the nuclear-powered *Ulyanovsk*, was terminated in 1992 when she was within a few months of being launched. She was to have been fitted with steam catapults and arrester wires. However, the Russian Navy lacked funds to

The Russian aircraft carrier *Admiral Kuznetsov* pictured being monitored by the British Royal Navy Type 45 destroyer *Dragon* as she transits the English Channel in May 2014. Russia's carrier-based naval air power is currently limited to this single ship and a limited number of SU-33 jets, the latter being in the course of replacement by MiG-29K strike fighters also operated by the Indian Navy. *(Crown Copyright 2014)*

TABLE 8.3: WORLD AIRCRAFT & HELICOPTER CARRIERS BY COUNTRY – PROJECTED 2020 NUMBERS

| COUNTRY | AIR GROUP FIXED WING & HELICOPTERS | | | | | | HELICOPTERS ONLY | | | CLASSES |
| CONFIGURATION | CATOBAR | | STOBAR | STOVL | | | | | | |
TYPE	CVN	CV		CV	CVS	LHD	CVH	LHD	TOTALS	
United States	11	–	–	–	–	10	–	–	21	*Ford*, *Nimitz*, *America*, *Wasp*
Russia	–	–	1	–	–	–	–	–	1	*Kuznetsov*
India	–	–	2	–	–	–	–	–	2	*Vikrant*, *Kiev* (mod)
China[1]	–	–	1	–	–	–	–	–	1	*Kuznetsov* (mod)
Brazil	–	1	–	–	–	–	–	–	1	*Clemenceau*
France	1	–	–	–	–	–	–	3	4	*De Gaulle*, *Mistral*
United Kingdom	–	–	–	2	–	–	–	–	2	*Queen Elizabeth*
Italy[2]	–	–	–	1	1	–	–	–	2	*Cavour*, *Garibaldi*
Spain	–	–	–	–	–	1	–	–	1	*Juan Carlos I*
Australia	–	–	–	–	–	–	–	2	2	*Juan Carlos I*
Egypt	–	–	–	–	–	–	–	2	2	*Mistral*
Japan	–	–	–	–	–	–	4	–	4	*Izumo*, *Hyuga*
South Korea	–	–	–	–	–	–	–	2	2	*Dokdo*
Thailand	–	–	–	–	–	–	1	–	1	*Chakri Naruebet*
TOTALS [3]	12	1	4	3	1	11	5	9	46	

Notes:

1 China has additional aircraft carriers of an unknown configuration under construction so as to increase overall numbers post-2020.

2 Italy will replace its current CVS, *Giuseppe Garibaldi*, with a new LHD post-2020.

3 Turkey will join the carrier club with the commissioning of a new LHD of the *Juan Carlos I* type in 2021.

pay for her completion and she was broken up on the slipway.

The *Kiev* class were soon withdrawn from service, although the last – the modified *Admiral Gorshkov* – was offered for sale to India. After years of negotiations, a sale was finally agreed in 2004 as part of a deal in which the ship itself was donated but India had to pay refit and modernisation costs at the Russian Sevmash Shipyard. It took a further decade and a near-tripling of the estimated cost to eventually complete her in 2014.

No large aircraft-carrying warship has been completed for the Russian Navy since *Admiral Kuznetsov*'s delivery. She currently operates a variant of the Sukhoi Su-33, given the NATO reporting name 'Flanker D', as well as various Kamov Ka-27 'Helix' helicopter types. Only twenty production Su-33 aircraft were built before funding ran out; several of these have been lost and about a dozen are thought to be currently serviceable. They are operated by the 279th Aviation Regiment based at the Severomork-3 airbase near Murmansk. Two Su-33UB two-seat trainers were also procured for use with a training unit ashore and a small number, perhaps as few as

five, Sukhoi Su-25 UT two-seat aircraft are used for deck-landing training. Embarked time has been limited, barely allowing pilots to maintain deck-landing proficiency and the skills required by aircraft handlers and engineering staff must be only adequate to allow a viable operational capability. To add to *Kuznetsov*'s problems, her aging machinery is considered unreliable and Ukrainian firms – now subject to a government ban on arms sales to Russia – are still the only source of major replacement components for steam turbines, gearboxes and boilers. During recent deployments from her Northern Fleet base to the Mediterranean, *Kuznetsov* has been accompanied at all times by a tug in case she broke down.

The most pressing need facing Russian carrier aviation is fielding a replacement for the dwindling number of operational Su-33s. Local media reports suggest deliveries of twenty MiG-29K single seat and four MiG-29KUB two seat fighters ordered in 2012 were completed around the end of 2015. These will form a second naval aviation regiment prior to the eventual withdrawal of the Su-33.

China: China has moved closer to bringing its first

carrier, *Liaoning* into operational service. After the long tow to China in 2001, she spent ten years in Dalian shipyard being examined, inspected, modernised and rebuilt to an improved design for STOBAR aircraft operations. Initial aircraft trials took place after commissioning in 2012, with a prototype Shenyang J-15 'Flying Shark' strike fighter of the People's Liberation Army Naval Air Force (PLANAF) making the first arrested landing. A series of developmental deployments with an increasingly operational bias have taken place with up to six J-15s embarked and analysts believe that around ten or more have been delivered to date. When disembarked, the jets operate from the naval air station at Huludao in Liaoning Province, which has facilities for an air wing of twenty-four aircraft and a dummy flight deck with a 'ski-jump'.

Reportedly based on the Russian Su-33 airframe, the J-15 is a big aircraft with a maximum take-off weight of 27,000kg (60,000lbs). Its two WS-10A turbofans give a combined total thrust of 270kN (61,000lbs) in full afterburner, giving the J-15 an electrifying performance with a thrust-to-weight ratio better than unity and a top speed of Mach 2.4

This is considerably in excess of any Western naval fighter although, of course, the use of full after-burner to achieve it would dramatically reduce endurance and provide a spectacular 'beacon' for heat-seeking missiles. It has one internal 30mm cannon and twelve external hardpoints capable of carrying a wide range of air-to-air, anti-ship and anti-radiation missiles, electronic countermeasure pods and both laser-guided and 'dumb' bombs. It is believed over twenty J-15s could be embarked when sufficient aircraft have been completed.

The remainder of *Liaoning*'s air wing will also include a number of helicopters, including Z-8YJ Black Cat airborne warning and control aircraft. Like the J-15, these are due to reach operational maturity in the near future. Licence-built derivatives of the French Super Frelon helicopter are already in service and embark regularly to give the carrier a viable anti-submarine capability.

There have been ongoing reports that China is building two new indigenous carriers of around 60,000 tons displacement; the first is said by Chinese media to be under construction at Dalian and the second at Jiangnan. Photographs published from September 2015 onwards confirmed that construction of a carrier-type hull at Dalian is relatively well-advanced.

France: France is a good example of a navy that knows exactly what it wants and works methodically to get the most from its limited budget. In spite of rumours that both India and China ultimately plan to build nuclear-powered aircraft carriers, thus far

Prototype Shenyang J15 strike fighters undergoing trials on the PLAN's first carrier *Liaoning*. (Simon Yang)

France is the only country outside the United States to have actually built one. Conceived during the last years of the Cold War and laid down in April 1989, *Charles de Gaulle* suffered from a protracted construction and trials period in an era of defence austerity and was not commissioned until 2001. A planned sister was never proceeded with, although – until 2013 – there were ambitions to procure a

second, conventionally-powered, carrier designated *Porte-Avions 2* (PA-2). The French Government paid the British Government for the right to base it on the *Queen Elizabeth* class design although, from the outset, it was to have steam catapults and arrester wires.[10] The French 2013 Defence White Paper terminated this plan for the foreseeable future, although DCNS continues to offer ships derived from its own work on the PA-2 project to potential export customers such as Brazil and India. The lack of a second carrier is the major weakness in French naval aviation.

Charles de Gaulle has operated an air wing comprising Rafale M omni-role fighters, Super Etendard-Mod. (SEM) strike aircraft, E-2C 'Hawkeye' airborne command and control aircraft, and helicopters for plane guard and search and rescue duties. With the planned retirement of the

The Rafale M will be the sole strike fighter in *Marine Nationale* service following the imminent retirement of its remaining Super Etendard jets, a type which gained fame in Argentine service during the 1982 Falkland Islands War. Current plans envisage an operational force of around forty Rafale Ms in three squadrons, two of which are normally embarked on deployments by France's sole aircraft carrier, *Charles de Gaulle*. (Dassault Aviation – S Randé)

Super-Etendard in 2016, strike and interception duties will be handled solely by the Dassault Rafale M, which is slightly modified from the aircraft in service with the French Air Force. Three squadrons or flotillas – 11F, 12F and the re-equipped 17F – are located at *base d'aéronautique navale* (BAN) Landivisiau in Brittany, with two normally embarked and the third recovering from or preparing for operations to maintain the optimum operational tempo.

Three versions of the Rafale have been delivered to the navy to date and earlier aircraft are being progressively upgraded to the current, F3 standard. It is not clear how a reduction from 286 to 225 in the number of Rafale jets to be procured for both the *Aeronavale* and *Armee de l'Air* that was announced in the 2013 White Paper will impact the total of naval variants ultimately acquired. However, it seems an operational force of around forty aircraft is envisaged around the turn of the decade. The enhancement of aircraft to the planned 3R standard will enable the use of the Meteor air-to-air missile and the HAMMER air-to-surface weapon. Other advances include AESA radar and improved electronic warfare capability.

Brazil: Brazil's carrier-based naval aviation capability is limited by reliability issues impacting its only carrier, *São Paulo*, which was docked in the Arsenal da Marinha do Rio de Janeiro in 2015 for a comprehensive hull inspection.[11] She was originally commissioned for the French Navy as *Foch* in 1963 and the Brazilian Navy has contracted DCNS to provide assistance in a number of upgrade programmes. However, plans to install a new diesel-electric integrated propulsion system and modernised catapults may not be viable given the ship's age. There are longer-term ambitions for two new carriers in the 50,000-ton size bracket under the *Programa de Obtenção dos Navios-Aeródromos* (PONAE) project that is scheduled for implementation from the late 2020s onwards.

When operational, *São Paulo*'s air wing will comprise a mix of AF-1 Skyhawks, Grumman S-2 Trackers and C-1 Traders, as well as SH-3A/B Sea King, SH-60B Sea Hawk and utility helicopters. Twelve of the veteran Skyhawks, originally acquired second-hand from Kuwait in the 1990s, are being modernised by Embraer with Elbit APQ-145B radar and an improved ECM/ASM package. They are armed with Sidewinder air-to-air missiles, two 20mm cannon and a variety of 'dumb' bombs and

Four F-35B STOVL variant Joint Strike Fighters taking part in a refuelling exercise in March 2015. The aircraft nearest the camera is in British markings. The F-35B will deploy operationally from the first new *Queen Elizabeth* class aircraft carrier from 2020. *(Lockheed Martin)*

rocket pods. The first was re-delivered during 2015 and the aim is to retain the modernised aircraft in service until 2025. The Trackers/Traders are newly acquired second-hand airframes also being modernised; they will carry out COD, air-to-air refuelling and early warning roles.

United Kingdom: The United Kingdom is not currently a fixed-wing carrier operator following the withdrawal of *Ark Royal* and the entire Joint Force Harrier as a result of the 2010 Strategic Security and Defence Review (SDSR). However, it will return to fast jet operation at sea with the operational deployment of the F-35B STOVL variant Joint Strike Fighters from *Queen Elizabeth*, the first of two new ships, by 2020. The new British carriers' design process was over-complicated and expensive, betraying the obvious fact that the project team – and their political masters - were uncertain as to how best to proceed. The selection of an adaptable design initially configured for STOVL jets and helicopters but supposedly capable of reconstruction to STOBAR or CATOBAR (catapult assisted take-off

but arrested recovery) configuration was intended to allow potential operation of the widest possible range of naval aircraft. However, it proved impossible to implement this flexibility in a cost-effective and timely manner when SDSR 2010 decided to equip the second ship, *Prince of Wales*, with EMALS and AAG to allow CATOBAR operation.[12] In 2012, it was determined that the F-35B and STOVL operation was, after all, the preferred way forward. *Queen Elizabeth* was officially named by Her Majesty Queen Elizabeth II on 4 July 2014 and is due for completion by the end of 2016 prior to the commencement of trials. *Prince of Wales* will follow around two years later.

Given the considerable period of time between the disbandment of the former Joint Force Harrier and the completion of *Queen Elizabeth*, it was fortunate that the US Navy generously agreed to provide support to 'keep the art alive' until the first new carrier is ready. Since 2010, a number of British pilots have flown F/A-18E Super Hornets from US Navy carriers and many other officers and men have served in US Navy carrier-based roles to gain 'big deck' experience under a bilateral agreement. Uniquely, the British Government has elected to operate F-35B Lightning II units as a joint force with roughly equal numbers of Royal Navy (RN) and Royal Air Force (RAF) personnel in units that are to be commanded alternately by RAF and RN officers rather than under RN-controlled naval air squadrons. The Lightning II is the first British aircraft to have no British designation allocated to it (as in Sea Harrier FRS 1; Sea King ASaC 7); the US designation F-35 is used in every reference.

The original intention was to acquire as many as 138 F-35Bs and the 2015 SDSR confirmed this remains the ultimate intention. These are being acquired in small batches, with four trials and ten production aircraft ordered as at the end of 2015. The first British F-35B unit to form was 17 Squadron at Edwards Air Force Base in California where it matures British operating techniques with the type and forms part of its joint operational test team (JOTT), working with United States and Dutch aircraft to develop Block 3 software. The first operational British unit, 617 Squadron RAF is to form at MCAS Beaufort in 2016, after which it is to spend two years training in America before moving to its planned United Kingdom shore base at Marham in Norfolk in 2018. A second unit, 809 Naval Air Squadron (NAS) will form after 617 and move to Marham in 2019. It is tentatively expected to become the United Kingdom training unit in addition to deploying operational detachments to carriers. Three periods of F-35B acceptance and proving will take place in American waters from 2018. The last is to culminate with an operational readiness inspection with part of 617 NAS embarked in late 2020. After its successful conclusion, IOC for both ship and squadron will be declared, ending a ten-year gap in British naval aviation capability. SDSR 2015 indicated an intention to have two squadrons of up to twenty-four F-35Bs available for carrier embarkation by 2023.

British F-35B squadrons will not embark as dedicated squadrons like those in US Navy carrier air wings but will, instead, provide detachments on an 'as-required' basis to form tailored air groups (TAGs) for specific operations or exercises. They cannot be in two places at once, however, and there are concerns that the British Ministry of Defence (MOD) may see land-based operations as normal with embarkation as an occasional exception, running the risk that ship and air wing operational

standards will not be easy to maintain at the required level. In September 2015 Rear Admiral Keith Blount, the RN Assistant Chief of Naval Staff (Aviation, Amphibious Capability and Carriers) stated that he expected 'the US Marine Corps to operate and work from the deck of the *Queen Elizabeth* class aircraft carriers … to get the most bang for the buck we can for the UK taxpayer'.

The TAG concept envisages the *Queen Elizabeth* class's F-35B being supplemented or even replaced by a wide range of rotary assets as dictated by specific operational demands. For example, a force-protection package of Merlin HM2 helicopters could fulfil anti-submarine and airborne early warning roles, whilst RAF Chinook and British Army Apache and Wildcats helicopters could join RN helicopters as part of a littoral manoeuvre package. The planned withdrawal of all Sea Kings from service on 31 March 2016 would have left the RN with no airborne surveillance and control (ASaC), capability for the first years of *Queen Elizabeth*'s life but this gap has been averted by funding the retention of seven Sea King ASaC 7s in 849 NAS until September 2018 with two flights, each of two aircraft, designated 'Palembang' and 'Normandy' available for embarkation as part of a TAG. The remaining three aircraft will train observers and maintain tactical development of the role as part of a headquarters flight. Project 'Crowsnest' is to provide a replacement by the end of 2018 comprising a re-packaged and upgraded version of the ASaC 7's Cerberus mission system as a roll-on/roll-off mission fit for the RN Merlin helicopters recently upgraded to HM 2 standard. Ten of these outfits are to be manufactured and all thirty Merlin HM 2's are to be modified to enable them to be installed rapidly as an alternative to the anti-submarine warfare equipment with the rear workstations swapped for ASaC-specific consoles. To date the MOD has made no comment on how many aircraft will be fitted with 'Crowsnest' systems on a regular basis to maintain 849 NAS aircrew currency, training and allow a regular contribution to TAG deployments.

Italy & Spain: The two remaining members of the fixed-wing carrier 'club', the Italian and Spanish Navies, both have small air wings of AV-8B Harrier II Plus aircraft, which are also operated by the USMC in the amphibious support role. Indeed, the difference between the capabilities of light carriers with STOVL fighters and the big-deck amphibious

carriers described below have become somewhat blurred and both may be given new designations that reflect the wide range of operational options they offer.[13]

The Italian Navy's Harriers can operate from the two light carriers *Giuseppe Garibaldi* (commissioned 1985) and *Cavour* (commissioned 2009) to give a balanced STOVL strike fighter capability for both fleet and amphibious operations, although the former ship is now principally used in the helicopter support role. It is planned that the existing aircraft will be replaced over the next decade on an approximate like-for-like basis by fifteen of the STOVL F-35B variant of the United States Lightning II Joint Strike Fighter.[14]

Following the withdrawal of the sole Spanish carrier, *Príncipe de Asturias,* in 2013, Spain's Harriers embark in the amphibious assault ship, *Juan Carlos I*. This is capable of 'swing' operations in either the sea control or amphibious roles although command, control and ammunition stowage arrangements are slanted towards the latter. Twelve AV-8B Harrier II Plus aircraft remain operational. It is likely they will serve well into the 2020s given current lack of funds to acquire replacement F-35Bs.

THE F-35 LIGHTNING II

The Lockheed-Martin Lightning II Joint Strike Fighter design was selected in 2001 as the principal future combat aircraft for the United States' armed forces after the X-35 demonstrator beat Boeing's rival X-32 design in competition. Designated the F-35, development of the new strike fighter was expected to be complete in around ten years but is still far from complete as of the end of 2015. It is fair to say that the work needed to bring the aircraft's software and systems to maturity was seriously underestimated. There are three variants, all single-engine, single seat aircraft:

■ The 'A' for use ashore with the US Air Force and a number of export customers.
■ The 'B' STOVL variant for use ashore and afloat by the USMC, British RN and RAF, and the Italian Navy and Air Force.
■ The 'C' for the US Navy. This has larger wings and is optimised for catapult launch and arrested recovery.

The 'A' and 'C' tyes were heavily penalised to achieve commonality with the 'B' and – without it – they could well have emerged earlier as very different, twin-engined, aircraft in both single and two-seat versions. Many American analysts now believe that it would have been both cheaper and more efficient to have designed two different aircraft, one conventional and one STOVL.

The F-35 programme envisages completion of as many as 2,457 F-35s for the United States, of which 2,443 will be production aircraft. Of this latter total, 1,763 are 'A' variants earmarked for the United States Air Force, 340 'B' variants for the USMC and 340 'C' variants (260 for the US Navy and eighty for the USMC). It is expected several hundred more aircraft will be completed for export customers. Total orders to date amounted to a little over 250 aircraft as at the end of 2015 – all ordered under low rate initial production (LRIP) contracts – so production is still in its relative infancy. Total programme costs for the United States alone are currently estimated to be around US$400bn in cash terms. There have been concerns about significant overall programme cost growth and the likelihood all planned procurement will be completed must be treated with some scepticism.[15]

In spite of the problems, however, considerable progress was made with the project in 2015. In July, VMFA-121, the 'Green Knights' based at Marine Corps Air Station (MCAS) Yuma was declared to have reached IOC. Its aircraft have Block 2B software, which lacks the ability to use external weapons stations but does allow limited use of the internal weapons bays, surveillance and combat manoeuvring capability. All US Navy, US Air Force and British aircraft are to have Block 3F software before they reach IOC, allowing the use of a wider range of weapons stowed both internally and externally together with full transfer of imagery and data. The USMC training unit VMFAT-501, 'Warlords', trains USMC and British personnel on the F-35B and the US Navy has formed its own training unit, VFA-101, the 'Grim Reapers' which is to be based at Naval Air Station Lemoore in California once its own training is complete.

BIG-DECK AMPHIBIOUS SHIPS

Vertical envelopment using embarked helicopters to land marines on objectives ashore evolved from the mid-1950s onwards. The first amphibious carrier, the American *Thetis Bay* (CVHA-1), was an escort carrier conversion which entered service in 1956; in the same year two hastily-converted British light

TABLE 8.4: F-35 JOINT STRIKE FIGHTER VARIANTS

AIRCRAFT:[1]	F-35A	F-35B	F-35C
Configuration:	Land-based	STOVL	CATOBAR
Length:	15.7m	15.6m	15.7m
Wingspan	10.7m	10.7m	13.1m
Max Take-off Weight:	c.32,000kg	c.27,000kg	c.32,000kg
Engines:	1 x F135-PW-100	1 x F135-PW-600	1 x F135-PW-100
	191kN	191kN	191kN
		Includes RR lift fan	
Maximum Speed:	Mach 1.6	Mach 1.6	Mach 1.6
Max G-load:	9	7	7.5
Range:	1,200NM+	900NM+	1,200NM+
Principal Sensor:[2]	AN/APG-81 radar	AN/APG-81 radar	AN/APG-81 radar
Weapons:	1 x internal 25mm cannon	2 internal bays[3]	2 internal bays
	2 internal bays	(2 hardpoints each)	(2 hardpoints each)
	(2 hardpoints each)	7 external hardpoints[4]	7 external hardpoints[4]
	7 external hardpoints		
	c.8,200kg capacity	c.6,800kg capacity	c.8,200kg capacity
Crew:	1	1	1
Number:	1,763 planned	340 planned	340 planned
	Additional export orders	Additional export orders	

Notes:

1 Data has been compiled from a range of manufacturers and US Department of Defense documentation. It demonstrates the compromises inherent in building variants of a common design, with the range, payload and manoeuvrability of the F-35B STOVL variant particularly impacted by the space and weight taken by the need to incorporate a lift fan into the design.

2 Although the AN/APG-81 active electronically-scanned array (AESA) is the F-35's principal sensor, the ability to fuse data provided by the aircraft's advanced electronic warfare suite with information provided by the APG-71 to provide a comprehensive tactical picture should not be overlooked.

3 The internal bays on the F-35B are smaller than on the other two aircraft.

4 The centreline hardpoint on the F-35B and F-35C variants is reserved for a gun pod containing the 25mm cannon installed internally on the F-35A.

A 2013 publicity shot of the three variants of the F-35 Lightning II Joint Strike Fighter. The conventional, land-based F-35A is shown to the right of the picture, the lift-fan equipped F-35B STOVL variant in the centre and the carrier-optimised F-35C, with larger wings, to the left. (Lockheed Martin)

The *Wasp* class amphibious assault ship *Essex* (LHD-2) pictured in company with the aircraft carrier *Theodore Roosevelt* (CVN-71) during a transit of the Arabian Gulf in August 2015. The US Navy's amphibious assault ships – which will soon host F-35B STOVL Joint Strike Fighter aircraft – are arguably second only to its nuclear-powered aircraft carriers in the aviation support they can deliver. *(US Navy)*

A MV-22B Osprey from Marine Medium Tilt Rotor Squadron (VMM) 163 pictured on exercises in October 2015. The Osprey has the vertical landing abilities of a helicopter but can travel much more quickly in level flight. *(US Navy)*

fleet carriers, *Ocean* and *Theseus*, carried out the first operational helicopter-borne assault during the Suez Crisis. Their success led the British to convert two larger carriers, *Bulwark* and *Albion*, into amphibious assault ships which both operated with success; the US Navy converted several *Essex* class carriers into amphibious ships and built seven smaller ships of the *Iwo Jima* class specifically for the role. Today's big-deck amphibious carriers in the US Navy are much larger and operate STOVL fighters and tilt-rotor assault aircraft as well as amphibious helicopters. However, a number of smaller ships are operated by other navies, with the widespread adoption of commercial shipbuilding standards making these a relatively affordable proposition.

The latest US Navy amphibious carrier, the 45,000-ton *America* (LHA-6), offers such a powerful 'cross-over' capability that she arguably represents a greater concentration of air power than any other warship except a nuclear-powered aircraft carrier. Unlike previous US Navy LHA and LHD type amphibious assault ships, she has no well deck for landing craft because the design emphasised aviation facilities. Her amphibious air wing can include AV-8B Harrier STOVL attack fighters, MV-22 Osprey tilt rotors and CH-53E Sea Stallion, AH-1Z Viper and MH-60S Sea Hawk helicopters. A sister-ship *Tripoli* (LHA-7), ordered in 2012, is to have a heat-resistant flight deck allowing her to operate with F-35Bs from the outset. A projected third ship is to have the well deck re-introduced, however, in order to allow heavy vehicles and equipment to be brought ashore by landing craft. This reversion is difficult to understand given the recently-announced USMC concept of operating amphibious aircraft from mobile forward arming and refuelling points, known as M-Farps, ashore. The aircraft will return to US Navy or Allied carriers positioned over 100 nautical miles out to sea only when necessary for maintenance. The new Sikorsky CH-53K King Stallion, which flew for the first time in 2015, will be central to the sort of mobility the marines envisage, being able to carry a 27,000lb load over a 110nm mission radius. It is difficult to imagine landing craft operating in a timely or effective fashion over such distances. The US Navy amphibious carriers also have the potential to operate in the 'sea control' role, when they would embark an air group of up to twenty-two F-35Bs and twelve SH-60R anti-submarine helicopters. However, unlike British carriers, American amphibious assault ships have no ski-jump since the

USMC has elected to retain the flat deck to maximise the space available for helicopter operations.

Other amphibious assault ships currently in service are largely of European design, of which the Spanish-designed big deck ships of the *Juan Carlos I/ Canberra* type are arguably the most capable. These are now in service with Spain and Australia, whilst a slightly modified variant is under construction in Turkey for delivery by 2021. The ships are equipped with both a well deck and 'ski-jump'. However, although the Spanish Navy operates AV-8Bs from its single ship, proposals for Australia to procure a small batch of F-35Bs for embarkation in its own pair of vessels appear to have foundered in the face of the Royal Australian Air Force's (RAAF's) limited enthusiasm. Another popular design is the French 21,000-ton *Mistral* class, which can embark 700 troops, sixteen helicopters and armoured vehicles but are not intended for STOVL operation. Three are currently in service with the *Marine Nationale*. Two more ordered by Russia would have given the Russian Navy its first new major warships for over two decades and transferred important technologies to the project team believed to be working on a new carrier design. However, Russian's annexation of the Crimean peninsula and continued support for rebels in Ukraine forced France to cancel the deal and the ships have now been sold to Egypt. Meanwhile, 2015 saw the Italian Navy issue a US$1.2bn contract to Fincantieri for the construction of a 22,000-ton big-deck amphibious carrier for delivery in 2022. It is to have a well deck for landing craft and five helicopter spots on deck for Merlin/NH-90 sized aircraft. It will be able to embark 1,000 troops for long periods. Elsewhere, South Korea has commenced construction of a second *Dokdo* class LHD that might be adapted for STOVL operation.

The core of USMC fast jet aviation is formed by its six operational AV-8B Harrier Marine Attack Squadrons (VMAs) plus a training unit, with the last due to retire in 2025. The AV-8B has been employed as a strike/attack aircraft but the USMC hopes to improve its air-to-air capability with low-cost upgrades that it expects to transform the big-deck amphibious ships into light carriers capable of a wide range of tasks, possibly replacing CVNs in some deployments. If funded, the upgrades will include the carriage of AMRAAM missiles for use against targets beyond visual range detected by the type's APG-65 radar; citing the RN use of the missile on its Sea Harriers after 1995 as a valuable precedent.

Helicopter assault capabilities are now largely in the hands of the MV-22B Osprey tilt-rotor aircraft. This hybrid can take off and land vertically but achieve a top speed of 305 knots in level flight over a mission radius in excess of 250 nautical miles with twenty-four Marines or a 9,000kg (19,840lb) internal load. It has now completely replaced the CH-46E Sea Knight 'Phrog' and will ultimately equip eighteen operational Marine Medium Tilt-Rotor (VMM) squadrons and a training unit. It has revolutionised the way ship-to-objective assaults can be carried out. The US Marines plan upgrades that will enhance its capability still further, including the V-22 aerial refuelling system (VARS); a roll-on/roll-off probe-and-drogue refuelling kit which contains 4,536kg (10,000lbs) of fuel in addition to the aircraft's own tanks and can trail its drogue through the after cargo door to extend the radius of action of F-35Bs, AV-8Bs and other V-22s. A similar process of renewal is seeing the CH-53K King Stallion being developed as a more capable heavy-lift helicopter to replace the CH-53E Super Stallion in the HMH Marine Heavy Helicopter Squadrons. The AH-1Z Viper 'gunship' helicopters, which give close-air support for Marines on the ground, are already replacing the AH-1W Super Cobras in the HMLA light attack helicopter squadrons.

No other navy has the comprehensive range of aviation support assets provided by the USMC, instead often relying on tailored air groups drawn from a range of services to provide the requisite capability. For example, the RAN plans to embark TAGs in its new *Canberra* class ships comprising MRH-90 assault helicopters and Tiger gunship helicopters drawn largely from Army Air Corps (AAC) units to supplement its own aircraft. Army CH-47D Chinooks could also be embarked to provide a heavy lift capacity. A derivative of the European NH-90, forty-six MRH-90s were built by Australian Aerospace. Forty are operated by the Army Air Corps (AAC) and a further six by the RAN's 808 NAS using aircraft rotated from AAC stock and finished in the standard grey/green/black camouflage. They provide regular embarkations which are reinforced, as necessary, by the AAC. The MRH-90 can carry twenty troops or a 4,000kg (8,818lb) external load over a combat radius similar to that of the MV-22B but at a speed of only 160 knots.

A similar approach is adopted with respect to the United Kingdom's amphibious capability which will

US Marine Corps MV-22B Osprey aircraft seem embarked on Spain's amphibious assault ship *Juan Carlos I* in October 2015. The use of big-deck amphibious ships to provide second-tier navies with a meaningful aviation capability is increasingly popular, with the Spanish-design also sold to Australia and Turkey. *(US Navy)*

transition to the *Queen Elizabeth* class carriers when *Ocean* is withdrawn from service in 2018 at the end of her planned twenty-year life. A significant TAG can comprise a variety of RN, AAC and RAF helicopters including Merlins, Apaches and Chinooks. The core of the capability is provided by a fleet of twenty-five Merlin HC 3 helicopters transferred from the RAF to the RN to replace the veteran Sea King HC 4s. They are being progressively upgraded to a 'navalised' HC 4 standard with new power-folding main rotors, a folding tail pylon and a 'glass cockpit' under a programme that will not be finally completed until 2022.

SEA-CONTROL HELICOPTERS

The use of helicopters at sea expanded rapidly from the 1950s onwards. The RN 'Tribal' and *Leander* classes were among the first to operate a manned helicopter, the Westland Wasp HAS 1, in what was termed the medium anti-submarine torpedo-carrying helicopter (MATCH) role from smaller

surface escorts in the early 1960s. Italy's *Marina Militare* deployed larger helicopters for anti-submarine duties from specially-designed 'helicopter cruisers' from 1964. At around the same time the US Navy deployed the innovative, unmanned drone anti-submarine helicopter (DASH), flown remotely from a console in the parent destroyer. This concept relied on immature technology, however: a number were lost and the system was soon withdrawn. Later, in the Gulf War of 1990–1, the potency of missile-armed helicopters in the anti-surface role against fast attack craft and other small surface combatants was demonstrated in an operational environment.

Today, large sea-control helicopter types operate from both carriers and other surface warships. Of these, the Sikorsky/Lockheed-Martin SH-60/MH-60 Sea Hawk series, the AgustaWestland AW-101 (named Merlin in RN service), the NFH variant of NH Industries NH-90 and the Kamov Ka-27 series are probably the most significant types.[16] All have been widely exported.[17] A number of smaller

helicopters are also deployed in sea-control missions, of which the British Westland Lynx and its replacement, the AW159 Wildcat, are probably the most well-known. A notable recent development is the return of unmanned technology, increasingly in conjunction with manned types. For example, 2015 saw the embarkation of a flight equipped with an MH-60R Sea Hawk variant and an unmanned MQ-8B Fire Scout in the Littoral Combat Ship *Fort Worth* (LCS-3). Maintenance personnel were qualified to work on both types and the four pilots were each trained to fly the MQ-8B from a console in the ship's combat information centre (CIC) as well as the MH-60R. The MQ-8B proved ideal for extended surface searches and for the illumination of targets for Hellfire missiles from the MH-60R when both were airborne The MH-60R was found to be more useful during dynamic situations but with two pilots and more limited endurance, crew fatigue became a factor more quickly. Deck-landing trials of the improved MQ-8C were carried out on the

TABLE 8.5: SEA-CONTROL HELICOPTERS IN SERVICE 2015

AIRCRAFT:[1]	MH-60R SEA HAWK	NH90 NFH	AW-101 MERLIN[2]	CH-148 CYCLONE	KA-27 'HELIX'	AW-159 WILDCAT[3]
Manufacturer:	Sikorsky	NH Industries	AgustaWestland	Sikorsky	Kamov	AgustaWestland
Country:	United States	European Consortium	Italy/UK	United States	Russia	UK
Length:	15.3m	16.1m	19.5m	17.1m	11.3m	12.1m
	19.8m (rotors)	19.6m (rotors)	22.8m (rotors)	20.9m (rotors)	15.8m (rotors)	15.2m (rotors)
Main Rotor Diameter:	16.4m	16.3m	18.6m	17.7m	15.8m (twin)	12.8m
Max Take-off Weight:	10,700kg	10,600kg	15,000kg	13,000kg	12,000kg	6,000kg
Engines:	2 x T700-GE-701C	2 x RTM-322[4]	3 x RTM-322	2 x GE CT7-8A7	2 x Isotov TV3-117V	2 x LHTEC CTS800-4N
Maximum Speed:	140 knots	162 knots	167 knots	165 knots	145 knots	157 knots
Hover Ceiling IGE:	4,500m	3,200m	3,400m	2,700m	Not known	2,300m
Max Endurance:	3.5 hours	5 hours	6 hours	3.5 hours	Not known	2.5 hours
Principal Sensors:	AN/APS-147 radar	Thales ENR radar	Blue Kestrel radar	AN/APS-143 radar	Radar	Seaspray 7400E radar
	AN/AQS-22 dipping sonar	Dipping sonar[5]	Type 2089 dipping sonar	HELRAS dipping sonar	Dipping Sonar	FLIR
	AN/AAS-44 FLIR	FLIR	FLIR	Star Saffire 3 FLIR		
Weapons:	Torpedoes, missiles, MGs	Torpedoes, missiles, MGs	Torpedoes. MGs	Torpedoes. MGs	Torpedoes, depth charges	Torpedoes, missiles, MGs
Crew:	3/4	3/4	4/5	4	2+	2+
Number:	c.300 planned (USN)	c.130 ordered to date	30 HM2 Merlins (UK)	28 ordered (Canada)	c.80 operational (Russia)	28 ordered (UK)
	Additional export orders	Excludes NH90 TTH sales	10 ASW AW-101 (Italy)		Additional Ka-27/28 exports	8 ordered (S Korea)
			Excludes other variants			Excludes AH1 variant

Notes:

1 Data has been compiled from manufacturers' documentation and other publicly available information. Due to considerable variations in published information, data should be regarded as indicative only.

2 Data relates to Royal Navy HM2 Merlin variant; Italian aircraft are fitted with GE engines and are additionally equipped with air-to-surface missiles.

3 Data relates to Royal Navy HMA2 variant. South Korean variant also has dipping sonar.

4 Some helicopters are fitted with two GE T700-T-6E engines.

5 Type of dipping sonar differs across national variants.

destroyer *Jason Dunham* (DDG-109) in late 2014 and the type is expected to reach IOC in 2016. It has the same avionics as the 'B' but a larger airframe, based on the Bell Jetranger. This gives it superior endurance and load-carrying capability.[18]

The three big Western sea-control types have similar sensors including the folding lightweight acoustic system for helicopters (FLASH), which is known as the AN/AQS-22 in the US Navy and Sonar Type 2089 in the RN. All carry active and passive sono-buoys and use acoustic processors to analyse their results; in the RN Merlin this is the AQS-903A, in the NH-90 it is the TMS-2000 and in the MH-60R the AN/UYS-2A. All three also have powerful surface search radars. The Blue Kestrel in the Merlin is typical, with 360-degree coverage and software capable of reading the automatic identification system (AIS), transmitted by the world's merchant ships. An electro-optical/infra-red imaging system for the passive, long-range identification of contacts is common to all types. However, the Merlin is unusual in having three engines which make it thirty per cent heavier than the others, which each have two. Whilst it has six hours' endurance compared to the Sea Hawk's three and a half and the NH-90's five, the extra complexity increases the type's cost of ownership by a considerable margin. This may explain why the RN has procured the smaller and more economical Wildcat for operation from destroyers and frigates. NH-90 customers have suffered some disappointment over delayed development and late deliveries but the Royal Netherlands Navy began operating the type in 2010 and the French version, the Caiman, was declared fully operational in March 2015. All three types can be armed with anti-submarine homing torpedoes and depth charges but the Merlin is the only one of the three without an air-to-surface missile capability.

The primary sea-control helicopter in use with the Russian Navy is the twin-engined Kamov Ka-27 which has been given the NATO reporting name 'Helix A'. It differs from Western helicopters in having two co-axial contra-rotating main rotor systems mounted one on top of the other, removing the need for a tail rotor. Systems are comparable with those in the Western helicopters and include a VGS-3 dipping sonar, Osminog 'Splash Drop' radar, sonobuoys, an ESM outfit and a magnetic anomaly detector (MAD). Armament includes up to three APR-2 homing torpedoes; nuclear or conventional

The NH Industries NH-90 helicopter has both tactical transport and sea control versions. The latter has proved popular with a large number of European navies and is starting to overcome a delayed and troubled entry into service. Aircraft from the Royal Netherlands Navy (foreground) and French *Marine Nationale* have been amongst the first to become operational. *(Anthony Pecchi/Airbus Helicopters)*

A Merlin HM 1 helicopter pictured in 2013. The British Royal Navy is now transitioning to thirty modernised HM 2 variants and the Italian Navy also uses the type. Its three-engined configuration increases range, capability and reliability but makes it more expensive to operate. *(Crown Copyright 2013)*

depth bombs and air-dropped mines. Similar Ka-27s are operated by a number of navies, including the Indian and Chinese fleets.

The AW159 Wildcat HMA 2 is significantly lighter than the large sea-control helicopter types and provides an effective small-ship helicopter capability, being able to operate from small decks in rough conditions. It has a maximum launch weight of only c.6,000kg (13,200lbs) compared with the Merlin HM 2's c. 14,500kg (32,100lbs). It shares a common airframe with the AAC Wildcat AH 1, and has an avionics management system (AMS) that fuses sensor data into the aircrew's 'glass cockpit' displays and provides accurate navigation and position information. The normal crew comprises a pilot and observer, whilst sensors include a Selex Seaspray 7400E AESA radar which has air-to-air, air-to-surface, air-to-ground and ground moving-target modes that can detect people moving on land or produce two-dimensional, high-resolution images for target identification. A Wescam MX-15DI electro-optical/infra-red passive imaging system is used to search for targets, identify them, provide range data and laser-designate them if necessary. All the images displayed in a given sortie are stored in the AMS and can be downloaded and studied after the flight. The Wildcat has a helicopter integrated defensive aids system (HIDAS) which prioritises and highlights serious threats and dispenses the most effective coun-

termeasures from the on-board store of chaff and flares. Wildcats can be armed with homing torpedoes, depth charges and a door-mounted gun and have been designed to take the Britain's future air-to-surface missiles in both light and heavy designs. South Korea, the first export customer for the new helicopter, also specified FLASH dipping sonar, to further improve anti-submarine capabilities.

Amongst other shipboard helicopters with more limited sea control capabilities, the Chinese Harbin Z-9 – a licensed variant of the French Eurocopter Dauphin – is in widespread service with the PLAN and has been sold to other fleets. A large number of legacy helicopter types also remain operational around the world. For example, the Royal New Zealand Navy (RNZN) has recently replaced its SH-2G Seasprite helicopters with eight of the improved SH-2G(I) version for service in its two frigates and a support ship. The old helicopters have been sold to Peru for further service.

SHORE-BASED MARITIME PATROL AIRCRAFT

Whilst a wide range of maritime patrol aircraft (MPA) are currently in service, 'high end' MPA operations continue to be dominated by the US Navy's P-3 Orion, which first entered service as long ago as 1962. More than 550 P-3 Orions were procured for the US Navy alone and total produc-

The US Navy's maritime patrol concept envisages using unmanned MQ-4C Triton aircraft to complement the manned P-8A. It appears the unarmed Tritons will be used to maintain continuous surveillance of broad areas of ocean, with the P-8A Poseidon aircraft being used for more specific tasking, including the anti-submarine role. *(Northrop Grumman)*

tion has been around 750 when exports and licensed production in Japan is taken into account. Although the latest P-3C update 4 variant is now being steadily replaced in the US Navy's VP patrol squadrons by the new P-8A Poseidon, around ten squadrons continue to operate the older type. Current overseas operators include Argentina, Australia, Brazil, Canada, Chile, Germany, Iran, Japan, New Zealand, Norway, Pakistan, Portugal, Spain, South Korea, Taiwan and Thailand. Apart from Japan, all these operate fewer than twenty aircraft each.[19]

The new P-8A Poseidon uses the airframe and engines of the very successful Boeing 737 airliner and is assembled on the same production line to minimise the cost of development and ownership. Its IOC was achieved on time in 2013 and at the predicted cost. By 2016 the US Navy will have six P-8A squadrons in service, with more following at approximately six-monthly intervals. The programme of record calls for the eventual procurement of 117 aircraft. The type has the same AN/APY-10 radar as the P-3C update 4, accessed through an integrated, open-architecture system with 'glass' screens at every crew station including those of the pilots. Radar modes provide imaging, detection, classification of both ships and targets on land and the aircraft also has a passive, high-resolution electro-optical/infra-red camera; both active and passive sonobuoys; an AN/ALQ-213V electronic warfare management system and countermeasures dispensers. The P-8A can remain airborne for up to ten hours. To conserve fuel, it operates at up to 40,000ft and a new range of weapons and sonobuoys have been developed that can be dropped from this height, including the high-altitude anti-

An Indian Navy P-8I variant of the US Navy's P-8A Poseidon maritime patrol aircraft, which is steadily replacing the legacy P-3C Orion. *(Boeing)*

TABLE 8.6: 'HIGH END' MARITIME PATROL AIRCRAFT IN SERVICE 2015

AIRCRAFT:[1]	P-3C ORION	P-8A POSEIDON	BREGUET ATLANTIQUE 2	IL-38 'MAY'	TU-142M 'BEAR'	KAWASAKI P-1
Manufacturer:	Lockheed Martin	Boeing	SECBAT/Dassault	Ilyushin	Tupolev	Kawasaki
Country:	United States	United States	France[2]	Russia	Russia	Japan
Length:	35.6m	39.5m	31.7m	40.2m	49.5m	38.0m
Wingspan:	30.4m	37.6m	37.5m	37.4m	51.1m	35.4m
Max Take-off Weight:	63,000kg	86,000kg	46,000kg	66,000kg	188,000kg	80,000kg
Engines:[3]	4 x Allison T-56 A14 TP	2 x CFM56-7B TF	2 x RR Tyne Mk21 TP	4 x Ivchencko AI 20M TP	4 x Kuznetsov NK-12M TP	4 x IHI F7 TF
	3,700 Kw each	120 kN thrust each	4,500 Kw each	3,200 Kw each	11,000 Kw each	60 kN thrust each
Maximum Speed	410 knots (750km/h)	490 knots (900km/h)	350 knots (650km/h)	350 knots (650km/h)	500 knots (925km/h)	540 knots (1000km/h)
Max Altitude	28,000ft (8,500m)	41,000ft (12,500m)	30,000ft (9,100m)	36,000ft (11,000m)	44,000ft (13,500m)	44,000ft (13,500m)
Range	3 hours on station	4 hours on station	4 hours on station	4,000nm maximum	7,000nm maximum	4,300nm maximum
	1,350nm from base	1,200nm from base	1,500nm from base			
Endurance	16 hours	10.5 hours	18 hours	13 hours	17 hours	10 hours
Weapons	Total 9,000kg	Total 9,000kg	Total 9,000kg	Total 9,000kg	Total 20,000kg	AGM-56 Maverick
	AGM-65 Maverick	AGM-65 Maverick	AM39 Exocet	Freefall bombs	AS-17 Krypton	AGM-84D Harpoon
	AGM-84D Harpoon	AGM-84D Harpoon	GBU-12 LGB	Torpedoes	Torpedoes	ASM-IC
	AGM-84K SLAM ER	AGM-84K SLAM ER	MU-90 torpedoes	Depth charges & mines	Depth charges & mines	Torpedoes
	Mk 54 torpedoes	Mk 54 torpedoes	Depth charges & mines	2 x 23mm cannon	Depth charges & mines	
	Depth charges & mines	Depth charges & mines				
Crew	11	9	12	8	10	13
Number:	c.750 produced	117 planned for USN	28 produced	c.40–60 produced	c.100–225 produced	c.70 planned.
	c.120 operational USN	Up to 12 India	c.20 operational	c.30 operational Russia	c.25 operational	
	c.200 operational overseas	Up to 12 Australia		5 operational India		
		9 planned for UK				

Notes:

1 Data has been compiled from manufacturers' documentation and other publicly-available information. Due to considerable variations in published information, data should be regarded as indicative only. In particular, sources differ significantly on numbers of Russian MPAs produced.

2 Original Atlantic produced by a multi-national consortium.

3 TF = turbofan; TP = turboprop.

submarine warfare weapon capability (HAAWC), a Mk 54 torpedo modified with precision wing kits to allow it to glide over considerable distances. Similar, but smaller, wing kits are fitted to sonobuoys and, together, they allow the release of weapons and sonobuoys at considerably greater ranges from a target datum than a conventional low-level drop. The Poseidon has enjoyed early export success, with both India and Australia agreeing contracts for up to twelve aircraft each. The Australian P-8As will be virtually identical to the US Navy's aircraft but the Indian P-8I incudes Indian supplied electronics and a magnetic anomaly detector. In November 2015, it was announced that the United Kingdom would be the aircraft's fourth customer, with a planned purchase of nine for the RAF in place of the former Nimrods scrapped under the 2010 SDSR.

The increasing importance of UAVs is demon-

A French *Marine Nationale* Atlantique 2 (ATL-2) maritime patrol aircraft. Around fifteen of these will be maintained in service in the longer term. *(Dassault Aviation/C Cosmao)*

strated by the US Navy's broad area maritime surveillance system (BAMS), which has been evolved to complement the P-8A in US Navy service. The unmanned airborne element of this system is the Northrop Grumman MQ-4C Triton. The concept involves a succession of Tritons flying from forward operating bases (FOB), to orbits at up to 55,000 feet, searching large areas of ocean. The aircraft's key sensor is the AN/ZPY-3 multi-function radar with an active electronically-scanned array which has a number of modes capable of obtaining high-definition pictures of ships which can be compared with its on-board recognition archive and AIS. Images and identities are transmitted in near real time to a remote command centre in the United States and to task forces at sea. The MQ-4C is also fitted with an AN/ZLQ-1 ESM package with a 'library' of known radar emitters to provide target identity. Link 16 provides secure communications and the aircraft also carries communications relay equipment to facilitate secure communications between ships over extended distances. The MQ-4C flight path is autonomous but operators in the command centre select the orbit to be searched and the aircraft's height. Individual MQ-4C sorties can last for over twenty-four hours; the type has a fatigue life of 51,000 hours and airframes are capable of spending up to eighty per cent of their forward-deployed time airborne. The first unit, VUP-19 the 'Big Red', formed in 2013 at NAS Jacksonville, is expected to deploy its first detachment in late 2016 or early 2017. Australia has already committed to buying an undisclosed number of MQ-4Cs to complement its own P-8As.

The JMSDF also currently operates a large air fleet of over eighty P-3 Orions, largely built under licence in Japan. However, it is now procuring a Japanese-designed and built aircraft, the Kawasaki P-1, to replace them. The new aircraft is equipped with radar, electro-optical sensors, electronic warfare systems and sonobuoys of Japanese design but which are compatible with those of the USN. Like the P-8A, the P-1 can remain airborne for ten hours and it can carry a broad range of weapons including torpedoes, depth charges, mines, air-to-surface missiles and bombs.

Amongst other 'high-end' MPA operators, the Russian Navy continues to fly small numbers of MPAs that date from the last years of the Cold War, including the Ilyushin Il-28 'May', several of which have been upgraded with improved sensors under

the 'Sea Dragon' programme with new search radar and improved weapons. The Tupolev Tu-142M 'Bear' has been in service since 1972 and is used for very long-range ocean surveillance with an endurance of seventeen hours which can be extended by in-flight refuelling. Some have been upgraded to Tu-142J standard with an electronic intelligence system and VLF radio capable of communicating with submerged nuclear-powered ballistic-missile submarines. Tu-142s can carry up to eight AS-17 'Krypton' anti-shipping missiles on under-wing pylons as well as torpedoes, depth charges and bombs in an internal weapons bay. Elsewhere, the Breguet Atlantic (ATL-1) – originally developed to meet a NATO requirement – remains in service with the French *Aeronavale* as the modernised Atlantique 2 (ATL-2). Around twenty are currently operational and it is envisaged that fifteen will be further upgraded for extended service. They have a Thales Iguane multi-mode radar and an infra-red camera under the nose, vertical and oblique cameras and a Sadang acoustic data processing system that can monitor up to sixty-four sonobuoy channels simultaneously. Weapons, carried in a bomb bay and on underwing hard-points, include Exocet air-to-surface missiles, MU-90 torpedoes, depth charges, laser-guided bombs and mines. A handful of the original ATL-1 type also remain operational in Italy and Pakistan.[20]

In addition to these high-end MPAs, many navies and coastguards operate smaller aircraft with more limited capabilities, frequently in support of coast-guard type search and surveillance missions. Examples of this type include MPA variants of the Airbus CN-235 transport aircraft and the Brazilian Embraer EMB-145MP regional jet. Somewhere between the two types – offering greater weapons carrying potential but still suffering limitations in terms of range, speed or payload – are the stretched C-295 derivative of the CN-235, the ATR-72 ASW version of the Franco-Italian regional airliner and the proposed SAAB 2000 Swordfish MPA. It is possible that this compromise solution may prove attractive to some forces looking for a P-3 replacement but unable to justify the cost of transition to the P-8A.

CONCLUSIONS

Despite concerns over their cost, there seems little possibility that the US Navy will cease building nuclear-powered aircraft carriers in the foreseeable future. All new warships are expensive but the capa-

bility the CVN air wings give the United States to project power across the globe is just too important to relinquish easily in the foreseeable future. Elsewhere, big, flexible warships with a flight deck capable of operating STOVL fighters, tilt-rotors and helicopters have already been built for a number of medium-sized navies and such designs – including the upgrade or replacement of existing ships – is likely to be an area of increased interest in future.

Several navies have operated warships together as a coalition in this century and, now that they are used to working together, it is possible that aircraft will embark regularly on allied carriers as part of a fully integrated task force. French Rafales have occasionally embarked in US Navy carriers, for instance. It is very likely that USMC and Italian Navy F-35s will be seen on *Queen Elizabeth*'s flight deck after 2020.

Unmanned combat air vehicles have already shown their potential for surveillance operations but it remains to be seen how they will be integrated with manned aircraft on strike operations. They are unlikely to be cheap to procure but will not need the kind of human continuation training that manned aircraft require. Definition of the way forward for the US navy's proposed RAQ-25A is proving more difficult than first thought but – by the end of the present decade – its relationship with manned strike fighters should be clarified. It is sobering to think that, by then, the F-35C selected for development in 2001 will only just be coming into operational service with the US Navy after nearly two decades of development. It may, or may not, be the last manned carrier-borne fighter but by then its value in the network-enabled, digital battle-space will be better understood, as will its relationship with unmanned systems that were not even thought of when it was specified. The new generation of MPAs and sea control helicopters are unlikely to be replaced in the next two decades but will undergo a series of spiral developments to keep them effective.

As Western navies concentrate on high-technology systems with very high price-tags, however, it must not be forgotten that there will come a point where no matter how sophisticated, reliable and effective a weapons system is in isolation, it will always be vulnerable to low-technology opponents deployed in large numbers. The potential use of 'swarms' of relatively simple manned and unmanned systems to overwhelm high-technology opponents in littoral operations is an aspect of warfare worth watching out for in the years ahead.[21]

Notes

1. It is quite difficult to make accurate cost comparisons between different members of the *Ford* class given the impact of inflation over a lengthy construction period. For example, the US$12.9bn of cash outlays expended on *Gerald R. Ford* between 2001 and 2016 have been estimated as equating to around US$14.7bn in '2015 money' when adjusted for inflation. Similarly, the second ship of the class, *John F. Kennedy*, is expected to cost US$11.5bn in cash terms between 2007 and completion but this translates into 'only' US$10.6bn at 2015 prices. None of these figures take into account a further US$4.7bn of research and development costs that apply to the entire class. Much greater detail on this is provided in Ronald O' Rourke's regularly updated *Navy Ford (CVN-78) Class Aircraft Carrier Program: Background and Issues for Congress RS20643* (Washington DC: Congressional Research Service).

2. For example, Senator McCain, Chairman of the Senate Armed Services Committee, a previous Republican party nominee for the United States presidency and a former naval aviator, has been a frequent critic of *Gerald R. Ford*'s cost growth, stating that he 'fully expects the study of alternative aircraft carrier designs to provide real options'.

3. The rejection of the CVV concept was reflected in the ultimate vetoing of various STOVL carrier design proposals from the same era. These originated in the Sea Control Ship (SCS) that emerged from Admiral Elmo Zumwalt's 'high-low' force concept of the early 1970s and were later developed into various VSTOL support ship (VSS) designs for combined jump jet and helicopter operation. Although the US Navy eventually decided that these ships did not represent good value for money, the basic SCS design was sold to the Spanish Navy, which completed *Príncipe de Asturias* at Ferrol in 1988. The Thai *Chakri Naruebet* is also derived from this design.

4. The US Navy is currently required by law to retain a set number of operational aircraft carriers but this number is steadily falling. The requirement was first established by the FY2006 National Defense Authorization Act, which set the total at twelve ships. The number was soon reduced to eleven carriers. Subsequently, the FY2010 National Defense Authorization Act permitted a temporary reduction to ten ships between the decommissioning of *Enterprise* (CVN-65) and the delivery of *Gerald R. Ford*.

5. It is interesting to speculate whether a design based on the British *Queen Elizabeth* at 65,000 tons, with a requirement for manpower only around a quarter of that of the *Gerald R. Ford,* would have been attractive to the US Navy study if the option to complete the British ship with catapults and arrester wires had been taken forward.

6. A good overview of the past and possible future development of US Navy CVW structures is provided by David Barno, Nora Bensahel and M. Thomas Davis in *White Paper: The Carrier Air Wing of the Future* (Washington DC: Center for a New American Security, February 2014).

7. The 'C' and 'D' designations relating to the Hornet and the 'E' and 'F' designations relating to the Super Hornet refer to whether the aircraft are, respectively, single seat of two seat variants. As of the end of 2015, all Hornet squadrons in the CVW squadrons are believed to be 'C' variants.

8. Naval interest has centred on a specialised surveillance platform with some strike capability but Congress felt that, with a number of other new surveillance assets entering operational service, a long-range strike platform capable of the deep penetration of hostile airspace and the suppression or destruction of enemy air defences represented a more pressing requirement.

9. *Vikrant* – perhaps uniquely – has been launched three times to date. She was first floated out in December 2011 to free the dock for other work as her propulsion train was not complete. Formal launch took place on 12 August 2013. However, she was subsequently re-docked for further work on shaft lines and other underwater equipment before being floated out for a third time in June 2015.

10. DCNS quoted a construction cost for PA-2 that was less than the estimated cost of modifying *Queen Elizabeth* to take wires and catapults, demonstrating the importance of planning what you want at the outset.

11. There have been unconfirmed reports that structural defects have been found during this inspection. See Victor Barreira's '"Cracks found" in Brazil's aircraft carrier', *Janes's Defence Weekly* – 11 November 2015 (Coulsdon: IHS Jane's, 2015).

12. By 2012 the Alliance estimated that the cost of modifying *Prince of Wales*, on which fabrication had actually commenced, would be over £2bn compared with an initial expectation of c.£950m in 2010. Any subsequent reconfiguration of a completed *Queen Elizabeth* would be considerably more, perhaps as much as £4bn according to some commentators or more than the original cost of the ship. The reasons for these 'eye-watering' estimates were never explained in detail but may have had much to do with the need to generate – and route – the huge amounts of power required to make EMALS workable and the need for space to install AAG into a design that was not designed for it.

13. The question of characterisation is further complicated by the new JMSDF helicopter-carrying destroyers *Izumo* (DDH-183) and *Kaga* (DDH-184). Derived from the earlier *Hyuga* (DDH-181) class, they are large ships at 27,000 tons, comparable in size with the Italian aircraft carrier *Cavour* and significantly larger than the recently-retired British *Invincible* class. Their primary roles are anti-submarine warfare and humanitarian aid/disaster relief with a nominal air wing of fourteen anti-submarine and minehunting helicopters but could deploy the MV-22B Osprey tiltrotors that the Ground Self Defence Force has already ordered in an amphibious role. Future purchases of F-35B STOVL strike fighters can also not be ruled out as Japan slowly dismantles constitutional impediments to expeditionary warfare.

14. A further fifteen F-35Bs will be acquired by the Italian Air Force. It is possible that some form of joint operating arrangement with the Italian Navy's aircraft similar to that agreed for the United Kingdom's F-35s will be agreed.

15. Greater detail on the current status of the F-35 programme is provided in Jeremiah Gertler's periodically updated *F-35 Joint Strike Fighter Program RL30563* (Washington DC: Congressional Research Service).

16. Amongst other sea control helicopters in production, the CH-148 Cyclone developed from the S-92 by Lockheed Martin's Sikorsky division for Canada has suffered significant development problems. Production is therefore unlikely to extend beyond the twenty-eight units already on order.

17. The US Navy has a requirement for c.300 of the latest MH-60R variant sea control helicopter in addition to around 275 of the MH-60S utility version as it seeks to standardise helicopter types. Among recent export customers, Australia began to stand-up two squadrons to operate the MH-60R in 2014 following a decision to buy twenty-four to replace legacy Sea Hawks in 2011. Denmark has ordered also nine MH-60Rs and Saudi Arabia is reportedly looking to acquire ten, whilst India has purchased sixteen upgraded versions of the older S-90B. NFH 'frigate' variants of the NH-90 – built by the Airbus controlled NH Industries – are being delivered to seven countries, which have made commitments for over 130 units. The anti-submarine variant of the AW-101 is only operated by Italy and the United Kingdom, the latter currently upgrading thirty helicopters to an improved HM 2 standard. However, utility variants have been acquired by more than ten countries.

18. A large number of navies are looking at UAVs capable of operation from ships other than aircraft carriers, particularly for long-endurance surveillance. Some of these would appear to be similar in size and capability to the MQ-8C; for example the British MOD has awarded AgustaWestland a contract to evaluate the possible development of a future optionally manned/unmanned helicopter to operate alongside the Merlin and Wildcat. More popular are smaller types such as the Schiebel Camcopter S-100 rotorcraft – which has been tested by several European navies – and American fixed-wing designs such as the Boeing Insitu RQ-21 Blackjack and the smaller ScanEagle. Both the latter UAVs have seen considerable use with the US Navy and the RN is deploying a small number of ScanEagle detachments to frigates and auxiliaries operating in the Gulf. They are provided under a 'contractor owned and operated' deal and deployed by 700X NAS, which provides a safety officer trained to operate the vehicle from a console in the ship's operations room. Weighing only 21.7kg (48lbs), the air vehicle has an EO900 electro-optical/infra-red camera which can provide real-time images of shipping for up to eighteen hours. It is launched from a portable pneumatic catapult on the flight deck and recovered by being flown into a vertical wire attached to the launcher, engaging it with hooks fitted to its wingtips.

19. More information on the venerable P-3 – including regularly updated lists on fleet status – is contained in the P-3 Orion Research Group's website at: http://www.p3 orion.nl/index.html

20. Much greater detail on current 'high end' MPA types was provided in the author's 'World Naval Aviation: An Overview of Recent Developments' in *Seaforth World Naval Review 2016* (Barnsley: Seaforth Publishing, 2015) pp.154–74.

21. In this regard, experiments by the British RN in the use of simple 3D printed drones devised by Southampton University may be an interesting sign of things to come.

A major uncertainty with respect to the future of naval aviation is the role of unmanned aerial vehicles. UAVs have already shown their potential for surveillance missions but the extent they will be integrated with manned aircraft for strike operations remains a matter of conjecture. The US Navy intends to pair Fire Scout unmanned aerial vehicles with conventional manned MH-60R helicopters (top image) in operations from surface ships, maximising the strengths of each type. The new Littoral Combat Ship *Fort Worth* (LCS-3) carried out an early trial of the operating concept in 2015. Meanwhile, he Northrop Grumman-designed X-47B test aircraft has carried out successful take-offs and landings from a carrier at sea but the way forward for the planned operational unmanned carrier-launched air surveillance and strike System (UCLASS) is unclear. *(US Navy/Northrop Grumman)*

9.0:

Philip Grove

NAVAL MANNING

Naval manpower is the single most important factor in ensuring an efficient and capable navy. Without sufficiently technical and appropriately-numbered personnel, a naval service cannot function effectively, no matter what the sophistication of its vessels or air assets. Yet in the last half of the twentieth century manning levels and the calibre of men within the services often resulted in a somewhat schizophrenic attitude amongst many senior naval officers. Consequently major problems in performance during both training and in wartime conditions were experienced by most navies. This schizophrenia was especially bad at times of national economic hardship, when senior officers saw manpower as a plentiful source and not one to unduly worry them. In theory at least. On the one hand senior officers were often quoted lecturing new recruits as representing the key cornerstone of their navy, whilst on the other when problems arose with the retention of personnel there was an easy solution in simply recruiting more! Little thought was given to the issues of retaining the already-trained and performing personnel.

In the twenty-first century manning and manpower have been treated differently. This has been a necessary consequence of a series of significant economic, technological, political and social changes since the end of the Cold War. Before the end of 1989 and the collapse of the Berlin Wall, the navies of much of the world were tasked very differently to today. Moreover their composition differed very markedly from the naval services of the last few decades. For many navies conscription had provided the bulk of their available manpower – and this was almost wholly dominated by male recruits. What female personnel existed normally found themselves in shoreside billets, performing auxiliary tasks. The sea, as it had been for centuries, was very much a male domain. Conscription, the draft or national service as various nations termed it created large manning levels but often of low-performing and technically less capable personnel, usually with little knowledge of the wider world and even less of the importance of naval power. Conscription also varied in duration: from as little as nine months in the case of some navies to as much as six years in others, though the norm was usually two years. Professionalism was correspondingly low, with some navies having less than a fifth of their manpower levels made up of full-time volunteers. Training was rudimentary in many services and the ability of personnel to perform different jobs in a working environment was far from guaranteed. Essentially the civilian was drilled out but only the most basic of maritime skills drilled in. Then again, many navies in the world only performed mundane roles often solely involved with patrolling territorial waters, with day running as standard behaviour and little exposure to the more varied and demanding roles of a large, balanced ocean going fleet.

Even if a naval service belonged to one of the two main coalitions of the Cold War, the situation might not be much better. Although training here was somewhat different and, arguably, far more thorough, much of it was training for a war in the North Atlantic that was considered unrealistic by many and one that neither side could arguably win. Consequently deficiencies persisted. For example, at times only a modicum of interest was paid to training for critical roles, such as ship damage control.[1] The Royal Navy endured this situation during the Falklands War and experienced the repercussions of this failure at first hand. The Boards of Inquiry that were held following the sinking of four of their escorts during the campaign highlighted training as a significant factor and one in need of rectifying.[2] Vigorous improvements were subsequently implemented to the Royal Navy's Flag Officer Sea Training (FOST) command, originally established as far back

The Royal Canadian Navy frigates *Charlottetown* (foreground) and *Montreal* on an anti-submarine exercise in the North Atlantic in the autumn of 2010. Much training by the major navies during the Cold War was focused on North Atlantic scenarios, leading to deficiencies in other areas. *(Royal Canadian Navy)*

TABLE 9.1: TRENDS IN FLEET PERSONNEL NUMBERS

COUNTRY	1990	1995	2005	2015	OBSERVATIONS
Brazil	50.000	47,000	51,000	c.60,000	Conscription in place throughout. Currently 1 year. Includes c.15k marines.
China	c.300,000	265,000	250,000	235,000	Conscription in place throughout. Currently 2/3 years.
France	67,000	64,000	43,000	32,000	Conscription ended 2001. Excludes deployed civilian employees.
India	52,000	55,000	57,000	58,000	All volunteer.
Japan	46,000	46,000	46,000	45000	All volunteer. Excludes civilian employees.
United Kingdom	63,000	51,000	40,000	33,000	All volunteer. Trained personnel in 2015 c.30,000, including 7,000 RM.
United States - USN	609,000	454,000	366,000	324,000	All volunteer.
United States – USMC	197,000	175,000	178,000	184,000	All volunteer.

Notes:

Data drawn from government statistics and supplemented by published data. Due to significant variations in information and statistical processes, data should only be regarded as indicative and figures are also not fully comparable between navies.

Although naval manpower has been declining globally since the end of the Cold War, the trend is less apparent in many emergent navies. There are plenty of sailors evident in this image of China's Type 052B destroyer *Guangzhou*, pictured on a goodwill visit to Portsmouth UK in 2007. *(Conrad Waters)*

as 1958 but which had previously been more interested in the warfighting aspect of ships than their survival. The changes that were made have subsequently paid significant dividends, notably when the ships *Nottingham* and *Endurance* were both saved from sinking due to the training received by their crews.[3] This change has not just benefitted the Royal Navy, as the last decades have seen many other navies receive training from the FOST organisation, the majority returning for further instruction.

The improvement in damage control training is just one example of a number of revolutionary changes over the past twenty-five years that have impacted the ways navies recruit, educate and deploy their manpower. More specifically:

- Manning levels have generally diminished, but with lower numbers of personnel being balanced by these being typically more capable and adaptable than their predecessors.
- This change is reflected in generally heightened education levels amongst sailors as navies pursue a better and longer return from their recruits in comparison to the more limited return achieved from an average conscript of one or two years' service.
- The quota of women within naval services has drastically increased. Moreover, they have become an integral part of the front-line seagoing strength in many fleets around the globe. In some navies, female personnel now make up to a sixth of the overall strength.

Of the changes, the key trend amongst most navies has been a downsizing of personnel strength. For most of the Cold War, cheap and plentiful conscripts fuelled much of the military machinery of East and West, as well as almost all of the non-aligned world. However, since the early 1990s, naval manpower strengths have mostly diminished due to a series of reasons, the most important of which are highlighted below. Whilst the trend has been largely universal, there are a small number of fleets that have bucked it, as evidenced by Table 9.1.

THE IMPACT OF FLEET MODERNISATION

Since the end of the twentieth century, mass modernisation and reconfiguration of navies has taken place around the world. In North America and Western Europe, this rejuvenation has resulted in

TABLE 9.2: TRENDS IN SHIP COMPLEMENTS

COUNTRY	SHIP TYPE[1]	1960s–1970s		1980s–1990s		2000–CURRENT	
United States	Surface Escort (Destroyer)	Spruance (DD-963)	c.330	Burke (DDG-51)	c.300	Zumwalt (DDG-1000)	c.150
United States	Surface Escort (Frigate)	Knox (FF-1052)	c.260	Perry (FFG-7)	c.220	Freedom (LCS-1)	c.50+25[2]
United Kingdom	Surface Escort (Destroyer)	Type 82	c.400	Type 42 – B3	c.300	Type 45	c.190
United Kingdom	Surface Escort (Frigate)	Leander	c.260	Type 23	c.180	Type 26	c.120
France	Surface Escort (1st Rate Escort)	F-67 Tourville	c.300	FASM-70 G Leygues	c.240	Aquitaine (FREMM)	c.110
India	Surface Escort (Destroyer)	Raijput[3]	c.320	Project 15 Delhi	c.350	Project 15A Kolkata	c.325
India	Surface Escort (Frigate)	Nilgiri/Leander	c.260	Project 16 Godavari	c.310	Project 17 Shivalik	c.260

Notes:

1 The table is intended to give a broad indication of general trends in warship crew numbers, acknowledging the significant differences that can exist in the size, function and capability of ships within a common heading.

2 The US Navy's LCSs deploy with a core crew plus an additional, mission-specific crew.

newer, more technologically-evolved navies but has often come with a penalty in terms of fleet size. This is because an almost continual increase in costs has resulted in fewer, if larger and more capable, platforms entering service.[4]

Additionally, whilst modern technology incorporated within these new ships encompasses vast advances in weaponry and sensors compared to their Cold War counterparts, automation has also facilitated smaller manpower establishments onboard. The introduction of labour-saving devices has been ongoing for a long time but the pace of acceptance – and the resultant reduction in manning levels

achieved – have accelerated since the start of the century. Most notably, units such as the US Navy's littoral combat ships have a core crew sized at a third or less of those they replace. Over 300 personnel have been saved as a result of the introduction of the much-publicised automated weapons handling system in the British Royal Navy's Queen Elizabeth class aircraft carriers. Table 9.2 provides a broad indication of falling crew sizes from the 1970s to the present day in different classes of naval vessel.

The resultant reduction in overall numbers of sailors has not been a universal one, as some emergent navies – which are also undergoing large

modernisation programmes – have been expanding their manning levels at the same time as growing their physical assets. The need to allow for adequate support ashore to accommodate demands resulting from enhanced technology not encountered before has probably been as important as the requirement for personnel at sea in these fleets.[5] The fact that many of these fleets benefit from manpower costs that are cheaper than those faced by the more mature navies also partly explains this exception, although even some developing fleets are now suffering from wage inflation as economic growth fuels labour costs in the broader market.[6]

Significant reductions in overall naval manning have been achieved by the increased use of automation to reduce warship crew sizes. These images show three generations of US Navy frigate-sized vessels, the Mexican Navy's Knox class Mina – formerly Whipple (FF-1062) – first commissioned in 1970; the 1980's era Perry class frigate Rodney M. Davis (FFG-60) and the LCS Fort Worth (LCS-3), delivered in 2012. Over this period complement has shrunk from around 260 to a core of just fifty in the new LCS. (US Navy)

QUANTITY V QUALITY

Conversely, a need to control manpower costs has often been a key concern amongst the established fleets. This is a particular consideration in a comparatively highly paid, all-volunteer force. Equally, there is a recognition that the more highly educated and trained crew that a volunteer force allows means that sailors can multi-task between different functions in a way that would have been inconceivable to many of their conscript forbears. In effect, the ending of conscription by a number of navies over the last two decades has substantially reduced their manning levels, but provided a consequent increase in the skill base of the remaining recruits. The benefits of this are covered in more detail later.

FINANCIAL PRESSURES

Financial issues have also made an impact on personnel numbers. Almost all North American and European militaries considerably shrank with the ending of the Cold War and the imposition of the 'peace dividend' by government treasuries across the Atlantic Alliance. Navies were not immune to the process with both manpower and procurement being reduced. Sometimes this process was carried out far from efficiently, with simultaneous redundancy of experienced personnel and curtailment of new recruitment subsequently creating a series of manning shortfalls in specific areas, often those requiring highly technical skills.[7]

Heavy reductions in personnel were also seen as a necessary, if knee-jerk, reaction to a worrying trend that became apparent at the end of the Cold War of (reduced) defence budgets being swallowed up by personnel expenditures. For instance, in 1990 almost fifty per cent of the United Kingdom's defence budget went on pay and pensions compared with less than forty per cent today. For some countries, the equivalent figure was (and sometimes still is) as much as eighty or even ninety per cent of the total defence budget, naturally having a massive detrimental impact upon platforms, training, deployments and procurement. The fact that procurement costs themselves are under pressure has added to the impetus to achieve personnel savings.

CONSEQUENCES OF LEAN MANNING

Though manpower savings have been achieved, serious questions have been raised by a number of commentators and naval personnel about the effectiveness of ships with reduced complements, partic-

A damage-control party fighting a simulated fire on the US Navy aircraft carrier *Harry S. Truman* (CVN-75). There are concerns that the lean-manning practices increasingly adopted in modern warships will hamper effective damage control. *(US Navy)*

ularly in scenarios such as damage control and the conduct of humanitarian missions. The key area of damage control, whether in wartime or peacetime, requires 'spare capacity' in terms of adequately-trained personnel to deal with the emergency that may have arisen. Naturally, this is a much easier task for a ship with a complement that numbers in the hundreds rather than one of a hundred or less.[8]

Moreover, navies are often at the forefront of a nation's disaster response, using vessels involved in deployed missions such as anti-piracy, anti-terrorist and drug interdiction to facilitate a fast reaction to a crisis overseas. Naval assets are able to access the vast majority of the world's population centres and are sometimes the only platforms able to do so if destroyed land bases, airfields and infrastructure deny other forms of response. This was clearly demonstrated in the December 2004 and March 2011 tsunamis in the Indian Ocean and off Japan. However, this inherent flexibility could well be curtailed if the small crew complements increasingly seen meant few personnel could be spared to assist a response. One counter to this has been building ships – the US Navy's Littoral Combat Ship and

French *Aquitaine* FREMM frigates are examples – that combine small crews with the surplus accommodation to surge specialised personnel should this be desirable.

CHANGES IN NAVAL AVIATION

Naval vessels have not been the only fleet areas to experience manning adjustments, with naval aviation also seeing considerable manpower changes. Cost considerations, such as the expense involved in the training and maintenance of extra aircrew, together with technological developments, have helped to reduce the numbers of aircraft in many of the world's fleets and simultaneously lower aircrew strengths. However, once again, certain emergent naval powers, notably China and India, have been increasing the numbers and quality of their naval air assets.

Superficially, fixed-wing naval aviation has changed little since the end of the Cold War, with manned aircraft still employed as a key power-projection tool. Interest in carrier aviation has grown, with a number of new nations aspiring to join the carrier club. However, the most significant development has been alteration to aviator force structures amongst the existing members to achieve greater efficiency. For instance, in America the US Navy and US Marine Corps are replacing the four-seat Grumman EA-6B Prowlers used in the suppression of enemy air defences with two-seat F-18G Growlers.

However, it is, perhaps, the Joint Strike Fighter programme that has raised the most eyebrows, as there will be no twin-seat F-35s as a result of both cost and engineering considerations. Potential training issues arising from this will be resolved through increased use of training simulators and other platforms. In combat, the solitary pilot will be well supported by the new onboard systems, in theory eradicating the need for a backseat weapons operator. This is not totally ground-breaking, as the French Navy has followed a similar path with their Rafale M. Today the *Aeronavale* pilots operate alongside their *Armee de l'Air* counterparts (who maintain a considerable fleet of two-seater Rafales) and the US Navy for much of their training. Arguments about complexity and information overload have now been largely set aside due to the operational success of the Rafale's sophisticated systems, which have been proven in combat over Afghanistan, Libya, Iraq and Syria.

Crew numbers in naval helicopters have changed slightly but not fundamentally. When a Wessex crew is compared to a Sea King's, and the latter's to a Merlin or NH-90 there is little to choose. However, the numbers of machines in a service have decreased considerably since the Cold War as technology has created far greater capability from the assets remaining. For instance an entire squadron of Sea King ASW platforms would have been needed to close the English Channel whereas only one (possibly two) Merlin HM 1 helicopters would be required. The modernised HM 2 is even more capable and numbers are falling again. There has therefore been a diminishing number of ASW squadrons in most naval arms, though with something of a balancing increase amongst developing navies, who are acquiring this capability for the first time. Land-based maritime patrol aircraft have also seen some manpower reductions. Whilst in America and much of the world the P-3C Orion operates with a crew of eleven or twelve, its replacement in the form of the P-8A Poseidon operates with just nine. The growing number of twin turboprop 'lower end' patrol aircraft have even fewer.

However, it is the growing introduction of unmanned air vehicles (UAVs) that has presented the most questions, with many yet to be answered adequately. Do UAVs save manning and manpower costs or not? What are the challenges in terms of their running costs and growing complexity? Many believed in the 1990s that UAVs would be cheaper to procure and operate than conventionally, manned planes. Additionally, the loss of an UAV was thought to be potentially less troubling to governments due to the omission of a flight crew and a consequent lack of personnel to fall into enemy captivity or be killed. It was therefore thought that they offered both financial and political advantages.

Today, however, it seems UAVs and the more offensively-focused unmanned combat air vehicles (UCAVs) are as complex, if not more so, than their manned counterparts and are consequently as expensive. The United States' X-47 programme has achieved a number of notable firsts on board US Navy carriers but its follow-on programme is mired in uncertainty. European programmes such as the BAE Systems' Taranis technology demonstrator may show Europe's thinking on possible carrier-based UCAVs in the future but these are still in the early stages of development. To date, it seems that manpower savings from the current generation of unmanned vehicles is minimal as aircrew are still needed, even if they now more closely resemble teenage gamers rather than the pilots of old. Also, the increasingly sophisticated machines still need maintainers to keep them flying. UAVs have already found roles in fixed-wing and maritime patrol operations, such as the broad area maritime surveillance role envisaged for the US Navy's MQ-4C Tritons. However, they are often finding themselves flying alongside manned platforms rather than entirely replacing them, potentially placing further demands on manpower. Finally, UCAV operations have not given politicians the 'easy ride' that was initially envisaged given adverse publicity over 'killer drones'.

A NEW BREED OF SAILOR

As well as changes in technology, personnel have also greatly changed. The end of conscription for many now sees navies welcoming new recruits who possess a desire to be there rather than merely being sent. This brings dividends in terms of training and

A trend towards single-seat naval fast jets is changing aviator force structures amongst members of the 'carrier club'. France's *Marine Nationale* has now moved to this operating model, with all its navalised Rafale Ms ordered in single-seat configuration. Here a pilot awaits the catapult launch of his Rafale from the deck of *Charles de Gaulle* in May 2013. *(Dassault Aviation/S Fort)*

behaviour on the part of naval manpower. Their ability to assimilate information and perform in the working environment is greatly improved, with loyalty and efficiency materially enhanced. To ensure this continues navies have to remain capable of attracting the most skilled in the working population and retain them upon completion of initial training. Conditions, pay and incentives to remain have therefore improved throughout many navies. A number of services have also lengthened the term of enlistments to retain consistency and continuity. This has been particularly true for senior non-commissioned and commissioned personnel, maintaining a more experienced and professional manpower pool.

There has also been a realisation that it might be better to recruit younger sailors. This reverses the trend of the later Cold War years, when many believed that older, more experienced and better educated personnel would be advantageous. Less need for training and education, together with a worldly-wise attitude, was seen as being beneficial to navies. This view has now been challenged and – although there will be always a place for the latter type of individual – the need for younger, more malleable personnel who are able and willing to provide a long period of service is seen as an important requirement. Besides a greater return of service, together with more successful indoctrination, there is a recognition that, with the greater complexity of today's platforms and systems, a younger, more dextrous mind is needed.

Moreover, this technical dexterity needs to be complemented by a more knowledgeable recruit with an appreciation of the world they are operating in and, perhaps more importantly, why they are doing so. Consequently there has been an expansion in the education processes of many navies beyond the accepted technical realm – especially in political science, history, ethos and the culture of their service – to create a better understanding of why they do what they do. It is critically important for navies to educate their own personnel to the highest standards so they can think more laterally than their Cold War predecessors, who sometimes suffered from tunnel vision in their appreciation of naval power, and lost track of its many attributes. A thinking body of naval manpower is more likely to be successful not just in performing its many and varied duties but also in articulating the case of naval power to the political decision makers and purse-string holders. In doing

Sailors aboard the US Navy LCS *Fort Worth* (LCS-3) prepare to launch a MQ-8B Fire Scout UAV during an Asian deployment in 2015. Although seemingly offering manpower savings, UAVs still need to be flown and maintained. *(US Navy)*

so, they are more likely to ensure their service's future rather than reactively relying on an existence brought about by a known threat, as in the Cold War.

AN INTERNATIONAL OUTLOOK

A final trend that warrants discussion is the significant expansion in the international experience and outlook of personnel serving in navies across the globe. For all but the largest fleets, operations and training during the Cold War were increasingly focused upon a scenario centred in the Atlantic and dominated by submarine activity, notwithstanding the publication of the US Maritime Strategy of the 1980s. Experiences since 1989 have been drastically different and vastly more numerous due to the actual deployment of navies since the end of the Cold War on a range of 'live' operations resulting from a more unstable and less predictable international environment. Since 1989 navies have found themselves serving globally in a series of wars and interventions such as the liberation of Kuwait, the Balkans struggles, East Timor, Sierra Leone, Afghanistan, Iraq, Libya, and against Islamic State.

The willingness of governments to employ naval power as a 'first responder' to situations and often as the key and sometimes sole instrument to the emergent crises has brought considerable benefits to institutional learning.

Interventions have also witnessed the rise of international coalitions and this has also brought further dividends for today's naval personnel. Working alongside other navies, and not just neighbours and alliance partners but extra-regional and global powers, has deepened the experiences of many, particularly for what are termed developing navies. Training changes have had to be made, staff work improved and the complexity of coalition warfare and deployments understood. This is not just the case for western alliance nations. The wars on terrorism and piracy in the Indian Ocean and Arabian Sea extend worldwide to encompass South East Asia, the waters off West Africa and even on the Amazon Basin. Drug interdiction in the Caribbean involves local forces, the US Coastguard and three European navies.

In simple terms this has been fed back into the

training of new and existing manpower, where the bonuses of being trained and educated by personnel who have been on active deployments bring benefits beyond the previous theoretical knowledge imparted by many in the past. In contrast with the situation prior to 1989 and a situation where few navies had experienced real-life operations and actual combat scenarios, these opportunities have now become plentiful and commonplace. More importantly, international deployments are being experienced by navies beyond the traditional global 'blue-water' fleets such as the US Navy, British Royal Navy and French *Marine Nationale*. Today most European navies – and many in Asia – have deployed on counter terrorism, anti-piracy, peace enforcement, drug interdiction and even actual war alongside each other and far away from home. Others in Africa and Latin America have also experienced deployments far in excess of what they would normally have experienced in the decades after the Second World War, deepening the expertise of their naval personnel.

CONCLUSIONS

The changes in naval manning since the end of the Cold War have been many and profound. The decreases in manpower levels partly brought about by the end of conscription but also as a result of financial pressures and the growing process of automation have resulted in a growth in professionalism and individual effectiveness. The creation of professional forces has also been broadened by the arrival of female personnel in the frontline with most western nations allowing women onboard ships from the 1990s, and subsequently into air assets and even submarines.[9] These trends, combined with the growing use of naval power globally, has seen a deepening in the knowledge base and expertise of the personnel which has been fed back into new recruits. The likelihood of deployments decreasing in intensity in the years ahead is minimal. As such, it seems the experience of the world navies will continue to broaden.

There have been some developments which have bucked these general trends. Numerically, many of the world's naval infantry units, normally marines, have either remained static or actually increased over years. This has resulted from the desire of many nations wishing to develop capabilities to project power from the sea in greater strength than hitherto, possibly reflecting the increased importance of the

A Royal Navy engineering electrical technician manning a console in the ship control centre of the Type 45 destroyer *Diamond*. The greater complexity of today's warships means that technical dexterity is a key requirement of today's sailors, although a broader appreciation of the world is needed as well. *(Crown Copyright 2013)*

A boarding party from the Royal Norwegian Navy frigate *Fridtjof Nansen* inspecting a fishing boat off the coast of Somalia in the course of anti-piracy operations in 2013. Experience of international operations is now extending beyond the traditional blue-water fleets. *(Royal Norwegian Navy)*

The demands on sailors and marines from major land-based commitments have resulted in many gaining new experience and skills, for example in riverine patrolling. This image shows US personnel assigned to Riverine Squadron (RIVRON) 1 undergoing pre-deployment training in 2012. *(US Navy)*

littoral. Moreover the demands placed upon these troops from major land-based commitments – often linked to the so-called 'War on Terror' – have brought new experiences and skills for many, particularly with respect to riverine patrolling and counter insurgency. Other naval services have seen broader growth, usually due to the perception of greater regional threats such as those faced by the navies of Vietnam and the Philippines. Others still have grown as a result of peculiarly internal factors such as the Bolivian Navy, expanding in 2014–15 by an extra 2,500 personnel.[10]

Fundamentally naval manning has dramatically changed since 1989 in terms both of numbers and skill base. This trend is likely to continue as the demands placed upon naval power and the importance attached to the seas increases in the 'maritime century'.

Notes

1. In fairness, this was an understandable position in that it seemed pointless in investing limited resources in building ships that could survive attacks together with crews that were trained in dealing with any contingency when the rest of the world was plummeting into a nuclear abyss.

2. The Boards, held in the summer of 1982, highlighted a number of factors, such as poor damage-control equipment and large-scale use of non-fire retardant materials in addition to deficiencies in damage-control training.

3. On 7 July 2002, the Type 42 destroyer *Nottingham* ran aground on Wolf Rock near Lord Howe Island between Australia and New Zealand. Although five compartments were flooded from a c.50m-long breach to the hull, she was kept afloat and ultimately repaired. On 16 December 2008, the ice patrol ship *Endurance* was saved from sinking after suffering an engine-room flood whilst transiting the Straits of Magellan. Although returned to the United Kingdom, she has not been repaired.

4. For example, the Franco-Italian 'Horizon' and associated British Royal Navy Type 45 air-defence destroyer programmes ultimately delivered only around a half of the units initially envisaged. The US Navy's *Zumwalt* (DDG-1000) destroyer programme saw even more radical

curtailment as a consequence of ballooning costs.

5. Interestingly a number of more-established navies have transferred some of their maintenance work that was previously carried out by service personnel to contractors, either the initial providers of the platform or third-party contractors, in an attempt to save costs and service manpower levels.

6. There have been ongoing reports in India that steadily rising personnel costs are starting to distort the overall defence budget. Amongst recent commentaries on this problem is Laxman Kumar Behera's *ISDA Issue Brief: India's Defence Budget 2015-16* (New Delhi: Institute for Defence Studies & Analyses, 2015).

7. For example, in May 1994, only sixty 'Young Officers' joined Britannia Royal Naval College as opposed to the normal 100–120. Of those sixty some twenty were from allied navies, twenty were long-time senior rates from within the service, whilst a further ten were short-term junior rates. Only ten were new recruits for the service.

8. A number of technological innovations have been devised to help alleviate this problem, such as the use of personal organisers to alert crew to potential system and damage control issues in the Dutch *Holland* class OPVs.

Nevertheless, there are a number of indications that the trend toward lean manning may have been pushed too far. A widely-reported Government Accountability Office report on the minimally-manned US Navy LCS *Freedom*'s inaugural overseas mission suggested that the crew struggled to get adequate sleep in spite of assistance from specialised mission module personnel embarked for the deployment and from outside contractors. See *Deployment of USS Freedom Revealed Risks in Implementing Operational Concepts and Uncertain Costs GAO-14-447* published by the Government Accountability Office, Washington DC, in July 2014.

9. The Royal Navy's first front-line female crew members deployed in the summer of 1990, with the first female submariners successfully passing their courses in 2014. The US Navy began their first female submariner training in 2015. However, Scandinavian countries have been at the forefront of women in front-line naval posts with Norway deploying its first women in submarines as far back as 1995.

10. This is not a bad increase for a land-locked nation, though the reason was purely to raise pressure on Chile to return the northern Bolivian territories lost in the War of the Pacific (1879–83) and thereby regain direct access to the world's oceans.

GLOSSARY

A2/AD: Anti-Access/Area-Denial. Strategies adopted by countries such as China and Iran to counter potential US Navy expeditionary (q.v.) operations in their littoral (q.v.) waters.

AAG: Advanced Arresting Gear. A new US Navy system using energy-absorbing water turbines (twisters) in replacement of traditional hydraulic systems used to assist aircraft recovery on CATOBAR (q.v.) and STOBAR (q.v.) aircraft carriers.

ABM: Anti-Ballistic Missile. A missile system designed to intercept ballistic missiles, forming part of a BMD (q.v.) system.

ACC/SES: Air-Cushion Catamaran/Surface-Effect Ship. Combines the flexible air cushion of a hovercraft with the rigid twin hulls of a catamaran, used to achieve both high speed and good levels of survivability.

ADF: Australian Defence Force.

Aegis: An automated US-developed combat system built around AN/SPY-1 phased arrays (q.v.), a command and decision system, a weapons control system and a display system, first introduced into operation in 1983.

AESA: Active Electronically Scanned Array. A type of phased array (q.v.) radar also known as an active phased array radar or APAR (q.v.). AESA radars use individually energised transmitting and receiving modules to form and direct their radar beams. In comparison, earlier-generation passive phased arrays rely on a single energy source. Both types of phased array offer significant advantages over earlier, mechanically-directed radars, but AESAs are more flexible and reliable.

AGS: Advanced Gun System: A new long-range, automated 155mm gun system capable of firing both conventional and guided munitions being developed for the US Navy's *Zumwalt* class.

AIP: Air-Independent Propulsion. A propulsion system that allows submarines to operate underwater without the need to come to the surface periodically to replenish the air supplies that are required by traditional diesel-electric propelled boats. It is currently typically used to refer to diesel-electric submarines equipped with an auxiliary AIP plant to supplement their main propulsion system.

AIS: Automatic Identification System. An automatic tracking system used to locate and identify ships. It was originally developed by the International Maritime Organization (IMO) for collision-avoidance but is increasingly used to facilitate maritime security. AIS has to be fitted to most commercial ships.

AMDR: Air and Missile Defence Radar. A new US Navy AESA (q.v.) radar – designated AN/SPY-6 – that will replace the existing AN/SPY-1 passive phased array: see Aegis.

AMRAAM: Advanced Medium Range Air-to-Air Missile. Designated AIM-120 by the US Armed Forces, AMRAAM is a development of the older Sparrow series and is designed to engage other aircraft at beyond-visual range

AMS: Avionics Management System. Known as a Flight Management System or FMS on civilian airliners, an avionics management system is a computerised system that automates a number of in-flight tasks.

AOR: Auxiliary Oiler, Replenishment. An oil tanker capable of replenishing ships at sea.

APAR: See AESA. APAR is also used to refer specifically to the Thales Nederland multifunction APAR radar, which uses AESA technology.

ARCI: Acoustic Rapid COTS (commercial off-the-shelf) Insertion. A 1990s US Navy programme to upgrade the sonar systems used in its submarine fleet by enhancing the computer hardware and software them rather than the sonars themselves.

ASEAN: Association of Southeast Asian Nations.

ASV: Autonomous Surface Vehicle.

ASW: Anti-submarine warfare.

Asymmetric Warfare: Typically refers to conflicts between opponents with unequal military resources where the weaker participant uses unconventional tactics and/or weapons to exploit its enemy's vulnerabilities. Asymmetric tactics often form part of A2/AD (q.v.) strategies.

ATFLIR: Advanced Targeting Forward Looking Infrared. A US Navy multi-sensor targeting pod developed by Raytheon Corporation and used on the Hornet and Super Hornet strike fighters. US Navy designation is AN/ASQ-228.

AUV: Autonomous Underwater Vehicle.

Blue Water: Open-water or oceanic. A blue-water navy has the ability to conduct sustained operations across the world's oceans far from its home base.

BMD: Ballistic Missile Defence. See also ABM.

CATOBAR: Catapult Assisted Take-Off But Arrested Recovery. Also referenced as Catapult Assisted Take-Off Barrier Arrested Recovery. The aircraft launch and recovery system used in 'conventional' aircraft carriers under which aircraft are launched with the assistance of a catapult and recovered with the use of arrester wires on which a hook suspended from the aircraft is caught.

CEC: Cooperative Engagement Capability. A system initially developed by the US Navy under which individual sensors and weapons systems on individual ships and aircraft are networked together to provide an integrated group-wide capability.

CEPP: Carrier Enabled Power Projection. A British Royal Navy concept developed for use with the *Queen Elizabeth* class aircraft carriers under which differently comprised air groups – a tailored air group or TAG – will be embarked dependent on the specific mission envisaged.

CG: Guided-missile cruiser.

CIWS: Close-In Weapon System. A point-defence system providing short-range protection against enemy aircraft or missiles.

CMF: Combined Maritime Forces. A multinational naval partnership of thirty-one nations under US Navy leadership undertaking maritime security, counter-terrorism and counter-piracy operations by means of three task forces (CTF 150, CTF 151 and CTF 152) in the Indian Ocean, Arabian and Persian Gulfs, and neighbouring waters.

CNO: Chief of Naval Operations. The most senior naval officer assigned to serve in the US

Department of the Navy, acting as deputy to the civilian Secretary of the Navy.

CODAG: Combined Diesel And Gas. See Chapter 5, particularly Note 4.

CODLAG: Combined Diesel-Electric And Gas. See Chapter 5, particularly Note 4.

CODOE: Combined Diesel or Electric. Under this arrangement, a diesel propulsion system is typically supplemented by electric power for low speed but fuel-efficient operation. It features in several modern offshore patrol vessel designs.

CODOG: Combined Diesel or Gas. See Chapter 5, particularly Note 4.

COGAG: Combined Gas and Gas. See Chapter 5, particularly Note 4.

CS21: *A Cooperative Strategy for 21st Century Seapower.* An important US Navy strategy document first published in 2007. An updated version: *Forward, Engaged, Ready: A Cooperative Strategy For 21st Century Seapower Refresh* – often abbreviated as CS21R or CS21-2015 – was published in 2015.

CV: Aircraft carrier. Typically refers to an aircraft carrier capable of carrying out a wide range of fixed wing and rotary operations. A nuclear-powered aircraft carrier is designated a **CVN**.

CVS: Support carrier. Typically a smaller aircraft carrier with more limited or non-existent strike capabilities. May be restricted to helicopter operations only.

DBR: Dual Band Radar. A new US Navy radar originally planned for installation in the *Ford* class aircraft carriers and *Zumwalt* class destroyers. It combines two sets of radar arrays operating in different radio frequencies. Due to cost considerations, it will now only be used in the first *Ford* class carrier. See Chapter 6.2, Note 4.

DDG: Guided-missile destroyer.

EEZ: Exclusive Economic Zone. An area of sea where the relevant state has exclusive rights to maritime resources under the United Nations Convention on the Law of the Sea (UNCLOS) regime.

EMALS: Electromagnetic Aircraft Launch System. A new US Navy launch system for CATOBAR (q.v.) equipped carriers, using a magnetic field to propel an aircraft launch carriage in place of the long-established steam catapult.

EMPAR: European Multifunction Phased Array Radar. An electronically-scanned array produced by Italian company Finmeccanica. See further

Phased Array.

EMRG: Electromagnetic Railgun. See further the section on Weapons Systems in Chapter 5.

ESSM: Evolved Sea Sparrow Missile. US Navy designation is RIM-162. It is a significantly enhanced development of the RIM-7 Sea Sparrow and is used primarily for defence against anti-ship missiles.

Expeditionary: Typically used to refer to operations undertaken or equipment capabilities used far from a country's hone base. See also Blue Water.

FAC: Fast Attack Craft.

FFG: Guided missile frigate.

FSG: A missile-armed light frigate or corvette. Typically a smaller and less capable ship than a fully-fledged frigate. A non-guided missile-armed light frigate or corvette is termed an **FS**.

FLASH: Folding Lightweight Acoustic System for Helicopters. A widely-used family of dipping sonar systems developed by predecessors of the French Thales defence conglomerate and widely used internationally.

FOST: Either **Flag Officer Sea Training**, a British Royal Navy training command, or *Force Océanique Stratégique*, the French submarine-based nuclear deterrent.

GDP: Gross Domestic Product. A measure of a country's economic output, based on the value of the goods and services produced over a particular period, typically a year.

GP: General Purpose. Typically refers to a surface escort designed to carry out a wide range of missions rather than one optimised to carry out a specific role.

GPS: Global Positioning System. A US government-owned but widely-used satellite-based navigation system.

GRP: Glass Reinforced Plastic. A term for fibreglass used in boat- and shipbuilding.

IFEP: Integrated Full Electric Propulsion. Also known as Integrated Electric Propulsion or **IEP**. Propulsion is provided by electric motors using electricity generated by a ship's engines rather than by direct mechanical drive from the engines themselves.

Informationisation: The process of an economy or society becoming information-based or dependent.

IOC: Initial Operational Capability. In the US military, this is the date when at least one of the intended users of a system is able to employ and

maintain it. The UK military refer to achieving an Initial Operating Capability, when the relevant system is available in its minimum usefully deployable form. The date this is achieved is the In-Service Date (**ISD**).

JMSDF: Japan Maritime Self-Defence Force.

JSS: Joint Support Ship. A multi-role naval auxiliary capable of undertaking both replenishment at sea and logistical support/transport for amphibious operations, for example the Dutch JSS *Karel Doorman*.

JTIDS: Joint Tactical Information Distribution System. A US/NATO network radio-based data communications system allowing rapid and secure transfer of information between different allied units, initially used to support the Link 16 tactical data exchange network.

KPN: Korean People's Navy. The navy of North Korea.

LaWS: Laser Weapon System. A prototype laser weapon – designated AN/SEQ-3 – currently being trialled by the US Navy.

LCAC: Landing Craft Air-Cushion: A US Navy hovercraft used as a high-speed landing craft.

LCS: Littoral Combat Ship: A US Navy corvette-sized surface combatant optimised for operations in littoral waters. It is being built to two different designs.

LHA/LHD: Amphibious assault ship. Typically a ship which combines the aircraft facilities of a CVS (q.v.) or LPH (q.v.) with the well deck of an LSD (q.v.) or an LPD (q.v.). However, some recent US Navy LHAs have omitted the well deck.

Littoral: This is defined by the US Navy's operational concept as being '… composed of two segments. The *seaward* portion is that area from the open ocean to the shore that must be controlled to support operations ashore. The *landward* portion is the area inland from the shore that can be supported and defended directly from the sea.' Other definitions vary widely.

LPD: Landing Platform Dock. Also termed an Amphibious Transport Dock. A development of the LSD (q.v.) with greater emphasis on equipment and, particularly, troop-carrying capacity.

LPH: Landing Platform Helicopter. Also known as a helicopter assault ship. An amphibious ship designed to land troops and equipment primarily by helicopter and thus omitting the well deck found in some other amphibious ships.

LSD: Landing Ship Dock. Also commonly termed

a Dock Landing Ship. An ocean-going vessel that can carry smaller landing craft in a well deck.

Maritime Domain Awareness: An understanding of events within a given maritime area that might impact security or safety.

MCMV: Mine Countermeasures Vessel.

Moore's Law: A prediction of the rapid increase in computing power. See further, Chapter 1, Note 5.

MPA: Maritime Patrol Aircraft

NAS: Typically refers to a **Naval Air Station**, a land based naval airfield or similar facility. In the British Royal Navy's Fleet Air Arm, it refers to a **Naval Air Squadron**, with the term RNAS being used for a Royal Naval Air Station. The Indian Navy uses the term INAS to refer to its own air squadrons.

NTDS: Naval Tactical Data System. A US Navy computerised information system developed during the 1950s and deployed onboard warships from the 1960s onwards. It allowed data from various sensors and other sources (e.g. communications links) to be displayed so as to provide an overall tactical 'picture' for command and control purposes.

ONI: Office of Naval Intelligence. The US Navy's maritime intelligence agency.

Optimal Manning: Typically refers to a reduction in the number of crew required to man a given warship category through use of a combination of, e.g., new technology, flexible working arrangements, improved training and enhances shore-based report.

OPV: Offshore Patrol Vessel.

PAAMS: Principal Anti-Air Missile System. A European surface-to-air missile system using the Franco-Italian Aster missile.

Phased Array: A type of radar that uses electronics to form and steer its radar beams. A phased array is far more flexible than a traditional mechanical radar, with one array being able to carry out a range of functions (e.g. detection, target indication and fire control) that previously required several separate radars. The AN/SPY-1 radar associated with the Aegis Weapon System (q.v.) is the most well-known example of the type. See also AESA and APAR.

PLAN: People's Liberation Army Navy.

Q-Routes: A network of specially-designated shipping routes kept clear of mines and other obstructions.

QDR: Quadrennial Defense Review. A US Department of Defense review of strategic objectives, threats and resources carried out every four years.

RAM: Rolling Airframe Missile. A surface-to-air missile system providing short-range 'point' defence against missiles and other targets. Its US Navy designation is RIM-116.

RAN: Royal Australian Navy.

RFA: Royal Fleet Auxiliary. A civilian-manned fleet providing logistical support to the British Royal Navy.

ROKN: Republic of Korea Navy. The navy of South Korea.

SAN: South African Navy.

SeaSwap: A US Navy term for the rotation of crews on surface combatants. The aim is to increase hull usage, reducing the number of hulls required for a given operational requirement.

SDR: Strategic Defence Review. A highly-regarded but poorly-implemented British defence review dating from 1998. Subsequent defence reviews have carried the term Strategic Security and Defence Review (SDSR).

SGR: Sortie Generation Rate. The number of individual combat missions that can be carried out in a given period, typically twenty-four hours. One sortie represents one mission by one aircraft. An aircraft carrier's SGR, for example, is therefore represented by the number of combat aircraft it can carry multiplied by the number of sorties each aircraft can carry out in a day.

SIGMA: Ship Integrated Geometrical Modularity Approach. A modular design system developed by the Dutch Damen Schelde Naval Shipbuilding Group. See further, Chapter 5.

SLOC: Sea Lines of Communication. The primary maritime routes between a country's ports and those of its major partners.

SOSUS: Sound Surveillance System. An extensive underwater submarine detection network comprising large sonar arrays developed by the US Navy and its allies to detect Soviet submarines passing through certain naval choke points during the Cold War.

SRVL: Shipborne Rolling Vertical Landing. A technique for STOVL (q.v.) aircraft under which vertical thrust from an aircraft's engine and lift from its wings allows a rolling landing using only its brakes, thus eliminating the need for arrester wires and allows more fuel/equipment to be carried than when landing vertically.

SSBN: Ship Submersible Ballistic Missile Nuclear Powered. A nuclear-powered strategic submarine carrying ballistic missiles.

SSDS: Surface Ship Defense System. A computerised command and control system often found in US Navy ships that are not equipped with Aegis (q.v.).

SSGN: Ship Submersible Guided Missile Nuclear Powered. A nuclear-powered submarine with a main armament of (non-ballistic) guided-missiles. Typically used to refer to Soviet-era Russian designs that were principally used as missile-carriers.

SSK: Ship Submersible Hunter-Killer. Originally used to refer to US Navy submarines specially-designed to hunt other submarines. Now generally used to refer to diesel-electric patrol submarines that do not have the range and speed of SSN type nuclear powered attack submarines (q.v.).

SSN: Ship Submersible Nuclear Powered. A nuclear-powered attack submarine.

Stanflex: Also known as Standard Flex. A Danish-developed system that mounts a range of weapons and other equipment in standardised containers that can be fitted in pre-prepared slots and rapidly swapped between warships, allowing them to be swiftly re-assigned to different missions.

STOBAR: Short Take-Off Barrier Arrested Recovery. An aircraft carrier operating system under which aircraft are launched with the assistance of a ski-jump but recovered conventionally using arrester wires.

STOVL: Short Take-Off and Vertical Landing.

TLAM: Tomahawk Land Attack Missile.

UAV: Unmanned Aerial Vehicle.

UCLASS: Unmanned Carrier-Launched Airborne Surveillance & Strike. A proposed US Navy programme to develop an autonomous UAV (q.v.) for use on aircraft carriers.

UKCSG: United Kingdom Carrier Strike Group.

UNASUR: Union of South American Nations.

UNCLOS: United Nations Convention of the Law of the Sea. See also EEZ.

USCG: United States Coast Guard.

USMC: United States Marine Corps.

USV: Unmanned Surface Vehicle. See also ASV.

UUV: Unmanned Underwater Vehicle. See also AUV.

VLS: Vertical Launching System. A system comprising a number of cells that both house and launch one or more missiles.

WMD: Weapons of Mass Destruction.

Contributors

Richard Beedall: Born in England, Richard is an IT Consultant with a long-standing interest in the Royal Navy and naval affairs in general. He served for fourteen years in the Royal Naval Reserve as a rating and officer, working with the US Navy and local naval forces in the Middle East and around the world. In 1999 he founded *Navy Matters*, one of the earliest naval websites on the Royal Navy. He has contributed to *Seaforth World Naval Review* since the initial 2010 edition, and has written on naval developments for many other organisations and publications, including *AMI International*, *Naval Forces*, *Defence Management* and *Warships IFR*. He lives in Ireland with his wife and daughters.

James Bosbotinis: James Bosbotinis is a specialist in contemporary maritime strategy. His research focuses particularly on the navies of Great Britain, Russia and China, naval force developments, and the connections between maritime strategy and national policy. Dr Bosbotinis attained his PhD in 2014 from King's College London, where his research examined the development of the forthcoming *Queen Elizabeth* class aircraft carriers and the implications for British maritime strategy. He has published widely on issues including the development of UK maritime airpower, Russian maritime doctrine and naval modernisation, and China's evolving strategy. Dr Bosbotinis is an Associate Member of the Corbett Centre for Maritime Policy Studies, King's College London

Alastair Cooper: Alastair Cooper is a public servant and a RAN reservist. He is the author of several articles and chapters on Australian naval history and military strategy. He has served at sea and as the research officer to the Chief of Navy, worked in private sector telecommunications, the Department of Defence, the Department of the Prime Minister and Cabinet and the Attorney General's Department. The views expressed are his own.

Hartmut Ehlers: Dipl.-Ing. Hartmut Ehlers, born and raised in Lübeck, Germany, is married. He graduated from high school in 1967 and, in, 1977, commenced a 38-year-career as a naval architect in the naval projects & design departments of the Blohm & Voss Shipyard and the MTG Marinetechnik GmbH, design bureau, retiring in 2015. The ten years in between saw him employed as a shipyard probationer, serving in the Federal German Navy and merchant marine, and studying naval architecture at the Technical University of Hannover. Dipl.-Ing. Ehlers, FGN (R), is a member of ASNE and RINA.

Norman Friedman: Norman Friedman is one of the best-known naval analysts and historians in the US. The author of over forty books, he has written on broad issues of modern military interest, including an award-winning history of the Cold War. In the field of warship development his greatest sustained achievement is an eight-volume series on the design of different US warship types. A specialist in the intersection of technology and national strategy, his acclaimed *Network Centric-Warfare* was published in 2009 by the US Naval Institute Press. The holder of a PhD in theoretical physics from Columbia, Dr Friedman is a regular guest commentator on television and lectures widely on professional defence issues. He lives in New York.

Philip Grove: Philip D Grove is currently Subject Matter Expert in Strategic Studies for the University of Plymouth at Britannia Royal Naval College, Dartmouth. He is also Head of Maritime Aviation in the new Dartmouth Seapower and Security Centre. His principal research interest concerns naval aviation and its contribution to security. He has contributed to a number of publications, most recently *Turning the Tide: The Battles of Coral Sea and Midway* (University of Plymouth, 2013) and with Duncan Redford co-wrote *The Royal Navy: A History Since 1900* (Tauris, 2014). Besides his Dartmouth teaching he has acted as a visiting lecturer to various Royal Navy units. Furthermore from 1996 to 2013 he delivered modules at Plymouth University, whilst more recently he has given talks at various international conferences.

David Hobbs: Commander David Hobbs MBE RN (retired) is an author and naval historian with an international reputation. He has written eighteen books, the latest being *The British Carrier Strike Fleet after 1945*, and has contributed to many more. He writes for several journals and magazines and in 2005 won the award for the Aerospace Journalist of the Year, Best Defence Submission. He also won the essay prize awarded by the Navy League of Australia in 2008. He lectures on naval subjects worldwide, and has been on radio and television in several countries. He served in the Royal Navy for thirty-three years and retired with the rank of Commander. He is qualified as both a fixed and rotary-wing pilot and his log book contains 2,300 hours with over 800 carrier deck landings, 150 of which were at night. For eight years he was the Curator of the Fleet Air Arm Museum at Yeovilton.

John Jordan is the regular illustrator for Seaforth's *World Naval Review*. A former teacher of modern languages, he is the author of two major books on the Soviet Navy, and has recently co-authored a series of books for Seaforth Publishing on the French interwar navy: *French Battleships* (2009) with Robert Dumas, *French Cruisers* (2013) and *French Destroyers* (2015) with Jean Moulin. He is currently preparing a technical history of the French battleships of the 1890-22 era. A book about the impact of the Washington Treaty of 1922 on the major fleets, *Warships After Washington*, was published by Seaforth in 2011.

Mrityunjoy Mazumdar: Mr Mazumdar has been writing on naval matters since 1999. His words and pictures have appeared in many naval and aircraft publications including *Jane's Defence Weekly*, *Jane's Navy International*, *Naval Forces*, *Ships of the World*, the USNI's *Proceedings* and *Warship Technology* published by the RINA. He is also a regular contributor to the major naval annuals like *Combat Fleets of the World*, *Flotes des Combat*, *Jane's Fighting Ships*, *Seaforth World Naval Review* and *Weyers Flotten Taschenbuch*. Mr Mazumdar lives in Vallejo, California with his wife.

Jack McCaffrie: Jack McCaffrie is a Visiting Fellow at the Australian National Centre for Ocean Resources and Security at Wollongong University, where he was recently awarded his PhD. He retired from the RAN in February 2003 on returning from his final posting as Naval Attaché, Washington. His recent work includes co-authoring *Navies of Southeast Asia: A Comparative Study* and (as a Visiting Fellow at the RAN's Sea Power Centre) writing the second edition of the RAN's doctrine publication *Australian Maritime Operations*. His current work includes a history of the Pacific Patrol Boat Program and a history of defence policy and the RAN's development from 1955 to 1983.

Chris Rahman: Dr Chris Rahman is Principal Research Fellow (Associate Professor) in Maritime Strategy and Security at the Australian National Centre for Ocean Resources and Security (ANCORS), University of Wollongong. He is an academic strategist, with a research focus on maritime strategy, strategic theory, Australian defence policy, China, and the strategic relations of the Indo-Pacific region; as well as contemporary issues in maritime security, including technology applications such as vessel tracking. He is currently co-ordinating a major project on the history of the Pacific Patrol Boat Program for the RAN and manages the ANCORS Vessel Tracking Initiative in collaboration with industry and Australian government partners.

Ian Speller: Ian Speller is Director of the Centre for Military History and Strategic Studies and a senior lecturer in Military History at the Department of History at the National University of Ireland Maynooth. He also lectures at the Irish Military College. His main research interests are naval history, maritime strategy and expeditionary warfare and he has published extensively in these fields. His publications include *Understanding Naval Warfare* (2014), *Small Navies. Strategy and Policy for Small Navies in War and Peace* (2014), *Amphibious Warfare*, co-authored (2014), *Understanding Modern Warfare* co-authored (2008) and *The Royal Navy and Maritime Power in the Twentieth Century* (2005).

David Stevens: David Stevens joined the RAN in 1974 and specialised in anti-submarine warfare. Highlights of his service included an exchange posting in the Royal Navy and seagoing staff appointments in both the 1991 Gulf War and 2003 Iraq War. He resigned from the permanent navy in 1994 to become the Australian naval historian, a position that he held until the end of 2014. He has now retired from full time employment, but remains an Adjunct Associate Professor at UNSW Canberra

and a Senior Visiting Fellow at the University of Wollongong. His new history of the RAN in the First World War, *In All Respects Ready*, won the 2015 Frank Broeze Memorial Maritime History Book Prize.

Geoffrey Till: Geoffrey Till is Emeritus Professor of Maritime Studies at King's College London Chairman of the Corbett Centre for Maritime Policy Studies. Since 2009 he has also been a Visiting Professor and Senior Research fellow at the Rajaratnam School of International Studies, Singapore. His *Understanding Victory: Naval Operations from Trafalgar to the Falklands* was published by ABC-Clio in 2014 and he is currently working on a fourth edition of his *Seapower: A Guide for the 21st Century*.

Scott Truver: Dr Truver directs Gryphon Technologies' Team Blue National Security group. Since 1991 he has supported the production of several USN strategic publications, including *… From the Sea*, *Naval Doctrine Publication 1*, *FORWARD … From the Sea*, *2020 Vision* (never published), *A Maritime Strategy for the 21st Century* (never published), *Sea Power 21*, and *A Co-operative Strategy for the 21st Century Seapower/Refresh*. He has provided similar support to several USCG strategic publications. He has lectured at the US Naval Academy, Naval War College and Naval Postgraduate School, among other venues. His further qualifications include a Doctor of Philosophy degree in Marine Policy Studies and a MA in Political Science/International Relations from the University of Delaware.

Conrad Waters: A lawyer by training but a banker by profession, Conrad Waters was educated at Liverpool University prior to being called to the bar at Gray's Inn in 1989. His interest in maritime affairs was first stimulated by a long family history of officers in Merchant Navy service and he has been writing articles on historical and current naval affairs for over thirty years. This included six years producing the 'World Navies in Review' chapter of the influential annual *Warship* before assuming responsibility for *Seaforth World Naval Review* as founding editor. Conrad is married to Susan and has three children: Emma, Alexander and Imogen.

INDEX

Page numbers in *italic* refer to illustrations, in **bold** to tables.

7 de Agosto (Colombia) 178, *178*

Absalon (Den) 80
Absalon class 141, 169
Abu Dhabi (UAE) 133
Adelaide (Aus) 107, *156*
Admiral Gorshkov class 84, 88–9, *89*, 150, 173
Admiral Kuznetsov (Rus) 83, 149, 226, *226*, 227
Admiral Nakhimov (Rus) 89
Admiral Panteleyev (Rus) *83*
Afghanistan 18, 19–20, 30, 58, 214
Africa 120, 121; navies **120**
Agosta class 78, 200
aircraft carriers 14, 24–5, 46, 147, **150**, **154**, 205, 220, 221, **227**, 231,
Akizuki (Jpn) *175*, *176*
Al Rasikh (Oman) *133*
Al Shamikh (Oman) *185*
Al Shamikh class 186
Albion (GB) 159, *160*, 232
Alexander Otravosky (Rus) *90*
Algeria 121
Alrosa (Rus) *85*
Alvaro de Bazan (Sp) 78, *78*, 165
America (US) 232
America class 158, *159*
Améythyste (Fr) *196*, 165
amphibious warships 7, 46–7, 147, 153–60, **154**, 158, 231
Anchorage (US) *53*
Andrea Doria (It) 76, *76*, 167
anti-submarine warfare 104, 135, 144, 216–17, 234
Anzac (Aus) *108*, *123*
Anzac class 106, 107, 108
Anzio (US) *30*
Aoife (Ireland) *25*
Aquitaine 70, *72*, 74
Araguari (Brazil) *185*
Arco (US) *8*
Argentina 39, 56, 138, 145
Argyll (GB) *157*
Arihant (India) 125, 126, 190, 191
Ark Futura (Den) *9*
Ark Royal (GB) *31*, 58, 60, 230

Arleigh Burke (US) *165*
Arleigh Burke class *48*, *50*, 164
Armidale class 108–9
Artful (GB) *55*
Ashland (US) *43*, *53*
Asia 12, 13, 14, 22–3, 25, 137; fleet strengths **91**
Askold (Rus) *135*
Astute class 194–5, *195*
Atlantic Conveyor (GB) 162
Australia 31, 91, 105, 145; Australian Defence Force 106–7; and East Timor 107; *Plan Pelorus* (2015) 105, 107, 109; Royal Australian Navy 91, 105–9, 153; RAN carriers 233; RAN force structure 106, **106**

Baden-Württemberg (Ger) *55*
Bahrain 66, 133
Baltic 79, 217; navies 79–80
Bangladesh 128, 137
'Barracuda' (Fr) 71, *195*, *196*
Baynunah (UAE) *132*, 133
Berlin (Ger) *80*
Berlin 702 class 37, *188*
Bernard Webber class 186
Berthof 'Legend' class *182*, 186
Blas de Lezo (Sp) *167*
Bosnia 18, 30
Brandenburg class 169
Braunschweig class 181–2
Brazil 13, 23, 25, 37, 39, 129, 192, 196; carriers 229; *Marinha do Brasil* fleet strength **38**
Britain: *Defence Industrial Strategy* (2005) 68; and India 120–1; and Libya 62, 203–4; military expenditure 24, 56, 57, 58, 63, 220–1; shipyards 69; and US 28 *see also* Royal Navy
Bulgaria 81, 82

California (US) *193*
Canada 36–7; Canadian Forces Maritime Command 36; Royal Canadian Navy 36–7, 159
Canberra (Aus) 105, 107, *156*
Canberra class 153, *158*
Cantabria (Sp) *79*
Cape St. George (US) *42*
Carabiniere (It) *76*

Carlo Bergamini (It) 76, *175*
Carrera (Chile) *201*
Cavour (It) 32, 76, 150, 153, *153*, 156, 230
Centurion class 193
Chafee (US) *164*
Chakra (India) 125, 192
Changbai Shan (China) *98*
Charles de Gaulle (Fr) 6, *6*, 69, 70, *70*, 71, 72, 74, 196, 228
Charlottetown (Canada) *241*
Cheonan (RoK) 91, 116, *116*
Chevalier Paul (Fr) *170*
Chile 39
China 7, 12, 22–3, 44, 93, 63, 205–6, 215; and Africa 121; and India 122, 123, 124; and Indian Ocean 121; island chain strategy 94–5; 'Malacca dilemma' 98; Maritime Safety Administration 144; and Middle East 130; and Pakistan 128; and People's Liberation Army 94; and piracy 97–8, 121; and Russia 99; ship-building 135, 144, 146, 174–5; and SLOC 93, 97, 98; and South Korea 115, 118; and Soviet Union 206; territorial disputes 91, 92, 93, 94, 95, 110, 114; and Taiwan 95, 214; and US 44, 91, 214
China People's Liberation Army Navy (PLAN) 12, 13, 14, 22–3, 25, 32, 91–104, 178, 205–6; anti-air warfare 215; anti-submarine warfare 104; carriers 99–100, **227**; force structure **96**, 99, 10; submarines *94*, 99, 103, 191–2 197; surface combatants **101**, 174–5
Choules (Aus) 107
Chung-Hoon (US) *50*
Clyde (GB) *185*
Cold War 27–9, 248; effect of end of 8, 12, 16, 30, 34, 40, 56, 135, 136–7, 248; and NATO 20, 28
Cole (US) 19, 33, *205*, 206
Collins class 106
Colombia 39
Connecticut (US) *190*, *209*
Constellation (US) 16
Co-operative Strategy for the 21st Century Seapower (CS21,

2007) 2, 44; (CS21R, 2015) 24
Cornwall (GB) 69, *188*
Coronado (US) *181*
Crimea 84, 174
Cuba 16, 36

Daishandao (China) 102, *103*
Daring (GB) 60, *140*, *170*, 171, *212*
Darwin (Aus) *26*
De Ruyter (Neth) *167*
De Zeven Provinciën (Neth) 163
De Zeven Provinciën class 168
Defender (GB) *41*
Denmark 80, 139–40, 206
Descubierta class 78
D'Estienne d'Orves class 73
Diamond (GB) *9*, *247*
Diligence (GB) 178, *188*
Dimitry Donskoy (Rus) *193*
Dokdo (RoK) *119*, 157, 158
Dolphin class 200
Dragon (GB) *24*, *130*, *226*
Dreadnought (1905) (GB) 135, 146
Dreadnought 2050 14, 142, *142*
Duncan (GB) *61*, 171
Durance class 74, 187

East Timor 31, 107
Egypt 121, 130
Endurance (GB) 56, *242*
Enterprise (US) 46, 221
Erfurt (Ger) *76*
Essex (US) *232*
Europe: fleet strengths **54**; navies 20, 21, 54–5, 70–82
European Union 20, 21, 32, 39, 54, 55, 77, 121, 178

Falklands Conflict (1982) 12, 28–9, 56, 162, 171, 214, 241
Fassmer-80 177, *178*
Finland 80
Firebolt (US) *130*
Fitzgerald (US) *212*
Flyvefisken class 139–40
Ford class 148, 152
Formidable (Singapore) 138, *172*
Formidable class *92*
Forth (GB) *61*
Fort Worth (US) 19, *182*, *216*, 234, *243*, *246*
Forward from the Sea (US, 1994) 18, 43

France 54, 120, 129; carriers 228–9; and Egypt 130; and Libya 72; and NATO 70, 71; military policies 70–1; naval exports 172; sale of *Mistral* to Russia 83, 85, 233 *see also* Marine Nationale
Freedom (US) 19, 49, *50*, *138*, 180–1
Freedom to Use the Seas: India's Maritime Military Strategy (2006) 124
FREMM (Frégate Européenne Multi-Mission) class 70, 71, *71*, 138, 171; exports of 171–2
Fridtjof Nansen (Norway) *22*, *247*
Fridtjof Nansen class 80, 165, *178*
... From the Sea (US, 1992) 18, 41–3
Fundamentals of British Maritime Doctrine BR1806 (1995) 30, 57

George H. W. Bush (US) *41*, 147
George Washington (US) 32, *164*, *221*
Gepard (Ger) *177*
Gerald R. Ford (US) 46, *46*, 148–9, *148*, *149*, 221
Gerald R. Ford class 147–8
Germany 80, 168, 171, 172
Giuseppe Garibaldi (It) 74, *74*, 76, 153, 230
Global Reach, Global Power (US, 1990) 41
Gold Rover (GB) *62*
Gomati (India) 16, 146
Gotland class 143, 201
Gravely (US) *165*
Greece 81–2; Hellenic Navy 81–2
Guangzhou (China) *242*
Guaiqueri (Venezuela) *141*
Gulf War (1990–1) 18, 29, 30, 57, 122, 177, 209, 234

Haikow (China) *102*
Hakuryu (Jpn) *200*
Halifax (Canada) 36, *36*
Hamburg (Ger) *80*, 168
Härnösand (Sweden) *181*
Harpers Ferry (US) 46, 49
Henry M. Jackson (US) *51*

'Heroine' class *201*
Hessen (Ger) *80*
Heybeliade class 82, *82*, 182
Hobart class 106, 107, 165
Holland (Neth) *34*, 178, *186*
Holland class 55, 80, 182–3
Hopper (US) *215*, *216*
Horizon class 171
'Horizon' project 72
Huntington, Samuel P., 'National Policy and the Transoceanic Navy' 40
Hyuga (Jpn) 32, *113*, *155*
Hyuga class 158, 176

Illustrious (GB) 31, 57, 58, *59*, 65
Independence (US) 49, *50*, 181
Incheon class 118, 176, 178
India 23, 25, 33, 120, 137, 173, 190, 206; and Britain 120–1; and China 123, 124; and Pakistan 128; shipbuilding 146; and Soviet Union 122, 123; and US 120
Indian Navy 23, 123–8; carriers 149–50, 224; *Maritime Capability Perspective Plan (2012–17)* 127; Maritime Doctrine (2004) 124–5; naval aviation force structure 127, **127**; naval force structure 123, 125, **126**, 125; OPVs 137; piracy 124; submarines 23, 125, 191–2
Indian Ocean 23, 121; navies 120, **120**, 122; piracy 32, 121; and PLAN 121
Indonesia 92, 93
Intrepid (Singapore) *92*
Invincible (GB) 56, 59, 151
Iran 69, 121, 131, *131*
Iraq 18, 19, 29, 30, 32, 54, 58, 72, 120, 133, 211, 213, 214
Ireland 22, 25, 33
Iron Duke (GB) *61*
Isaac Peral class 78, 210
Ise (Jpn) *110*, *203*
Iskandar Muda (Indonesia) *140*
Islamic State (IS) 32, 63, 72
Israel 23–4, 130–1, 134, 163, 190
Italy 74–7, 205; carriers 230; shipbuilding 75–6
see also Marina Militare

Iver Huitfeldt class 80, *141*, 169–70, *169*
Izumo (Jpn) *110*, *159*, *203*
Izumo class 113, 158

James (US) *137*, *182*
James Joyce (Ireland) *184*
Japan 23, 91, 93, 121, 137, 201; and Australia 111; and India 111; naval aviation 158; National Defense Program Guidelines 111; and piracy countermeasures 111; shipbuilding 144, 175; and South Korea 114, 119; territorial disputes 93, 110, 114; and US 91, 110, 111
Japanese Maritime Self Defense Force (JMSDF) 13, 91, 110–14, **112**, 238; submarine and mine warfare 113–14
Jian (China) *101*
Jinan (China) *23*, *26*, *93*
John C. Stennis (US) *170*
John F. Kennedy (US) 46, 148–9, 221
John Warner (US) *51*
Joint Support Ship 159–60
Juan Carlos 1 (Sp) 20, 76, 78, 153–4, 157, 230
Juan Carlos 1 class 134, *155*, 157

Kalaat Béni Abbès (Algeria) 121
Kamorta (India) *145*, 146, 178
Karel Doorman (Neth) 7, *7*, *21*, 55, 159, 160, *161*, 178, 189
Kawasaki P-1 238
Kearsage (US) *32*, *47*, *188*
Kent (GB) *68*
Kerkyra (Greece) *81*
'Kilo' class 131, 202, *202*
Kitty Hawk (US) *16*
Kolkata (India) *124*, 163
Kolkata class 163, 173, 174
Kongou (Jpn) 163, 165
Kosovo 18, 30, 74
Kursk (Rus) 85, 89
Kuwait 28, 29, 133

La Fayette (Fr) *137*, 138, *138*
La Fayette class 70, 72
L'Adroit (Fr) *72*, *73*
Lake Erie (US) *215*
Lancaster (GB) *62*
Lanzhou (China) *101*, *103*
Lassen (US) *92*

Latin America 36–7; fleet strengths **37**
Le Triomphant (Fr) *71*
Lebanon 131
Lekiu class 172, *172*
Lewis and Clark (US) 187, *188*
Liaoning (China) 22, 102, 149, 226, 227, 228, *228*
Libya 21, 29, 31–2, 62, 72, 74, 203–4
'Lider' class 88, 89
Limburg (Fr) *33*
Linyi (China) *97*
Littoral Combat Ships 19, 49–50, 132, 137–8, 178–82, **179**, 206–7, 243
Los Angeles class 51, 193
Luoyang (China) *12*

Makin Island (US) 46, *53*, 158
Makinami (Jpn) *111*
Malaysia 92, 121
Maldives 122, 129
Marcellariu (Romania) *44*
Marina Militare (Italy) 32, 74–7, carriers 233; force structure **75**, 76; helicopters 234
Marine Nationale (France) 54, 70, 71–4, 156, 204–5; bases 71; carriers 72, 74, 228; force structure 71–3, *73*; personnel 245; submarines 71, 72, 195
maritime patrol aircraft 236–8, *237*, **237**, 245
Maryborough (Aus) *109*
Masa Verde (US) *160*
Maud (Norway) 188, *189*
MEKO (Mehrzweck-Kombination) 13, 138, 141, 145, 360; exports of 139, 172; modularisation 139, 169; MEKO 140 145; MEKO 200 134, *134*; MEKO A-200 129
Méndez Núñez (Spain) *35*
Meteoro class 78, 178, 183–4, *183*, *186*
Mexico 37, 39
Middle East 120; and China 130; navies **120**, 130; and Russia 130; and US 130, 133
military expenditure 8–9, **9**, 203, 206
Mina (Mexico) *243*
mine warfare 13, 54, 74, 113–14, 144, 177, 208–9, 217–19, *217*

Mistral (Fr) *157*
Mistral class 71, 72, 83, 85, 130, 156–7
MKS-180 141–2, *141*
modularisation 139–41, 181, 206
Montford Point (US) 47, 161
Montreal (Canada) *241*
Myanmar 123, 128–9

Nasr (Pakistan) *128*
National Security Strategy (UK, 2010) 59
National Security Strategy and Strategic Defence Review (UK, 2015) 62–3
National Strategy for Maritime Security (UK, 2014) 62
NATO 6, 27, 28, 6; Frigate Replacement Programme 165–6; navies 20, 21; recon-figuration of navies 204; and Turkey 134
naval aviation and air forces 14, 213–15, 220–4, 244, 245
navies 12–14; aviation force structures 245; command and control 211–12; conscription 55, 241, 244; constabulary role of 14, 33–4; co-operation 6, 20; costs 206, 244; expen-diture on 8–9; fleet moderni-sation 242–3; fleet strengths **10**, 12; international opera-tions 246–7; key role of 6, 27–30; personnel 8, 14, 241–8, **242**; reconfiguration of 204; ship complements **243**; training and education 231, 242, 245, 246–7; women personnel 241, 242, 247
see also specific countries and navies
Nerz (Ger) *177*
Netherlands 21, 80–1, 159, 169; and Germany 168; Royal Netherlands Navy 55, 80, 147
Nevada (US) *191*
Newport class 107
Nimitz class 46, 147
Noor (Iran) *131*
Normandie (Fr) 130, *171*
North Korea 13, 14, 91, 93, 116
Norway 80
Nott Defence Review (1981) 28
Nottingham (GB) *232*

Oaxaca class *184*, 185
Ocean (GB) 58, *60*, 65, 159, *204*, 232, 234
Ocean Shield (Aus) 107
offshore patrol vessels (OPVs) 55, 137, 141, 177–8, 186, **187**
Ohio class 51, 191
Oman 133
'Oscar II' class 88
Otto Sverdrup (Nor) *175*
Oyashio class 201

Pakistan 121, 122, 124, 128
Pasadena (US) *8*
patrol vessels 33, 92, 182–6
Paul Hamilton (US) *52*
Peru 39
Phalanx (US) 215
Philippines 91, 92
piracy 21, 22, 32–3, 54, 97–8, 111, 115, 120, 121, 124, 132, 246, 247
Poland 80
Ponce (US) 144
Porte-Avions 2 (PA2) 228
Porter (US) *44*
Portugal 81
Prince of Wales (GB) 65, 67
Principe de Asturias (Sp) 78, 230
propulsion systems 142–3, *143*, 169

Queen Elizabeth (GB) 65, 67, 229
Queen Elizabeth class 55, 67–9, 151–3, *151*, *152*, 243
Qingdao (China) *99*

Rahav (Israel) *131*
Rankin (Aus) *108*
Ranvijay (India) *122*
'River' class 185
Rodney M. Davis (US) *243*
Romania 82
Ronald Reagan (US) *110*, *203*, *220*
Rotterdam (Neth) *81*
Royal Navy 13, 28, 54, 56, 59, 205, 214; Armilla Patrol 56, 66; bases 65; carriers 67, 205, 214, 229–30; changing role of 56, 57; expenditure cuts 56–9; Fleet Air Arm 65; force struc-ture **64**, 65; manpower short-ages 67;

Maritime Doctrine 30; naval construction orders (1990–2015) **66**; operations 66–7; organisation of 65–6; personnel 67, 242, 243–7; public relations 69; reduction of 57, 58–9, 60, 63; Royal Fleet Auxiliary 187; submarines 68, 194; surface combatants **61**; vessel replenishment 203, 188–9, *189*; women personnel 242, 247

Rubis class 70, 72, 195–6

Russia 12, 63, 84, 85, 172–3, 200–1, 206, 233; and China 99; legacy of Soviet period 83–5; and Middle East 130; and Ukraine 84

Russian Navy 13, 22, 25, 83–90; carriers 89, 226; Maritime Doctrine 86; naval force structure **86**; order of battle 87; personnel **87**; purchase of *Mistral* class 83, 85; submarines 88, 191, 197, 209; surface combatants 88–9

Sabha (Bahrain) 133

Sachsen class 169

Sahyadri (India) *140*

Saif (Pakistan) *128*

Salvatore Todaro (It) 200, *200*

Samuel Beckett (Ireland) *186*

Samuel Beckett class 184

San Antonio class 47, 158

Santa Maria class 78

São Paulo (Brazil) 13, 39, 229

Saudi Arabia 11, 35, 132

'Scorpène' class 39, 92, 196, *201*, 202

Sea Hawk (US) *33*

Sea Power 21: Operational Concepts for a New Era (US, 2002) 20, 42, 43–4

Seawolf (US) *190*, 192–3

Seawolf class 51, 209

Sejongdaewang-Ham (RoK) 118, 165

Sekiryu (Jpn) *114*

Serbia 30, 211

Sevastopol (Rus) *84*

Severodvinsk (Rus) 197

Shakti (Kuwait) 146

Sheffield (GB) 58, 162

Shiloh (US) *47*

shipbuilding 135–6, 144–6

Shivalik class 173, *175*

Sierra Leone 21, 31, 57–8

Sindhurakshak (India) 126

Singapore 92, 93, 121

Sirius (Aus) *105*

Skjold class 178, 180, *180*

Slava class *84*

Somalia 7, 21, 32–3, 120, *247*

Soryu (Jpn) *200*, 201

South Africa 121, 129

South China Sea 91, 92, 93, 94, 95, 105

South Korea (Republic of Korea) 13, 23, 91, 114, 115–19, 121, 178, 233; and Australia 111; and China 115, 118; and Japan 114, 119; naval aviation 117, 158; naval force structure 115–16, **116**, **117**, 119; navy 115, *115*, *178*; shipbuilding 135, 144, 176; submarines 118

Sovremenny class 83, *88*, 89, 100, 174

Spain 201, 205; *Armada Española* 77–9, *77*; air-defence escorts *78*; carriers 230

Spearhead class 160

Spioenkop (South Africa) *121*

Spruance class 164, 206

Sri Lanka 33, 122, 129; and Tamil Sea Tigers 33, 129

Stan Patrol OPVs 186

stealth technology 138–9, 141, 169, 208

Steil (Nor) *180*

Steregushchy class *88*, 173

Stockdale (US) *8*

Strategic Defence and Security Review (UK, 1998) 57, 151, 221; (2002) 58; (2010) 55, 59, 151

Stuart (Aus) *108*

submarines 12, 51, 55, 135, 190–202, 216; AIP 55, *79*, 197–8, 217; diesel-electric **199**; nuclear-powered 23, 28, 190–7, **194**, 216; passive detection of 216; and piracy 33; propulsion of 143; reconnaissance 208

Suffren (Fr) 72

Suffren class 195–6

Supreme (Singapore) *92*

surface combatants 13, 48, 162, 174

Sweden 80, 201

Sydney (Aus) *108*

Syria 32, 72, 130, 131

Tabar (India) *123*

Tahya Msr (Egypt) 130

Taiwan 18, 22, 91–2, 93, 94, 95, 214

Taizhou (China) *205*

Tapajo (Brazil) *39*

Tarawa (US) *18*

Tarkash (India) *173*

Te Mana (NZ) *140*

terrorism 19, 20, 22, 33, 54, 206, 246, 247

The Way Ahead (US, 1991) 18

Theodore Roosevelt (US) *15*, 147, *232*

Thetis Bay (US) 231

Theseus (GB) 232

Thor Heyerdahl (Nor) *11*

Ticonderoga class 47–8, 162, 164

'Tide' class 187

Tidespring class 37, 69

Tireless (GB) *57*

Tobruk (Aus) 106, *107*

Tomahawk (US) *210i*, 211

Tonnerre (Fr) 72, *155*

'Tribal' class 234

Trident 191, *192*

Trikand (India) *173*

Triomphant class 191

Tripoli (US) 158, 218, 232

Triumph (GB) *60*

Tromp (Neth) *168*

Tula (Rus) *88i*

Turgutreis (Turkey) *139*

Turkey 81–2, 130, 133–4, 145, 146, 153

Tyne class 185

U 1 (Ger) 144

U 31 (Ger) 144

U 32 (Ger) 200

U 33 (Ger) *198*

Ukraine 82, 84, 89, 173, 206

Ulyanovsk (Rus) 83, 226–7

Umkhonto (South Africa) 215

United Arab Emirates 132–3

United States 9, 11, 14, 16–18; '1–4–2–1' concept 43; and Australia 92; and Britain 28; and China 91, 214; Defense Strategic Guidance (2010/2012/2014) 44; foreign policy 29; and India 120; and Japan 110, 111,130; and Middle East 130, 133; military expenditure 9, 11–12, 41, 220–1; 'Pivot to Asia' policy 23; 'Pivot to the Pacific' policy 12, 91; and Saudi Arabia 132; shipbuilding 164

United States Navy 14, 40–6, 204, 214; '600-ship fleet' 40; amphibious warships 46–7, 158–9; bases 48, **48**; carriers 147, 221, **222**, **223**, 233; core capabilities 20; expenditure on 18–19, 164–6; fleet strength 18–19, *37*; force structure goals 45–6, **45**; Littoral Combat Ships 49–50, 137, 180–2, 206–7, 243, 244; Marine Corps 18, 42, 43, 233; Marine Expeditionary Units 20, 46; Maritime Strategy 16–17, 29, 40, 204, 214; submarines 51, 190; surface combatants **163**, 164; warships **49**

unmanned vehicles 8, 14, *15*, 25, 144, 207, 214, 224, 234–5, 237–8, 245

Valour class 172

Vanguard (GB) 67

Varyag (Rus) 83, 149, 226

Victorious (GB) *192*

Vietnam 33, 91, 92, 95, 211

Vigilant (GB) *27*

Vikramaditya (India) 90, 124, 125, *125*, 126, 150, *225*

Vikrant (India) 128, 149–51, *149*, 150, *151*, *225*

Vikrant II (India) 224–5

Vincennes (US) *162*

Viraat (India) *124*, 125, 225, *226*

Virginia class 51, 192–5

Virginio Fasan (It) 76

Visby (Sweden) *137*, 139, *225*

Visby class 80, 180, *181*

Vishnal (India) 225

Vladivostock (Rus) *84*

Warramunga (Aus) *12*

warships 13–14, *17*, 47, 114, 135, 162–4, 177; accommodation on 135, 141, *141*; building of 144–6; constabulary vessels 177; design of 135–9; minor and auxiliary 177–8, 186–9; propulsion 142; replenishment 203; volume growth 140

Wasp class 46

West Virginia (US) *192*

Whidbey Island (US) 46–7

Wiesel (Ger) *204*

women personnel 241, 242, 247

'Xia' class 99

Xuzhou (China) *101*, *103*, 175

Yemen 32, 132

Yi Yang (China) *26*

Yuri Dolgoruky (Rus) 191

Zaporizhhya (Ukr) *85*

Zeeland (Neth) *183*

Zumwalt (US) *136*, 139, *207*

Zumwalt class 49, *50*, 144, 164, 165, 206